To my Son Mike
Love mom
Michael Thelu

Only 317 Survived!

Printing Partners, Inc.

Authors: USS Indianapolis Survivors
Book Acquisitions Editor: Mary Lou Murphy
Copy Editor: Heidi Weas Muller
Graphic Designer: Brian Kingen
Proofreader: Mary Lou Murphy
Publishing Director: Joel O'Brien
Copyright © 2002 by USS Indianapolis Survivors Organization

Printed in the United States of America
Cover illustration by John Gromosiak

Printing Partners
929 W. 16th Street
Indianapolis, IN 46202
www.printingpartners.net

ISBN: 0–9725960–0–3

02 03 04 05/987654321

ONLY 317 SURVIVED!

FOREWORD

In downtown Indianapolis on the local water company canal, on August 2, 1995, a national memorial was dedicated to the officers, chiefs and men of the USS *Indianapolis* (CA-35). A local coalition of reserve and retired navy veterans had worked with the survivors for six years to raise almost 1.5 million dollars to accomplish this task. On a very hot day in August, we had expected a crowd of hundreds, but thousands attended. When the memorial was unveiled, those of us present realized that this was a form of closure for many who had lost loved ones in this great tragedy at the end of World War II. The citizens of Indianapolis quietly and proudly appreciate such veterans as the men of the USS *Indianapolis*. The Midwestern core values of integrity, hard work and love of freedom drew our Congress to name great warships after this city.

It is vital for those of us still in the service, our fellow citizens and our children to honor those whose courage and dedication have kept our nation and many other nations free. We owe a great debt of gratitude to those who have served and sacrificed like the men of the USS *Indianapolis*. We have the responsibility to pass on untarnished to those who come after us the ideals for which our veterans have served, suffered and too often died to preserve.

About once a month I drive by the memorial. Rarely does it stand alone. Sometimes a jogger stops to read about this historical ship and crew. Sometimes I see parents explaining the monument to their children, talking of heroism, tragedy, history and sacrifice. On several occasions I have seen a couple or a family placing a flower or a note at the base of the granite. I never interrupt, as it is their time of peace knowing their loved ones are remembered and that their ship is at last moored in its home port. Many families of those lost to us now finally have a headstone for the men still at sea. The memorial to the USS *Indianapolis* is here forever, and thankfully a grateful nation has truly remembered.

The recollections and remembrances in this book are not written by professional writers. These are the officers, men and family members of those who survived the tragic sinking of the ship. What do all these people have in common? The answer, of course, is that they are veterans of the United States Navy who have given of themselves in the service of their country. These remembrances will be read with the deepest interest by those who have served or continue to serve at sea. The spirit that guided the actions of these men lives on in the traditions we carry forth in the United States Navy. Tradition is something that cannot simply be written down and filed away for another day. Tradition embodies the values that can never be replaced by hardware. Tradition is that essence of the human spirit that is passed on when older warriors like these men look a young sailor in the eye and say, "We did our part. It's your turn now."

To carry on these traditions we must continue to honor the officers and sailors like the men of the USS *Indianapolis*. The best way to honor the service of these veterans is to ensure that their sacrifices were not in vain. We must not forget the lessons that America's wars in the 20th Century have taught us, lessons paid for with our shipmates' blood. The lesson that the forces which defend our nation must have the capabilities to meet not only crises that we can anticipate, but also the unforeseeable threats to freedom that are certain to rise in an uncertain world.

Now we can stop all engines, lay about smartly and drop anchor to pay homage to our shipmates whose stories are remembered here.

George Donald Steel
Captain, United States Naval Reserve

★ ★ ★ ★ ★ ★ ★ ★ ★ ★

Captain George Donald Steel, United States Naval Reserve

Captain G. Donald Steel was born in Lansing, Michigan and was appointed to the U.S. Naval Academy in 1971. In 1980, Captain Steel was released from active duty and affiliated with the Naval Reserve.

In his civilian career, Captain Steel serves as president of Planned Investment Company of Indianapolis, Indiana. He is actively involved in the community, including being past president of the following organizations: Indianapolis Kiwanis Club, Navy League, USO Council, Reserve Officers Association Chapter and the Indianapolis Securities Traders Association. He was also president of the USS *Indianapolis* Memorial Campaign and the Veterans Day Council of Indianapolis. He is the chairman of the Salvation Army of Indianapolis.

Captain Steel is authorized to wear the Meritorious Service Medal (2 awards), Navy Commendation Medal (2 awards), the Navy Unit Commendation, Battle "E" (2 awards), the Joint Meritorious Unit Award, Navy Unit Commendation, Armed Forces Service Medal, National Defense Service Medal (2 awards), Sea Service Ribbon (3 awards), Navy/Marine Corps Overseas Service Ribbon, the Armed Forces Reserve Medal, the NATO Service Medal, the Navy Rifle Marksmanship Ribbon, and the Expert Pistol Medal.

Captain Steel is married to the former Alison A. Fisher of Pittsburgh, Pennsylvania. They reside with their five children, Shawn, Eric, Grace, Kathleen and Corinne in Indianapolis, Indiana.

FOREWORD

The first time I heard the story of the USS *Indianapolis* was March 17, 1979, when I met my favorite survivor, Paul J. Murphy. This is what he told me. He was a survivor of the USS *Indianapolis,* and that ship delivered the atomic bomb components to the island of Tinian. Four days after they left Tinian, they were hit by two torpedoes and his ship sank in about 12 minutes. They had no time or way to send an SOS and no one came to look for them. After four days and five nights, they were accidentally spotted in the water by a plane that was searching for enemy submarines. The pilot saw an oil slick and began to make a bombing run. As they got closer to the water they noticed many heads bobbing, and men began to wave.

Mary Lou Walz Murphy

The pilot radioed for help and a PBY was sent out. You will learn of these forgotten sailors' experiences and rescue as you read their very own stories.

We married in 1987 and in 1995, Paul was elected chairman and I was elected secretary (truly an honor) of the USS Indianapolis Survivors Organization. Since that time, Paul has spoken frequently to schools, service clubs, churches, and military groups. We volunteer about twenty hours a week, sending frequent newsletters, planning reunions, and designing, ordering, housing, and shipping USS *Indianapolis* merchandise.

In May 2002, several survivors were together and the "book issue" was being discussed again. One survivor said, "We should have written our own book twenty years ago." After that comment, I said, "It is not too late. If survivors send me their stories, I'll put them together, we will get a publisher, and all 317 survivors will be recognized." None of us are professional journalists. Their stories are exactly as they remember this 57-year-old tragedy. Nothing has been left out. Nothing has been added. As I typed their stories—often in the quietness of the very early morning hours—sometimes I would laugh, sometimes I would cry, and many times I thanked God that I was married to one of these great American heroes.

One early morning I was so touched at how many of the survivors expressed their appreciation to the rescue crews. I felt I needed to call one of my favorite rescue crew members and share with him the feelings of the survivors in their chapters regarding the wonderful care and compassion of the rescue crews. Before I hung up the phone, we were both in tears. A few days later I received a letter from him, and I'd like to share it with you.

Dear Mary Lou:

Thank you so much for your early telephone call. I regret that we could not have visited longer. I think it would have helped both of us. I too, would like to suppress the emotions when I speak now before a group, but the memory of the suffering floods back and I lose control for a short spell. It seems after 57 years one could handle speaking about the event. But instead I still feel their flesh as it moves from the bone structure as I lifted them from the sea. I can hear that deep groan that comes from one who is in great agony. I know he is depending on me to get him aboard and in spite of his agony he bears with me. Once he has been placed on the deck of the LCVP I reach for the next one and this time it is the life jacket that I tug and say to myself, "Thank God, this one has a jacket." You steel yourself to the cries and the deep groans because it has to be done. Your adrenalin flows and you can lift mountains. Sure, you can suppress it, but when you meet a survivor and he emotionally thanks you, tears flow and your speech stumbles.

The crew on the *Bassett* in most cases were the same age as the survivors they were helping. These crew members had no special training. Yet they stood by every bunk and did whatever was needed to bring the survivor around to reality. You know this because you have read their letters.

Looking in the logs of the ship I learned that most all of the ships' crews, at this stage in the war, were young men in their late teens or early twenties. Do you realize how many would never have seen their twenty-first birthday had the invasion scheduled for November 1, 1945 occurred? If there ever was a ship to be honored or a crew to be thanked it is the USS *Indianapolis*. Though tragically lost after completing its mission, the world is a safer place because of the USS *Indianapolis*. A ship is only as great as its crew and the leadership its commanding officer instills. I am delighted that the captain's name has been cleared and the crew is recognized with the Special Ribbon.

Because of the reunions I have met so many now on a personal basis. On top of that I have met you and your favorite sailor, Paul Murphy, who I hold as very dear friends.

My best, always,
L. Peter Wren
LCDR USNR ret

Lt. Wren was on the USS *Bassett* during rescue and is also the author of two books relating to the rescue: *Those In Peril On The Sea* and *We Were There*.

May the names and memories of those who perished in the sinking of the USS *Indianapolis* and those shipmates who have followed them into eternity be forever etched into our hearts and minds. May God continue to richly bless the remaining 112 survivors living today.

Mary Lou Walz Murphy
Secretary, USS Indianapolis Survivors Organization

FOREWORD

The story of the last voyage of the USS *Indianapolis* and its sinking into the depths of the Pacific Ocean is one that I think should be told by all of those who survived.

Their story is remarkable because it is they, who in the waning days of the Second World War, served aboard the ship that carried the weapon that ultimately ended the war. And it is they who endured unthinkable horrors in a harrowing ordeal at sea.

It is a story of bravery, of tragedy, of triumph, and of extraordinary young servicemen who lived in an extraordinary time.

After such intense experiences in their youth, it is hard to imagine that as these men emerged from the waters of the Pacific, they had most of their lives left to live. They returned to America and established careers, raised families and were active in their communities. Yet, they never lost touch with their fellow sailors from the USS *Indianapolis*, or the families of those still at sea.

They chose Indianapolis as their place to reunite, to gather, to celebrate and to mourn. And for that, I am truly grateful. As the ship was once the pride of the United States Navy, its sailors remain the pride of this city. Their legacy lives on not just every July, but every day.

Indianapolis is home to a national memorial to the men of the USS *Indianapolis*. It stands prominently along the Downtown Canal Walk, where countless residents and visitors pause to remember the scarifies of the "Greatest Generation." It is a memorial in which I take great pride.

During the summer of 2002, I had the opportunity to honor Jimmy O'Donnell, the only survivor of the USS *Indianapolis* from the city of Indianapolis and a retired city firefighter. In an emotional ceremony, where Jim was surprised by his many friends and loved ones, several of his fellow survivors joined him with laughter and tears.

As I looked over the crowd that morning, I was struck by the diversity of the people looking back at me—young and old, military officers, firefighters and police officers, veterans in street clothing, children—all there because of these courageous survivors, and in this instance, Jim O'Donnell. After the ceremony, members of the audience quietly approached the survivors, asking them to sign books and hats, or just to thank them for their service to our country. I found that display of appreciation from the people of this city gratifying, but not surprising. For these men—survivors—are a tangible link to values that we as Hoosiers and Americans prize.

For those survivors who returned to life back home, I commend their quiet drive to tell their story. And I applaud their outstanding efforts to honor those still at sea. May you remember them as you read this book.

Bart Peterson
Mayor, City of Indianapolis

INTRODUCTION

Named in honor of the capital city of Indiana, the heavy cruiser USS *Indianapolis* CA-35 was launched on November 7,1931, having been christened by Miss Lucy Taggart, daughter of the late Senator Thomas Taggart and former mayor of the city of Indianapolis, Indiana.

Commissioned on November 15,1932, she was 610 feet, 4 inches long, making her 6 feet longer than the battleship *Arizona*. The *Indianapolis* was armed with nine 8-inch guns, and had a secondary armament of eight 5-inch guns.

Beginning her 13-year career as the flagship of the Scouting Force, prior to World War II she served several times as President Franklin D. Roosevelt's ship of state. On May 31,1934 while on board, the president reviewed the fleet off New York. The president also made a "Good Neighbor" cruise to South America. He was the first serving president to visit South America.

When the Japanese struck Pear Harbor on December 7,1941, the *Indianapolis* was at Johnson Atoll, 750 nautical miles southwest of Hawaii. Heading back toward Hawaii she joined Task Force 12 and began searching for the Japanese carriers that attacked the islands. Having no luck in locating the enemy, the *Indianapolis* arrived at Pearl Harbor on December 13, 1941, joining Task Force 11 for further action against the Japanese. On February 20, 1942 the *Indianapolis* had her first encounter with the enemy when the Task Force was attacked by enemy bombers near the Bougainville Islands in the Solomons. At least 16 of the attacking 18 bombers were shot down. During this time, the USS *Indianapolis* received her first battle star.

She went on to earn a total of 10 battle stars during the war:

- Bougainville & Salamaua-Lal Raids (February 1942)
- Aleutians (March 1942)
- Gilbert Islands (November 1943)
- Marshall Islands, Kwajelin & Majuro-Eniwetok Atolls (January-February 1944)
- Yap, Palau,Ulithi, Woleai (March-April 1944)
- Marianas-Battle of the Philippine Sea, Saipan and Guam (June-August 1944)
- Tinian Island (July 1944)
- Western Caroline Islands (September 1944)
- Japanese Home Islands, Honshu, Nasei/Iwo Jima (February 1945)
- Okinawa (March 1945)

It was at Okinawa on March 31,1945 that the *Indianapolis* was struck by a single-engine plane. It crashed into the port side of the aft main deck, killing the pilot instantly, with the wreckage toppling into the sea. Though little damage was caused to the deck, the pilot released a bomb from a very low altitude, which plummeted through the deck armor, tore through the bottom of the ship, and exploded in the water under the keel. Nine men were killed and twenty-nine wounded.

After temporary repairs at Kerama Retto, the ship limped back for major repairs at Mare Island, California at Vallejo. After almost two months the work was completed. Steaming into Hunters Point, she picked up her top-secret cargo, unknown to all aboard the ship. Proceeding at top speed to Tinian Island in the Marianas, the *Indianapolis* was carrying the components of the atomic bomb that was to be dropped on Hiroshima. The bomb was to be known as "Little Boy." (The bomb was dropped on August 6, 1945 by the *Enola Gay*, piloted by Colonel Paul W. Tibbetts.) Invading the Japanese home islands could have possibly cost millions of lives, as the Japanese would not surrender and were willing to sacrifice their lives for the emperor.

Leaving Tinian Island after being refueled and replenished, the *Indianapolis* proceeded to Guam and arrived on July 27. Receiving new orders, the ship's captain, Charles B. McVay, set course for Leyte to begin gunnery training with the battleship *Idaho* for the planned invasion of Japan. The destroyer escort *Underhill* had been torpedoed along the same route the *Indianapolis* was planning to use to get to Leyte only four days earlier. This information was not relayed to McVay. In fact, he requested an escort, which is normal procedure for a capital ship, but it was denied as not being necessary.

On July 30, a few minutes past midnight, a Japanese submarine commanded by Lt. Commander Mochitsura Hashimoto fired a spread of six torpedoes at the *Indianapolis*, the first blowing off a large section of the bow. The second struck amid ship, rupturing fire mains and penetrating a fuel tank and a powder magazine. The ship began listing sharply. The order to abandon ship was given. In a few minutes she slid silently beneath the waves.

Approximately 300 men went down with the ship. Some 900 more–many just partly clothed or naked–donned kapok life jackets, leaping into the thick black-fuel-oil-covered ocean. A handful of rubber rafts provided refuge for some. Others just clung to debris. Many were badly burned. Besides the vomiting and nausea caused by the oil, a number died from shark attacks, which began with the dawn. The men were without food or drinking water for almost five days. The sharks were always there!

Early in the morning of August 2, while on routine patrol in a twin-engine PV-1 Ventura, Lt. Wilbur Gwinn noticed a long black streak of oil in the water below him while testing a new antenna. Dropping to a lower altitude to get a better view, he noticed small black bumps on the surface, which took the shape of waving arms and heads! Radioing his base on Palau Island his position and what he had spotted, a PBY-5A from Palau piloted by Lt. Adrian Marks took off with survival gear and headed for the location where the men were discovered. While en route, Marks radioed the skipper of the *Cecil J. Doyle*, Commander W. Graham Claytor Jr., who proceeded immediately for the scene! In the meantime, upon seeing men in the water attacked by sharks, Marks landed his seaplane in the choppy water (open-sea landings were against regulations). Shutting his engines down, he proceeded to rescue 56 men. Some men were placed on the plane's wing and strapped down with parachute cord.

The *Cecil J. Doyle* (DE 368) arrived at midnight and took aboard the men rescued by Marks' PBY-5A. Other ships involved in rescue and recovery operations were the *Madison* (DD 425), *Dufilho* (DE 423), *Helm* (DD 388) *Alvin C. Cockrell* (DE 366), *Bassett* (APD 73), *Ringness* (APD 100), *Register* (APD 92), *Ralph Talbot* (DD 390), *French* (DE 367) and the *Aylwin* (DD 355).

Of the ship's complement of 1,197 men, 317 were rescued and 880 died. It was the worst tragedy at sea in our navy's history.

An inquiry held on August 13 on Guam concerning the loss of the ship resulted in court-martial proceedings which were held in Washington D.C.. Lasting from December 3 to December 19, 1945 the court tried McVay on two charges. He was first charged for failure to issue and secure the execution of orders for the abandonment of the USS *Indianapolis*. Secondly he was charged with negligence in "Suffering a Vessel of the Navy to be Hazarded" by neglecting and failing to cause a zigzag course to be steered when visibility conditions and information concerning enemy submarines required him to under the danger from submarine attack. Only convicted of the second charge, McVay was not indicted for losing the *Indianapolis*. The prosecution produced as a witness Commander Mochitsura Hashimoto, the officer in charge of the submarine that sank the *Indianapolis*. He stated he would have sunk the ship whether it zigzagged or not. United States Navy submarine skippers testifying for the defense substantiated Hashimoto's claim.

Carrying the weight of the tragedy on his shoulders for years took its toll. On November 6, 1968 using his own service revolver, McVay took his own life.

In the late nineties, hearings were held in Washington D.C. concerning Captain McVay's court-martial. "Please help us restore our captain's good name," said Paul J. Murphy, a survivor and chairman of the USS Indianapolis Survivors Organization who attended the hearings. Through the efforts of many others in 2000, the House of Representatives overwhelmingly passed a resolution exonerating McVay. The United States Senate also exonerated him. Despite the above, Captain McVay's court-martial still remains.

On August 2, 1995, a national memorial was dedicated in Indianapolis, Indiana to honor this great ship and its crew. Work is now underway to obtain a location for a proposed USS *Indianapolis* Memorial Museum, also to be located in Indianapolis. The tragedy of the USS *Indianapolis* CA-35 must never be forgotten.

This is the story of the men who survived the sinking of the ship and their ordeal.

John G. Gromosiak
USS Indianapolis Honorary Survivor

THE MEN OF THE USS INDIANAPOLIS

On the high seas she sailed
"Old Glory" blowing in the breeze
What so proudly we hailed!

With young men who so gallantly will have served
In time of war – some will become unnerved!

On that fateful day July 30th 1945
A great ship will sink
And many a man will no longer be alive!

Two torpedoes struck and she quickly slid beneath the waves
And for almost five days and nights they hoped and prayed
But no rescue seemed in sight!

Until an angel appeared in the sky
A plane piloted by Wilbur Gwinn
Only God knows why – only God knows why!

Later Adrian Marks landed his plane in the sea
Saving 56 men born in the "land of the free!"

And the ships came and let it be said
To rescue men – and honor the dead!

Let the story of the USS *Indianapolis* forever be told!
To all those both young and old – both young and old!

> John G. Gromosiak
> USS Indianapolis Honorary Survivor

WE DEDICATE THIS BOOK TO THE RESCUE CREW

Lt. (jg) Wilbur C. Gwinn "Our Angel", pilot of the PV-1 Ventura bomber. He accidentally spotted us on a routine enemy submarine search.

"I felt groups could help each other and had a chance to fight off the sharks; but, it was like being God, deciding who lives and who dies. It was horrible, the fury and dismay of those we passed by. It was the hardest thing I ever had to do and it haunts me to this day." Lt. Adrian Marks, pilot of the PBY.

WE DEDICATE THIS BOOK TO THE RESCUE CREW (cont.)

USS *BASSETT*
Commanding Officer Harold Theriault
Picked up 148 men

USS *CECIL DOYLE*
Commanding Officer W. Graham Claytor
Picked up 94 men

USS *DUFILHO*
Commanding Officer A. H. Nienau
Picked up 1 man

USS *REGISTER*
Commanding Officer John Furman
Picked up 12 men

USS *RINGNESS*
Commanding Officer William C. Meyer
Picked up 39 men

USS *RALPH TALBOT*
Commanding Officer Winston S. Brown
Picked up 23 men

Other Ships Participating in the Search and Rescue:

USS *Aylwin,* Commanding Officer K. F. Neupert
USS *Cockrell,* Commanding Officer M. M. Sanford
USS *French,* Commanding Officer LCDR Reginald Chauncey
USS *Helm,* Commanding Officer CDR A. F. Hollingsworth
USS *Hollandia,* Commanding Officer Calvin E. Wakeman
USS *Madison,* Commanding Officer Donald W. Todd
USS *Tranquility,* Commanding Officer Captain Mullins

NAME	ADAMS, LEO H. S1
STREET	
CITY	
STATE	
PHONE	
ENTERED SERVICE FROM	Atlantic City, NJ
PICKED UP BY	USS *Bassett*
DIVISION	
DOB	

FAMILY

EXPERIENCE
  Unable to contact any family members.

NAME	AKINES, WILLIAM R. S2
STREET	215 Bonnavue Dr
CITY	Hermitage
STATE	TN 37076
PHONE	615 889 7227
ENTERED SERVICE FROM	Chattanooga, TN
PICKED UP BY	USS *Doyle*
DIVISION	1st Division
DOB	12/6/27

FAMILY
Spouse: Margaret Bell Akines
Children: Sandra Akines Smith (Buddy), Bill Akines Jr. (Kathy), Ramona
Cherry Riling (David), Marina Gregory Frizzell, Tina Cherry Adams (James),
William (Butch) Cherry
Grandchildren: Jeff Barton, Mike Gregory, Jason Gregory, Kim Merritt,
Christie McArthur, Bill Akines III, Chris Riling, Rachel Riling, Lindsay Riling,
Bobby Akines, Sarah Akines, Brian Morrison (deceased), David Cherry, Austin
Welker
Great-Grandchildren: Jayme Gregory, Kelsey Gregory, Sydney Gregory
(deceased), Dustin Merritt, Joey McArthur, Drew McArthur

EXPERIENCE:

I was born to Roy Litton Akines and Ada Lee Akines on December 6, 1927. I turned 17 on December 6, 1944, and anxious to take care of my mother after my father died in 1942, I joined the navy on February 8, 1945. I had seven weeks of training at Great Lakes, Illinois, then went to Mare Island, California to board the USS *Indianapolis*. She was in dry dock, being repaired from damage done by a kamikaze attack at Okinawa on March 31, 1945.

When we sailed from Mare Island on July 16, I had been aboard ship about 4 months. My actual sea duty was about 16 days. Our first mission was top secret. No one knew what we were carrying in the crates brought aboard just as we were ready to sail. Very mysterious! Later we would learn it was the most destructive weapon known to man...the atomic bomb.

IT IS MY BELIEF THAT DROPPING THAT BOMB ENDED WORLD WAR II, SAVING MILLIONS OF LIVES.

My duties on ship were as follows: my general quarters station was in the powder magazine for the forward number one 8-inch gun turret. I stood my watches as quartermaster on the bridge and steering aft, four hours on, eight hours off, seven days a week.

When the ship was hit, I had been off duty about 15 minutes. Because it was too hot to sleep below, I slept topside by the number one 8-inch gun turret. Sleeping topside probably saved my life because the second torpedo hit my compartment area.

When I abandoned ship, I was with a large group of swimmers, probably 200 men. This later was known as Dr. Haynes' group, as he was a hero among many heroes.

After four days of panic, quest for survival, and great fear, we were spotted by a plane on a patrol mission. That alone gave us new hope for life as the plane turned and made several passes over us, dipping his wings in acknowledgement. We knew our prayers had been answered and that rescue was close at hand. A short time later a PBY seaplane flew over us just above the water. After a couple of passes the pilot brought the plane quickly to a stop on the water and began to taxi around, picking up men from the water and securing them on the plane. At that point, we were all within hours of death.

Lt. Wilbur Gwinn piloted the first plane. Lt. Adrian Marks (of Indianapolis) brought that "beautiful" PBY in to carry us out of the jaws of death and home to a country we all loved so much, even though we thought we were the "forgotten sailors." We call our saving pilots our "angels."

There is no way I can describe my feelings at that point of our rescue. I did give sharks and other dangers much thought as the rescue was under way.

My greatest jubilation came after dark. We were looking toward the sky and could see a great beam of light that appeared to come down from heaven. I for one am convinced it came from God, although it came to us from the first ship to arrive on the scene. This happened to be the ship that picked me up out of danger after one hundred and eight hours.

My rescue ship was the USS *Cecil J Doyle,* and I am forever grateful to the men of that great ship.

The adrenaline from knowing that the planes and ships were on the way gave us strength to live those next 18 hours. To survive and be able to tell about our experiences was truly a miracle.

CHAPTER 3   SURVIVOR ALLARD

NAME	ALLARD, VINCENT J. QM3	
STREET		
CITY		
STATE		
PHONE		
ENTERED SERVICE FROM	Omak, WA	
PICKED UP BY	USS *Ringness*	
DIVISION	NAN Division	
DOB	1/13/18	Deceased 2/91 Omak, WA

FAMILY
Children: Ron Allard (Donna), Glenn Allard (Mary Anne), Shannon Allard Allen (Leonard), Kim Allard Sprowls (Scott)
Grandchildren: Laurie Allard, Ron Allard, Brandon Allard, Duston Allard, Afton Allard, Vincent Allen, Dewayne Allen, Mike Allen, Kara Sprowls

EXPERIENCE
Respectfully submitted by Survivor Allard's son, Glenn.

Dear Mr. Murphy:

Thank you for the letter requesting information about my father, Vincent J. Allard, QM3. As you are aware, Dad passed away in February 1991. However, his memory will never be far from me.

Dad never talked much about the navy. But you always knew he never forgot about the time when the torpedo hit his ship. I have read most of the books that have been written and must say they sure are contrary to what my father stated. Everyone has their own account of what it was like in the water four days and five nights.

If I can be of any help to you, please let me know.

Respectfully,
Glenn Allard
(Survivor Vincent Allard's son, Glenn, was named after a very close friend and shipmate, Survivor Glenn Morgan.)

CHAPTER 4   SURVIVOR ALTSCHULER

NAME	ALTSCHULER, ALLEN H. S2
STREET	
CITY	
STATE	
PHONE	
ENTERED SERVICE FROM	Los Angeles, CA
PICKED UP BY	USS *Doyle*
DIVISION	
DOB	Deceased 12/94

FAMILY

EXPERIENCE
Unable to contact any family members.

NAME	ANDERSON, ERICK T. S2
STREET	
CITY	
STATE	
PHONE	
ENTERED SERVICE FROM	Vallejo, CA
PICKED UP BY	USS *Doyle*
DIVISION	
DOB	Deceased 12/96

FAMILY

EXPERIENCE

Unable to contact any family members.

CHAPTER 6 SURVIVOR ANDREWS

NAME	ANDREWS, WILLIAM R. S2
STREET	
CITY	
STATE	
PHONE	
ENTERED SERVICE FROM	Munhall, PA
PICKED UP BY	USS *Bassett*
DIVISION	
DOB	Deceased 11/91

FAMILY

EXPERIENCE

Unable to contact any family members.

NAME	ANUNTI, JOHN M. M2
STREET	
CITY	
STATE	
PHONE	
ENTERED SERVICE FROM	Duluth, MN
PICKED UP BY	USS *Bassett*
DIVISION	A Division
DOB	1/1/25
	Deceased 10/99 Duluth, MN

FAMILY

Widow: Kathleen Anunti
Children: Kathy Anunti Mathias, Linda Anunti, John Anunti, Jr.
Grandchildren: Kathy Cortes, Matt Mathias, Mark Anunti, Drew Anunti, Michael Anunti Arkulary, Daniel Anunti Arkulary
Great-Grandchildren: Nick Cortes, Madelyn Cortes

EXPERIENCE

Respectfully submitted by Survivor Anunti's widow, Kay, and family.

John Anunti was born January 1, 1925 in Duluth, Minnesota. In 1942, he was 17 years old and with his courage, patriotism and fortitude, he enlisted in the navy. He soon became a welding instructor at the Advanced Welding School in Treasure Island and was sent to the naval training station in Farragut, Idaho. As a metal smith second class, John was sent to serve on the USS *Indianapolis* in 1943.

While aboard the *Indianapolis*, John participated in several battles, including Tarawa, Kwajalein, Enowitok, and Palau.

He took part in carrier air strikes on Japan, Guam, Saipan, Tinian, Iwo Jima and Okinawa. John got lucky in the battle at Okinawa, where he survived a direct hit on the *Indianapolis* by a Japanese kamikaze.

He got very lucky again, very lucky, in the year 1945. Out of 1,197 men aboard the USS *Indianapolis*, John was one of 317 men who survived what is known as the worst naval disaster in American history.

This is his story of what unfolded on the night of July 30, 1945, and how he survived the shark-infested waters of the Pacific Ocean for the following five days.

John was on deck patrol aboard the *Indy* from 10:00 p.m. until midnight. The night skies offered partial visibility, meaning stars were dimly visible through the overcast sky. When he made his first round, everything was secure. He could see no lights showing, no gear adrift; all ports, doorways, and hatches were secure. It was a normal night aboard the ship. Hundreds of men, as usual, had hauled up mattresses, blankets and cots to sleep on deck as the ship was carrying twice as many men as normal, and it was much more comfortable to sleep on deck than in the inferno below.

During his second round, John noticed light streaming from an open porthole on the starboard side of the ship, far forward in the officers' area. He immediately reported it and then went forward to find the source. As he came closer to the room he believed was the source of the light, he heard men's voices. He was now near the aviators' rooms, and as he entered the room, he found three fly boys playing cards. John entered the room and told them, "Secure that porthole right away, light is showing through," and "knock off the noise too." The men did as told as they all knew and liked each other. John finished his round and was relieved of patrol duty shortly thereafter. He headed for the showers.

While in the shower, he was rocked off balance and everything went dark. Scrambling to his feet, he felt his way through the darkness to get to a passageway to see what was happening. He found total chaos. Men were running in every direction. He could hear screaming. He found a man who had been badly burned and was in immediate need of medical attention. He grabbed the man and started for sickbay. As they neared that area, John saw that the floor was filling with water and was inaccessible. Men were screaming from the sickbay area and there was no way to get to them. John hurriedly turned and with the injured man headed in the opposite direction. He found a first-aid station and left the badly burned man to receive help. John realized he was not too far from his locker, so he ran to it to finally get some clothes on.

Everything was happening in seconds. John, now with pants on, could smell the smoke in the air. He raced for the deck of the ship and began grabbing for water hoses to fight the fire, but there was no water to fill those hoses and fight those fires. Injured men were everywhere. Among the chaos on deck, John remembered seeing a marine officer waving a gun in the air, shouting that he would shoot anyone who tried to jump overboard. No one knew what to do. No one could receive any orders, as all communication systems were down.

The ship was heaving and tilting. Despite the warning from the marine officer with the gun, men started jumping overboard by the hundreds. John reached in his pocket for his knife and cut a floater net and a life raft loose. He realized that he too would have to jump soon. The ship was unquestionably sinking. He knew that if he didn't jump soon, the sinking ship would create a vacuum effect and suck him down with it. There was no time for John to find a life jacket—he had to jump and jump now! He remembers hitting the water and his mind telling him to swim as fast as he could away from the ship. He swam, but it wasn't fast enough. The ship was going down and he could feel the ship sucking him down with it.

He took one last gulp of air and down he went, too. He didn't have any idea how far under the water the ship pulled him, but John recounts swimming against the current with every ounce of his strength to try to get to the surface. He thought his lungs would burst before he could reach the surface.

The *Indy* sank within 12 to 15 minutes after it had been hit by what we now know were two torpedoes sent by a Japanese submarine. This submarine had the *Indianapolis* in its sights and had perhaps used the light streaming from the aviators' cabin as its target for launching those torpedoes.

John was by himself that first night. Without a life jacket and totally spent from the struggle to free himself from the pull of the ship as she sank, he spent the night floating on his back as much as possible.

As dawn approached and offered light to see by, John found a floater net floating in the ocean. (He liked to think it was the one he cut loose.) He grabbed it and used it as a flotation device. He also found a shipmate and shared the floater net with him. As the day wore on, John was sure a ship was on its way to pick them up, because he saw a plane pass overhead and seem to come back and circle the area. He also thought someone must have gotten an SOS off before the ship went down. As the day wore on, he found other stragglers and other small groups of men. The most injured were placed in the floater net, and the other men would hang on to the outside of the net. The men stuck together and waited to be rescued.

Day two brought sharks. John noticed the sharks swimming just outside the rim of the oil slick caused by the ship sinking. He felt he and the men were protected by that oil slick because it appeared that the sharks wouldn't swim into the oil. Because the slick was only about 4 feet deep, John tucked himself into a ball. "Eventually I had to stretch my legs out and as I did, I just stood up on something. I thought it was a piece of debris until I realized I was being moved along in the water. I stood up on one of those sharks." Contrary to popular belief today about shark attacks (that you should stay still and avoid sudden movements), the men from the *Indianapolis* found that if they stayed in groups and kicked and screamed the sharks would stay away. The men learned that if one person swam away from the group by himself, he would be eaten by a shark.

By day three, many men were swimming away from the group. Men began to hallucinate and see mirages. As the men baked in the sun with no food or water, John recalled that he himself saw a mirage of an A & W Rootbeer stand floating in the water. Luckily for John, he was still sane enough to know not to swim to it. He also remembers talking to an electrician who told him that he had a pump hooked up under the water and that he just had to dive under, flip a switch, and then he could pump all the water away so they could walk to shore.

The oil from the ship was also creating havoc for the men. It literally covered them. John said it was about two inches thick on his body. The oil burned their eyes and made them bake in the hot sun.

By the fourth day, most of the injured men had died and now many others had been eaten by sharks. When a man died, a life jacket would be freed up for one who was without. Men were losing all hope of being rescued.

But it was on this fourth day that the men were found. John saw a plane, a bomber to be exact. It made two passes over him and then opened up its doors and dropped by parachute what looked to him to be a whaleboat. He stated, "It was a beautiful site watching that whaleboat float down to the sea." He then knew that they had been spotted and that help would be on its way. John, however, was too exhausted and too occupied with an important duty to swim to the whaleboat. John was holding up his friend, Chuck Tawater, and encouraging him to "hold on a little while longer, help was on the way."

After over 100 hours in the water, John was finally picked up by the USS *Bassett*. The *Bassett* lowered a stretcher down and hauled him on board. Lying on the deck, John remembered a doctor examining the man next to him. The doctor asked the man if he had pain anywhere, and the man replied that his back hurt. The doctor turned him over and much to everyone's

Survivor Tawater, Kay Anunti, Survivor Anunti

surprise, the man had two large shark bites on his back.

John was placed in a bunk aboard the *Bassett* and fed spoonfuls of sugar water and orange juice. He was extremely dehydrated but thankfully hadn't suffered any other major injuries. From the *Bassett*, John and his surviving crewmates were sent to a naval hospital in the Philippines, where he was treated for the dehydration and ulcerated sores on his skin caused by the oil and salt water. He stayed there for approximately seven days. From the Philippines, the men were flown in a hospital plane to Guam and put in Fleet Hospital 114 where they stayed for a week before finally being sent to the submarine rest camp for further recovery. When the recovery was complete, the men were loaded into an aircraft carrier and flown to San Diego where they were met by a band and given survivor's leave.

Through this horrendous ordeal, the one thing John felt bitter about was the fact that the U.S. Navy decided to court martial his captain for the sinking of the *Indianapolis*. John felt strongly that the charges made against his captain were poor and that the navy was looking for a scapegoat. John testified in Washington at the court martial proceedings and always supported his captain, believing that "the skipper didn't do anything wrong."

John returned to Duluth, Minnesota where he married Kathleen Schiel and had three children. He continued his welding career as a certified pipe fitter and a licensed steam fitter. In 1968, he moved his family to Littleton, Colorado. There he spent countless hours playing with his six grandchildren and telling them endless stories of his days of survival in the ocean. "I wouldn't talk to my children, at first, about what happened on the *Indianapolis*. But I felt obligated to tell my grandchildren whenever they got curious. They needed to know about the sacrifices that were made." His grandchildren considered him a true hero and would beg him to tell them his stories of survival.

Never forgetting his crew members, the terrible mistakes made by the navy (including the court martial of his captain) or the four days and five nights spent in shark-infested waters, he thanked God daily that he was one of the 317 survivors.

John received the Purple Heart and numerous decorations for the battles he served in. He was proud to have served on the USS *Indianapolis* and truly looked forward to attending all the reunions and the memorial dedication.

John passed away on October 18, 1999, but those wonderful stories he passed on to his grandchildren will be passed on to his great-grandchildren, and he will be remembered as the true hero he was for generations to come.

Survivors John Anunti, Paul Murphy, unknown and Grover Carver.

CHAPTER 8 — SURVIVOR ARMISTEAD

NAME	ARMISTEAD, JOHN H. S2
STREET	
CITY	
STATE	
PHONE	
ENTERED SERVICE FROM	Memphis, TN
PICKED UP BY	USS *Register*
DIVISION	
DOB	Deceased

FAMILY

EXPERIENCE

Unable to contact any family members.

CHAPTER 9 — SURVIVOR ASHFORD

NAME	ASHFORD, JOHN T. JR RT3
STREET	
CITY	
STATE	
PHONE	
ENTERED SERVICE FROM	Lubbock, TX
PICKED UP BY	USS *Doyle*
DIVISION	
DOB	Deceased 12/88

FAMILY

EXPERIENCE

Unable to contact any family members.

NAME	AULT, WILLIAM F. S2
STREET	3004 21ST NW
CITY	CANTON
STATE	OH 44708
PHONE	330 453 6154
ENTERED SERVICE FROM	Louisville, OH
PICKED UP BY	USS *Bassett*
DIVISION	RADAR
DOB	8/25/19

FAMILY
Spouse: Verena (Married 62 years)
Children: William F. Ault Jr. (deceased), Richard Ault, Steven Ault
Grandchildren: Melinda Ault, Gina Ault, Steven Ault, Tricia Ault

EXPERIENCE

This is transcribed from documents written by me around 1962-63, relating my life and experience during the sinking of the USS *Indianapolis* during World War II.

I was born August 18, 1919 in Canton, Ohio. I have two sisters older than I and a brother and two sisters younger than I. When I was seven years old, my family moved to a small farm near Louisville, Ohio. I spent my youth in Stark County and went to a country school where each teacher had two grades. While attending Louisville High School, I played guard on the football team and was elected captain my senior year. When I graduated in 1937, jobs were scarce and I worked for Stark County road maintenance. My wife and I were married January 25, 1941 and her father was a foreman at Timken Roller Bearing Co. He got me a job as a helper on the electric fes (furnace).

On June 23, 1944, at the age of 25, I was drafted into the navy and left for boot camp at Great Lakes. Five of us that had been in boot camp together were sent to radar training school at Ponta Loma, California. I was assigned to the USS *Indianapolis* and went aboard December 30, 1944, while she was tied up at the San Diego destroyer base. We left the States on January 1, 1945.

On a regular watch I stood duty at the sky search radar and plotting table, which was on the aft gun deck. During general quarters my first station was a talker in CIC. Later, my station was changed, and I operated the fire control radar on the forward main battery, 8-inch guns.

I took part in the landings on Iwo Jima and the carrier air strike on Tokyo. We were in the task force that was to make the invasion on Okinawa; however, we were hit by a suicide plane on Sunday morning, March 31, 1945, the day before the invasion was to start. (The Okinawa invasion eventually started on Easter morning.) This disaster sent the *Indy* back to the States for repairs and a complete overhaul. During the time in dry dock at Mare Island naval yard in Oakland, California, I was allowed to go home on leave and see my son for the first time. He was seven months old.

On July 16, 1945, we left for the South Pacific, carrying components of the atomic bomb to be dropped on Hiroshima on August 6, 1945. On July 29, a group of us from the radar division had been playing cards all afternoon. When chow time came around in the evening, we didn't bother to eat because not too many of the fellas cared for the cold cuts we always had on Sunday evenings.

I had just gone on watch at 11:45 p.m. Sunday night, July 29, and had checked my radar set and checked in with the gun crew to make sure everything was okay. When the guns weren't being used, we kept the fire control radar on a stand-by condition. During this time I had nothing to do but keep in contact with the gun crew by telephone.

It was shortly after midnight when the torpedoes hit. With the explosion, the lights dimmed and then went out. When we stepped outside, portside, the ship was already beginning to list to starboard. There were quite a few men standing on deck waiting for some word to be passed over the loudspeaker as to what had happened and whether they should go to their battle stations or abandon-ship stations. The word was never passed because the power had been knocked off. When no word was passed, an officer standing with us told a couple of sailors to break out the life preservers. We all put them on and about this time the ship was listing 45-60 degrees to starboard.

The officer told us that we had better leave the ship, so a couple of lines were tossed overboard and we could almost walk down the side of the ship at that time. I grabbed the line and went over the side, walking and slipping until I was close enough to the water to jump. As soon as I hit the water, I started swimming as hard as I could to get away from the ship, as I had always heard that the undertow from a sinking ship would pull you under. I swam maybe 50 to 100 yards from the ship and then glanced around to see what was happening. The only part of the ship that was out of the water was the fantail, with the 4 screws sticking out of the water. I started swimming again to get as far away as possible and the next time I looked, the ship was gone. Many things had gone through my head as I was going over the side of the ship into the water. I thought for one thing that my time had come, and I was wondering what my wife and son would do.

At that point, I felt I was the only one left. No one else was near me, and all this had happened in about 15 minutes. All I could think of was surviving. I heard voices a short time later and swam around until I spied a few men clinging together. Some were sick from swallowing salt water, but our biggest concern at that time was that if we had been sunk by a sub, it would surface and open fire on us in the water.

After the initial shock of sinking had worn off, we were beginning to group together in the water. I had made up my mind that if I did lose my life in the water, I would be one of the last to go. I think this determination was what kept me from losing my sanity, which is what many of the men did.

When I went overboard I was wearing a blue denim shirt, dungarees, shoes and socks. Some of the men had on only shorts and no shirts and some, I think, had on even less. I had no injuries and didn't get sick from swallowing sea water, but some of the men weren't as lucky. During the sinking, a few life rafts had floated away from the ship, and each one had one or two men on it. In the group I was in, we tied the rafts together, and the ones who couldn't get in the rafts hung onto the sides.

I don't remember whether it was the first night or after daylight of the first day when we found the floater net, but it was a real life saver. We tied all the rafts–three or four–to the floater net. That way we had a place to hang on and it wasn't as tiresome as hanging onto the rafts. Also, during the first night we kept finding more men, and we were running out of room for them to hang on.

I didn't think we would be picked up that night, but I was sure that when daylight came help would be there. We all thought that an SOS had been sent out and help would come quickly.

That first night seemed like it would never come to an end, but finally daybreak came and everyone began looking for our rescue ship. We saw planes flying overhead and tried to signal them, but they never knew that we were down there. As the day progressed we began to wonder if we would be rescued by nightfall. Our spirits were very low.

During this first day, we checked to see what supplies we had aboard the rafts. We had three casks of water and a few malted tablets. The water, we found out later in the day, was brackish and not drinkable. We also had a rocket gun and a few rockets.

During the day, the sharks would come around and when anyone yelled "Sharks," everyone would splash the water, kick their feet, and make noise to try to drive them away. As long as we floated in the oil slick, which would come and go, the sharks wouldn't bother us. I guess they were afraid of darkness, and the shadow from the oil slick kept them away.

In some ways the nights on the water were better than the days, because at night we didn't worry about the sharks, and we didn't have the sun beating down on us. Our kapok life vests were beginning to get soaked, and we kept sinking lower in the water. We all knew that a kapok vest was supposed to be good for 48-72 hours.

The second night I was hanging on to the floater net and dozed off for a short time. When I woke up, there was no one around me–I had let go of the net while I dozed and had floated away from the group. I didn't know which way to swim to rejoin them and I was trying to decide what to do when I heard their voices. It didn't take me long to rejoin them, and from that time on, I kept myself tied to the net.

I think my only other narrow escape from death came on the last day we were in the water. Many of the men were becoming delirious and were seeing drinking fountains, soda fountains, or coffee urns under the water. Some thought they saw the ship's mess hall where the drinking fountain was. One of the men told me he was going below to get a drink and wanted me to go with him. I agreed, and he went under the water. I started to follow but when the water went over my head I had enough strength left to realize that there was nothing there but water.

I don't remember much about the rescue except that when the crew on the LCVP pulled me aboard, I thought my arms would give out before I got on board. I don't know if I walked or was carried to a lower bunk. While I was laying or sleeping there, I was awakened by the man above me whose urine was running through the bunk on to me. I looked about and saw a crewman nearby. He saw that I was awake and asked me if I would like him to try and clean me up. I agreed. He took me into the shower and washed me first with diesel fuel. One wash wasn't enough, so he was washing me again when he said, "My God, I have a blond!"

This is where my writings ended.

Further information submitted by sons Richard and Steven is as follows:

The men were rescued after a plane spotted an oil slick by accident and came in for a closer look. They had spent 4 and one-half days, 105 hours in the water. Our dad was one of the lucky few to survive. After the rescue, he went to the U.S. Field Hospital 114, then to USN Base Hospital 18. After recovery, he went to the U.S. Navy Separation Center in Toledo, Ohio, where he received an honorable discharge February 4, 1946. He received the Purple Heart, Asiatic Pacific Medal (2 stars), Victory Medal, American Medal, Combat Action Ribbon and Navy Unit Citation Ribbon. He retired from Timken Roller Bearing on January 1, 1983.

Survivor William Ault, Survivor Allen Altschuler, Survivor Robert Gettleman, September 26, 1945.

NAME   BALDRIDGE, CLOVIS R. EM2
STREET
CITY
STATE
PHONE
ENTERED SERVICE FROM   Waco, TX
PICKED UP BY   USS *Bassett*
DIVISION
DOB   Deceased

FAMILY

EXPERIENCE
   Unable to contact any family members.

NAME   BARTO, LLOYD P. S1
STREET   2960 Via Alhama
CITY   Temecula
STATE   CA 92592
PHONE   909 693 4380
ENTERED SERVICE FROM   Gile, WI
PICKED UP BY   USS *Doyle*
DIVISION   2nd Division
DOB   10/28/24

FAMILY
Spouse: Mary Lou
Children: Bruce Barto and Beth Barto Siapkas
Grandchildren: Alex and Dimitri

EXPERIENCE
   I was assigned to the USS *Indianapolis*. My duty was in the number two turret,
Second Division. On Sunday night, July 29, 1945, we had been playing poker
and had just finished. I went to the shell deck of number two turret to sleep,
which is where I slept every night.
   Shortly after midnight, there was a huge explosion. It knocked me down,
knocking the wind out of me. I was in pain—my right leg was bleeding badly. I

finally made it up the gun platform to the turret and opened the side hatch. It was like daylight! We were already listing. I looked forward to the bow and was surprised to see it had been blown off. You could see a white wake where we had spun in a circle. I reached up above in the air duct where I had hidden a blow-up type rubber vest. This vest saved my life.

I tried desperately to abandon ship. The life line was thick with sailors. I crawled over top of them, jumped off the ship and landed on my back. Looking back, I realize I could have just walked off the side. I swam with my tube not inflated for a long way. I tried blowing up my tube; however, just a little air got into it. I started vomiting black oil and bile. Fortunately, someone grabbed me and blew up my tube. I hope whoever it was made it out safely.

I thought we would be picked up the next morning. After all, we were the flagship of the Fifth Fleet. Night came! Then another night! The third day was terrible with sharks under and all around us. Everyone was starting to get delirious. The fourth day was chaos! From hundreds of men...we were now down to small groups.

It was a long time before we got a raft dropped by planes. A PBY landed and was picking up survivors. They threw out a line to grab on to but each time I got on the PBY, they would throw me back in the water. All I wanted was a sip of water they were giving the rescued sailors. I have had many bad dreams about this. I later found out the reason I was not pulled on, they were saving the lives of the sailors in bad shape. That bad dream finally left me, and I am glad they were helped first.

I was in the same group as Dr. Haynes the entire time. He was a real leader and hero. When they dropped the life raft, we had to blow it up. We had to work together to get everyone on the raft. Dr. Haynes and I got in the same raft. If someone touched you, your skin would fall off, and there was a lot of fighting going on.

While we were in the raft, I looked at the sailor next to me. He was dark from all the black oil on his face and we didn't recognize each other. He turned out to be my best friend from Hurley High School, Charles Bruneau, gunners mate, third class, Fourth Division. We had joined the navy together. He was in bad shape and did not say a word. I put my arm around him to hold him up. He stopped moving. I called Dr. Haynes. He said, "Charles is dead." We had to put him overboard. I never had the heart to tell his parents he almost made it. I told them I did not see him.

LAS Charles "Chuck" Bruneau on left and Survivor Lloyd Barto on right, 1943.

Hours later we saw a light in the darkness. We were still getting delirious and thought it was a

Japanese submarine coming to smash us. It
turned out to be the USS *Doyle*. When they
took us on board, we were given spoonfuls of
water that tasted like sugar. Later they covered
me in salve and wrapped me in sheets.

A sailor was assigned to look after me to
make sure I couldn't crawl to a scuttlebutt for
water. His name was Doyle. He was the
younger brother of marine pilot Doyle who
was known for diving his plane into the stack
of a Japanese ship and sinking it. I had heard
all about this pilot from my older brother, Captain Gordon Barto, wingman for
Major Joe Foss, World War II Ace.

After my discharge, I went to business college in Ironwood, Michigan, and
graduated. I got a job in Milwaukee, Wisconsin and worked as an inspector for
the green military cans that we needed for the Korean War. They were used for
goods, water and gas. Later I went back to Ironwood and met Mary Lou and we
got married. We decided to move to Los Angeles, and I went to work for the
greatest company in the United States, Dunn-Edwards Paint Corp. I became a
division manager and went into sales and became the first "Million Dollar
Salesman" in that division. After working there for 38 years with the nicest
people, at the age of 65, I retired.

CHAPTER 13   SURVIVOR BATEMAN

NAME	BATEMAN, BERNARD B. F2
STREET	
CITY	
STATE	
PHONE	
ENTERED SERVICE FROM	Cleveland, OH
PICKED UP BY	PBY - USS *Doyle*
DIVISION	B Division Boilermaker Striker
DOB	12/2/26 Deceased 9/99 Columbia Station, OH

FAMILY
Widow: Frances

EXPERIENCE
Unable to contact any family members.

NAME   BEANE, JAMES A. F2
STREET
CITY
STATE
PHONE
ENTERED SERVICE FROM   Eatonville, WA
PICKED UP BY   USS *Bassett*
DIVISION
DOB   6/22/27
                  Deceased 11/00 Puyallup, WA

FAMILY
Widow: Tae Im
Children: Steve Beane, Dave Beane, Jenny Beane Sparks
Stepchildren: Myung Ja Chamness, Keum Sik Hwang, Nora Keller, Lisa Meyer, Lynn Cobb
Grandchildren: Shon Beane, Heather Beane, Josua Beane, Olivia Beane, Amanda Sparks, Bradley Hwang, Ali Hwang, Robyn Hwang, Tae Keller, Sunhi Keller, Noelan Meyer, Aidan Meyer

EXPERIENCE
Respectfully submitted by Survivor Beane's widow, Tae Im.

James Beane was born on June 22, 1927 on a stump ranch in western Washington. Jim was used to the hard, physical labor needed to work the land and, in truth, preferred it to school work. During his sophomore year, he left high school and worked odd jobs until he was old enough to join the navy.

After boot camp in Idaho, Jim was assigned to the USS *Indianapolis*. On his first cruise, the *Indianapolis* was hit by two Japanese torpedoes that demolished the sleeping quarters he had left only moments before. Jim rushed to the deck and barely made it off the ship before it went down. Jim and two of his shipmates grabbed hold of a fire hose floating in the debris. Over the next five nights and four days, they watched over each other, talking and encouraging one another to hang on, to stay awake and live. At one point, Jim said that he woke up breathing water, submerged, and was yanked back by one of his friends.

Later that night, as the men were talking, Jim noticed that the man who had saved his life was nodding off. Thinking his friend was sleeping, he shook him. His friend tipped over; a shark had bitten off his legs.

The nights were the worst, Jim said, because of the sharks. During a feeding frenzy, the water would smell like blood and you would never know who would be hit next. More men died from shark attacks than from exposure or from the torpedo hit itself.

The second man sharing the fire hose with him became so thirsty he drank ocean water. He went crazy and swam off one day before they were rescued. Jim didn't know why he was the only one of the three to survive, but he commented once that every day after those days at sea was a bonus in life.

Jim rarely talked about his experience on the *Indianapolis* or the following days he spent adrift in the open ocean. But those days and nights formed much of his independent and unflinching approach to life. As his brother Bill once said, "Jim went ahead in civilian life with more guts than a government mule."

Fifty-five years after the sinking of the USS *Indianapolis*, Jim Beane passed away on November 11, 2000.

CHAPTER 15   SURVIVOR BEATY

NAME	BEATY, DONALD L. S1
STREET	2665 Sycamore Beach Rd
CITY	Angola
STATE	IN 46703
PHONE	260 833 1525
ENTERED SERVICE FROM	Ft Wayne, IN
PICKED UP BY	USS *Bassett*
DIVISION	5th Division Fox Division
DOB	1/20/25

FAMILY

Spouse: Blanche Beaty
Children: Barbara, Kenneth, Carolyn and Kelly
Grandchildren: Seven

EXPERIENCE

I have often felt that I had a unique navy experience being from Indiana and ending up on the USS *Indianapolis*! I turned 18 on January 20, 1943, graduated from high school on June 14, 1943, and was sworn into the navy on July 5, 1943. My boot camp was at Great Lakes, Illinois. After nine weeks of training, I was allowed to go home for a week. When I returned, I was put on a train to San Francisco, California. There I boarded the USS *Louisville* as a passenger and went to Pearl Harbor. In

September, I was assigned to the USS *Indianapolis*. Within a few weeks I was at Operation Tarawa. I knew the navy needed men, but not that fast. I participated in eight of the ten operations, the last being Okinawa. I am proud to have been a member of the crew that delivered the atomic bomb.

The following paragraph is a statement that we were required to write for the navy on August 9, 1945.

I had just gone on watch in the radar room of Dir 43 & 44. It was located directly below mount number three on the boat deck. I had been on watch about 20 to 25 minutes when I heard three explosions. I tried to push the door open at once but 40-mm cans had fallen against it. Two other fellows and I finally were able to push it open. One man went back in to man the phones. When the ship started to list, more cans began to block the door. I worked for several minutes getting it clear enough to get the one man out again. After he was free, we all grabbed a life jacket. The ship was about 20 degrees by this time. I climbed up to gun eight. I lost my grip and fell back against an ammunition elevator box. When I turned around, I saw the water was already halfway up the ship. I walked right over the bathtub into the water. This was off to the starboard side. I swam through many 5- and 40-mm shells to about forty feet from the ship. At that time, I joined a group.

CHAPTER 16   SURVIVOR BELCHER

NAME	BELCHER, JAMES R. S1
STREET	
CITY	
STATE	
PHONE	
ENTERED SERVICE FROM	Abbeville, AL
PICKED UP BY	USS *Ringness*
DIVISION	O Division
DOB	10/27/26
	Deceased 5/01 Waynesboro, VA

FAMILY
Widow: Toni

EXPERIENCE
No response from family.

NAME	BELL, MAURICE G. S1
STREET	5805 Woodgate Rd
CITY	Mobile
STATE	AL 36609
PHONE	251 661 8299
ENTERED SERVICE FROM	Bell Wood, IL
PICKED UP BY	USS *Bassett*
DIVISION	7th Division
DOB	2/17/25

FAMILY

Spouse: Lois
Children: Beverly Bell Gros (Richard), Bonnie Bell Hall (Ray), David Bell
Grandchildren: Sherri Williams Bailey, Floyd Ray Hall III, Mary Leigh Williams
Covington, Amanda Kay Hall, Kathy Williams Simpson, Tammy Williams
Great-Grandchildren: Joshua Hall, Jordan Bailey, Austin Williams, Kyle Bailey,
Coby Simpson, William Hall, Landon Bailey, Cameron Simpson

EXPERIENCE

I was drafted in June of 1943. I chose the navy and went to Great Lakes naval training station at Great Lakes, Illinois for boot camp. After completion of boot camp, I was taken to a camp near Oakland, California. I got a troop ship and went to Pearl Harbor, Hawaii. There I boarded the USS *Indianapolis*, a heavy cruiser, which was to be my home for the next two years.

My job aboard the *Indy* was to man the 20-mm anti-aircraft guns. I stood watch and was a lookout for enemy planes and ships. The first battle I participated in was at Tarawa. I participated in eight of the ten major battles.

My most memorable battle was at Okinawa. I was on lookout watch when a plane came from behind a cloud, and it seemed like it was coming straight toward me. The plane landed on the port side. The engine and bomb went through all decks. The bomb exploded underneath, blowing a large hole in the hull. A temporary patch was made at Kerama Retto. We limped back to Mare Island, to the dry dock for repairs. It took about two months for the repairs to be completed at Mare Island.

After repairs were completed, we moved to Hunters Point, California, and I was assigned to help load a huge crate on board the *Indy*. We fastened it securely in a port hangar but had no idea what was inside the crate. It was guarded by marines all the time. We made a record run to Tinian, unloaded the crate onto a barge, and it then was taken to the Air Force base where the *Enola Gay* was waiting.

We left for the Philippine Islands. On Sunday night, July 29, 1945, just after midnight, I was sleeping in my bunk. A loud explosion knocked me out of my bunk. I slipped on my clothes and went topside to get a life jacket. I got the next to last one from a sack on a deck. I went to port side, which was the high side, and I got on the screw shaft which was just forward of the port screw. It was there that I jumped into the dark waters of the Pacific.

I swam as fast as I could to get away from the ship because I was afraid of the suction taking me down as the ship sank. One man jumped shortly after I did. He had been in the shower and didn't have any clothes or a life jacket. I helped him until we could find something to hold on to. Later he got some clothes and a life jacket. He was one of the survivors. We got into one of the larger groups of men who were in the water. The first thing that was so horrible was the fuel oil that covered the water. Every breath I took made me so sick I vomited everything I had in my stomach. We were all black from the fuel oil covering our bodies. We did what we had to do to survive the ordeal at sea. I never gave up hope.

I was picked up by the USS *Bassett* at daybreak on the morning of Friday, August 3, 1945. I was taken to Samar Base Hospital in the Philippines. After a few days, I was flown to Guam Base Hospital, and it was there that I found out what it was that I helped load aboard the USS *Indianapolis*. It was components of an atomic bomb, which was dropped on Japan to end the war. We all received a Purple Heart.

I returned to the United States aboard the USS *Hollandia,* and we landed at San Diego, California. We had a ticker tape parade downtown. I returned to Chicago, Illinois, where I had duty at Navy Pier until my honorable discharge on December 3, 1945 at Great Lakes naval training base, Illinois.

For the next ten years, my wife and I lived in Elmhurst, Illinois where we had our three children. In February 1955, we moved to Mobile, Alabama, where we still live. During the last several years, I have been privileged and honored to speak to thousands of boys and girls in middle schools and high schools across the nation. I went to Sacramento, California in April of 2002 to speak to eight large classes of history students to tell my story. I have also been speaking to many organizations and churches in my area, as well as four major television networks. Many articles and columns have appeared in the local newspaper. I am so very thankful to be able to speak. I have told my story to my three children, six grandchildren and eight great-grandsons.

I believe history is important, and as I speak to the boys and girls they seem to be very interested in what I have to say. They have expressed their feelings and thoughts about what I have to say in their letters to me, and that is very rewarding. They call me a hero, but the real heroes were those who died at sea.

NAME   BENTON, CLARENCE U. CFCP
STREET
CITY
STATE
PHONE
ENTERED SERVICE FROM   Seattle, Washington
PICKED UP BY   USS *Bassett*
DIVISION
DOB   9/16/16   Deceased 82

FAMILY
Widow: Neota
Children: Constance Benton, Patricia Benton
Grandchildren: One

EXPERIENCE
Excerpted from the *Los Angeles Times* dated Friday, July 29, 1955:
"Clarence U. Benton, 38, remembers the sinking well. Benton, a civil and
electrical engineer, related the story from his desk in the Los Angeles City Hall,
where he has been serving as deputy director of civil defense. He was chief fire
controlman on the USS *Indianapolis* and now lives in Reseda with his wife, Neota,
and two children, Constance, 7, and Patricia, 5.

"I reached the boat deck aft," he began quietly. "The ship had already heeled
over 40 degrees. There was that ominous groaning and grating of metal, which is
the death rattle of a ship breaking up. We had no communication with the bridge.
Shells from our deck guns were bouncing around the deck like tenpins. Their fuses
were set and I kept expecting one to go off. We kept tossing them overboard until
I knew the ship was doomed. I ordered the men around me to abandon ship."

The endless ordeal in the water had commenced, where as the days passed,
several hundred more would die of burns, shock, thirst and exposure. Others in
their madness would shed life jackets to slip underwater, searching for an imaginary
island where beautiful native girls waited with cooling drinks.

Today, Clarence Benton is a man dedicated to his role in the nation's civil
defense program. For his heroism in caring for wounded men in the water, and
calming others about him, he was awarded the Navy and Marine Corps Medal.

In his present job, he has been responsible for the design and installation of the
communication system used by civil defense in this area.

He feels that had the USS *Indianapolis* been readied for sea with all life rafts
properly equipped, there would have been more survivors, just as alert civil defense
program would save countless lives, should we be subjected to a surprise attack
similar to the one which sank the USS *Indianapolis*.

NAME   BERNACIL, CONCEPCION P. FC3
STREET   256 School St
CITY   Livermore
STATE   CA 94550
PHONE   925 447 1670
ENTERED SERVICE FROM   Oakland, CA
PICKED UP BY   USS *Bassett*
DIVISION   Fox Division
DOB   12/14/

FAMILY

Spouse: Leola Gurie Bernacil "Lee"
Children: Janet Bernacil Bearson (Glenn), Art Bernacil (Marcia), Dan Bernacil (Michelle), Jeff Bernacil (Anita)
Grandchildren: Joe Bearson, Jeff Bearson, Michael Bernacil, Todd Bernacil, Daniel Bernacil, Devin Bernacil, Jeffrey Bernacil, Jason Bernacil

EXPERIENCE

I was born and raised in Santa Ilocos Sur (northern Luzon), Philippine Islands. My parents have passed on, but my three sisters and younger brother still live in the Philippine Islands. I am the second child and first son. During my teenage years, I emigrated to the United States to live with relatives and work in central California.

On July 11, 1942, I joined the U.S. Navy and I was honorably discharged on November 8, 1945 after three and one-half years in the military. I was sworn into the navy at the Federal Building in San Francisco and did boot camp at Camp Decatur in San Diego. After boot camp I was sent straight to fire control school at Newport, Rhode Island for 16 weeks of training.

My first ship was a destroyer, the USS *Ellis*, used for escorting convoys of American troop ships to the war in Europe. On the *Ellis*, I made two round trips to North Ireland and one to Algiers. In between convoy duty, the *Ellis* patrolled the Azores for German submarines. We also patrolled the Caribbean Islands off the coast of Florida.

On my last round trip from Europe, we docked at the Brooklyn navy yard where a notice awaited me to attend advanced fire control school at Washington, D.C. for 20 weeks. I went home on leave before reporting to D.C..

My relatives had moved from Salinas to Pleasanton, California, to work at Jackson 7 Perkins Rose Nurseries when I went home on leave the latter part of 1943. It was in Pleasanton that I first met Lee, and we became engaged in May 1944.

When my training at advanced fire control school was almost complete, the war in Europe was waning and appeared it would soon be coming to an end. I asked for and was granted a transfer to the Pacific. (Later, Lee told me I should have stayed in the Atlantic!) It was then that I was assigned to that famous USS *Indianapolis* and went aboard in November 1944. That was the same time that Captain Charles Butler McVay III boarded as our skipper.

On the *Indy*, I participated in the last two major battles of World War II, Iwo Jima and Okinawa. It was at Okinawa the *Indy* got hit by a kamikaze, killing nine men instantly. I experienced my first burials at sea. The ship's damage was so extensive it was ordered back to the San Francisco Bay area for repair at Mare Island. To keep me busy during that time, I was assigned temporary work at the Treasure Island Fleet Post Office.

While the ship was being repaired, it occurred to me to suggest to Lee that we should get married! She absolutely refused getting married before graduation from high school in June. I asked when it would take place; she said, "On June 15." I responded, "Okay then, how about June 16?" She said, "Do you realize how hard it is planning a wedding in such short time?" After all was said and done, the wedding took place on June 16...exactly one month before the USS *Indianapolis* sailed under the Golden Gate Bridge and into history!

On July 16, 1945, the *Indianapolis* was ready to return to the war zone. We pulled out of Mare Island that morning and made a short stop at Hunters Point to pick up cargo for delivery to Tinian Island in the South Pacific. A large, canvas-covered crate was hoisted onto the *Indy's* deck and bolted down securely on the hangar deck located about five feet from the ladder that I always took to climb up 20 feet to get to my 40-mm director. We shoved out of San Francisco, making a quick stop in Hawaii to refuel and pick up more supplies, then continued to Tinian Island in the South Pacific.

We arrived at the Tinian navy base on July 26, 1945 and anchored offshore where personnel boarded the *Indy* to remove the cargo and take it inland. Our next stop was at the Guam CINCPAC headquarters, where Captain McVay was to get his orders to take the *Indy* and his crew of 1,197 men to Leyte. It was at Guam where Captain McVay requested a destroyer escort to complete the last 1,300 miles of the trip to the war zone. The surface operations officer of the day, Captain Oliver Naquin, denied Captain McVay's request for an escort! Reasons given Captain McVay were that an escort was not necessary and that all battle-ready destroyers were at Leyte in preparation for the invasion of Japan.

The USS *Indianapolis* was Admiral Spruances' flagship of the Fifth Fleet in the Pacific theater of war, and although it was a very fast ship, it had NEVER traveled unescorted in the war zone, for it was not equipped to defend itself against submarines. In addition, four days before the *Indy* arrived at Tinian, an American ship had been torpedoed by a Japanese submarine and sunk on the same path the *Indy* would be taking to Leyte. That information was WITHHELD from Captain McVay.

The big question still remains: If Admiral Spruance had been scheduled to take the *Indianapolis* to Leyte himself, instead of Captain McVay, would the admiral have been denied a destroyer escort to take his flagship of the Fifth Fleet safely through the war zone?

Thus, the inevitable happened! Shortly after midnight on July 30, 1945, a Japanese submarine spotted the "unescorted" USS *Indianapolis* sailing alone in the wide-open Pacific like a "sitting duck" ready for the kill!!

That fatal night of July 30, 1945, I was scheduled to do the midnight watch, and I stopped at the galley for a cup of warm soup before heading up to my station to relieve the watch ten minutes before time, as was the custom. When I arrived, Ensign Blum, my spotting officer, was not yet there. I took the phone from the watch and told him to go down and get some sleep to be ready for the early morning gunnery practice we were to participate in at Leyte Gulf. He said, "Okay!" and left.

A few minutes later the *Indy* took its first hit. I tried contacting the sky control officer, the radio shack, and the captain of the anti-aircraft battery attached to my director, but I got no response. The ship's communication system was completely dead. Then I heard Ensign Blum climbing up the ladder to our station. When he arrived, I told him, "Ensign Blum, we got hit!" He didn't seem to believe me. I gave him the phone to contact the same stations I had called and he also got no response. I asked him to look at the second stack where flares were shooting out—then he believed.

The *Indy* then was hit by a second torpedo (the deadly one that hit like a direct shot to the heart), and the ship began to jerk violently and creak distressfully. It started listing on the starboard side, then began pointing down bow first. Ensign Blum panicked and suggested we jump off. I said, "No, Ensign Blum, the body of the ship is not yet under water; why don't we wait until the water reaches us, then we could jump off and swim like in a swimming pool." I'm glad Ensign Blum agreed. Had he not, I doubt we would have lived to tell the story. When the water reached us, we counted 1-2-3 and jumped off the ship, swimming as fast as we could to get away from the suction of the ship. I looked back only once and saw the *Indy's* fantail standing straight up! Our ship was as long as a football field, and it sank within 10-12 minutes.

Just to set the record straight, historian Dan Kurzman, who wrote *Fatal Voyage*, turned the tale completely around on page 85 of his first edition, making it appear I was the one who panicked and suggested we jump off the ship before it was safe to do so! (Shouldn't historians be factual about what they write?)

Ensign Blum and I eventually became separated in the water, but we wound up in the same large group that Dr. Lewis Haynes and Chaplain Thomas M. Conway were in. Dr. Haynes had a most difficult time treating injured men with the few medical supplies on hand. Father Conway worked very hard trying to console so many men in the water, praying with them and over them, until he was so exhausted he "gave up the spirit" on the third day. We couldn't understand why the navy did not search for us after the third day at least.

On the night the *Indy* sank, I was not wearing a life jacket when I went on duty. I did not take off my shoes when I jumped into the water. Soon my shoes were soaking wet and weighing me down. I had to remove them fast. My friend, Paul Murphy (another third class fire control man), saw me in the water without a life jacket and yelled out to me, "Bernie! What are you doing without a life jacket on? Here!" And he threw me one of two life jackets he had found floating in the water. I credit him for saving my life because I would not have lasted long without the life jacket he threw at me, which I wore the entire time in the water. "Thanks, buddy! You were one of my 'guardian angels', too." (Today, Paul Murphy is a four-term chairman of the USS Indianapolis Survivors Organization and a mighty good one, too!)

At about 3:00 in the afternoon of the fourth day, a plane flew over us and dropped down the message, "Hang on, you will be rescued in the middle of the night." An hour or so later, a B-17 bomber flew over us and dropped down a whaleboat by parachute. Many men, who were in the water on floating lines, began swimming toward the whaleboat.

Another friend of mine from our Fire Control Division was Douglas French (whom we called Frenchy). We found each other in the water on the first day and floated together on a floating line until that fourth day. When we saw the men on the floating lines swimming to the whaleboat, he said, "Come on, Bernie, let's go too!" I told him we couldn't make it because we were too exhausted, but he kept insisting. Then he took off swimming by himself to catch up with the other men. I don't know if any of the men ever reached the whaleboat because it was getting dark and we could not see them. Frenchy was never seen again. When we were rescued by the USS *Bassett*, he was not among us.

Two years after the war, Frenchy's wife wrote me, asking if I knew anything about her husband because she felt he may still have been alive on some island in the Pacific. It was so sad to tell her what I knew. In March of 1946, Frenchy's first child was born. Her name is Susan Douglas Harter, now from the state of Florida. As her mother had done 55 years before, Susan wrote a message on the *Indy* web site on the internet, requesting anyone who may have known her father on the *Indianapolis* when it was sunk in 1945 to please contact her by the email address listed on the *Indy* website. Just by chance, my wife Lee happened to read her message on the internet and told me about it. She thought the person inquiring might be the daughter of my friend, Frenchy, who was lost at sea. We contacted Susan, and she was overwhelmed to hear from someone who knew her father in the navy 55 years ago. Susan grew up to be a beautiful young lady, and she looks just like the father she never knew!

In the late morning hours of the fifth night, we were finally rescued by the USS *Bassett*. We will never forget the compassionate way the *Bassett* crew treated us. They placed each of the survivors on stretchers on the deck. They fed us warm liquids slowly to adjust our stomachs after having had nothing to eat or drink in four days and five nights. They washed us down with kerosene oil to remove the black crude oil that was on our bodies from head to toe. They even gave up their own clean, comfortable beds that we might get some much needed sleep for our weary bodies. They were true Samaritans to us. "Thanks, *Bassett* crew! We will never forget your kindness!"

It was not until we were at a base hospital at Samar, Philippine Islands, that we learned what we had delivered to Tinian Island on the *Indy* was a TOP-SECRET CARGO. It was the components of the atomic bomb that was dropped by the *Enola Gay* over Hiroshima, Japan, which led to the end of World War II in the Pacific.

After the war it was unfortunate that the navy chose to place the blame on Captain McVay for the loss of the *Indianapolis* and 880 men, plus the needless suffering caused to 317 survivors. Captain McVay was court-martialed in Washington D.C., even after Captain Hashimoto testified at the trial that he could have sunk the *Indianapolis* whether it had been zigzagging or not!

This is my story as a Purple Heart veteran and survivor of the USS *Indianapolis*. GOD BLESS AMERICA FOREVER AND EVER, AMEN!

CHAPTER 20   SURVIVOR BITONTI

NAME	BITONTI, LOUIS P. S1
STREET	27690 Jean Rd
CITY	Warren
STATE	MI 48093
PHONE	810 754 3633
ENTERED SERVICE FROM	Detroit, MI
PICKED UP BY	USS *Ringness*
DIVISION	5th Division
DOB	9/18/24

FAMILY

Spouse: Mary Bitonti (deceased)
Children: Phyllis Ann Bitonti Mercier, Louis Bitonti, Sam Bitonti (deceased), Andy Bitonti, Mark Bitonti
Grandchildren: Cristine Mercier, Chris Mercier, Erik Mercier, Mary Bitonti, Katie Bitonti, Andrew Bitonti, Mark Bitonti, Anthony Bitonti

EXPERIENCE

I was born in Star City, West Virginia, one of fourteen children. My father worked in the coal mines, and we lived in a small four-bedroom home in a mining community. We moved from West Virginia to Michigan in 1929 when two of my father's brothers lost their lives in a mine explosion in Monongah, West Virginia. Monongah is a small town between Clarksburg and Fairmont in the northern part of the state, not very far from Pennsylvania.

I entered the military because of my brother's involvement. One of my older brothers was drafted into the army in 1941. In 1942, two of my other brothers were drafted into the army. I thought I would join so as not to be left behind. I selected the navy over the army. Everyone thought I was too small to get in, but they were wrong. I was accepted into the navy.

After enlisting I was sent to Great Lakes naval base, Chicago, Illinois for my seven-week basic training. It wasn't as tough as I first thought. When basic training was over, I had a seven-day furlough then reported back to Great Lakes. I was then told to go to Camp Pleasanton in San Diego, California. That very night, I was to get liberty in San Diego, but the commanding officer canceled all liberty and shipped us to San Francisco. I went aboard the USS *Portland*, the sister ship of the USS *Indianapolis*. We then proceeded to Hawaii, where I immediately boarded the USS *Indianapolis*.

My first battle took place at Tarawa, within two weeks of being a new sailor. I didn't even have a permanent duty assignment yet–I was cleaning the smoke stacks.

Between 1943 and 1945, I was a crew member aboard the USS *Indianapolis* during eight of the ten battle stars she was awarded. They are: Bougainville, Aleutians, Gilbert Islands, Marshall Islands, Asiatic-Pacific, Marianas, Tinian, Western Caroline, Japanese Home Islands and Okinawa Gunto. (The only two I was not involved in were Bougainville and Aleutians).

In the summer of 1944 I did some work as catapult operator, but that did not last for a long time. I went back on the guns, and I manned my posts until the last possible moment, when the ship was rolling on her side. When in the water, we all watched our home fade away into the deep black ocean forever.

I am a survivor and proud American. I am blessed to meet with the other survivors at our reunions in Indianapolis, Indiana. They also floated in the waters that summer of 1945.

NAME	BLANTHORN, BRYAN S1
STREET	Box 77 Slash 1 Ranch
CITY	Grouse Creek
STATE	UT 84313
PHONE	435 747 7412
ENTERED SERVICE FROM	Grouse Creek, UT
PICKED UP BY	USS *Talbot* tr USS *Register*
DIVISION	5th Division
DOB	12/29/19

FAMILY

Spouse: Barbara (Bobbie)

Children: Patricia Blanthorn, Peggy Blanthorn, Dale Blanthorn, Paul Blanthorn, Bruce Blanthorn, Lloyd Blanthorn (deceased), Janet Blanthorn, Sammie Blanthorn, Corie Blanthorn

Grandchildren: 9 granddaughters, 17 grandsons

Great-Grandchildren: 6 great-granddaughters and 15 great-grandsons

Great Great-Grandchildren: One great-great-granddaughter

EXPERIENCE

Respectfully submitted by Survivor Blanthorn's family.

Bryan was born December 29, 1919, the son of George Blanthorn and Emma Lucas. While growing up he always wanted to be a cattle rancher. He attended school, grades 1 through 8, at Grouse Creek, Utah. At quite a young age he helped with the farm work, when it was all done by hand. Early to bed and early to rise was the motto. There was no electricity or TV. He remembers helping to raise a big garden, milk cows and do other chores on the farm. He went to school on the band wagon pulled by horses, sleigh riding in the winter and horseback riding in the summer time. His best friends were George Gellingham, Mervin Tanner, Grant Frost and Kendell Kimber. After Grouse Creek School, he attended Box Elder High School for one year and Logan High School for two years. Bryan married Afton Paskett on August 27, 1938. Their children were Patricia, Peggy, Leroy, Paul, Bruce and George. Bryan and Afton were later divorced.

On May 23, 1944, Bryan joined the navy as a selective volunteer and attended gunner school at the naval training center in San Diego, California. He was assigned to the USS *Indianapolis* in November 1944 with Captain Charles Butler McVay as commander of the ship. The first battle they saw action in was Iwo

Jima. Bryan was glad to be on the ship rather than going on the beaches with the marines and army. He said it looked like the whole island was on fire. Planes were dropping bombs and the ships were shooting shells. From there, the war front continued toward Japan. It was at Okinawa that the *Indianapolis* was hit by a suicide bomber. It did not take a direct hit. One wing of the plane had a bomb attached to it. The bomb went through one end of the mess hall, and Bryan was in the other end. As it went out the bottom of the ship it exploded. It caused considerable damage and caused the ship to list to one side. The damage was such that they had to return to San Francisco for repairs. When the repairs were completed, the *Indianapolis* was chosen to carry components for the atomic bomb from San Francisco to Tinian in the Marianas. Ten days and 5,000 miles later they delivered their cargo. From there they went to Guam for fuel, supplies, etc. Their next assignment was to report to the Gulf of Leyte for training, before joining the U.S. Fleet. While journeying there they were hit by enemy torpedoes and the ship sank.

The following is Bryan's account of that ordeal. Bryan, at age 82, is still mystified about why he survived the sinking of the USS *Indianapolis*. Out of a crew of 1,197, only 317 men lived to tell the horrifying story of bobbing in the shark–infested ocean for five days without food or fresh water. "I can't explain it," Bryan says softly. "And no one can. People from all walks of life survived." His wife, Barbara, offers an explanation, "He told his kids that getting back to them helped him survive."

Bryan had just finished his watch and was getting ready for bed when he heard the explosion of the torpedoes hitting the ship's ammunition magazine. It was 14 minutes past midnight. "I jumped back into my clothes and grabbed a new life jacket from near my bed," he recalls. "If I'd still been on watch I'd have had a small life jacket that just fit around my waist. They said the life jacket would only last 72 hours. We proved them wrong. They lasted 105 hours. That's how long I was in the water."

Bryan ran on deck to go to his battle station, but communications had been destroyed and the ship was burning. Within ten minutes of being hit, the *Indianapolis* rolled onto its side. "I scrambled onto the high side. I was right over the screws. Men were jumping into them. So I went forward and waited for a clear spot in the water. I was one of the last ones to jump into the ocean. I was not very far from the ship when it went down, but I do not remember feeling any suction. The sea was so rough. It seemed we were under water as much as we were on top during the night.

The next morning I was so ill from ingesting oil, fuel and salt water, I vomited all day. There was nothing there to come up, but I couldn't stop wretching. I thought I was going to die. My throat was so sore I couldn't swallow. That was good, because as days passed and the floating men became frantic with thirst, those who couldn't resist drinking the sea water died. "From what I saw, if they drank some salt water, within a few minutes they started to foam at the mouth, and then it was all over for them." Bryan knew from his childhood ranching experiences in Grouse Creek that he could work on the range all day without a drink of water and survive.

About 200 men floated together in his group. They had eight-foot square float nets with corks on the ropes to keep the nets afloat. "We put the wounded and burned on the nets," Bryan said. The first day they were certain rescue would come any minute. But instead of help, sharks arrived. For several nightmarish days, the sharks ate both living and dead. Bryan remembers he fell asleep, drifted away from his group and woke to see a shark swimming toward him. "I was raised out of the water," he says. "The shark went right underneath me. Then it turned around and came for me again. I was still raised out of the water. I believe in angels and God or whatever you want to call it," Bryan says. As the men floated hour after hour, we did a lot of talking and a lot of praying. After the third day, we were no longer lucid. We couldn't talk to each other. It's hard to remember.

Finally on the fourth day, an aircraft pilot and crew who were testing a new trailing antenna looked down and saw them. Rafts were dropped to the survivors. Seven men, including Bryan, shared one raft. "I don't think we could have survived without the raft," he said. A plastic sheet was included in the survival gear to collect water if it rained. Luckily it did rain and they had fresh water for the first time in four days. "We went into it like pigs," Bryan remembers.

Finally, as the fifth day began, ships arrived to pick them up. Of 200 men originally floating together in Bryan's group, only 17 were alive, but just barely. Bryan remembers seeing a ship maneuver near his raft. A man was getting ready to come down to help them aboard, but Bryan beat him to it. "With a surge of adrenaline, I went up that rope like a monkey. I hit the deck and stood up and looked around, then I folded up and collapsed."

He was showered and given water and put to bed. For ten days, intravenous fluids nourished him. He recuperated for a month in the hospital in Guam. "The saltwater sores took a long time to heal," he said.

He has only been able to speak openly about the event during the last few years. Tears well in his eyes when the memories from more than 57 years ago flood back vividly. He has been reluctant to talk about the sinking because what the survivors endured was so incredible he thought people would think he was making it up. It was just something you didn't want to talk about.

After his honorable discharge, Bryan returned to ranching at his native Grouse Creek, Utah. Later he worked as a state trapper for four years. Then he worked for J. R. Simplot Co's cattle ranches for 16 years. After 13 years as manager, he retired, but continued ranching for himself.

Bryan married Barbara Jane Archibald on April 24, 1961. They were sealed in the Temple on September 22, 1965. It was difficult for Bryan to even tell Barbara about his experience. Shortly before they were married, he gave her a book about the sinking, telling her, "Read this and you will know what's wrong with me." Bryan and Barbara have three children: Janet (stepdaughter), Sammie and Corie.

Today, Bryan can tell his story but feels frustrated he can't fully convey the experience.

CHAPTER 22　　　　　　　　　　　　　　　　　SURVIVOR BLUM

NAME	BLUM, DONALD J. ENS
STREET	35 Sheridan Rd
CITY	Scarsdale
STATE	NY 10583
PHONE	914 723 4423
ENTERED SERVICE FROM	Scarsdale, NY
PICKED UP BY	USS *Bassett*
DIVISION	Gunnery
DOB	4/16/24

FAMILY
Spouse: Sandra

EXPERIENCE
Almost 56 years ago, I was dumped into the Pacific Ocean in the middle of the night without a life jacket. More on that in a moment. This account is written for my descendants and any others who might be interested. Certainly the occurrence left an indelible scar on my memory and has affected my life whether I like it or not.

Years ago, I thought about writing my story but stopped when it started to bring back to me thoughts and memories of that time. I knew of no stories that had been published by survivors which seemed to me to be truthful. The few I had seen were about others or were made up and were promotional. I have not yet seen any stories that either depicted what happened or what the survivors thought and did during the four-plus days it took to pick us out of the water.

First, a short explanation of what led up to the incident. I had graduated during World War II from Stevens Institute of Technology (an engineering school) in October 1944. I had turned 20 that spring. I was one of the younger graduates, having been promoted through a year of my primary and secondary school years. I started at Stevens in the fall of 1941. School started early for us since there was a "get-acquainted" period on campus for several weeks before classes began in September. That summer I had worked as a machinist in a factory.

On December 7, 1941, the Japanese hit Pearl Harbor in a surprise attack. President Roosevelt declared war on Japan and also Germany, an ally of Japan at the time. The U.S. had been preparing for war in Germany, and some of my friends had joined the armed services. My brother Roger had graduated from MIT in the spring of 41 and was in the navy, having joined the NROTC in college. There was a local draft board, but since I had been under draft age at the time, I did not have to register. In 1942, however, it appeared that I would have to register for the draft when I turned 18 in April of that year. If the draft board called me up, I would have had little choice as to which service I was assigned.

Rather than take a chance, I decided to join the navy ahead of the draft since some of my engineering education—no matter how little—could be of some use. The navy put me in the inactive reserve since they really wanted me to stay in college and learn more about engineering. They called me to active duty in July of 1943 and sent me back to Stevens to a naval training program called V-12. Most of the college was turned into a training base. College professors taught the usual engineering courses, and a few naval people taught calisthenics, marching, ball playing and other programs. I was commodore of the college yacht club, and since this was a water-connected activity, I was encouraged to continue sailing and competing with other teams in sailing regattas and to teach others to sail.

College courses were compressed. I was rushed through without stopping, and we missed all the usual vacations. Christmas vacation in 1943 was only two days. Immediately after graduation in the fall of 1944, I was sent to midshipman's school at Columbia University—not to the engineering section, but to the deck officers school. I was trained then in navigation, damage control, some gunnery, and seamanship and recognition of foreign airplanes and ships. All courses were learned by rote. No thinking was allowed, except I was able to do some in navigation. After this training, I received a commission in the navy as ensign.

I then was assigned to gunnery school in Washington D.C. for two months of intensive memory course learning about new radar-assisted gun directors being installed on ships. These directors, when aimed by a person, would calculate lead angle required to fire a projectile at a moving object. It would correct for ships' speed and trim. Radar set in the range. Corrections for wind, target maneuvering, and other factors would be entered by the control officer if he saw that the tracers were not hitting the target. Ultimately that was to be my job. I graduated from this school at the end of May 1945. During my stay in Washington, President Roosevelt died and there were many formal ceremonies connected with Truman's taking over the office.

I then was ordered to go to California to the naval commandant in San Francisco for further transportation to the USS *Indianapolis*. I took the four-day train ride across the country. Although air service was available, it was only used by high-priority passengers during war time. I met on the train several other new ensigns and army lieutenants on similar orders, and we all were assigned to the last car on the train, the observation pullman car. It was a fun ride.

Reporting to the navy upon arrival in San Francisco, I was advised to take a local bus to Mare Island navy yard where the USS *Indianapolis* was undergoing repairs. The ship had been damaged in a kamikaze attack in the Pacific and was in dry dock. I reported aboard as I had been trained to do in midshipman's school and was told to go to the captain's office somewhere forward; a sailor would carry my sea bag and travel val pac. I had carried them for many miles. I was greeted by another new ensign in the corridor who said, "My name is Woolston. What is your date of rank?" When I told him March 8, he was crestfallen and walked away without so much as a "welcome aboard." Subsequently, I learned that I outranked him by a few days, and I learned rank meant everything on that ship. I checked in the office and found out I would be in the gunnery division.

I learned I would be staying in the navy yard bachelor officers' quarters across the other side of the navy yard. I checked in there, got a room, and returned to the ship next day. I went to the gunnery department and met the gunnery officer, who recommended I meet the captain. The captain spent at least one minute with me. On my way back to the gunnery officer (I hardly knew the way), I was accosted by a supply officer, Harvey Bernard, who told me I was to go to Seattle the next day to an ammunition handling school. He had a copy of my orders, since he had to provide me with transportation vouchers and directions. He also told me to look up his family there when I got a chance. Another ensign, John Howison, would go with me, as well as a few enlisted men. I have no idea how the enlisted men went there, but they were not in the sleeper section I was in during the overnight journey. I must say the scenery was magnificent.

We reported to the naval training base at the school and were told to go to a hotel in town for billeting. This turned out to be a nice setting. The enlisted men I learned traveled in coach and were billeted in dormitories on the base.

I did look up Harvey Bernard's parents who insisted that I come to the house for dinner. They were nice people and introduced me to others and I had a very good time.

I almost failed the course at ammunition handling school because I was so tired of memorizing with no letup, and I was having a good time elsewhere. When I got back to the *Indianapolis*, Harvey Bernard had been transferred. Subsequently though, Harvey got married in New York, where he knew no one. His mother suggested I be asked to be best man at his wedding, and I was. This was the second time I had met Harvey. As a coincidence, a few years later, Mrs. Bernard came through New York with a friend, Mrs. Lurie and daughter Elise, who was related to my wife Sandy. Small world.

When I returned to Mare Island and the *Indianapolis*, the ship was floating, and

I was told to move aboard. The next day we set out for a shakedown trip over one 24-hour period. The ship was a mess from all the yard work–yard work was even being finished while we shook down. We were told we would leave the next day for the Pacific. I had the watch that Saturday and could not leave or make liberty. We had returned from the shakedown to Hunters Point yard, but I never put my foot on land there. Sunday at noon I was relieved of duty but told not to go on liberty since we would be leaving the next morning, July 16, 1945. I saw a box delivered and welded to to our hangar deck. A lot of people were coming aboard whom I did not know–I knew almost no crew at that point. Among those who came aboard was a friend from Stevens who was there for transportation only. Another face I knew was a friend from Scarsdale, Tom Brophy, whom I had not seen aboard before. He was part of the crew and knew about as many as I.

On the morning of July 16, we left Hunters Point, headed for I knew not where...but I assumed it was the Pacific theater.

After we passed under the Golden Gate Bridge, there was an announcement over the PA system from the captain saying we were headed for Pearl Harbor and that we would be going at high speed. We were cautioned to stay away from the forward part of the main deck, because we could have waves coming over the bow. I had been told that on leaving the west coast, there often are large wave buildups that can wash over the bow. The "old hands" said this was not unusual. I did not know what was usual or unusual since I had never been at sea on a large ship before. We picked up speed, and I noticed the bow wave was constantly coming over the bow. I was told we were doing about 32 knots, which was fast for this ship, with 15 knots the usual speed.

I was assigned a watch station on sky control for the aiming of the 40-mm guns. There were six quad 40s–three on port and three on starboard. There were two directors, each one aimed electrically–the three quad 40s on port or starboard. Two officers were assigned to sky control at the same time. Each had a director pointer–a seaman to keep the target in his sights. The officer was to watch where the shells went and to set in corrections. That was my job on watch. On general quarters (when the ship is in full fighting condition), each of the six gun mounts was attached to its own director so that I would only be correcting for the fire of one set of quads. That director was located amidships but high up above the guns. It was possible to turn the director in such a manner that we could shoot ourselves. Luckily someone thought of that and the director trigger would become inoperative if the gun was aimed to hit part of the boat.

Standing watch lasted for two or four hours at a time. Watches were split up into four hours from midnight to 4:00 a.m. Then there were two two-hour dog watches until 8:00 a.m. for meals, then two four-hour watches and two dog watches, and then one four-hour watch until midnight. Every third watch was mine. There was little to do except talk to the director pointer next to me with whom I stood watch. My director pointer was from the Philippines and spoke only some English. It seems he had emigrated to the United States and joined the navy, after which the Japanese attacked and overran his homeland. He had not heard from his family for two years.

When off watch, we ate and also did some work writing reports or seeing that repair work was going on. Due to our high speed and vibration, bolts and screws on the after-gun mounts became loose and constantly had to be tightened. The gun crews–those who would load and get rid of empty shell casings–had to be trained so they could do their work in the dark. Those who were old salts said they had never experienced the vibration for so long.

As we approached Hawaii, a target-towing plane arrived and we practiced firing the guns at the target. At least I would see the guns fired. For this I was at my general quarters station. I wore ear muffs and still the noise was deafening. Then the 8-inch guns were fired at a towed surface target. I thought the front of our ship was coming off since the turret from which the guns protruded tipped way back and the deck under the muzzles formed waves in the deck. There was a lot of recoil, and I felt the whole ship jump sideways. My ears still ring from this.

Many of the crew, including officers, seemed to be seasick during the run to Honolulu. They did not show up for meals. We were rolling and pitching, but I thought this was normal. Anyway, I was told that it is not unusual for so many to become seasick. I was one of the few who was not. But with little regular sleep and a lot to do, I got quite tired. We arrived in Pearl Harbor after 72 hours at sea, which is still a speed record. I did not know it was that fast a trip. We went in directly to the fuel dock, and fuel lines were already on cranes ready to connect to our tanks. Later I was to learn that this was most unusual. Normally, I was told, we would have had to wait in line to get to the fuel dock and then our crew would have had to get the lines aboard.

I had made a date with Brophy to see Pearl Harbor, but we were told not to leave the ship. Normally, a short stay in Pearl was part of the fun. This was not to be. We pulled away from the dock and set out to sea again. My friend from Stevens had disembarked at the fuel dock for transportation elsewhere.

After leaving Pearl, we were told that we would be going a bit slower west to the Marianes. We now traveled at about 25 knots, and the ship quieted down. Water still came over the bow, but not quite so often or so much. We had more room in the wardroom, since most of the passenger officers had been left at Pearl.

There were two army officers wearing gunnery devices still aboard. Since I had had a course in ballistics at Stevens, I engaged them in small talk and wondered why they seemed to know so little about ballistics. I noted though that one of them was in his cabin most of the time. I also noted that when we had had two little fires aboard due to oily rags left by the yard, these two passengers were at the scene of the fires before most of our crew. They had learned their way around the ship very well.

Seven days after leaving Pearl, we approached Tinian in the Marianas. We had some target practice, then entered the harbor and anchored. I wondered what this island looked like, but again no one was allowed off. Along side came LCVP, a little tank landing craft, with several admirals and generals aboard. Our boatswain was ready to lower the big box off the hangar deck but was waved aside. What was wanted was the little box in the army passengers' stateroom–the guts of the atomic bomb. The "army passengers with the gunnery devices" I learned many days later, were physicists connected with the Manhattan project. They were never in the army, which explained their lack of ballistic knowledge. The large box was later removed on the second trip by the LCVP but without all the brass. It contained gun parts.

We then weighed anchor and went overnight to Guam. We were not allowed off the ship that night or the next when we loaded ammunition. I had to supervise some of the loading. When I saw that the wood slide that was being used to slide the ammo cans up onto deck from the lighter alongside was in need of a couple of nails, I went to get them and was about to hammer them in when I was notified from the bridge that officers did not do that sort of thing. I got a carpenter's mate for the job. Such was the way the navy did things. Of course, I had a steward to make my bed and clean our cabin every day. He also saw to it that my laundry got to the laundry and returned to my bureau with the fresh things at the bottom of the pile.

After we had ammunition aboard, we left Guam for Leyte for training purposes. With all the new personnel, including me, we did not yet know how to really fight the ship. I had never seen it done. My training in college did not prepare me for this. We cruised along at 15 knots. The vibrations had stopped, and it felt as if we were going very slowly, but this was the standard speed. I had one of the dog watches (4:00 – 6:00 p.m.) and was scheduled for the midnight to 4:00 a.m. watch. I napped after dinner and was late getting up for my watch. We were supposed to be on station 15 minutes before stated time. I woke at ten to midnight, rushed through the ward room where I made myself a sandwich and went up on deck to relieve one of my roommates on watch. My roommate headed back to the room for some sleep. The time was just before midnight.

While I was finishing my sandwich, there was a terrific explosion forward. I saw a flash of flames coming out of the forward stack. The ship lurched. All went quiet. Fans that always made a lot of noise were suddenly silent. I called on my sound-powered phones to the gun mount near the bridge to see if they could tell what was happening. I thought a boiler had exploded. Very shortly there was another explosion, and flames again came out the forward stack. I thought it was the second boiler in the boiler room. Then the cruiser, all 10,000 tons, started a turn to the left, and went down by the bow somewhat. I sent one of the director pointers for life jackets. He climbed down the ladder. My director pointer and the other ensign stayed on sky control. Via the sound–powered phones orders came from the bridge. We were told to load all guns and shoot at anything we saw in the water. The gun mounts reported they had no power and would aim the guns by hand.

Now the ship was listing to starboard rather noticeably. I thought one of the boiler rooms probably was flooded. We stayed on perhaps a 20-degree list while the ship kept moving forward in a circle. Then rather suddenly the ship went over to about 45 degrees, and I slipped and fell inside the protective shield around the director. I saw aft that one of the lifeboats attached to davits on the stern was being dragged under the water. I also told crew that were aft to abandon ship. My director pointer now was standing on the director itself asking if he should dive. "Now, Mr. Blum?" he asked. I said, "No, not yet. Wait until we are closer to the water." Shortly, I put my hand in the water from where we were standing watch which had been high up near the top of the second (after) stack, usually about 50 feet above the water. I said, "Now" to my director pointer and I followed. Water was at my level. The ship had turned over on its side. I had been on the low side. Subsequently, I learned that the other officer I had been with had walked down the high side of the ship to get into a life raft. He did not even get wet.

I remembered that the best thing to do when abandoning ship was to get away since there could be suction. I swam through the inky darkness as fast as I could–possibly 50 yards. I looked back to see the port propeller still turning, coming down on me. It was probably 25 feet away and above me. I immediately turned and swam as fast as I could. I was a motivated swimmer. I turned to look back when I came up for air and the ship was gone. Here I was! Alone in the ocean! Midnight, water warm–almost too warm, and I threw up the sandwich I had been eating.

I saw only blackness. I wondered if this was a dream and whether I would wake up to find this was not really happening. Of course it must be a dream! I wondered where my life jacket was and whether I would be reprimanded for not having it with me. All seemed so quiet. Of course it could not be happening. I knew how to swim and I don't think I panicked at the time. I smelled fuel oil around me but saw no flames. From water level, my field of vision did not seem great but I could not see much in the blackness of the ocean. It must be a dream. In about 15 minutes, I had arisen from my bunk, made a sandwich, proceeded to my watch station and relieved the prior watch, saw explosions (two), and now was swimming in darkness in the middle of the Pacific Ocean, ALONE. All was quiet. Now what?

Soon I heard someone nearby call me to join him and another man on a blow–up rubber life preserver–the kind one wears around the waist in the hopes that it will never be used. When inflated this preserver is about six inches in diameter and about three feet long - like a big sausage. I joined the two and held on, sometimes putting the end of it under my arm when I got tired of holding on with my hand. This was not so good, since it left less for the other two to cling to. I also slipped off it often because I was on the end. It had been lubricated with fuel oil.

We discussed whether an SOS had gone out. We wondered where we were. One said we were north of the Island of Yap, a Japanese-held island. Possibly it was 50 miles south. All three of us were tired by dawn. We knew that the navy would miss us and send rescue boats for us very soon. Slowly, I became aware this was not a dream or a practice situation. It was very real. I was awake and very uncomfortable. Most of the night had been spent shifting hands holding the "sausage" and in a way treading water. My arms were very tired.

When it got lighter at dawn, I spotted an unused Mae West–type life jacket floating near us, and I swam for it and put it on. Letting go of the "sausage" to swim a distance was a conscious decision after spending perhaps five or six hours just holding on a slippery tube. The ship had had two extra sets of jackets on board, and this one probably had just floated free. I went back to the other two still holding on the rubber preserver. We then spotted more life jackets and the other two each got one. The Mae Wests would hold us up without having to hold on. After a while spent discussing our predicament, we assured each other that help was on the way and we would certainly be picked up soon. The sun was coming up.

Perhaps about noon or later, we saw a group of men on some life rafts. We swam over to them. There were probably 100 men with four rafts. Slowly we picked up more men who had been alone or in smaller groups. By night there were about 150 men, most with life jackets, and some of them were in the rafts. Some in the rafts did not have jackets. The rafts were built to hold about ten standing in the center on a wood–slatted rope floor. I thought it might be nice if I could get on a raft and rest for a little while. I found out that those on the rafts were reluctant to give up any space. Several sailors tried by pushing to get on a raft. Perhaps they made it, but no one was giving up space without a fight. I decided not to try to get aboard and use up what little strength I had after almost a day in the water. We would be rescued very soon anyway. Someone started the Lord's Prayer. I did not really think it necessary because rescue was to be soon at hand. Besides, I really did not understand the need or the purpose. These sailors were making a wish together as if that would be better than independent wishes. I was wishing very hard myself.

There were some drogues of water among the rafts, one or two, and some cans of Spam. These were passed around. We soon learned that to get water out, you had to float the drogue and suck on the spigot while holding your breath under water. If we lifted the drogues up, we would go under water. Most of the water I got was salty. If I got more than two swallows I would be surprised. Among the 150 people there was not much to go around. I have not the slightest idea if these wood drogues or kegs were full to start.

I had tied myself to one of the rafts using one of the ropes along its side. I found that if I tied myself at the end of one of the ropes, I would be away from the people fighting for space on the rafts. Also, there seemed to be another officer with us, but I did not know him. I had been recognized as an officer but that did me no good because there was little I could do.   There was little any of us could do.

There were a few flares packed 12 to a container. I noted that for the space inside, more could have been contained therein. Someone unfamiliar with the need had decided a dozen would be enough, even though the container would hold 14.

At some point, I don't know when, a floater net appeared. This is an easier thing to hold to, but for support, the life jacket is needed. The body is submerged in the ocean. I found that one of the little cork floaters attached to the net was just enough buoyancy to keep my face above the water in case I went to sleep. After 24 hours in the water, I got sleepy and certainly I was tired. There were reports of rescue ships on the horizon but I could not see them. It was a wishful illusion. Several planes were observed or at least reported.

What was the conversation during this first day? We talked about when we would be picked up. The Lord's Prayer seemed to be said often during this time with some audible prayers for rescue and some cursing about the inconvenience. I really never knew all the words and now many were talking of heaven. This was an idea that did not register with me. If the Lord was to rescue us, why had He put us here?

We saw several planes fly over at very great height, I would guess at least two miles up. We could also hear them. We had several cans of flares and someone on the rafts fired some into the sky. They must have gone up fifty feet, and they came back down still illuminated. The fireball must have been in the air for five seconds. I wondered at the futility of it all. Anyway, I thought that the flares might be better used to attract ships or planes at night. Later it was brought to my attention that we were in the company of some menacing fins close by.

I had never seen sharks before, but I had seen pictures in a movie. I had heard lots of stories. This was to become a very real threat. I began to think I might be shark bait. It did not worry me so much when I could see that they were circling us at a distance—It was when they dove under us. We could see them swim under at very close range—maybe a few feet away. One of the sailors drifted away from the group, about 25 feet away. While I was watching, his head went under and I did not see it again. Made one wonder who was next. I felt that it was important to stay as a group. When the fins appeared, we would hit the water with cupped hands, hoping the noise would frighten the fish away. The day ended with many recitations of the Lord's Prayer. I was determined that as long as I could see others, I was okay.

The cans of Spam seemed to attract the sharks. I noted that a small piece accidentally dropped would attract a shark very quickly. It would not drop more than two or three feet below us when a shark would swim by to get it.

Night was very long. We had hoped that at least we would see airplanes looking for us. We knew, however, we would be overdue in Leyte on Tuesday and the navy would certainly be out looking for us.

When the ship went down, fuel oil floated up. We all were covered with oil, and no one was recognizable. During the night, someone came up to me, apparently having seen the officer devices on my shirt. He said he needed his money back. (He thought I was keeping some of his money as some sort of safe-keeping device.) He said he needed it now since he said he was going on liberty. I assured him I did not have any money, particularly his. I did not know who he was, and I thought he had mistaken my identity. All of a sudden he was on top of me pushing me under water. I decided he was delirious and got away from him and swam to the other side of the group. He followed me there but soon tired of the game. He started swimming away from the group, and I did not see him or at least recognize him again. He was a real threat to my life—worse than sharks.

After dark I heard reports of lights on the horizon. I was wishing, but I could not see them. Someone said he was thirsty and was going below for a drink from the scuttlebutt. Someone else said, "Don't go. The ship is not there. You are imagining things." It was impossible to talk a delirious person out of this type of idea. This pattern seemed to be happening more and more.

During the night, I got cold. This was a relief from some of the heat of the day, but I started to shiver. This seemed to keep me a little warmer. I kept thinking it would be nice to be home, and also, I wondered what was going on there. I had a sister in the army in Europe and a brother in the navy, and I wondered what they must be doing. What would they think of my being dropped off into the ocean. I remember my mother's victory garden, which I had helped plant that spring. I knew it had lots of tomatoes, more than could be consumed. One of them might be nice to eat.

Come to think of it, I had not eaten or had a drink of water for two days or so. I was passed a box of malted tablets. I tried one but it was covered with fuel oil. I spit it out. The tablets were in a large container—as I remember the top was big enough to get my whole hand in. Lots of oily wet hands had been in it before mine.

Amazingly, I still seemed to have some spit, and I did once in a while urinate. Perhaps some sea water was entering through my skin. How long would I survive without fresh water? I remember stories about sailors who drank sea water from the "Rhyme of the Ancient Mariner." "Water, water, everywhere but not a drop to drink."

There was talk of seeing lights and being picked up. Some of the planes that had flown over probably had reported seeing the oil slick and would radio this to the rest of the navy. Several people recited the Lord's Prayer again. I did not really think this would help, but I had nothing better to suggest. I thought that with a few leaving the group, I should help bring them back. I tried doing this for a few but it was only temporary. They would swim away again. At night it was difficult knowing who was swimming away. Bringing them back was a frustrating exercise. These people were delirious. I was tiring and everything became an effort.

The next day, not much was happening except more people were reporting seeing ships on the horizon or seeing smoke from a ship. It was disappointing looking at cloud patterns to determine what they were looking at. The sharks were circling our group. The look of their fins was not nice, but it was worse when they went under because then we could not tell where they were. I felt and saw one brush my leg. I think I must have pulled my legs up just in time. Anyway the shark lookout was getting anxious.

During the heat of the day, when the sun was almost overhead, the oil slick on the water sometimes became inches deep. Sometimes there would be little oil or very thin amounts. When it became thick (about one or two inches), it became very hot and would burn about my face. The life jacket I was wearing was rubbing against my skin and it was full of fuel oil. I would push away the oil, and water would take its place to cool my skin. Frequently the oil would be back in a few minutes. This was a constant annoyance during the wait.

Sleep was beginning to overtake me. I would nod off and then find myself with my face in the water and would get a snoot full. I would force myself to stay awake. Some sailors thought they would drink the sea water. This they were warned against, but thirst overcame them and they would drink and tell everyone how good it was. It was not long before those people disappeared. They went mad. They could not relate to where they were. There was nothing anyone could do to get them back, and they would swim off and disappear. Disappearing was not hard. Our field of vision was very limited—only to the next wave. We had some rolling waves, I would guess about 3 feet higher than the trough of a wave. Sight lines were only about 40-50 feet or so. Even when on top of the wave we could see only the top of the next wave. The water was rough, and we went up and down. Thinking of water to drink and tomatoes from home began to be an obsession with me.

Nights were very long, although it was summer, and days and nights were about the same length. Only the nights took forever. I am not sure whether I got any sleep for more than a few minutes or not. Since I had tied myself to the rafts and nets, I was not in danger of drifting off. I noted that some who disdained tying on did drift off. There was more talk of heaven and whether possibly we had arrived there. I had had little knowledge of an after world and no desire to visit or to find out if there really was one. Possibly it was because I had heard many of the different theories on the subject. Could this have been the River Styx? Where were the harps? I just decided that as long as I could see others, I was still okay. I really had no place to go, but I seemed to be the exception. It seemed some were looking forward to where they might be going.

On the afternoon of the third day, there were a lot fewer people around. Airplanes flew over and never saw us. The common thought that people in a group were more likely to be seen from above began to evaporate. There were fewer and fewer people around that were coherent. After listening to them, I was not always sure whether they were sane or not. I had to think several times before I realized they were hallucinating. But in their hallucinations, I began to think that I would enjoy what they were saying. It took a conscious effort to sort out what was real and what was not. I heard stories of what heaven was like; were we actually there? Was not the water good to drink? People seemed to drift off faster. That night, there became space on one of the rafts for me. For the first time, I had my shoulders somewhat out of the water. There was not enough room to sit on the edge of the raft, only to stand on some of the now broken wood and rope bottom. Anyway sitting on the edge of the raft made it sink and that was not very comfortable for anyone.

On the morning of the fourth day, there were even fewer of us. I counted forty people and four rafts. Then I decided that most of the forty were out of their minds. I rounded up ten who seemed to be sane enough and we took one raft and separated from the rest. It was getting too difficult to sort out the hallucinations and the real world. We separated the raft and at least got over the next wave. The excuse for leaving the pack was that we would sail to land somewhere. There was a sheet or tarpaulin and a paddle. For a while we held it up and pushed the raft away from the rest. It did not move well but it got us out of sight of the others. Was there safety in numbers? No way! We had separated ourselves from a group that was starting to fight over their hallucinations. It was a raw case of survival of the fittest.

When away from the larger group, we sane ones—at least we thought we were still thinking okay—made a deal that if any of us were to hallucinate we were to be shoved from our raft. Seeing or talking of imagined things could not be tolerated by us. That is why we had left the larger group.

Some of the wood pieces forming the dropped bottom were broken. At one point, one of the sailors bopped a shark swimming under us with a piece. I did not think this was a good idea. Sharks could fight better than we could. This scared me a lot. Fortunately the shark did go away. I think we were very lucky. These sharks were possibly eight or ten feet long and in the middle maybe 18 or 24 inches thick. They moved and could turn very quickly.

After some time, I got a sock on the jaw. I looked at the person who did it, and he said I should watch out what I was saying. Perhaps I was talking in my tired stupor. I remembered our deal, and believe me I was very sharp after that. I did not allow myself to think of sleep or even a short doze. It scared the hell out of me.

Whether being separated helped someone see us, we do not know. We were very glad to see a plane fly over us later that day, probably about noon. The same plane turned and came back over us and waggled its wing. At least we now knew someone missed us and maybe help would really be on its way.

Soon we saw what looked like a bomber fly over us. When it was directly over us we noted a whaleboat strapped to the bottom. It was dropped a ways away, and it floated down on parachutes to the water. The landing was over the horizon, which was not far away. I then listened for the sound of its engine, to no avail, because as I later learned it had no fuel aboard.

A few hours before sundown, another plane flew over. This time it dropped a package near our little group. It inflated to a rubber raft when it hit the water. It must have been 50 feet from us, but being downwind, it was drifting away steadily. I asked among our group who had the strength to swim for it. A marine said he could, and we saw him do it, and climb aboard. I asked that he row back, but he was unable to figure out how to row. We called out instructions which he did not follow. I decided enough was enough and I swam for it, only now it was not such a short swim. I got there but did not have the strength to get myself aboard. The marine helped me. I then assembled the oars, put them in the oarlocks and said to him, "Row." He said that he never had rowed and did not know how. I finally rowed back to the group. Rowing a rubber raft is not easy, even in the best of circumstances, and I did know how to row.

Eight of us got on the rubber raft built for two. The balsa raft that we had been on now had two on it, and they could lay out on the side. It had become somewhat water-logged and was not very buoyant. We found a few cans of water and some Charms candies on the rubber raft. We all shared the water very quickly, and I noted that no one cheated or took more than his fair share. I was somewhere near the middle of the pilot's raft athwart ships so that my legs were over one side and my head over the other. Some one was on top of me. The others were parallel across. In this position, I fell fast asleep–really passed out from exhaustion.

Some time later, maybe eight hours later, I was awakened by some excitement. It was dark. There was a little landing craft circling us. There was a large search light trained on us. The sun had been up when I had fallen asleep. When the motor boat was down light from us, I noted two sailors holding machine guns aimed at us. They were wondering who we were. Where did the Dodgers come from? By this time I had slipped back into the water. I did not want to be shot at. Someone must have given the right answer to the question, and the craft soon picked us up. Questions started right away. Where did we come from? They were surprised that we were from the cruiser USS *Indianapolis*. Someone helped me out of the water and onto the craft. Fifty years later, I got a letter from Peter Wren, the ensign who had pulled me out of the water. He had remembered me.

Shortly we were alongside a destroyer transport named USS *Bassett*. We came alongside near the stern, where there was a cargo net over the side. The idea was for us to climb up about ten feet to get aboard. I got the idea and climbed like a homesick angel, but I noted no others could or would try. They had to be lifted aboard in a litter basket. As soon as I landed on deck, a sailor from the *Bassett* asked that I accompany him to the bridge to talk to the captain. On the way, I saw the scuttlebutt and made a straight line for it. I drank and drank and drank.

The sailor got impatient with me and said we had to go right away to see the captain. I turned away to follow him but when I was about five feet away, I turned and went back for more water. I had had nothing much to drink for over four days.

A few minutes later I was on the bridge. From my memory this was now about 2:00 or 3:00 in the morning. The captain asked what ship I was from. He had not been told. How many others were in the water? I did not know.

I had known that there were about 30 or so in the group we had left but did not know where they might be. (They also were picked up by this rescuer.) The captain said that he would keep the lights on because he did not want to run over anyone. Radar apparently had picked us up, but would not show up a single person if alone. I saw no other lights anywhere although the radio between ships kept going. No other ship turned on its lights. Perhaps this is why the *Bassett* picked up half of the survivors. There were reported to be seven ships in the vicinity. As an aside, the ship had been named for Edgar Bassett, a Scarsdale flier who had been killed at the beginning of the war. I probably had met him. There were several Bassett families in Scarsdale. My sister Betty thinks she knew him. Roger says he did know him.

The captain offered me something to drink, and I asked for tomato juice. A steward was sent for it and after a delay of about ten minutes, he emerged with a bowl of hot soup. Just what I did not want. I threw it overboard and sent him for juice, which came quickly.

I then went down to the main deck and saw that a lot of the canvas bunks were occupied by some pretty oily sailors. Some had passed out, and some were sucking on orange slices. Some were being fed sips of water at the direction of a doctor who had come aboard. He had said that too much water suddenly would not be good. I did not tell him I had drunk my fill and then some. The men were being looked after very well, and I decided I could use some rest. I looked for a place to sleep and found one that was labeled Troop Officers' Quarters. I went in to find a well-ventilated space with soft mattresses and flaked out after removing my oily clothes.

I slept until at least 10 a.m. and went to the head. I had ulcerated sores on my shins and face. On the way back past chief's space, I was asked in for coffee. It was laced with alcohol and because I had not eaten for four days, it went to my head. I took a lay down until lunchtime. I then got up and was shown the shower room. I was given a pail of kerosene to wash with and some soap and a towel. After scrubbing with kerosene, soaping off, and then rinsing, I felt cleaner. A few wipes with the towel indicated otherwise, because by that time, my skin was very sore. Someone gave me skivvy shorts.

Somehow I had saved my wallet in which was a one-dollar bill. This is still in my possession in the little black box with the combination on the front, although the bill has decayed. A two-peso bill, the American money issued for the Philippines was signed by the crew of the airplane (now called a short snorter) that flew a few of us to Guam from Samar.

Lunch was in the ward room. I don't remember what was served, but I really had gotten out of the habit of eating. I was not very hungry as I remember, but I was really tired.

After lunch I went to look at the rescued who were still pretty much comatose. Some were being given liquids with a needle, some were bandaged, some were pretty passed out. All were covered with oil. I strayed out on deck into the sunshine and made small talk with some of the ship's crew. I learned we were going to Samar in the Philippines, but I had no idea where that was.

That night I went back to my quarters. A few of the others who had been rescued also found the room and had bunked down. I looked at my bunk of the night before, and oil was coming out from the bottom of the mattress. I chose an oil-free one. It was hot, and I sweat black oil from my skin. My face and shins were a complete mess of infections and pus and were very sore. My hair (I had some then) was matted flat to my skull. These were minor things compared to the other people, so I did not bother to have my injuries attended to. The doctor was very busy.

We arrived in the Philippines the next morning. I was on the first boatload going ashore and was escorted to a jeep for a ride to the hospital. I noted the driver was in a hurry, and every bump pained not only me in the front seat but the men behind who had no clothes on at all. Of course they had sores too. I ordered the driver to slow down and take it easy, which he did. He thought he was an ambulance driver, which in a way he was. He took us to a fly-screened, wood, one-story building with beds. This was the hospital.

Many of the other survivors were transported on stretchers. They were in poor shape. One who made it to the hospital died. This was really the first time my mind dwelled on the fact that I had been in a life-threatening situation, in particular a threat to mine. On the rafts at sea, I always took a positive attitude that I was okay as long as I could see others. Even though I knew others had left the raft, I did not dwell on whether they were alone, had joined another group elsewhere, or that they might have been eaten by sharks.

This attitude apparently helped me a lot. I knew I had no place to go so I stayed around. I kept thinking positively. Those who had another place to go seemed to be willing to give up and leave. I think that is why I survived while so many others did not. I also had been in pretty good physical condition when I went into the water, but so were most of the others.

One of the corpsmen at the hospital gave me a Red Cross survivor kit of toilet articles. A doctor gave me some stuff to put on my face to help with the infection. I put it on my shins too. I showered and a lot more oil came off. New sheets on the bed were made oily just as soon as I lay on them for a while. The same happened to others.

We were put on a "forced" liquid diet of all kinds of juice, which was very nice. However we were not allowed out of the building. Marine guards were there to see that we did not leave or talk to others about our experience or to any not in the medical corps. One exception–a priest came to talk to his boys and a minister to his. Two rabbis came to talk to me. Not really having had a previous occasion to talk to people of the cloth, I knew not what to say. Was there anything they could do for me? I thought a few minutes. One question, given that I had never seen anything of the Philippines, was whether they could get me a jeep to see the Island. They said that was possible but I would have to arrange to get out of the hospital myself. If I could, they would arrange it. I could not get out. The other thing I asked was for a party to celebrate our rescue. This they did arrange.

A few hours later there was a knock at our building's back door. In came two washtubs filled with ice. They were shoved under my bunk with the directions not to touch until the "guests" arrived. In a few minutes, several off-duty nurses arrived to help us celebrate. The tubs were filled with beer and soda. We partied. Of the survivors in Samar, five were officers. We shared the refreshments with the rest of the survivors but only a few could walk to our space.

My director pointer, Conception Bernacil from the Philippines, also was picked up by the *Bassett*. I only knew he had been rescued after I saw him in the hospital. After a couple of days, he said to me he was going to go AWOL and look for his family–his parents from whom he had not heard since the Islands were captured by the Japanese. I suggested he not go although I would see what little I could do for him. I told him I understood his feelings. I called the rabbis and they came down to talk with him. He gave them the names of his parents and his hometown, and they arranged with the Red Cross to look for his parents.

A day or two later the parents were located. I arranged that he get a month's leave to visit them, as well as transportation back to the States when leave was over and to draw some of his pay. He worked with the staff travel people to get to his island. Conception's leave would start when we were allowed to leave the hospital and when he was well enough to travel.

News came to us at the field hospital in the Philippines, that an especially powerful bomb had been dropped at Hiroshima, some kind of nuclear device. We did not understand what it was, nor did we associate this news with our trip to Tinian. I did know that there was a theory that a lot of energy was inside particles. This was associated with theory of disassociation of atoms and valences. A college professor at Stevens had been Irving Langmuir, who demonstrated that particles could disassociate. He had been at General Electric when I was in college, and my father had had him as an instructor.

For 25 years, I did not see or hear from Bernie, my director pointer. We met again at a reunion in Indianapolis, my first. He was thankful that I had arranged a leave for him and had gotten the Red Cross to find his parents. The way he showed his thanks was to hug me like I had never been hugged before. He literally took my breath away. He had become a farmer in California.

A few officers and men, those well enough to travel, were given orders to go to Guam for a court of inquiry to report what had happened. This group included me. The trip to Guam on a C-47 cargo plane was my first airplane ride. Other than for the pilot and copilot and navigator, there were no seats. We had been given a pair of cotton pants and shirt, shoes, and socks. The pants rolled up on the bottom, since there were no tailors. We sat on the cargo deck of the plane, and I had found a tarpaulin in the rear to sit on. After we were airborne, it became quite cold, and I began to wear the tarp. Someone got the bright idea to tell the pilot to fly lower, because we were all freezing (The pilot had heat in his cabin.) He did go lower, and we did not expire from the cold. As I looked out one of the windows at the endless water, I decided that getting to Guam in an airplane was better than the way we had gotten to the Philippines.

We arrived in Guam and were ferried to Base 18 Hospital, where we were assigned bunks in a large ward. I was in one of the beds near the center along with some officers whom I cannot remember. At the end of the ward were some men in rather poor shape. Most of these people were from the *Indy*, but they had been picked up by other ships and had arrived much earlier.

Walking around the hospital and going to the mess buiding for meals were encouraged. The meals were awful. Imagine reconstituted dried lima beans for breakfast! Hot coffee also was served with canned milk–this in the tropics. Lunches were salami sandwiches with bug juice. Dinners were frequently macaroni in glue, sometimes with liver or other expendable food. Although the patients got bad food, the staff did eat better. Vegetables such as squash, beets, peas and sauerkraut were canned. Not fresh, but that was not expected. Frozen did not exist.

The court of inquiry was rather bazaar to me. I was asked what the weather was at the time of attack–I did not remember. Had I seen any homosexual acts on any of the rafts while we waited? I did not know what they meant. Did any person on the rafts do anything wrong? I could not have recognized my best friend covered with oil. Did I have any suggestions for better survival gear? I sure had a few things to say about the water drogues and large economy malted tablet containers.

While in Guam, I received from home a care package which included some snacks like canned hot dogs. My mother thought I would need this nourishment since such items were in scarce supply at home. Luckily they came in handy when I visited a marine uniform supply building. I traded the can and some crackers for marine fatigue pants and a shirt and arranged to have the pants made into shorts and the sleeves cut off the shirt above the elbow. There were no officer clothes available, and I reasoned that I might as well have shorts to keep cool on this tropical island. The following day I was made mail officer. I was told to take the Jeep with some enlisted men to the mail building, and to handle the classified mail. Since I had a petty officer with me who knew the routine, I could leave the group at the appointed building and then drive off to find some of my friends on the island.

The story of our loss and rescue was the news of the day on Guam. I was invited to several ships for meals during the time my men were sorting mail. The meals were orders of magnitude better than hospital food. I also found some of my friends on other ships. One friend was on the USS *Portland*, a ship very much like the *Indy*. I surprised him in his stateroom. He thought I was a ghost, since he thought I had been lost. His name was Dick Hammer from I think Owatonna, Minnesota. Some day I will look him up again.

Returning with the jeep full one afternoon, I saw a friend with whom I graduated from Stevens standing guard at the hospital gate. He could not be an officer because he wore glasses or for some other silly reason. (In college, he had been an all-American lacrosse player.) Anyway, I greeted him as a long-lost friend, which he was. We arranged to meet later. I was advised that officers in the navy do not fraternize with the enlisted men–this one of my good friends.

One afternoon after picking up four men at the post office, I heard a siren ahead. Thinking there might be some action, I sped up to find a car with an admiral in it. Of course to catch it I had to have exceeded the speed limit, and to go faster than an admiral was a breach of etiquette. Of course it was noted I had destroyed an enlisted man's clothing by cutting off the sleeves and pants legs, and the worst infraction–I was out of uniform. (Of course, he did not advise where I could get a uniform or where I could get money to pay for it if I found one.) Also, there were too many people in the jeep. Probably the worst thing for Nimitz was that he had loaned the jeep for use by us survivors. It had CINCPAC Commander in Chief Pacific on the front, which meant I could go almost anywhere on the island without being questioned.

Two people came to Guam from Tinian to visit us survivors. These were the two "officers" who had accompanied the atomic bomb elements in their cabin. They were paying respects to the captain and the survivors. When they spotted me, they were happy to explain that they were physicists from Columbia University and not ordinance people. They had thought that I was about to blow their cover and tried to avoid me while aboard the *Indianapolis*. I did not imagine at all what they were up to. Even the captain had not been told what was in the radium carrying case in their stateroom.

On this subject there are several books and docudramas in our tape library. One "recent" book, *Abandon Ship,* was reissued with a supplement to the effect that Congress absolved the captain of the conviction of the court martial. Since the captain had committed suicide thirty-five years previous, it did him no good.

Shortly after Nimitz blamed me for all the wrong moves with the jeep, the captain removed me from the mail detail. I had been having a good time. Right after that, the well survivors were transferred to a remote area in Guam where there was a rest camp. My replacement on the mail run, also a junior ensign, hated the job since he now had to drive about 40 miles each way over rough roads. He also had a lot more sorting to do since some survivors were still in the hospital.

We had quonset huts, an officers' club, tennis courts if you could play with bare feet on an asphalt surface, a skeet range, horse shoes, etc. Drinks cost a dime each and included beer, coke, and scotch. Life became more normal, but a bit isolated. There were beach picnics where some enlisted men made a fire, cooked dinner, and served it at tables set up for us on the beach. The enlisted men got to eat while sitting on the sand. The food was okay at the rest camp.

A week of this rest camp living, and then V-J Day came. We were told we were going home. Three weeks later we were in San Diego after a ride on a "jeep" carrier. The war was over. Getting transportation home was up to us to arrange.

It took me four days to return to Scarsdale from San Diego. The plane I arranged to take first was canceled for two days because of icing conditions over the Rockies, and then I got the first one out only to be held in New Mexico for a night, then on to St. Louis, and then to New York. The airplane company put me up in a nice hotel and paid for my meals. They supplied a hostess to see that I was treated properly and paid for meals while I waited two days.

A condolence call on the Brophys was required since Tom had been lost. My parents and I knew them; they had been neighbors when they moved to Scarsdale. This was the tough part.

The Brophys wanted to know what had happened to their son and went to see the captain when he arrived in Washington, long before the rest of us survivors got back. He had flown from Guam. The Captain brushed the Brophys off, claiming an important meeting. They followed the captain by taxi to a cocktail party in the Shoreham Hotel. A few minutes later they were talking to Secretary of the Navy Forrestal, a personal friend. He arranged a conversation with President Truman and vowed they would "get" the ship chauffeur for this very unfeeling brush off. And get him they did. This can be read about in various books.

In a weak defense of the captain, I received many letters (more that 100) from relatives of non-survivors wanting to know what had happened and whether I had known whomever it was they lost. Since I had known very few officers and almost none of the men, I was not much help. I hated getting those letters. I felt so helpless. Should I have made up stories of what they wanted to hear? I still get inquiries to see if I can tell stories or something about lost fathers or grandfathers.

I had to call on the Brophys many times. They asked me about various investigations I had been to. I noted they seemed to know a lot of what had been talked about in the investigations. They had been given permission to inspect a lot of what seemed to me confidential information. I think the whole affair would have been covered up but for the Brophys.

A family friend, an ex-navy man and lawyer, visited me after I got home. He advised me to say little to any investigators and to forget most of what happened. He felt the navy was looking for a scapegoat, and he did not want it to be me. After watching the movie about the *Iowa* recently, and the explosion of a gun turret, I saw a demonstration of how the navy still operates.

At the court martial of the captain, I met the mother of one of the deceased. She asked me directly why I should be alive while her son was lost. I still do not have the answer to that question and certainly, none that I would have told her. I thought she was a southern Baptist, and I got the feeling it was also an anti-Semitic question but I will never know for sure.

The captain was convicted of "endangering the ship by not zigzagging." I had not cared for the captain, but this seemed to me at the time to be outrageous. To what purpose? Although the captain lived only about an hour's drive from home, I never went to see him after I got out of the navy. I never called any survivors that I knew lived locally, and they never called me.

After 25 years, I went to a reunion of survivors in Indianapolis. I recognized only two officers. The visit was somewhat of a downer. I really had not known anyone aboard ship; why should I want to revisit the scene? I had planned not to revisit, but someone called on the telephone from the survivors' committee saying mail to me had been returned, and they were calling all Blums in Westchester. (We had moved from Hartsdale to where we are now.) That made me think that I could go to put a period on the end of the affair. We did have dinner there with the pilot of the plane that spotted us. We also had dinner with a farmer, a sheet metal worker and a school bus driver and their wives. Sandy said when it was over that she infrequently had dinner with people like this. I recognized almost no one.

There were several widows and children of non-survivors there. They were looking for some kind of solace which I am afraid I could not give them. They must have suffered their losses more than I could imagine. When do people get to go on with their lives?

After 15 years more, Dan Kurzman, author of *Fatal Voyage*, asked me to go with him to the fortieth reunion. He had arranged to have dinner with the captain's two sons. We did go, but I really wondered why I went. Now 56 years later, we are all over 75. I will go again.

The captain's sons had tried to get the navy to rescind their father's conviction, but they were stonewalled. In 1998, Congress asked the navy to review the circumstances of the court martial. The navy reported back that it had reviewed the conviction, and found it to be proper.

Meanwhile, a twelve-year-old boy from Florida, Hunter Scott, won second prize for his class history project about the sinking of the *Indianapolis*. He brought it up to a senator from Florida, who introduced a bill to absolve the captain. After several influential people joined the fray, the bill was passed in the fall of 2000 and signed by President Clinton. Our survivors' organization helped, but the kid got done what no one else could.

In the meantime, how did the navy help us survivors regain our lost possessions? They gave us checks for what we said we lost as long as what was lost was required for our jobs. We lost only used uniforms and accessories so everything had to be depreciated. The enlisted men were issued a new sea bag of clothing. As an officer, I had to buy uniforms where they were sold at retail. Since I did need a pen to write reports, they paid for that. I really did not need a watch so I was not compensated for the one I lost, which had been given to me by my parents upon graduation from college. My class ring from college was also lost but not paid for. Although new shirts cost about 3 or 4 dollars then, the ones I lost were used and worth only about 50 cents in the second hand store. The navy gave me only what used shoes might be worth. The navy lost a multi-million dollar ship and they gave us back very few personal items. The non-survivors I think got nothing. Of course, the navy could not make up for the loss of 880 lives. That is what war is about.

I have been contacted by a number of people wanting information about the ship. Among them were The Discovery Channel; Dan Kurzman who wrote *Fatal Voyage*; Newcomb, who wrote *Abandon Ship;* and only recently (2001) The History Channel. Also I was contacted by Peter Wren, who picked me out of the water and wrote *We Were There* and *Those In Peril On the Sea* (both books are about the USS *Bassett,* the ship that rescued many of us).

I have given a number of talks about some of these experiences. It does not seem to get any easier. Recollection of what happened during the sinking and immediately after still bothers me. I think of all the lives lost and the callous attitude of the navy people particularly. One friend, a navy buff, still thinks that the captain got what he deserved and was very guilty of endangering the ship. He felt that way until more recently when he read some of the speeches given in Congress. Now he is confused.

Unanswered at this late time are questions about why the ship was not missed. I think twice as many men would have survived if there had been some effort to find us after the *Indy* did not show up in Leyte when scheduled. There are reports of SOS signals being received by several ships. Had we been rescued the morning after the sinking, probably 900 men could have survived. Was not this negligence worse than "endangering the ship?" Cruisers did not carry anti-submarine gear. Why was the decision made to not have an escort when the port director knew there had been submarine activity in the area we were to travel? These are questions that never will be answered. The people concerned, all senior officers then are not alive today.

I do not believe what was said by the navy about the "homosexual" sailor who reportedly blew up the *Iowa*. Battleships are obsolete, particularly those with the 16-inch guns with bagged ammunition. Rockets are faster, more accurate and pack a bigger wallop. The navy has been reluctant to give facts about the sinking of a Japanese fishing boat by a surfacing U.S. submarine. The captain of the sub is not to be court martialed because, I believe, the testimony would bring out a lot of facts the navy wants to keep to themselves. In contention now is a U.S. Navy spy airplane that was damaged in the air by a Chinese airplane in patrol of China's borders. Will we ever hear the truth?

A question I have asked some of the groups I talk to about the sinking is whether we should have dropped the atom bomb. The younger groups–those who had teachers too young to be around during World War II–generally say "no." Their teachers apparently want to rewrite history. Many of the teachers think that a soldier's or sailor's life is not worth as much as a civilian's life. Of course most of the service people were civilians in uniform. In my opinion, dropping the bomb was least costly in lives, both Japanese and American. Unfortunately the second bomb was neccesary to convince the Japanese government that we meant business.

A good friend, Henry Gruff, a former professor of history at Columbia University, was part of the secret army group that was breaking the Japanese radio codes. He said that after the first bomb was dropped, the emperor wanted to surrender for the welfare of his people. The head military officers objected and would not stop fighting. After the second bomb, the emperor ordered the military to surrender. The top military people thought by surrendering that they would lose face and wanted to fight to the last Japanese. The top Japanese military did subsequently commit suicide rather than give up. This Henry had learned early on, but only now–50 years after the surrender–is the information available.

December 2001

At the August 2001 reunion, I talked with Peter Wren from the USS *Bassett* which had a reunion at the same time. He told me that while he and two other LCVPs were out picking up survivors, the captain of the *Bassett* gave orders to vacate the area because he thought there was a submarine in the vicinity. He was to abandon the LCVPs. He gave orders to turn off the lights. Wren said at one point he lost the *Bassett* in the dark. I am told that the others on the ship "mutinied" and stopped the ship, turned on the lights, and continued the rescue. I hope to talk Wren into writing about this and to add it to the book he published about the rescue. We had noted that the name of the *Bassett,* which picked up about half of the survivors, did not appear on the memorial in Indianapolis while other ships were mentioned. This should be an important story.

I gave a talk to some of my Stevens buddies in Hoboken in October 2001. I could look out the window and see smoke rising out of the remains of the World Trade Center buildings. It was daunting.

NAME	BOOTH, SHERMAN C. S1
STREET	3122 So Holly St
CITY	Nampa
STATE	ID 83686
PHONE	208 468 0899
ENTERED SERVICE FROM	Avondale, AZ
PICKED UP BY	USS *Bassett*
DIVISION	5th Division
DOB	9/2/23

FAMILY
Spouse: Myrtle

EXPERIENCE
I entered the navy November 19, 1942 and was sent to Camp Decatur at San Diego, California for training (BWKS). After that, I was sent to Mare Island at San Francisco to board the USS *Indianapolis,* which was in port for heavy armor.

We left for the Aleutian Islands to bombard Kiska and one other island. It was almost continuous fog for nine months. We had to pull a spar behind us to alert the ship behind us that it was getting too close. One time during the nine months (the only time to see land) we pulled in at Attu. Most of our time was spent patrolling the Bering Sea with two other light cruisers.

I was standing watch on the port side when I spotted a torpedo wake coming straight toward the ship, and I froze—couldn't say a word! All I could do was point. Someone on the bow reported it in time for the ship to be turned toward the torpedo enough that the torpedo just glanced off. It pushed the side in about three feet, but it didn't go off until it sank.

After nine months in the Aleutians, we went back to San Francisco for more range finds and heavier armor and improvements to radar. After the repairs, which took about two weeks, we left for Pearl Harbor. From there we went to Terrawain Island to help in bombardment. A Japanese submarine went in as close to shore as possible and then went down to the bottom. When our marines went in for a landing, they were like sitting ducks for the sub. As soon as we figured out what was happening, the sub was blown out of the water. From there we went to the Marshall Islands to bombard. Everything went fairly normally, except two of our battle ships collided out in the open waters. One of them was cracked almost in half...someone wasn't paying attention!

I think Peleliu was next. We just by-passed Truck Island because there was only one way in...same way out. It would have cost too many lives to take it over, cut off their food supplies, and starve them into surrendering.

Then we went to the Marianas which consisted of Saipan, Titian and Guam. The first two islands went as expected, but Guam was something else. By that time propaganda was being spread so fast you didn't know whom to believe. The people were convinced that we would kill all the men and children and rape the women and then kill them. We made what we thought was a surprise attack and killed a lot of people at water's edge. After the marines landed, we pulled in to about five miles from shore and dropped anchor. The island had cliffs about 300 feet high, straight up from the edge of the water. After sitting at anchor for a while, we noticed movement in the cliffs through our binoculars. There was a cave about midway from top to bottom. The older men and women would bring their children to the entrance and push them off and then jump themselves.

We also found that the surprise attack that we had made was no surprise at all. I was told that the army had given two sots to approximately 1,200 people, told them to take them back to prison camp (12 miles away), and be back in 30 minutes. As they marched them out on the beach, we shot them down with our 40- and 20-mm weapons. They didn't have a chance. That was really sad to me. There were so many bodies floating in the water, even though we were five miles out to sea. We couldn't move without running into bodies.

From there we went to Iwo Jima. We patrolled one side of the island, and to our left there was an old, inactive volcano. There was a large section of flat land, just open space, no trees, and then I could see the hill or mountain where the marines placed the American flag. This volcano had tunnels dug into the side the navy couldn't hit with their ammo. We could shell two-thirds of the volcano but not the other one-third. (That one-third was where the tunnels were dug in the side of the volcano.) They also had guns mounted on tracks in the tunnels, and when our marines and army went ashore, they waited until they were close enough and then started firing. It was like they were shooting ducks on a pond. The army and marines lost a lot of people.

After Iwo Jima, we joined up with the task force and went to Japan. The weather was cloudy and foggy. We went in to within 30 miles of shore. Our planes would go out to approximately 50 miles then go above the clouds and go inland. We got by that way for about three days. Then they all hit the USS *Franklin* aircraft carrier. I think that was the worst damage that I had ever seen to one ship. The first two or three planes hit dead center. After that it was no problem as she was out of commission. One of our ships towed her for three days at 3 miles per hour. The first attack on Japan was so unexpected that their troops had been doing calisthenics.

From there we went back to Okinawa to help bombard the same. After a few days, we got hit by a kamikaze. It hit us near the port side near the rear gun turret. The body of the plane and one bomb went over the side. The other bomb went straight through the ship and out the bottom, hitting the drive shaft to the forward screw (prop). Immediately after we were hit, we went to what we called suicide harbor, which was off the southern tip of Okinawa (near where Ernie Pile the news reporter went down). We stayed there several days while the hole in the side was repaired temporarily. Somehow we managed to get back to Mare Island at San Francisco for major repairs.

We stayed there long enough for them to repair the damage and put the ship in tip-top shape. It took several days to bring aboard supplies. We couldn't help noticing that there was no rush to get any of it done, which was unusual. Typically they wanted supplies loaded "yesterday." After a day or so our work seemed to come to a crawl. Then just before we left a lot of white-collar people came with something we knew was important, because they were protected with all kinds of security. They brought something aboard, and they did not want us to know what it was. It raised our curiosity. Rumors were started as to what was in the box, placed in a hangar on the port side, with marine guards at both ends. The rumors were ridiculous, including one that it was toilet paper for General MacArthur. Then someone else would think of another rumor.

Anyway, we left and headed out to sea with some of the white-collar people who had escorted the box aboard. When we got to Pearl Harbor, some of them got off. The others stayed aboard until we got to Tinian, where the box was unloaded.

From Tinian, they told us we were headed to Guam and would get orders from there. When we left Guam our destination was Leyte in the Philippines. We had slowed our speed considerably. We knew the important cargo was off.

The weather was hot, and the ship didn't have refrigeration. When it got too hot for you to sleep, you could take a blanket and go topside. At approximately 16 knots, it was fairly cool. Topside is where I slept at night. We placed a blanket on the steel deck with our life jacket for a pillow. Several of my friends and I picked a spot by the forward smokestack two decks above the main deck. We didn't have far to go when they blew general quarters. Everyone tried to sleep at the same place every night so that the person you were to relieve on watch knew where to find you so you could take his place on watch. Watch in the navy is the same as "guard" in the army or marines.

On July 30, 1945, shortly after midnight, I heard an explosion and at the same time was thrown about 6 feet in the air. I came down with my blanket still over me. In fact, I came down tangled up in my blanket, while my best friend who had been sleeping just 4 feet away from me had come down on his feet. He ran straight into the fire that was caused when the first torpedo hit the aviation gasoline. The flames came up around the smokestack like a large welding torch. I heard him call for help one time and that was the end of him. I went in the air the second time and when I came down I rolled off the deck onto the next deck below. That knocked the flame off me. After everything had cleared, I went back up the ladder and saw about 40 people that had been burned. The flames had burned their clothes off and cooked them completely.

I went to the fantail of the ship and went below to the third deck, where my assigned sleeping quarters were. The lights were out on the starboard side. I went to the port side where the lights were still on, and there were four or five people there. I was shaken up so much that I sat down and leaned my back against a wall locker and lit a cigarette. I didn't get comfortable. Someone standing said, "I think I'll go topside. I think this thing is going down." When I sat down, the ship had been on an even keel, but when I stood up about two or three minutes later, it was listing to starboard about 15 to 20 degrees. I headed for topside myself and was followed by a kid we called "Halfhitch." By the time we got up the ladder and to the entrance of the mess hall, the ship was listing about 30 degrees. We had a space of about 40 feet with nothing to hold on to until we got to the ladder to topside. I ran slightly to the high side so that I could grab the rail on the ladder. At that time Halfhitch had grabbed hold of my feet so I hand walked the ladder, pulling both of us to topside. We managed to make it to the high side of the ship, as we were taught. I saw sailors jumping over and going into the screws, which were still turning. Doing this made hamburger out of them.

I went back to the bulkhead, and on the way the ship suddenly listed, which caused a piece of steel sheet (about 4 inches by 8 feet and 3/16-inch thick) to slip. It had been placed on the outside of a lifeboat to protect it from the blast, when they fired the 8-inch guns. Just before the metal fell, there were some poles, including a boat hook that caught Halfhitch's legs and caused him to fall. When he fell, the metal fell on him with such force that it cut off his head, which rolled to where he was looking at me. I saw that and figured it was time for me to get off.

I walked to the top of the wall and had to jump about 3 feet to the water. I didn't go underwater. I started to swim away, knowing that I had got off on the wrong side. The life line on port was turning down fast enough to catch me and take me under. I swam as fast as possible. I swam until it should have taken me under and looked back and saw that the ship was moving forward so fast that it was some distance from me. It had turned completely and was bottom up, sticking out of the water about 250 feet, going down slowly. I looked around at the situation I was in and got really scared. Just like that I had lost a home and had no neighbors to go to.

I found an empty container and pushed it up through the front of my life jacket, just high enough for me to lay my head on it. The reason for that was I was in the hot oil just about 4 inches below my nose and was getting sick. I laid my head on the container and tried to go to sleep. I got too sick to die and started vomiting. Later, a wave came along and washed my head off the container, which left my head in a position that when I vomited it went straight up. Occasionally a wave would come over my face and wash it off. After everything that could had come up, I began to feel a little better and somehow managed to get my head back on the container. I went to sleep until about sunup. I heard some people talking and I swam to where they were.

I have to tell you this so that you can understand the situation I was in. There were about 60 black men aboard ship, and in those days there was segregation in the worst way. These men took care of the officers as mess stewards, etc. When I was swimming to the group, not knowing what I looked like, I thought that I had got into the wrong group. When I swam closer, I found that they were some of my buddies and that I was just as black as they were. So I joined the group and strapped myself to them so that I couldn't drift away. I also found some people from my division—some from the compartment that I slept in! I asked one guy that I used to run around with when we were in San Francisco whether he had been hurt in the incident at midnight. He said, "No." I said, "Are you sure?" Again he said, "No." He said that he didn't think they got out an SOS, and he didn't see how they could find us in such a big ocean. I tried to get him to think of what he was going to do when this was over, but he said he couldn't. That was all he would talk about, and he talked about it to himself. He worried himself to death in three to four hours. That proved to me that the brain could only stand so much stress before snapping. That is nature's way of stopping the pain.

There weren't too many things happening the first day, with the exception of a lot of people who had been burned or injured. The explosion had run off all the sharks and fish. They didn't bother us until later that night, and then I think it was because of the blood in the water from the injured men.

The next morning was something else. There were sharks everywhere. I didn't see how anything could survive with so many sharks around. It reminded you of a bunch of minnows in a lake, feeding on a piece of bread.

When reading this, you would think getting sick the first time that part would be all over, but that isn't true. Every day when the sun got hot, you got sick again because the oil stayed with you. You couldn't vomit anything, so there was nothing but bile. I think that is worse.

The first day out, there was someone without a life jacket. I gave him the ammunition container that I had stuck through the front of my life jacket. That kept him afloat until we could find him a life jacket, which wasn't a very long time, because some of the ones who had been burned really badly began to die. When a man died, we would remove the life jacket, push him away from the group, and let his life jacket float on top of the water so it could dry. Then it could be used by someone whose life jacket was water-logged to the point it would not hold him up. When you pushed someone away that wasn't moving, he would last about a minute, because the sharks would hit the body...just like the minnows in the lake did to the bread. The sharks were like a bunch of vultures, waiting for someone to die or get tired and stop moving.

There were funny things also if you have a sense of humor. One of the larger guys was swimming around the group checking on how others were doing. All he had on was a life jacket and a pair of boxer shorts. He was talking and got careless and started to drift away from the group. He had drifted about 12 feet away when we saw a shark head toward him. He started to yell. He headed for the group, but the shark came so close that it took the whole seat of the shorts, and he had what looked like a knife cut across both cheeks. I had to laugh, but he didn't think it was very funny. When he made it to the group, he started pushing people under like bobbers until he got to the center where he stayed until we were picked up. I would somehow wind up at the edge of the group and would tease him by trying to get him to trade places with me. He would say, "To hell with you; I'm staying right where I am."

The sharks were continually checking to see if they could find someone dead or not moving. I don't think I saw them eat anyone who was moving. Once they hit a man though, he could move all he wanted and they would eat him anyway.

The second day started a little differently. People began to get thirsty–really thirsty. There were about 150 guys in our group, which had only one life raft. The water in the kegs had not been changed in so long that you couldn't drink it. If the raft had any food, I didn't know it. The men began to imagine things, like the ship being only 10 feet below us with plenty of water just for the taking. I don't know whether that was caused by thirst or by drinking salt water. I found by observation that anyone who got just a little water in his mouth would go crazy in about 15 minutes, and he was sure to die in about 45 minutes.

While you were trying to sleep, the sharks kept bumping the backs of your legs, and if you moved your legs apart, sometimes they would swim between them. You would try to see how high you could climb, but there was nowhere to go. You would kick or do anything you thought would do any good.

I noticed a really good friend of mine would go underwater occasionally and come back up immediately. I asked what was wrong and found that he had to stand or kneel on the straps of his life jacket. When he went to sleep, his feet would slip off the straps and he would go under. He was so short that when he sat in the life jacket, water would come over his face. I put his feet on the straps and he would sit on my lap and lay his head on my life jacket and sleep. He slept about five hours the first time–he was that tired. After that, I would let him sit in my lap until I got tired, then make him move, then let him back. Sometimes he would ask to get back. That went on until the fifth day, when we found a water-logged life jacket and put it on the straps of the first life jacket for him to sit on.

On the third day, a guy in our division who used to curse about every other word started praying the most beautiful prayer I have ever heard in my life. His prayer lasted three to four hours...then his brain snapped and that was all for him.

I sized up my situation and decided to swim to another group not too far away, because too many bad things were happening where I was. So I started to swim. I got about 60 or 70 feet, and all of a sudden I saw sharks in front of me, then 4 or 5 on each side, 2 or 3 behind, and 8 or 10 under me. I changed my mind really quick! I turned gradually, swimming at the same speed, and returned to my former spot. I decided that it wasn't such a bad spot after all, and I stayed there the rest of the time. That was also the day that I began to really get scared, because some of the larger guys were dying for some reason or another and I was so small in comparison. Also, most of them were in good physical condition, weighing 200 to 250 pounds and I only weighed 155 pounds.

At the end of the third day there were between 150 and 175 people in our group, but the next morning there were about 60. We had to sit there and listen to these guys describe all kinds of objects—islands, ships and boats nearby—of which they were hallucinating. We would try to wake up to see if anything was real, just to be disappointed again.

On the fourth day, a boy from Oklahoma saw the sharks eat his best friend. I suppose that was more than his brain could stand. He took his knife which was about 12 inches long, placed it in his mouth (like Tarzan did in the movies), and started chasing sharks. They would stay just far enough ahead of him that he couldn't touch them. He would go under for long periods at a time, making us wonder whether he would come up. I don't know how long this went on, but sooner or later, I noticed that he wasn't around. Every day there seemed to be more people drinking the salt water. Also, more being eaten by sharks.

It was about 10:00 a.m. that day that they found us. Lt. Chuck Gwinn spotted us in the water and flew over several times, dropping something each time to let us know that he saw us. That was the most beautiful plane that I had ever seen in my entire life. It still is a beautiful plane. It was a navy Ventura. Lt. Gwinn dropped rubber rafts and a boat, which most of the guys in our group were too weak to swim to or too weak to get in if they could swim that far.

During the first four days, when I had tried something, it had seemed to be wrong, so I was content to stay where I was. I had been safe so far. If one swam to a boat or raft and was too tired to climb or couldn't hold on and stay still, a shark would sample him, thinking he was dead. If a shark hit a person, the rest would join in and that was it. I'm sorry to say, but that was the way it was. After the first shark bit you, odds were it didn't matter whether you were dead or not, they would eat you anyway.

I saw the PBY that flew over and landed in the water. I also learned that you couldn't judge distance in the water. An object that would appear to be 50 yards away might actually be 250 yards away. Several of the guys would see the plane and think that it wasn't very far away. They would pull off their life jacket, start swimming toward the plane, but they were too weak to make it. That was the end of them.

Things like that—people being overcome by thirst, drinking the salt water, and hallucinating—finally got you to the point where you would ignore most of them and try to rest as much as possible. Things were happening so fast that I had trouble distinguishing the difference between facts and mirages.

I thought they would pick us up that day, not knowing or caring how, as long as they did. Thinking back, it would have been impossible; there were no ships in the vicinity at the time.

The next morning, our group was much smaller and things kept happening much faster. I was getting too tired to keep up, and I also was getting to a point that I didn't care. I finally began to wonder if they were going to pick us up. I didn't have enough information to sort things out in my mind.

Things got so bad that I didn't see the ships that came in. If I did, I thought it was a mirage and ignored it. They picked us up out of the water some time between 10:00 p.m. and 1:00 a.m. the next morning. The barge came up next to the group. Someone unfastened the straps that were holding us together. There were two large men on the side of the barge who picked us out of the water and dropped us in the barge like a sack of potatoes. We were too weak to stand. The USS *Bassett* picked me up.

When they got back to the ship, one or two tried to climb the ladder but couldn't. They put us in a stretcher and took us aboard one at a time. The first thing they gave me was a hot cup of soup. It was so good that I gulped it straight down and I heard someone yell, "Don't give them any more hot soup!" Not knowing what had happened, the next morning, I knew why—the hot soup had burned my throat and I could hardly swallow. At the same time, the guy asked me what I wanted to eat—anything I wanted, and if they didn't have it, they would try to get it.

Before the sinking, when we carryed supplies aboard, we would carry a few cases of Spam and cheese down to the compartment and hide them in wall lockers. When we couldn't eat what they served, we would go to the baker, who would give us all the bread that we could eat. We would go to the storage on top deck to get onions, and we would eat Spam, cheese, and onion sandwiches.

When he gave me a choice of what I would like to eat, I asked for a Spam sandwich, which was as good as cake and ice cream would have been to a child. He gave me the sandwich, but I couldn't take a bite of it. The guy began to cry, thinking that I had lockjaw. He called the doctor, who told him to give me some gum. I chewed the gum about 30 minutes, and that did the trick.

After we had had enough to eat, they decided to clean us up. They put us in a wheelchair and took us to the shower room, which had several showers. They used grease, oil, or anything to try to cut the oil. When they got down to the skin, and the skin began to come off, they would have to change to some kind of bath soap. I just laid there and enjoyed being cleaned up. They rolled me over every which way until I was clean.

When they got us back to bed, I think I slept until the next day. Every time one of us moved, they would be there to see if we needed something. They treated us like we were kings.

They took us to Samar in the Philippines to a hospital there. When we got to the hospital, they wouldn't let us talk to anyone except the staff, like doctors, nurses and Red Cross workers. Everything had to be kept secret. They kept us there for a week or so to get ready to fly us back to a submarine base on the south side of Guam Island.

On Guam, they wouldn't let anyone see us because we were so skinny. I weighed 155 pounds when we were sunk, but when they picked me up I weighed 129 pounds after I was cleaned up. I never dreamed of eating so good. We would go through the chow line for breakfast, and they would have eggs any way you wanted–pancakes, toast or whatever. They gave us bacon, sausage, or ham. The whole chow line was that way. When it came to noon meal, they would feed us the same as breakfast, and when we got to the table, they would have three pies and three gallons of ice cream. When one was empty, they would replace it with another. All we did was eat and sleep and play for one month. I gained back all the weight I had lost in one month. I think everyone else did the same.

They did everything they could for our benefit, some good and some not so good. For instance, they had a tank which they would fill with ice cubes and water. When someone ran a really high fever from the infection of the sores, it would take about five guys to put him in the tank. I didn't have to contend with that, because my fever stayed fairly normal. Thank God!!

They kept us at Guam until we had gained back most of our weight and most of our sores were healed. (All the survivors had sores from head down.) After they did what they wanted to with us, they put us on the USS *Hollandia* and sent us to San Diego, California.

It took somewhere between 12 and 15 days to make it to San Diego. The first weekend I was there I went to Long Beach, where I had a girlfriend. That would have been all right, except when I got back to San Diego and caught a taxi from there to camp, the taxi had a flat on the way and I was two minutes late. They restricted me for two weeks. After that I got to go home.

NAME	BRANDT, RUSSELL L. F2
STREET	
CITY	
STATE	
PHONE	
ENTERED SERVICE FROM	Clifton, IL
PICKED UP BY	USS *Bassett*
DIVISION	
DOB	Deceased 10/96

FAMILY

EXPERIENCE
Unable to contact any family members.

NAME	BRAY, HAROLD J. JR. S2
STREET	400 Vista Ct
CITY	Benicia
STATE	CA 94510
PHONE	707 745 5706
ENTERED SERVICE FROM	Ramsay, MI
PICKED UP BY	USS *Bassett*
DIVISION	Rodger Shipfitter Shop
DOB	6/15/27

FAMILY
Spouse: Stephanie J. Lopes Bray
Children: Harold J. Bray, Jr., Patricia Ann Bray Peterson, Deborah Bray Morris, Lindsay Axtman Hicks, Patricia J. (PJ) Axtman
Grandchildren: Scott Peterson, Terra Peterson Apman, Bobby Graham, Sarah Bray, Ryan Benjamin Bray
Great-Grandchildren: Jacob Peterson, Cassandra Peterson, Rico Graham, Anthony Graham, Gabriella Graham, Socorro Graham, Johnathan Gomez Bray, Justyna Bray

EXPERIENCE

This is an account of my service as I remember it. I was born and raised in a small mining town in northern Michigan, the Great U.P. The war started when I was about 14 years old, so I had to wait to get into it. I turned 17 in 1944 and I enlisted in the U.S. Navy. I left home for boot camp in Great Lakes, Illinois in January 1945 and ended up in a dental company. I had 16 weeks of boot training. Because I had had two years of ROTC in high school, I was made a squad leader (big deal). All that meant was that I got up to get up the others...no more volunteering for me!!

I left boot camp April 12, 1945 (the day President Roosevelt died) and went home on a nine-day boot leave. I returned to Great Lakes, caught a troop train, and ended up at Camp Stoneman, California to wait for assignment. While at Camp Stoneman, I volunteered for mess cook, because they ate first.

May 12, 1945 rolled around and assignments were posted. Eleven others from my boot company and I were assigned to the USS *Indianapolis*. She was under repair at Mare Island naval shipyard in Vallejo, California. She had taken a hit from a suicide bomb at Okinawa, but came all the way back to Vallejo under her own power after being patched up out there somewhere. When I first saw her, I could not imagine anything that big and that heavy being able to float.

The months and days that followed were spent training, firefighting, standing watches, and learning to drink navy coffee. While the ship was getting repaired, we lived in the barracks at the north end of the island and rode a train to the ship every day. During my stay at the yard, I was assigned to the repair division (Rodger Division).

The ship was looking good—new paint, some new guns. It was a very exciting time for this old country boy. Then we had sea trials. That was great! We then went back to the yard and repaired what was broken during the sea trials. Around July 14, all hell broke loose. The yardbirds took all of the equipment off our ship—in a big hurry!! On July 15 we were out of Mare Island and into Hunters Point in San Francisco.

Everything was very hush-hush and secret. A crate was loaded and put in the port hangar. There was a lot of speculation as to what was in it, but all of the guesses were later proven wrong. As soon as our secret cargo was loaded, we hit the high seas running at top speed for 32 knots. We were traveling so fast the ship was taking water over the fantail. We made it to Pearl Harbor in 73-74 hours, and we still today hold the speed record for that type of ship.

We unloaded some passengers at Pearl and proceeded to Tinian in the Marianas where this mystery cargo was unloaded. Then we were off to Guam where we loaded more stores and ammo because we were headed to the Philippines and then Japan. We left Guam on July 28 without an escort, which the skipper was told he did not need. Everything was going along nicely—training during the day, standing watches at night. It was pretty warm during the day and night, so the second night I decided to sleep topside. I took a blanket and my pillow and got under number one gun turret (8-inch gun). I felt pretty safe there with a nice cool breeze. There were sailors sleeping all over the decks and gun tubs.

It seemed as if I had just drifted off when I was awakened suddenly by the ship shaking. I don't remember hearing any explosion. I looked up from where I was sleeping and saw the number one stack on fire and appearently melting. My first thought was that a boiler blew. I reached for my shoes and saw them disappear over the side of number one gun turret. I thought that I had better get to my battle station; however, as I tried, the fire and smoke filled that passageway. I crossed the quarterdeck, which was crazy with wounded and screaming men. When I made my way back aft through the port hangar, someone was in the carpenter shop throwing out life jackets. I grabbed one and continued aft.

When I got to the fantail, I saw a sailor standing there badly wounded. I gave him my life jacket and went back and got another. When I got back to the fantail, that sailor was gone, but Frenchy was there. By that time the ship was listing badly and Frenchy kept saying, "You better go! She's going down!" but I was in denial. How could anything that big and beautiful sink? Well, when the mast was in the water, I figured it was time to go. (I don't know what happened to Frenchy, but much later at one of our reunions we got back together.)

I pulled myself up and climbed over the life line. By that time she was on her side and one of the screws was out of the water and still turning. I ran down the side of the ship until I got to the quarterdeck, and that is where I jumped off. It was still pretty far to the water. I hit the water and at about that time someone hit me and drove me down. It seemed like a long way, but I came back up and hit the surface swimming. I swam up to a sailor sitting on a rolled up crash net. We somehow got it unrolled and flattened out. As we were swimming away from the ship, I looked back in time to see the *Indy* stand on her bow and slowly disappear beneath the waves. Even as she was going down, there were sailors falling off her until she went under. A little while later there was an underwater explosion. We started to gather up survivors. A group came by with a raft, and we tied the crash net to it so we could stay together.

There was a lot of speculation and conversation about what had happened and how long it would take to find us. Everyone thought we would be picked up the next day or in a few hours. Well, none of that came to be true.

The first day in the water was pretty horrific for this first-time sailor. Sharks—I had not in my wildest dreams thought I would ever be that close to those creatures, but there they were! The men with bad wounds or burns did not last very long. During the day the sun was very hot, and at night it was very cold. After a while, the men developed saltwater sores and blisters and they would drink the salt water and get blisters inside their mouths and throats. We saw airplanes go over us everyday. We shot flares, but got no response from the air.

Around the third day some of the guys started to act and talk kind of strange, so I stayed to myself as much as I could. At night I would get up in the middle of the net, so if I did happen to fall asleep I wouldn't float away.

We lost a lot of good young men the first three days in the water. I think it was on the fourth day that I was hanging on the side of the net and this sailor came floating by–his mouth and tongue were just full of saltwater sores. I grabbed him and tied him as best I could to the net, but he got away during the night.

The next day the "angel" showed up. What a wonderful sight that was! He flew over, dipped his wings, made another pass, and dropped what I thought was a can of water. I proceeded to swim out to it. When I got there I found it was a sub detector or locator. After discovering that with great disappointment, I spotted another raft a short distance away and I swam to it. It had two men on it but it did not have a bottom. Well!! I got on it and watched the activity unfold. Pretty soon, more planes came and dropped more supplies. Then night came, and some time during the night the two guys that were on the raft with me disappeared. I don't know what happened to them. They might have gotten a rubber raft that one of the planes dropped.

Early the next morning this big spotlight lit up all around me and a voice said, "Hey, sailor! Can you climb aboard?" I said, "Hell, yes!" But I could not. One of those guys came over the side and gave me a boost into the nice dry Higgins boat. This boat was from the USS *Bassett*. They rescued over 150 of us that night–the most of any of the rescue ships. After a preliminary exam on board the *Bassett*, we were taken to a naval hospital in Samar, Philippines. After treatment and a few weeks of R&R, we were flown to a navy hospital on Guam and then to a submarine rest camp for more R&R.

We were shipped home on the USS *Hollandia*, an aircraft carrier. We arrived in San Diego, California and were issued new clothing and a 30-day survivor leave. After that, the navy let us choose where we wanted to be stationed. I chose Grosse Isle Naval Air Station just outside of Detroit. I was honorably discharged on August 6, 1946 at Great Lakes, Illinois.

CHAPTER 26   SURVIVOR BROWN

NAME	BROWN, EDWARD J. S1
STREET	P O Box 4225
CITY	Dana Point
STATE	CA 92629
PHONE	
ENTERED SERVICE FROM	Sioux Falls, SD
PICKED UP BY	PBY - USS *Doyle*
DIVISION	4th Division
DOB	10/16/25

FAMILY
Children: Five
Grandchildren: Nine

EXPERIENCE

In Sioux Falls, South Dakota on October 16, 1925, I was born during one of history's greatest Great Plains blizzards. Eighteen years later, to the day, Uncle Sam called me into the service of the U.S. Navy. In March of 1944, after a short six-week boot camp in Idaho, I was sent to San Francisco where I was assigned to the USS *Indianapolis* at Pier 14.

We sailed for Hawaii and saw the disaster of our battleships' remains in Pearl Harbor. All of a sudden I realized that I was no longer a young high school kid. As we sailed from Pearl Harbor past Diamond Head, our division officer told us that we were now in enemy territory on our way across the Pacific (some five thousand miles) to engage the enemy, the Imperial Japanese Navy.

We invaded Saipan, Guam, and Tinian and met the Japanese navy in the first battle of the Philippine Sea on June 19, which became known as the "Marianas Turkey Shoot." The Fifth Fleet shot down 402 enemy planes in that little skirmish. We were at Peleliu, Iwo Jima, and Okinawa, where we took a kamikaze hit. We then headed back to the States for an overhaul.

We picked up the atomic bomb "Little Boy" at Hunters Point in San Francisco and sailed to Tinian in a record ten days. We were a member of Commander Flynn's aviation crane crew. I lowered the bomb onto the awaiting barge and into the hands of the 509th Bomber Squadron. Therefore, the USS *Indianapolis* and the *Enola Gay* were the team that ended World War II.

My duty aboard the *Indy* was to man the 5-1/4-inch anti-aircraft gun number 7 on the starboard-side after-boat deck, which the Fourth Division manned. The marines manned two of these gun mounts as well. At one point during the "Turkey Shoot," my gun fired 57 rounds of 5-inch shells at one Japanese plane before we hit it just off the bow of Admiral Mitscher's carrier, which was steaming directly behind us during that air battle.

I often have been asked, as all of the survivors have, "What did you do all day and night while you were floating in the largest expanse of the world's greatest ocean a million miles from no where?" Day and night, night and day, we were freezing cold at night and boiling all day long. I remember one day when the ocean was really calm, I think it was the third day, I lowered my head sideways to look at the level of the water and it looked like a pane of glass. I did not do that too many times, because tilting my head sideways meant I was taking water into my mouth. The other times we were riding the swells up and down all day and the swells splashed the waves into our mouths at night when we tried to get a few minutes of shuteye.

One afternoon, I remember Danny Spencer, Dr. Haynes, and I were drifting along, and Danny said, "Hey, Big Ed, what are you thinking about?" and I looked at them and started to sing that ol' song of Bing Crosby's, "Give me land, lots of land, under starry skies above, don't fence me in...." They sang along with me for a few minutes, and it gave us a wee bit of relief for the moment.

At our first reunion in 1960, we chuckled about another humorus event. When the first life raft was dropped to us, Danny and a bunch of other guys scrambled aboard. Danny pulled out a fishing line from the survivor's kit and yelled out, "Stand by mates, I'm going to catch us a fish to eat." He was buck naked and goofy as a loon. There was no bait on his hook, and Doc and I damned near drowned laughing.

At the time another raft was dropped, and I started to swim after it. Soon I found out I was out of gas and I just quit swimming. It was at that moment that I heard the voice scream at me, "Grab the ring, grab the ring." I found the life ring in front of me, and I grabbed it. I was pulled aboard Captain Adrian Marks' PBY and I was a SURVIVOR!

I am very grateful to have been one of the survivors and am very grateful for all the love I have received from the families of the crew over the years, especially Danny Spencer's kids and my dear friend Jerry Rowden, who is my beloved adopted son.

I am retired from a career in sales and have met many wonderful people all over the United States, Canada, and Mexico. I have kept in touch with these friends over the years.

Occasionally, when I sit in silence, I toast some of my closest "buddies" whom I lived with aboard the *Indy*. I think about what great guys they were and how many laughs we had together aboard that Happy Warrior, the *Indy* Maru.

We were a happy crew, you know. We did win the war, didn't we!!

Survivors Ed Brown, Daniel Spencer, Louis Erwin. Reunion 1960.

NAME   BRUNDIDGE, ROBERT H.   S1
STREET
CITY
STATE
PHONE
ENTERED SERVICE FROM   Des Moines, IA
PICKED UP BY   USS *Ringness*
DIVISION
DOB   Deceased 94

FAMILY

EXPERIENCE

Respectfully submitted by Survivor Brundidge's son, Brian.

The following was written by my dad in 1947, as he remembered it.

May the memory of those men who did not see rescue never be forgotten. May the cause that they died for never be lost. It is the duty of we who lived to see that this will be done.

It was a typical summer night. Hot. Steamy hot and very humid. We were just a few degrees above the equator. It was impossible to sleep below deck, and my sleeping compartment was three decks below the main deck. I obtained a folding cot and set it up in the breezeway of the starboard hangar. I removed my clothing down to my undershorts. I had only been asleep a few minutes when I was suddenly awakened by a heavy explosion—a blast so strong that it threw the ship into the air and bounced the seaplane into the air and down on top of me. The wing strut hit me across the back with such force that the legs of my cot collapsed. I quickly put on my clothes and life jacket. I proceeded to the quarterdeck just forward of the hangar door where I had been asleep. The first thing I noticed was fire coming from the forward stack and from the hatch. Water was splashing onto the starboard side of the deck and bursting into steam as it hit the red hot steel.

There were several men that had been sleeping on the deck here. It seemed they could not move from the place they were sleeping. They were all just sitting up in place and screaming in intense pain. They were literally being cooked alive on the red-hot deck. This is the most horrible thing I will ever have to remember. It was totally dark, and the only voices were of the men screaming on the deck with the added voices of panic-stricken crew members wanting to be told what to do.

I went to my battle station on the port side of the ship. By this time the starboard list of the ship had slanted the deck so the five-inch mounts were no longer operational. I determined the list of the ship to be so much that it was only a matter of time before it would capsize. It was now time to abandon the ship. As I slowly made my way through the darkness I could hear the frenzied calls for help from the newer members of the crew. Most of these men had come aboard just as we left the States. They were not trained for emergency situations. Some were only 17 years old. After four short weeks of boot camp, they were sent aboard the USS *Indianapolis* to be trained at sea.

Now there were men shouting and begging for a life jacket. One man beside me was frantic in the search. "I can't swim!!" he shouted. "I don't have a life jacket!" I took my jacket off and gave it to him, as I could swim. I decided to go over the port side of the ship on the high side at that point. Just as I moved to grasp the life line, the ship suddenly rolled over on her starboard side.

One of the men I knew was beside me now, and we started to walk over the superstructure as a large piece of sheet metal slipped from its rack and struck him in the back of the neck, decapitating him. After this, I walked up the side and stepped into the dreaded, dark, and scary water. (Remember, the ship now lay on her side in the water.) Everything I owned while in the navy was on this ship. Now she would take all with her to the bottom of the ocean. My thoughts now were of one thing. SURVIVAL!!

I swam as fast as I could, as I remembered from training that the suction would pull anyone under. My back injury was now starting to pain me. I also reminded myself if there was fire on the water the swimmer must swim under. I found two water casks, but they were empty. However, they did float, and since I had given my life jacket away, I could use them as a life preserver until morning when I thought we would be rescued.

There were men all around me in the water. Some were yelling and screaming. From somewhere ahead of me I heard voices calling, "This way, we have a raft." I swam in the general direction and soon I felt someone pulling me aboard a life raft. As I was attempting to clear my eyes of diesel fuel, I looked in the direction of the ship just as the stern and propellers slipped beneath the sea.

As we awaited the coming of morning, I thought back on the events that led us to this place. Just 15 days ago we had been in San Francisco Bay, where we had loaded aboard one of the strangest things–it was a crate of unknown contents. Then came the speed run to Pearl Harbor and then to Tinian, where we unloaded the strange cargo and the guards that came with it. We still had no idea as to the crate's contents. And what had just happened? Did the ship explode on its own or was it hit by a Japanese submarine?

The coming of daylight allowed us to look about and attempt to assess the overall situation. We could no longer see or hear any other men. We were the only survivors known to us. Nineteen out of 1,197. I prayed this was not so. As a group, we decided to preserve the safety of the four rafts by cutting them apart. We had fairly strong life–saving equipment. It was decided to have in each raft one man that was a seasoned and trained sailor. I and some others had attended the survival school in the yards. I was assigned to the raft with the three other sailors and the marine. The marine had been on brig duty when we were hit and he had escaped with his .45 automatic. It could possibly be useful as a signal device in case we needed to draw attention. We divided the rations that were available. Each raft took one can of Spam, one bottle of malt tablets, and two packs of hardtack biscuits. Surely we would be rescued in a few hours.

I attempted to recall the names of my raft mates. I can remember that one man had a light complexion...maybe even red hair. He was from West Virginia and was becoming very sunburned. He had no shirt and his back was very red. I remembered to associate his name with "Payne." I never knew his first name. There was one man from the Carolinas. I believe he was from the Fifth Division...his name was Outland. The oldest, I believe, was a seaman from Detroit. His name was Gray. And then the marine. I don't remember his name or where he was from. I only remember that he was a cocky marine. A marine with a .45 automatic. Then there was me. A farm boy from Iowa, raised on the streets of Des Moines.

As time wore on, it became more apparent that we would not be found on this day, or the next day or the next. And so we survived hour to hour, day to day in the belief of rescue coming.

While not having been a deeply religious man, I must give credit to the power of prayer. We were five men from different parts of the United States and of different beliefs and religions. We constantly prayed to our God for rescue. I will always believe, firmly believe, the one reason that we were able to face this ordeal and, in time, to survive was the power of these prayers. Without God, we surely would have been lost.

We saw a search plane, but then it was gone. Later we heard the roar of a plane as it appeared over the near swells, flying close to the surface of the water. I noticed a dye marker and smoke bomb on the surface, and then I knew. We had been found. At long last we had been found. Suddenly there appeared from over the horizon the bow of a huge ship. It sure looked huge to me. On the bow was also the ship's numbers–APD 100. This, we found out later, was the USS *Ringness*. As we passed by the after-part of the ship a man on deck threw a heaving line toward us. It fell short of the raft and in my panic of being left, I grasped the ball of the line and held tight.

Our raft of five was the last rescue after naval enemy action–not only of the USS *Indianapolis* but of World War II. This makes me possibly the LAST MAN RESCUED ALIVE FROM THE SEA BECAUSE OF ENEMY ACTION DURING WORLD WAR II. My sea ordeal had lasted for more than 120 hours and now had come to an end aboard one of our own ships, a ship I will never forget. GOD BLESS ALL WHO RESCUED AND AIDED IN THE RESCUE OF OUR USS INDIANAPOLIS SURVIVORS.

NAME	BUCKETT, VICTOR R. Y2
STREET	2345 Longboat Dr
CITY	Naples
STATE	FL 34104
PHONE	239 643 0068
ENTERED SERVICE FROM	Rye, NY
PICKED UP BY	USS *Doyle*
DIVISION	NAN Navigation
DOB	4/10/22

FAMILY

Spouse: Dottie
Children: Bonnie Jean, William, Barry
Grandchildren: Kyle (U.S. Navy/USS *Nicholas*), Lucas, Trevor, Evie, Wesley

EXPERIENCE

Naval Service: September 1942 – February 1946
Awards: Purple Heart, American Theatre Ribbon, Asiatic Pacific Theatre Ribbon (9 Stars), Victory Medal, Good Conduct Medal, Navy Unit Citation Ribbon, and Combat Action Ribbon

I was born in Mamaroneck, New York, a suburb of New York City, the only child of Ethel Kennedy Buckett and Victor Buckett. I was part of a loving and very close family. It was with heavy hearts that my doting parents said good-bye when I enlisted in the navy on September 5, 1942. However, they understood, as my father had served in the U.S. Army during World War I.

After boot training at Great Lakes, Illinois, I was sent to Treasure Island in San Francisco. Within a short time, I was put on a merchant ship for my first sea voyage, ending up in Pearl Harbor, Hawaii. Within two months, I was assigned to the USS *Indianapolis* where I served until our fatal voyage.

While on board, an officer asked if I would like to be a quartermaster striker in the "N" Division. For a period of two years eight months, I remained in the "N" Division until our ship was sunk. Because I could type, I became a yeoman. My duties were the navy log and the war diary.

Every day the officer of the watch on the bridge would write down what had happened during his watch. At the end of each day I would get the log of the previous day and type the data. Afterwards, each officer would have to check what I had typed and sign off on the data. When all the officers had signed their watch, I would then have to go to the captain, who would check the log and sign it. I did this every day.

The war diary was more of the happenings of the ship, such as battles, bombardments and so on. It was sent out once a month with the log to the Navy Department in Washington, D.C.. I served in this capacity under three captains. Captain Charles McVay earned my greatest respect.

My time aboard ship was basically a happy time. I had many friends who would come to my office after hours, and we would talk or play cards. I would also spend time colorizing black and white portraits of their families or girlfriends. Other times, we would go to the movies in the hangar. I also sang with a little band that was formed aboard ship. Of course, there was always the gedunk stand and great ice cream to eat.

After I came aboard ship we headed for the Aleutians and were involved in the ATTU operations. That was cold territory, and we were up there for a long time. We were up there so long that we actually ran out of food. We finally left the north and headed for the Pacific where we participated in eight more battles. We saw action in the Gilberts-Marshalls campaign, the Marianas, Iwo Jima, and Okinawa. Our ship bombed nearly every enemy stronghold in the Pacific.

In March 1945 while fighting in Okinawa, a suicide plane hit us and damaged the ship, killing nine of the crew and injuring 26. A gaping hole was cut into the ship from the main deck, through the mess hall and into the hull. We also lost one propeller. Most of the guys who were killed or injured were having breakfast. I was just heading there when the ship was hit. Sadly, I was in the party that took our men to the island for burial.

The ship was sent back to Mare Island in California to be repaired. It was there that we were assigned to carry the components of the atomic bomb, guarded day and night in our hangar by marines. By July 1945, the ship was ready to go again.

The *Indy* took off on a speed run for Tinian. After our cargo was unloaded in Tinian, we headed to Guam for orders, which sent us heading to Leyte in the Philippines to pick up Admiral Spruance and his staff. Unfortunately, we never made it because we were torpedoed and sunk by a Japanese submarine and that is where our horrors began.

My office at this time was in the catapult tower. I would put a mattress down and sleep on the desk. When the ship was hit, the explosion knocked me off my desk. I got up, got dressed, and went down to the quarterdeck, where there was a great deal of confusion. No one knew what had happened but the ship was starting to list. Commander Lipski was on the quarterdeck, burned very badly, but he was telling the men to get their life jackets on and prepare to abandon ship. I helped pass out some life jackets when the commander told me to get one for myself. I went to get my jacket and also tried to look for my buddy, Ed Alvey, who had his office in the tower. I couldn't find him and hoped he was okay. I was very concerned for him because just before we sailed from San Francisco he was married, and I was his best man. He never made it.

When I got back to the quarterdeck, the ship had already rolled over on its side. Commander Lipski gave the order to abandon ship, and I walked down the side of the ship and jumped into the water. Knowing that the suction of the ship could pull you under, I swam out as far as I could. Someone yelled, "There she goes!" as the *Indy* stood straight up and disappeared.

When the ship went down, it caused a huge wave that covered us all with diesel oil. Having swallowed a lot of diesel oil and looking like Ole Black Joe, we were all out in the ocean on our own. Someone asked me if I had a life jacket. I said, "Yes, but it is a Mae West and I don't have it blown up yet!" He was wearing a kapok jacket and said, "Blow your jacket up." I did and from that time on all I did was lay across it. Only once did I have to add air to it, but that was no easy task—I couldn't turn the valve with my hands as they were so water-logged that my skin came off. I had to open the valve with my teeth. I was in what was probably the largest group of swimmers with Dr. Haynes.

On the first day, our hopes were high about being rescued. Weren't we expected in Leyte? Weren't we to have a plane come out with a sleeve for gunnery practice? We thought it would not be long. Little did we know no one was looking for us. We just vanished. To this day, I can't believe that an admiral with a staff of a hundred men did not question where his flagship was when it did not arrive. Too much was ignored and forgotten. Why did so many men have to die?

As days passed, many things became big problems. Every moment was painful. The thirst was incredible. I dreamt I was in a room full of watermelons. The salt water ate at your skin. The nights chilled you to the bone. The sun baked our diesel-caked faces. Hunger passed but thirst was always there. Some would start to drink the salt water and go mad or hallucinate. I don't know who it was, but one man thought the water down below was real cool and fresh. Down he went and I pulled him up a couple of times and told him not to do it again. That was the last time I saw him.

Then there were the circling sharks. They were everywhere! Luckily only once did one pass directly through my legs. If anyone drifted away from the group, that was it for him.

To be frank, I don't know how many of us made it. For me, maybe it was that I was fully clothed except for shoes. I even had my wallet with two two-dollar bills in it. I still have one of them. My other thought was that I was a good athlete in school and maybe that helped, but most of all, I had a strong determination to live and a strong belief in God. He was always with me.

The days were warm, and the water temperature was in the 80's with slight rolling swells. About the third day, because of the sun and salt water, I had temporary blindness. As time went on, it cleared up. Nights were bad because your body temperature dropped, causing chills. You didn't dare sleep for fear of going underwater by slipping off the life jacket. And of course at night, no one would ever spot you slipping under water. The sharks seemed to go away at night, maybe because you couldn't see them as well.

After four days, when we all thought there was no hope left, along came our "angel," Chuck Gwinn. When his plane flew overhead, everyone's hopes jumped sky-high. We knew someone finally had spotted us in the water and we might make it after all. Chuck radioed in that he saw men in the water. Adrian Marks, flying a PBY, landed his plane against regulations. Although many of the men were able to get aboard the plane, their weight was too much, and the plane could not take off. Finally, we knew help was on the way, but we didn't know how long it would take.

At one point I tried to get onto a raft that the planes had dropped, but someone pushed me off. When they did that I lost my life jacket, so I just held onto the raft. Somehow during the night, I managed to get aboard the raft and just passed out. The next thing I saw was a beam of light coming our way. It was the search lights directed up to the sky from the USS *Doyle* to let us know they were on their way.

The USS *Doyle* was my rescue ship, and as it pulled close to our raft, I made it up the ladder to the deck of the ship. When I reached the top I caved in. The men and officers on the *Doyle* were wonderful. The first thing I remember is that they gave us a spoonful of sugar water and then took us to the shower, as we still were covered with diesel oil. As I removed my pants, I noticed that my legs were raw where the flesh had rubbed off in the salt water. After offering us a shower, some new clothing, and oranges to eat, they gave us their bunks. I just slept for a while, and when I woke up I was close to the water fountain. I just drank and drank and drank.

We were taken to Peleliu and later transported to the hospital ship *Tranquility*, which took us to the hospital in Guam. While I was in the hospital, Captain McVay came to me and asked if I was well enough to work. At that point he assigned Otha Havins and me a jeep that we drove up into the hills of Guam to an office, where we worked on the records of the ship and the ship's crew. Little did we know at that time that some Japanese still were up in the hills of Guam. Every day we would see marines bring them out of their caves in the hills.

When the survivors were well enough to go home, they transported them by ship. However, I flew back from Guam with Captain McVay and Lt. McKissick. En route, the captain got off the plane in Hawaii, while Lt. McKissick got off in Olatha, Kansas, leaving me all by myself. The plane continued to Cleveland where it was grounded by fog. I decided to go into Cleveland to try to get home another way.

As I was walking, an MP stopped me and said, "Are you in the navy? If you are, you are out of uniform." At that point all I had on was a blue dungarees shirt, trousers, and seabee shoes. I told him I had been on the USS *Indianapolis,* and he immediately said to come with him to see what he could do. We went to the dispersing office, where they gave me money, chits for clothing, and a train ticket home. Having done all that, I made it home for a wonderful leave with my parents. Their joy was indescribable, as they didn't know what to expect.

After my leave, my orders were to report to the USS *Dauntless,* a flag ship in Washington, D.C. I thought, "Oh my God, I have to go to sea again!" It just so happened that I had to report there but was assigned to the U.S. Navy Bureau in Washington, D.C. It was there at the Navy Department that I had to work on all the records of the ship's crew.

Captain McVay was also at the Navy Department and would receive many letters from parents and wives of deceased crew members. Some letters were bad, but we answered most of them. Others wrote to ask if someone could come and talk to them about their loved ones. The captain asked me if I would go and visit with them and tell about the ship and what had happened. I said I would be glad to go and remember traveling to New Jersey and Pennsylvania visiting with parents, brothers, and sisters. Even though I may not have known their loved one, I told them all that I could to relieve their minds.

The trial of Captain McVay was a travesty. It should never have happened. The captain was a scapegoat for the navy. Over 700 ships were sunk during the war, and no captain was ever court martialed. Why Captain McVay? I was called to testify at the trial in Washington, D.C. I testified on the captain's behalf. An American sub captain and the Japanese sub captain testified zigzagging only helps a little. Such a waste of a good man!

Near the end of my enlistment, the navy offered to make me a chief yeoman, if I stayed on. But I wanted to go home, so I received my discharge on Valentine's Day, 1946 in Lido Beach, Long Island.

It was fortunate that I decided to leave the service because I met my wonderful wife, Dottie. We have three great children (Bonnie, Billy, and Barry) and five super grandchildren.

Over the years, we have missed only two reunions of the survivors and their families in Indianapolis and have had a great time at the two reunions in Colorado. The survivors share a bond like no other.

Dottie and I love to travel and have covered a lot of territory. We see our children and grandchildren often, and we love to play bridge and go boating (when the boat runs). I also continue to play golf and shuffleboard at least once per week. I still collect stamps (for 70 years), collect paperweights (I have 150 now), and still sing in the church musicals.

One of the most memorable times in my life was speaking to the fifth grade core group of children at Aiken Elementary School in South Carolina. They had been were studying about famous trials and came across the trial of Captain McVay and the sinking of the USS *Indianapolis*. They were so intrigued by the story that their teacher mentioned it to our daughter, who taught there. When Bonnie said I was a survivor and was coming to visit, they were so excited to think they would meet a "real hero." The school was decorated with welcomes, and they arranged television and newspaper coverage for the event. I was on stage from 9:30 a.m. until noon answering questions. Every one of those kids wrote me a letter that I have today and will always treasure. It was a wonderful day for me.

God bless Chuck Gwinn, Adrian Marks, and all the rescue ships that picked us up and–especially for me–the USS *Doyle*. They were wonderful!

All the survivors are great guys and I hope they all live to be 105 with me standing by their side.

Left, Lt. Kramer, center Worthington and right, Survivor Vic Buckett. Others unknown. A little band they had aboard ship, June 1943.

NAME	BULLARD, JOHN K. S1
STREET	
CITY	
STATE	
PHONE	
ENTERED SERVICE FROM	Chicago, IL
PICKED UP BY	USS *Doyle*
DIVISION	
DOB	2/20/26 Deceased 5/94

FAMILY
Widow: Shirley
Children: Five

EXPERIENCE

Respectfully submitted by the Anunti Family.
John was born February 20, 1926 in St Louis,
Missouri. He joined the navy on February 20, 1942
and went to boot camp at Great Lakes Training Station
in Illinois. John went aboard the USS *Mann* in the
European theater of operations and later went aboard the USS *Indianapolis* in the
Pacific theater of operations. While on the USS *Indianapolis,* he participated in
the invasions of two of her ten battles, Iwo Jima and Okinawa.

On March 18, 1946 he was honorably discharged and married his wife, Shirley,
in 1949. John retired and was living in Phoenix, Arizona at the time of his death
in 1994.

NAME	BUNAI, ROBERT P. SM1
STREET	4851 Washington
CITY	West Roxbury
STATE	MA 02132
PHONE	617 323 8661
ENTERED SERVICE FROM	West Roxbury MA
PICKED UP BY	USS *Doyle*
DIVISION	SM 1st Class
DOB	12/2/12

FAMILY
Spouse: Leila

EXPERIENCE

I joined the navy to see the world. Since we were too busy fighting a war, I didn't see the world.

Upon my retirement from the Bank of Boston, I joined an AARP group for a trip around the world in 49 days. We visited London, England; Frankfurt, Germany; Istanbul, Turkey; Zurich, Switzerland; Tel Aviv, Israel; Amman, Jordan; Cairo, Egypt; New Delhi, India; Kathardu, Nepal; Bangkok, Thailand; Singapore, Malaysia; Hong Kong, Mainland China; Tokyo, Japan; and Honolulu, Hawaii. When we arrived back to America, I kissed the ground. We are home where the American flags fly proudly.

CHAPTER 31

NAME	BURDORF, WILBERT J. COX
STREET	
CITY	
STATE	
PHONE	
ENTERED SERVICE FROM	Gibbon, MN
PICKED UP BY	USS *Bassett*
DIVISION	
DOB	Deceased

FAMILY

EXPERIENCE
Unable to contact any family members.

NAME	BURTON, CURTIS H. S1
STREET	
CITY	
STATE	
PHONE	
ENTERED SERVICE FROM	Kewanee, IL
PICKED UP BY	USS *Register*
DIVISION	
DOB	Deceased

FAMILY

EXPERIENCE

Unable to contact any family members.

CHAPTER 33 SURVIVOR CAMPBELL

NAME	CAMPBELL, HAMER E. Jr. GM3
STREET	
CITY	
STATE	
PHONE	
ENTERED SERVICE FROM	Wilmington, OH
PICKED UP BY	USS *Talbot* tr USS *Register*
DIVISION	
DOB	Deceased 3/71

FAMILY

EXPERIENCE

Unable to contact any family members.

NAME	CAMPBELL, LOUIS D. AOM3
STREET	
CITY	
STATE	
PHONE	
ENTERED SERVICE FROM	Richmond, CA
PICKED UP BY	USS *Doyle*
DIVISION	
DOB	11/24 Deceased 6/99

FAMILY

Widow: Barbara Livingston Campbell
Children: Kathy, Bruce, Michael, Patrick, Susan and Bonnie
Grandchildren: Kathy Had Deanna, Deanna Had Paul

EXPERIENCE

As remembered by Survivor Campbell's daughter, Bonnie.

My dad was born in Nebraska in November 1924. He came to Richmond, California as a teenager and made Richmond his home. He went into the navy, and he soon was on board the USS *Indianapolis* CA-35 as an aviation ordnance man.

He told me that he wanted to make the navy his career; however, that all changed when the *Indy* went down. Part of my dad went down with her. He was never the same, physically or mentally.

In 1948, he married Barbara Livingston. He had met her when he was in school, and they had eight children. I was the youngest. As I got a little older, I could hear screaming in the night. It was my dad! I did not know for many years why he was having bad dreams.

He told me one day that he had been on the USS *Indianapolis* and that she had been sunk, taking many crew members down with her. He hated himself for some of the things he did. He cried when he told me how he had to take life jackets off the sailors when they died. He never did get over that, and he never forgot the screams of his buddies.

I think we kids were the only kids on the block that could drink anything we wanted before going to bed. Dad always told us that we could have all the water we wanted.

As time went by, the ties between my mom and dad came to an end. I did not see my dad for quite some time—until I was out of high school. I had a drawing that I had done of the USS *Indianapolis*. When he came by years later to see us, I gave him that drawing. That was the last time I was to see him. In 1999, alcohol took him down.

I have attended several reunions. The USS Indianapolis Survivors Group makes me feel like family when I am with you. I will always keep you in my prayers. Again, thank you for asking me to complete "Chapter 34."

CHAPTER 35   SURVIVOR CARTER

NAME	CARTER, GROVER C. S1
STREET	
CITY	
STATE	
PHONE	
ENTERED SERVICE FROM	Rotan, TX
PICKED UP BY	USS *Bassett*
DIVISION	
DOB	Deceased

FAMILY

EXPERIENCE
Unable to contact any family members.

CHAPTER 36   SURVIVOR CARTER

NAME	CARTER, LINDSEY L. S2
STREET	23770 Vasser
CITY	Hazel Park
STATE	MI 48030
PHONE	313 398 1688
ENTERED SERVICE FROM	Pinonfork, KY
PICKED UP BY	USS *Doyle*
DIVISION	3rd Division
DOB	12/20/24

FAMILY

EXPERIENCE

I would like to tell you the story about my life on the USS *Indianapolis*. It started back in 1942, when I wanted to serve in the navy. I had my brother lie about my age, and he forged my parents' signatures on the forms. I was actually 16 years old at the time I joined the navy. On September 9, 1942 I went in, and in December 1945 I was honorably discharged.

My boot camp was at Green Bay, Illinois and on November 26, 1942 I was assigned to the USS *Indianapolis* as we left port on our first voyage to Alaska. On my 17th birthday we sank an enemy cargo ship. I got to see the fantail go under and it was exciting to have this moment on my birthday. My position at this time was the Third Division. My duties were in the shell deck for general quarters, 20-mm for AA, gun watch on the 40-mm and on the fantail with the marines. When we got back to Hawaii, I had the duty of number two lifeboat.

When we were in Hawaii, we were told not to stay the night, but I did anyhow. The next day I went before Captain McVay for a court-martial. He asked me, "Why?" All I could do was say, "I don't know." Being the good captain that he was, all I got was two weeks of hard labor scrubbing pots and pans.

We set sail to the Mariana Islands. I took Captain McVay and Admiral Spruance fishing. We had two sailors with us at the time. When we went to the Officers' Club, Captain McVay sent us a coke and something to eat. After we got back to the ship, Captain McVay asked the cook to fix up whatever we wanted to eat. The next morning we were hit by a suicide plane on the port side. Thankfully, I was asleep on the starboard side of the ship. The compartment was flooding fast. Unfortunately, we did have some causalities, and several men had to be buried at sea.

Another injured sailor died while we were in port and a priest, myself and two other men buried him on the island.

Then we got new orders to take a secret cargo to Tinian Island. That night after dropping off our cargo, I could not sleep in my bunk as it was so hot. I took my hammock, went up to the fantail, and tied my hammock from rail to rail. I had drifted off to sleep when suddenly I was thrown from my sleep onto the deck of the ship. There were loud explosions. When I got to my feet, I learned that we had been hit by one torpedo, and then another. I went where the lifeboats were and started to get them ready to put in the water. At that moment someone said to me, "We are not going to sink." I could see the propellers coming out of the water. There was no more time left! I had to get off the boat. I did not want to sink with her. As I jumped over the side, I yelled back, "If we don't sink, come back and pick me up."

After I went over the side, I swam about 50 feet and turned around to look at the ship. I saw some men still on the ship. The fantail came up and out of the water. Within minutes, the ship was gone. Here we were in the water! All of us were full of oil, some burned, others just in pain. The first day we all tried to get together in groups. At that time, a marine captain said he would shoot the first man who did not look straight into the sun for Japanese planes. The next day he was gone.

Other guys around us started to lose it and would dive into the sea, coming back up and telling us the *Indy* was there. They wanted us to go with them to get fresh orange juice and water. I actually started to follow with four others. Two had dived down when Dr. Haynes came to us and said there was no ship down there and for us to go back to the group. The other two never came back up.

I met a friend that had a rubber belt like mine. We stuck together, telling each other that we would make it and not to give up. We took turns, one sleeping while the other made sure he stayed awake. After three or four days, he looked at me and said, "I can't take this anymore." We started to pray, and that is when he gave me his life belt...then he went down. I tried, but I could not reach him. I gave his belt to another, hoping he would make it. I have tried to remember his name but just can't. I know with the good Lord's help, I will see him again.

I have never talked about this part of my life because it has hurt so much to think about this. This is the first time in my life I can tell you what happened that day. I do believe we all survived this tragedy by the grace of God. We who did survive will never forget our fallen brothers at sea and the ones still alive today.

CHAPTER 37   SURVIVOR CARTER

NAME	CARTER, LOYD G. COX
STREET	Unknown
CITY	
STATE	
PHONE	
ENTERED SERVICE FROM	Holdenville, OK
PICKED UP BY	USS *Bassett*
DIVISION	
DOB	

FAMILY

EXPERIENCE

Unable to contact any family members.

NAME	CARVER, GROVER C.
STREET	620 McClellan
CITY	Monterey
STATE	CA 93940
PHONE	831 373 4634
ENTERED SERVICE FROM	San Francisco, California
PICKED UP BY	USS *Bassett*
DIVISION	4th Division
DOB	3/9/24

FAMILY
Spouse: Bea
Children: Two daughters
Grandchildren: Five
Great-Grandchildren: Seven

EXPERIENCE

I was born in a rural farm house in Simpson, Louisiana into a family of twelve children. The farm was removed from civilization. I can remember seeing my first airplane...a biplane.

When I was in my teens, I was encouraged to enter the CCCs to learn through on-the-job training. It was a good program, much like job training of today. I traveled to and settled in Union Creek, Oregon. This is very close to Crater Lake and I was very impressed. I had quarters and meals and learned various skills. I also had time for recreation–I played in the snow. All this came with a small stipend. I liked the experience.

When I had some leave time, I ventured to Oakland, California to visit the family of my oldest brother, who had sea duty. I liked it there, so I stayed. I was about 17 years old at the time and was a waiter at the famous First and Last Chance, the place Jack London hung out and wrote some early works on the edge of the Estuary between Oakland and Alameda. I did not know at the time that I should have been 21. No one knew that I was so young and no one asked!!

I obtained work at Kaisers Shipyard in Richmond, California. While working one day, I mentioned to an elderly lady how I wished I could get a nice home-cooked country meal. "I know just the place," she replied and she showed me the way. The spunky old gal was my future wife Bea's great aunt. The place with good chow was at Bea's parent's Ranchito. They piled five rambunctious kids in my Chevy...3 were Bea's little cousins and my little niece and nephew. After that excursion, I was glad to return to work (I worked swing shifts).

Then one day it was time to report to the draft board. I thought employment could defer my being drafted, but that was not so. I recalled soldiers crawling around in mud, bitten by red bugs and mosquitoes, using helmets for shaving, and all those memories, so I hotfooted it over to the navy recruitment center. In a mere three days, I was in and went to Farragut, Idaho for boot camp. I did not mind boot camp and was soon assigned to the USS *Indianapolis*. We sailed to the Aleutians, and I remained on the ship through all subsequent campaigns.

While in the navy, I married my blushing, red-haired bride, Bea. The date was November 9, 1944 in Oakland. When we were in Mare Island from May through July 1945, we shared a quonset hut with Dan and Sis Spencer. We remained friends thereafter.

The USS *Indianapolis* was sunk July 30, 1945. I was part of the largest group in the water, and we were rescued by the USS *Bassett*. The greatest encouragement I received was from Chief Clarence U. Benton and one Bos'n Mate, Louie DeBernardi. They both survived but are now gone.

After many days and nights of waiting, Chuck Gwinn, our "angel," came from the heavens above to find us. We all went to a new hospital on Samar Island.

When I came home, I received the good news that Bea and I would be parents in April 1946. I separated from the navy, was in the Reserve, and did not have a set length of time to serve.

I built a structure we called home. During the process, Marius Teulliere, the Frenchman up the street, asked me if I would like a job. On January 1, 1946, I became an apprentice carpenter at Carmel's famous M.J. Murphy Construction Company. It became famous for building Coast Highway One from Carmel south to Hearst Castle. We also made pews for several early Californian missions. After forty years, I retired and was given a nice retirement party at the local Elks Lodge.

With the assistance of other survivors in the area and Chuck Gwinn, two mini-reunions were held in California. The first was held in San Diego and featured a floral drop from a helicopter off the beach in memory of those lost at sea. The second was at Vallejo and consisted of Napa Valley and San Francisco tours and a barbeque.

Bea and I also attended two mini-reunions in Colorado in 1998 and 2000. Activities included a tour at NORAD in Colorado Springs (now closed to the public), the Air Force Academy, cookouts at the Murphy's home in Estes Park, cookout brunches in Rocky Mountain National Park near Estes, Rockies' baseball games, Ocean Journey, Denver Mint, and complementary meals at the VFW Post 9565, American Legion Post 11-11, and Eagles Club as well as many other activities. The highlight was the dedication of a memorial to the USS *Indianapolis* near a small lake in the city park of Broomfield. The morning of July 30, 2000 started with a brunch at the Rundus Funeral Home, followed by a police escort of white limousines delivering survivors and families to this special occasion. Peter Wren, of the USS *Bassett*, was the guest speaker. His very emotional speech told of the horrible condition of the survivors when they were rescued after five days in the water. (Peter Wren is the author of *Those In Peril On The Sea* and *We Were There*.) I have always enjoyed seeing other shipmates. Dr. McKissick signed his Christmas cards, "SHIPMATES FOREVER."

Since retirement, life has been good...I have no complaints.

CHAPTER 39   SURVIVOR CASSIDY

NAME	CASSIDY, JOHN C. S1
STREET	
CITY	
STATE	
PHONE	
ENTERED SERVICE FROM	West Springfield, MA
PICKED UP BY	USS *Doyle*
DIVISION	Radio
DOB	1/23/27
	Deceased 4/01 Ft Riley, FL

FAMILY

EXPERIENCE

Unable to contact any family members.

CHAPTER 40   SURVIVOR CELAYA

NAME	CELAYA, ADOLFO V. F2
STREET	977 Schulman Ave
CITY	Santa Clara
STATE	CA 95050
PHONE	408 727 5855
ENTERED SERVICE FROM	Tuscon, AZ
PICKED UP BY	USS *Bassett*
DIVISION	
DOB	

FAMILY

EXPERIENCE

The story I am about to tell is a very difficult one, one you may not be willing to print. However, I feel very strongly that at some point it should be told.

It begins after our rescue following five days at sea, and while we were on our way to the States aboard the aircraft carrier USS *Hollandia*. The very first morning at roll call, the officer of the day singled me out for work detail moving heavy boxes. The second day the same officer singled me out for the same work detail. Then, on the third morning, when this same officer of the day again singled me out of the 300 survivors, I told him I was not feeling well and was suffering from a backache.

I explained that there were others who had not been called to work duty and asked to be excused. The officer of the day accused me of refusing an order. I told him again that my back was hurting from lifting the heavy boxes the past two days. The officer of the day (who incidentally, was one of the survivors) took me to sick bay, and gave me a reprimand, which was a captain's mast.

I was given five days bread and water. After two days, when all the survivors were getting off the ship with the band playing, I was taken off the ship by three shore patrolmen with guns at their side. I was taken to a barracks in the morning. I was taken to breakfast at the mess hall. At 10:00 a.m. two MPs showed up and said the navy had made a mistake by giving me breakfast and I would have to start my five days of bread and water again. I spent seven days on bread and water in a small cage with a mattress on the floor. To this day, I have nightmares about this incident. To me, the five days in the water were nothing compare to the injustice I suffered at the hands of the officer of the day. Yes, I still remember his name and he is still living.

This story will explain why I never go to any of the reunions. I'm still afraid of what I might do or say if I came face to face with that officer.

NAME	CENTAZZO, FRANK J. SM3
STREET	158 Park Ave
CITY	Warwick
STATE	RI 02889
PHONE	401 738 6035
ENTERED SERVICE FROM	Providence, RI
PICKED UP BY	USS *Doyle*
DIVISION	C Division
DOB	12/3/24

FAMILY
Spouse: Rhoda

EXPERIENCE

I have been asked by our organization to write a short story about my life on board the USS *Indianapolis* from December 1943 to the day of its sinking on July 30, 1945.

What follows is a brief story about Frank J. Centazzo and the ill-fated cruiser, USS *Indianapolis*, which was torpedoed by Japanese submarine I-58 on July 30, 1945. However, before I begin I must go back in time to December 7, 1941. Four days earlier I had celebrated my 17th birthday and was thinking of joining the service. My problem was that one of my brothers had been in the regular army since 1939 and my oldest brother was classified as 1A for the draft. Another older brother was 19 years old and wouldn't register until his 20th birthday. I could never convince my dad that I wanted to enlist. I agonized for months, and the opportunity to confront my Dad and seek his approval became more difficult as the war progressed and my country was suffering huge losses everywhere...the Pacific and Europe.

Suddenly the president announced that men could register for the draft at age 18 to increase our military strength and enable recruits to be trained earlier for active duty. This gave me the opportunity I was looking for. A day after my 18th birthday on December 3, 1942, I volunteered and was able to choose the branch of service I desired. My choice was the U.S. Navy. A few months later I was examined, and shortly thereafter was inducted into service. My boot training was in Newport, Rhode Island, from March 9 to mid-June 1943.

My dad could not understand why I was "drafted" before my older brother. I didn't dare reveal to him what really did happen while I was in service and after my honorable discharge on November 21, 1945.

Following my boot training in Newport, I was ordered to signal school located at the University of Chicago. Upon my completion of the intensive course, I was on my way to Camp Shoemaker in California to await further assignment. I spent three weeks living in barracks. Most of the time it was cold and rainy. Was this really sunny California?

In early October I was told that I had been assigned to the destroyer USS *Downs*, but I didn't complete the order. I had been admitted to sick bay for one week with a severe case of tonsillitis. I guess I was not destined to serve on a destroyer. If so, what was my next order going to be? I received the answer in mid-December 1943. I was transferred to Mare Island and for the first time I had a look at a huge ship, neatly camouflaged. What a sight! I was told that it was a heavy cruiser–CA 35–which had been commissioned in 1932 and named the USS *Indianapolis*. Was this ship to be my home for the duration of the war?

After I received permission to board the ship, I was directed to my assigned bunk and locker, in a compartment in the stern of the ship below the water line. The brig also was located nearby. Soon after, I made my way to the signal bridge where a warm welcome awaited me. I instantly felt at home with the shipmates who greeted me, and also with the others I met later in the day. I felt like I had been on board for a long time and not like a new arrival.

Shortly after Christmas, we were on our way. I remember going under the Golden Gate Bridge and wondering how long it would be until I once again would see this glorious sight. The waters began to get rough and my legs got wouldwobbly. How long would it take before I would get my sea legs under me?

We arrived at Pearl Harbor, and I saw some of the damage, including part of the USS *Arizona*, which was still out of the water. My shipmates filled me in regarding the *Indy's* participation in the Aleutians and the ship's whereabouts before and after Pearl Harbor.

The next stop was Tarawa. It was a small island and capturing it took a heavy toll. I went ashore and it was a sight that I can still see in my mind. A day later, I saw the destroyer USS *Downs* anchored. I was told that a man-maneuvered suicide torpedo had hit the side of the ship and caused substantial damage when our forces were invading the island. This ship was the assignment I missed. "Lucky me"!

The following 16 months were busy ones. The ship was involved in 7 more major battles and air strikes. The Carolinas, Marianas, Iwo Jima, Guam, Okinawa, and Saipan were some of the high spots. The *Indy* was the flagship of the Fifth Fleet under Admiral Raymond Spruance. We sure were busy, busy, busy. I'll allow historians, correspondents, book authors and others to give all the details and statistics for each of the battles. My reflections will be few and only those that I still see.

My first was when the ship took a dozen or so Japanese prisoners on board to be questioned. They were showered down and much to my surprise took over my bunk and all the others in the brig area. I had to find other lodging.

Another sight that still haunts me occurred at Saipan. After a one-week bombardment, the island was secured. During the next few days I saw dozens of Japanese soldiers, women, and children jump into the ocean from one of the cliffs, and their bodies were floating by the ship. They had all feared we would torture them if they were captured.

Another adventure was when we had air strikes on Japan—some carried out by the Doolittle Raiders. Hundreds of Japanese planes were sent out to find and destroy us. Flares were dropped over us for hours, and we didn't know if they would be followed with bombs.

One sight that I relish was the raising of the United States flag on Mt. Surabachi in Iwo Jima. I was on the long binoculars on the signal bridge, and all I can say is "What a show!" How proud I was to be an American and to be a part of the victory. It was costly.

The last one I'll write about took place at Okinawa. We shelled the island for a whole week, in the latter part of March 1945. The Japanese were sending out planes every day. It was a shoot-out. A few of our planes were mistakenly shot down. On the final day of March, we secured from battle stations and a few minutes later a plane was flying toward us. It managed to hit our port side AFT. The wing had a bomb mounted on it, and the bomb went through the deck and other compartments and exploded under the ship, rupturing the screws on the port side. The casualties were, I think, 9 dead, and 19 wounded. We had to go into the atoll for emergency repairs, and a few weeks later had to depart for San Francisco for further repairs. The once invincible *Indy* saw its first damage after ten major battles. Was this the beginning of the end for *Indy*?

Our journey back was slow and arduous but uneventful. It took more than two weeks. We went into Mare Island for repairs and a long-overdue overhaul. I remember staying in barracks for weeks. The nice part is we were expecting leaves during this time—mid-April to mid-July 1945.

During this time in port, while the ship was undergoing repairs and having new radar equipment installed, hundreds of shipmates were being transferred and new recruits were coming on board to replace them. Close to 25 percent of the crew left. Another surprise was that leaves were canceled and we got the ship readied for departure. The ship left Mare Island and proceeded to Hunters Point to take on a huge crate and a couple of canisters. Repairmen were still on board, but we departed from San Francisco on July 16 and made a high-speed run to Pearl Harbor. We took on supplies and other new crew members. All of the repair personnel left the ship. Within a few hours we left Pearl Harbor and headed for Tinian. The huge crate and the two canisters were unloaded. We couldn't guess what was in the crate.

The captain then alerted the crew that we would leave Tinian and proceed to Apra Harbor in Guam. We expected that we would have Admiral Spruance and his flagstaff of over 100 come on board. Only three personnel came on board, one of whom was a signalman striker named James Madison Flynn. He came to the signal bridge and asked, "Anyone here from Rhode Island?" I answered in the affirmative. That was the first and only time I saw Flynn. He did not survive. Many years later his uncle, state senator Flynn, and I dedicated a memorial site in Bristol in his honor. Signalman second class Scoggins was disappointed that his replacement didn't come aboard. He was trading his place with a signalman stationed in Apra Harbor. Approval of the exchange was late.

Soon we were on our way to Leyte. There was a need to train our new shipmates, some 350 sailors. A battleship was to meet us for battle exercises upon our arrival. We were scheduled to have 17 days of training. On Saturday morning, July 28, we steamed out of Apra Harbor. No escort was needed. We expected to reach Leyte in three days on July 31, 1945 at 11:00 a.m.

Sunday was a relaxing day. Chaplain Conway was providing service, a Mass celebrated first. Afterward there would be a Protestant service. In the afternoon, Dr. Haynes and Dr. Modisher set up and began giving the crew our first round of cholera shots in the mess hall. Later in the day, the sea was choppy and rough. Visibility was poor. I had the 8:00 to 12:00 p.m. watch. We were on a zigzag course at 15.7 knots. I remember entering in the logbook that we ceased zigzagging and increased speed to 17 knots. The rest of the watch passed on with no significant problems.

I was relieved from watch at midnight, July 30, and prepared the area forward of the signal bridge to sleep. There was a mattress cover on the deck and for my headrest I used my rubber life belt, which only took a few seconds to inflate. My shoes came off so I lay there, got onto my side, and said my prayers.

Suddenly there was a terrific explosion lifting the ship out of the water. I looked over the shield of the signal bridge (port side) and to my astonishment about 60 feet of the bow was no longer with the ship. As I went to speak to other mates who were on watch, another explosion occurred. The ship was not in control, heading to port side and listing on the starboard side where the second explosion took place. Fire and smoke erupted on the starboard side in the passageway where the officers' quarters were. All communications were knocked out.

Captain McVay was on the bridge just above the signal bridge awaiting word from his damage control officer, Commander K. C. Moore. Commander Moore appeared and told the captain that the hole on the starboard side was huge and water was pouring in where the bow was hit. The captain ordered the commander to take another look and to ascertain whether the ship could be saved. A minute later the executive officer, Commander Flynn, appeared and told the captain that the damage was so severe that the ship couldn't be saved and recommended that the skipper give orders to abandon ship. Captain McVay agreed with his executive officer and asked him to pass the word to abandon ship.

Before I went to my battle station on the port side, I helped Bob Bunai put all the code books in a leaded canvas bag. Kenly Lanter and others also assisted. We then proceeded to climb the ladder to the lower deck and jump off the high side (port side) into the sea, which was covered with heavy oil from the ship's ruptured tanks. One of the mates in the water needed assistance with his life jacket. Much to my surprise it was signalman second class David Singerman, my buddy. We swam as fast as we could to get away from the sinking ship. I heard yelling and screaming from shipmates who were too injured to jump into the sea or who were reluctant because they didn't know how to swim. I looked back when I was fifty yards away in time to see only the stern of the ship out of the water and the screws still churning away.

I joined one group of survivors (about sixty men), not realizing that this was only one of several groups within close proximity. Almost immediately I heard marine captain Parke asking us to be on the lookout for buoys which may have a telephone to call for help. He said the navy did this because of downed pilots who crashed into the sea. Dr. Haynes told us not to vomit and to try to hold the food we had eaten as long as possible. We would need the strength! My thoughts were, "For how long?" I didn't think that any SOS was sent.

Nevertheless, I was sure the navy would be looking for us because we were supposed to arrive at Leyte within 36 hours. Could I last that long in open sea with no raft, no provisions of any kind? How could I rest? Was I strong enough to endure a few days in the water? Would there be sharks to contend with?

I tried to find my fellow signalman, by swimming from one group to another. No luck! Nausea set in fast. I was cold but determined to make it no matter what. Nearby I saw Lt. Commander Lipski with his hands out of the water because they were scorched–so were his eyes. We took turns caring for him and pulling him back when he drifted away.

I talked to Commander Haynes who inquired how I was doing. He asked about my left leg, which had been injured when we got hit by the kamikaze on March 31, 1945. I was surprised that he remembered treating me in sick bay. I prayed with my buddy Father Conway, who had my leave extended in May so I could complete my Confirmation. Father Conway continued to go to each of us, giving us hope and praying with us to be rescued.

I never did find Robert Bunai, but I did find Paul McGinnis. We helped each other so we could get some rest. It seemed like an eternity, but only one hour had passed. I saw one sailor with a lighted flashlight trying to signal a ship in the distance. I knocked it out of his hand and said that the light might be from the submarine that sank us. I went back to join with Paul and prayed that we would be all right until dawn.

As the sun rose on the eastern horizon, it already was warming us. Unfortunately, the glare it made on the water and oil was unbearable. I quickly tore part of my shirt so I could cover my eyes, which were burning from the salt, the oil, and the glare. We kept searching the horizon for any sign of a ship, which may have been using the peddie route. I didn't dare swim away from the oil slick. It gave us some protection from sharks, or so we thought, until we heard of some attacks being made on seamen on the outer rim.

As the day went on, our thirst slowly became greater. Most did not think about drinking the seawater. Planes flew over us at midday but were too high to spot us. We all believed the area would be swarming with planes looking for us. When they didn't see the *Indy* arriving in port Tuesday morning, they would come looking. That thought gave us strength to stay alive until morning.

Commander Lipski could not hold on, and Dr. Hayes released him from his life jacket and his body drifted away. During the night, many more slipped away–the badly burned and injured. As the night wore on, we held each other to keep warm and to remain awake so no one drifted away from the group. During the night, it was easy to slip away, to give up and end it all.

The next morning gave us hope of rescue. Kapoks became logy and men were emerged in the water up to their chins. We all had hopes that by nightfall we would be on a ship and into warm dry sacks after washing off all the oil. The sun felt a lot warmer this day. My blindness continued. We couldn't make out the sailor next to us because faces were swollen and oily. Thirst became an acute condition from dehydration. Some started to take sips of the salt water, then more and more and then suffered a horrible death. When night came, our hope of rescue died. Men started to hallucinate...seeing ship lights and diving down to get a cold drink from cook Spinelli who was passing it out on the ship's fantail. Most of these men were in a world of fantasy.

Wednesday was a day of celebration. The *Indy* was just below the surface and gedunks were available. Many of the men took advantage of this treat. Also, an island with an airstrip and a hotel was discovered. About fifteen men were in line doing the dog paddle, waiting for their turn to go on the island and sleep in a bed for one hour. The hotel had only one bed available. Scoggins asked me to join him and two others to swim to Palau which was a few hundred miles westward. I passed up the invite. I never saw Scoggins again. Many men swam off and never returned.

Captain Parke swam around trying to hold the group together. Later that night he sank beneath the sea, exhausted. Father Conway was saying prayers and thrashing the water when he collapsed in delusion and expired in Dr. Haynes' arms. Father Conway had been between McGinnis and me. We had to use restraint because he was delirious but he managed to slip away from us.

The night was one of terror. Fighting broke out. Demented men were victims of shark fear–everyone became the enemy. One shouted, "There's Japanese on this line," and all hell broke loose–men were stabbing the people next to them, fighting with whoever was close. Toward morning it became quiet. I guess those of us who remained became exhausted to a point of no return. This was our last hurrah. Less than one hundred men left out of four hundred, and some with their faces down on the water...more dead than alive.

Toward noon on Thursday we prayed an awful lot when we found the strength to do so. A noise that sounded like a plane was heard, but the plane was too high to spot us. But then the plane flew lower and lower. He dipped his wing. We shouted and kicked our feet in the water. Some shouted with joy, while others could only grunt or didn't move at all.

Soon a raft, some life jackets, and other survival gear fell from the plane. I swam to retrieve a water can, but it had burst upon hitting the water. I swam back to my small group with the can and showed them it had burst; otherwise they would have thought that I drank all the water and would have turned on me. The plane continued hovering and that comforted us. We put some of the most weary and injured on the rubber raft. The rest of us hung onto the sides.

Another Ventura plane came into view, and soon the first one flew back to its base. A few hours later a PBY glided down as if to land, and by God it did land safely after three bounces on the water. The plane then went right by us and stopped quite a way from us.

Within a few hours, more planes appeared and dropped more rafts and other survival gear. At long last, help was on the way. Could we hold out until the ships came to rescue us? Sleep was the enemy. We were so tired. We had had no sleep for eighty hours. Shortly after midnight, a huge searchlight had illuminated a cloud overhead. Or was this light from the heaven above?

A ship was close to us by early morning–the USS *Doyle*, a destroyer escort. It lowered a raft and started to pick up pitiful looking men who had escaped the ravages of shark-infested waters for four and one-half days–five nights and four days of horror. They were not aware of who we were or what ship was lost. Only when we were on board did they realize that we were survivors of the ill-fated heavy cruiser CA-35, the USS *Indianapolis*, flagship of the Fifth Fleet under the command of Admiral Raymond Spruance. It turned out to be one of the most important rescue missions of the navy and the end of one of the most prolonged battles of men against the sea. The *Doyle* also took fifty-odd survivors from Adrian Marks' PBY.

Once on board, sailors washed the oil from our bodies, placed us in bunks, and gave us something to drink. I couldn't take anything because my throat and stomach were inflamed, but I did sleep until a blast from a five-inch gun woke me. Before I could jump from my sack, a sailor watching out for me said they had had to sink the PBY. It couldn't take off in the open sea and a wing had been badly damaged when it landed. I returned to sleep until we reached Peleliu of the Palau Island group.

By the way, the first survivor I met when they took me on board the *Doyle* was Robert Bunai. What a great surprise it was for both of us.

Lt. Commander W. Graham Claytor commanded the *Cecil J Doyle* (DE 368). He was a cousin of Captain McVay's wife, Louise, and he later became secretary of the navy.

Lt. Commander Gwinn, who piloted the Ventura land-based plane that accidentally found us became our "angel" and an honorary survivor of the

Survivors Organization for life. While alive, he and his wife, Norma, attended all of our reunions.

The morning of Saturday August 4, we found ourselves at Base Hospital 20 in Peleliu. We only stayed in the hospital for two days. We boarded the hospital ship, *Tranquility* on Monday morning. Once on board, I thought of the two shipmates that managed to survive but later died. (Shipman and Harrison had funeral services and were buried in Peleliu.) One surprise was meeting Chuck Gwinn, our "angel." That night, movies were shown topside and the ship was lit up like a Christmas tree. I couldn't keep my eyes on the screen. To this day, I cannot remember the name of the movie, what it was about or anything...my eyes were looking seaward.

We arrived at Guam on Wednesday. The following week Admiral Spruance pinned Purple Heart medals on his shipmates of the Fifth Fleet flagship. Shipmates who were not ambulatory were visited by the admiral and received their medals while in bed. It was announced that a second A-bomb had been dropped on Nagasaki. The first was dropped on Hiroshima with the message "The little boy—this is for the men of the *Indianapolis*."

There wasn't much to do on Base Hospital 18 on Guam. Friends from Admiral Spruance's staff visited and we were free to walk around. A few nights there were alarms that went off. Some Japanese were hiding in caves and would come out at night to do damage.

On Wednesday, August 15, the war ended. It was Tuesday night in Washington, August 14. President Truman gave the news to a happy gathering assembled outside the White House.

At this time, the navy released the news that the USS *Indianapolis* had been lost in the Philippine Sea as the result of enemy action and that had the next of kin of casualties had been notified. The greatest disaster at sea in the history of the United States Navy and the navy used two dozen words in its news release. The story was purposely delayed until the news that the war had ended was announced. Ironically, families who had lost a son, a brother, a husband, or an uncle received the telegrams on this day. The families of the survivors received a different telegram.

"A report just received shows your son _____ has been wounded in action 30 July 1945. Diagnosis, emersion (or exhaustion from over-exposure). Prognosis, good. Your anxiety is appreciated and you will be furnished details when received. You are assured that he is receiving the best possible medical care and I join in the wish for his speedy recovery. Communications may be addressed to him, % U.S. Base Hospital (Guam, Samar, or Peleliu). To prevent possible aid to our enemies, please do not divulge the name of his ship or station unless the general circumstances are made public in news stories."

All the newspapers on August 15, 1945 were full of stories of the *Indianapolis'* sinking.

I started to gain some of the forty pounds I had lost when we were given one week of rest and relaxation at the submarine rest camp on the island. After a few more weeks (in early September), we boarded the escort carrier *Hollandia*. The carrier arrived in San Diego on September 26, and the city turned out to celebrate our return. A Jeep parade up Broadway that included the navy band and city officials was warmly greeted by all that gathered to watch.

We all received a thirty-day survivor's leave after being checked out in San Diego. I went to the train station and the clerk asked me for a civilian fare for my ticket. I said, "Hell no, I am a navy man." (I had forgotten I was in civvies.) I showed him my leave papers and he adjusted the price accordingly. I think it was a four and one-half day trip to the East Coast.

After my leave, I reported to the Fargo Building in Boston for assignment. None was given to me as I had sufficient points to be discharged. After three weeks, confirmation arrived and I was a civilian on November 21, 1945.

My joy was short-lived, because I read that the navy was going to court-martial my skipper. I immediately mailed to Captain Cady (McVay's defense counsel) a copy of my news article which had appeared on the front page of one statewide newspaper. I did receive a subpoena from the president to appear at the Washington navy yards, but it came days after I was supposed to be there (the navy couldn't find me). I wired Captain Cady a short statement in defense of McVay. The court martial commenced on December 3, 1945, the day of my twenty-first birthday.

The verdict reached was unjust. Our Captain was not guilty of any charge. All the survivors were incensed with the results, especially having Hashimoto of the I-58 submarine testify at the trial.

All the survivors were committed to have the navy expunge the records of the conviction and exonerate Captain McVay.

I have written dozens of letters over the years to my congressional delegation urging them to overturn the conviction. Nothing was ever found in the rules or regulations which could be used to do this, although at one time my senator's office suggested that if a joint resolution from both branches passed simultaneously, the conviction could be overturned.

Nevertheless, I have to give credit to my congressional delegation who answered my letters and tried to help. Some of my letters were three pages long. Thanks to Senators Pell and Chafee (who was secretary of the navy before he was elected to the Senate) and Congressmen Ron Machtley, Patrick Kennedy and Jack Reed (who is now a United States senator).

And kudos to other survivors who have not relinquished the commitment, and special thanks to Senators Warner and Smith who championed the last attempt and were successful this past year in exonerating our captain. Last but certainly not least, my thanks to the young Hunter Scott, who lit the flame and carried the torch to Congress and showed the way. The national attention he received was sensational and captured the hearts of many congressmen and senators.

NAME	CHAMNESS, JOHN D. S2
STREET	
CITY	
STATE	
PHONE	
ENTERED SERVICE FROM	Malvern, AR
PICKED UP BY	USS *Bassett*
DIVISION	
DOB	Deceased

FAMILY

EXPERIENCE
   Unable to contact any family members.

NAME	CLARK, ORSEN N. S2
STREET	
CITY	
STATE	
PHONE	
ENTERED SERVICE FROM	Phillipsburg, KS
PICKED UP BY	USS *Talabot* Tr USS *Register*
DIVISION	
DOB	Deceased 11/86

FAMILY
Widow: Iona Griffith Clark
Children: Orsen Jr., Ona, Robert, Tony, Dave, Larry, Terri
Grandchildren: Christina, Kara, Michael, Orsen III, Dave Jr., Alicia, Brandon, Morgan, Malissa, Michael, James, Daniel, Timothy
Great-Grandchildren: Catherine, Tyler, Savannah, Christopher

EXPERIENCE
   No additional response.

NAME	CLINTON, GEORGE W. S1
STREET	5215 Buford Jett Ln
CITY	Balch Springs
STATE	TX 75180
PHONE	972 286 6111
ENTERED SERVICE FROM	Rosedale, MS
PICKED UP BY	USS *Doyle*
DIVISION	
DOB	1/19/22

FAMILY

Spouse: Dorothy Mae Clinton
Children: Walter George Clinton
Grandchildren: Stephen Clinton, Sarah Clinton, Kristen Clinton, Jonathan Clinton

EXPERIENCE

Respectfully submitted by Survivor Clinton's son, Walter George Clinton.

My father, George Clinton, has worn an Indianapolis survivor's cap every day of his life for the last 20 years or so. It has always brought questions from people he meets, most of whom have had never heard of the tragic ship. Recent books and movies have heightened the awareness of Americans concerning the contribution of the *Indy* to the ending of World War II and of the terrible plight of her crew members.

A few days ago, someone met Dad for the first time. After about 15 minutes the gentleman noticed Dad's ever-present cap and asked, "Were you on the *Indianapolis?*" Dad replied, "Until it sank." That reply was typical of the tongue-in-cheek conversational style that has always endeared me to my father.

Unfortunately, Dad suffered a stroke shortly after the 1995 USS *Indianapolis* survivors reunion, so I hear fewer of those witticisms than I once did. He has also found it increasingly difficult to remember the facts about the sinking. On some days he knows the dimensions of the beloved ship to the inch, but on most days he doesn't even remember major events like the kamikaze attack that brought the ship to San Francisco for repairs or even the details of his rescue. Fortunately, Dad has related a fair amount of information to me over the years. He also gave an interview in 1976 that contained some interesting facts and opinions. This interview was printed in the Greenville, Mississippi *Delta Democrat-Times*. In this chapter I will focus on the details which he had previously mentioned to me while also including some direct quotations taken from that article.

Dad volunteered to serve in the navy immediately after Pearl Harbor. He said that he did this so he could choose which branch of service to be a part of. If he thought that the navy would be easier than the other branches, he did not realize what lay in store for him as the war drew to a close! He was assigned to service in the Pacific theater, since ethnically he was part German and the navy did not want to cause him to fight against possible relatives.

I believe he was assigned to the USS *Indianapolis* immediately after finishing boot camp. On board the *Indianapolis*, Dad had several jobs. An early duty as a messenger was short-lived. One of the officers asked him to relay a message, but by the time he arrived at the destination, he had forgotten the message. He says that they never asked him to do that again! During part of the war he worked on number one gun turret. He was a range-finder trainer. This means he was responsible for left/right movements of the gun. (A range finger pointer is responsible for up and down movements). He said the range finders were a backup for an electronic system. Late in the war I think he was working in the carpentry shop. One of the jobs he had prior to the war had been a carpenter's apprentice.

Just before midnight on July 30, 1945, Dad was asleep in his bunk. "They fired six torpedoes and two hit us. I had the 4:00 to 6:00 a.m. watch, so I was asleep. The jar woke me. It knocked me out of my bunk. I went to the front of the ship and met a bloody man who said the boiler had exploded. When I got up to the top deck the ship was listing to the starboard. I went to the carpenter shop where I worked to get my life jacket, but it was gone."

He and another sailor found some spare life jackets. Each took one and threw the rest in the passageway. When Dad got back up to the top of the ship he attempted to jump off the port side but it was listing so badly he slid down to the starboard side. He managed to jump clear of the ship just as she sank. "I turned from white to black from all the oil in the water and stayed that way until we were rescued."

Dad said there were nine life rafts in the water but "we never saw them." A 15-mile-per-hour wind kept the water so rough there were whitecaps all the time. It only rained once in the four days that they floated helplessly in the water. "We had two 250-foot lines and used them to tie our life jackets together. There were about 150 in my group to start with. (I think some of these numbers may be a bit different from some I have read in books on the sinking.) All we had to eat were some malt tables and a crate of potatoes someone caught as it floated past." During the entire four days all he ate was one malt tablet which "made me more thirsty than ever" and "a nibble" off one potato.

Dad said he figures being a small man was an advantage, since his stomach wasn't as big as some of the others and he didn't miss food as much. "I went from 120 pounds down to 90," he said. One key difference between Dad's recollections about the ordeal and most others' that I have read is in the role that sharks played in the death of many of the crewmen. He figures that most of the men who died in his group died from drinking salt water or from starvation.

Some men in other groups told stories about being attacked by sharks, but my father didn't remember having that problem. "Probably because there were so many of us," he said. Whenever someone thought they saw one of the deadly fish, they'd slap the water and make loud noises to scare it away. "I heard stories about men floating around in life jackets with nothing left from the waist down because the sharks had eaten their legs off, but I didn't see any of that."

One major similarity between Dad's version of the story and others that I have read was in the role of dementia. "One guy had a daydream and said the water down deep was fresh. He'd swim way down to where it was cool and he really thought he was drinking fresh water." Dad also got to the point where reality and fantasy were indistinguishable. Once he imagined he saw half the ship still afloat and that he went on board to get water. "I passed the water around to all my friends and when I went to drink some, it was all gone. Then I woke up." Another time he saw a mirage—an island with palm trees and a hot dog stand with a girl selling hot dogs, hamburgers, and drinks. He and a friend started to swim toward the "island" and several friends called them a bunch of quitters. He turned around to explain where he was going but when he looked back the island had disappeared. Disappointed, he swam back to the men who had just saved his life.

Dad claims that the worst part of the four days in the water was "there was nothing to do. You couldn't sleep because the waves kept you awake. Once I got strangled and I also got seasick for my third time." I also remember Dad saying that he had noticed a pattern in the waves as he floated in the water. Every seventh wave was higher than the six that preceded it. He said that he got so accustomed to that pattern that even when he was semi-dozing he would lift his head every seventh wave so as not to get splashed.

On the third day, the men had a bitter disappointment when they sighted a mail plane flying overhead, but it didn't see them. Off and on they'd see flares shot by survivors on the life rafts, but they never saw the rafts.

Finally, after what seemed like weeks, just before nightfall on the fourth day, the pilot of a PBY amphibious plane spotted the oil slick and survivors floating in the water. "First he dropped us some plastic bags with tablets to turn salt water to fresh water. One of them busted and I never got any water until I got on board the plane." They were taken to a hospital ship where they took baths and were fed broth, he remembers. Then after spending several weeks in a hospital in Guam, he returned to the Untied States on the aircraft carrier USS *Hollandia*. "I got a Purple Heart because they treated me for saltwater ulcers on the backs of my legs."

Dad told a reporter that he'd never had any psychological effects from the terrifying experience, but then he admitted, "I'm a pretty calm guy." During those four days did he ever feel like he might not make it? "Oh, no. My mama told me to come home. I couldn't die!"

After the war, Dad went to work for the U.S. Gypsum Company. He worked as a deckhand and an engineer on a towboat called the Weatherwood. Many have expressed surprise that after such a terrible ordeal on the ocean he would chose to spend the rest of his working life on a boat. However, to him it seemed perfectly natural. I also note that he never showed any sign of fear of the water and was a good swimmer.

Beginning in 1970 he became a regular and faithful member of the First Free Will Baptist Church. In his spare time he played his harmonica. Over the years he built up a repertoire of almost 300 songs, which he played by ear at church or in front of a grocery store, anywhere where there were people who would listen. He also made plans to build a boat. He had an idea for a boat that would be like a catamaran except that it would have three enclosed hulls instead of two. He didn't know it, but he was dreaming of a design that is known as a trimaran. One of his best friends told him that it would never work, but this only fueled his determination to do it.

After he retired from working at USG he had some time to build his boat. He made it out of materials that he had collected in years of riding around Greenville Mississippi on his bicycle. He suspected that the hull of his ship might not be completely waterproof, so he filled the hull with empty water jugs. This he said, would make his boat unsinkable. (I don't think he wanted to relive another sinking experience!)

Eventually, he actually finished the construction of his boat. It had one mast and a sail. He towed it on a trailer that he pulled with his bicycle to the nearest water that he could find. I came down to visit him from Cleveland, Mississippi, where I lived at the time, and the boat, though a bit funny looking, was actually functional.

I have always been proud of my father for the role he played in the war effort. And now the more I hear about the story the more amazed I am that he survived. He has been an example to me of patience and optimism in the face of difficult and uncontrollable circumstances. Even now as I see him exhibiting calmness and humor in the face of increasing health problems, I see once again... what it means to be a survivor.

NAME	COLEMAN, ROBERT E. F2
STREET	2775 Fairway Dr
CITY	Baton Rouge
STATE	LA 70809
PHONE	
ENTERED SERVICE FROM	West Monroe, LA
PICKED UP BY	USS *Talbot* Tr USS *Register*
DIVISION	
DOB	

FAMILY
Spouse: Sylvia "Sid"

EXPERIENCE
No response.

NAME	COLLIER, CHARLES R. RM2
STREET	
CITY	
STATE	
PHONE	
ENTERED SERVICE FROM	Fayetteville, TN
PICKED UP BY	USS *Bassett*
DIVISION	RM2
DOB	10/07/16
	Deceased 8/81 Nashville, TN

FAMILY
Widow: Louise Dyer Collier
Children: Charles Dyer, Hal Collier, Suzanne Collier Little, Gary Collier
Grandchildren: Nine

EXPERIENCE

Submitted by Survivor Collier's daughter, Suzanne Collier Little.

After the military, Charlie lived in Nashville until his death in August 1981. He worked in the wholesale grocery business. He also co-owned several grocery stores in his hometown of Fayetteville, Tennessee. After obtaining his real estate license, Charlie sold commercial real estate.

Charlie was an avid golfer. He maintained a single digit handicap, and he won several tournaments at his golf club. He also enjoyed all sports. Charlie especially enjoyed watching his three sons playing high school football. He was a deacon at Vine Street Christian Church and served on several committees at the church.

Charlie was proud to be a navy man and pleased to be a survivor of the USS *Indianapolis*. His favorite book was *Abandon Ship* by Richard Newcomb. He read this book several times and was always willing to share his experience with family and friends.

The family of Survivor Charles Collier is very proud to be a part of the USS *Indianapolis* story. We consider Charlie and ALL the 317 survivors heroes. To him, he was just doing his duty for our country.

CHAPTER 47   SURVIVOR COSTNER

NAME	COSTNER, HOLMER J. COX
STREET	
CITY	
STATE	
PHONE	
ENTERED SERVICE FROM	Tecumseh, OK
PICKED UP BY	USS *Doyle*
DIVISION	
DOB	Deceased 1/81

FAMILY

EXPERIENCE

Unable to contact any family members.

NAME	COWEN, DONALD R. FC3
STREET	
CITY	
STATE	
PHONE	
ENTERED SERVICE FROM	BOISE ID
PICKED UP BY	USS *Doyle*
DIVISION	
DOB	Deceased 3/78

FAMILY
Spouse: Gladys Cowen

EXPERIENCE
Family did not respond.

NAME	COX, LOEL DENE S2
STREET	203 Williams Dr
CITY	Comanche
STATE	TX 76442
PHONE	915 356 3132
ENTERED SERVICE FROM	Sidney, TX
PICKED UP BY	USS *Bassett*
DIVISION	NAN Navigation
DOB	4/12/26

FAMILY
Spouse: Sara Lou
Children: One son, Lowell Dean (Terry)
Grandchildren: One grandson, Jeff

EXPERIENCE

I am a survivor of the worst naval sea disaster in history. Serving aboard the USS *Indianapolis*, I was just 19 years old when the ship began the first leg of its final voyage, to deliver the atomic bomb that would subsequently be dropped on Hiroshima. The ship was to proceed to the Philippines. We were advised that no escort was available so we set out alone. On July 30, 1945, just after midnight, the USS *Indianapolis* was torpedoed by the I-58 Japanese submarine.

For years, I could not discuss the events that unfolded over the next few days. However, later I found it easier to discuss the events, because it is important to share my story as we must learn from history. Sometimes it has seemed like a bad dream.

Before all of that, at Okinawa, the USS *Indianapolis* was hit by a kamikaze, which knocked off two propellers. We came back to the United States to be repaired, after which we were to begin gunnery practice. Instead, a big box was put on board and we headed for Tinian. We made it in ten steaming days, and that is still the record for a surface vessel. We did not know what was in the box. I even leaned against it. A smaller metal container was brought on board and carried to the captain's quarters. That was not common knowledge; however, we learned about it later. We think that was the uranium part of the bomb. Scuttlebutt, or gossip, concerning the contents of the box ran rampant. My favorite story was that it was a big box of scented toilet paper for General MacArthur.

After we left the bomb at Tinian we came back to Guam and took on supplies. We were told to join the battleship USS *Idaho* in the Philippines for gunnery practice. Our ship carried no sonar equipment, so we depended on escorts, like destroyers. We asked for an escort but were told that there was none available. The captain was assured that the route was safe. He was not told that one of our ships, the USS *Underhill*, had been sunk by an enemy sub just five days earlier on the same route. Zigzagging to avoid enemy fire is left to the discretion of the captain. If it was very dark, it wasn't unusual for a ship to cease zigzagging. Captain McVay III gave orders to stop zigzagging and told the officer of the deck that if the weather cleared to start zigzagging again.

When I went on watch at midnight, I went to the bridge. The captain had a little cubicle that he slept in on the bridge. He happened to be sleeping up there that night. When I got up there, it was pitch dark. Then the clouds began to break a little bit and I could see some of the moon. Then it would cover back up, so we were not zigzagging at that time. My duties on the bridge were either to steer the ship, be on the telephone with the engine room, or to be lookout. On this night, my duties were to communicate with the engine room. So I went up to the bridge and took headphones.

After five or ten minutes, there was an explosion. We had been hit by a torpedo. I was blown up into the air about five feet and landed on my stomach.

As I started to get to my feet, I looked up and saw debris, water, flames, and everything up above me. The bridge was 81 feet from the water line, so that indicates how powerful the explosion was. Suddenly, we were hit by another torpedo. This one hit right in the middle of the ship, and it hit the ammunition magazine. There we were in the middle of nowhere, by ourselves, and WHAM! We were wondering what happened. We really didn't know if it was our own ammunition that had blown up or what. We didn't know it was a torpedo. We didn't know anything.

The explosions knocked the captain out of his bunk and he came up and took charge. I was told to get the captain a life jacket, so I got one and helped him into it. All power was out. We couldn't contact any lookouts, the engine room, or anyone. Captain McVay called the damage control officer and had him check on the ship. In about five minutes he came back and said we were beginning to list badly and that there was damage and blockage and he could not reach anyone in the engine room. The captain told him to check some more...that time he came back and said, "Captain, we are sinking." By this time we were lying down on our right side at such a degree that one could nearly walk down the smoke stack. The Captain said to pass the word to abandon ship. I took him at his word. I had heard how when a ship sinks it could suck you down and under. I also had heard that the captain will go down with the ship. I was with Captain McVay. When he said to abandon ship, I left him. I ran to the port side, the high side. There was a passageway one deck down. I reached over and grabbed a hook, swung out over the main deck, hit the hull, and then the water. It was about 40 feet from where I swung out.

The first thing I remember thinking when I came up was that I had lost my cap. I had swallowed a bunch of oil and water, and I began to vomit. I began to swim as fast as I could to get away from the ship. I was still concerned about the suction. When I looked back I saw the ship had already laid completely over on her side. The stern was coming up, and it just went straight down. I could see the propellers still slowly turning and men still jumping off. It took only 12 minutes for the ship to sink, and it was 610 feet long.

I swam out a little farther and came upon this sailor, all by himself. He was one of my best buddies. He had been flash burned and somebody had put a life jacket on him and pushed him overboard. His name was Clifford Josey. He lived only an hour or two.

I've been told there were rafts...I never saw any. When the moon came out, I found a little group of about 30 men, and we stayed together. We knew we'd be safer in a group than alone. When daylight came we were cold and shivering. I still had my shoes and clothes on. One guy next to me said, "I wish you'd take those shoes off, you keep kicking me." I then pulled my shoes off. We figured we'd be found pretty quick. People should be looking for us. We had high hopes.

As the day wore on, the sun began to take its toll. It got so hot that the sun was just blistering. It was so hot, we prayed for darkness. When darkness came, we got chilled and began to shake. The water was so cold. Then we prayed for sun. We had oil all over us. Some people say that the oil helped us. I guess it did, but when that hot sun would beat down on us, we nearly fried. It was a terrible ordeal.

Unfortunately, there were bigger ordeals to come. We saw sharks from day one. After a short while they became aggressive. With our legs dangling, we became easy targets. We'd hear men scream and then the water would turn red. The sharks were getting us. A shark got one of my buddies who was just a couple feet from me. The shark's tail and the water just covered me up–I was that close. If the sharks took a man's leg, or just bit him, sometimes he would float back up; some did and some didn't. Of course, they were all dead. We'd take their life jackets and their dog tags.

After a couple of days with no food or water, some men began to hallucinate. Several men drank the salt water and died. A potato floated by, but I was so afraid that it had salt water in it that I decided not to eat it. I saw a man undo his life jacket and slip beneath the water "to return to the ship for a drink of water." Men also started saying they knew there was an island, and they'd swim off...never to be seen again.

Every day we would see airplanes fly over us. Finally, after five nights and four days, a pilot saw us. It was the happiest day of my life! I heard an airplane motor. I looked up and saw a PBY plane just above the horizon. We all started to scream, kick, and splash, but he just kept going. In about 30-60 minutes, we heard the motor again. It was coming from the other direction. It looked like the same plane but it was closer to us. We started yelling and kicking again. We thought that he was on patrol and if he didn't see us, that was it. That could be our last chance!

Just before dark we heard the motor again, and this time he was closer. Just then he turned and flew right over us. There was a guy in the door of this plane, waving to us. We realized that we had been found! The hair on my head stood straight up. I WAS SO HAPPY!

The men still faced hours in the water and some died before they could be rescued. Later that night there was a bright light shining. It was like a light from heaven! It was a big flood light shining down on the water. One of the rescue vessels had turned on its flood lights to give us hope. I lost consciousness for a while. The next thing I remember was a bright light shining in my face and a strong arm pulling me into a little boat that took me to the USS *Bassett*. With a little help, I still had enough strength to climb a rope ladder. I got on the deck, took two steps, and fell on my face. Someone picked me up and carried me to a canvas-covered bunk. They laid me face down with my hands under me. I fell asleep and don't know how long I slept. When I woke up, my hands stuck to the canvas. When I rolled off it nearly pulled the skin off.

Two sailors from the *Bassett* took me and washed me down to get the oil off. I had sores all over me. They looked like burns, and the skin was just coming off. When I got to the hospital, they took tweezers and took strips of my skin off my shoulders from where my life jacket had been. I lost all my body hair, fingernails, and toenails. I had basically been pickled in salt water.

While we were in the hospital, we received word of the atomic bomb. They brought a newsletter that said, "This is what you men were carrying and it's been dropped by the *Enola Gay*." That was the first time we knew what we had been carrying. We also learned that of the original 1,197 men on the USS *Indianapolis*, only 317 survived.

The end of the war did not bring an end to the suffering for the survivors. Not only did we have injuries and scars both physical and emotional, but we discovered that our captain was being blamed. I was called to Washington to testify.

They court-martialed our captain. They said he didn't give proper "abandon ship" orders. I was standing beside him when he did. The navy found him guilty of not zigzagging. They even humiliated him by bringing the commander of the Japanese submarine, Mochitsura Hashimoto, over to testify. Ironically, his testimony supported Captain McVay. Hashimoto said it would not have made any difference if the captain had been zigzagging or not.

I honestly feel Captain McVay was just a scapegoat. Even though the U.S. had lost 700 ships during World War II, he was the only captain court-martialed. He received hate mail from some families of men who had died. Eventually it became too much for him to bear and he took his own life in 1968.

For years survivors and many people wrote letters to Congress asking that Captain McVay be exonerated. I also went to Washington and visited with senators. Finally in October of 2000, the president signed a bill that both houses had passed, exonerating Captain McVay and saying he should not have been tried and was not at fault. In July 2001, the navy added the congressional declaration to McVay's military service record. The *Indianapolis* crew received the Navy Unit Citation.

In August 2000, the Discovery Channel sent Kurt Newport and four survivors, including myself, to the Pacific Ocean for 32 days to look for the ship. Unfortunately, we did not find it.

The survivors have a reunion every other year in Indianapolis, Indiana. We have erected a beautiful monument to the USS *Indianapolis* in the city of Indianapolis. Survivors and friends collected donations of 1.3 million dollars from individuals and companies...no government money.

What would the world be like if the 1,197 men of the USS *Indianapolis* had not succeeded in their final mission...a staggering, sobering thought!

Survivor Cox and wife Sara Lou

Survivor L. D. Cox

CHAPTER 50   SURVIVOR CRANE

NAME	CRANE, GRANVILLE S. JR. MM2
STREET	4273 Hwy 35E
CITY	Dermott
STATE	AR 71638
PHONE	870 538 5746
ENTERED SERVICE FROM	Galveston, TX
PICKED UP BY	USS *Bassett*
DIVISION	Master At Arms
DOB	8/26/26

FAMILY
Spouse: Mary V.
Children: Jack Walton, Anita Cooke, John Stephen
Grandchildren: Jacqueline Marie, Jennifer Lauren,
John Stephen II, Julianne

EXPERIENCE

I was born in El Dorado, Arizona. I joined the service before I graduated from high school in 1942. I enlisted in the U.S. Navy and my boot camp was at San Diego, California. After boot camp, I was sent to our ship, the USS *Indianapolis*. I participated in eight of ten campaigns that were all "thriller battles."

On July 30, 1945, the night the ship was sunk, a small group of men held a prayer meeting and Bible study. I was in that group. Later I took my cot topside and tried to sleep. Awakened at midnight, I was bounced out of my bed in the hangar. Shocked out of my wits, I went to my battle station on the fantail of the ship, where I rounded up a large group of men under my command.

The ship began to go sideways to the right after the attacks. Most of the men wanted to go overboard. I said, "NO! We've been hit by the enemy before." We had never heard the command of the captain, or any one else, to abandon ship. Soon after, we had no choice but to jump off and start swimming for our lives. But that wasn't the hardest ordeal that we had to go through.

I got away from the ship and turned to see the *Indy* going down bow first. Many men were jumping off and some were hitting the "screws" as they were still turning fast. I felt guilty for not letting them off the ship or telling them to jump before it was too late.

It was about 12:30 a.m., July 30, 1945. I began to swim in the moon-light. Because of the oil slick, I could not see very well. The oil covered the 800 men in the water, and we were sick from it. Some had life vests but some did not. A few rafts had been released, as well as a few nets. All of us were sure that we would be rescued soon after the sinking. It was cold at night and very hot during the day. We saw planes on each of the five days that we were swimming without food or water.

Sharks were around us all the time. They were drawn to the survivors, who were disappearing by the droves. It was reported that 880 men died and never reached land. Those that were badly injured were the first of the crew eaten by the sharks, and we saw them descending into the deep. And if any of the men would drift off from one of the group that had formed, the sharks would get them and take them under. We watched our close shipmates die before our eyes.

The men in the groups that were yelling and kicking to scare off the sharks were miles apart. I was in the largest group of men in the water. About half died while we were out there in the sea. Some of the men gave up and wanted to die. Many drank salt water and a few hours later were gone.

We started to pray aloud. However, being a Christian, I prayed all the time out there. I made no bargain with God if he would deliver us. I had dealt with fear and God's safety before. I was ready to die, but I wanted to wait until God's time to go to meet Him. I continued to swim and catch onto anything that floated, including cans, boxes, or water-logged life vests. I was one happy young man when I saw a Ventura bomber flying over us in the water. The pilot, Wilbur

Gwinn, was our "angel" from God as he circled over us and gave the radio broadcast to the American base. The message was that he saw many men in the water. Not knowing at the time who we were, a navy PBY, piloted by Lt. Adrian Marks, was sent to find us. He was the first aircraft that came to rescue us from the water. After seeing us being eaten by sharks, he landed his sea plane close to us, which gave us great hope.

When the USS *Bassett* came to pick us up, those in my group knew that our prayers were finally answered. We were pulled out of the sea throughout the night. It had seemed longer than five days. All of us were so exhausted that we hardly knew what was going on. Many men drowned trying to get rescued.

A boat came for me from the USS *Bassett,* and I was pulled in. I barely remember being transferred to the USS *Bassett.* Once aboard, I thought one of my limbs was gone, but I was not sure. The good crew members of the *Bassett* carried me half alive to one of their bunks, treating me well with "red-carpet" care. I thank the dear Lord for them and all the other rescue men that helped the survivors.

To what do I attribute my survival? To me it wasn't luck. The God of my salvation was with me and delivered me. Not what I deserved, by any means, but the grace of God to be usable in his service. I've been trying to serve Him by being a pastor and teaching for a long time...remembering how thankful I should be just to be alive and back home with my family.

CHAPTER 51   SURVIVOR DANIEL

NAME	DANIEL, HAROLD W. CBMA
STREET	
CITY	
STATE	
PHONE	
ENTERED SERVICE FROM	Des Moines, IA
PICKED UP BY	USS *Bassett*
DIVISION	
DOB	10/29/20
	Deceased 2/02 Hayward, CA

FAMILY
Widow: Le Cam Trinh

EXPERIENCE

Respectfully submitted by Survivor Daniel's widow.

Harold was born in North Platte, Nebraska and graduated from high school in 1938. He joined the navy shortly after graduation, went to Great Lakes Naval Training Center for boot camp, and boarded the USS *Oklahoma*. In 1939, Harold was transferred to the USS *Indianapolis*. He remained on the USS *Indianapolis* until it met its fate on July 30, 1945.

His next tour of duty was the naval training center in San Diego, California as a company commander/physical ed instructor until early 1949, when he was transferred to the USS *Valley Forge*. Late in 1949 he was selected to attend electronics school at Treasure Island, California and spent 13 months at school. When that training was completed, he was transferred to West Pacific COMSERON 3 to Mobile Electronics Tech Unit #3. In 1952, he returned to Treasure Island as an electronics instructor and was advanced to VO-1 in 1957. He was transferred to the USS *Salisbury Sound* as EMO. In 1960 he was transferred to Pac Res Fleet, Brementon, Washington and retired from the navy January 31, 1961.

Harold retired from civilian life in May 1991 and died February 8, 2002 in Hayward, California.

CHAPTER 52   SURVIVOR DEBERNARDI

NAME	DeBERNARDI, LOUIE BM1C
STREET	
CITY	
STATE	
PHONE	
ENTERED SERVICE FROM	Sacramento, CA
PICKED UP BY	USS *Bassett*
DIVISION	
DOB	3/16/18
	Deceased 11/89 Sacramento, CA

FAMILY
Widow: Florence
Children: Louis DeBernardi (Rose Ann), Joseph DeBernardi (Wendy)
Grandchildren: Haley DeBernardi, Kimberly, Jeremy
Great-Grandchildren: Delitah

EXPERIENCE
Respectfully submitted by Survivor DeBernardi's widow, Florence.

Louie never talked much about his military experience. The family found out more when they attended reunions of the survivors.

He was born March 16, 1918 in Nevada City, California and died November 6, 1989 in Sacramento, California. He entered the navy on December 14, 1940. He served most of his time on the USS *Indianapolis*; however, he also served on the USS *Eucalyptus*. On December 6, 1941, he left Pearl Harbor for Australia.

The night the ship was sunk, he had just started his watch. He helped with life jackets and jumped from the high side. He always said that he had $120 in his socks when he jumped in the water.

He received the Asiatic-Pacific (10 stars), American Theater, American Defense (1 star), Good Conduct, World War II Victory Medal, Purple Heart, Combat Action Ribbon and the Navy Unit Citation. He was honorably discharged January 11, 1947.

Louie enjoyed the *Indianapolis* reunions and kept in contact with many of his shipmates. During his retirement, he traveled some, spent time working on "projects" at the cabin, fished, and enjoyed his friends in La Porte, California.

CHAPTER 53   SURVIVOR DEWING

NAME	DEWING, RALPH O. FC3
STREET	
CITY	
STATE	
PHONE	
ENTERED SERVICE FROM	Columbus, ND
PICKED UP BY	USS *Bassett*
DIVISION	FOX
DOB	10/11/13 Deceased 1/99 Bismarck, ND

FAMILY
Widow: Helen

EXPERIENCE

Respectfully submitted by Survivor Dewing's widow, Helen.

Ralph was drafted into the service early in 1944. He was a farmer and had two small daughters. He did not want to use these reasons as excuses to not serve his country. He made a choice of the navy and went to Farragut, Idaho for his boot camp training.

After completing boot camp, he began fire control school at Lake Union, Seattle, Washington. He was there about three months and then went to Camp Shoemaker in California for further training.

Ralph's wife, Helen, and two daughters joined him in Seattle in July and followed him to Shoemaker, which was a few miles from Mare Island. He boarded the USS *Indianapolis* December 6, 1944 and was proud to be a part of the crew.

The USS *Indianapolis* was involved in the invasions of Iwo Jima and Okinawa and many other battles. He witnessed the burning of a large ship and also the raising of the United States flag at Iwo Jima. A kamikaze hit the ship and nine men lost their lives...one was his good buddy. The ship returned to Mare Island, California for repairs.

At this time, he learned he was to become a father again. He made a bet with two shipmates that it would be another girl...it was a boy. The bet was for a dinner. Helen made an old fashioned farm-type dinner of roast beef, mashed potatoes, and apple pie. The two buddies were Forest Gaither from Indiana and Smitty from Iowa.

During the repairs, Ralph made a trip back to North Dakota to visit his elderly parents, family, and friends. When the repairs were completed, USS *Indianapolis* received orders that she would be leaving July 16 to go to Tinian. Helen, two sisters, his mother-in-law, and three small children watched the *Indy* sail out of Mare Island to go to Hunters Point.

Ralph had been in sick bay with a sore throat, and at about 11:00 a.m. on July 29, he begged the doctor to let him out. He went to his bunk and fell asleep. Ralph awoke about 11:30 p.m. and prepared to report to his midnight watch in a position high above the bridge. He went on duty five minutes before midnight, and shortly thereafter the ship was hit by two torpedoes. He heard "abandon ship" and slowly crawled down the side of ship, being careful to avoid the screws below.

Later Ralph realized there had been another miracle. The sick bay was in the fore part of the ship, and that is where the torpedoes hit. He said prayers of thankfulness that the doctor had released him earlier.

After the ship sank, Ralph was with several shipmates who had a floater net.

They were in water, but they kept together by the net. One day, with the sun burning hot on his fair skin (Ralph was a redhead), he swam to a small raft and asked to come aboard for a few minutes. Because he had lost his white hat, he took off his dungarees and shorts and wrapped the shorts on his burning head. He put his dungarees back on and went back to the net.

Ralph was always thankful for his dear friend and shipmate, Paul Murphy. Ralph had slipped away from the net, and Paul missed him and swam out to get him. Several hours later, Paul heard Ralph's voice calling, "Paul, Paul, help me." Paul swam out again, brought Ralph back, and tied him to the net. Ralph always felt that God had a hand in this. He and Paul became life-long friends.

By the third day, Ralph realized that many of his shipmates were disappearing. He said he never heard the Lord's Prayer said by so many people and so often. He prayed often to be able to go home to his wife, two daughters, baby son, and elderly parents. He experienced the disappointment of so many, as they would see planes fly over and disappear, but no one came to rescue them. After 96-plus hours in the ocean, Ralph eventually was pulled aboard the USS *Bassett*. He said so many times that he wished he knew the name of the sailor on the USS *Bassett* who gave him his bunk, water, and oranges. The USS *Bassett* took him and other shipmates to the Philippines.

In the hospital, they were given Red Cross candies and doughnuts, etc. To this day, Helen, still has the box the candies came in. It also includes the oil-soaked wrist watch, and an ID bracelet from Helen, and it shows oil damage.

Ralph arrived in California with other shipmates. The barber on the ship came from our hometown of Columbus, North Dakota. It was a heartwarming reunion. It may have been illegal, but the barber ordered a set of blues and a white cap in Ralph's size, so he had a dress uniform when he arrived in San Diego. A few days later, Ralph and his family boarded the train and went back to North Dakota. In November he was honorably discharged. Ralph received the Purple Heart and some battle ribbons.

Ralph never spoke of his ocean experience until after the first survivors' reunion in 1960. He felt a close bond to all the survivors. He attended all the reunions and in 1995, nineteen Dewing family members attended the dedication of the memorial.

CHAPTER 54 SURVIVOR DEZELSKE

NAME	DEZELSKE, WILLIAM B. MM2
STREET	
CITY	
STATE	
PHONE	
ENTERED SERVICE FROM	Colerrainie, MN
PICKED UP BY	USS *Doyle*
DIVISION	
DOB	Deceased 1/79

FAMILY

EXPERIENCE

Unable to contact any family members.

CHAPTER 55 SURVIVOR DONNER

NAME	DONNER, CLARENCE RT3
STREET	UNKNOWN
CITY	
STATE	
PHONE	
ENTERED SERVICE FROM	
PICKED UP BY	USS *Bassett*
DIVISION	
DOB	

FAMILY

EXPERIENCE

Unable to contact any family members.

NAME   DOUGLAS, GENE F2C
STREET
CITY
STATE
PHONE
ENTERED SERVICE FROM   Bucyrus, MS
PICKED UP BY   USS *Bassett*
DIVISION
DOB   Deceased 12/89

FAMILY

EXPERIENCE
  Unable to contact any family members.

NAME   DRAYTON, WILLIAM H. EM2C
STREET   5619 Bayshore Rd #132
CITY   Palmetto
STATE   FL 34221
PHONE   941 722 1945
ENTERED SERVICE FROM   Philadelphia, PA
PICKED UP BY   USS *Bassett*
DIVISION
DOB   6/4/21

FAMILY
Spouse: Louise
Children: William Drayton (Catherine)
Grandchildren: William Drayton, Christopher
Drayton, Craig Drayton
Great–Grandchildren: Ashlie Drayton, Cierra Drayton

EXPERIENCE

I was asleep on the second deck on the night we were hit. Quickly, I went up to the electric shop. By then, the water was already on the quarterdeck. I went across the passage to the filters. The ship started to list. Holding onto oxygen tanks, we worked our way to the turret, then the bulkhead. All that time, Baker was calling, "Come on, Drayton!" We walked off the ship and into the water together. After swimming a short distance, I turned to look back. He was gone. I never saw my buddy Baker again. The next time I looked back, the *Indy* was going straight down.

On the third day, I gave up on being saved. I started to swim away when a shipmate, Coleman, told me to wait. He took a life jacket from a deceased crew member and gave it to me. During that time, I learned what the words to the Lord's Prayer meant. To this day, I don't remember being rescued. I only remember asking for a cigarette. I don't remember being hungry or thirsty all the while I was a prisoner of the water. I never talked about it and never went to any reunions, until the submarine SSN 697 *Indianapolis* was launched. I didn't attend any more reunions until the dedication of the memorial in 1995. I HAVE NOT MISSED ONE SINCE.

CHAPTER 58   SURVIVOR DRONET

NAME	DRONET, JOSEPH E J. S2
STREET	P O Box 279
CITY	Cameron
STATE	LA 70631
PHONE	318 775 5542
ENTERED SERVICE FROM	Cameron, LA
PICKED UP BY	USS *Bassett*
DIVISION	I Division
DOB	8/10/27

FAMILY

Spouse: Hazel
Children: Pamme, Terry (deceased), Rhondanea (deceased)
Grandchildren: Terry Joseph Dronet Baldwin

EXPERIENCE

The last of eight children (six boys and two girls), I was born on August 10, 1927 in New Iberia, Louisiana. My father was killed in an auto-train accident near New Iberia about six months after I was born. I attended elementary school in Jefferson Island, where we lived until I was 17. I attended and graduated from New Iberia High School in May 1944. Shortly after graduation, I went to work for the Pennsylvania Shipyards, Inc. in Beaumont, Texas as a machinist helper.

After I had worked there for two or three months, a navy recruiting officer was after me to join the navy. I kept putting him off because I wanted to save a little money to go to college, as I had received a scholarship to attend Louisiana State Normal College. He persisted in his recruiting efforts, even promising my mother and I that the navy would send me to college after boot training. This, I learned later, would not be the case. Mom finally agreed to let me join if they agreed on the schooling.

I was 17 on August 10 and on August 18 I was sworn into the U.S. Navy in New Orleans. I went through boot training in San Diego, California for 13 weeks, after which I was given a seven-day leave to go home. Ironically, my boot company commander was Boy Gary from Earth, Louisiana, which is a small town near where I was from. I did not know him prior to entering the navy, but I did know his sister. He did not show me any special favors and I did not expect any even though we were from around the same place.

When I returned from my seven-day leave, I was sent to Shoemaker, California for about two weeks. I knew then that what the recruiting officer had promised would not come through, because when you were sent to Shoemaker, it was usually to be assigned to a ship to go overseas. I made very good grades on my tests, but somehow the navy must have been in need of additional men overseas. Shoemaker was so crowded that you would practically be in line all day for chow. By the time you were through with breakfast, it was time to stand in line for lunch, and then stand in line for supper. I had a few night passes to go into town and did go to San Francisco and Oakland.

On December 1, 1944, I was assigned to duty on the USS *Indianapolis* (CA-35), a heavy cruiser at Mare Island, California. I really had a funny feeling when I approached the ship, as I had not realized that ships were that large. Then I found out I was the only one from my original boot company being assigned to the ship. This would be rough not knowing anyone when going aboard. The ship was being repaired and reconditioned, as she had just returned from combat in the Pacific.

We were about forty men going aboard at the same time, and we were each given a hammock to sleep on that first night. The hammocks were hung in one of the airplane hangars, and while we were sleeping that first night, the strings to my hammock and quite a few others were cut, and we fell on the hard deck. I figured this was some kind of initiation from some of the older crew, and I did not think anything of it. It didn't happen again, as the following day we were assigned to our regular bunks.

The *Indianapolis* was the flagship of Admiral Raymond Spruance, commander of the Fifth Fleet in the Pacific, which was attached to the mighty Task Force 58.

I was assigned to the small arms department aboard ship, and I soon made quite a few friends. One of my best friends at that time was Gunners Mate First Class Miller, who was in charge of the small arms department. He gave me my first nickname aboard ship. I was perhaps the youngest boy aboard the *Indianapolis,* having turned 18 less than four months prior to coming aboard, and Miller called me "Tender".

We stayed at Mare Island shipyard for repairs for about two weeks, during which time I had a few overnight leaves in San Francisco and Oakland. After repairs, we went off the California coast on a shakedown cruise. The first day out, I got sort of dizzy, but got over it pretty quickly and never did get seasick again. A week or so later, we went off the coast of San Diego for gunnery practice. After this we went to San Diego where we spent Christmas and New Year's. I did get somewhat lonesome for home this time of the year, and I was used to drinking a few beers once in a while. I couldn't buy beer in California due to the requirement to be 21. In Louisiana, you can buy if you are 18 or wearing a uniform.

After January 1945, we left San Diego for Honolulu, where we were to get some more fuel and groceries. I was assigned my first battle station, which was three decks down, handling the 5-inch shells in elevators to the top deck. I did not like this station. I preferred to be topside in case we ever were hit by the enemy.

I'll never forget my first liberty in Honolulu. I thought I was an old salt by then, and as soon as I got off the bus into the city, I had my hat cocked on the back of my head. An SP spotted me right off and asked if I knew how to wear a sailor cap. It was too late then, and I was given a slip to report back to my deck officer. I was really disappointed not being able to stay in town. From then on, I never forgot how to wear my cap square on top in Honolulu. I finally went into town later, only to find out that it was crowded all the time, which I did not enjoy.

Shortly thereafter, we joined the famous Task Force 58, and we had Admiral Spruance aboard with the flag of the Fifth Fleet. We made two air strikes on Tokyo, and my watch then as always was as a lookout. It was so cold then (in February and March) that we had to wear face masks to keep warm. After the air strikes, we returned to an island called "Mog Mog," which was sort of a recreation island. We went ashore for swimming, baseball, and even a few beers.

After this, we went to Iwo Jima to bombard the hell out of it prior to the invasion. By this time, I was transferred to the 8-inch guns on deck as a trainer. I liked this battle station because it was on deck. I remained in this battle station throughout the Iwo Jima battle. Of course, when we were not shooting at the island, I still had my lookout watches. The way we had bombarded the island for two weeks prior to the landing of the marines, I thought we had flattend it. But we later found out that the Japaneses were practically buried all over the island.

After Iwo Jima, we went again back to the West Caroline Islands and to "Mog Mog" Island for some more recreation. Then came the Okinawa campaign. By this time, I had been transferred and was an ammunition passer for the 40-mm anticraft guns. I liked this station better than the rest because I was definitely on deck and could see all that was going on. I remained at this battle station until the sinking.

During our steady bombardment of Okinawa, we were hit by a Japanese kamikaze (suicide plane), which destroyed our fresh water converter. The day before the landing at about 7:00 a.m., I was eating breakfast on the forward starboard side of the galley when we heard the 20-mm guns go off. Before general quarters could be given to the crew, I heard a loud crash and explosion. As a result of the hit, nine comrades were killed, seven were wounded, and a large hole on the side of the ship was made. The ship started to list slowly and finally stopped because the compartments involved were shut tight. The next day the dead were given a funeral aboard and were buried ashore nearby. Because of this incident, we missed the landing on Okinawa which I was looking forward to seeing. We spent three days in a cove about ten miles from Okinawa, where we were being given a patch-up on the hull. Underwater welders worked night and day. We were in danger of Japanese planes especially at night, with the lights on. We were lucky and no planes came. When the patch-up was completed, we started back toward San Francisco. We had only enough water for cooking and drinking purposes. We were forced to take baths in salt water because the converter had been destroyed. The journey was very slow, and we were traveling all alone, no escorts at all. When we finally made it to the Mare Island repair yard, we were given 22 days' leave. I was very happy to get it.

After the ship was completely repaired and radar was installed on the 20-mm guns, we went to San Francisco for supplies. During the night, three crates were brought aboard. One was fairly large and the other two were smaller. The two small boxes were taken to the captain's quarters. The large one was placed in one of the airplane hangars, and marines stood guard. We had marines aboard the *Indianapolis* manning the 5-inch guns.

We left that morning at full speed toward Honolulu, where we fueled up and left immediately. During the voyage, I told my buddy Tommy Meyer that the contents of the crates must be some kind of "secret weapon" because marines were watching it day and night, and we were traveling at full speed constantly. The *Indianapolis* broke a speed record for ships during this trip. We arrived at Tinian about ten days after leaving San Francisco.

At Tinian the crates were unloaded, and we went to Guam for fuel and groceries. That night, we saw a movie on the quarterdeck. The morale of the crew was very high, because we had been told we were going to Leyte Island in the Philippines to join the Third Fleet for gunnery practice. We were anticipating that later we might get to go to Manila for liberty.

When we left Guam on Friday, July 27, 1945, everything seemed to be okay. My battle station at this time was furnishing ammunition to the 40-mm gun crews. My watch was as a lookout. My rate was seaman, second class in the "I" Division (deck). As mentioned earlier, I had had two battle stations prior to getting on the 40-mm. I was first assigned to loading elevators with 5-inch shells, three decks below the main deck. I then was transferred to the 8-inch guns as a trainer. I also had been attached to the small arms crew for about three months.

I was very happy after leaving Guam, because I had received mail from Mom, my girlfriend, and my brothers. I had one brother on a destroyer in the Pacific, one in the infantry in France, one in the field artillery in Italy, and one in England. I knew Mom was taking things hard with five boys all overseas at the same time. All of us were volunteers, except the older brother in the navy. I did not blame him for not signing up, as he had a wife and two children. The rest of us were single at the time of joining.

On Sunday, July 29th, there appeared to be more crewmen desiring to go to church services than before. I really did not know why until today. It seemed that something was telling us to pray especially hard that day. The Catholics were busy relieving the Protestants on watch so that they could attend their services and later the Protestants relieved the Catholics so they could attend Mass.

We also had a very good meal that day. If I remember right, we were served fried chicken with all the trimmings. Of course, on Sunday nights we were served cold cuts from the ship's soda fountain.

I was to go on watch at 4:00 a.m., and I wanted to get some sleep early. It was too hot to sleep below decks, so I brought my blanket and pillow and slept on the forecastle of the main deck in front of the 20-mm guns on the starboard side. I did not have any trouble getting to sleep.

I was awakened suddenly by an explosion that sent me into the air about one to two feet. I found myself sitting and confused. I felt a little pain in my right foot and touched it to find blood. It must have been a shrapnel wound. As soon as I got up, another explosion was felt. All the lights were out, and so were all the engines. I did not know what had happened or what to do. The nearest I could figure was that there had been one explosion right below where I was sleeping on the forecastle and another in the mid-part of the ship.

I went aft to my battle station, where I met some of my buddies. Some said the boilers had blown up, and others were not sure of anything. I had a feeling that it might have been torpedoes, but I tried to tell myself it could not be true. I did not even put a life jacket on, because I really did not believe she would sink with the compartments closed. Everything was quiet; no one knew what to do. All communications were out. Everything was at a standstill.

The ship began to list a little, but we did not pay too much attention because we had listed at Okinawa from the kamikaze hit without sinking. She started to list a little more, and I decided to put a life jacket on. Some of the men that were below decks advised that they thought we were hit at the bow and close to mid-ship forward. In that case, the first torpedo had hit right below where I was sleeping.

The ship began to list more and more. Still we thought she would stop, but just in case, we started throwing over cork nets, as they were easier to cut loose. All of a sudden, she started to list further to starboard at a faster rate, and we thought it best to get off. Captain Charles McVay did not call out to abandon ship, at least I never heard the word if it was given. An effort was made to send an SOS from one of the planes aboard ship, but the pilot said he didn't believe the message went through.

By this time, the ship had a good list, and we could hardly stand on the aft deck. I started to the port side but could not make it because it was getting too steep. I tried again and failed. I then knew I was going to go down, with the ship falling on me. I made my last try, saying to myself, "If I miss, I'm gone." Surprisingly enough, I do not know where I got the strength. I finally caught the side with my fingernails and pulled myself over. I sat on the port side of the ship and just let myself slide down to about 10 feet from the water. I was not a very good swimmer and thought the ship's suction would pull me down before I could get away from it. I started swimming but could not make any headway. The ship was going all the way over. You could hear the noise of the equipment falling inside the ship.

I looked up and saw someone I recognized. You never know too many on a cruiser with 1,197 men aboard. It was coxswain Smitty from Oklahoma. I told him I could not get away from the ship, and he said he could not either. He was a short, small man; however, he was a fair swimmer. He suggested that if we both went together we could probably make it. I held him by the shoulders, and he swam with his arms and I kicked my feet. We finally got away from the suction, and when we turned around, all we could see was the aft part of the ship going down. We kept looking until she was no longer there. We kept swimming until we saw a group of men, and we joined them.

The water was thick with oil. We were all black. I prayed fire would not start on the water and luck was with us–no fire started. The water was warm and not very rough, just long lazy swells. When we joined the group, I thanked Smitty for his help because he had probably saved my life. I began to think that if the Japanese submarine (which probably had hit us) came up and started to machine gun us, we would not stand a chance.

The group had only a cork net–no lifeboats. The net was rolled in a bundle in the middle and stretched out all around. There were about five or six fellows that were burned pretty bad, and they were laid on the high part of the net. The rest of us were in the water to our necks, holding on to the net to stay in a group. We got along fairly well the remainder of the night, with the exception of two or three comrades suffering from severe burns. We tried to comfort them the best we could.

When daylight came, we counted 124 men in our group. We had high hopes that a plane would spot us that day and we would be rescued soon. The first ordeal had passed, as certainly the Japanese submarine would not come up to shoot us down. By mid-morning the question of drinking water was entering our minds. We had two water kegs attached to the cork net. We figured this would certainly last long enough–at least until we were rescued. One keg was opened, but to our sorrow, it was empty. The other was opened and it contained salt water. We then began to worry because we knew we could do without food for a while, but not without water.

About 12:00 noon the first day, a plane passed over our heads, and we waved garments to try to attract his attention. He was flying low, and we certainly thought he had spotted us. To our surprise, the plane kept going until it was beyond the horizon.

By mid–afternoon, the three or four men who were badly burned died. We had an informal funeral by praying out loud. We took their life jackets and dog tags off and let their bodies drift away. We gave the dog tags to our deck officer for safe keeping.

The water was very warm with no rain in sight. As a rule in the South Pacific, you may get showers about two or three times a night. We were hoping this would happen, but it had not happened yet. The second night in the water was quite cool.

The best I can remember, we had about three cans of Spam and we opened one. As soon as it was opened but before anyone could taste it, the sharks were upon us. I heard a few cries of pain from some who were bit. We then decided that perhaps the sharks had smelled the meat and that drew them to us. The Spam was thrown away, rather than risk being attacked again. This did not do any good, as the sharks were upon us every three or fours hours.

I remember being taught in boot training that if you are in shark-infested waters and they strike, you should lay flat on your back and not move a muscle. I did this the whole time the sharks were coming at us. I could feel the swish of the water under me. Unfortunately, some of the men were not so lucky and died as a result of the sharks.

I had not slept a wink since the sinking. The next morning we were really getting thirsty, and by midday, it was getting very hot. We kept telling each other not to drink the ocean water because it could kill you. I kept my courage. Some could not, and soon we were losing comrades right and left. We prayed harder and louder for rescue. Certainly, we thought, someone should be looking for us by now. I said to myself, "Someone has to care for the crew of this ship." Some of the boys I knew aboard ship who never went to church services and were always using abusive language were the ones who prayed the most and the loudest. As one of our friends would die, we would all pray together and let his body go. The Lord's Prayer was the most frequently used.

The sharks hit us again and again and on the second afternoon, we lost three more to the sharks. Some were bit and survived. I had been lucky so far. Planes were passing over us day and night but did not seem to spot us.

On the third day, without sleep, water, or food, we all began to see different mirages. I had heard of this, but I never dreamed it would happen to me. On the afternoon of the third day, the deck officer shouted, "I see an island over there about a half mile away." I looked but could not see a thing but water. He kept this up for about 10 minutes, until about 25 men agreed with him. I myself thought I could see it at times, but I did not want to leave the group in case I was wrong. These men decided to swim for the so-called island against our advice. We told them we would eventually drift to the island if it was actually there. They left, and we never saw them again.

The group was rapidly reducing in size as a result of sharks, burns, and attempts to swim for the "island." The main reason we were losing men was that many could not stop themselves from drinking salt water, which eventually killed them. Thirst is a terrible ordeal to survive.

On the fourth day, I was really getting weaker. I could hardly hold on to the cork nets. My life jacket was beginning to get water-soaked, and I was beginning to sink in the water a little deeper. I was told before that the average use of a life jacket was 72 hours, and I knew that time was about up. I was so thirsty that I would let the salt water come in and out of my mouth, using all the will power I had not to swallow. I knew the consequences if I did. I was not hungry anymore, just terribly thirsty. I had not slept a wink as yet. I could not take the chance of letting loose from the net. Planes were still passing over us, but none spotted us. Men were still dying from exhaustion, thirst, and hunger. I knew my turn was coming and I prayed almost continuously. I also kept thinking of home, of Mom, who worked so hard to let me finish high school and of her high hopes that I would go to college, and of my other brothers who were overseas.

By noon on the fourth day, I had just about given up all hope of being rescued. We tried our best to keep the morale up, but in our hearts we knew it would take a miracle by God for us to be rescued. The *Indianapolis* had made frequent voyages alone in the Pacific—why, we do not know. It seemed that no one cared for us.

At approximately 4:00 p.m. on the fourth day, we heard a plane. I said to myself, "This is the last chance. By tomorrow, we will all be dead." Sometimes we wished we were dead. It would be so easy then, no pain, no thirst, and no worrying. The plane kept getting closer, and we were praying and hoping. All of a sudden we noticed the plane coming down closer to us. Of course we knew we were not the only group of survivors—I believe there were four or five other groups.

The plane tipped his wings a few times, and we knew he had spotted us. We were overjoyed. If only he could land in the water close by so we could get aboard. I knew this was impossible even if the plane was amphibious, because we were too many and too weak to swim to it. We noticed the plane dropped rafts and other supplies. The first was too far from us, and none of us dared try to swim the distance because of weakness. A small parachute with what appeared to be a small water jug did drop close by and started to drift toward us. One of the strongest left the group and started to swim toward the jug about 25 yards away. He came back with a pint of fresh water.

We were then only 30 men left in the group, and we passed the water from one to the other, just more or less wetting our lips. The survivors cooperated well in that not one drank more than his share.

We then noticed that the plane landed in the water near another group of men, and we could see some going aboard. I wish I could have gone too, but I knew it was impossible. We knew then that the pilot had radioed in for ships to come pick us up. Four more men died during the night, and it wasn't until about 3:00 a.m. the next morning that we began to see searchlights. I was contented, and I passed both my arms through the net. I must have fallen asleep for the first time. I guess I slept for about 15 minutes, because I was beginning to see the searchlights come closer. The ships had to be careful not to run over the survivors, as we were scattered all over.

The next thing I heard was a landing barge coming toward us, and it stopped about 25 yards away. I could see two men dive in the water and swim toward us. This was a happy day. I must have passed out, because when I came to I was being pulled to the landing barge by someone and he kept saying, "Take it easy." I never realized how weak I was until I was laid in the barge. I tried to stand up but could not. I gave up and just sat down. The first thing I asked for was a cigarette and was given one by the crew. I puffed twice and that was enough. What I really wanted was water.

We really had lost many of our shipmates since the sinking. In our particular group, we had counted 124 the first day, and when we were picked up, there were only 26 left. This was indeed a terrible loss...one which possibly could have been avoided.

We were taken aboard a destroyer escort. A water fountain was on deck, and we were told to drink all we wanted. This was contrary to what I thought they would allow us to do. I started to drink, but surprisingly enough I could not drink more than three swallows. We were taken inside, where we stripped off all our clothes and laid on a canvas bunk. We were told by the crew that some of the survivors were taken aboard another ship. I was so tired and weak that I could not sleep.

A few minutes after we were aboard, one of the crewmen brought us each a fresh orange cut in half. This was the most delicious thing I had ever tasted. Shortly after this, we were brought a coffee cup full of hot soup. I ate about half of this and was no longer hungry. The men assigned to the DE were sure nice, in that they tried to make us as comfortable as possible.

I slept fairly well for about two hours and when I awoke, I was taken to the shower for a bath. I was too weak to wash myself, so two other fellows helped me. One would hold me up and the other used either kerosene or diesel to remove the oil off my body. After this, I was soaped down and cleansed thoroughly. I was given clean underclothes and was put back to bed on clean sheets. After this I rewarded myself with the long sleep I really needed.

The next day we arrived at Samar, where I was taken to a field hospital for medical treatment of shock, saltwater sores, and the shrapnel wound in my right foot. We learned there that there were only 317 survivors out of 1,1997 aboard at the time of the sinking. Some survivors were taken to a hospital on the island of Peleliu, because one hospital could not take care of all of us at one time.

The main thing I wanted to do was write to Mom and all my brothers to let them know I had made it through okay. I knew that by now they had heard on the radio that the ship had sunk with 100 percent casualties, and they would be worried not knowing whether I had survived. Mom, I knew, had already received a telegram advising her that I was wounded in action, but I wanted to write her myself to tell her how I felt. I did manage to write to all during the seven days I was in this hospital.

On about the third day we were at this hospital, the date was August 10, 1945—my birthday. I was only 18 years old. One of the nurses found out, and she had a birthday cake baked for me. This made me just as happy as I could be to have someone think of me this way, especially so far away from home. On this date we also learned that an atomic bomb had been dropped on Japan and that the war was about over as far as the Japanese were concerned. We also learned that our proud ship, the USS *Indianapolis*, had delivered the atomic bombs to the B-29s in Tinian just three days prior to the sinking.

After staying in this hospital at Samar in the Philippines about seven days, we were flown to a base hospital in Guam. This was the first time I had ever flown on a large transport plane for such a distance. We made the trip fine. There were nurses aboard who treated us like royalty, always trying to do their best to make us comfortable. We stayed at the Base Hospital in Guam about three weeks as the saltwater sores were slow in healing. While at the hospital and when we were strong enough to walk around, we all were presented with the Purple Heart.

After leaving the hospital, we were taken to a submarine rest camp on Guam for about four weeks. We really had it easy there. All we had to do was eat, sleep, and play some type of sports. We had a recreation center, which had all kinds of amusements furnished by the Red Cross. The time spent there was like a vacation and we enjoyed it. But we were really looking forward to going home on leave.

After our stay there, we boarded an aircraft carrier escort to take us to the States. We arrived at San Diego where we were greeted by the people of the city with great honors. We were given liberty the first night, and all the people were so nice to us.

We then were sent to Camp Elliott near San Diego for a few days, and then we were given a 30-day survivor leave. This was a happy day for me, knowing I was going home.

My orders were to report to the U.S. naval repair base at New Orleans after my leave was up. I succeeded in getting assigned to this base as ship's company and remained there until my honorable discharge on June 15, 1946.

CHAPTER 59   SURVIVOR DRYDEN

NAME	DRYDEN, WILLIAM H. MM1C
STREET	
CITY	
STATE	
PHONE	
ENTERED SERVICE FROM	Edwardsville, AL
PICKED UP BY	USS *Bassett*
DIVISION	M Division
DOB	10/28/20
	Deceased 6/02 Winston, GA

FAMILY
Widow: Claudine

EXPERIENCE

I was raised in Cleburne County, east-central Alabama, in a farm family of five boys and three girls. I was the second-oldest child. My older brother was in the Marine Corps aboard the USS *New Orleans* at Pearl Harbor on December 7, 1941.

I joined the navy in late January in Birmingham; however, they kept sending us home as there was no place else to send us. On March 9, I took the oath and was sent to San Diego. After three weeks of boot camp, I was sent to Treasure Island. Shortly after I got off the bus, there was a change in orders. I reboarded the bus for Mare Island and went aboard the USS *Helena* for two days. In April I was transferred to the USS *Indianapolis*.

On my first trip we escorted a convoy to Melbourne, Australia. We spent one night and I got to go ashore. On our return, we stopped at Pago Pago American Somar to give stores and fuel to destroyers. This was when we learned of the Coral Sea Battle and the loss of the USS *Lexington*. From Somoa we went to Pearl Harbor for supplies, fuel, and our orders. We left Pearl Harbor in late May and were in an assist position for the Battle of Midway but did not participate.

We got patrol duty out of Kodiak along the Aleutian Islands, while bases were besieged. After taking Kiska and Attu, we went back to Pearl Harbor where we were assigned to Admiral Raymond Spruance as his flagship. In the fall of 1943, we started island hopping, retaking Tawara and Makin in the Gilbert chain and continuing right across the Pacific. In February 1945, we were involved in the invasions of Iwo Jima and the first carrier air strike on the Japanese mainland. In March we were involved in the invasion of Okinawa when we got hit by a suicide plane. We went back to Mare Island for repairs.

On July 16, 1945, we left San Francisco with the atomic bomb. On July 26 we delivered it to Tinian and then went to Guam for supplies and orders. We were ordered to Leyte Gulf and about halfway there we were sunk. The only way I can figure I came through was determination, faith in the navy, and above all, divine power. I was picked up by the USS *Bassett*. We went to Samar, then Guam, then Camp Dealy, and eventually to San Diego. I had several leaves and was honorably discharged November 15, 1945.

After the service, I was restless and could not get my feet on the ground. I did not know what I wanted to do. I got a job on a construction site with American Bridge, a division of U.S. Steel. This turned into a 20-year job. I frequently moved to new job sites, including the eastern half of the U.S. and Bogota, Columbia in South America. I also built the first tall building at Epcot for Disney World in Orlando. I married a lovely lady, Claudine, whom I knew before the war. I quit American Bridge, moved to Atlanta, where I worked for a local company, and retired in 1982.

Survivor Dryden submitted this chapter one month prior to his death on June 28, 2002. God rest his soul.

CHAPTER 60   SURVIVOR ECK

NAME	ECK, HAROLD A. S2C
STREET	3323 Constance St
CITY	New Orleans
STATE	LA 70115
PHONE	504 899 1425
ENTERED SERVICE FROM	New Orleans, LA
PICKED UP BY	USS *Bassett*
DIVISION	7th Division
DOB	8/11/26

FAMILY
Spouse: Genevieve (Jenny) Trenticosta Eck
Children: Patrick Eck, Maria Eck Bullard
Grandchildren: Jennifer Eck, Emily Eck, Jenna Bullard, Mia Bullard, Olivia Bullard, Trent Bullard

EXPERIENCE
I was born in New Orleans, Louisiana on August 11, 1926. I was the youngest of three children born to loving German parents, and I grew up in a household in which three generations all lived together. I spent my summers at a local swimming pool and became an accomplished swimmer and lifeguard. At the time, I didn't realize how this experience would affect my life, but I soon found out.

In 1944, at the age of seventeen, I begged my parents to sign the waiver allowing me to enter the navy. I knew that as the war progressed, it was only a matter of time before I would be drafted. I figured that if I didn't enlist on my own, they would choose a branch for me, and I wanted to join the navy. My parents were quite hesitant, because my older brother was already serving in the army, and they resisted my requests for months and months. Finally, two weeks before my eighteenth birthday, my father relented and went with me to the enlistment office.

After three months at boot camp in San Diego, I came home for a two-week leave before my first assignment...the USS *Indianapolis*. As I announced this to my family and friends, I was so proud because I already knew so much of the history of this great ship.

I left with great pride in December of 1944, leaving my family hoping and praying for my safe return. I boarded the *Indy* at Mare Island, California. I was assigned to a battle station toward the bow of the ship at one of the 20-mm anti-aircraft gun mounts. My job was to hustle ammo to the loaders for the guns. I participated in the battles at Iwo Jima and the raid on the Japanese homeland, as well as the kamikaze attack on the *Indy* at Okinawa in which we lost nine sailors. The *Indy* was badly damaged by this attack, and we returned to the States at Mare Island for repairs. I knew we would be back, because Japan had to be invaded in order to end this war. By July 14, 1945, the *Indy* was ready for action.

At this time, I remember "secret cargo" being loaded onto the *Indy*. We all wondered what was in this crate, and we all made our speculations about what it might contain. Some guessed it was secret germ warfare, and others joked that it was General MacArthur's toilet paper. Unknown to us, the cargo contained the critical components of the new atomic bomb. All I knew is that we were traveling at record-breaking speed across the Pacific Ocean. We arrived at Tinian and the secret cargo was immediately unloaded. Our new orders were to proceed to Guam, and then on to Leyte in the Philippines for gunnery training. On the morning of July 28, we left Guam on the 1,200 mile journey to Leyte.

It was hot and humid, and quite uncomfortable—even for a New Orleans boy. On Sunday evening, July 29, I went to my rack below deck. I felt like I had just fallen asleep when I was thrown out of my rack a few minutes past midnight. I didn't know what had happened, but everyone was yelling to get topside, so I grabbed a kapok life jacket and started moving. My first thought was to go to my battle station, but the ship was already listing, making it nearly impossible to walk. The first torpedo had hit near the bow and the second one hit 180 feet from the bow. This second one was the killer. It ignited a fuel tank and severed water main lines as well as the electric power. The orders to abandon ship had been issued, and I just stepped over the rail and slid into the water.

Once in the water, I swam as hard as I could away from the ship. I now realized how fortunate I was to have had the lifeguard training! I swam about 100 yards and looked back. The stern of the ship had risen, and I noticed how the props were turning slowly. It just slipped into the sea. Hard to believe my eyes...just 15 minutes earlier I had been asleep on that ship! I will never forget that sight or forget the feeling I had at that moment. I just stared at the surface where she once was. Many men around me were screaming in pain but I seemed to be okay. I was covered in oil and my eyes burned, but I was okay. The first thing I thought about was whether the sub that torpedoed us would surface and kill us all now.

I spent the first night freezing cold in that water, just hugging my life jacket. I knew that after dawn, our rescue would arrive. I swam to a large group of men that were holding onto a cargo floater net. The wounded men were placed into the net and everyone else held on. I did not know anyone in the group. Someone counted and there were 124 men in this group. We thought we were the only survivors.

As daylight came, the sun got hotter and hotter. I tore my shirt to make a cap to cover my head. We all talked about how we were certain we would be rescued that day. Some said they thought we would be found the next day but at least they would come for us. We agreed that worst-case scenario would be that we would be reported missing on July 31 when we didn't arrive at Leyte.

As we talked about our rescue a guy next to me nudged my shoulder and said, "Hey, look at that!" At first I didn't know what he was talking about, but then I saw it...a large, grayish brown fin circling the group. Everyone started yelling "SHARK!" and bunching up tighter in the group. There soon were hundreds of fins around us. The first attack I saw was on a sailor who had drifted away from the group. I heard yelling and screaming and saw him thrashing...then I just saw red foamy water. Next thing I knew, other sharks started attacking the poor guy, too. I was frozen with fear. My legs dangled in the water and were constantly being bumped by the sharks swimming below. I curled my legs up under me as close as I could. The sharks would come and go, but the fear of them was always there.

We talked about the best thing to do when the sharks started to circle again. Some said to stay very still and let them pass, while others said we should thrash around and beat the water to frighten them away. We tried everything. Sometimes it worked; other times it didn't.

Many of the injured men who had been placed on the floater net had died. We removed their jackets and set them free. This was very difficult for me because their bodies were quickly followed by sharks. I thought about the rescue ships. I thought about home. I thought about my old neighborhood. I thought about my group of friends nicknamed the "Tornadoes." I thought about my mother and father and our corner grocery. I just wanted a large cool drink of water!

On the second day, we faced the job of freeing those that didn't make it through the night. Again, the sharks showed up and the floating dead were taken in a feeding frenzy. Planes passed that day, and we yelled and screamed and waved but no one noticed us. We huddled together at the end of the second day, encouraging each other that surely we had been missed at Leyte and rescue was on its way. The days were hard because of the heat and sharks. The nights were so cold and dark...many more men died.

On the morning of the third day, I was shocked to see the condition of the other guys around me. They were hallucinating from being so dehydrated. We were hungry and thirsty. On our bodies we had huge sores that made us miserable. I remember a fellow survivor who floated up to me and told me to look at the tag on my kapok life jacket. I looked down and saw that it read "Good for 48 hours." Some men started to drift away from the group, telling us they were going to an island or a ship or to land that they saw just ahead. I remember one guy who started taking off his life jacket and telling me that the ship was just below the surface and that we could go to the water fountain. I tried to restrain him, but he just slipped away and never came back. By now, over half of the original group was gone. I was floating in the most horrible sea you could imagine. There was blood and oil mixed with parts of bodies and half-eaten corpses still floating in their life jackets. And I was only 18 years old!

On the fourth day, many people had given up hope. My life jacket was so water-logged that only my head was out of the water as the jacket sunk deeper. I just hung onto that floater net, and my mind drifted. By nightfall, I was more dead than alive. I thought this was the last night of my life. I just prayed.

The next thing I knew, I saw a huge beam of light that looked like it was coming from the sky. The rescue ships were shining their searchlight into the cloud so that we could see them coming, and it gave us hope. I couldn't believe my eyes. Some of the others saw this too. Some started yelling, "They're coming, they're coming!" I didn't know if it was heaven opening up for us or our rescue. Either way, this had to end.

The next thing I remember was waking up with a light shining in my face and hands grabbing me. I was being pulled from the water onto a LCVP and being placed in a wire basket. I could hear myself moaning and crying but that's the last thing I remember. I found out later that of the 124 men in my group, 26 had survived and were rescued by the USS *Bassett*. God bless those men! That

searchlight that night saved my life. It helped me dig up that last little bit of
courage to not give up.

I have no idea how much time passed, but when I awoke, I was clean but had
no recollection of how that had happened! A kind sailor on the *Bassett* handed
me a fresh orange. That was the best gift I have ever been given. I thanked God
that I was alive and went back to sleep. I regained full consciousness in a hospital
on the island of Samar. We were issued Purple Hearts in the hospital. I was very
sad when I heard that only 317 survivors had been rescued. I was so sad because
I remembered what happened to so many of them.

My family had followed my whereabouts through news clippings and my
censored letters. Eight months had passed since I had left, and several days
following the news of the Nagasaki bombing, my father received a cryptic
telegram–just two lines–informing him that his son, Harold, was "missing in
action." He did not have the heart to share the news with his family, so he kept
it to himself, hoping. I was instructed to write a letter home, but not to mention
any details of the sinking. I gave them very few details other than the facts that
the ship was sunk and I was okay. They just thought that since I was such a good
swimmer, I must have swam to a nearby island. They had no idea what I had just
experienced.

In September, we were put on the aircraft carrier USS *Hollandia,* and we
headed toward home. I arrived in New Orleans in October and finished out the
last year of my enlistment there. I was honorably discharged in the fall of 1946
and entered the New Orleans Fire Department. I never talked much about the
experience.

Captain McVay lived in New Orleans for awhile, just about five blocks from
my house. One day I ran into him and hesitantly introduced myself. He looked
like he didn't want to talk about it. He just asked me how I was and told me to
take care of myself. I guess he felt the same way I did. It was over and I didn't
want to talk about it. I knew about the court-martial of Captain McVay, and I
thought it was horrific. How could they do this to him? He was a wonderful
captain and I certainly would not place any blame on him for the tragedy.

I raised a family and made a career as a firefighter. I tried not to talk about the
Indianapolis. I just told my wife a few little details, and I lost touch with my
shipmates. When I was young, I just kept telling myself that that was war and
things like that happen in a war. But as I grew older, what had happened to me
began to work on me. I opened up a little more and started answering a few of
my family's questions.

Then in 1960, I attended the first reunion of the survivors. That's when I came
to grips with the whole thing. My best friends in my life are those who are my
fellow survivors and those who were part of the rescue, especially my angel,
Chuck Gwinn. What I didn't know at the time (but soon found out) was that it
was navy pilot Chuck Gwinn who by chance flew his Ventura over us, first
spotted us in the water, and radioed for our rescue. He saved my life. I thank

God every day for him and all those involved in our rescue. I was more dead than alive and would not have survived another few hours had they not come when they did.

I live every day of my life remembering the men that did not survive. I think about them during every major event or holiday. I think about the lives that they never had; I think about the children and grandchildren that they never had. When people want to know how I survived, I just tell them that God and the devil got together. God said I wasn't good enough to come to heaven yet. And the devil said I wasn't bad enough to come to hell...I had been an altar boy back in New Orleans! So they didn't want me in heaven and they didn't want me in hell, and that's why they just let me stay right here. I always figured that God had a plan for me...and that's how I live my life.

CHAPTER 61   SURVIVOR ERICKSON

NAME	ERICKSON, THEODORE M. S2C
STREET	
CITY	
STATE	
PHONE	
ENTERED SERVICE FROM	New Canada, MN
PICKED UP BY	USS *Doyle*
DIVISION	
DOB	Deceased 12/97

FAMILY
Widow: Mary Virginia
Children: Judith Erickson Zink (Edward), Terrence Erickson (Therese), Mary Candace Erickson Butcher (James William), Lawrence Wise-Erickson (Dianna), Jean Erickson (Mitchell Franklin), Leonard Erickson (Mary), Elizabeth Erickson-Quilling (John), Richard Erickson (Michele)
Grandchildren: Danika, Jared, Tamara, Nichole, Michelle, Tina, Shannon, Keely, Mark, Mathew, Kristin, Teresa, Jennifer, Rohni, Dawn, Theodore, Jeremy, Justin, Colleen, Cynthia
Great-Grandchildren: Brenna, Sean, Jessika, Victoria, Shannon, Victoria, Stephanie, Joshua, Katrina, Constance, Thomas, Alexander, Jordan, Victoria, Scott, Jessica, Drew, Taylor, Camryn, Samantha, Kyle, Sara

EXPERIENCE

Respectfully submitted by Survivor Erickson's family.

Our family grew up with the story of the *Indianapolis*. Dad didn't talk about his experiences until the time of the first reunion in 1960. After that he went to every reunion until his death in 1997. We feel that the best way we can share our father's story is through his own words. This chapter, Ted Erickson's story, is comprised of excerpts of speeches he gave to school groups about the *Indy*.

One of his eight children, Candy, was born while Ted was in the water. She was always very special to him. Thoughts of his family and unborn child kept Dad alive in the water. The story of the *Indianapolis* is also about the wives, girlfriends, and mothers that were at home. Our mother waited at home with two babies and one on the way. Then, women "at home" endured days and weeks of fear and years of loving support when these sailors came home.

In Loving Memory, The Theodore Erickson Family

Ted's Experience

"In San Francisco, we picked up big, big heavy boxes. They told us they were packages but didn't tell us what they were. Both of these packages were put into the port hangars. The morning we left San Francisco, it was very, very foggy. We pulled underneath the Golden Gate Bridge. I had driven over it many-a-time, but never under it. After we got out about seven miles, we started picking up speed. We could feel the vibrations from the fantail all the way to the front. The boilers were really taking off. We broke all speed records going to Pearl Harbor. The water was rough. My watch was the 5-inch gun on the quarterdeck, close to the packages. I used to sit on them or close by them on coils of rope. On watch we would take turns on the railing, watching over the side to see if we could see submarines or ships. You could see a ship about seven miles away.

"We arrived in beautiful Pearl Harbor where the water and sky were blue. We didn't have to wait. They docked us immediately and we took on fuel. The part I could never understand is why we took all-weather gear when we were going to the South Pacific, where it is nice and warm. We were expecting shore leave where we could go for a rest period and have a couple beers. We were only there three or four hours, and we didn't get a chance to go to shore.

"After we loaded fuel and supplies, we headed to Tinian at a pretty good speed. The packages were unloaded at Tinian. We didn't learn that it was the atomic bomb until we were in the hospital at Guam.

"We left Tinian for Guam and got our orders. Orders were to go to the Philippines and have gunnery practice. Halfway to the Philippines, a Japanese submarine spotted us. It was a big, new submarine. We didn't know it was out there.

"It was Sunday night, July 29, 1945. I had taken a shower and grabbed a blanket and gone up on the deck to sleep. Our ship did not have air conditioning and it was very hot in the South Pacific. I laid the blanket on the deck and slept until it was my time to go to watch at fifteen minutes before midnight. It was dark. A few minutes after midnight, I heard an explosion. I heard the boom and saw all the flames from the center part of the ship going up through the smokestack. I knew something had happened.

"When the torpedo hit, I went down a ladder toward the fantail because I didn't have my rubber belt. There was a big mesh bag with some kapok jackets. I grabbed one and slipped it over my head. The ship was listing and started over on its side. I could hear some of the men that had gone before me yelling and screaming. They must have hit the screws down below. I went over as far as I could get, and then I dropped through the screws. I went down, down, down, and I didn't think I would ever come up. I was exhaling a little air every now and then to be able to breathe. When I got up the ship had bounced up and the bow of the ship was corkscrewing right down into the water.

"When I got out far enough I noticed a bunch of fellows in a group. There was one fellow with a broken leg. You know what a broken leg is like. They tried to hold him up out of the water as he didn't have a jacket on. You could hear him scream as the bones would grind against each other. Some of the men never had life jackets and would take off their dungarees and shake them in the air to pick up air pockets so they use them as life jackets.

"Everybody was getting sick because they had ingested some of that heavy oil. You didn't know anyone as we were all covered with heavy black oil.

"The next morning the waves were pretty high, and whenever we came to the top of the swell we could see the sharks off in the distance. We didn't have any water and we didn't dare drink the salt water because it would make you delirious. There were quite a few that drank the salt water and got delirious. They would imagine that could swim to an island. They never came back.

"We floated that way for several days and nights. By the second and third day it was very hot. The sun was beating down. I only had my shorts on, and I tore those off and wore them over my head as a deterrent from the sun. At night it was cold and you would shiver.

"I was getting pretty hungry. We had no food and no water, so I was going to see if I could catch a fish. We could see these little fish swimming by us all the time. I cupped my hands and tried to grab one but never did. I picked up a potato that was floating around in the water, but I never did eat it.

"Lt. Gwinn was flying on a patrol run with a new type of antenna. It was tangled so he was trying to untwist it, and as he was looking out the window he saw an oil slick. He flew a little closer and saw heads bobbing in the water. He radioed back for help.

"Lt. Marks came out with his PBY plane and landed in the water. It was the first time he had landed on rough water. The plane bounced and popped some rivets. Some of his crew took pencils and used them to plug the holes on the pontoon. As he taxied the plane, I don't know where his crew got their strength, but they picked men right up out of the water and put them on the pontoons and on the wings. He picked up 56 men. I was too far away to swim to the plane.

"Another plane came and dropped rubber rafts. There were twelve men in my group, and it was an eight-man raft. With all of us, the raft was floating under water. About midnight, the USS *Doyle* came and shined a big spotlight up in the air to give us hope someone was coming. I was picked up about 4:30 in the morning. The *Doyle* pulled right up to us and dropped a line down over my waist and hoisted me up to the deck. When I got to the deck, I thought I could just walk off, but I completely collapsed. They took me to a shower and washed all the oil off and gave me beef broth. They took me to a bunk where I could sleep. The kapok jacket I had been wearing was very water soaked.

"We went to Peleilu to a navy hospital ship there. I don't know how long I was in the hospital, but then we were taken to Guam to another hospital to recuperate.

"My wife was expecting our third child at the time. When I was in the hospital in Guam I contacted the Red Cross nurse to find out how my wife was. On the same day they let my wife know that I was wounded, she got a letter from me. The Red Cross told me I had a daughter and they brought me a little birthday cake–a "Happy Birthday" cake."

The Erickson family would like to thank Al Mueller, a teacher in Cakato, Minnesota for inviting the Minnesota survivors to speak to his classes annually.

CHAPTER 62   SURVIVOR ERWIN

NAME	ERWIN, LOUIS H. COX
STREET	4340 Duvall St East Ridge
CITY	Chattanooga
STATE	TN 37412
PHONE	423 698 2870
ENTERED SERVICE FROM	Chattanooga, TN
PICKED UP BY	PBY Tr USS *Doyle*
DIVISION	4th Division
DOB	3/1/25

FAMILY
Spouse: Thelma
Children: Son Louis "Kayo" Jr. and wife Brenda; Daughter Sandy and husband, Jerry

EXPERIENCE
I enlisted in the U.S. Navy when I was 17 years old. I took boot camp training in San Diego, California. After

boot camp, I was shipped to Pearl Harbor where I went aboard the USS *Indianapolis* (CA-35) in the Fourth Division, a deck division that manned the 5-inch guns. I started as a hot shellman and then was a pot loader, then a pointer, trainer, and rammerman.

I am very proud to have served aboard the USS *Indianapolis*. For over two years, the *Indy* was my home. The USS *Indianapolis* and her crew were one of the greatest ships in the U.S. Navy Fleet, earning ten battle stars. I am fortunate to have served aboard the USS *Indianapolis* on eight of those ten battle stars, starting at Gilbert Islands in 1943 until July 30, 1945, when the *Indy* went down.

I survived four days and five nights in the water in only a kapok life jacket. We would get very cold at night and very hot in the day. The sun and salt water in the day would burn your eyes and the glare on the water hurt very much. Every day I would get so thirsty for a fresh drink of water. Not having food didn't bother me too much, just my thirst for water. I would feel so bad when my shipmates would start to lose it after drinking salt water. They would go out of their mind, lose it, then disappear into the water. Sharks would take their toll. Day and night you could hear screams for help. We would do our best to help save our shipmates. It just was not enough.

I was in a group of 200-250 the first day. When we were picked up by Lt. Adrian Marks' PBY a few days later, there were only 56 men left in our group. The other shipmates were lost at sea. Later, we were transfered to the USS *Doyle*. I would pray every day and every night for help that we would all make it home safely. I also prayed for the ones that we lost at sea. May God bless them and their families.

After the war, I had enough points to get out of the service. I received my honorable discharge in 1946.

I married a wonderful woman, Thelma. We have been married for 56 years and have two wonderful children: Louis "Kayo" Jr. and his wife Brenda, and Sandy and her husband, Jerry. We are very proud of them all and love them.

I would like to thank so many people for their help in rescuing the survivors. Being 1 of 56 men rescued by the PBY, thank you Adrian Marks and crew, also to Wilbur Gwinn and crew. I would like to thank all the USS *Indianapolis* Survivors Organization officers and board of directors. Thanks to the ones that served our organization in earlier years and those in office now. Special thanks to Paul and Mary Lou Murphy for keeping us up to date on all that's going on and for spending countless hours working for our organization. Thanks to all the people that have supported our survivor reunions.

NAME   ETHIER, EUGENE   EM 3C
STREET
CITY
STATE
PHONE
ENTERED SERVICE FROM   Minneapolis, MN
PICKED UP BY   USS *Bassett*
DIVISION
DOB   Deceased 7/70

FAMILY

EXPERIENCE
   Unable to contact any family members.

NAME   EVANS, CLAUDUS GM 3C
STREET
CITY
STATE
PHONE
ENTERED SERVICE FROM   Henrietta, TX
PICKED UP BY   USS *Doyle*
DIVISION   3rd Division
DOB   1/15/25   Deceased 9/02

We Dedicate this Plaque to
Claudus Evans
*An Honorable Man
and
Purple Heart Recipient*

FAMILY
Spouse: Helen B.
Children: Marilyn and Claudia
Grandchildren: Todd and Troy

EXPERIENCE
   I have had a lot of good times in my life, including
serving in the U.S. Navy.
   One of the most unpleasant experiences was being
rolled out of my bunk in the middle of the night,

grabbing anything so I could get topside to find out what was happening. I was told the ship was sinking and to abandon ship as quickly as possible. I did not have a life jacket and had only a pair of shorts on. I swam for a while and bumped into a fellow sailor who had two life jackets. I do not remember his name, but we were together all the time until we were picked up five days later.

I guess he and I were supposed to live because we had help to survive this ordeal. We would swim to a different group every day, but returned to our original group each night. I guess the sharks were told to leave us alone.

He and I were in the group to get aboard the PBY when it landed close by. We emptied the keg of water that he carried real quick.

I always will have great respect for Captain McVay. I believe he was correct in his decision. If it were possible, I would serve under him again and be very happy to do so.

Survivor Evans passed away during the completion of this book on September 2, 2002. God rest his soul.

CHAPTER 65   SURVIVOR FARMER

NAME	FARMER, ARCHIE C. COX
STREET	111 Prospect Ave #30
CITY	Hot Springs
STATE	AR 71901
PHONE	501 620 4486
ENTERED SERVICE FROM	Houston, TX
PICKED UP BY	USS *Talabot* Tr USS *Register*
DIVISION	5th Division
DOB	3/3/23

FAMILY
Spouse: Alice

EXPERIENCE
No response.

NAME	FARRIS, EUGENE S1C (Radioman)
STREET	
CITY	
STATE	
PHONE	
ENTERED SERVICE FROM	Bethlehem, PA
PICKED UP BY	USS *Register*
DIVISION	
DOB	Deceased

FAMILY

EXPERIENCE

Unable to contact any family members.

CHAPTER 67 SURVIVOR FEAKES

NAME	FEAKES, FRED A01C
STREET	
CITY	
STATE	
PHONE	
ENTERED SERVICE FROM	Santa Cruz, CA
PICKED UP BY	USS *Register*
DIVISION	
DOB	Deceased 1/85

FAMILY

Widow: Katherine

EXPERIENCE

Unable to contact any family members.

NAME	FEDORSKI, NICHOLAS S1C
STREET	
CITY	
STATE	
PHONE	
ENTERED SERVICE FROM	Milwaukee, WI
PICKED UP BY	USS *Talbot* tr USS *Register*
DIVISION	
DOB	6/26/11 Deceased 10/92

FAMILY

Children: One son
Grandchildren: Three
Great-Grandchildren: One

EXPERIENCE

Submitted by Survivor Fedorski's daughter-in-law, Susan Fedorski.

Nick lost his brother, Greg (USMC), at Tarawa on November 20, 1943. Greg was buried at sea and received a Purple Heart posthumously. Nick was inducted into the navy January 14, 1944 and went into active duty January 21, 1944.

After the USS *Indianapolis* tragedy, Nick returned home to his wife, Della, in Milwaukee, Wisconsin. He worked at American Motors until his retirement. Nick and Della had one son. Nick passed away in 1992. He didn't want much in life; material things were not important. He didn't speak much of the tragedy and didn't care much to be near water.

After reading the book *Fatal Voyage*, by Dan Kurzman, I spoke with Nick about it and he relayed this story to me:

Because it was hot, he was sleeping near the sail locker topside. He said as they were abandoning ship, he was throwing kapok jackets overboard and handing them out to men. He jumped off the port side (the high side). He missed the spinning propeller, but many didn't. The last thing he saw of the ship was the propeller in the air. It was glowing like a beautiful sunset. It was the last thing to go down. The group of men he was with numbered 188. By the time they were rescued there were only 10 men left. Most were taken by sharks, drinking salt water, and hallucinations. On the fourth day a raft was dropped down to him by Lt. Adrian Marks' PBY. He was rescued by the USS *Talbot* and transferred to the USS *Register*. He received his Purple Heart in his hospital bed.

NAME	FELTS, DONALD BM1C
STREET	
CITY	
STATE	
PHONE	
ENTERED SERVICE FROM	Artesia, CA
PICKED UP BY	USS *Doyle*
DIVISION	
DOB	Deceased 91

FAMILY

EXPERIENCE
Unable to contact any family members.

NAME	FERGUSON, ALBERT CMM	
STREET		
CITY		
STATE		
PHONE		
ENTERED SERVICE FROM	Coeur D'Alene, ID	
PICKED UP BY	USS *Register*	
DIVISION		
DOB	6/21/18	Deceased 1/94

FAMILY
Widow: Georgianna
Children: Son Jeffrey Ferguson, Daughter Heather
Grandchildren: Kevin and Phillip

EXPERIENCE
Respectfully submitted by Survivor Ferguson's son, Jeff.
My dad died in January 1994 from complications following cancer surgery. He was a member of the USS Indianapolis Survivors Organization but never saw the

completed monument in Indianapolis. This story was assembled from excerpts of writings he was working on before he died. Thanks for the opportunity to share with others my father's memories about his service aboard the USS *Indianapolis*.

I was born June 21, 1918 in Libby, Montana but was raised in Coeur d'Alene, Idaho. My parents had immigrated to the U.S. from Scotland, so it came as little surprise to find myself in a ship's engine room years later. I was one of three children: I had a sister Peg and brother Ewen, who joined the army and slogged through the ground war in Europe.

I enlisted in the United States Navy December 2, 1940. The following year I graduated from Henry Ford Trade School as a machinist mate second class.

I first boarded the USS *Indianapolis* in June 1941. This magnificent gray lady was my first ship and her steam engine room was my home throughout World War II. My friends called me "Al" or "Fergy" and my soon-to-be wife called me "Bert".

I had the honor of standing watch as chief machinist mate as we steamed from Hunters Point outside San Francisco for the Marianas July 16, 1945. I wouldn't learn about the nature of our secret cargo for years, but my shipmates and I coaxed enough speed out of the engines to break all speed records and deliver that cargo to the island of Tinian in ten days. We participated in battle stations together at Bougainville, Attu, the Gilberts, Kwajalein, Eniwetok, Palau, Saipan, Guam, Honsu, Iwo Jima, and Okinawa.

When the *Indy* was stateside for refitting, I wed Georgianna "Nancy" Kidwell on May 7, 1945. I also left with her a chunk of the *Indy's* main teak deck that I had salvaged when parts of the rotten wood had been replaced during one of her overhauls at Mare Island. I had spent some of my free time whittling and carving the chunk into a sculpture of a hand. I had no idea how precious that piece of the *Indy* would become to me later, after the ship was sunk. (The little chunk of teak deck from the *Indianapolis* now belongs to Survivor Ferguson's son, Jeff.)

Midnight, July 30, 1945, I was relieved from my watch in the engine room. I stepped into the shower to wash away the day's grime and sweat. The shock of the torpedoes in succession threw me to the deck and against the sharp edge of a sink, slicing my calf open five to six inches—to the bone. Nothing was broken, so I was able to scramble out and up to the deck, but I was bleeding everywhere. A cook came up to me and handed me his pants to wrap around my leg. I never saw him again.

As the ship reared and slowly rolled, I stepped off the side and dropped into the water. By the time I broke the surface, the *Indy* was completely gone. I floated using a large, empty tin until I was scooped into a raft by some shipmates. One of them put a tourniquet on my leg, and the days of hope and despair began.

One of my raftmates was preparing to amputate my lower leg to prevent gangrene, but we were rescued before any impromptu surgery had to be performed. My group was a handful of sailors picked up by the USS *Register*. My leg was saved.

I stayed in the navy and returned to battle November 1952 off Korea, in the engine room of the destroyer USS *Thompson* (DMS 38) as an ensign. After that I spent three years at Subic Bay in the Philippines. After making lieutenant, I commanded Mine Squadron Three is Sasebo, Japan from 1958 to 1961. In January 1962 I transferred to the USS *Frontier* (AD 25) and retired from the navy January 14, 1964.

After I retired, I joined Stauffer Chemical Company in southern California and was in charge of plant maintenance for ten years. After that I ran a little printing operation more as a hobby than a business. Through it all I raised a son, Jeff, a daughter, Heather, and have given grandfatherly advice to my son's boy, Kevin.

My wife often suggested we take a vacation cruise, but I always told her the last ship I would ever be on would be painted gray. Sure enough, in autumn of 1982 my son and I took a father-and-son trip to England and Scotland, and we boarded an old British Cruiser anchored as a tourist attraction in the Thames in London. She bore the hull number 35, so I couldn't resist the tour. Climbing down through the engine room, my own memories flooded back: the smell of fuel oil, hiss of steam, rattle in the valves, wide grins of friends through oil-grimed faces. To borrow a phrase from literature, the memories reminded me...they were the best of times, and the worst of times, but times I wouldn't trade with another soul.

CHAPTER 71   SURVIVOR FITTING

NAME	FITTING, JOHNNY W. GM1C
STREET	
CITY	
STATE	
PHONE	
ENTERED SERVICE FROM	Kooskia, IA
PICKED UP BY	PBY tr USS *Doyle*
DIVISION	
DOB	Deceased 11/88

FAMILY

EXPERIENCE
Unable to contact any family members.

NAME	FLATEN, HAROLD J. WT2C
STREET	
CITY	
STATE	
PHONE	
ENTERED SERVICE FROM	Snohomish, WA
PICKED UP BY	USS *Bassett*
DIVISION	
DOB	2/23/23
	Deceased 11/00 Snohomish, WA

FAMILY
Widow: Ida
Children: Sheila Flaten Houck, Terry Flaten (Carolee)
Grandchildren: Elke McGarry (Rob), Stephanie
Foster (Adam)
Great-Grandchildren: Christopher McGarry,
Nicholas McGarry, Alyssa McGarry, Landon McGarry,
Kendall McGarry, Kellen McGarry, Ocean Foster

EXPERIENCE
Submitted by Survivor Flaten's granddaughter, Elke McGarry.

The following is written in memory of our husband, father, and grandpa,
Harold Flaten, who survived the sinking of the USS *Indianapolis*. Hap passed
away on Thanksgiving day of 2000 at the age of 77. Our family is not certain
that Hap would have wanted to or been able to fully describe his experience
aboard the *Indy* and those days in the water following the sinking, as it was very
difficult for him to relive it. Hap, would, if asked, describe his experience of this
event, and he did so throughout the years as an invited speaker at Kiwanis
meetings and also as a subject for his grandchildren's school reports. Our family,
as well as anyone who heard about this incident from him, had the greatest
respect for Hap and his fellow crew who experienced this tragic event.

Harold "Hap" Flaten was born in Park River, North Dakota on February 23,
1923 and moved to Washington state as a youngster. He married Ida on August
1, 1942. Hap was a young newlywed when he signed up to serve in the military
during the summer of 1943 and celebrated his first wedding anniversary while at
boot camp in Farragut, Idaho. Aboard the *Indy*, Hap was in charge of the
evaporation of distilled water that made steam to run turbines as well as the water
supply for the ship. During battle conditions, he worked on the fuel circuit and
the transferring of water.

Early in the morning of July 30, 1945, upon hearing the explosion caused by
the torpedoes, Hap and a fellow sailor ran down to secure the water tanks in the

airlocks. He and another shipmate discovered a man who had been badly burned by the explosion. They dragged the man to the mess hall and yelled for someone to give him the medical help he needed. Before leaving the man, Hap gave his own life vest to him, as the man was without. Hap then grabbed an extra life jacket and made a quick retreat overboard.

Once in the water, Hap knew that falling asleep would be fatal. He and another survivor agreed to guard each other to make sure they did not go to sleep. By the third day in the water, however, they could no longer trust each other. Hap remembers one hallucinating sailor who claimed that a woman was giving birth and needed help. The man swam off, never to be seen again.

After being rescued, Hap was taken to a hospital in the Philippines. His weight five days prior to the sinking of the ship had been a healthy 230 pounds. Now, he'd dropped down drastically to 147. His foot had to be treated because of a wound incurred by scraping it on his retreat from the ship. The minor cut turned major after it became infected in the water.

Hap was honorably discharged from the navy in 1945. In 1947, he began work at a petroleum products business in Snohomish, Washington, eventually taking over the business. In 1958, it was discovered that he had cancer. He fought cancer off and on for many years during his life. He was never able to attend a reunion of the *Indy* survivors, as it seemed that every time he was invited to a reunion event, he was in the hospital or in very poor health. Fortunately, he and Ida were able to enjoy traveling to Hawaii and Reno, among other places, during the times when he was feeling well. Hap was a good golfer and an even better bowler. He knew how to grow a great garden full of vegetables. Hap sold his petroleum business and retired in 1981.

As a final note, some years before Hap passed away, he'd made it known to his wife, Ida, that when he died, he would never want his ashes scattered over the ocean. The reason for this was that he'd "fought too hard to get out" of the ocean during those days in the water in 1945.

NAME	FORTIN, VERLIN L. WT3C
STREET	337 N Orchard Dr
CITY	Burbank
STATE	CA 91506
PHONE	818 846 7227
ENTERED SERVICE FROM	Burbank, CA
PICKED UP BY	USS *Talbot* Tr USS *Register*
DIVISION	
DOB	1/24/25

FAMILY

EXPERIENCE

I was born in Burbank, California in 1925. I spent most of my youth working with my dad raising horses. I never went close to the water until I joined the navy. I never learned how to swim.

When I was 17 and a half, I quit school to join the navy; however, the navy would not accept me until I was 18. So at 18, they took me to Farragut, Idaho for 16 weeks of training. They let us out in eight weeks. I got to go home for two weeks and then was assigned to the USS *Indianapolis* in 1943. I was assigned to the fire room, and that's where I spent most of my time aboard the *Indianapolis*.

In March of 1945, we were hit by a suicide plane. One of my buddies was killed. We buried him in Okinawa, then came back to Mare Island for repairs. In July we took off to deliver a special cargo which was a mystery to us. In ten days we dropped it off on the island of Tinian, then took off to the Philippines. It was during this time that we were sunk on July 30 at midnight.

I was sleeping down below that night. Usually I slept on deck but I had traded my hot iron for a fan. That was the first night I slept with a fan. We were traveling at full speed when we were hit. I only had time to grab a life jacket before I fell in the water.

I didn't know until long after the rescue how many had got off the boat, as we were strewn across several miles of the ocean. The swells were high enough to obscure everything that was in your immediate vicinity. I was with a group that kept together by a rope net anchored to the surface by cork floats. I had my feet wrapped over a float and a life belt around my waist. That's how I spent the next five days.

The sharks were under us all the time. They just kept swimming back and forth. A good buddy of mine had his heel bitten off. Mostly they went after the ones that drifted from the group. We had no food, which actually may have saved me. Some of the guys had tins of Spam, and I think the sharks were attracted to the smell when they tossed the empty tins aside. We did have water, but I think I had one drink. Somebody didn't put the plug back in, and that was that. It was one of those things where you thought you were going to be picked up right away.

The life belts were not designed for prolonged immersion. Some became water-logged and worked as a weight instead of a float. Some of the men couldn't release the fasteners, because their fingers were so blistered and swollen. The sharks took them below the surface.

I don't think I could have lasted another day. I was about to lay back and take a drink of ocean water. Some of the men died that way, diving down to take a "drink" or swimming off to an "island" to get a "hotel room." You just don't think! You don't know—and you can't believe—what is happening. Only 12 survived in our group. There were 16 of us when they dropped the life rafts, but four died before they picked us up.

By that time, I was nothing but pus. My skin had blistered. I had gone from 130 lbs to 80 lbs. We spent two days in a hospital on Peleliu. Then a hospital ship, USS *Tranquillity*, picked us up and took us back to Guam. There I spent four weeks in the hospital.

We came back to the United States on the USS *Hollandia*. I had a 30-day leave. At the end of 30 days I was reassigned to San Diego, where I spent my time until I got an honorable discharge in 1946. Then I went to work for the City of Burbank for 40 years. I am now retired.

CHAPTER 74   SURVIVOR FOSTER

NAME	FOSTER, VERNE E. F2C
STREET	19251 Brookhurst St #59
CITY	Huntington Beach
STATE	CA 92646
PHONE	714 968 6250
ENTERED SERVICE FROM	Detroit, MI
PICKED UP BY	USS *Bassett*
DIVISION	
DOB	11/11/26

FAMILY
Children: Janet Louise Foster Savidan and Boyd James Foster
Grandchildren: Scott Savidan, Summer Foster, Roxanne Foster

EXPERIENCE

I grew up in Detroit, Michigan and tried to enlist in the navy when I was 17 years old. I was turned down because they said I had a heart murmur. Three months later when I was 18, I was drafted. My basic training was at Great Lakes naval station in Illinois. Four weeks later I was sent to Shoemaker, California. Two hundred of us were assigned to the USS *Indianapolis*. We then waited four months for the ship repairs. I was a fireman second class.

The ship was loaded with a secret cargo and guarded by marines. We went to Pearl Harbor, where we dropped off 250 radio men. We headed for Tinian and dropped off our secret cargo. Our schedule was to head to the Philippines and join other ships and prepare to invade Japan. The weather was so hot, I decided to sleep on top deck. The night was cloudy with occasional moonlight.

Captain McVay decided we no longer needed to zigzag. The ship was open and fully lighted. A Japanese sub surfaced just as the moon came out, allowing them full sight of the ship. Two torpedoes hit us, and I washed over into the churning water. The only thing I found to grab onto was debris from the ship. I was determined to hang on.

I credit my survival with being an excellent swimmer, having grown up on Lake Huron where my folks had a summer cottage. My high school also had an excellent swim program. I was not afraid of the water, but of course, I was used to water with no sharks! I was very slender and didn't require a lot of food, which I think helped in those four days and five long nights without any.

After I was given a physical, I was given 30 days' survival leave with my parents. My father was a mounted policeman in Detroit. While on leave we received numerous calls from relatives of other men who didn't make it asking if I could give them any hope that they could be on some remote island or something. My mother kept a scrapbook of all the newspaper clippings and letters from friends thanking God I survived. Perhaps this scrapbook can go into the museum. Newspapers had headlines...WAR IS OVER...and way down at the bottom of the page...USS *Indianapolis* Sunk.

The only thing that makes my story somewhat of an addition to the other survivors is that after my leave, I was ordered back to California and assigned to the USS *Iowa*, then to Japan where I was assigned to the USS *Columbus*. Its orders were to go out to sea and sink the leftover Japanese Navy. One of the targets for sinking was the I-58 submarine which is the one that had sunk the USS *Indianapolis*. **"SWEET REVENGE"**

I was honorably discharged from the navy with a Purple Heart, and I returned to Michigan. A year later I married, and we had two children. When the children were 10 and 6, we moved to California where I still reside.

NAME   FOX, WILLIAM H. F2C
STREET
CITY
STATE
PHONE
ENTERED SERVICE FROM   Perth Amboy, NJ
PICKED UP BY   USS *Bassett*
DIVISION
DOB   7/4/25   Deceased 90
FAMILY
Widow: Mary Gregor Fox
Children: Marylou Fox Reynolds, William Fox, Timothy Fox
Grandchildren: Mathew Reynolds, Allison Reynolds, Crysteal Fox

EXPERIENCE

Respectfully submitted by Survivor Fox's family.

As a little sister, I was five years old when my brother Bill came home; he was very quiet. He never told us about his ship or what happened. Bill used to take my mother and me for long rides in the country and brought home my first pizza. He was a volunteer fireman for Highland Park, New Jersey.

In September of 1954, he married Mary Gregor. They lived in Perth Amboy, New Jersey. He continued to serve as a fireman at Earle Ammunition Depot. Bill and Mary had three children and moved to Neptune, New Jersey. He retired from Earle Ammunition and worked different part-time jobs.

Bill was awarded the Purple Heart in 1945 and the New Jersey Distinguished Service Medal in 2001. The Navy Unit Commendation Ribbon and the Combat Action Ribbon were awarded in 2001. He was interviewed by his local newspaper in 1958 and by Richard Newcomb, author of *Abandon Ship*.

Although he never spoke much about his experience, he did say that a lot of men drank the ocean water and went crazy. He told us that many of them said they saw islands and swam away. During the hospital recovery after the rescue, he said the men were fed chicken every day. He never ate chicken again.

When he saw the movie *Jaws* for the first time in the theater and the character "Quint" started talking about his experience surviving the *Indianapolis* disaster he got excited. He said, "That's the ship I was on." I remember that like it happened yesterday. He really got a charge out of it.

Bill died of cancer December 25, 1990, the same year the book *Fatal Voyage* by Dan Kurzman came out. He never got a chance to read it. In early 1991, the television movie *Mission of the Sharks* was aired.

Bill's son Timothy and his wife have complied a scrapbook from family photos, newspaper clippings, and his awarded citations.

NAME   FRANCOIS, NORBERT E.
                      F1C Machinist Mate

STREET
CITY
STATE
PHONE
ENTERED SERVICE FROM Green Bay, WI
PICKED UP BY   USS *Doyle*
DIVISION
DOB   Deceased 2/91

FAMILY
Widow: Bernadine Francois
Children: Jean Francois Martin (Tim)
Grandchildren: Mike Martin, Kathy Kozlowski
Great-Grandchildren: Zak Kozlowski

EXPERIENCE
   Submitted by Survivor Francois' daughter, Jean
Francois Martin.
   I am writing this chapter in memory of my dad, Norbert (Nubs) Francois,
fireman first class. My mom, Bernadine, is still alive and resides in an assisted-
living facility in Sarasota, Florida, near me.
   My dad had to quit school after the eighth grade to help support his family.
This didn't stop him from achieving whatever he set out to do. He built his own
home in 1940 and later built a cottage. He also helped my husband Tim and I
build a home. To help pay the mortgage on his new home, he volunteered to
work on the Alaskan Highway.
   Shortly after he returned home from working on the highway, he was drafted
into the service. He was considered an "old man" by most of his fellow
servicemen, as he was 30 years old. Actually he was too old to be "drafted," but
he chose to go anyway because he believed it was "his duty." They originally
wanted him to go on a submarine because he was only 5 feet 8 inches tall. He
refused to do it (he was very feisty) and told them he would only go into the
navy, on a ship. So away he went to the Great Lakes, Illinois training facility.
After leaving boot camp he boarded the USS *Indianapolis* and stayed with her
until the end.
   Mom and I went out to Mare Island navy yard in California to visit my dad
while the ship was in dry dock after being hit by a Japanese suicide plane in
March 1945. We had just returned home when Mom got word that his ship had
sunk and that he was in a hospital recovering.
   I do have a "souvenir" of his time spent in the boiler room. He made my

Mom and me matching stainless steel rings and a bracelet. I still have them. Luckily he had given them to Mom when we visited him, right before he shipped out on the last voyage.

Dad lost his best friend, Delbert E Dufraine, S1, "Duppy". He never saw him after the ship was hit. They later bought me a sailor doll, which I immediately named "Duppy".

Dad didn't talk too much about his time "in the water." I do remember, as I was growing up, that he didn't care much for swimming. Mom always said, "He had enough swimming during the five nights spent in the water after the ship went down."

She does recall his story of how he held up abandoned life jackets he found floating past, and as one would dry he would exchange the wet one for a dry one. He also gave some away if a fellow survivor was in need. He did pick up a can of Spam and was saving it for when he got really hungry, but an officer floated by and took it from him. He learned later that when this person opened the can of Spam, the smell attracted the sharks and he was killed. When the airplane landed, he also told of how in his haste to get on one of the pontoons, he was almost hit by one of the props. I guess it wasn't his time because after all that, he came home to us.

After Dad returned from the navy he worked as a welder for a steel erector company in Green Bay, Wisconsin until 1952, when he took a position working for the Wisconsin State Reformatory in Green Bay. He started in the boiler room and worked his way up to a special position of "jack-of-all-trades" in maintenance. He could fix just about anything, and this was recognized by his superiors, so they made a position and title just for him. Officially he was called a welder. He retired in 1976.

Dad enjoyed fishing, hunting, trapping, camping, and in his later years, he began carving decoys, something he had learned as a boy and a hobby which brought extra "fun money" and relaxation. He made dozens for Mom's "retirement fund".

In 1960 they bought property on Thunder Lake in Oconto County, in northern Wisconsin, and built a cottage which he planned to use for his retirement. He enjoyed fishing and relaxing on weekends and holidays. After he retired, they spent most of their time there. They did discover that it was too isolated for them in the winter, so they never did truly retire there. They also enjoyed yearly trips to Florida to visit friends, usually spending a month down there in the winter.

For ten years before Dad passed away, he enjoyed feeding "his geese" in his yard. Their house was on the banks of the East River in Green Bay, and one day Dad found a goose that had a plastic bottle holder stuck around his neck. He nicknamed him "Charlie". Dad rescued Charlie, and the next year the goose returned to nest with his mate. Each year more geese returned, and after awhile hundreds just stayed around most of the year. They knew Dad's voice and would come flying or swimming in to be fed. He went through many bags of corn and got help from neighbors and friends toward the cost of the feed.

Mom and Dad tried to make every *Indy* reunion, even some of the "mini" ones. They renewed friendships and kept in touch with many friends through letters, especially at Christmas time.

In May, 1990, Dad was diagnosed with multiple myeloma (bone cancer) and within days his kidneys failed. He survived for nine months but had to have dialysis three times a week, which he really hated. Dialysis left him totally drained for a day or two and about the time he felt better, he had to go back for another treatment.

He fought valiantly to the end. He was very angry and frustrated that "the big c" had to get him after all he had gone through in the war. What he really wanted was to live to see the change of the century, the year 2000. But on February 19, 1991, it was apparent that he had suffered enough. I begged Mom to "tell him it's okay to go," and when she did, he peacefully joined relatives, friends, and fellow shipmates who were waiting for him.

Sadly, he never got to see his grandson, Mike, become an exceptional artist and designer or his granddaughter, Kathy, become a devoted mother and part-time career woman. And last of all, he never got to meet his great-grandson, Zak, a delightful and mischievous little boy who, much like his great-grandpa, loves a challenge. He really would have enjoyed watching Zak grow...teasing and making him laugh when he got cranky, just like he did with his grandkids.

He is truly missed by his family and friends.

CHAPTER 77   SURVIVOR FUNKHOUSER

NAME	FUNKHOUSER, ROBERT M. AR2C
STREET	
CITY	
STATE	
PHONE	
ENTERED SERVICE FROM	Wauseon, OH
PICKED UP BY	PBY tr USS *Doyle*
DIVISION	
DOB	7/7/20 Deceased 2/76
FAMILY	

Widow: Jean
Children: Thomas Funkhouser

EXPERIENCE

Respectfully submitted by Survivor Funkhouser's widow, Jean.

The experience of my deceased husband, Robert M Funkhouser, at the time the USS *Indianapolis* was hit by a Japanese submarine on July 30, 1945 is described in the book *Ordeal By Sea* by Thomas Helm. I have requested that this be shared in Robert's chapter of the survivors book.

"Aviation Radio Technician Second Class Robert Funkhouser from Wauseon, Ohio, and his buddy Aviation Radio Technician Third Class John Ashford from Lubbock, Texas, were fairly new aboard the *Indianapolis*. They had spent Sunday evening helping to belt fifty-caliber ammunition for the OS2U scout planes carried aboard. The endless business of clipping the big shells in long metal belts had begun just after the evening meal of cold cuts and continued well into the night while others were watching the movies. When the job was finished, Funkhouser, Ashord and a few more made their way across darkened decks and sat around in the port hangar and entertained themselves with a little harmony singing. It was late when the last cigarette was snubbed out and the final song was sung. In all, it had been an evening of simple pleasure. One by one they settled themselves in crowded bunks and drifted off to sleep. Robert Funkhouser awoke as he felt the ship stagger under the impact of the torpedoes. His first thought was that she was going to roll all the way over, but he relaxed as she righted herself.

"Ashford," he shouted. "This is it!" Hurriedly he pulled on his dungarees, shirt and shoes. He was worried about his friend who had been trying to shake off a morbid dread of sinking ever since the *Indianapolis* had put to sea on her final voyage. Now the bad dream had come true. There were few if any men in the port hangar who had any serious doubts that the ship was bound for the bottom.

Funkhouser and Ashford tried to help launch a life raft, but it was a job for ten men and only four were present. When the vessel began falling over on her starboard side, they clawed their way through the life lines on the port side of the quarterdeck and walked down the hull and into the water. Both were wearing pneumatic tubes around their waists, but Funkhouser lost his as he was going through the life lines–a severe loss that could not be helped. He started swimming, or trying to swim, but the weight of his clothes and shoes dragged him down in the oil–coated water, first five and then ten feet. He kicked off his shoes and bobbed back to the surface. Next he squirmed out of his dungarees and then his shirt and finally he was swimming free.

With every tick of the second hand the *Indianapolis* was drawing closer and closer to her end. The torpedoes had torn great gaping holes in the starboard side. Later there were those qualified to voice an opinion who would say that the entire bow section had been blown off, but because those who knew for sure will never be heard from, it can only be surmised. Nevertheless, tons of sea water were pouring into the ship, bringing her down by the head and causing the lighter stern to rise slowly but inexorably out of the water. The roll was to the starboard in animated slow motion like a great lean whale beginning to sound.

Of course in the first few minutes there had been a feeling of shock and dismay from bow to stern and bridge to engine rooms, but the general belief was that the trouble could be quickly corrected and the ship would survive. There were those with a sort of sixth sense or those with a more realistic view of the situation because they had a clearer picture of what had happened, who knew immediately that the *Indianapolis* was going to sink.

Robert Funkhouser, who had lost his life belt as he left the ship, shouted for his friend, Ashford, who miraculously found him in the darkness and swam up to him. For a while the two clung together, depending upon the limited buoyancy of Ashford's pneumatic tube to keep them afloat. Funkhouser knew the life belt could hold one man fairly safely on the surface but not two, and he knew that if he continued holding onto Ashford, both would sink. He did not want to drown, but if he was going to, he was not dragging his good friend down with him. With a final word he turned loose and swam away, ignoring Ashford's demands that he come back.

An hour passed—or maybe it was only thirty minutes—and he was rapidly running out of strength. He had always been a pretty good swimmer and he knew all of the tricks: turn over on your back and float, make slow easy strokes with your arms and above all, conserve your energy. But this was different. The surface of the sea was coated with a thick blanket of slick, stinking fuel oil. If you opened your mouth a split second before your head was out and clear, you gulped a mouthful of the oil and the result was a spasm of uncontrolled retching. Funkhouser was in the final stages of a feeble dog paddle when he heard someone calling his name. It was Ashford again and he was not far away. "Come over here. I have a life jacket for you...a life jacket!" he shouted.

Drawing on the last few ounces of strength that remained in his body, he swam toward the voice of his friend. It was true! Ashford was bobbing about on the surface holding a fresh kapok jacket in front of him. Funkhouser put it on and hung limp for a few minutes while he caught his breath. Together the two began swimming toward the sound of other voices. In the moonlight of early morning they only knew that there were many men from the *Indianapolis* still afloat, but it was a comforting feeling."

NAME	GABRILLO, JUAN S2C
STREET	617 Meir St
CITY	Laredo
STATE	TX 78040
PHONE	
ENTERED SERVICE FROM	Laredo, TX
PICKED UP BY	USS *Bassett*
DIVISION	
DOB	

FAMILY

EXPERIENCE

No response.

CHAPTER 79 SURVIVOR GALANTE

NAME	GALANTE, ANGELO S2C
STREET	
CITY	
STATE	
PHONE	
ENTERED SERVICE FROM	Detroit, MI
PICKED UP BY	USS *Ringness*
DIVISION	
DOB	Deceased

FAMILY

EXPERIENCE

Unable to contact any family members.

CHAPTER 80 SURVIVOR GALBRAITH

NAME	GALBRAITH, NORMAN S. MM2C
STREET	
CITY	
STATE	
PHONE	
ENTERED SERVICE FROM	Chicago, IL
PICKED UP BY	USS *Doyle*
DIVISION	
DOB	Deceased

FAMILY

EXPERIENCE

Unable to contact any family members.

CHAPTER 81 SURVIVOR GARDNER

NAME	GARDNER, ROSCOE W. F1C
STREET	
CITY	
STATE	
PHONE	
ENTERED SERVICE FROM	Bolivar, MO
PICKED UP BY	USS *Doyle*
DIVISION	
DOB	Deceased

FAMILY

EXPERIENCE

Unable to contact any family members.
(Survivor Gardner's twin brother, Russel T. Gardner F2, was lost at sea.)

NAME	GAUSE, ROBERT P. QM1C
STREET	424 Doric Ct
CITY	Tarpon Springs
STATE	FL 34689
PHONE	813 937 3739
ENTERED SERVICE FROM	Miami, FL
PICKED UP BY	USS *Doyle*
DIVISION	NAN
DOB	1/20/20

FAMILY
Spouse: Norma

EXPERIENCE

First a word about the USS *Indianapolis*. She was a heavy cruiser, 610 feet long, Admiral Spruance's flagship for the Fifth Fleet. Her fame now rests on two facts:
1. She was the ship that carried the atomic bomb that was dropped on Hiroshima, thus ending World War II in August 1945.
2. Four days after unloading the bomb she was sunk, resulting in the worst U.S. Navy sea disaster in history.

About four months after Pearl Harbor, I joined the navy. I had grown up with boats because my dad owned a wholesale fish business. I worked jobs at a local hardware store and also as a teller in the local bank, but I would fish one of his boats when the fish were running. When I joined the navy at the age of 22, I passed the navigation test and was sworn in as a third class quartermaster. In the navy, a quartermaster aids in the navigation of the ship, not in supplies as is the job of quartermasters in the army. After three years in the navy, I was assigned to the USS *Indianapolis*. My station was on the bridge with Captain McVay.

We participated in a number of engagements: Iwo Jima, Kanachishima, and two air strikes on Japan. While bombarding Okinawa, we were hit by a kamikaze plane and eight of the nine men killed were from my NAN Division of 26.

We came back to the States for repair, and I was allowed to go home where I got to see my one-year old son and wife, NormaNeal. While on leave I went on one of Dad's boats and caught 4,000 pounds of mackerel, which helped pay some bills that had piled up after my son's birth. This little fishing trip also taught me something that saved my life when the *Indianapolis* sank. I'll tell you about that later.

My wife returned with me to San Francisco and lived in a quonset hut on Mare Island while the ship was being repaired. I made arrangements for her to go to San Diego, our next assignment for gunnery practice. The captain got on the air and said that all liberty was immediately canceled, and we would be heading back into the war zone early the next morning. I jumped ship and told my wife to go back to Florida instead of San Diego!

The next morning, a detachment of men and marine guards started loading some crates. It seemed that no one had any idea what was in the crates. Of the 1,197 men aboard, there were about 1,196 different guesses as to what was so important that we were making a speed run without even synchronizing our guns or testing anything. My guess was that the boxes contained inner-spring mattresses for the Marine Corps.

As we sailed out under the Golden Gate Bridge and approached the high span, I could see NormaNeal standing there waving as I steered the ship directly under her. I dared not look up and I sure couldn't wave back. Imagine, if you can, how I felt! The speed limit through the pass is about ten knots and we were doing about 25. We set a speed record to Honolulu, stopping just long enough to refuel and then heading right to Tinian. We unloaded the huge crates, still not knowing what was in them. Then we sailed to Guam, about a six-hour run.

Captain McVay got our orders to proceed to Leyte Gulf for aerial gunnery practice. He asked for an escort. A heavy cruiser has no sub detection other than sight. We sailed out of Guam on a Friday night. It is about a four-day run from Guam to Leyte. It was Saturday and we were about halfway when we got a radio message that a Japanese submarine had been sighted in our path. This was not unusual. The radio contact that had been made with the sub wasn't exactly in our line. It was maybe 100 to 150 miles off. A sub can travel that far in 24 hours.

That night as we started to turn in, the captain had me write in the night order books that if it was cloudy when the moon came up we were to continue on our course at 15 knots. If it wasn't cloudy, then we were to zigzag. Well, that was written in the night order book. The night watch would be changed at midnight when the 12:00 to 4:00 watch would begin.

Around 11:00 I went to bed topside in the catapult tower. I had been sleeping on a cot inside the tower because I had developed boils from the heat when I slept below deck. A few minutes after midnight a Japanese sub surfaced to recharge its batteries just as the moon broke out. We were not zigzagging. The moon broke out again for a minute and we were right there! The commander of the sub had never sunk a major ship before and those on the sub were really thrilled that they were going to get to sink a big one. The sub submerged and prepared to fire six torpedoes.

The first torpedo hit the bow part of the ship. It blew me off my cot and wedged me up under a hand rail. (The telegram they sent to my wife on the day the Japanese surrendered said I had been injured in action and had "contusion of the spine.") The second torpedo hit us midship where the magazine was located. That blew the ship wide open. What an explosion. We sank in about ten minutes.

I don't know how I got to my battle station on the bridge, but I did. No one was there and I couldn't see a thing from the bridge forward. The bow of the ship was gone and all power was knocked out. I went to the pilot house and the captain was there, along with the gunnery officer, the bugler, a quartermaster striker and two or three other guys. I said to the quartermaster striker, Allard, "We are fixing to sink." He had been on the ship for a number of years and he said, "No, this old ship won't sink. I was brought up on boats."

The captain knew we were in serious trouble and was trying to get an SOS off. We had two radio transmitters on board, one aft and one forward. He knew the bow had been blown off and that we had no power on the ship. We couldn't talk by phone to the aft radio transmitter so he kept sending a messenger, but the messengers didn't come back.

Captain McVay turned to Commander Lipski, the gunnery officer, and asked him to take command of the ship because he was going aft to make sure we got an SOS off. Captain McVay didn't have a life jacket. I took mine off and told him he'd better put it on because he was going to have to cross the well deck and it was awash. He thanked me, took it, and left the bridge. I didn't see him again for five days. That left me on a sinking ship without a life jacket, which is worse than being up a creek without a paddle. I turned to Allard and said, "We are fixing to sink and I don't have a life jacket." Allard said, "I'll get you one. I've been sitting on a whole stack of them playing poker down on the single bridge." He ran right down and came back with two. He said, "Take both, I've got one." About that time the gunnery officer said, "Hear this! Abandon ship! We are sinking!"

I had been told that when a big ship sinks the suction would pull you with it. I wanted to get as far away as possible so I started over the high side. I got hung up in some rigging and thought I was going to stay there. Finally, I got loose and crawled down the side of the ship to the water. The ship had listed so far to the starboard by then that I ran into the bilge keel on the way. That's a keel on each side of the ship that keeps it from rolling. I jumped from the keel into the water. No lifeboats could be seen. It was just a few minutes after midnight and it was dark.

I started swimming as hard as I could and got about 150 yards from the ship. I saw a fellow swimming near me who didn't have a life jacket. I told him I had two, which one did he want? He said, "I'll take that kind you blow up, because the other one is only good for 72 hours and we are going to be here a long time." As I handed it to him, I figured that was one of the biggest mistakes I ever made, but I learned later that the rubber kind didn't last near as well as the Mae West. Five days later there would be hundreds of empty life jackets floating in the sea around those of us still alive. Some men were eaten by sharks, though I didn't see that.

When the ship sank, it just stood on end and there were three or four hundred men standing on the fantail holding on to the life line that goes around the railing. When the ship upended, those fellows just floated off like flies. I don't think it sucked anybody under. Some men hit the propellers that were still turning and were killed. Some were battened down at their station in the engine room. I imagine three hundred or more were sealed in tight below deck as they tried to save the ship from being swamped. A bunch of fellows had been severely burned and you could hear them scream.

The first night some of us began to get together and form a group. I looked around and thought I saw somebody in trouble waving for help so I started swimming out to him. Just before I got there I saw that it was the dorsal fin of a huge shark coming right at me. I just kicked into reverse, not even bothering to turn around. I backed up to the group and said, "Fellows, we need to form a big circle and I want in the middle. There is a shark out there so big I couldn't see both ends at once!" One guy had a fifty foot rope that he had salvaged. Those of us with a Mae West life jacket ran the rope through the little rings and formed a circle.

The next morning we discovered we had an officer in our crowd. With everyone in a life jacket and covered with black oil, we all looked alike. One fellow said, "We need to count off and see how many we have here." There were 157 of us. We thought we were the only ones alive. Five days later we would discover there were several groups of men and three life rafts with a few men on each. Soon the officer spoke again, "You know, we really ought to be praying." I'd been praying since a little after midnight and I couldn't imagine that everyone hadn't. I sometimes call this "my 109th-hour conversation with the Lord." That is how long we were in the water.

The officer started off the prayer and told the Lord where we were and why he didn't want to die. He had things he wanted to do at home. Everybody that prayed, prayed virtually the same thing. When it came my turn, I corrected our location to the Lord, since I'd been keeping the log, and prayed about the same thing as the others, with one difference. When I finished my brief prayer, I said, "Lord, thank you, that we are going to be picked up."

The Lord had taught me that He does hear prayer and that He answers when we pray with faith, just as the Bible promises He will. The night of my fishing trip when I was home on leave I had figured out that I would need to catch 4000 pounds of mackerel to pay my bills, and I prayed that I could catch that many. In spite of the fact that our engine broke down soon after we struck the school of mackerel and we couldn't close the ends of the net to enclose the fish, and the fish around the hot engine box had to be thrown away, and we couldn't get in till the next day when someone came along and gave us a tow...in spite of all that, our fish didn't spoil because it was a very cold night, extremely cold for Florida! When we weighted out the fish they weighed not 3999 pounds, not 4001 pounds, but 4000 pounds, exactly what I had asked the Lord for. A few months later, I prayed again, "Thank you that we are going to be picked up."

A while after our prayer, the same officer said, "Listen up, all of you, I've got something to say. We are traveling alone and because we are the flagship, when we don't show up they will just think the 'old man' changed the orders (he was referring to Admiral Spruance) and he wouldn't have to tell anybody, so they won't look for us. We won't likely be found. So when we get tired we may as well give up and drown."

That made me mad! I didn't think that was any way someone who had just prayed should be talking, so I said, "I don't know about you, but I just prayed to a God who answers prayer and I expect to be picked up. In fact 1,196 of you might drown, but when the ship comes along to take us home, Gause is going to be hitchhiking a ride." In fact 880 men died, 317 came home. I don't suppose what I said set too good with him fifteen years later at our first survivors' reunion, but I learned that it made a difference to some of the men. Our officer didn't make it. I was there when the ship came along.

Lots of things happened during those five days in the water. Every day we all swam constantly. I don't know where we thought we were going. The land was 250 miles away and it was held by the Japanese. Actually, the nearest land was 2 1/2 miles from us but it was straight down. That was about the second deepest place in the Pacific.

Men's tempers grew short. No food. No sleep. No water to drink! Sharks all around us day and night. Fights broke out between men. Some had their shoes on. When you got kicked and the skin is knocked off in salt water, it hurts like the devil. We had all been bouncing up and down in those stiff life jackets for so long that all of the flesh was gone from under our arms and off the backs of our necks.

One day a fellow said, "There is plenty of fresh water 15 feet below. The salt water is only on the top." One guy pulled his jacket off and started diving. Some of us tried to talk him out of it but he just kept diving till at last he didn't come up. Things like that happened often.

I saw sharks swim around our group every day except one. They would come within three feet of us. We learned that if we screamed and yelled it scared the sharks away. If we splashed water they would come closer. You probably saw the movie *Jaws*. The leading character, Quint, gave as the reason for his hatred of sharks that he was on the USS *Indianapolis*. He says in the movie that he shook his buddy one morning and a shark had bitten him off at the bottom of the life jacket. I had related that incident, which had happened to me and maybe to others, to Tom Helm, author of *Ordeal By Sea,* and he included it in his book.

I never saw anyone get bitten by a shark. No one in our group got bitten in the daytime, but if a man drifted ten feet away from the circle at night we wouldn't see him again. Sometimes when someone drifted away or swam away at night, we would hear a blood-curdling scream and we would have to believe a shark got him.

Every day we would see planes fly over. Sometimes as many as five in a day. They were high and couldn't see us but oh how we yelled and waved and, yes, cried or cursed when they didn't turn back. Most of the men died of exposure and drinking salt water. Soon they would spit up green bile and go out of their mind, take off their life jacket, and drown. Out of the 157 men in our group, only 27 were still alive at the end of 109 hours.

On Thursday, four days into our ordeal, someone told another fellow that Gause had a canteen of fresh water in the left side of his life jacket. The guy took a knife and cut all the kapok out of that side looking for the canteen. Right after that I was separating two fellows that were fighting. One of them was a buddy of mine and I was trying to calm him down. A wave hit me in the face and I swallowed salt water by accident. There were life jackets everywhere and I had my buddy tie another one real tight to mine as I lost my mind. I swam off by myself and wasn't touched by a shark. That was a miracle. I began to come to my senses about 9:00 Friday morning. I didn't see another soul and thought the other 1,196 had drowned. After about an hour, I heard some men yelling, "Hey, Mulvey." I started swimming toward the voice.

I prayed a different kind of payer now...an urgent one. "Lord, I believe. I have faith that you are going to get me home. But you've got to get on the ball. I've done all I can do. It's up to you now." At that moment, I felt something solid under my feet. It felt like the bottom came up to meet me and I stood on solid rock where it was 2 1/2 miles deep. I rested. I rested so well that when the plane spotted us late that morning, I had strength enough to swim to the five-gallon water tank the pilot dropped about 100 yards away from us. Unfortunately, it had burst open and spilled all its precious cargo but I had to prove to the men that I hadn't drunk it. In a few hours we would have all the water we could drink.

The story of our rescue and of the brave pilots and captains of ships and planes that broke radio silence to get help to us as fast as possible is another whole story.

My most vivid and unforgettable memory is of a bright and shining light. By that time we didn't know if the ships could find us after dark. Many of the boys were out of their minds. At first we may have all thought we were delusional when we saw the light shining in the heaven above us. The captain of the USS *Cecil B Doyle* knew how close to death we all were. Not knowing whether the sub that had sunk us was still in the area, he nevertheless shined the ship's spotlight light on a low-hanging cloud to let us know that help was on the way. The light ricocheted from the cloud back to earth and looked like a beam from heaven.

While I was in the hospital on Guam, Captain McVay pinned Purple Hearts on all of us. He told me he would see to it that I got my chief's rating if I wanted to stay in the navy. I said, "Thanks, but no thanks. I have enough points to get out and I'm going to get out just as quick as I can and go home." And I did. I hitchhiked to Florida. At home at last, I learned that on the day the headlines screamed "Japan Surrenders," a small article at the bottom of the page announced that the USS *Indianapolis* had been sunk with 100 percent casualties.

(The sub commander came to the United States to testify against our captain at his court martial. He did testify that our ship was not zigzagging but that it had made no difference...he would have sunk it anyway.)

NAME	GEMZA, RUDOLPH A. FC3C
STREET	
CITY	
STATE	
PHONE	
ENTERED SERVICE FROM	Detroit, MI
PICKED UP BY	USS *Bassett*
DIVISION	Fox
DOB	Deceased

FAMILY
Spouse: Lillian

EXPERIENCE
Unable to contact any family members.

CHAPTER 84 SURVIVOR GEORGE

NAME	GEORGE, GABRIEL V. MM3C
STREET	
CITY	
STATE	
PHONE	
ENTERED SERVICE FROM	North Canton, OH
PICKED UP BY	USS *Bassett*
DIVISION	
DOB	Deceased

FAMILY

EXPERIENCE
Unable to contact any family members.

NAME	GETTLEMAN, ROBERT S2C (Radar man)
STREET	Unknown
CITY	
STATE	
PHONE	
ENTERED SERVICE FROM	Los Angeles, CA
PICKED UP BY	USS *Ringness*
DIVISION	
DOB	

FAMILY

EXPERIENCE

Unable to contact any family members.

NAME	GIBSON, BUCK W. GM3C
STREET	3209 Village Green Dr #235
CITY	Waco
STATE	TX 76710
PHONE	254 751 0978
ENTERED SERVICE FROM	Mart, TX
PICKED UP BY	USS *Bassett*
DIVISION	7th Division
DOB	6/13/22

FAMILY
Children: Stacey Gibson

EXPERIENCE

The USS *Indianapolis* (CA-35), heavy cruiser, flagship of the Fifth Fleet under Admiral Raymond Spruance, earned ten battle star citations. The tragedy of the USS *Indianapolis* stands as the largest single disaster at sea ever suffered by the United States Navy. This is my experience aboard the *Indianapolis*...the complete truth, without fanfare, without exaggeration, without misrepresentation. Actually, I cannot convey in words the horror I have seen and experienced and my recounting here is less than the real happenings.

This is my story:

I enlisted in the navy in 1942 and after completing basic training, I was assigned to the USS *Indianapolis* and served aboard until her sinking. My commander was Captain Charles McVay.

My first maneuver was to the Aleutian Islands where we patrolled the waters on the Bering Sea for Japanese ships and subs. We guarded the islands of Attu and Kiska. I was there more than six months without getting off the ship and saw the sun only a few times during that period.

From there we went to the South Pacific and participated in the invasions of Tarawa in the Gilbert Islands, Marshall Islands and Eniwetok. We were in the Battle of the Eastern Philippines (known as the Marianas Turkey Shoot) with the invasion of Saipan, Tinian, Guam and the Palau Islands. I encountered strafing, shelling, and air raids without cessation.

I was a gunners mate third class on the 20-mm in the second section of the Seventh Division, consisting of more than 60 men and officers. My gun was located about one-third of the way from the fantail in a spot commonly called "the Bathtub." There were four men assigned to each gun: the gunner, first and second loader, and ammo supplier. Alfred "Pago" Reynolds from Wanette, Oklahoma was in charge of my division. We jokingly called him "Pop" because he was 36 years old, and most of us were 22-23 years old and even younger. One of my good friends, E.J. Dronet from Cameron, Louisiana, was only 17 years old. Also from Texas in my division were good friends Tommy Meyers from Marlin and L.D. Cox from Comanche.

We were battle weary, but the war in the Pacific raged on. I would look at the black, swirling waters of the Pacific Ocean and feel it was ready to swallow me up any time. The Japanese kept coming and coming–with every one shot down there seemed to be two to take their place. Every now and then I would wonder if I would ever see the States, or Texas, or my folks back in Mart again. Sometimes their faces flashed before me in life-like realism.

We then headed for the major invasion of Okinawa where we were hit by a kamikaze on March 31, 1945. The hit was about 100 feet away from me. The explosion killed nine men and injured 26. The damaged ship returned to Mare Island navy yard in California for repairs. This took 6-8 weeks and I was granted a 12-day leave to go home.

While in the Mare Island dry dock, the U.S. Army loaded a secret cargo onto our ship. In the early morning hours on July 16, 1945, the "heart" of two atom-bombs (uranium-235) sealed in a small lead-lined metal container was welded to the deck in the admiral's cabin. It was guarded around the clock by U.S. Marines. The cargo was kept secret from all the crew, including the captain. We dropped our cargo at Tinian, but it was much later that we learned the bomb was assembled on Tinian and dropped on Hiroshima August 6, 1945, causing the Japanese to surrender.

As we left the California coastline, no one could know the truth of the ominous prediction made by one of my shipmates that the *Indy* was making her final voyage. As we sailed out of Oakland through San Francisco Bay, he made the remark to all of us, "You boys take a good look at the Golden Gate Bridge. Some of you will never see it again."

We had general quarters every day at sunrise and sunset as this was usually the time the Japanese attacked. This meant every man took his battle station, loaded and cocked his gun, and was battle ready. I was in the Bathtub with head phones on and got my usual call from the CIC who called all stations for a visibility report. I was on the 6:00-8:00 p.m. watch and told him it was clear as far as the eye could see. Even though it was 8:00 p.m., it was as light as day. We were on a straight course and you could see the ship's wake far across the horizon. When I left my watch at 8:00 p.m. it was smooth and clear as a bell.

I went below deck to my bunk, which was behind the number three mess hall. It was the first deck below the main deck, starboard side. I was about to sack out when one of my best friends, Orval Spindle from Palo Pinto, Texas, came by and asked me to go up on the bow to sleep with him since it was so hot below deck. I had just washed my blankets and didn't want to get them dirty again, so I told him, "Give me one of your old dirty blankets and I'll go with you." He told me to use my own blanket, so I stayed in my bunk. I never saw Orval again. Sixty feet of the bow was knocked off when the torpedo hit. The bow took a direct hit by one of the torpedoes fired by the *I-58* Japanese submarine commanded by Mochitsura Hashimoto.

Around midnight on July 30, 1945, there was a loud explosion and I either jumped from my bunk or was knocked from it. I immediately dressed and ran topside and uncovered and loaded my gun. I heard someone say the boiler had exploded. It was calm for a few seconds until the *Indy* started listing on her right side. I was not afraid that we would sink. I never thought we would go down. As she listed starboard and boxes began sliding, I started putting life jackets on the younger crew members. All that was left for me was an old jacket called a "horse collar," but I had no trouble putting it on since I had harnessed plenty of mules and horses in my lifetime. Tommy Meyers and I shook hands and made a pact that I would go see his folks back in Marlin if he didn't make it, and he would go see mine in Mart if I did not make it. I did not see Tommy again until we were rescued and in the hospital.

I had been taught to go off the high side of the ship if she started to sink. The bow was knocked off and she was taking on water. The *Indy* rolled on her side starboard. Pago Reynolds and I walked up the port side near the bulkhead, threw a cork net off her side, and jumped about three feet into the water. Everything not secured started falling off the deck as the ship rolled. The empty magazines, gun barrels, ammunition and ammo boxes all slid around us and something hit me in the back.

Once in the water I looked back and the *Indy* was right over me, bottom-side up. I knew then my time was up, but the giant ship turned away from me because her bow was gone. I started swimming as fast as I could and kept swimming until my strength completly failed me. I cried openly and was wondering when the suction would pull me under. I looked back the second time and the ship looked like it was a mile away. It was completely turned bottom-side up; the screws were the last thing I saw as the *Indy* slipped out of sight.

The USS *Indianapolis* and an estimated 400 of her crew went to their watery graves. Some of the crew were killed instantly from the blast while an undetermined number drowned below deck. I can remember seeing my shipmates jump off the *Indy* when her hulk was at least 300 feet in the air. They were screaming from the time they jumped until they landed in the water, and I never knew what happened to them. As the *Indy* disappeared from sight, I heard someone say, "There she goes." It was then I realized I was alone and had lost everything I had: my home for 2 1/2 years and many of my friends. The *Indy* was 610 feet long—twice the length of a football field and 66 feet wide at the quarterdeck, but she went down in less than 12 minutes.

We started trying to get together. We all wanted to be in a bunch, thinking we would have a better chance to survive. We found a net and I think it was the one Pago and I had thrown off. These nets were 8 to 10 feet long and had cork approximately every 18 inches. We stretched the net out as far as we could and put the most severely wounded and burned on the net the best we could. Little did we know then it would be our home and salvation for the next five days. As soon as we got it stretched out, sailors came from every direction trying to get a place on the net. Pago and I had to fight for a place to hang on. Everybody was jittery trying to find something to hang on to.

I was holding on to one boy who was badly burned. He was so severely burned he had to call out my name before I recognized him. He told me he was 17 years old, but he looked like he was only 15. He was from one of the southern states and had taken up with me only a short time before the sinking. He was a magazine handler on the 20-mm. I recall he had asked my opinion on a gambling pot he had collected. He wanted to know if I thought this was gambling and when I said, "Yes, I guess it is," he returned everyone's money. I believe he was a Christian who had lived a Christ-like life. He was not afraid to die; he did not fear death like the rest of us. He was so badly injured and I was helpless to aid him. His left leg was floating a little under the water and the bone was sticking out of the leg. He had a badly burned right arm and his face was covered in severe burns. He did not complain very much. I kept telling him help was on the way. I kept holding him on the net, thinking that if he did die I could hold on to his body to send back to his family. I held him on the net for two days.

The second morning when it was daylight, I knew he was still beside me, as I felt for him all through the night. When the sun came up I realized something had eaten his broken leg. Nothing was left but the bone sticking out in the water. He was dead, but still limber. I kept him on the net until some of the other sailors discovered he was dead. Somebody said, "We will say the Lord's Prayer." I did not know the words to the Lord's Prayer, but I followed along the best I could. After the prayer they all looked at me and I knew what their look meant. I knew it was something I had to do. I lifted the boy out of the net and rolled him over on his back. He floated off with his face in the water. I had taken his dog tags off and given them to another sailor to keep to send back to his family. This sailor later fell off the net and took the tags down with him.

I cannot think of this young blond kid today without reliving this horrible tragedy, although time has erased his name. I cannot talk about him without crying. I can only think that this young person's life was such a waste and of the grief his parents would have to endure. It is a loss you never get over but try to learn to live with.

I felt like the end was near for all of us. We did not know where any of the other crew members were. We learned later that the crew was scattered over 100 miles in open sea. Pago was the only other one I knew in the group. We kept reassuring the injured and ourselves just to hang on, we would be picked up as soon as it was daylight. We wondered if an SOS had been sent before the ship went down. We found out later one of the torpedoes hit the CIC, knocking out our communications completely. We also thought maybe one of the planes made it off. There had been four aircraft aboard the *Indy*, but unfortunately they were all tied down and went down with the ship.

The next morning we started counting off and discovered there were 167 in our group. During our time in the water others drifted into our group to hang on. The dead were pushed off the net to make room for those still alive. (When we were picked up there were only 32 of us remaining.) I heard somebody say, "Did they get an SOS off?" No one said anything. Nobody knew. No one could even guess the perilous situation we were in. I thought we would be picked up at daylight. I expected any minute to see a "tin can" (destroyer) pull up beside us and rescue us. My hopes were very high that we had not been left to die in the middle of the Pacific.

Thinking that we would be picked up as soon as it was daybreak, it was not too hard to keep encouraging the injured to hang on. We were so covered in grease and oil we didn't know whom we were next to. Some of the wounded had broken legs, broken backs, and broken arms and others were so badly burned you could not recognize them.

I heard and saw my shipmates scream in agony and terror. Many were burned beyond recognition. I grabbed the arm of an injured man above the elbow. His flesh came off and I was holding on to the bone of his arm. I heard screams, "Where are all my friends?" Every man was fighting for his own life. The screams were those of dying men. CONFUSION! PANIC! HELL!

Everybody was fighting for something—just something—to hang on to. Some were hanging on to five-gallon cans, ammo cans, anything that would float.

Many sailors in the water had no life jackets and they were climbing on top of each other. If a sailor had a life jacket, three or four men would be trying to climb on top of him. It was like rats swimming in a bathtub, with no way out and nothing to cling to. I was surrounded by screaming and panic.

The ocean was a black, swirling pit of blood and oil. The severely wounded and badly burned did not last long. I heard their dying screams pierce the night. My buddies' screams were blood-curdling as they gasped and died in agony. I was alive in HELL. I thought I was dreaming, but it was real. All the horrors we knew about hell were happening before my eyes and I was helpless to aid anyone. We each struggled for one more breath of life. I was covered with oil and blood. We were floundering around in a blood bath. The moon was shining brightly, but you could see only a short distance. The waves on the high seas are tall, even when it is calm. Everyone was covered in slime.

My injured back was hurting and I knew, had I not had the water to support me, I wouldn't have been able to stand. When I hit the water the first thing I did was kick off my shoes. We had been taught that shoes were extra weight in the water. Ironically, they floated back to the top. I was fully dressed with my horse collar life jacket.

I heard someone say, "Let's say a prayer." I do not remember ever having prayed before, but I prayed silently for the first time in my life. Don't let anyone tell you he cannot pray; even an atheist cannot deny the existence of God. We prayed for our lives to be spared. We prayed to God to ease our pains. We prayed to God not to forsake us, not to let us die, to save us. We prayed for His mercy. The soothing effects of prayer linked us together as we began to try to help each other. All of us tried to help everyone any way we could.

As we were bobbing around in the Pacific, I thought of all the ways my shipmates were dying. There were those who went down with sharks and it was over quickly. The wounded begged for help and we were helpless. Some of the deaths were drawn out and prolonged with agony, and we were only made aware of their slipping into the deep by seeing vacated life jackets. Others would have delusions about an island just a short swim away, where there would be refuge. We never saw them again. Another would dive for a drink of fresh water just a few feet below. There were others who just gave up—they lost the will to live and the fight to stay alive. It was so much easier to give up and die than to try to stay alive. The Pacific is scorching hot in the daylight hours and icy cold in the night. We experienced freezing as well as dehydration from the heat of the sun and lack of water.

We had wondered all along if the SOS went off. We all were looking for a rescue: a plane, ship, anything. We all thought help should have been to us by daylight if the SOS was sent. The longer we waited the more nervous we got. It was about 10:00 before anybody started talking. We decided the SOS had not been sent. To realize that help was not coming was a heartbreaking disappointment, one of the many disappointments we were forced to face in the days ahead.

As far as I know none of my gun crew survived. All the gunners' mates hung around a small area called the "gun shack" where we drank coffee and talked. One of my very good friends from this group, Joseph Durand of New Orleans did not survive. He slid under the number three 8-inch gun mount when we were hit, broke his back, then slid into the water. I feel a great sense of guilt that I never tried to locate his family to tell them what happened to him.

We had made it to another daybreak. I kept looking for that "tin can" coming to our rescue. I was already so weary from trying to hold my place on the net; I knew I had to preserve my strength until we were picked up. As dawn broke I could see debris scattered everywhere. Dead bodies were floating all around us. I was floating with only my shoulders and head out of the water.

I always figured I escaped the fish and sharks because they had plenty of dead bodies to eat. They liked the bodies that were still in the water. I had lived in the country all my life before joining the navy and those fish in the water eating on the bodies reminded me of hogs eating ears of corn. Small fish of all kinds were swarming around the bodies until a larger fish would tear the body in half and swim off. The smaller fish would eat what was left. They ate all the flesh off the bone. It was a battle of size, as sharks and great fish swept the half-eaten bodies out of sight. This is what I saw the first hour of daylight on August 1. I kept thinking I was dreaming. But it was real and I learned a lot about life and death in that first hour. I couldn't know at this time that it was going to get worse, that we were just starting on a long, floating journey.

From the time we hit the water sharks started attacking us. All of the five days I was in the water, sharks attacked men next to me, pulling them under. We tried splashing and screaming to scare them away, but a hungry shark smelling blood and death is not easy to scare. Without a warning a shark would grab a body and carry it off, or if they took only a piece of the body, we knew they would be back for the rest. We moved away as quickly as we could. We got away from anyone who was burned or smelled of blood, as this was a sure invitation for a shark attack. As soon as a man expired, we cut him loose from the net as bait for the sharks in the hopes they would not come back for us. We would say a prayer, cut them loose, and bury them at sea. When you hear the SCREAMS of someone being pulled away by a shark, it is a scream like nothing you have ever heard or will ever forget. You hear them screaming and there is nothing you can do to help them.

We began to settle down to help each other and the wounded. We all knew the badly wounded could not last much longer. We were scheduled for gunnery practice with the battleship USS *Idaho* at 10:00 on August 2 at Leyte Gulf. We thought if a plane came out for practice and couldn't find our ship they would start looking for us. I was a gunner's mate and knew this practice was scheduled. I passed the word around and this gave everybody a little hope. If we could last for 2 1/2 days, help would be coming—so we thought! We all knew when we were missed the fleet would be out looking for us!

We began to figure out how we could survive until help arrived. I think everybody figured out his own method of survival. Not one word was said. Everybody had their own thoughts–how to survive the 2 1/2 days. There was no doubt in anyone's mind that there would be help by 12:00 if an SOS was sent. We had two nets floating and we all knew it would be a long wait. We all knew we had two canteens of water. Nobody asked for any water, as we all knew it had to last.

There was a little Spam on the life raft, but an open can of Spam was an immediate invitation for a shark attack. They loved the smell of Spam. (I cannot eat Spam even today.) Imaginations ran wild and there was a lot of fighting among the men. Someone always thought another person was hoarding either food or water. I was continually thinking about a drink of water. The two canteens of water were not rationed and divided. The water disappeared and everyone thought one man drank it all. We had nothing to eat or drink for five days.

All of us talked out of our heads and lost consciousness. Pago Reynolds helped me the most when I was delirious by keeping me on the net out of harm's way. One sailor tried to keep all the dog tags from the dead for identification, but he later disappeared and did not make it. We knew that unless we helped each other, none of us would survive. My body was in the water the entire time, resulting in saltwater sores on my legs and arms. These scars are still plainly visible. When we were sunk I weighed 179 pounds but weighed in at 129 lbs when rescued.

There was only one life raft in my group. We drifted at least 60 miles and would occasionally drift into both live and dead shipmates. When we came across a dead body, we removed the life jacket and anything else that would help us survive. I could not remember anything for hours at a time, even a whole afternoon would pass. We had to constantly help keep someone from swimming off. I always thought I could see a ship coming toward us, but I never did dive down for water. I kept thinking about fried chicken and about being picked up by a destroyer. I never did give up completely. I always had a dim ray of hope that we would be missed and then picked up.

The incidents I am about to relate I tried to forget, but how can I not remember? This horror has seared my mind like a hot branding iron and I CANNOT forget it. A man in my division cut the throat of another sailor to drink his blood and quench his thirst. He did not survive. I saw another man cut the wrist of another man and suck his blood. Everybody yelled, "Look he's eating that arm!" I witnessed four or five incidents of cannibalism. The waves were so high you could not see straight across, but I would catch glimpses of one person eating another. Sometimes I would be only ten feet away from this. I do not know how to put into words the acts of cannibalism. How do you describe a horror such as this? I did not know anyone involved in this and I consider this my good fortune. It is something I can never forget.

Somewhere out there I lost some of my best friends: John L. Sipes of Tennessee, Herman E. Kron of New Orleans, Robert L. Shipman of Kansas,

James R. Lewis of Tennessee, Saul A. Ham of Oregon, and Richard H. Bollinger of New York. The survivors in my division still talk about them when we get together. I cannot forget their cruel deaths.

On the fourth day, an Army Air Corp bomber on patrol for Japanese subs saw an oil slick made by our sunken cruiser. The pilot was Lt. Chuck Gwinn, who attended all our reunions and was immediately renamed "the angel." Sadly he passed away in July 1993. He radioed that survivors has been sighted in the water and Lt. Adrian Marks, PBY commander (who also attended our reunions), received the message and immediately flew to the area. He had to make a dreadful decision—whom to take and whom to leave. He could not take them all. He decided to take the most severely injured and loaded his plane with the emaciated bodies.

Several ships were dispatched from the Philippines and I was picked up by the USS *Bassett* during the night of August 4, 1945. The *Bassett* picked up a total of 146 survivors and two bodies. Ed Kiser of Cobbs Creek, Virginia, was on the *Basett* and aided in my rescue. In October 1993, I visited him and met him for the first time in almost 50 years—a man directly involved in my rescue and without whose efforts I would not be alive today. I could only hug him and cry when we met.

We were told that all the dead floating bodies had their finger prints removed for identification at the point of rescue. I was brought aboard the *Bassett* on a stretcher and placed on the fantail. Someone gave me a Chesterfield cigarette—it seemed to open me up and was the best-tasting thing I ever remember. I was taken to Fleet Hospital 118 in Samar and then to Fleet Hospital 18 in Guam. From there I was sent to Camp Wallace near Galveston for several back operations and recuperation. After treatment I was sent to the navy hospital in Houston and then honorably discharged at Orange, Texas on December 16, 1945.

After 50 years, dates and faces lose their distinction, but the horror never goes away. I suffer long periods of depression and cannot shake the feeling. I am always grateful I made it, but it does not lesson the agony I feel for my lost shipmates. The older I get the more it bothers me. There is not one day that passes that I do not think about my days in the water, my lost friends, the shark attacks, and the cannibalism. I can still hear the screams. My wife tells me I cry out and yell in my sleep and that I talk to myself all the time. I relive these nightmares over and over. I am still extremely nervous and jumpy. My family told me when I first came home from the hospital and I was sleeping, no one would go near me or touch me as I was so nervous I would attack them. Words are inadequate to express my feeling and no one can really know the horror I have been through.

I went to work at General Tire and Rubber Company in Waco in January 1947. I worked four years straight without missing a day and without turning down any overtime. The manual labor of building tires and running a farm kept me exhausted and no doubt kept me from losing my mind. This horror has become part of my life, and I feel I have paid a high price for freedom.

NAME   GILCREASE, JAMES
STREET
CITY
STATE
PHONE
ENTERED SERVICE FROM   Baskin, LA
PICKED UP BY   USS *Bassett*
DIVISION
DOB   Deceased 8/01 Coushatta, LA

FAMILY

EXPERIENCE
Unable to contact any family members.

NAME   GLADD, MILLARD Jr S2C Machinist Mate
STREET
CITY
STATE
PHONE
ENTERED SERVICE FROM   Ogensburgh, KY
PICKED UP BY   USS *Bassett*
DIVISION
DOB   Deceased 5/92

FAMILY

EXPERIENCE
Unable to contact any family members.

NAME GLENN, JAY R. AMM2C
STREET
CITY
STATE
PHONE
ENTERED SERVICE FROM Van Nuys, CA
PICKED UP BY USS *Ringness*
DIVISION
DOB Deceased

FAMILY

EXPERIENCE

Unable to contact any family members.

CHAPTER 90 SURVIVOR GOFF

NAME GOFF, THOMAS G. SF3C
STREET P O Box 445
CITY Canal Fulton
STATE OH 44614
PHONE
ENTERED SERVICE FROM Homerville, OH
PICKED UP BY USS *Bassett*
DIVISION
DOB 11/15/06

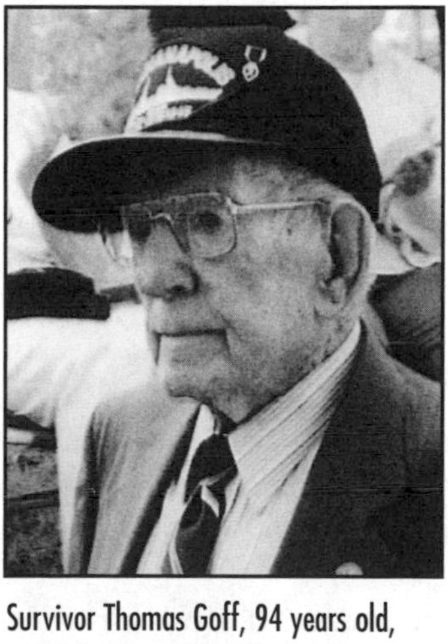

Survivor Thomas Goff, 94 years old, 2001 Reunion memorial service Indianapolis, Indiana

FAMILY

Spouse: Peggy Goff
Children: Sall Goff Hogan (Jim), Bobby Goff Swinehart (Jerry), Janet Goff Stefan (Mike)
Grandchildren: 15
Great-Grandchildren: 36

EXPERIENCE

Respectfully submitted by Survivor Goff's grandson, Joe Steffan.

I am one of the 15 grandchildren of Survivor Thomas Goff. I have been given the great honor of writing this chapter for my grandpa. The task will be difficult and I hope that I do justice to him.

Thomas Goff was born in West Virginia in 1906. As of this writing he holds the distinct honor of being the oldest living survivor of the USS *Indianapolis*. When Tom enlisted in 1943, he did not have to; he was 36 and just wanted to see what it was all about. Peggy still teases him about that. He found out, that is for sure!

Tom's list of citations includes the American Ribbon, Asiatic Pacific Ribbon with eight stars, Philippines Liberation Ribbon with one star, the Victory Medal, Purple Heart, Navy Unit Commendation Ribbon, and the Combat Action Ribbon.

On the night of the attack, fate was on Tom's side. He was topside that evening. Had he been down below in his quarters, which were two decks below and forward, he would not have made it out, as many didn't. Tom says that one of the things he will always remember is the way when the moon broke you could see the propellers still turning as the ship went straight down. In Tom's group they were floating in the midst of an oil slick. He talks of being covered in the black oil from head to toe. By the time they were rescued sharks were circling and very thick; two men in Tom's group did survive shark attacks with injuries.

Tom always wants to make sure that pilot, Lt. Wilbur "Chuck" Gwinn is given credit for being the first plane to spot the survivors. Tom suffered damage to his ears from the explosion, scars still remain on his head, and he still to this day has problems with his skin. Tom adamantly stands behind Captain McVay, believing he was a good captain and who did all that he could do.

Tom and Peggy have always enjoyed attending the yearly reunions of the survivors. Now Tom spends most of his time as a devoted husband caring for his wife. He has always been very proud of his three daughters and their families. In our small town, Tom talks about when he would go for walks it was almost constant that he would hear "Hi, Grandpa!" from every street corner. He wouldn't change that for the world.

Tom has always been a humble man, retiring from B.F. Goodrich in Akron, Ohio after 38 years of service. He moved to Florida, but then he and Peg decided to move back to Ohio to spend time with their children. Tom has always been the kind of guy who would give you the shirt off his back if you needed it, and I know that his generosity has been tested by us grandkids more than once! I speak for all of our family when I say that we are very proud of our husband, father, and grandfather!

We also are proud of every crewman of the USS *Indianapolis*. The gratitude that is owed to them can never be repaid. In our family, each of us kids has a bumper sticker that we display proudly stating that we are related to a survivor of the *Indy*. I think the most amazing experience has been that so many people now know what I'm talking about when I say I am related to a survivor of the USS *Indianapolis*. The *Indianapolis* and all of her crewmen have finally started to receive the recognition that they have not asked for but so deeply deserve. God bless each and every survivor of one of the greatest ships in history!

CHAPTER 91 — SURVIVOR GOOCH

NAME	GOOCH, WILLIAM L. F2C
STREET	
CITY	
STATE	
PHONE	
ENTERED SERVICE FROM	Martinsville, IN
PICKED UP BY	USS *Register*
DIVISION	
DOB	Deceased

FAMILY

EXPERIENCE

Unable to contact any family members.

CHAPTER 92 — SURVIVOR GRAY

NAME	GRAY, WILLIS L. F2C
STREET	
CITY	
STATE	
PHONE	
ENTERED SERVICE FROM	Ferndale, MI
PICKED UP BY	USS *Ringness*
DIVISION	
DOB	Deceased 60

FAMILY

EXPERIENCE

Unable to contact any family members.

CHAPTER 93 — SURVIVOR GREEN

NAME	GREEN, TOLBERT Jr. S1C
STREET	
CITY	
STATE	
PHONE	
ENTERED SERVICE FROM	Vale, OK
PICKED UP BY	USS *Bassett*
DIVISION	
DOB	Deceased 65

FAMILY

EXPERIENCE

Unable to contact any family members.

CHAPTER 94 — SURVIVOR GREENLEE

NAME	GREENLEE, CHARLES I. SK3C
STREET	
CITY	
STATE	
PHONE	
ENTERED SERVICE FROM	Waynesburgh, PA
PICKED UP BY	USS *Doyle*
DIVISION	
DOB	Deceased

FAMILY

EXPERIENCE

Unable to contact any family members.

NAME   GREENWALD, JACOB
                            1st Sgt USMC
STREET   3125 So Rene Dr
CITY   Santa Ana
STATE   CA 92704
PHONE   714 546 9024
ENTERED SERVICE FROM   Lincoln, NE
PICKED UP BY   USS *Bassett*
DIVISION   Marine
DOB   12/19/17

FAMILY
Spouse: Vivian E.
Children: Gary Greenwald, Jay Greenwald, Gail Greenwald Kubat
Grandchildren: Erica Denney, Jacob Greenwald, Ben Greenwald, Stephen
Kubat Jr., Matt Kubat
Great-Grandchildren: Lilly Greenwald, Malia Denney

EXPERIENCE
   I stayed in the U.S. Marine Corps for 26 years, retiring in 1966 as a major. I
served with ground forces in Korea, Taiwan, and Japan and at the Washington
Headquarters twice.

NAME   GRIFFITH, ROBERT L. S1C
STREET
CITY
STATE
PHONE
ENTERED SERVICE FROM   Pottsboro, TX
PICKED UP BY   USS *Doyle*
DIVISION
DOB   Deceased

FAMILY

EXPERIENCE
   Unable to contact any family members.

NAME	HANSON, HARLEY C. Machinist
STREET	
CITY	
STATE	
PHONE	
ENTERED SERVICE FROM	New York, NY
PICKED UP BY	USS *Doyle*
DIVISION	
DOB	Deceased 7/98

FAMILY

EXPERIENCE

Unable to contact any family members.

NAME	HARRELL, EDGAR CORPORAL MARINE CORP
STREET	725 Kesterson Ln
CITY	Paris
STATE	TN 38242
PHONE	901 642 9204
ENTERED SERVICE FROM	Murray, KY
PICKED UP BY	USS *Doyle*
DIVISION	Marine
DOB	10/10/24

FAMILY

Spouse: Ola Mae
Children: David Harrell and Cathey Harrell Tierney
Grandchildren: Joseph Harrell, Jana Harrell, Joshua Harrell, Joseph Tierney, Colin Tierney, Benjamin Tierney, Ross Tierney, Celeste Tierney
Great-Grandchildren: Kaitlyn Lea Vandygriff, Olivia Mae Harrell

EXPERIENCE

As a survivor of the largest casualty at sea in the history of the U.S. Navy–the sinking of the USS *Indianapolis* on July 30, 1945–I am honored to be able to tell

of my four and one-half day experience at sea.
Moreover, I am humbled to share with each reader
the amazing providence of almighty God who
provided, protected and sustained me those days,
and yes, even over the past 57 years.   Often I
reflect upon God's faithfulness to me summarized
in His word through the prophet Isaiah saying,
"Hast thou now known? Hast thou not heard,
that the everlasting God, the LORD, the Creator
of the ends of the earth, faintest not, neither is
weary? There is no searching of His
understanding. He giveth power to the faint; and
to them that have no might he increaseth strength"
(Isaiah 40:28-29). I pray that the following short summary of my ordeal at sea
will be a testimony of His infinite grace and mercy to all who placed their faith
in Him.

When I got off watch at midnight on that fateful night, I went below and got
my blanket and headed for the main deck forward to make a pallet on the deck
under the barrels of number one gun turret. I was all wrapped up in my blanket
and had just begun to relax on the hard deck floor when I heard and felt the first
massive explosion. In the amount of time it took Commander Hashimoto to say
"Fire one . . . fire two," there was a second explosion. Later we discovered he
had fired six torpedoes, hitting us with two, with two human torpedoes
("kaitens") ready to be dispatched in case they missed. The first torpedo cut
through the ship just forward of me, completely severing over 30 feet off the
bow, and the second was aft of me near mid-ship. There was also a third
explosion in the powder magazine under the number one gun turret. It was so
intense that it lifted the entire turret off its mooring and sat it over to the
starboard side. The previous night I had slept on top of that turret in a life raft
with a fellow marine named Munson. Unfortunately, he slept there again that
disastrous night.

As I made my way to my emergency station, I looked forward and noticed the
bow was completely cut off. I could hear and feel the bulkheads below breaking
from the massive water pressure as the ship continued to plow ahead with an
open bow. I knew then that we were going to sink. As I looked around, I saw
many men in shock from the massive explosions and fire. Some had flesh
hanging from their face and arms and where begging for help, but my orders
called for me to report to my emergency station for instructions, so I hurried on.
When I arrived, I realized that my life jacket was below deck in my locker. I
quickly asked my marine lieutenant Stauffer permission to cut down the large
canvas bags containing hundreds of jackets to which he replied, "Not until we get
word to abandon ship." But by then the bow was already under water and the
ship was listing to the starboard so severely that we could hardly stand on the
deck. The ship was sinking. We all knew it.

Suddenly a severely burned navy commander came from below deck causing someone to yell out, "Get the commander a life jacket." Immediately a sailor cut open the canvas bag, freeing the precious life vests. I reached in and grabbed one and put it on, but I did not fasten it in the straddle as yet. With almost unbearable anxiety, seconds seemed like hours as I waited for word to abandon ship. However, since the ship ultimately sank in twelve minutes, what seemed like hours could only have been a few minutes when suddenly word came that the captain had given the order to "abandon ship."

Immediately there was panic as many rushed to the high port side and jumped into the water. Too scared to jump and horrified as I watched men jumping on top of others, I hung on to the rail and prayed. I desperately needed hope and assurance as I looked out into what I thought could be eternity. But I will never forget that moment when the peace of God suddenly came stealing across my soul. As promised, the presence of the Lord was very much with me at that time because I previously placed my faith in Him as my personal Savior and confessed Him as Lord of my life in August of 1943.

Digressing for a moment, I volunteered for the marines, and after having been "sworn in" in Indianapolis, Indiana, I was sent back to my home in Kentucky before I reported for duty. During this time the Lord drew me to Himself on the first day of August 1943 while I attended a little church. That Sunday, after the sermon, the pastor gave an invitation then pronounced the benediction. I remained seated as most everyone left. Then the pastor came back and sat down by me and asked if he could help. I told him that I needed to get things right with the Lord and that I felt as if "today was my last chance." He turned to Acts 16:31, which simply says, "Believe in the Lord Jesus Christ and you will be saved." He then reminded me that, "God who cannot lie has made you a promise. And if you will place your faith in Him as your Savior—the One who paid the penalty for your sins on a cross—He will save you." In the quietness of that moment, by God's infinite mercy and grace, God forgave me of my sins and I experienced the miracle of the new birth in Christ.

With my faith as an anchor for my soul, combined with the ministry of the indwelling Spirit of God, I knew as I held on to that rail and looked out into the blackness of night that He was the mighty Sovereign who had ordained this moment. My life for eternity was in His hands. The sound of His voice heard through scripture gave comfort to my heart as he brought to my remembrance the words of Jesus in John 14:27, "Peace I leave with you, my peace I give unto you; not as the world giveth, give I unto you. Let not your heart be troubled, neither let it be afraid." I thought of Jeremiah, imprisoned in a cistern, crying out to the Lord who answered, "Fear not." With all this running through my mind, I released the rail and stepped into the mighty deep. Although my heart was secure with whatever God chose to do with my life, I remember having an overwhelming confidence that I was going to make it. And during the next four and one-half days, He revealed His presence to me over and over again.

As I swam away from the ship, I joined about 80 other men and together we watched as the *Indy* rolled over on her starboard side–the bow already under with her fantail sticking high out of the water. I will never forget watching her sink rather silently to her doom. Of the 80 in our group, there were 10 or more who were so badly injured and burned they did not make it through the night. One marine buddy lasted only a couple of hours.

When morning came that first day, we discovered that we were not alone. There were several sharks swimming all around us, but not appearing as though they would attack us. However, for protection's sake we fastened our life jackets to each other and tried to keep in a tight circle. But when someone left the circle, we would soon hear a blood-curdling scream as the sharks would mass in numbers in a feeding frenzy.

Perhaps an even greater problem was mass hallucination that came as a result of swallowing the salt water either intentionally because of thirst or as a result of getting strangled. Soon the water caused men to see strange things–islands, ships, planes, and even the ship down below. One sailor swam up to me and said, "I've just come from an island over there, and all your marine buddies are having a picnic, and we want you to come and join them." He swam less than fifty yards away when I heard that all-too-familiar scream and watched him disappear completely under the water. Then suddenly his kapok bobbed his remains back up to the surface.

I witnessed another sailor stabbing his shipmate thinking he had a canteen of water in his life jacket. Another thought his buddy was a "Jap" and he yelled out, "Jap! Jap!" while others joined together and drowned the innocent victim. Repeatedly I watched these kinds of horrific scenes, and by the end of the first two days our initial group of eighty had dwindled to about forty.

Thirst was agonizing, an inconceivable torture. Water was everywhere, yet not a drop to drink. But on the second day, God was merciful as He sent a little cloud over our beleaguered group allowing a few drops of water to soothe our parched mouths. It was also on this second day that my marine buddy Spooner wanted to give up and take his life. He had jumped from the ship head first into the thick oil that covered the water causing his eye sockets to swell into excruciating sores. Convinced no one was looking for us, he believed that if he could dive down into the sea far enough he would drown and be delivered from his misery. Refusing to let him go, I tied his jacket to mine and would not let him loose until the next morning after I insisted that he vow to fight for life as long as he had breath.

By noon the third day there were only seventeen of us left. Dehydration, hallucination, and the sharks had taken their toll. However, it was on this day that once again God proved Himself powerful on our behalf. We had just finished a long prayer vigil when we saw five of our shipmates approaching our group. They had one arm locked onto a make shift-raft consisting of some old crates and a couple of 40-mm ammunition cans. They also had gathered several life jackets off deceased sailors and had them on the raft drying out.

Knowing that my kapok was nearly water-logged, I saw joining them as a wise option. They said that since we were swimming all the time anyway, why not direct all our energy swimming toward the Philippines? That made sense to me, so I told Spooner that I was going with them to which he responded, "Harrel, if you go, I'm going too," so five sailors and two marines headed off for the Philippines.

Sometime later that afternoon we spotted what looked to be a crate on our starboard. Driven by survival, curiosity and no doubt compelled by God, I swam away from the group to discover what was in those containers. To my utter dismay and joy, I reached in to find some potatoes—rotten potatoes. As I squeezed my new-found treasure, the rot oozed between my fingers until I felt the solid core in the middle that offered a little nourishment and water. Stuffing my pockets, I swam back to our little group to share the divine provision. That night Lt. McKissick and some other sailors who had also decided to swim toward the Philippines hoping to be spotted joined us. Together we dined on half-rotten potatoes and rejoiced in God's mercy toward us.

To my utter dismay, the next morning, the fourth day, I discovered that I was not with the raft or Spooner, but was only in the company of McKissick and one other sailor. Unfortunately, later that day—about an hour before Wilbur Gwinn spotted us from his plane—the sailor dropped his head into the water and slipped into eternity. After the heroic water landing of the seaplane, Adrian Marks first rescued McKissick, then me. And to my astonishment, the first person I recognized when they put me in the plane was my buddy Spooner. By God's grace we had survived.

Immediately after the rescue, I was transferred to the USS *Doyle* then shipped to Peleliu and to Guam via the USS *Tranquility*, where I spent some time in the hospital. When I arrived back at Marine Corps Base, San Diego, on October 2, 1945, I was expecting to leave for home on the 4th, but due to a perforated appendix, I was admitted to the naval hospital in San Diego. Twenty-nine days later, after 11,800,000 units of penicillin, they finally operated. Unfortunately, I never got my survivor's or rehabilitation leaves. I then was honorably discharged on February 16, 1946 at Great Lakes naval base.

God in His providence protected me from the sharks, gave me water from heaven on the second day, provided me with a spare life jacket and a potato feast on the third day and finally on the fourth day, with hope almost gone, He dispatched His angels to direct our rescue. To God be the glory. In conclusion, over the years I have had many opportunities to travel all across our great nation to not only tell of my survival experience, but also of the purpose and mission of the Survivors Organization; namely, to get our good Captain McVay exonerated of the false accusations made against him. We all rejoice knowing that our persistence and travail was finally rewarded on July 13, 2001.

I wish to thank each of you of the USS *Indianapolis* for all the years of camaraderie and friendship. May God richly bless you in all you do for His glory.

CHAPTER 99 SURVIVOR HARRISON

NAME	HARRISON, CECIL M. Chief Gunner
STREET	
CITY	
STATE	
PHONE	
ENTERED SERVICE FROM	New York, NY
PICKED UP BY	USS *Doyle*
DIVISION	Fox Division
DOB	Deceased 8/97

FAMILY

EXPERIENCE

Unable to contact any family members.

CHAPTER 100 SURVIVOR HART

NAME	HART, FRED Jr. RT2C
STREET	
CITY	
STATE	
PHONE	
ENTERED SERVICE FROM	San Bruno, CA
PICKED UP BY	USS *Ringness*
DIVISION	
DOB	Deceased 6/71

FAMILY

EXPERIENCE

Unable to contact any family members.

CHAPTER 101 — SURVIVOR HATFIELD

NAME HATFIELD, WILLIE N. S2C
STREET
CITY
STATE
PHONE
ENTERED SERVICE FROM Salt Lick, KY
PICKED UP BY USS *Register*
DIVISION
DOB Deceased

FAMILY

EXPERIENCE

Unable to contact any family members.

CHAPTER 102 — SURVIVOR HAVENER

NAME HAVENER, HARLAN C. F2
STREET
CITY
STATE
PHONE
ENTERED SERVICE FROM Decatur, IL
PICKED UP BY USS *Bassett*
DIVISION
DOB Deceased

FAMILY

EXPERIENCE

Unable to contact any family members.

NAME	HAVINS, OTHA ALTON Y2C
STREET	
CITY	
STATE	
PHONE	
ENTERED SERVICE FROM	Shafter, CA
PICKED UP BY	USS *Ringness*
DIVISION	
DOB	2/18/23
	Deceased 10/97 Clovis, CA

FAMILY

Spouse: Billie Havins

Children: Steven Havins (Kimberly) and Carl Havins (Laurie) (Carl was named after Survivor Havins' best friend on the ship who was lost at sea...Carl Lloyd Arnold)

Grandchildren: Sean Havins (Leigh Ann), Cheree Havins Manicki, Ginger Havins Steiner (Larry), Anne Havins

Great-Grandchildren: Raicheal Havins, Bandon O. Alton Havins, Kylie McAdams Havins

EXPERIENCE

The following was received from Survivor Havins' widow, Billie.

"I am sending a copy of my husband's notes on what happened on the night when the ship USS *Indianapolis* sank. He was at one time going to write a book, but for some reason he just couldn't do it. Al spent most of his time answering letters and phone calls from people who had lost loved ones. Some calls were long distance, some were in the middle of the night. He just wanted to help give peace and encouragement when he could. For several years, Al and Angel (Wilbur Gwinn, pilot of PV-1 Ventura bomber), went around northern California telling the story of the *Indy* to different groups. This was one of the main reasons Al wanted to write a book.

Paul, you asked me if you could print Al's notes in a book the USS Indianapolis Survivors Organization was trying to put together. I would be very pleased to give you (Paul Murphy, Chairman) and you alone permission to print these notes in that book. My permission is not given to any one else to be used in any other way without my written permission.

These few pages are very precious to the boys and me. So we would appreciate it if you print these notes that you would print all of them."

Love to all from "My Al" and wife
Billie Havins
2257 Goshen Ave
Clovis CA 93611
559 325 1732

April 10, 1993
Dear Kimo and Charles McVay:
I'm sorry this is so long in coming, but here it is, such as it is, it's a quickie.
There's a lot that could be filled in during each day, but I hope I have given you
enough to form a picture in your minds, of what your dad went through those
five days, only to be set up and then have his life and career shot from under
him.
Hope you fellows are well, likewise your families. We love you.

This material was pulled from an outline I'm doing for a book. When finished
the book will be dedicated to my wife, Billie Havins, my two sons, Steven Alan
Havins and Carl Lloyd Havins. I reserve the right to its use for all endeavors in
the future.

Alton Havins

SINKING OF THE USS *INDIANAPOLIS*, CA 35
DAILY LOG APPROXIMATELY 0010, JULY 30, THRU AUGUST 3, 1945.
SURVIVORS 317 - LOSS OF LIFE 880
BY O. ALTON HAVINS, SURVIVOR

I was awakened by violent vibrations and bouncing of the ship. Water struck
my face, apparently from the explosions. I experienced the same sensation as I
did when we were struck by a suicide plane. I dressed, buckled my life belt on,
headed for my battle station, fire control, in bow of ship.
Crossing the quarterdeck, I found a man, badly burned. I took him into the
port hangar, bedded him down, covered him with blankets and told him I'd find
medical help. A lot of men slept on the quarterdeck at night. Consequently,
adequate blankets were available to use for the burned victims. When I returned
to the quarterdeck, I found several men, all severely burned. I took another one
to port hangar, bedded him down, and continued my search for medical help.
It was important that I get to my battle station. If there's a fire and it's
neglected it invites disaster. There were so many wounded I chose to take a few
moments to help. I did not know most of my battle station was gone...blown
away by the first explosion. What remained was on fire.
My best friend was having difficulty with his life belt. I assisted in inflating it,
helped him through the life lines and told him to jump. I never saw him again.

Reports from survivors in his group said he disappeared the third night. Many men were already in the water, some blown overboard by explosion, others struck by waves and washed over. Some escaped through the hole in the hull, perhaps others realized the ship was beyond help and jumped overboard.

Our speed had slowed to a snail's pace because the starboard engines had been knocked out. She was diving bow first into the black waters below, no one realizing the ship was mortally wounded. I returned to the task at hand, trying to save my ship, and helping the injured. Moments later, I realized the ship was in real trouble. Water was standing about fifteen feet up on the quarterdeck. About eight minutes had passed since first explosion. With water standing on deck I realized we had lost her. She began rolling to starboard real fast, settling quickly by the bow.

The plane in the port hangar broke loose from its mooring and fell on injured men I had just put there. Tool boxes, spare parts, and bunk beds began falling through the guard rail from above and were falling on the injured men. List to starboard now so deep I could no longer stand. My feet slid from under me. I had to crawl on my belly to the life lines, about fifteen feet away and above my head. Sliding into water on starboard side was of great concern to me. I knew when you abandon ship to keep cool, leave from the high side, and swim into the wind. Becoming entangled in lanyards dangling from flag deck or being struck by the superstructure as the ship rolled wasn't high on my list of priorities. I reached life lines just as she rolled on her starboard side, the bow diving still deeper into the water, the superstructure forward is completely submerged. About ten minutes had passed since first explosion.

Things were happening real fast! There was no time to dilly-dally with decisions. I had to make one real fast. Run with it or swim, whatever fit the occasion. I pulled myself through life lines, standing on outside of hull, I began preparations to "abandon ship." Until that moment, no thoughts of or plans to abandon ship had been made. The superstructure was doing a good job of pulling her over and down.

The next couple minutes was pretty much every man for himself. There was very little, if anything, we could do for each other. The ship was almost completely upside down and still rolling, hole in bow, scooping up water, pulling her deeper and deeper into the sea. Standing at the keel, exposed above water, I removed my life belt, inflated same, and secured it around my waist. Now I'm as ready, physically and mentally, as I will ever be to "abandon ship."

Men were clinging to the bottom of the ship as best they could. I walked along keel yelling for them to move away, that the ship was lost. I have no way of knowing, but many probably were without life jackets, some unable to swim, every one no doubt confused and frightened. No one moved away. This wasn't the time to try reasoning with them. Having nothing else to cling to, they refused to move away. I jumped over their heads and swam into the wind, hoping I was heading in the direction of the Philippines–not that I thought I could swim the 500 miles, but what the heck, there wasn't anything else to hang around for.

I estimated ten or eleven minutes have now elapsed since first explosion. I swam only a short distance when a man came up behind me and to my left. He grabbed me around both arms. He had no life support and his strength was like a vise. I realized I had a very serious problem and there was only one that could help. I said, "Lord please take note, I have a problem." The next thirty to sixty seconds seemed like an eternity. First I needed to break his death hold so I could keep our heads above water. Unable to free myself from his grip, we were repeatedly pulled under water. When we broke surface the first time, I glanced at him and saw he was inhaling water. I wasn't unaware, until later, there was a hole in my life belt and all the air had escaped. Waves were about eight to ten feet high and making the situation very difficult, even without the above-mentioned problems.

We were pulled under a second time. The man's strength was great, and I feared I would be unable to break his grip and free myself. He was fighting to hold on; I was desperately struggling to break loose. My lungs were screaming for air. I was burning oxygen fast, trying to fight our way to the surface. Kicking my feet frantically, I had only a moment to replenish my lungs with fresh air before the next dive. It was very dark but I could see his oil-covered face. Our heads were only inches apart. I glanced over my shoulder again at him and realized he was in very serious trouble. Instead of air, he was taking in oil and water.

I prayed, "Lord, I still have a problem, you can lend a hand any time." We were pulled under a third time. His strength began to fade. With one more burst of strength, possibly my last, I was able to break his hold around my arms. Breathing a sigh of relief, believing my life belt to be inflated, I said to myself, "Thanks Lord." And to the sailor, "Hold on fellow, we'll make it yet." When he relaxed his grip his arms slipped to my waist. His strength was failing but he was now clinging to my waist. I was able once again to practice what was now my most favored sport, swimming.

With my friend in tow, I headed out. Just where we were going I didn't know, but we were on our way. Glancing back I saw he was still struggling to breathe. My thoughts were if we can only get a little further away before the ship blows, I'll stop and hold his head above water. The possibility of the ship exploding was a real concern to me. If she blew, being so close to her, both of us would surely die. A moment later his grip relaxed, his arms slid over my hips, now he was holding both legs, below the knees. This situation was every bit as serious as when he held my arms. I could no longer use my feet to kick and break to the surface. Now he was dead weight. I could no longer help him or myself. I was in more trouble than before. His head was no longer visible above water. My strength was fading fast. My need for help had reached the critical point. Again I asked, "God, please take note, the situation is deteriorating fast."

The man released his grip. My legs were free. I turned to help but he was gone. The sea had engulfed him and he was swept away by the waves.

The man needs help! The engine room may blow! The ammunition could explode! These and many other possibilities flashed through my mind. What should I do? A decision had to be made, and quick. If I dive in search of this man and the ship explodes, both of us are dead meat. At best, the chance of finding him was next to zero. If I found him, would he be dead or alive? Would I die trying to save a dead man? With my strength almost drained, in a state of confusion, I did the only thing my mind was capable of communicating to my body..."GET OUT OF HERE!" The decision I made, right or wrong, I knew I'd have to live with the rest of my life. This just might be the last decision I ever made!

The ship was just beyond where the man once was. She was standing on her bow, fantail towering above me, and was diving straight down, fast, with one screw still turning. Another quick search was made for my friend. Not finding him, I glanced once more at the ship. The fantail stood high above me, about two hundred feet tall. If she fell in my direction I would be taken down with her. No contingency plans were in place for this kind of problem. In about five seconds she was gone! Completely consumed by the sea! Only boiling foam remained! I turned and swam fast. I was expecting an explosion at any moment which would probably kill me or, in case of fire, turn me into a burnt offering.

My ship, my home for almost three years, dropped like a rock. She was no more. It only took seconds for her to disappear. Now all alone, feeling I was pretty much in control of everything, I quickly formulated a plan. At the center of that plan was survival. How this was to be effective, I wasn't sure—only that it could and would be with the help of God. To survive I had to have God's help, and He gave it. I'm sure glad God hung around.

Chance of an explosion now was remote. She had been gone for a couple of minutes. I quickly surveyed my surroundings the best I could, looking and listening for sounds from other survivors. With no sign of life, I resumed my newly adopted hobby, swimming. At this juncture I thought I was the only survivor. This was a frightening thought. Seeing and hearing no one for the next fifteen or so minutes, I really believed I was the only survivor. The reality and presence of God now filled my mind and heart. I no longer felt I was in control—quite the contrary. I knew God was with me and had control of everything. I was convinced God would somehow effect my rescue. Just when and how wasn't clear. There have been times when I've felt all alone, but nothing to compare with the feeling I now had. All my shipmates dead, my life jacket deflated. "Lord, whatever it is you have in mind, please let me in on it." Now it's just God and me.

My mind couldn't fathom my situation. Believing I was the only survivor, I reasoned it would be a while before I'd be found. One man in a big ocean. I had nothing to signal passing ships or planes if and when they came. Yes, things seemed to be getting worse by the minute, not better. My body was deep in the water. I was not yet fully aware my life belt was useless. My prayer was, "Lord, move in real close please, and let's get out of here."

Over the next twenty minutes or so, I accepted the fact there were no other survivors. I resisted, very strongly, the thought I might never be found. With death all around me how could I escape its clutches? Yes indeed there was a tough job ahead. I kept telling myself I'd be found. I was unwilling to accept death. Somehow God and I would work this thing out. Fear never overcame me. I was just having difficulty sorting things through. God helped me keep cool. I knew I shouldn't run scared, or swim in this case. My parents taught me to always keep cool, that fear was an enemy if not controlled. God made it possible for me to keep cool.

It was difficult to accept the fact the ship was gone. I kept swimming, putting distance between me and her just in case the odds were stacked against me and an explosion or fire occurred. Besides, it seemed the logical thing to do. With nothing important to do there, I set a course and a steady pace in what I thought was the direction to Leyte Gulf. According to my watch it was past midnight, in fact my watch stopped at 0023 hours. There was no moon or stars and no signs to direct me. I never was one to remain idle for long. This was no exception so traveling was the logical and next best thing to do. The presence of God was with me. He kept my fear under control. I really didn't know what direction I was going, or where I was going, but I was on my way. This kind of situation was very new to me. I found myself revising my plans on a minute-by-minute schedule or as the situation demanded.

Probably thirty minutes had passed when I heard a voice calling, "OVER HERE." Again I heard the voice, "OVER HERE! I HAVE A CARGO NET." Needless to say, this was sweet music to my ears. God was providing a way out. I called back, "Keep yelling so I can find you." The wind and high waves made it difficult to home in on a sound. Within ten minutes, having changed direction several times, I found the man and cargo net. We quickly identified ourselves and our physical condition. Both of us kept yelling, and within ten to fifteen minutes we picked up three other sailors. Now we were one God and five sailors.

Everyone was rational, no hysteria, no serious injury, but all were dazed at what had happened, whatever it was that had happened. We kept calling to those we hoped were out there. After a couple hours or so it was evident we were it. Torpedoes, suicide plane, mines, ammunition exploding, the list went on. It was conceivable that any of these could have happened. Talk seemed to ease the shock we felt. We still yelled out occasionally just in case some one was out there. Several hours had passed when we spotted a life raft. No occupants. With cargo net in tow, we swam to it. A quick survey told us the raft was badly damaged, no floor, no sea rations, no paddles, just the ring. We unrolled the cargo net, folded it twice and slid it under the raft. This would get our bodies out of the water and away from sharks and would help us maintain our balance.

The thousand pounds of combined weight made the raft ride deep in the water.

I informed our group of the target plane that would be out later that day for target practice. This made everyone feel better. Not knowing the exact time we sank, it seemed reasonable to think the pilot would spot us. We didn't reason it out that we were one hundred sixty miles from proposed rendezvous.

Approximately six hours had passed; it was beginning to grow light on the horizon. The waves were still high, more like swells, very few were breaking. We were on top of a large wave, and at that moment we saw another raft in the distance, with occupants. They also saw us and we began waving, yelling. Neither group had oars so it took a while before we came alongside. It was Captain McVay with two very sick men and two rafts.

Things were looking up. The skipper and his crew of two had also accepted the fact they too were the only survivors. We pulled the three rafts together, shook hands, laughed, and yes...cried a little. The skipper inquired about our condition, did we see others, any sea rations. We told him there were none. The skipper told us he had some rations, a piece of canvas, a flare gun and three flares.

My regular watch station was on the bridge. I was a phone operator for the captain so he and I knew each other. He inquired about our physical condition, where we were when we were hit, what happened around us, how we escaped, how many we thought got into the water, other information relevant to our situation. We were very glad to see our captain.

The three rafts were lashed together most of the day. The skipper talked to each man, asking about martial status, number of children (if married), where we lived, education, naval training, our job, division, were we career people, things of that nature. He told us of his family, his career. If it's possible for a full captain to be a regular guy, then I must say Captain McVay was a regular guy. Following his in-depth fact-finding inquiry, he told us how he was swept overboard by a wave. He shared with us his feelings after he found a raft, but was unable to find other survivors. He then made a statement that shook every one. QUOTE: "YOU KNOW, THE CAPTAIN IS SUPPOSED TO GO DOWN WITH HIS SHIP!"

DAY ONE

Spent trying to figure out what had happened. In the afternoon the skipper directed the three rafts be tied on long lines, allowing us to drift in a wider pattern. This gave us a better chance of being spotted from the air. Day one brought two sharks. They remained with us for the duration. The five men on my raft remained together for the four nights and five days. The skipper remained with the two men he had when we found him. I suppose there was a bond between us since we had come this far together.

There was no sleep for anyone the first or second night. By mid afternoon it appeared that everything that need be said had been said. We were covered with black oil. It was in our eyes. With the hot sun beating down on us, it kept us pretty well occupied the first day. We kept close tabs on each other through the second night, to make sure all went well. The days were very hot; the nights were cold.

DAY TWO

Began with counting our visitors, the sharks. The three were now five, then prayer with the skipper. A nice warm sun was welcome, it drove the chill from our bodies. By mid-day, every day, the sun became very hot. The skipper checked in with each of us frequently through the days ahead, and every morning led us in prayer. This was part of his duty in the absence of a chaplain.

The sun melted the oil in our hair. It ran down our face and into our eyes. The waves were now rolling swells, smooth like glass. The glare off the water caused much pain in and around the eyes. Day was quite peaceful, except for the heat and burning eyes. We kept our distance from our five hungry sharks.

EARLY MORNING

We heard yelling in the distance, and on top of a wave we spotted a life raft with one occupant. With no oars, and rowing into the wind, it took several hours to reach him. By his yelling we thought he was badly wounded. We labored hard and long to reach him, only to find him well, but practically out of his mind. We threatened to throw him overboard, but the skipper thought this was a very bad idea. He was very persuasive. The raft was in tact except for provision.

MID AFTERNOON

The skipper directed our rafts pulled close and he gave each man two malt tablets, and a piece of Spam, half-inch square. We rolled it around in our mouth, rubbed it on our lips, and after a while would squeeze it with our tongue then swallow. During the day I found an onion and scooped it up, tucked it away in my shirt for future use. Jay Glenn and I, both in Aviation Unit, were members of a barber shop quartet. In the afternoon we sang a couple courses for the men such as "I WANT A GIRL JUST LIKE THE GIRL THAT MARRIED DEAR OLE DAD'. 'DON'T SIT UNDER THE APPLE TREE WITH ANYONE ELSE BUT ME." The captain expressed his thanks. During the day we bumped into a large block of butter. It didn't last long, but long enough for us to cover the exposed parts of our body with it. We found a 40-mm ammunition can and took it aboard to catch water, if it rained. There were no planes or ships today. P.S. It never rained either.

DAY THREE

Began by counting noses, men and sharks, and praying with the skipper. Talked of rescue. We reasoned the plane had not reached us because we were not where we were supposed to be. We were one hundred sixty miles away from our planned position. It was obvious an SOS message never got off the ship. It was also very obvious we weren't even missed. The skipper tried to be upbeat, hoping to convince the men, and himself, that we would be found. Mid-afternoon we saw a ship in the distance. The very tip of superstructure could be seen. A flare was fired with no results. A plane also was spotted but he was many miles away. No flare was fired. We had two flares left. Glenn and I once again warmed up our vocal cords and sang a couple courses. We sang to the crew twice, once on day two and once on day three.

Mid-afternoon the skipper served lunch, a piece of onion, (he had taken possession of all food), two malt tables, a half-inch square of Spam. Skipper had a fish hook and line, so we took it out, baited it with Spam, crossed our fingers and prayed. The bait didn't last long, so we used dry hook. Low and behold we landed a big one, probably five inches long. We agreed the fish was poisonous, so we used the rascal for bait. Actually this was a pretty good day. It was fun fishing even with one hook. The excitement was good. No luck; our friends of the deep also knew the bait was poison. Everyone was trying to put on a good face in a bad situation. Everyone went all out to keep the spirit alive.

The highlight of our five-day voyage happened today. We needed moisture and without letting the skipper in on our plans, we decided to kill a shark. One man had a navy pocket knife, so he was elected to bring home (aboard) the bacon. We remained real still till one shark came within a foot of the raft. We didn't have to wait long, and then he struck out. With all his strength he hit the shark square between the eyes with the knife. We were sure there would be shark meat on the table tonight. Then the surprise of a lifetime. The shark threw up his tail and struck him alongside the head. The blow sent the man flying through the air, across a raft, into the water and into faces of other sharks. This frightened them and they scattered. After a few minutes they were back, one sporting a big gash between his eyes. The captain suggested we refrain from trying that again. Actually it was an order, but he did it like the diplomat that he was.

The captain told us we had drifted out of the shipping lane, making our chances of being seen less possible. Night fell after what was thought to be a pretty good day. During the day several men had fallen asleep, falling backward into water. The sharks would scatter for a few minutes, then they were back. We gave support to each other, hoping to prevent this from happening again. During the night men on our raft would slide into the warm water for a while. When it became cold we would climb back on raft, thus freezing, again sliding back into water. This continued for the remainder of voyage.

DAY FOUR

We welcomed the nice warm sun. The five sharks were still with us. One plane was spotted many miles away. No flare fired. Roll call, prayer with the skipper. We began to talk about the seriousness of our situation. No one could hold out much hope for rescue, not even the captain.

MID-AFTERNOON, PROBABLY TWO P.M.

Our rafts were pulled close. We were given our daily rations of food. Portions were smaller this time. We had to make them last awhile longer, three, four days, maybe longer.

Couple hours after our fabulous hunger-quenching feast, we spotted a large cardboard box near by. We paddled over, and took it aboard. It was a box of

Lucky Strike cigarettes. We ripped open the box and gave each man a carton to search through. I found one cigarette, half of it smokable. After much persuasion the skipper finally agreed to our request to rip off the collar of a kapok life jacket, put it in the 400-mm ammunition can and fire a flare into it. For the next hour or so we almost forgot about our troubles. What excitement there was. Those who smoked had two drags from the butt. The skipper didn't smoke, but he was pleased at the excitement this created.

MID-AFTERNOON, PROBABLY FOUR OR FIVE P.M.

After our big meal and smoke out, we spotted a plane very low, very far away, circling in the same general area. This meant one thing! There were survivors! We had been found! Our rafts had drifted about twenty-five miles from the group. Another party of six was found in our vicinity that we hadn't been aware of. The skipper was poised to fire the last flare if things began to go bad. An hour or so later, just before sundown, a large plane came into view. It was making a systematic search. We knew we were the object of their search! Every time the plane made a turn it came closer. He was definitely moving toward us! We took turns standing on the raft, held by others, waving the piece of canvas. We could only stand for a short time. Each man was willing to take his turn. Talk about excitement! It was rampant on our rafts. We knew we were going home to our loved ones. Night fell before we were spotted. The plane turned and faded into the distant night. This was heart-breaking! But we knew he would return the next day, take up his position and that we would be found by mid-day.

There were searchlights over the horizon all night. One pointed straight up. So we still felt good. This was the longest night of all! Skipper cautioned us to stay calm, keep away from sharks, and we would make it. The night was long, but we were ready for day five. No one slept that night.

DAY FIVE

Nose count, men and sharks, prayer with the skipper. Breakfast was offered. There were no takers.

Soon after sunrise the plane was back. Excitement filled the air! Then... another bad moment presented itself. The plane was there, but he was on the other side of us and his search pattern was taking him away from us. Our greatest fear became a reality! We had drifted into an area he had searched the day before. We waved frantically, but the plane kept moving away. The captain was ready to fire our last flare. But waiting, hoping, that the plane would turn in our direction. If he fired the flare now it would not be seen.

The naked sailor didn't participate in our endeavor to attract the plane. He looked behind us, and speaking in a low, unexcited voice he said, "Fellows, do I see a ship bearing down on us, or am I hallucinating?" We turned quickly, focusing all of our attention on whatever it was that was coming up behind us. At first we weren't sure we saw what we were seeing. No one moved for a couple seconds, then we knew it was the real thing, a ship bearing down on us, I mean straight at us, at high speed. At this point everyone was ready to try walking on water. What a beautiful sight that was.

The radar aboard the *Ringness* had locked in on the 40-mm can. Suspecting it to be a submarine, they made haste to protecting the rescue of survivors. With cargo net hanging over starboard side, and men already coming down the net to assist, the ship pulled alongside our rafts. We were met topside by a sailor with cigarettes. Two men, one on each side, carried us inside and put us in the most wonderful bed we had ever seen. The medics were on deck to give aid where needed. We were promised food on the double. In the interval we were given small portions of water, followed by lots of good strong navy coffee.

We were unable to walk so they carried us to the shower. We were stripped of our clothing, washed down with a solvent, showered with soap, given clean clothing, returned to a clean bunk, another cigarette and cup of coffee. Soon we had all the steak, potatoes, string beans and corn we could eat. The skipper was taken forward. I saw him the next day just before we reached port and he disembarked. This was the last time I saw Captain McVay. I sent him a telegram of support during his KANGAROO-COURT MARTIAL. I wasn't at the reunion he attended."

Alton & I were married six months after he was honorably discharged, and after two sons, Alton could not forget the promise he made to God while in the water and on the raft looking into the eyes of five or more sharks. One Sunday afternoon while washing his car and listing to Charles Fuller on the car radio, Al turned to me and said, "What would you think if I went to Bible college and studied to be a minister? I was so surprised that I just said, "Sure, if that is what you want." That was the first time he told me of making a promise to God.

We packed our things and went to Michigan to tell my parents he was going to study to be a minister. He settled on a Bible college in Ft. Wayne, Indiana.

He was a person that needed to help people, not condemn or put them down. One of his passions was his interest in young people that had their lives ahead of them. So many things could hurt and lead them astray. He would tell them often you can never take the holes out of your life, but you can keep from putting them in there. At one church he had a motorcycle club for the young people after church on Sunday night. They rode all over Phoenix and in the mountains, with me hanging on for dear life. It also was a good hobby for our boys. Many of the young people wrote to us after we left telling how much it meant to have their minister care enough to keep them together and teach them what the Bible taught, so they could have fun and still be God-loving people.

We had churches all over, from Michigan to California. He was sent many times to a church that had a problem to help them to look on the good side and start loving instead of hurting one another and the church. He was the kind of man that if God said it, he would believe it, live it, and teach it.

When his health began to go he went to the hospital to be the minister of the ill. He would pray, talk, and stay all night if a family needed him. All people were important people to him and he wanted to be a friend that would help in time of trouble. He also was a wedding pastor. He would counsel couples before marriage, perform weddings, and continue to help as long as they needed him. He always wrote a letter or two later to make sure things were going well for them.

When at the last he was bed–ridden, he had three nurses, a head nurse, and a doctor to help him. You can bet that he made sure that all went to church and learned about just how good the Lord was to us all.

The Lord came and took him home early on the 14th of October. You can bet that he is riding his Harley motorcycle all over heaven telling people just how good God is to prepare heaven for those that love and accept Him.

He was interested in the young married couples so much that we both went into counseling. It lasted for forty years, and we never charged because that was a God–given gift to us. I still have many people call me (since Al has passed) just to thank us for the work that helped to make their married life so much better.

HE KEPT HIS PROMISE TO GOD AND BECAME A MINISTER.

The USS *Indianapolis*, (CA-35). This is the last known photograph to be taken of this famous ship. *Indianapolis* is shown in the harbor at Tinian Island just after off-loading the world's first operational atomic bombs.

NAME   HAYNES, LEWIS L. Lt. Commander
STREET
CITY
STATE
PHONE
ENTERED SERVICE FROM   Chelsea, MA
PICKED UP BY   USS *Doyle*
DIVISION
DOB   4/27/12
                Deceased 3/01 Naples, FL

FAMILY
Widow: Margaret P. Haynes
Children: John, Henry, Christopher, Mary Elizabeth, Virginia
Grandchildren: 14

EXPERIENCE

Respectfully submitted by Survivor Haynes' widow, Margaret.

My husband, Lew, passed away in March 2001, just before his 89th birthday. He dearly wanted to make 90 but it was not to be. However, he had a full and wonderful life–he touched so many people, both personally and professionally. We had been married just over thirty years and he was the dearest husband with the sweetest disposition. He was a caring father to five children who loved him dearly. He is missed by us every day.

He was very proud to have served on the *Indianapolis*, and like all the survivors he was traumatized by the events that took place. I don't think a night went by when he didn't "tread water" in his sleep. He found the reunions emotionally draining. It would break his heart when various family members of those who perished would ask him for memories of their loved ones and whether he knew how they died. He had so many sleepless nights after recalling the tragedy to the various people who wanted to hear his stories.

And yet Lew was not defined by the *Indianapolis* experience. He accomplished so much in his life. He had a distinguished medical career and was a fine surgeon who also was involved in various successful research programs.

He loved the navy–he was so proud to have been in the service. He retired in 1965 and after 12 years' association with the Lahey Clinic in Boston, he retired again and spent many happy years in retirement, playing golf and fishing. I am so glad he was able to have those years. He surely deserved them.

The *Indianapolis* story will never be forgotten nor will my husband's role, and for that I am appreciative to the authors who have chosen to write of those tragic events.

NAME	HELLER, JOHN T. S2
STREET	255 W 14 Mile #105
CITY	Clawson
STATE	MI 48017
PHONE	
ENTERED SERVICE FROM	Detroit, MI
PICKED UP BY	USS *Ringness*
DIVISION	Deck Div
DOB	11/6/27

FAMILY
Children: Linda
Grandchildren: Aaron, Kristen

EXPERIENCE

I turned 17 years old November 6, 1944. I talked my mother into letting me quit high school and joined the navy January 29, 1945. After seven weeks in boot camp at Great Lakes, I got one week leave and then went back to Great Lakes. There we boarded a train and it took five days to arrive at Mare Island. I saw the USS *Indianapolis* for the first time and she was in dry dock. I was very proud to be assigned to her and watched as she was put into the water. We went to Hunters Point and waited there as a large crate was put on deck. Then we delivered this crate to Tinian.

The night of the sinking, I had a helmsman watch from four to eight which gave me all night to sleep. I was there when Captain McVay came in and told the officer of the deck he would be turning in. I was on a zigzag course and the captain told the officer of the deck to resume straight course. The officer of the deck turned to me and said to resume regular course. At eight o'clock I was relieved and went below and ate. It was so hot below I went topside and watched the sun go down. I was only 5'2" tall and weighed 111 pounds. There was lots of room in the trainers booth and it was also cool. I soon fell asleep.

Shortly after midnight, I woke up when the torpedo hit and climbed out on the deck. My feet were burned when I hit the deck and I did not know what was going on. The officer of the deck was yelling to turn out the lights where we had been sleeping. Someone cut a row of life jackets off the side of the turret. I grabbed one and put it on. Men were screaming all around and many were wounded. The ship listed to one side and I went into the ocean. After landing in the water, one of the planes started to roll over on me and another sailor. We finally got away from it. When we looked up we could see the *Indy* in the distance, plowing through the water on its side. The sky was all lit up with fire as it finally rolled over. I saw men on top and the screws were still turning as it went straight down. From then on...it was a big ocean.

NAME	HENSCH, ERWIN F. Lt.	
	(USNR 184602)	
STREET	7297 LAKESIDE PK DR NE	
CITY	REMER	
STATE	MN 56672	
PHONE		
ENTERED SERVICE FROM	Fergus Falls, MN	
PICKED UP BY	USS *Doyle*	
DIVISION	Assistant Chief Engineer	
DOB	3/30/20	

FAMILY

Spouse: Helen
Children: Judith, Susan and Thomas
Grandchildren: Seven

EXPERIENCE

After 19 months in the Aruba/Curacao area in the Dutch West Indies aboard a YMS minesweeper, I reported aboard the USS *Indianapolis* in the fall of 1944. It was about the time that Captain McVay took command. Commander Degraves was the chief engineer and Lt. Redmayne was the assistant chief engineer. I was assigned as the electrical division officer. My duty station was the engine room. Since this was my first experience on a steam-powered ship, I had a lot to learn. Dick Redmayne, my boss, was very patient throughout my learning process, for which I thank him. He became the chief engineer, relieving Mr. Degraves in July, 1945, and I in turn became the assistant chief engineer.

The best and most accurate way for me to describe my experience during the ship-sinking event is to repeat the official accounting I wrote to the navy in August 1945, which follows.

I was in my bunk in room P on the starboard side on the main deck just aft of number one turret. First thing I knew was that I was awakened by an explosion and by the time my feet hit the deck I heard and felt another explosion. I went out into the passageway and headed aft. The passageway was filled with men and was very crowded and smoke filled. I couldn't get through there so I came back forward. I started down the ladder into the warrant officer's quarters—about frame 30, but that was also in the same condition. I felt fresh air come from forward on the main deck. I saw that I couldn't get to my battle station so I headed for the forecastle deck and entered the forecastle deck through the escape hatch just aft of the forward head on the main deck. I got up on the forecastle and looked forward and saw that part of the bow forward of the anchor windlass was blown off. I also saw that we were taking a list to starboard and going down by the head. On the port side there were a number of men injured and lying on the deck. They were sliding to the starboard because the ship was listing to starboard. I know that one or two of these men were carried off the ship with us and I don't know what happened to the rest of them. When I could see that the ship was listing fast and turning over, I jumped overboard after getting a life belt from one of the fellows who had an extra one. I had accidentally grabbed a gas mask instead of a life belt. When I left the ship I had on a pair of pajama bottoms and they tore off when I hit the water and swam away. Upon looking back I could see that the ship had capsized and was sinking with the stern end up. I could see a plane about midships (one of the *Indy* SOCs) and the plane also appeared to be sinking. I presume that the ship was hit approximately at midnight and sank between 0010 and 0015. I noticed several small areas which appeared to be several square feet in area which were aflame but after a few minutes I saw nothing more of these areas.

It appeared to me that we received two torpedo hits—one way forward on the bow on the starboard side, and one on the starboard side just forward of number one stack.

On the following day, July 30, 1945, we tried to keep the men in a large group as much as possible and when evening came there were approximately one hundred and seventy five (175) men in that group. Shortly after dark we saw some lights—about three or four in different positions all around us. There was a red light with an arrow pointing down which appeared to be stationary. There were also two white ones like that. There was one red light with no arrows—it looked like a masthead on a ship. We yelled "ahoy" and tried to make as much noise as possible. One of the men had a one-cell flashlight which he waved in the air but nothing resulted from this. The following day in the morning we saw a plane come in about four or five thousand feet. We waved and splashed water and tried to attract its attention and about a mile away from us he looked as though he saw us and he appeared to change course about twenty or thirty degrees and went off in another direction. Everyone seemed quite confident that he had seen us.

On the night of July 31st, we still had a fairly good-sized group, about one hundred men, but many of them were showing signs of hysteria and were inclined to wander off by themselves. Between then and the time we were picked up this situation became constantly worse and a good percentage of the men were out of their mind. It was almost impossible to keep them together. One person would come up with some story about an island he had sighted, or the discovery of fresh water, or something like that. Immediately a number of the men would follow him and never return. One story was that the stern end of the ship had come to the surface again and that food and water were available. The men would go out and search for the ship, sometimes in groups and sometimes individually. No amount of persuasion would keep them from doing so. Some became angry when questioned as to whether or not they had seen anything out there.

On the morning of the second of August a search plane discovered us and after a couple of hours there were a number of other planes patrolling the area. Towards evening they had dropped a number of rubber life rafts, some of which contained water and "K" rations. Between the time we went over the side and that time, we had had practically no food and water. We had two raw potatoes on the second day and two biscuits and an ounce of water on the fourth day after the planes had dropped the water and rafts. Much of the water was lost when it was dropped because the containers broke and we were still without water except for one or two gallons which had to be used for possibly one hundred men. On the evening of August second, I left the main group with one of the electrician's mates to try to get the electrician's mate aboard one of the planes. He had been given morphine shots and his condition was very bad and his eye sight poor. Dr. Haynes decided that it would be best to get him to the plane fast and by the time we got to the spot they had stopped picking up men. We managed to board a rubber raft someone had found.

During the night we picked up Lt. Reid and several other men, which made a total of eight men on that raft. Throughout the night the search planes were over us all the time and we waved the paddles and rigged a sail with a piece of canvas that had been used for a sea anchor to attract attention. Finally one of the searchlights picked us up and we were taken aboard a whaleboat and from there to the *Cecil J Doyle* (DE 368).

Upon arrival on board the *Cecil J Doyle* we were given a small amount of sugar water and washed as much of the fuel oil off of us as possible. Later we were given some beef broth and coffee and put to bed. The care they gave us on the *Cecil J Doyle* was excellent. We were aboard the *Doyle* from the morning of the third till the morning of the fourth, at which time we were brought to the hospital.

After hospitalization in Guam Base 18 Hospital and Camp Daily Hospital, I accompanied Capt. McVay to Washington, D.C., assisting him in cleaning up ship's records and writing letters of condolence. During this time (several weeks) Helen and I became rather well acquainted with him and his wife. His tragic death some years later was therefore a shock to us.

The Indy Survivors Organization under the leadership of Giles McCoy and Paul Murphy has done a magnificent job in building a beautiful monument and in getting legislation through the U.S. Congress which exonerates Captain McVay. Forming the Second Watch to carry on the efforts of the organization has also resulted from their efforts.

As Paul would say, "Smooth Sailing."

NAME	HERSHBERGER, CLARENCE L.
	S1 Firecontrol
STREET	24 High Ridge Ave
CITY	DeLeon Springs
STATE	FL 32130
PHONE	386 985 3755
ENTERED SERVICE FROM	Elkhart, IN
PICKED UP BY	USS *Bassett*
DIVISION	Fox Division
DOB	10/7/25

FAMILY
Spouse: Juanita

EXPERIENCE

My name is Clarence Hershberger and on October 7, 1925 I was born in a farmhouse just outside Nappanee, a small town in Indiana's Elkhart County. I spent most of my life around Elkhart County. I attended school in Elkhart until 1941 when I had to quit school and go to work. This was just two weeks before the attack on this country by the Japanese. At that time, I very much wanted to enlist and serve my country. However, I found it next to impossible to get either of my parents to sign for me to enlist. I had to wait until I was 18, two years later, when I was required to sign up for the draft.

That was what I had been waiting for; I no longer needed my parents' consent. I had heard that those that volunteered would be allowed to request the branch of the military they wanted. I also had noticed that many girls I had been around seemed to like the marine dress uniform, so I volunteered for the marines. A few weeks later in November, I was ordered to report to Indianapolis for my physical. The marines turned me down because I had fallen arches in my feet. My second choice was the navy.

I then was sent to Great Lakes naval training near Chicago for six weeks. Upon completion of training, I was told that I would go to signal school. Two hours before I was to leave for signal school, I was informed I was going to fire control school in San Diego. After finishing fire control school in early April, I was transferred to Treasure Island to await my assignment, which was the USS *Indianapolis*.

The rest is history...

After my honorable discharge, I returned to Elkhart and worked as a wood worker in a trailer factory and cabinet shops.

NAME	HIND, LYLE L. S2C
STREET	
CITY	
STATE	
PHONE	
ENTERED SERVICE FROM	Jasper, MN
PICKED UP BY	USS *Bassett*
DIVISION	
DOB	Deceased 9/96

FAMILY

Widow: Deloris

EXPERIENCE

Unable to contact any family members.

CHAPTER 109 SURVIVOR HINKEN

NAME	HINKEN, JOHN R. Jr. F2
STREET	
CITY	
STATE	
PHONE	
ENTERED SERVICE FROM	Norfolk, NE
PICKED UP BY	USS *Bassett*
DIVISION	
DOB	Deceased

FAMILY

EXPERIENCE

Unable to contact any family members.

NAME	HODGE, HOWARD H. R2C
STREET	
CITY	
STATE	
PHONE	
ENTERED SERVICE FROM	Lyndhurst, NJ
PICKED UP BY	USS *Ringness*
DIVISION	
DOB	

FAMILY

EXPERIENCE

Unable to contact any family members.

CHAPTER 111 SURVIVOR HOOPES

NAME	HOOPES, GORDON H. S2
STREET	
CITY	
STATE	
PHONE	
ENTERED SERVICE FROM	Yankton, SD
PICKED UP BY	USS *Bassett*
DIVISION	
DOB	Deceased 1/85

FAMILY

EXPERIENCE

Unable to contact any family members.

NAME   HORNER, DURWARD R. Gunner Warrant Officer
STREET
CITY
STATE
PHONE
ENTERED SERVICE FROM   Vallejo, CA
PICKED UP BY   USS *Bassett*
DIVISION
DOB   Deceased 3/89

FAMILY

EXPERIENCE
  Unable to contact any family members.

NAME   HORVATH, GEORGE J.
                          F1 Motor Mach Mate
STREET   4632 W Cholla St
CITY   Glendale
STATE   AZ 85304
PHONE   602 843 9285
ENTERED SERVICE FROM   Cuyahoga Falls, OH
PICKED UP BY   USS *Bassett*
DIVISION
DOB   9/8/20

FAMILY
Spouse: Alice Mae

EXPERIENCE
   I was born September 8, 1920 in Wesbore, Wisconsin. My married life started
September 26, 1941 and my wife presented me with two boys. My military draft
number came up in April of 1944. After my physical in Cleveland, Ohio, I was
asked which branch of service I would like...army, navy, or marine corps. I chose

the navy. My boot camp was at Great Lakes, Illinois, and when I finished I attended basic engineering school at Great Lakes and then diesel school in Richmond, Virginia.

My first sea duty was on the USS *Chester*, a heavy cruiser, where I fired boilers. At Iwo Jima, the *Chester* was rammed by one of our own ships and had to return to the States for a much-needed overhaul at Mare Island. After the overhaul, I was transferred to Treasure Island for reassignment and on June 26, 1945, I was assigned to serve on the USS *Indianapolis*. My job was in the deck of the evaporator room making fresh water for shipboard use. The *Indianapolis* had just finished being overhauled at Mare Island, having suffered a kamikaze hit at Okinawa. Having cut short her sea trials, the *Indianapolis* tied up at Hunters Point in San Francisco Bay, where a large crate was brought on board and secured and guarded on the hangar deck. A small cylinder guarded by two army officers was taken into officer country.

On July 16, 1945, the USS *Indianapolis* set off on a record-breaking run from Frisco to Pearl Harbor. There was much conjecture as to what might be in the two items we were transporting. After refueling at Pearl Harbor, the *Indianapolis* set off again at high speed and on July 26, 1945 made landfall at Tinian. There, the two mysterious packages and the army officers were off-loaded. The *Indy* then proceeded to Guam to refuel, and there she received orders to report to Leyte. Captain McVay requested an escort for the journey but none was available. After the war we learned that the *Indianapolis* was sailing through an area where a Japanese sub had sunk an American Navy vessel just four days earlier. This information was not given to Captain McVay.

Sunday evening, July 29, 1945, I sacked out under number three gun turret because it was so hot below deck. We were awakened shortly after midnight by an explosion. Another explosion sent flames skyward. I quickly pulled on my pants, shirt and shoes and ran forward to the hangar deck. In a few minutes, wounded men were brought to the hangar deck from the forward areas. We knew something terrible had happened, and strangely enough, there was no information from the PA system. About this time my buddy, John Hoogerwerf, who was by my side, said he was going forward to get something from his locker. I never saw Hoogerwerf again. More wounded were brought to the hangar deck as the *Indianapolis* started listing to starboard.

Remembering my life jacket was hanging in the evaporator room, I scrambled down three decks to get it. Luckily, the ship's lights were still functioning, but there was a frightening tilt to the deck...the evaporator room. With some difficulty, I hurried up two decks to the mess hall and from there to the main deck. The main deck list was so severe when I reached it that it was difficult to stand, but I did manage to grab the port railing and hang on.

When the ship rolled over and the main deck was perpendicular to the water, I slid down the hull just forward of the screws into the ocean. When I surfaced, my instincts told me to get away from the ship, so I swam as fast as I could away from the ship to avoid the suction. The *Indianapolis* was rapidly filling with water, and it was a terrible sight to watch her slide straight down into the ocean.

Once in the water, the problems mounted for all who survived. Fuel oil was everywhere and some men didn't have life jackets. I got the shakes and vomited the fuel oil I had swallowed. Two shipmates combined to hold me up while one of them inflated my life belt, which was the pneumatic type.

Monday dawned clear, and the sun was a welcome sight. My group of about 250 men was headed up by the engineering officer. We had a floater net, a raft, and mostly swimmers and some wounded in our group. The wounded were put on the raft. Most of my time was spent on the floater net. During that first day our spirits were high because we fully expected to be sighted or picked up by Tuesday at the very latest. Little did we know there would be no search for the *Indianapolis*. Navy policy deemed *Indianapolis* able to take care of herself in all situations. That policy has changed!

As the day wore on the heat rose and thirst began to bother some in our group, but there was no drinking the ocean water yet. It was disheartening when several planes flew over and did not notice us. Some sharks were seen but didn't bother us. We kicked and thrashed to scare them away. A severely wounded sailor died and his life jacket was removed, and his lifeless body was shoved out into the open ocean. It was a relief when the sun went down, but the night was chilly.

Tuesday...the ocean seemed to moderate, but it soon got hot again as the sun rose. Some of the men became irritable. Some wanted more time on our lone raft. The raft was so crowded it floated about a foot under water. The kapok and pneumatic life jackets were rubbing sore spots on our necks and chins. Oil was also an irritant. Thirst was now a real problem. Some talked about "straining" the sea water or "evaporating" it in their hands to make it potable. I thought of opening the refrigerator at home for a cool drink of water. Tuesday started out as a day of hope, but that hope faded when we were not rescued.

Wednesday...many lives were lost. A rumor started that the *Indianapolis* was lying just below the water surface and there was fresh water aboard. As the word spread a kind of frenzy affected many men who dived down to the ship and never came up again. By now some were starting to drink the sea water. One sailor, when we tried to restrain him from drinking sea water, turned on us like an angry animal and kept drinking. He died soon after. Wednesday night was a night of terrors. To some every shape in the dark was an enemy. Several fights broke out but toward dawn calm returned. For those floating face down the ordeal was over.

Thursday...most of us dozed. I had a strange emphatic feeling that everything was going to be just fine. I fell asleep but when my head hit the water, I sputtered awake. It was hot again, and possibly about noon a plane flew over.

This was just one of many that flew over. Then there was some excitement as the plane seemed to be turning, and then we realized the plane did change course and was looking over us. We were found by accident by pilot Wilbur Gwinn and his crew, who were on submarine patrol. They saw the oil slick and came down to investigate. Seeing many men in the ocean, they radioed our position to others.

A navy PBY piloted by Lt. Adrian Marks arrived on the scene by late afternoon and when he realized the plight of the survivors, some being harried and eaten by sharks, Marks landed the PBY in the open ocean. By nightfall they had 56 survivors inside and on the wings of the PBY. A second PBY also landed and managed to pick up only a couple of survivors.

Meanwhile other aircraft arrived at the scene and were dropping survival gear. A survival craft was parachuted down from a B-17 near our group, and I knew there should be water on that craft. I swam for it but soon tired and stopped to rest on my life jacket. While resting, I glanced down in the water and saw a huge shark with big teeth looking me over. I prayed, "Not now, Lord," and finding new strength, I paddled on to the boat. Thank God the shark didn't bother me. Two sailors were already in the boat and helped me into it. There were pint cans of water on board and I downed one real quick and then I lay down and slept.

Sometime in the night we saw a light off in the distance. The USS *Doyle's* skipper turned on his searchlights and turned them skyward to give us some encouragement and let us know rescue was near.

The USS *Bassett* picked me up early in the morning. I was able to walk to a shower room where I scrubbed with diesel fuel and soap. This was after a huge drink of orange juice. It was great then to lie down in a bunk and go to sleep. The *Bassett* picked up 152 survivors and delivered them to Samar in the Philippines. After recuperating on Samar and healing our wounds and bruises, which had been aggravated by the salt water, we were flown by DC-3s to a submarine rest camp on Guam. It was almost like a vacation on Guam. The chow was great. A baby-flat top, the USS *Hollandia*, transported us to San Diego, where we all scattered and headed home on a 30-day survivors leave. Sometime in February 1946 I received my honorable discharge from the navy at Great Lakes and headed home for good.

I sometimes wonder why I was one of 317 who survived the sinking of the USS *Indianapolis*. Eight hundred eighty men were lost at sea. Some people tell me I was lucky because God was looking out for me. God didn't cause the others to die. It was a man-made catastrophe. I really don't feel that God would pick who would die and who would live!

NAME   HOSKINS, WILLIAM O. Y3C
STREET
CITY
STATE
PHONE
ENTERED SERVICE FROM   Neosho, MO
PICKED UP BY   USS *Ringness*
DIVISION
DOB   6/18/09   Deceased 50

FAMILY
Widow: Maxine Hoskins
Children: Carla Churchill, Max W. Hoskins, Aliece Kronawetter
Grandchildren: Jonathan Hoskins, Amber Hoskins, Russell Hoskins (Lindsay), Scott McEachern (Dena)

EXPERIENCE
Respectfully submitted by Survivor Hoskins' oldest daughter, Carla Churchill. Our father, William O. Hoskins, was born and raised in Baxter Springs, Kansas. He was the oldest of three brothers and graduated from Western Military Academy, Alton, Illinois in 1928. Then he attended two years at Kansas State Teachers College, Pittsburgh, Kansas.

Our father met my mother in college and they secretly married in Phoenix, Arizona, on December 16, 1932. Mother returned to Idaho and completed the school year, acting as a single teacher so she would not lose her job. They reunited in Joplin, Missouri the following year.

I was born in 1937 and my brother in 1940 and my memory of these years before our dad enlisted in the navy are cloudy. At some point we moved to a farm near Neosho, Missouri, and our maternal grandparents lived with us. Our parents had never had previous farm experience. Our father enlisted in the navy in 1944 or 1945. At the age of 34 or 35, he was much older than most of the other sailors. He was called "Pop" aboard ship because of his age.

After my father left for the navy, my mother took an office position at Camp Crowder, Missouri. My grandparents managed to keep the small farm running. I remember we had a boaring garden and mean chickens.

The USS *Indianapolis* was hit by a kamikaze in the attack on Okinawa March 1945. The ship returned to dry dock in California for eight weeks to be repaired and our father came home on leave. He hitched a ride on a motorcycle from California to Missouri. I remember when our father's ship was hit and sunk by a Japanese submarine, that there was great confusion and unrest at our house for several days as we did not know if he was dead or alive. Even after news of his survival and rescue reached our family, we did not know his condition for some time. I was only eight years old and my brother was five.

Our father was eventually moved to a military hospital in Oklahoma City. I remember that he would sometimes leave his bed looking as if it was occupied and take the train to Neosho to spend the weekend with us. I am certain that this was not acceptable behavior but under the circumstances, I wonder if punishment was often less severe or non-existent.

After his discharge, he returned back to the farm. His civilian life began back on the farm. This was not a good situation for him. He soon took a civil service job at Camp Crowder. This only lasted a short time and he transferred to Kansas City and only came to the farm on weekends.

During these years, I remember people contacting my father wanting to know if he knew their lost loved ones. Eventually he accepted a civil service position at Fort Campbell, Kentucky. He worked in the Quarter Master office on base. My father, mother, brother and I moved to base housing. Fort Campbell was active and exciting as the home of the 11th Airborne Division. My sister was born December 14, 1948 in Hopkinsville, Kentucky. My father continued to experience a restless life. He had many friends and spent numerous hours with them at the American Legion Club. His sense of family responsibility seemed to be an ongoing challenge for him.

Toward the end of September of 1950, my father was not feeling well; however, he continued to work. He took me to my music lesson on Saturday of that week, and later that day was admitted to the hospital in Hopkinsville for observation. That was my last time I saw my father. His condition seriously deteriorated that week and he was moved to a veterans' hospital in Louisville, Kentucky. He died October 3, 1950 of hepatitis and uremia poisoning.

Our family life was changed forever. For unknown reasons our father had cashed in his $10,000 government insurance policy several months before his death. We were homeless and without adequate or sufficient living funds. Fort Campbell let my mother complete her 1950-1951 teaching contract.

As a strong person our mother took an aggressive position trying to prove that our father's death was related to his USS *Indianapolis* experience. She believed this to be a reality but lost the battle with the government as she could not prove her beliefs. She did learn that legislation had been passed shortly before his death that would count his military service years toward his social security. This entitled us to the lowest level of benefits. Life was not easy.

As an adult I became more curious about our father and his war experiences. Richard Newcomb's book *Abandon Ship* had always been in our living room but was never really shared with us. I read it as a young adult and began to want more information. After college, I moved to Denver, Colorado, and taught for the Denver public schools for 21 years. During these years I was single, married, divorced, and single again. My priorities at the time didn't seem to focus on family history. After a new marriage in 1981 and a move to Lima, Ohio, I had occasion to spend an unbelievable afternoon with Paul Stillwell, director of history at the U.S. Naval Institute at Annapolis, Maryland. He found incredible information for me about the USS *Indianapolis*. He gave me pictures that I had never seen before. We corresponded and he sent me additional information. Shortly after this, my good friend Mary Strandburg, a Denver public school principal, told me about one of her teachers, Tammy Brown. Tammy's mother, Mary Lou Murphy, was married to USS *Indianapolis* survivor Paul Murphy. This was very interesting to me, and when I returned to Colorado in 1996, I made contact with them.

This was a very important turning point in my life. Mary Lou and Paul Murphy are truly heroes in pursuing information for our father's chapter. They have never given up their dedication to make the USS *Indianapolis* story a true part of our history for the past, present and future. I admire and respect all that they have unselfishly given toward this goal. They opened my mind to a new world. I realize that I knew so little about the USS *Indianapolis* tragedy and my father's experiences. Little had been shared with me and my siblings. This was an emotional awakening in my life. I attended my first reunion in 1999. What a powerful experience! Words are difficult to express the true depth of feeling that I experienced while in Indianapolis. One morning at sunrise, I walked by myself from the hotel for my first view of the USS Indianapolis national memorial. There are no words that I can put on paper to describe my emotions of that solitary morning visit. My father's spirit was so alive behind his name etched on the memorial.

I left Indianapolis so full of enthusiasm and energy, which I shared with my siblings. I realize that their younger ages and different life experiences gave them a different perspective than mine. Our 92-year old mother seems somewhat detached from the true story. She has lost all hearing; thus communication is extremely limited.

In May 2002, I was excited and stimulated when I received news from the Murphys about the book.

I had ideas that would involve my mother, siblings, and myself contributing to my father's chapter. I came to the realization that I couldn't implement that plan. Around August 1, I received a special note from Mary Lou with samples of chapters to give me ideas and to encourage my participation. She reported that the response had been overwhelming and the publisher's deadline was August 24. This has been a long and difficult journey for my entire family. We have each been affected differently. I now realize after 57 years that I can be responsible only for my own level of interest and participation.

As our father's chapter, Chapter 114, closes, I wish to share that a grandson of our dad, Seaman Apprentice Russell W. Hospkins, 21 years old, graduated from boot camp training at the Great Lakes Naval Recruit Command Center in May,

2002. This is the same place our dad completed his training 58 years ago. A number of survivors were in attendance at Russell's graduation as they dedicated the new swimming pool building named for the USS *Indianapolis*.

I end this narrative with a loving tribute to our father's tenacity in surviving the USS *Indianapolis* tragedy in order to return to his family. I regret that he had such a short number of years and that readjustment seemed to be impossible for him. He made special contributions to his family, friends and colleagues in his limited number of years on earth.

Seaman Apprentice Russell W Hoskins
Great Lakes Boot Camp Graduation,
May 2002. Grandson of Survivor
Hoskins.

CHAPTER 115   SURVIVOR HOUCK

NAME	HOUCK, RICHARD E. EM3C	
STREET		
CITY		
STATE		
PHONE		
ENTERED SERVICE FROM	Columbus, OH	
PICKED UP BY	USS *Doyle*	
DIVISION		
DOB	1/23/17	Deceased 2/02

FAMILY
Widow: Estelle Houck (deceased)
Children: None

EXPERIENCE

Unable to contact any family members.

Respectfully submitted by Paul J. Murphy, Chairman, USS Indianapolis Survivors Organization.

Survivor Richard Houck and his lovely wife, Estelle, spent many hours throughout the years helping our organization. They both served on original committees to organize the first reunion and were very involved with our memorial in Indianapolis. We are forever grateful. May they rest in peace.

CHAPTER 116　　　　　　　　　　　　　　SURVIVOR HOWISON

NAME	HOWISON, JOHN D. Ensign
STREET	4570 Pinebrook Cr #303
CITY	Bradenton
STATE	FL 34209
PHONE	941 795 3007
ENTERED SERVICE FROM	New Albany, IN
PICKED UP BY	USS *Bassett*
DIVISION	
DOB	11/3/21

FAMILY
Spouse: Joyce (deceased)
Children: Beth and Nancy
Grandchildren: Four

EXPERIENCE
Enlisted in Louisville, KY November 9, 1942
Boot Camp – Great Lakes naval base
Storekeeper School – Toledo, OH
PT Boat Training – Suncook, NH
V–12 – Dartmouth College
Midshipmen School – Cornell University
Small Craft Training Center – Miami, FL
USS *Indianapolis*
Officer's Ordnance School – Washington, D.C.
Bureau of Ordnance – Washington, D.C.
Released from active duty May 10, 1946
Graduated from Indiana University February 1947
Employed by International Harvester Co February 1947 to October 1982
Dresser Industries from October 1982 to March 1986
Retired to Bradenton, FL in March, 1986

NAME	HUBELI, JOSEPH F. S2
STREET	
CITY	
STATE	
PHONE	
ENTERED SERVICE FROM	Chicago, IL
PICKED UP BY	USS *Bassett*
DIVISION	
DOB	Deceased

FAMILY

EXPERIENCE

Unable to contact any family members.

CHAPTER 118 SURVIVOR HUGHES

NAME	HUGHES, MAX M. PFC Marine
STREET	
CITY	
STATE	
PHONE	
ENTERED SERVICE FROM	Wilderville, OR
PICKED UP BY	USS *Doyle*
DIVISION	Marine
DOB	Deceased 98 Medford, OR

FAMILY

EXPERIENCE

Unable to contact any family members.

NAME	HUPKA, CLARENCE E. Baker 1C
STREET	Box 303
CITY	Cook
STATE	NE 68329
PHONE	402 864 2821
ENTERED SERVICE FROM	St Mary, NE
PICKED UP BY	USS *Talbot* Tr USS *Register*
DIVISION	Commissary
DOB	2/7/22

FAMILY

Spouse: Helen

Children: Michael Hupka (Marlene), James Hupka (Loretta), Randy Hupka (Teresa), Robert Hupka

Grandchildren: Rhonda Beadle (Duane), Sheila Racine (Lance), Melissa Mosser, Lindsey Hupka, Jeff Hupka, Josh Hupka, Katie Hupka, Kellie Hupka

Great-Grandchildren: Jessica Beadle, Jordon Beadle, Riley Racine

EXPERIENCE

My name is Clarence Hupka. I was born on February 7, 1922. I grew up on the farm and helped my dad. I enlisted in the navy in October 1942 and took four weeks of boot camp training at Great Lakes, Illinois. I applied for cook and baker's school and was accepted and received my schooling at the University of Wisconsin, which was a good duty, living in dorms. I received a third-class rating as a baker.

In May 1943, I reported to Bremerton, Washington, then went on to Alaska to report for duty aboard the USS *Indianapolis*. I served on her until the day she was sunk by a Japanese submarine on July 30, 1945.

The *Indianapolis* was the flagship for Admiral Spruance and was involved with most of the bombarding of islands in the Pacific. The ship was equipped with three 8-inch turrets, several 5-inch guns and several 40-mm guns. It carried a crew of 1,197. We made several trips back to the States for repairs and supplies. Mare Island at Vallejo, California was the shipyard. I was able to get home several times during my time aboard.

After securing several islands like Peleliu, Guam, Okinawa, and several others, the *Indianapolis* was at Okinawa during the invasion. While there, one morning at about 7:00, a Japanese plane dived down at the ship. I was in the wash room cleaning up to help serve breakfast. Luckily the plane missed hitting me by about 50 feet. The plane hit the edge of the ship and fell off into the sea, but not until one bomb went down through the ship, damaged one of the screws, and flooded compartments below. We lost nine lives at that time.

The ship had to start back to the States for repairs, which took about two weeks' travel. After two months at Mare Island, the captain was called for a meeting at headquarters and was asked if he could leave ahead of time–and that it was top secret information. We were to make a delivery to Tinian Island. No one knew what was aboard, but it was guarded around the clock by marines. We unloaded at the island, not realizing until later that it was some parts of the atomic bomb which was dropped on Japan.

After that the ship went to Guam and then the captain got his orders to go to Leyte in the Philippines. The captain asked for an escort but was told that he didn't need any because the waters had had no reports of subs operating in the area. He also was told he could use his own discretion on whether to zigzag.

During this time, a certain Japanese sub (*I-58*) was on the way to these waters looking for a large vessel to destroy.

We had left Guam traveling at a speed at which they wouldn't be able to hit us with torpedoes. The night was partly cloudy with a half-moon We didn't know that a sub had spotted us around 11:30 and was waiting for us to come his direction, until he could fire six torpedoes, hoping some would hit.

At 12:14 a.m., July 30, 1945, two torpedoes hit the bow section and damaged all communications. No word was passed as to what had happened. I was knocked out of bed, which for me was topside. I could hear screaming and loud voices at the bow. I knew it was serious.

Not long afterwards the ship listed starboard. I and another cook at the galley wondered what to do. By that time another list of the ship made our decision to abandon ship. After we barely made it topside, we went to the port side, slipped on life jackets, walked down the side of the ship into the water, and started swimming away as fast as we could. I thought that the suction of the water would pull me down with the ship, but this did not happen. This all took place within 12 minutes. I looked back and saw the fantail of the ship disappear. Thank God I was still alive and the water was covered with oil and the night had darkened.

Luckily I came upon some men that were clinging to a floating net, and I stayed with them. I vomited most of the night because of the oily water I had taken in. It was almost impossible not to get some water in your mouth. By daybreak, I was feeling much better. However we did not know whether we were going to be found or picked up, and the sharks were plentiful. Some of the fellows were injured by them.

Monday went by, Tuesday was getting bad, and by Wednesday, we had lost lots of men. Some died of exposure, while some took in too much salt water, became delirious, and swam off, thinking they saw islands and girls in the distance. They were wrong, but no one could keep them from leaving. They would swim off never to be seen again.

On Thursday, while a pilot and his crew from Peleliu were patrolling the area, they were having antenna trouble. While he was at the tail of his plane looking down at the water, he spotted an oil slick on the water below. He went down to find out what it was then spotted men in the water. He had to go back to Peleliu for fuel, where he reported what they had found. They came to the conclusion that the men could be survivors of the *Indy* because no one knew what had happened to the ship.

On Thursday afternoon, late, a plane spotted my group and dropped a small raft. I and two other fellows went for it, hoping to find something to eat or drink. We found nothing. We spent that night in the raft, and at 5:00 on Friday morning we were picked up by a ship that took us to Peleliu for treatment. Later we boarded a hospital ship and went to a hospital on Guam.

I was lucky and had no injuries. After a month at Guam, I went to San Diego, California and was honorably discharged on January 1946 with a first class baker's rating.

After being discharged, I worked in a bakery and eventually went into farming. I married my wife, Helen, and we have four sons. Within the last ten years, I have spoken to many high school classes, especially history classes, and to community organizations. It was difficult at first to talk about the USS *Indianapolis* but now it is much easier.

I wouldn't take a million dollars for the experience, but I also wouldn't want to go through it again for a million dollars.

CHAPTER 120   SURVIVOR HURLEY

NAME	HURLEY, WOODROW E. GM2C
STREET	
CITY	
STATE	
PHONE	
ENTERED SERVICE FROM	McCrory, AR
PICKED UP BY	USS *Bassett*
DIVISION	
DOB	Deceased

FAMILY

EXPERIENCE
Unable to contact any family members.

NAME	JACOB, MELVIN C.
	PVT 1st Class USMC
STREET	5218 Brookside Dr #306
CITY	Madison
STATE	WI 53718
PHONE	608 241 0430
ENTERED SERVICE FROM	Detroit, MI
PICKED UP BY	USS *Bassett*
DIVISION	Marine
DOB	4/10/26

FAMILY
Spouse: Betty
Children: Donald and Diane
Grandchildren: Melinda Jacob, Matt Jacob and Jennifer Mickey

EXPERIENCE
One thing that kept me going while in the water was the time I heard we would get a 30-day survival leave. The anticipation of going home made the days go by much faster.

NAME	JACQUEMOT, JOSEPH A. S2C
STREET	
CITY	
STATE	
PHONE	
ENTERED SERVICE FROM	North Bergen, NJ
PICKED UP BY	USS *Doyle*
DIVISION	
DOB	Deceased 95

FAMILY
Children: Joel Jacquemot

EXPERIENCE
Unable to contact any family members.

NAME	JAMES, WOODIE E. COX
STREET	2335 E Evergreen Ave
CITY	Salt Lake City
STATE	UT 84109
PHONE	801 485 8850
ENTERED SERVICE FROM	Mobile, AL
PICKED UP BY	USS *Doyle*
DIVISION	1st Division
DOB	1/13/22

FAMILY

EXPERIENCE
I was born Woodie Eugene James on November 13, 1922 in Gilbertown, Alabama and joined the navy September 11, 1942. In June of 1943 I was assigned to the USS *Indianapolis*, First Division.

Sunday, July 29, 1945 was a quiet day. The sea was

running five or six-feet waves, just a beautiful day. I didn't do too much...read a book, did a little tinkering as usual. Had the 8:00 to 12:00 p.m. watch and got off just at midnight. A guy relieved me about quarter to twelve. I went down through the galley and had a cup of coffee. Then I went to my compartment, got a blanket off my bed, and went back up on deck. I slept under the overhang on the first turret. My battle station was inside it, so in case general quarters sounded, I slept underneath it. Just got laid down good, using my shoes for a pillow as usual, and the first torpedo hit. I was up and down between the deck and the overhang of the turret like Yankee Doodle Dandy. I wondered, "What in the hell is going on?"

I got out of my blanket and started to roll out from underneath the turret when the other torpedo hit. Another Yankee Doodle deal, all over the place. I started to walk forward to see what I could see, and what I saw was about sixty feet of the bow chopped off, completely gone. Within a minute and a half, maybe two minutes at the most, the bow started to go down. It filled up with water that fast. Everything was open below deck, and the water just flooded in. We were still under way, just scooping water. Complete chaos, total and complete chaos all over the whole ship. Screams like you couldn't believe and nobody knew what was going on. The word got passed down, "Abandon ship!" It had been maybe five minutes and we were really down in the water, so we proceeded to abandon ship.

Jim Newhall and I went over the side holding hands. I got tangled up in the life line alongside the ship. I got untangled and surfaced. I was all alone so I swam out away from the ship, probably fifty yards, maybe one hundred yards, I don't know. I flipped over on my back, looked back, and about two thirds of the ship was in the water, bow first and leaning to the right, the propellers still turning. In the silhouette of the sinking ship I could see guys jumping off the fantail like crazy. I went over the side with a life jacket. I pulled it off and gave it to one of the younger officers that was screaming his head off that he didn't have one.

Anyway, there I was lying on my back looking at that, and no life jacket. I didn't hear anybody around me so I was just kind of floating and relaxing when lo and behold, a potato crate floats by. Potatoes were packaged in wooden crates then. It was just an empty potato crate, made a good buoy to hold on to...worked as well as a life jacket I guess. Then pretty soon I heard some voices. I yelled, and who answered me but my buddy Jim Newhall. So I swam over to where he was, and there was quite a group of them. It was chaos...everybody talking and a lot of the guys wounded, burned. We tried to do the best we could.

Day 1

The next morning we counted heads the best we could. There were about 150 people in the group. We were scattered around quite a bit. Well this isn't too bad, we thought, we'll be picked up today.

They knew we were out here—after all we were due in the Philippines this morning at 11:00, so when we don't show they'll know. If they didn't get a message off (but we're sure they got a message off) they'll still know where we are so no sweat, we'll be picked up before the day is over. So the day passed, and night came and it was cold. IT WAS COLD. The next morning the sun came up and warmed things up...then it got unbearably hot, so you started praying for the sun to go down so you could cool off again.

Day 2

The sharks showed up. In fact, they had showed up the previous afternoon, but I don't know of anybody being bit. Maybe one on the second day, but we just know we'll be picked up today. They've got it all organized by now; they'll be out here pretty soon to get us, we all thought. The day wore on and the sharks were around. Come nighttime, nobody showed up. We had another night of cold, praying for the sun to come up. What a long night.

Day 3

The sun finally did rise and it warmed up again. Some of the guys had been drinking salt water by now, and they were going bezerk. They'd tell you big stories about the *Indianapolis*. She's not sunk, she's just right there under the surface. I was just down there and had a drink of water out of the drinking fountain and the gedunk is still open. (The gedunk was the commissary where you buy ice cream, cigarettes, candy, and what have you). "It's still open," they'd tell you. "Come on, we'll go get a drink of water," and then three or four guys would believe this story and go with them.

The day wore on and the sharks were around, hundreds of them. You'd hear guys scream, especially late in the afternoon. Seemed like the sharks were worse late in the afternoon than they were during the day. They fed at night too. Everything would be quiet and then you'd hear somebody scream and you knew a shark had got him.

It didn't ever get any cooler in the daytime. In fact, Newhall asked me, "James, do you think it's any hotter in hell than it is here?" I said, "I don't know, Jim, but if it is, I ain't going."

We were hungry and thirsty, with no water, no food, no sleep. We were getting dehydrated and water-logged and more of the guys were going bezerek. There were fights going on so Jim and I decided to heck with this, we'll get away from this bunch before we get hurt. So he and I kind of drifted off by ourselves. We tied our life jackets together so we'd stay together. Jim was in pretty good shape to begin with, but he was burned like crazy. His hand was burned; he couldn't hold on to anything, couldn't touch anything.

Day 4

Then the next day arrived. By this time I would have given my front seat in heaven and walked the rotten log all the way through hell for just one cool drink of water. My mouth was so dry it was like cotton. How I got up enough nerve to take a mouth full of salt water, rinse my mouth, and spit it out I don't know, but I did. Did it a couple of times before the morning was over. That's probably why I ended up with saltwater ulcers in my throat. When we got picked up my throat was bigger than my head.

Anyway, we're out there in the sun praying for it to go down again, then lo and behold there's a plane. Course there had been planes every day since day one. They were real high and some of the floaters had mirrors that tried to attract them, but nothing. Anyway, this one showed up and flew by and we thought, "Oh hell, he didn't see us either. He's gone." Then we saw him turn and come back and we knew we had been spotted. What a relief that was.

So he did...he came back and flew over us. It was a little PV-1 Ventura bomber. The plane was out on submarine patrol when he spotted us. He radioed back to his base and instead of sending some help out, the navy sent one plane out. One PBY that came out and circled and radioed back to the base that there was a bunch of people in the water and he needed more assistance and more survival gear. The pilot ended up landing in the water and picked up a lot of guys, the single guys, one or two guys that were together...so the afternoon went on.

Late in the afternoon before dark there was another PBY on the scene. He dropped survival gear and a little three-man rubber raft. Jim and I tried to swim to it. He made it but I didn't. I was just so worn out from holding him up and hanging on to him all day and the night before, I just couldn't make it, but he did. About the time he got on it there were two other guys—three of them total—and that's all it was made for, three.

Anyway, in another direction were two more guys in the water. The two guys in the raft told Jim, "We'll go over there and pick those two up." Jim said, "No, we're going to pick Woodie up, then we'll go get those two guys." They said, "Nope, we're going to do it the other way."

Now the raft contained those little aluminum oars that come in two pieces. Jim put one of them together and threw the other one overboard. He said, "Okay you guys, I don't want to be mean, but we're going over to get Woodie and you guys are going to do the paddling by hand. If you don't, things are going to happen with this oar that you ain't going to like." So they came over and picked me up, and that's why I owe Jim Newhall my life. If it had not been for him, I wouldn't be here telling this story.

So they picked me up and then we went and got the other two guys. Now there's six of us on this raft. It's getting pretty crowded, but we run onto three other guys and we pick them up. Now there's nine of us on this little raft. It's just about dark and we figure we'll make it through the night one way or another. About midnight or a little bit before, there was a light shining off of the bottom of a cloud, and we knew then we were saved. That was the spotlight of the *Cecil Doyle*. The navy was on the scene...there was a ship coming. You can't believe how happy we were, guys screaming and yelling, "We're saved, we're saved!"

Morning of Day 5

The *Doyle* arrived on the scene and started picking survivors out of the water a little after midnight. It was daylight the next morning when the *Doyle* came alongside our little raft. Boy, what a happy day that was...my feet on the deck again.

We got on deck and asked the officer of the day permission to come aboard, which was navy tradition. All I had on was a boatswain pipe hanging around my neck on a lanyard, and I pulled it off and gave it to one of these guys. Why? I don't know, I was just happy to give anything I owned for being rescued, I guess. Anyway, they gave me one spoonful of sweetened water and assigned a guy to get me cleaned up because we were all covered with oil. Had been oily for a days, which was a blessing. Had we not had the oil on us like we did, the sun would have really ruined us. It was a good thing we had the oil on.

So I went to the shower and got cleaned up the best as I could. I asked the guy, "Is this shower fresh water or salt water?" He said, "Fresh water." I turned my head up to it, opened my mouth, and tried to drink that shower dry. After we had got what junk we could off of me, they gave us clothes (dungarees of course) and found us a bed. All the crew were just the nicest people in the world. They gave up their beds and everything.

I had noticed when I was showering that my legs were burned. Both legs were burned on the back, from halfway between the thigh and the knee to halfway between the knee and the ankle. I went to sleep and didn't see the doctor. (They had one doctor aboard and a couple of corpsman, but they had more important things to do than take care of me.) There had been many men in worse shape than I was, but they tried to help.

I went to sleep; I don't know how long I slept. I had gone to sleep on my back with my knees drawn up. I woke up and all that burn had matted together, and I couldn't straighten my legs. I spent the rest of my time (until I got aboard the hospital ship) on a stretcher. They wanted to move me around so they put me on a stretcher.

Three days later I got aboard the hospital ship and my legs were still bent and matted together. I remember going aboard the hospital ship. They hoisted us up and I was still on the stretcher. The doctor was standing on the deck directing traffic—this one goes to the emergency room, this one goes to the ward—and it got to me and he sent me to the emergency room. I got in there and they laid me on the operating table on my stomach and started to give me a shot. I said, "Doc, no shot, it ain't going to hurt any worse than it hurts already, so if you got something to do, you do it." The doc said, "Do it to you, son?" and the nurse handed me a wet folded-up towel and said, "You better hang on to this." The doctor put one hand on my ankle, one hand on my buttocks and straightened my leg and I thought my head would go through the roof and as weak as I was, I just about twisted that towel in two. Then he did the same thing to the other leg. They picked all of the scabs off with tweezers, laid gauze on it, put on some

229

kind of ointment, and it stayed that way. They changed it every few hours and put stuff on it again. This was in the morning, before noon. We spent the rest of that day, that night, and the next day, and night aboard the *Tranquility*.

We got into Guam to a U.S. navy hospital. They transferred us off the ship and over to the hospital. We were there for five weeks or so and they would tweezer my legs and put gauze and ointment on frequently. To this day, I don't know what they used on my legs but I have no scars. On the back of one leg I have a scar that is maybe an inch long. That's the only thing I have from it.

They finally discharged us all from the hospital. They kept us all in the hospital–the whole crew–until everybody was able to move out. Then they moved us down to what they call the submarine R & R camp. We thought we'd died and gone to heaven. This was not the navy. You went to bed when you wanted and got up when you wanted. You went over to the kitchen and told the cook what you wanted to eat and how you wanted it fixed, like a downtown cafe.

I was discharged on the third day of December 1945, and that was the end of my navy career. I'm glad. I wouldn't want to do it again, but if I had to I would, even at my age. I would gladly serve my country again.

Having said all that, let's go back to the first explosion, where God put in his hand and gave me a guardian angel. He got me off the ship, found me a potato crate, joined me with my shipmates and dear friend Jim Newhall, taught me the twenty-third Psalm and its meaning, gave me strength, guided Wilbur Gwinn to find me, watched over me and guided me to this day, and still does. All that I am I owe to my God, for without him there would be no survivors.

NAME	JARVIS, JAMES K. AMM3
STREET	3222 Oaklynn St NW
CITY	Uniontown
STATE	OH 44685
PHONE	330 699 5963
ENTERED SERVICE FROM	Weston, WV
PICKED UP BY	USS *Doyle*
DIVISION	V Division AVIA Metal Smith 3rd C
DOB	11/4/21

FAMILY
Spouse: Dorotha L. (Butcher) Jarvis
Children: Susan Dian Jarvis Wasiniak
Grandchildren: Melissa Clara Wasiniak

EXPERIENCE
Boot Camp – Sampson, NY January 1944
Aviation Metalsmith School – Norman, OK
Advanced Base Aviation Training – Quonset Pt, RI
CASU 6 – Alameda Naval Air Station, CA
SOSU 3 – Alameda Naval Air Station, CA
SCI Training School – Memphis, TN
Assigned to the USS *Indianapolis* April 1945

Shortly before being picked up by the USS *Doyle*, I was able to get on the raft with Dr. Haynes. There were nine men on the five-man raft. Dr. Haynes and John T. Ashford were the only ones I knew. I always wondered who the other six were.

NAME	JENSEN, EUGENE W. S2C
STREET	
CITY	
STATE	
PHONE	
ENTERED SERVICE FROM	St Paul, MN
PICKED UP BY	USS *Ringness*
DIVISION	3rd Division
DOB	10/1/26
	Deceased 7/00 Minneapolis, MN

FAMILY
Widow: Maxine Jensen
Children: Cynthia, Monica, Jeannie and John Jensen
Grandchildren: Taylor Sweeney, Samantha Sweeney, Katherine Sweeney, John Sweeney, Nichole Jensen, Celestsine Jensen, Athena Jensen, Cody Jensen
Great-Grandchildren: Makayla Sweeney

EXPERIENCE
Respectfully submitted by Survivor Jensen's widow, Maxine.

Eugene W. Jensen (Gene) passed away July 28, 2000 at the age of 73. I am Gene's widow, Maxine. I am writing about Gene's experience from a videotape and what he told me.

Gene was 18 years old and getting ready to graduate from Monroe High School in St Paul, Minnesota. He completed all the requirements to graduate in June of 1945. His draft number hadn't come up, but he decided to enlist in the army before his high school graduation. When he went to Fort Snelling in Minneapolis to be sworn into the army, they said they needed 20 men for the navy. My husband's family had a summer cottage on Clearwater Lake in Annendale, Minnesota where he spent all his summers. He loved the water and was an exceptional swimmer. He raised his hand and was sworn into the navy on February 19, 1945. For basic training he went to the Great Lakes naval training base in North Chicago, Illinois.

Gene was assigned to the USS *Indianapolis* while it was in dry dock at Mare Island, California being repaired after being hit by a Japanese kamikaze plane. After repairs the ship was dispatched to pick up a secret cargo in San Francisco. When the ship arrived in San Francisco the cargo was loaded onto the ship. No one knew what the crates contained. The ship proceeded to the island of Tinian where the secret cargo was delivered. Much later it was learned the USS

Indianapolis had delivered the atomic bomb. The *Indy* left the island and proceeded to the island of Guam for further orders. They were directed to proceed to Leyte Gulf in the Philippines. After receiving their orders, the *Indianapolis* left Guam unescorted.

They were about 600 miles into their trip. The night of July 29 was a very warm evening and trying to sleep below deck was impossible. Gene had permission to string his hammock between the life line and the fantail. It was a beautiful night, with a full moon and a slight breeze. It was after midnight when the first torpedo hit and threw him into the air. Then the second torpedo hit. He dressed quickly and even saved his white sailor hat, which he put in the top of his uniform. The hat later proved to be his only protection from the sun.

Gene decided not to jump from the ship into the water. He was at the end of the ship and close to the wake of the propellers. He waited as long as he could then started to climb down the chain ladder. When he was a third of the way down, two sailors fell on him and his right leg got caught in the chain ladder. He was hanging, dangling head down. He tried to get his leg loose and couldn't. The propellers were getting further and further away. He reached up with his left hand, said a prayer and pulled again. His leg came loose and he fell headfirst into the ocean. Gene had to make a decision quickly—swim to the left or to the right. He decided to swim to the left and made the right decision. He came upon four rafts that were tied together. Including him, there were nineteen men on the rafts. He always felt being on a raft helped save his and the other sailors' lives.

Thirst was the main problem—even more than hunger—because having all that water around you and not being able to drink it was unbearable. But then a little hope came to the men on the rafts. In the distance they saw what looked like a water container. The only trouble was that there was a shark that kept circling around the rafts. If someone tried to swim out to see what the object was, he could be attacked by the shark. As quickly as the shark appeared, it disappeared. My husband said he would swim out to what they hoped would be a water container. He removed his clothes (so he could swim better) and swam out to the object. To his disappointment it was an empty container. He returned to the rafts and put his clothes on. He was back for just a few minutes when the shark reappeared and stayed by the rafts until the USS *Ringness* rescued them on the fifth day.

Gene said when he saw the ship coming to rescue them it was the most wonderful thing he had ever seen. The men were brought aboard the *Ringness* and were given water. From that moment, water never went to waste in Gene's presence. Second, the sailors were asked, "Do you have anything of importance you want us to keep for you?" My husband said, "Yes, in my pocket watch there is a twenty-dollar bill my father gave to me when I left for the service." He reached into his pocket and pulled out a white piece of paper—the color was all gone but the men had a good laugh, just what they needed at the time. The survivors were well taken care of by everyone on the *Ringness*. The doctor that took care of the men did everything he could and did it very well. When Gene left the ship, the doctor (who had gotten to know my husband very well) said, "Gene when you get to the States take two aspirin and stay away from the salt water!" Adversity can never take away the wonderful medicine of laughter. Gene told his father, who was also a doctor, "God bless that doctor and God bless the *Ringness*!"

On July 7, 1946, Gene was honorably discharged from active duty and returned home to St Paul, Minnesota. He was nineteen years old. He completed his studies at the University of Minnesota and the Minnesota School of Business. His first business was Tuesday Motors, a sportcar lot that fired the dreams of many young car enthusiasts. He then organized Speedorama, which was the first car show in Minneapolis. In between his successful sportcar business and his auto show, he was involved in many other business ventures.

Gene and I had known each other for 60 years and were married for 52 years when he passed away. We raised a family of three daughters and one son of which he was very proud. Then when the grandchildren came he felt an extra dividend was added to his life.

He was a kind and gentle man who loved God, his family, his home, friends, music, his dogs, meeting weekly for coffee with his cronies, a good political discussion, and special talks with his children and grandchildren. He taught his children and grandchildren the importance of being objective and open-minded, always to respect yourself and others. He was a fair man that never judged anyone and respected people as they were. A loving and devoted husband, father, loyal friend, mentor to many; he brought grace, wit, and compassion.

During his lifetime he never forgot the bravest men he ever knew...his shipmates!

Survivor Jensen's high school graduation, 1945

Survivor Jensen with former Governor of Minnesota Harold Stassen.

The USS *Indianapolis* survivors receive the Purple Heart from Admiral Raymond A. Spruance.

Speedorama, the first auto show in Minnesota.

NAME	JOHNSON, WILLIAM A. S1
STREET	
CITY	
STATE	
PHONE	
ENTERED SERVICE FROM	Midway, TX
PICKED UP BY	USS *Doyle*
DIVISION	
DOB	Deceased

FAMILY

EXPERIENCE

Unable to contact any family members.

CHAPTER 127 SURVIVOR JONES

NAME	JONES, CLINTON L. Cox
STREET	
CITY	
STATE	
PHONE	
ENTERED SERVICE FROM	Boise, ID
PICKED UP BY	USS *Bassett*
DIVISION	
DOB	Deceased

FAMILY

EXPERIENCE

Unable to contact any family members.

NAME   JONES, SIDNEY SK3C
STREET
CITY
STATE
PHONE
ENTERED SERVICE FROM   Danville, KY
PICKED UP BY   USS *Doyle*
DIVISION   Store Keeper
DOB   5/22/09   Deceased 11/84

FAMILY
Widow: Lola (deceased 2/02)
Children: Dewey Jones, Clayton Jones, Esther Jones Sallee and Bernard Jones
Grandchildren: Scott Jones, Cheryl Jones, Steven Jones, Holly Jones and Joseph
Sallee

EXPERIENCE
   Respectfully submitted by Survivor Jones' grandson, Joseph Sallee.
   Sidney Jones was born May 22, 1909 in Fentress County, Tennessee, the first of
nine children born to Bertha and James Jones. Sidney was one of five siblings
who served in World War II. He left school at the age of nine to work in a local
sawmill. This was done to help care for his younger siblings. He also spent time
carrying water for local railway workers as well as doing other odd jobs.
   November of 1943 brought sad news to the Jones family. Sidney's youngest
brother, Sgt. Covely Jones, was reported missing when the plane he served on as a
gunner went down in the English Channel. The family prayed that he would be
found alive, but as time passed that hope turned to a quiet acceptance that their
loved one had paid the ultimate sacrifice.
   The loss of his brother would be a primary reason for Sidney Jones' decision to
volunteer for service in World War II. Jones enlisted in the navy in January 1944.
He was 35 years old when he arrived for training at Great Lakes naval training
station in Illinois. He was eventually assigned to the USS *Indianapolis* and would
serve on her until she met her fate at the hands of a Japanese submarine. He
would participate in many of the ship's engagements with the enemy. These
included the assaults on the Marianas Islands, Iwo Jima, and Okinawa. The attack
made by a kamikaze pilot against the ship was a memory he shared with family
from time to time.
   Sidney rarely spoke in depth of the event that had such an impact on his life.
What is known is that he came from below deck and entered the water with a
life belt. He became attached to the group that included Dr. Lewis Haynes. His
right hand was injured at some point in the disaster. It was later determined to
be broken, and would eventually result in the partial amputation of one finger.

He spoke of the immense thirst that was brought on by the heat, and the desire to drink of the water that surrounded him. Later in life he would always appreciate a cool glass of water or iced tea. Such a simple thing he never took for granted again. He watched as many of his shipmates died and was helpless to do anything. The heat, the cold, the sharks, and the loss of hope were all elements that combined to make him wonder if he would survive. He often questioned why he survived when other good men did not.

Following his rescue from the water Jones recuperated in a hospital. His hand would continue to give him problems. Doctors did all they could to save his hand, and for the most part they were successful. Final analysis required only the partial amputation of one digit.

Survivor Sidney Jones and wife, Lola

While the physical injuries from the disaster would heal, it was the emotional and mental trauma that would last a lifetime. Sidney Jones returned home, but part of him remained in the Pacific Ocean. He would struggle with nightmares for the rest of his life...dreams that would not go away, and the fear of waking up in the middle of the ocean. The trauma would also result in a lifelong battle with depression and alcohol. However, there was never enough liquor to drive away the ocean.

Jones was honorably discharged from the navy on December 29, 1945. He returned to work for Southern Railways. In the mid 50's he retired from the railroad and moved to New Lebanon, Ohio where he went to work with his brother contracting, constructing, and selling houses. Jones would attend the first survivor's reunion in 1960, and remained a strong supporter of the reunions until his death. He was proud to have served on the USS *Indianapolis*. He was also a believer in Captain Charles B. McVay and was always of the opinion that the captain did what was best for his men.

By 1974 Sidney Jones had moved to Danville, Kentucky, where he had previously lived while working for the railroad. He was grandfather to five and enjoyed spending time with his grandchildren. He was an avid fisherman and woodworker. He continued to work even when he was calling himself "retired." Carpentry work and small projects for family members kept him busy during his time off. He began work as a security guard for the American Greetings Corporation in Danville not long after moving there.

Sidney died on November 23, 1984 at the age of 75. At the time he was still working security for American Greetings. He is buried in Bellevue National Cemetery in Danville, Kentucky. Sidney Jones was a simple man who persevered through extraordinary circumstances. He, like all men who served their country, is a hero in the truest sense.

NAME	JURKIEWICZ, RAYMOND S. S1C
STREET	
CITY	
STATE	
PHONE	
ENTERED SERVICE FROM	Hamtramck, MI
PICKED UP BY	USS *Ringness*
DIVISION	
DOB	Deceased Hamtramck, MI

FAMILY

Widow: Jane

Children: David Jurkiewicz, Caroline Jurkiewicz, Raymond Jurkiewicz, Daniel Jurkiewicz, Michael Jurkiewicz, Leslie Jurkiewicz Enald

Grandchildren: Steven, Mathew, Raymond, Lavinia and Rita

EXPERIENCE

Respectfully submitted by Survivor Jurkiewicz's widow Jane and family.

Raymond never really spoke of the horrors he and the other men experienced because of the torpedoing of the USS *Indianapolis*. We mostly learned about it through reading books on the subject, especially *Do No Harm,* and by seeing stories about it on television. We learned all this after his death. He died suddenly in his sleep from a massive heart attack on November 18, 1983 at the age of 59.

He worked at the Fisher Body Plant in Detroit in the skilled trades department and was the recording secretary of the UAW Local 337 at the time.

Raymond was a wonderful and good husband and father. He loved his family very much and was loved by them. Raymond belonged to the St. Florian Catholic Church in Hamtramck, Michigan. He served as an usher there for many years and belonged to the Ushers' Club. He also belonged to the Dad's Club of St. Florian High School and helped to raise funds for athletic equipment by volunteering a lot of his time.

Roy was well liked and respected by everyone. May all the dead of the USS *Indianapolis* rest in peace.

NAME	JUSTICE, ROBERT E. S2
STREET	3710 Eberly Rd
CITY	Hartville
STATE	OH 44632
PHONE	
ENTERED SERVICE FROM	Left Hand, WV
PICKED UP BY	USS *Bassett*
DIVISION	2nd Div
DOB	7/19/24

FAMILY

EXPERIENCE

No response.

NAME	KAY, GUS C. S1
	(formerly Katsikas)
STREET	7601 W Belmont
CITY	Elmwood Park
STATE	IL 60707
PHONE	708 453 2344
ENTERED SERVICE FROM	Chicago, IL
PICKED UP BY	USS *Bassett*
DIVISION	
DOB	11/5/26

FAMILY
Spouse: Beatrice

EXPERIENCE

I joined the navy when I was 16 years old. I forged my mother's signature to get enlisted. After boot camp I was transferred to Hunters Point, California, where I was put on a troop transport ship headed for Pearl Harbor. I told the captain of that ship that I was only 16 years old and wanted to go back home.

The captain said, "Wait till we get to Pearl Harbor and we will make arrangements for you to go home," but that day never came. When I was at Pearl Harbor I was assigned to the USS *Indianapolis*, a heavy cruiser. I was a gun pointer on the ship.

While on the *Indianapolis* we encountered several combat situations. The ship was hit by a kamikaze and nine men were killed. We were ordered stateside for repairs. After the ship was repaired our next mission was to deliver a component of the atomic bomb. It was a secret mission and we did not know what we were carrying. The bomb was delivered to Tinian. After dropping it off, Captain McVay told us it was the atomic bomb. We left Tinian that morning at 11:45.

I was on the 40-mm gun on deck that night. Lucky for me my relief was late. I heard an explosion and then a second explosion followed. The ship was capsizing fast. We manned the guns but the ship was listing too quickly. I slid down the side of the ship and had to jump into the water.

There was fire, oil, and debris all around me. I bobbed up and went under the water to swim away as fast as I could. I was in my shorts with a kapok around my shoulders. There were men around me, and we swam to a floater net that was in the water. Little did I know that the floater net was to be where I spent the next five days. The one thing that I remembered from a survival test from basic training was, "Do not drink the water!"

In my group there were approximately 129 men. Every day the number of men afloat dwindled. Men who drank the water were hallucinating. Some took off their life jackets to swim away to an imaginary island. Many men were suffering from open wounds on their bodies. The sun was brutally hot in the day and the water freezing cold at night.

On the fourth day some men said they saw PT boats coming to rescue us. As these images came closer we realized that they were sharks. The sharks stalked us for three hours and then in a matter of minutes, 63 men were eaten. The screaming and crying still haunts me today. One shark brushed by my side and I thought I was next. There were limbs and blood everywhere; I was swimming in a pool of blood. When the sharks finally swam away I was in a state of shock and too weak to even talk.

That afternoon a B-24 plane spotted us in the water. He circled and dropped a shark repellent in the water so that the sharks would not attack again. We stayed in the circle of orange-colored repellent. One of the shipmates next to me said, "Gus, I have all the water and food that we need, come with me." I said, "Did you drink the water?" I told him that we might get rescued soon. But he swam away and the sharks attacked him.

Now there were 18 men left in my group. We waited and waited...finally the next day came and we were rescued. There were only seven men left in my group. The USS *Bassett* was the ship that rescued us. I remember we were hoisted out of the water in a net, like fish scooped out of the water. Our bodies could not be touched and we were too weak to stand up.

My next recollection was that I was on the ship, and the first thing that came out of my mouth was the word "water" —to think I was in water for five days and could not drink any of it. The ship took us to Samar in the Philippines, then we were flown to Guam where I found there were 316 more survivors. When I saw my buddies Mike Obledo and Louie Bitanti, Mike said to me, "Greek, we knew you were still alive!"

Meanwhile back at home, my Greek-born mother went to get her citizenship papers. The judge asked her many questions about the United States. She could not answer. All she could reply was, "I don't know." The judge said, "If you cannot answer these questions then you cannot get your citizenship papers." Then the judge asked her, "How many stars are on the American flag?" She replied, "There are three stars." The judge said, "If there are 48 states why are there only three stars?" My mother said that the president of the United States had sent her a flag with three stars for her three sons fighting overseas. The judge said, "Give this lady her citizenship papers and take her out to dinner."

When I came home I went on with my life, like we all did. I have a wife, two beautiful daughters, and five grandchildren. How fortunate I am! Very often I think of all my brave shipmates who did not have the chance to come home and have a wife, children, and grandchildren. It's a miracle that 317 men survived.

CHAPTER 132   SURVIVOR KAZMIERSKI

NAME	KAZMIERSKI, WALTER J. S1	
STREET		
CITY		
STATE		
PHONE		
ENTERED SERVICE FROM	Kewanee, IL	
PICKED UP BY	USS *Bassett*	
DIVISION		
DOB	7/13/20	Deceased 8/96

FAMILY
Widow: Mary
Children: Julie Ann

EXPERIENCE
Unable to contact any family members.

NAME   KEES, SHALOUS E. EM2C
STREET
CITY
STATE
PHONE
ENTERED SERVICE FROM   Montgomery, WV
PICKED UP BY   PBY tr USS *Doyle*
DIVISION
DOB   7/4/19   Deceased 10/95

FAMILY
Widow: Mabel
Children: Michael Kees, Gregory Kees, Sherry Kees
Grandchildren: Seven

EXPERIENCE
   Unable to contact any family members.

NAME   KEMP, DAVID P. Jr. SC3C
STREET
CITY
STATE
PHONE
ENTERED SERVICE FROM   Sparta, WI
PICKED UP BY   USS *Ringness*
DIVISION   Cook
DOB   12/14/24   Deceased 4/85

FAMILY
Widow: Nita Mae Aucoin Kemp
Children: Thomas David Kemp, Mary Kathryn Kemp, Ronald David Kemp,
Joanne Pearl Kemp, David Poole Kemp, Bonnie Lee Kemp, Michael John Kemp,
Kathy Louise Kemp
Grandchildren: David, Billy, Cheryl, Troy, Kelli, Jeff, Christine, Shelly, Todd,
Dixie, Melissa, Dana, Alison, Jenni, Carlee, Brandon, Josh, Katie
Great-Grandchildren: Morgan, Mara, Kaden, Trey, Teryn, Jacob

EXPERIENCE

Respectfully submitted by Survivor Kemp's son, Thomas David Kemp.

This chapter is dedicated to the memory of my father, David P. Kemp Jr., who served his country with honor and courage; to my grandmother, Violet Kemp, who meticulously kept the information on the USS *Indianapolis* and supported the efforts of the survivors; and to my mother, Nita, whose zeal for telling the story of the survivors has never faded for a moment in all these years.

My dad, David P. Kemp Jr., was one of the 317 sailors rescued from the Pacific Ocean after the sinking of the USS *Indianapolis* during World War II. Their rescue was a God-given miracle in that, having spent five horrifying days and nights in the ocean, they were accidentally discovered by a navy pilot on a routine mission.

My father never spoke to us much about his ordeal in the water, nor did he ever complain, but he always commented that the person he most wanted to meet was the pilot who had spotted the survivors in the water. The two men had phoned and written to each other. But it wasn't until 15 years later (July 28, 1960) that Dad had that wish granted. Mr. and Mrs. Wilbur Gwinn were coming to our house in Angelo, just outside of Sparta, Wisconsin for a face-to-face meeting with Dad and our family. Dad was the happiest man in town that day.

Much interest in the get-together was expressed by the town and press. A local reporter asked the big question: "What would you say to a man whose sharp eyes were responsible for rescuing you from an ordeal of five days and nights swimming in the Pacific Ocean filled with sharks?" The reporter never seemed to get a direct answer from my father; it was Gwinn who was first to respond.

"Actually, I had little to do with it. It was just an act of God that I spotted them. Well now we don't feel like strangers; we felt we knew one another because we had been in contact for so long," Gwinn said. "First we met each others' wives. And then we talked about our families all through dinner. It wasn't until after dinner that we finally got around to talking about the sinking. And then it was mostly about Dave's experience in the water."

Dad and Mr. Gwinn kept in contact for many years after this first face-to-face meeting, and they attended many of the reunions together.

The experience of my father after the sinking is almost beyond comprehension. It was a very hot night. My father got up and went to the galley, made a Spam sandwich, and went up on deck. Whatever caused him to wake up and go to the upper deck saved his life. Had he remained asleep he would have been trapped below deck.

After it was struck, the ship went down in 12 minutes. My father spent the first two days swimming alone in the water. It was during the second night that he heard voices and swam toward the sound, finding four shipmates on a raft. The men, most of them stripped of clothing, were without food or water for five days before their rescue. One of the men had a hatchet and killed a shark, but

244

after the men had chopped off only a few hunks of meat, another shark grabbed the carcass.

Two of the men became delirious and made frequent attempts to jump off the raft. They were hauled back each time, my father said. Dad finally removed his only remaining piece of clothing, his shorts, and tearing them into rags, tied one of the delirious men onto the raft. Long before this, the man's life preserver had become water-logged beyond usefulness, and he had abandoned it.

"It was the hand of God that directed our plane over those men," said Gwinn reverently, and my father, who said and heard many prayers during those five grim days, added with equal reverence, "Amen."

Pilot Lt. Wilbur Gwinn, "Our Angel," and Survivor David Kemp

My father was a very private man and shared very little with his family about those days. I read his first letter to his parents after the sinking. It was dated August 9, 1945, and it was written from a navy base hospital somewhere in the Pacific. Security was so tight in those days he was not even permitted to tell his parents his location. Almost every other paragraph told his parents that he was doing fine and that he hoped to be back to work soon. He also expressed concern that he had missed sending his brother a birthday card. Never once a mention of his ordeal at sea. Most of my information about his ordeal came from news articles and books that have been published since.

It wasn't until after I had spent a year in Vietnam during the late 60's that I understood the reason for the silence. You see things that you never thought could happen and endure things you never thought you could; and you do it all for your country and your fellow man. When the end of day comes and you are one of the fortunate to survive, you bow your head and pray for those who will not be at your side tomorrow, that they are held at peace in the hand of God. These were very personal times to me and I never shared them with anyone except my God. So, I know now my father's reason for sparing us youngsters from the horror of war.

The "Navy Hymn"–Eternal Father, Strong to Save–was a favorite of my father, so I offer it in reflection here...not only for my father, but for all those who have served our country at sea and for those who still do.

Eternal Father, strong to save
Whose arm hath bound the restless wave,
Who bidd'st the mighty ocean deep
Its own appointed limits keep;
Oh, hear us when we cry to Thee,
For those in peril on the sea!

Whose voice the waters heard
And hushed their raging at Thy word,
Who walked'st on the foaming deep,
And calm amidst its rage didst sleep;
Oh, hear us when we cry to Thee,
For those in peril on the sea!

Most Holy Spirit! Who didst brood
Upon the chaos dark and rude,
And bid its angry tumult cease,
And give, for wild confusion, peace;
Oh, hear us when we cry to Thee,
For those in peril on the sea!

O Trinity of love and power!
Our brethren shield in danger's hour;
From rock and tempest, fire and foe,
Protect them wheresoe'er they go;
Thus evermore shall rise to Thee
Glad hymns of praise from land and sea.

— Amen

CHAPTER 135   SURVIVOR KENLEY

NAME	KENLEY, OLIVER W. Radar 3C
STREET	
CITY	
STATE	
PHONE	
ENTERED SERVICE FROM	Chicago, IL
PICKED UP BY	USS *Doyle*
DIVISION	
DOB	Deceased 4/80

FAMILY

EXPERIENCE

Unable to contact any family members.

CHAPTER 136 SURVIVOR KERBY

NAME	KERBY, DEO E. GM3C
STREET	
CITY	
STATE	
PHONE	
ENTERED SERVICE FROM	Mt Zion, WV
PICKED UP BY	USS *Bassett*
DIVISION	
DOB	Deceased

FAMILY

EXPERIENCE

Unable to contact any family members.

CHAPTER 137 SURVIVOR KEYES

NAME	KEYES, EDWARD H. COX
STREET	
CITY	
STATE	
PHONE	
ENTERED SERVICE FROM	Antigo, WI
PICKED UP BY	USS *Doyle*
DIVISION	
DOB	Deceased

FAMILY

EXPERIENCE

Unable to contact any family members.

NAME	KING, A C. S1
STREET	
CITY	
STATE	
PHONE	
ENTERED SERVICE FROM	Murray, KY
PICKED UP BY	USS *Doyle*
DIVISION	
DOB	Deceased 97

FAMILY

EXPERIENCE

Unable to contact any family members.

CHAPTER 139 SURVIVOR KINZLE

NAME	KINZLE, RAYMOND A. BK2C
STREET	
CITY	
STATE	
PHONE	
ENTERED SERVICE FROM	Chicago, IL
PICKED UP BY	USS *Bassett*
DIVISION	S Division
DOB	Deceased 1/00 Santa Rose, CA

FAMILY

EXPERIENCE

Unable to contact any family members.

NAME	KIRKLAND, MARVIN F. S1
STREET	
CITY	
STATE	
PHONE	
ENTERED SERVICE FROM	Tampa, FL
PICKED UP BY	USS *Bassett*
DIVISION	
DOB	Deceased

FAMILY

EXPERIENCE
  Unable to contact any family members.

NAME	KISELICA, JOSEPH F. AMM 2C
STREET	
CITY	
STATE	
PHONE	
ENTERED SERVICE FROM	Forrest City, PA
PICKED UP BY	USS *Talbot* tr USS *Register*
DIVISION	Victor
DOB	5/18/21
	Deceased 11/00 Hartford, CT

FAMILY
Widow: Ann

EXPERIENCE
  Unable to contact any family members.

NAME   KITTOE, JAMES W. F2
STREET
CITY
STATE
PHONE
ENTERED SERVICE FROM   Cuba City, WI
PICKED UP BY   USS *Bassett*
DIVISION
DOB   4/5/21   Deceased 7/96

FAMILY

O'Donnell
Brandt, Kuryla and Kittoe

EXPERIENCE
Unable to contact any family members.

Pictured submitted by O'Donnell

NAME   KLAPPA, RALPH D. S2
STREET   2727 W Mitchell St #2
CITY   Milwaukee
STATE   WI 53215
PHONE
ENTERED SERVICE FROM   Milwaukee, WI
PICKED UP BY   USS *Ringness*
DIVISION   1st Division
DOB   8/4/27

FAMILY
Spouse: Alice
Children: Scott and Nancy Wison; Frederick and Rebecca Thorpe
Grandchildren: Aubrie and Ashlie

EXPERIENCE
Respectfully submitted by Survivor Klappa's wife, Alice.
Ralph suffered a stroke as we were returning from the survivors' reunion in
Indianapolis in 1999. That is why I am writing for him. He is in a nursing

home at the present time, doing well. Although he can't talk, we have a way of communicating.

He always looked forward to the reunions in Indianapolis, enjoyed seeing all of his buddies and their families. Ralph always said that if they hadn't been rescued, they wouldn't have had children and grandchildren to carry on their name. It made him sad when he would reflect on all his shipmates that didn't survive.

Ralph was dedicated to clearing his captain's name. He spoke to various elementary schools and organizations, wrote many letters to our congressmen, and was so glad when it finally happened. He felt it was all worth it. He is also glad that the crew of the USS *Indianapolis* is finally getting the recognition they deserve.

I remember whenever a reporter called him for news about the *Indianapolis*, Ralph would say, "I didn't know how to swim then...and I still don't know how, but I did survive. I guess I was meant to live...only God knows the answer."

God bless all of my shipmates who didn't make it and "till we meet again, rest in peace."

CHAPTER 144   SURVIVOR KLAUS

NAME	KLAUS, JOSEPH F. S1
STREET	721 N SUNSET #144
CITY	BANNING
STATE	CA 92220
PHONE	909 849 5890
ENTERED SERVICE FROM	Cleveland, OH
PICKED UP BY	USS *Ringness*
DIVISION	2nd Division
DOB	3/28/25

FAMILY
Spouse: Faye Francesca
Children: Bonita Zupan and Norma Wible
Grandchildren: Terry Zupan, Tisa Weisz, Judson Wible, Gerald Wible, Leslie Wible
Great–Grandchildren: Ashley Zupan, Julia Zupan, Jacob Zupan, Robert Weisz, Nina Weisz, Noah Weisz

EXPERIENCE

I was sleeping in the shell deck of turret number two when the explosions woke me. I opened the hatch. The passage ways were filled with fire. I climbed up through the turret and came out on the comm deck. I yelled up to the bridge, "The passageways by the ward room are filled with fire." After five to ten seconds, the bridge yelled back, "Cut loose all life rafts and prepare to abandon ship." I went down to the forecastle to jump off the high side. Just as I grabbed the life line the moon came out.

A marine was laying on the deck about four feet from me. He asked me to help him. I picked him up. His left arm was broken. He asked me to blow up his life belt. While I was doing this, the water generated from the bow going down came up and hit us. I blacked out. I don't remember anything. Then I was swimming in the water near a life raft. The men on the raft yelled at me and that woke me up. I do not know what happened to the marine. He did not survive.

On the raft with me were Glenn Morgan and Joseph Moran, a radioman. This was the first time we learned that no message got off the ship. We prepared ourselves to be out there for 14 days. We were very lucky to be picked up before that time.

CHAPTER 145   SURVIVOR KOCH

NAME	KOCH, EDWARD C. EM3C
STREET	
CITY	
STATE	
PHONE	
ENTERED SERVICE FROM	Denison, IA
PICKED UP BY	USS *Bassett*
DIVISION	2nd Division
DOB	Deceased

FAMILY

EXPERIENCE

Unable to contact any family members.

NAME KOZIARA, GEORGE S2
STREET
CITY
STATE
PHONE
ENTERED SERVICE FROM Oil City, PA
PICKED UP BY USS *Ringness*
DIVISION
DOB Deceased

FAMILY

EXPERIENCE

Unable to contact any family members.

CHAPTER 147 SURVIVOR KREIS

NAME KREIS, CLIFFORD E. S1
STREET
CITY
STATE
PHONE
ENTERED SERVICE FROM Kalamazoo, MI
PICKED UP BY USS *Ringness*
DIVISION
DOB Deceased 96

FAMILY

EXPERIENCE

Unable to contact any family members.

NAME	KRUEGER, DALE F. F1
STREET	56715 849 Rd
CITY	Winside
STATE	NE 68790
PHONE	402 286 4966
ENTERED SERVICE FROM	Winside, NE
PICKED UP BY	USS *Bassett*
DIVISION	Forward Engine Room
DOB	7/4/23

FAMILY

Spouse: Lois

Children: Diane Miller, Dean Krueger (deceased in 1999 at age 44)

Grandchildren: Cory Miller, Wendy Miller, Jodi Miller, Jason Krueger, Townya Krueger, Ryan Krueger

EXPERIENCE

In the winter of 1944, I entered the U.S. Navy. After boot camp at the naval training station in Great Lakes, Illinois, I was given the rank of fireman second class, meaning I would work in a ship's engine room. I was assigned to the heavy cruiser USS *Indianapolis*, and we were on our way to Tinian. We were to deliver a secret cargo. Later, we found out it was the atomic bomb. It was so hot a buddy and I decided to sleep on deck, which probably saved our lives. About midnight, the *Indianapolis* was hit by two of six torpedoes. The sound was like a tremendous thunderhead. In just minutes the ship tilted and water swamped the main deck. We scrambled to get our life vests on.

Not realizing the PA system had been knocked out, we waited for the captain to give the "abandon ship" orders. When the ship turned nearly sideways, my buddy and I decided to take a short run and jumped into the water. We swam very fast because we feared we could get caught in the ship's suction as it sank. Exhausted and covered with oil, I looked back and saw the fantail standing straight up in the air, and just like that it slipped away.

I was in a large group of about 30 men in a floater net. My buddy and I were separated during the ordeal. I remember the huge swells of the pitching sea but was convinced that we would be rescued soon. We prayed that the navy would send rescue ships. We were tempted to drink the salt water after several days without water. I remembered in training school we were told never to drink it. Many did, and it caused their tongue to swell and cracked their lips. They got very sick and hallucinations started. Some suffered terrible burns and the salt water left open sores. During the day the blistering sun burned our scalp and at night the water temperature rapidly plummeted. Many men died every day.

On the fifth day a navy pilot on a submarine patrol accidentally saw the floating men as he investigated the oil slick. The first rescue ship finally arrived. By now, the life vests were so water-logged we struggled to keep our faces above water. When we finally were rescued, we didn't have the strength to stand. I am happy to say my buddy was also rescued on the same boat.

Due to a combination of communication errors, military protocol, and scheduling bureaucracy, the navy had never sent a search party to look for us—even though we had not reached our destination on time. Although all of us experienced a great tragedy, I have never been sorry I joined the United States Navy. Nothing is too great to protect freedom for our country. Until the last few years I have not been able to talk much about my experience. It would just bring back bad memories, especially of those who died on our raft and had to be released.

I hope that some day I will be able to see a movie based on our true experience.

CHAPTER 149   SURVIVOR KRUEGER

NAME   KRUEGER, NORMAN F. S2
STREET
CITY
STATE
PHONE
ENTERED SERVICE FROM   Poynette, WI
PICKED UP BY   USS *Ringness*
DIVISION   5th Division
DOB   Deceased 4/00 Portage, WI

FAMILY

EXPERIENCE
   Unable to contact any family members.

NAME   KURLICH, GEORGE R. FC3C
STREET   459 Georgiana Way
CITY   Wadsworth
STATE   OH 44281
PHONE   330 336 7135
ENTERED SERVICE FROM Akron, OH
PICKED UP BY   USS *Ringness*
DIVISION   Fox Division
DOB   9/29/25

FAMILY
Spouse: Mary Lou Kurlich

EXPERIENCE
Survivor Kurlich did not wish to participate.

NAME   KURYLA, MICHAEL N. Jr. COX
STREET   1500 So Armore #214
CITY   Villa Park
STATE   IL 60181
PHONE   630 833 4007
ENTERED SERVICE FROM Chicago, IL
PICKED UP BY   USS *Register*
DIVISION   4th Division
DOB   9/10/25

FAMILY
Spouse: Lorain Kuryla
Children: Michael Kuryla III (Evelyn),
Diane Kuryla Schnurstein (Frank), Jody
Kuryla Bierzychudek (Thomas)
Grandchildren: Paul Bierzychudek,
Matt Bierzychudek, Julie Bierzychudek,
Michael Kuryla IV, Ashley Kuryla

EXPERIENCE (Typed from a Newspaper Article)

I joined the navy at the age of 17 and attended boot camp at the Great Lakes naval training station north of Chicago, Illinois. Shortly after boot camp I was shipped out to Camp Shoemaker in California, then to San Francisco, where the USS *Indianapolis* (CA-35) was anchored in the harbor.

The *Indianapolis* was the largest ship I had ever seen. Having grown up as a young boy during the depression in Chicago, seeing the magnificent ship was one of the greatest moments of my life. I hadn't ever seen a boat much bigger than a canoe for most of my life—the biggest thing I had seen was a barge some way offshore on Lake Michigan. Not only was the *Indianapolis* larger than this barge, but I got to see it sitting right there in the bay before me.

I was assigned to the Fourth Division, a deck division. Quickly I learned that the way to get by on board the ship was to shut my mouth and do all the work that was handed to me. The more work that my petty officers saw me doing, the more chances for advancement I was given. I advanced from seaman second class, coxswain third-class, petty officer in charge of the fourth section. We maintained the gun decks, with the five-inch 25-caliber gun mounts. I was in charge of the boat deck and served as a pointer on the 5-inch 25–caliber director above the bridge, "sky forward." I served under three commanding officers, Captain N. Vytlacil, Captain E. R. Johnson and Captain Charles McVay III.

The *Indianapolis* was the flagship of the Fifth Fleet, Task Force Fifty-Eight, commanded by Admiral Raymond Spruance. The *Indianapolis* earned ten battle stars from March of 1942 through April of 1945.

Star 1   Pacific Raids, 1942. Air Action off Bougainville, February 20, 1942. Salamaus-Lai Raid, March 10, 1942.

Star 2   Aleutians Operations. Attu Occupation, May 25 to June 2, 1943.

Star 3   Gilbert Islands Operation, November 20 to December 8, 1943.

Star 4   Marshall Islands Operation. Occupation of Kwajelin and Majuro Atolls, January 29 to February 8, 1944. Occupation of Eniwetok Atoll February 17 to March 2, 1944.

Star 5   Asiatic-Pacific Raids, 1944. Palau, Yap, Ulithi, Woleai raid March 30 to April 1, 1944.

Star 6   Marianas Operation. Capture and Occupation of Saipan June 11 to August 1944. Battle of Philippine Sea June 19-20, 1944. Capture and Occupation of Guam July 21-23, 1944.

Star 7   Tinian Capture and Occupation July 24-25, 1944.

Star 8   Western Caroline Islands Operation. Capture and Occupation of Southern Palau Islands, September 6 to October 14, 1944.

Star 9   Iwo Jima Operation - Fifth Fleet Raids. Honshu and Nansei Shoto 15-16, February 25; March 1, 1945. Assault and Occupation of Iwo Jima February 15 to March 6, 1945.

Star 10   Okinawa Gunto Operation. Assault and Occupation of Okinawa Gunto March 17-25, 1945 Operation March 26 to April 1945.

I was on board for eight of the battles in which the USS *Indianapolis* earned battle stars. During the battle for Okinawa, the *Indianapolis* shot down six kamikaze planes and was credited for two more. Early in the morning of March 31, 1945, a Japanese kamikaze plane broke through the low clouds, survived a wall of anti-aircraft fire and crashed into the port side of the afterdeck of our ship.

Just before the plane impacted the ship, it released an armor-piercing bomb that penetrated the deck, crew's mess, and crew's compartment. It barely missed the fuel tanks and went straight through the hull of the ship to eventually explode in the sea beneath us. Nine men lost their lives and 26 more were injured in the kamikaze attack.

After making emergency repairs, we limped back to Mare Island ship yards in Vallejo, California under our own power. We were expecting to simply be making repairs in dry dock. After our overhaul and a few days of sea trials we put into Hunters Point navy yard, San Francisco, and to our surprise the entire crew was quarantined to the ship.

It was 3:00 or 4:00 a.m. on July 16, 1945 when we heard the message over the PA system: "Now hear this, heads of departments prepare to get underway!" A lot of security was around, and two trucks could be seen approaching the ship from the docks. As we prepared to get underway, news eventually filtered down that one of the trucks contained a large crate and the other a small metal container. The large crate was brought aboard the ship and put into the port hangar. The small metal container was welded to the deck in the admiral's cabin. We cast off and sailed at 8:30 a.m., passing under the Golden Gate Bridge and out into the Pacific Ocean. A lot of scuttlebutt was going on among everyone on board trying to guess what was in the large crate.

The *Indianapolis* made a speed run to Pearl Harbor (which was 2,091 miles away) in 74 1/2 hours, a record that stands to this day. From Pearl Harbor, the ship traveled at 29 to 32 knots to Tinian Island in the Marianas. The island was home to a B-29 air base, where the large crate and metal container were off-loaded. Until much later, that was the last we heard about the crate and container.

With the mission completed, we sailed from Guam south to Leyte on the east coast of the Philippines where we were to join the battleship USS *Idaho* for gunnery practice and training. We were expecting to rejoin the Fifth Fleet off Okinawa for the invasion of Japan.

As the watch changed at midnight on Monday, July 30, visibility was poor. I had just gotten off watch when I went down below for a cup of coffee and then returned topside to the hangar deck with my buddy, Paul Knoll from Muskegon, Michigan. We stood at the shield next to the 5-inch gun mount. It was a very dark night and the moon was behind the clouds; you could not see your hand in front of your face it was so dark. Once in a while, the moon would come out from behind the clouds, and looking aft I noticed that the ship was on a straight course; we could tell by the wake trailing out behind the ship. Paul and I decided to sleep on the deck, which was much cooler than below. We used our shoes like pillows on the hard metal deck.

All of a sudden there was a loud explosion. My body felt the sting from the explosion on the metal deck, and then I was thrown into the air. Before I could regain my senses I was thrown into the air for a second time. As soon as we could get to our feet, Paul and I put our shoes on. I looked up forward and I could see my battle station in flames. The ship was damaged forward of the quarterdeck, and we expected that this was just the beginning of an attack. Paul and I rushed to positions on the gun mount, opened the ready box that contained the 5-inch shells, loaded, and waited to open fire. There was no more of this attack to come; the two explosions that rocked the ship were all it took to send it on its way to the bottom.

There was a time when my bunk on the ship was below decks right up against the outer bulkhead. I used to lay in bed all night worrying that if the ship were ever torpedoed I might be on the receiving end of one coming straight in through the bulkhead. I guess it was a strange bit of luck that I had made my bed on the deck of the ship when at 12:14 a.m. the *Indianapolis* was struck by two of six torpedoes fired by the *I-58* Japanese submarine.

Fatally damaged, the ship listed quickly to starboard and sank in under twelve minutes. The first torpedo hit the bow, blowing it clear off the ship. The second torpedo struck near mid-ship on the starboard side adjacent to a fuel tank and a powder magazine. When the fuel and powder magazine exploded, it split the ship to the keel and knocked out all electric power.

Paul and I cut down canvas bags from the bulkhead that contained the kapok life jackets and began passing them out to everyone we could find. Someone passed the word to release the life rafts on the boat deck. I told Paul that I was going down to the boat deck to release the life rafts and I'd see him later. The life rafts were on the port side of the ship secured to a metal stanchion. The ship was listing to starboard such that the pins that held the rafts were binding the lines. With no other way to release them, I cut the rafts loose with my knife, knowing they would come up to the surface when the ship sank.

Having released all the rafts I could, I tried to get to the high side of the ship to avoid being trapped beneath the ship as it sank, but the list was so bad that I started to slide back down to the low side. Realizing I would not be able to reach the high side of the ship in time, I grabbed the first line I saw and hung on for dear life. By this time the ship was on its side and beginning to turn over. The deck of the ship that had been the only solid ground for me to stand on just a moment before was now above me. I remember just doing my best to hang on while everything was falling down around me. I was afraid but stayed as calm as I could to plan an escape route out from under the doomed ship. The superstructure was on my left, so I decided to go to the right when the ship was on top of me. I inhaled all the air I could hold, and with my feet and hands I shoved down from the deck and swam to my right, but it was all in vain as the suction took me back to the deck. I tried again with all my might, but I could no longer hold my breath. I started to black out.

They say your life goes before you—and I saw my mother, father, six sisters, brother, and the street I lived on back in Chicago. I said the Act of Contrition and was prepared to die. I blacked out.

After who knows how long, I miraculously bobbed to the surface of the water and regained consciousness. I saw the stern and the screws slowly turning, and desperate men hanging onto the screw guard. It was just a moment more and she went down to the bottom. Before I realized what had happened, I was holding on to something; it was a raft with a seaman from my section onboard! He helped me onto the raft and, having found a sanctuary if only for the moment, I vomited all the oil and sea water I had swallowed.

We tried our best to help other sailors around us that night. Eventually we gathered with other sailors floating in the sea and a few other groups with rafts of their own. In not too long we accumulated four rafts full of sailors all floating together. I remember having spent the better part of a day clinging onto the raft next to me to try to keep us all together. Within a day my efforts to keep the rafts together were for nothing as the sailors decided to head off in their separate ways in hopes of being spotted.

We expected to be rescued from the Philippine Sea the next morning; a ship the size of the *Indianapolis* does not just fall off the map. As the nights and days went by with no sign of rescue, conditions only got worse. We had no food or water—the most important thing we needed adrift in the open Pacific. (Without water our chance of survival beyond a few days was slim.) Our throats went dry, and we could hardly swallow and would choke with just the effort of breathing. It took a lot of will power not to drink the salt water. Many who did died. Oil coated the sea, making many survivors sick. Having no protection from the elements, the sun felt extremely hot as it beat down on us and we hoped for cooler temperatures. The night brought cooler temperatures, but it would grow so cold that we could only hope for the sun to rise again. We prayed at every waking moment to the Lord for rescue. I had always carried my rosary in my pocket, but to my surprise I found it around my neck on the second day I spent in the water. Having found it still with me after the ordeal of the sinking, my faith was renewed that I would survive and be rescued.

The shark attacks began at sunrise of the first day and continued through the entire time we were in the water. Between shark attacks and exposure, many of the wounded men began to hallucinate and slowly went mad.

Piloting his navy PV-1 Ventura bomber, Lt. Wilbur C. "Chuck" Gwinn was having trouble with his radio antenna wire when he glanced down to see what the problem was and instead spotted a huge oil slick. Thinking he had found an enemy sub in the water below, he dropped to a lower altitude to prepare an attack, but to his surprise he spotted many people in the oil slick. Having radioed his base at Palau, a Catalina PBY flying boat was sent out with navy pilot Adrian Marks and his crew to investigate. It was reported to Adrian that sharks were eating the men in the water, so he disobeyed orders not to land in the open sea and brought his plane down. Adrian Marks and his crew alone saved 56 of the survivors.

Many rescue ships began to reach the area to pickup survivors and the bodies of our shipmates who gave their lives for our country. On the final night in the water I saw searchlights piercing the clouds above us and sweeping over the water. I have always compared those beams of light coming down from the sky to the beams of heavenly light often shown in religious paintings and stained glass windows. It was those beams of light that convinced me that we were finally being rescued. On the next morning, the USS *Register* (APD 92) arrived to pull me from the water. We lost 880 men and only 317 survived the five nights and four days in the water.

It wasn't until after the *Enola Gay* dropped an atomic bomb on Hiroshima, Japan that we had a guess as to what it was that had been in that large crate. We were floating on board the hospital ship USS *Tranquility* in Agana Harbor at Guam when we were told of the news. After a second atomic bomb was dropped on Nagasaki, Japan surrendered, ending the war.

NAME	LANE, RALPH CMM
STREET	
CITY	
STATE	
PHONE	
ENTERED SERVICE FROM	Fairfield, IL
PICKED UP BY	USS *Bassett*
DIVISION	
DOB	Deceased 1/86

FAMILY

EXPERIENCE
Unable to contact any family members.

NAME	LANTER, KENLEY M. SM3C
STREET	P O Box 832
CITY	Thomasville
STATE	GA 31799
PHONE	229 226 5030
ENTERED SERVICE FROM	Thomasville, GA
PICKED UP BY	USS *Ringness*
DIVISION	C Division
DOB	4/14/24

FAMILY
Spouse: Carmen
Children: Kenley Lanter Jr., Joe Lanter (Mary Ann), Debra Lanter Rogers (Dannie), Linda Lanter Chastain (Jimmy)
Grandchildren: Kara Lanter, Matthew Lanter, Calla Chastain, Kenley Chastain, Prescott Hughes

EXPERIENCE
I was born and grew up in Thomasville, Georgia. I had a brother who served in the army right before Japan bombed Pearl Harbor. I went to Fort McPherson to be inducted into the army. While I was there I saw the army boot camp boys picking up cigarette butts and candy wrappers and I thought, this is not for me.

So I and another boy from Thomasville got the chief to send us over to the navy. I was inducted into the navy in 1943.

I was shipped off to Great Lakes, Michigan, where I went to basic training or boot camp, as the navy called it. It was there that I learned to take orders...like picking up cigarette butts and candy wrappers! After boot camp, I attended the University of Illinois for signal school. I was trained in visual communications, which included things like semaphors, flashing lights and pennants.

The following March, I was shipped out to California and checked in at Treasure Island. It was at Pier One, Navy Pier that I first saw the USS *Indianapolis*. It was the biggest thing this Georgia boy had ever seen. Our ship was the commander of the Fifth Fleet, which meant it was the flagship of Admiral Spruance.

After boarding the *Indianapolis*, I participated in Asiatic-Pacific raids, Yap, Palau, Ulithi, Woleai, Marianas "Turkey Shoot", Saipan, Tinian, Guam, First Battle of the Philippine Sea, Western Carolines, raids on Japan, Iwo Jima and Okinawa.

In Okinawa, the suicide planes were becoming commonplace. A Japanese kamikaze that was heading straight for the *Indianapolis's* superstructure, which housed the signal bridge, navigational bridge and gun deck, was spotted and fired on by the 20-mm gun. The plane missed us, but the bomb ripped through the mess hall. A fellow by the name of Johnny Diamond, whom I had just relieved on watch, was sitting at the same table that I had been sitting at earlier. The bomb tore through the table and cut his big toe off. The *Indianapolis* was also damaged by the Japanese kamikaze plane, right aft of the quarterdeck on the port side, killing nine sailors. I had the sad honor of being on the burial detachment on Kerama Retto, Nansei Shoto, for my shipmates. While the ship was anchored and getting patched up, the captain had the motorized whaleboat circle the ship to look for possible suicide boats.

One night our own sailors and marines got trigger-happy and fired at us several times. The boat captain had had enough, took the radio from me, and told the OD we were coming in. We did and I never had that duty again. With our patch on, we limped back to Mare Island, California for repair of the damage done by the kamikaze.

Because my father was ill, I was given first leave, which was 28 days. Even though my father had not improved, I had to return from leave. I had been back in California about two or three days when my mother wired to tell me that my father had passed on. I got an emergency leave to go home, and the Red Cross helped me catch an army flight out of San Francisco to Washington, D.C. After getting bumped off another flight I had to catch a train, so I regretfully called my mother to tell them to go ahead with the funeral. After finally getting home three or four days later, I had to return to Mare Island. Another group already had left on their leave and after they had returned, all liberties and leaves were suddenly canceled.

We pulled out of Mare Island and went around to Hunters Point, which was right at the opening of the San Francisco Bay. There at Hunters Point a huge crane brought aboard a big crate that was stowed in the port hangar, where we normally kept an airplane. Two guards were put on the hangar, and we pulled our lines in, went out in the bay, and dropped anchor for the rest of the day. Early the next morning, we sailed under the Golden Gate Bridge. My battle station was the signal bridge, which was just under the navigational bridge where the captain was. That morning, from high atop Knob Hill Navy Tower, I received a message so far out; I had to switch over to the carbon light because it was larger and brighter than the twelve-inch light. That was the last message received from the States to the USS *Indianapolis* by visual communication.

We ran what seemed to be almost wide open to Pearl Harbor, where we stopped only to refuel and to put off and take on a few passengers. After that, we didn't see land for six days, and after ten days arrived in Tinian. The *Indianapolis* made the fastest speed recorded by a ship from the United States to the Marianas Islands, ever. After the cargo in the port hangar was removed on Tinian, we moved down to Guam for a couple days. There we received orders and pulled out for the Philippine Islands.

The second night out from Guam, I remember, it got really hazy and hot down below. I had the 4:00 to 8:00 a.m. shift, so I decided to go topside to the signal bridge and sleep where it was cool. At five minutes past midnight, a blast lifted me up off the deck, and about the time I came down to hit the deck, I went back up again. I scrambled to my feet and looked forward, in front of the number one turret. I could see that about 50 to 90 feet of the bow was missing and fire was coming out from the aviation gasoline. I thought someone might have thrown a cigarette butt in the powder magazine. As I had been taught in boot camp, I put on my shirt and shoes.

After that, a second explosion went right through the center of the ship, under the main mast. The ship began to list about thirty-five or forty degrees to starboard. The skipper came down from the navigational bridge and ran into the engineering officer right in front of the number one stack where the signal bridge was located. The captain was informed of how badly the ship was damaged, and because all power was off, Captain McVay gave orders to abandon ship by word of mouth.

After hearing him say that, I grabbed my kapok and strapped it on, then went over to the com desk and helped get the secret publications and stuff them into a lead bag. This was done so that the secret publications would go down with the ship and not fall into enemy hands. I tried to get into the hatch to the CIC, to get my New Testament and black onyx cross that my uncle had given me on my last cruise, but the dogs wouldn't open. I bowed my head, asked the Lord to take care of me...He took care of me then, and many more times and is still doing so.

The ship was listing at about forty-five degrees. I climbed down the port side superstructure. When I got to the hull, the ship had rolled over on the starboard side, so I walked down the hull to the water. Johnny Diamond was in front of me. I got him in the water, telling him we had to get away from the ship. I never saw Johnny again. He didn't make it. There were a lot of injured men in the water that just didn't want to get too far from the ship for one reason or another, but I started swimming away. I had learned to swim as a boy (at the YMCA in Thomasville) and spent a lot of time outdoors, so already I was a lot better off than some of the boys. I turned back, only to see the fantail go down with one of the huge props still turning. I wiped the oil off the face of my watch—it had been twelve minutes from the first explosion till the ship sank. I spotted one of our airplanes (that probably had been on the catapult on the ship) floating in the water. I started swimming toward it, thinking I could get to its radio, but the plane sank before I could get to it.

Later that night I found a raft at about the same time as some other guys. We also found a bag of kapok life jackets and slung them out in every direction, because we each had one. One of the guys was J. J. Moran, a radio man. I asked him whether he had gotten an emergency signal off. He said he thought he had but didn't know for sure. There were a lot of injured men. Lt. Freeze was badly burned and died the first day out. Harold Shearer had a bad gash on his hip from hitting a mooring ring when he jumped from the ship. We let him lay in the raft.

The days were so hot you couldn't wait for the sun to go down, and the nights were so cold you were praying for the sun to come up. The second night out we could see a big, dark shadow looming across the horizon that we thought could be a ship. So I used my one cell emergency light that was attached to my kapok to signal for help. He sent something back to me that I couldn't make out, so I asked for a repeat. He sent some more gibberish. I asked a boy in the raft (who was a radio man) if he got it. He and I talked it over with the group and finally decided that it could be a Japanese sub and we didn't want to get picked up by him! So we dashed the light and laid low until he finally passed on by. We couldn't believe that someone wasn't looking for us.

On the third day, lashed to the underside of the raft we found a canvas bag containing a little bit of water and a first aid kit. We found two syringes of morphine and after reading directions, I gave Harold Shearer (who was in a lot of pain) a shot that seemed to ease him off a little. We managed to tie them all together. At that time, we really thought someone would be there to pick us up soon. We rationed the water, giving each man an ounce a day and the injured fellow two ounces a day.

In the canvas bag we also found a fish hook and line with some malt crackers you could set and use for bait. Someone caught four little blue fish, and I cut them into squares with a knife that I had on my belt. We hesitated to eat them because we knew there were poisonous fish in the waters around the Philippines, but we decided to go ahead. We divided the fish between us. We also found a flare gun. Glenn Morgan and I shot one when we heard planes flying over, but the planes didn't see us. They seemed like they were on a flight plan and maybe too high to see the flares, so after the second one wasn't seen, we saved the last one for a last-ditch effort.

By the fourth day a cloud bank had rolled in and we could see lights flashing in the sky that night. We didn't know it at the time, but we had been spotted by a PV-1 Ventura bomber flown by Wilbur Gwinn earlier that day when he had been out on a routine hunt for subs. When we saw the lights we really began to think surely we were going to be found. We couldn't see ships or anything–just the lights swishing back and forth in the clouds–but it gave us hope.

On the fifth day the water was rough. The waves were fifteen to twenty feet from the top to the bottom of the swells. It misted rain. I was able to catch a little water by opening my mouth, but not much. Then a plane started coming over. It had spotted some of the other guys in the water, but it didn't seem to have spotted us. We were really worried that we wouldn't be seen by the plane, so we yelled and waved as much as we could. He finally got to us, dropped a dye marker near by, and then came back and waved his wings at us. Everybody in the crew of the plane was leaning out of this big door where they evidently loaded bombs, and they were all waving at us. It was then that we knew our prayers had been answered and we were going to be picked up. At about noon, an AP 100–the USS *Ringness*–came by and picked us up. I was carried to the Palau Islands where I caught a hospital ship to the navy hospital in Guam.

After two or three weeks in Guam, I got liberty and was able to go over to the big air base there and spend some time with Emory Milton, brother of Red Milton, who had taught me to swim at the YMCA in Thomasville. He had tried to visit me in the hospital, but we had missed each other. Eventually I was transferred back to the States.

I finished my tour of duty in Norfolk, Virginia. It was there that I read in the newspaper that the navy was charging Captain McVay with inefficiency and negligence of duty. I told the chaplain at the base in Norfolk my story of the captain. After getting permission the chaplain called Washington and told them that he had a man in Norfolk that could tell a different story than the one they were hearing out of Washington about Captain McVay. They immediately cut my orders and I flew to Washington, where I waited three weeks until the court-martial began.

I and several other men were in Washington to testify on behalf of our Captain. We knew that he was getting a real raw deal from the navy, but to our disbelief, he was unfairly court-martialed anyway. While waiting in the hallway outside the courtroom, we watched as marine guards escorted in a Japanese man. We were shocked to learn later that the Japanese man we had seen was Lt. Commander Hashimoto of the submarine that had sunk our ship. And unbelievably, the navy had had him brought there to testify against Captain McVay! I was discharged at the rate of SM 3C in January of 1946.

I now live in Thomasville, Georgia where I own my own communications business. I attended my first survivors reunion in Indianapolis in 1975. Over the years, my wife Carmen and I (and occasionally some of my children) have tried to be there as much as we could for the reunions. We were happy to have been present for the dedication of the USS *Indianapolis* memorial. My son Joe is the president of the Second Watch. I have felt strongly and participated in every way to exonerate our captain, whom I have always felt was not at fault in the tragedy of events that led to the sinking of the USS *Indianapolis* and the rescue of her crew.

CHAPTER 154   SURVIVOR LaPAGLIA

NAME	LaPAGLIA, CARLOS GM2C
STREET	
CITY	
STATE	
PHONE	
ENTERED SERVICE FROM	Tempe, AZ
PICKED UP BY	USS *Bassett*
DIVISION	
DOB	Deceased

FAMILY

EXPERIENCE
Unable to contact any family members.

CHAPTER 155   SURVIVOR LAWS

NAME	LAWS, GEORGE E. S1
STREET	P O Box183
CITY	Manchester
STATE	IL 62663
PHONE	217 587 2711
ENTERED SERVICE FROM	Springfield, IL
PICKED UP BY	USS *Bassett*
DIVISION	2nd Division
DOB	5/24/26

FAMILY
Spouse: Eve
Children: Carolyn Laws Rodden and Peggy Laws Fitzgerald
Grandchildren: James Briggs, Kathryn Fitzgerald, Kevin Fitzgerald

EXPERIENCE

Respectfully submitted by Survivor Laws' grandson, James Briggs.

The first time I saw the *Indianapolis*, boy, to me it was a beautiful ship and a big ship. It reminded me of the stories my father told when I was young...about being on a ship to England. Ever since hearing those stories, I had wanted to be in the navy. I was working at a garage when I was 16 and my dad didn't like me working there. One week before I turned 17, he came to the garage and asked if I wanted to go to town with him. As we were walking by the navy recruiting office, we stopped to look at the pictures in the window. He asked if I was interested in joining the navy. We went in and talked to the recruiter and dad signed for me to join.

After four weeks of basic training and three weeks at Camp Shoemaker, I was stepping off a bus in San Francisco, staring at the USS *Indianapolis*. A group of us went aboard and were mustered out into different divisions. I was put in the second division which was in charge of cleaning the quarterdeck. We were out at sea when my division officer asked if I would like to be a helmsman. Two of us shared a four-hour watch, alternating between two hours on the bridge and two hours on the steering half. I had the 12:00 to 4:00 a.m. watch on the night the torpedoes hit.

I relieved the watch early that night because I was wide awake and anyhow, I enjoyed it. I sat down on a five-gallon can just after midnight and cracked open an issue of *Time* magazine. Before I could even begin reading, the first torpedo hit. I flew up in the air, came back down, and hit the deck. I had no sooner hit the deck than another torpedo hit. Back up I went. I tried calling the bridge and the lines were dead. I went through the sleeping quarters, into the mess hall, onto the port side, crossed over the starboard side, and went through the hatch. The machine shop was right there. I saw lots of smoke and fire up ahead. I thought, "This is no place for me," so I got out of there. The ship began to list, going very slowly, until it was lying just about on the starboard side. It was still in motion, swinging to the left.

We went to the rear deck. There were a lot of people there, and many without life jackets. There were 2,500 kapok life jackets hung up around the ship. I saw one guy on a ladder trying to get to them. I gave him my knife and he cut two packs of them and everyone started grabbing them. The ship had listed to such a degree that if you looked over the side of the ship, you could see the prop sticking out of the water.

"Abandon ship, abandon ship!" an officer yelled. "Over the side, abandon ship, get away from the ship!"

I began sliding down the ship. I reached the waterline, where moss had built up on the side of the ship. It was like greased lightening. I slid down that moss and was in the water in nothing flat. I got a good swallow of salt water and fuel oil and it made me very sick. I was fully dressed and a fellow shipmate said to get rid of my shoes as they would draw you down. I kicked my shoes off. From there on, it was one terrible thing. When I looked up at the ship, it was going away from me, rolling over onto the starboard side. The nose went down, then the bow. The fantail was left sticking straight up in the air and then, like slow motion, it went right on down. I thought, "Oh my god, there goes my home."

We began grouping people together. They were so black, you didn't know who they were unless they identified themselves. A lot of men were talking, but it's hard to say what they were talking about. After a couple of days, they began talking about islands and saying the ship wasn't really sunk. Hallucinations. They saw hotels, and I don't know what else.

Sharks...I had never seen so many in all my life. You'd hear a guy scream, go to help him, and find half of him there and the rest of him gone. It was terrible. I think the only reason I survived was the fuel oil all over my body. I was covered in it.

Late in the third day, I began thinking I wouldn't make it. Then the fourth day came and it was the hardest. I figured nobody would find us. The fifth day came and I didn't even know why I was still there. During the fifth afternoon, I saw a bomber flying over with an 18-foot boat attached. They waited until the boat was close enough to swim to yet far enough away that nobody would be hit, and they dropped it. Three of us swam to the boat. I could reach it but was too weak to pull myself over. When I finally did get in, I passed out.

The next thing I remember was boarding the USS *Bassett*. The waves were so strong that the boat would rise to the *Bassett's* deck level, and then dip until you could see the screws underneath the ship. They'd pull somebody aboard, and then wait for it to rise again. When we dipped down and I saw those screws, I knew I was getting out. The next time it came up, I reached up and grabbed a life line. Just as the rescue craft began going down, an officer saw my weak fingers pulling away. He grabbed both my arms and husked me up on the deck. He asked if I could walk and I said, "Yes, sir." He told me to go through the hatch. I got just one foot away from him before my legs gave out. I fell straight down. He grabbed me under the arms again and carried me. I bet his uniform was just black with oil. I bet all of them were. But they saved us and I was grateful.

I didn't realize how black I was until they put a mirror in front of me. All I could see were eyeballs and teeth. But when I woke up, I was in clean clothes and the oil had been cleaned off. We were eventually transferred to a hospital in Guam. It was there (while we were watching a movie) that the announcement came: The war was over! I wondered why that couldn't have come 16 or 18 days sooner. In a way, though, I'm glad I went through everything. It was an experience that a lot of people had.

After I got back to America, people asked if I was sorry that I helped take the atomic bomb to Japan. I'm not sorry, simply because of the atrocities the Japanese were causing. By ending the war, we saved many, many lives.

I stayed in the navy after the war, serving on the USS *Sabine*. We traveled to

Pearl Harbor, Japan, and China. I was never nervous about being back on a ship and in fact, liked it. Sailing was the reason I joined the navy in the first place. It's what I had dreamed about, ever since I was a young boy, listening to my father tell stories about being on a ship.

CHAPTER 156   SURVIVOR LEBOW

NAME	LEBOW, CLEATUS A. FC3C
STREET	Box 96
CITY	Memphis
STATE	TX 79245
PHONE	806 259 2427
ENTERED SERVICE FROM	Abernathy, TX
PICKED UP BY	USS *Bassett*
DIVISION	Fox Div
DOB	2/8/24

FAMILY
Spouse: Joan Lebow
Children: (Previous marriage) Sonja Rosson (Bobby), Cleata Ann Crutchfrield (Roy), Gerald D. Lebow (Louise)
Grandchildren: Trisha Hughes (Russell), Tracy Lebow, Pepper Pippin, Timothy Pippin, Jeffrey Reeves
Great-Grandchildren: Kayla Hughes, Kenon Hughes, Austin Lebow

EXPERIENCE
I was inducted into the navy in Lubbock, Texas on February 12, 1943. The seven men inducted that day were sent by train to boot camp in San Diego, California. After boot camp, I spent several months in general detail at the destroyer base in San Diego. During this time, I attended range finder school and graduated with the second highest mark in my class, so I was promoted from S 2C to FC 3C, skipping S 1C.

In early December, I got sailing orders to go to Pearl Harbor. We left San Diego on a minesweeper. A bad storm came up and the little ship was ordered to put in at San Francisco. It took three days to make the trip and I was too sick to die for the entire trip. I was never seasick again after that. I spent 30 days on Goat Island as a shore patrolman. The only job I had was to deliver a prisoner back to San Diego that had jumped ship there. When I got on the train with the

6'2" prisoner handcuffed to my 130 pound frame, the 2 SPs on the train laughed and asked who was escorting whom. They kept a close eye on us the entire trip.

In the first week of January 1944, I left Goat Island on an LST and made it to Pearl Harbor ten days later. After three days there, I was called to go on the USS *Indianapolis*. I remember when we pulled onto the dock thinking, "What a sleek, good-looking ship." As soon as the last man of our detail cleared the gangplank, it was lifted and we set sail for the adventure of this ole country boy's lifetime.

We headed back to the Gilbert Islands, the Marshalls, then the Asiatic-Pacific raids at Palau and Yap. Then on to the Marianas where we captured Saipan, Guam and Tinian. Then to the Western Carolines where we took the Palau Islands. In February and March 1945, we were in the raids on Honshu and Nansei Shoto, then the occupation of Iwo Jima and on to Okinawa. I received eight battle stars on my Asiatic-Pacific ribbon for all of these major battles. As a range-finder operator, I had a ringside seat with a perfect view of all the landings and the action taking place. The toughest, bloodiest, most horrifying landing was at Iwo Jima. It is nothing short of a miracle that our marines were able to take the island considering the obstacles and conditions that prevailed. I was proud of them and could not have been prouder than I was on the morning of February 23, 1945 when I watched them raise the American flag on Mt. Suribachi.

From Iwo Jima we went back to continue our bombardment of Okinawa for the landing coming up there. On the morning of March 31, 1945, we were hit by a kamikaze. After getting patched up a little, we hobbled to Vallejo and dry dock for major repairs.

In June I was home on leave. The day before I was to go back to the ship I was at my parents' house in Abernathy, Texas. I was playing touch football with some of my brothers and sisters in the front yard. I went into the house for a drink of water. My mother got up from the porch and followed me in. She asked, "Cleatus what's wrong?" I said, "Oh, nothing." She said she knew something was bothering me, so I told her that I was really dreading returning to the ship because I felt like something awful was going to happen. She said, "I wish I could go with you, but I can't, but we know who can." I answered, "Yes, mama, Jesus can go with me."

I returned to the ship and history has recorded that we delivered the atomic bomb to Tinian Island. We went to Guam and left there for the Philippines.

July 30, 1945 was much like any other Sunday in the war zone. We knew Captain McVay had requested an escort ship but had been told there were no enemy subs along our route, so we were not too worry. Nevertheless, there was an air of expectancy on the ship.

I had passed my written test for FC 2C a few weeks earlier, but one of the CPO's in my division was reluctant to give me the test on practical factors. Our division officer was sure I could perform the work because I stood watch with him on much of the equipment I had to operate. He gave me the test that afternoon and I passed. He said the paperwork would be completed the next day.

He then asked me to move from my quarters in the after-part of the ship to a compartment up forward near the sick bay and the powder magazine for the two forward 8-inch gun turrets. I told him I had to go on watch at 1600 hours (4:00 p.m.) so he said it was okay to wait until morning.

I was in my bunk when we were hit. If I had been in the one up forward I would never have seen another morning on this earth. Our after-compartment was not damaged by the blasts, so I was able to slip on my shoes, shirt, pants, and an inflatable life belt before I went up to the main deck, across the quarterdeck with all its chaos and confusion and then up to the fire control workshop. There I started passing out life jackets to the men on gun watch on that deck and put one on myself. Smitty and Gaither and I went down one deck to help push a lifeboat off. The ship listed hard to starboard and I told them we better get out of there. We were going up the ladder to the next deck when it rolled hard again and sent the lifeboat crashing against the bulkhead behind it, crushing several men.

By then, we realized there was no option but to abandon ship, so the three of us climbed over the gunwale and walked down the side of the ship. I never saw either one of them again. By the time I hit the water and started swimming, I was scared and shaking, but I remembered my mother saying we knew who could go with me, so I prayed a little prayer, "Lord help me." Immediately a calm feeling of peace enveloped me and I was no longer afraid. I knew I was going home, either to heaven or back to Abernathy and it didn't matter which because He was in control. I am sure this kept me from succumbing to the almost irresistible and fatal desire to drink my fill of good old salt water straight from the ocean.

Yes the sharks came, and the hot sun came by day, the cold wind by night. Thoughts of home came with enough pleasant memories to sustain us, along with the morning and nighttime recital of the Lord's Prayer by our entire group. Then the airplane finally came, the one that we had been praying for for five days, piloted by Wilbur Gwinn. Then Adrian Marks came and landed his PBY near us and picked up 56 men. Then the ships came to pick up the decimated hanger–on who would not give up.

The hallucinations came in the twilight of the day we were found. I swam away from our group to where I saw survival gear being dropped from planes that morning. I did this two times and a friend, Clarence Hershberger from Indiana, swam out and pulled me back. He asked, "What are you doing?" I said, "Can't you see those crates of airplane parts out there? We can put one together and fly home."

After resting a little, I became lucid once again and remember a boat from the USS *Bassett* picking us up and taking us to their ship. It took us to Sumar to a hospital. Next stop was Guam where we spent 30 days at a submarine rest camp. I never knew the navy had chow that good anywhere!

We shipped to San Diego on the USS *Hollandia*, went home for a 30-day survival leave, and then back to California where I was honorably discharged on November 11, 1945.

I worked 35 years for GTE and contracted with them for ten more years. I am presently retired and enjoying it. Survivor Jimmy O'Donnell said it very well when he said, "Don't ever give up." I am going to add,

"Remember who can go with you."

NOT LOST AT SEA
I gave my country my very best
I fought and prayed and passed the test
I proudly went where duty called
For a brief time I was stalled
By a torpedo blast that shattered the night
I knew right then that things were not right
Then the sun arose on a bloody sea
And I knew things were not right for me
By that day's setting sun
I knew my life's race was run
With a smile on my face and peace in my heart
I knew this world I would soon depart
And my spirit would rise like an eagle on high
And I would be in my mansion in the sky
I was really NOT LOST AT SEA
So shed no tears over me
My work was done here on earth
So the Lord took me home to my Heavenly berth

Dedicated to the memory of all the sailors
of the USS *Indianapolis* who were Lost At Sea
July of 1945
Cleatus Lebow, Survivor

SURVIVOR'S PRAYER
As the waves rolled over the *Indy*, asleep in the deep
The Lord gave us a miracle to keep
He gave us the chance to serve Him for many more years
And we remember the lost comrades as we shed sad tears

Lord, we thank you for added days
We work to glorify You in all your ways
May the miracle of survival live in each heart
We pray you will guide us to do our part

We give glory and honor to You
And strive to serve you in all we do
Thanks for the miracle of survival from the sea
Thanks for Your love and grace and for saving me

Survivors' Reunion August 7, 1995
Cleatus Lebow, Survivor

CHAPTER 157   SURVIVOR LEENERMAN

NAME	LEENERMAN, ARTHUR L. RDM3C
STREET	1601 W Point Dr
CITY	Mahomet
STATE	IL 61853
PHONE	217 586 4873
ENTERED SERVICE FROM	Sibley, IL
PICKED UP BY	PBY Tr USS *Doyle*
DIVISION	Radar
DOB	7/5/24

FAMILY
Spouse: Ethel
Children: Cynthia Cooper, Gregory Leenerman
Grandchildren: Jason Eaton, Ryan Cooper, Emma Leenerman, Kristen
Leenerman

EXPERIENCE
I was born and raised in Sibley, Illinois, a small town (pop. 399) in the farm
country of central Illinois. In 1878, 17,641 acres of farmland around Sibley was
owned by Hiram Sibley from New York. Later, his son Harper Sibley inherited
this land. Barns were painted red and the houses yellow. At one time, Sibley had
the largest ear-corn crib in the world. It held 125,000 bushels. While in high
school, I worked on some of the farms for the tenants. My maternal grandfather
also owned 1,392 acres within four miles of Sibley. My father worked for the
Shell Pipeline Corporation, retiring after 37 years.

I graduated from high school in 1942, and received my 1A Draft Notice when
I turned 18 in July. I worked at the Joliet Illinois Arsenal Plant. (My uncle was
killed there in 1942 when a boxcar load of mines exploded.) Before being
inducted into the navy at Great Lakes training camp, I attended boot camp in
June and July of 1943. After boot camp and a short leave, I was sent to the
receiving camp at Shoemaker, California.

In early September 1943, I went aboard the USS *Indianapolis*, anchored in San Francisco Bay. The ship proceeded to Pearl Harbor, Hawaii. I was sent to the hills of Hawaii to train on army radar. The ship had gone out on gunnery practice and returned. I returned aboard the ship. They tried to use me on the number three gun turret, but I could not understand the gunnery sighting system. I was then sent to aft CIC to operate the radar and stayed there the remainder of my time on the USS *Indianapolis*.

In November of 1943 the ship went on the Gilbert Islands (Tarawa) operation. In 1944 we went on the Kwajelin and Eniwetok operation, then to Palau, Yap and Ulithi raids, then to Saipan and Guam, which included the Battle of the Philippine Sea...(the Marianas Turkey Shoot—our ships and planes shot down 402 enemy planes). Also in July 1944, we participated in the capture of Tinian Island and in September the Western Caroline Islands operation.

In February 1945, the *Indy* escorted the aircraft carriers to the Japanese home islands and particiated in the capture of Iwo Jima. In March, while on the Okinawa operation, we were hit by a Japanese kamikaze plane which disabled two of our propellers (screws). We limped back to the islands just south of Okinawa and a hole in our bottom side was patched with some concrete. We proceeded back to Mare Island naval repair center at Vallejo, California. After being repaired, we proceeded to Hunters Point naval harbor on the San Francisco side of the bay.

At Hunters Point on July 15, 1945, we received a secret cargo that was later ascertained to be the first atomic bomb. Our ship delivered it to Tinian Island where General Tibbets, the pilot of the *Enola Gay*, dropped the bomb on Hiroshima. After leaving Tinian Island, we proceeded to Guam where we received orders to go to the Philippine Islands for training for the invasion of the Japan.

While traveling unescorted—at about the halfway point—the USS *Indianapolis* was struck by two torpedoes at about ten minutes past midnight on July 30, 1945. I had been relieved from duty late that night and was at the head on the main deck aft when we were hit. I went to the fantail for a life vest and went to my general quarters station (CIC radar aft). The ship immediately began to list to the starboard side. I told my friend, Ray Kozik, "This thing is going to sink." We slid down the port side and jumped off the bilge keel. We were in salt water and oil and I immediately vomited. Eventually I ended up with a group of shipmates (150 or so) that had gathered around a floater net. I didn't see my friend Ray again.

We thought we would be rescued soon but of course that didn't happen. Our group dwindled down to about 50 or 60. On the fourth day about noon, after suffering from hunger, thirst, sunburn, and saltwater ulcers, we were accidentally spotted. The pilot was Lt. Wilbur Gwinn in his PV-1 Ventura bomber. He dropped inflatable rubber life rafts and we knew we would be rescued. I tried to get in one of the life rafts but couldn't. My life jacket was soaked and heavy. I didn't want to remove it but I finally did and was able to get in the raft.

In the meantime, Adrian Marks, flying a PBY 5A arrived, broke all navy rules, landed in the water, and started to pick up survivors. I passed out in the life raft and was tied to the PBY. The rescue ships arrived early in the morning, which I did not know. I was the last one taken from the PBY because they thought I was dead. I barely came to when I was taken aboard the USS *Cecil F Doyle*. At the island of Peleliu, we were taken aboard the hospital ship USS *Tranquility* and then to the base hospital on Guam. At the hospital, I was visited by a high school friend, Raymond Enghausen. He was notified by the Red Cross that I was there. To this day, we do not know who notified the Red Cross. After the hospital and rest camp, we were sent home for leave by the way of San Diego on the small carrier *Hollandia*. Lo and behold, who was on the ship...Raymond Enghausen.

After a thirty-day leave, I was sent to Shoemaker, California and received shore patrol duty at Stockton, California. I was honorably discharged on February 18, 1946 in California. I rode home from Los Angeles, California with my uncle, John Hinrichs, and Dean Lindholm.

I was aboard the USS *Indianapolis* for eight of its ten battle engagements. At the reunion in Indianapolis 2001, the navy presented us with the Navy Unit Commendation and Combat Action Ribbon.

CHAPTER 158   SURVIVOR LOCKWOOD

NAME	LOCKWOOD, THOMAS H. S2C
STREET	
CITY	
STATE	
PHONE	
ENTERED SERVICE FROM	Columbia, MO
PICKED UP BY	USS *Doyle*
DIVISION	
DOB	Deceased

FAMILY

EXPERIENCE

Unable to contact any family members.

USS *Indianapolis*
Survivors
Archive

Survivors and their wives at the first reunion in 1960.

Survivors at the 1980 Reunion.

Survivors at the 2000 Reunion.

Survivors' wives at the 2000 Reunion.

MINI REUNION BROOMFIELD, COLORADO 2000

Girl Scout Escorts: Lauren Brown, Ashley Roddy, Jessica Klingensmith, Kristina Majzner, Melissa Seelig

USS Indianapolis Memorial, 2nd and Main Street, Broomfield, Colorado

Lost at Sea Sam Miller and Survivor Paul Murphy, Tijuana, Mexico December 31, 1944

1944 Cartoon by Harry Todd Hickey, Radioman 3/C, who was Buried at Sea Sunday, August 5, 1945 by the Destroyer USS *Helm* DD 388.

LAS Thomas Leon Barksdale FC-3

USS *Indianapolis* (CA-35) 1932-1945 Still at Sea....

Funeral services were held on the quarterdeck for two of the nine sailors killed from the Japanese suicide attack on the *Indianapolis* on March 31, 1945. Commander Joseph A. Flynn, the executive officer, is shown with back to camera. Donald F. Mack, the bugler on duty, stands to Commander Flynn's left. Glenn Morgan stands (back to camera) over the body of Richard Kucenback, second group, last one to the right. Chaplin Lieutenant Thomas Conway is shown presiding over the ceremony. As pallbearers, the twelve shown in this picture transported these two bodies in a Higgins boat across the bay for burial at Kerama Retto.

Bridge

Alidade

Signal bridge

Last point I touched of the USS Indianapolis

40 millimeter quad gun turret

My Escape by Glenn Morgan

When I arrived on the bridge with quartermaster Ralph Guye, the only officer on the deck, Lieutenant Orr, and the bugler of the watch, Donald F. Mack were visible. I asked Lieutenant Orr what we could do. He said word had been passed to abandon ship. I asked bugler Mack if he was going to sound "abandon ship." "When somebody orders me to do so," he said. I saluted Lieutenant Orr and told him I would see him later. I climbed over the steel railing as shown (the ship had at least a 45-degree list at that time). I jumped to the signal bridge then down the bulkhead and into the 40-mm gun mounts. There, the water caught me and swiftly pinned me to the first gun breech. By then the ship was on its side. As the ship sank, the 40-mm gun barrels were vertical. I grasped the barrel while I was submerged and I passed it through hand over hand. When I felt the flash funnel, I swam away. As I looked back, Ralph Guye was nowhere to be seen.

August 15, 1945 on Guam, some *Indianapolis* survivors are being awarded the Purple Heart by Admiral Raymond A. Spruance, Commander of the Fifth Fleet. Glenn G. Morgan is shown in the foreground, with Joseph J. Moran and Louis P. Bitonti. Joseph Moran was accidentally electrocuted some seven months later.

USS Indianapolis cooks

First row: Roy Kingle, Keith Owen, Clarence Hupka, David Kemp. Second row: Fernando Sanchez, Sal Maldonado, Morgan Mosely, John Spinelli

In happier days, a night on the town in San Diego. From left to right: Robert S. Owens Jr., QM3, Arthur A. Labuda QM3, Ralph L. Guye, QM3, Marion J. Scaap, QM1, Edward W. Alvey, AerM2, Glenn G. Morgan BGM2 and Vincent J. Allard, QM3.

A USS Indianapolis Officer and cooks posing for a picture

USS *Indianapolis* (CA-35)

USS Indianapolis Memorial located on the canal in Indianapolis, Indiana.

Visitors and Survivors' families pay tribute to the USS Indianapolis Memorial.

NAME	LOFTIS, JAMES B. Jr. S1C
STREET	
CITY	
STATE	
PHONE	
ENTERED SERVICE FROM	Alton, VA
PICKED UP BY	USS *Doyle*
DIVISION	
DOB	2/8/25
	Deceased 3/90

FAMILY
Widow: Eleanor
Children: Elizabeth Loftis Brusig, Mark Loftis
Grandchildren: Andrea Brusig, Alexandra Loftis, Isabelle Loftis

EXPERIENCE
Respectfully submitted by Survivor Loftis' family.

Reprinted from a newspaper article in 1970.

J. B. Loftis, a Brookneal resident, is one of the few survivors of the greatest single disaster at sea in the history of the United States Navy. The disaster was the sinking of the USS *Indianapolis*, torpedoed by a Japanese submarine in the Philippine Sea in World War II, with a loss of 880 lives. The *Indianapolis* sailed from San Francisco on July 16, 1945 on a highly secret and important mission—she carried the atomic bomb that was to be dropped on Japan. The mission was accomplished, the bomb delivered, and the *Indianapolis* sailed on alone to her unsuspected doom.

James graduated from Turbeville High School. As soon as he reached the proper age he was drafted and assigned to the navy. His father served in the navy during World War I. Life aboard a battle cruiser, however, can be strenuous and severe at times, especially if your ship is in action against the enemy. He spent eight weeks at Great Lakes Training Station, then went to Camp Pendleton in California. From there he was routed directly to Pearl Harbor, and upon arriving there was assigned to the cruiser, USS *Indianapolis*.

"First, we were in action around the Marianas Islands, including Saipan and Guam, then to Iwo Jima and to Okinawa. At Okinawa the *Indianapolis* was struck by a suicide plane and disabled. We were returned to the United States for ship repairs. After these repairs were made, we were ordered to Tinian where we unloaded our cargo of supplies. Imagine our surprise after the destruction of Hiroshima when we learned that the nice-looking crate we unloaded at Tinian contained the atomic bomb.

We were ordered to Guam and on Saturday morning, our ship steamed out of the harbor of Tinian bound for the Philippines. About 12:15 a.m. on Monday, July 30, 1945, we were hit by a torpedo fired by a submarine. The torpedo struck our ship in the forepart and tore it practically in two. The ammunition we were carrying was detonated. The ship seemed to rise completely out of the water, then settled back and sank quickly. I was on the second deck. The jolt was terrific and I had no idea it was as bad as it was. I dressed, put on shoes and ran on deck. The ship was listing badly by that time. I dashed back to my compartment and put on a life jacket. By the time I returned to the deck, the ship was lying at such an angle that it was difficult even to stand erect. No order to abandon ship came. The signal system had been knocked out by the terrific explosion. Our ship was doomed!

When struck, the *Indianapolis* was around 600 miles off the coast of the Philippines and almost that far off the shores of Guam. We kicked around in the water for three or four days. All radio communication was knocked out by the blast; consequently no calls for help could be sent out. Perhaps it was well we did not know what our plight was, for it would have only added to our terror and suspense. The thirst was terrible—unbearable to some. I saw many fellows deliberately take a deep swallow of the briny water and in what seemed only a matter of minutes would begin screaming in their delirium, foam at the mouth, throw their arms wildly about, glare madly into space then with one last wild croak, sink to their death. This was salt poisoning. Many developed hallucinations.

For some reason, perhaps in answer to my earnest prayers, I was able to hold my reasoning faculties under fairly good control. I would take a good mouthful of sea water, rinse it around, then spit it out. I was only one swallow from madness, then eternity.

We saw several planes go over. They did not know our predicament and did not look below. But thanks be to God, one day when hope was nearly gone, a plane spotted us. The pilot did not know whether we were Americans or Japanese. He circled. We shouted at him and he recognized us as friends. The plane was commanded by Captain Adrian Marks. He risked his own life and the lives of his whole crew, for his airship could land on water but could not take off; however, he took the long chance. He sent calls for help.

Some in our group were in pretty bad shape. Out of 350 of my group who were washed off the deck of the ship, only 30 were still alive. We were helped aboard the plane and stretched out on the wings. In about ten hours we sighted one of the three destroyers coming to our rescue. Can you imagine the feeling in our hearts as the speck on the horizon grew larger and larger as it came nearer and nearer!

All of us were quickly transferred to the ship. Some were in pitiful condition with salt burns practically all over their bodies. My dungarees rubbed a raw spot under my knees which later developed into painful and rather severe salt sores. The sores ate deep into my flesh but gradually healed. I was in a hospital in Guam for three weeks. All of us who survived were given Purple Hearts.

I am not overly religious but I called on my Maker as earnestly as any young fellow ever did. I am sure all the others did the same. Lying there in the middle of the Pacific Ocean with nothing but water in sight reminded me of the quote, "Water, water, everywhere, but not a drop to drink."

It is true that one never knows how good life is until he has looked death squarely in the face. My parents received a telegram stating that I "was wounded in action."

While in the hospital, all of us survivors agreed to meet every five years in Indianapolis, Indiana for a reunion. So far, I have been unable to attend, although I do hear from several of the fellows occasionally. As everyone who reads this story will know, I am thankful to be alive and safely back in America. I can sing with more feeling than ever, "God Bless America, my home, sweet home."

CHAPTER 160　　　　　　　　　　　　　　　　　SURVIVOR LOPEZ

NAME　　　　　　　　　LOPEZ, DANIEL B. F2C
STREET
CITY
STATE
PHONE
ENTERED SERVICE FROM　　Sacramento, CA
PICKED UP BY　　　　USS *Talbot* tr USS *Register*
DIVISION
DOB　　　　　　　　Deceased 6/88

FAMILY

EXPERIENCE
　Unable to contact any family members.

NAME	LOPEZ, SAM S1C
STREET	717 Thomas
CITY	Monongah
STATE	WV 26554
PHONE	304 534 3217
ENTERED SERVICE FROM	Shinnston, WV
PICKED UP BY	USS *Bassett*
DIVISION	1st Division
DOB	9/27/24

FAMILY

Spouse: Joanne
Children: Linda Lopez Gandy (James), Sam Lopez Jr. (Joyce)
Grandchildren: James Gandy, Bryan Gandy, Shawn Lopez, Shane Lopez

EXPERIENCE

I was born and raised in the small town of Shinnston, West Virgina, one of eight boys and four girls born to Pete and Mary Lopez. I and two of my brothers served our country during World War II.

The heavy cruiser USS *Indianapolis* was the pride of the United States Navy and was chosen to be the flagship of the Pacific Fleet. The ship took part in the battles of Saipan, Tinian, Guam, Iwo Jima, Okinawa and the key battles of Midway and the Philippine Sea.

I enlisted in May 1943 and was assigned to the USS *Indianapolis* in August 1943. We were engaged in the Battle of Okinawa and were hit by a Japanese kamikaze pilot. The damage was severe; we lost nine members of our crew, and we were pulled from Okinawa for repairs.

On July 16, 1945 the *Indianapolis* was assigned the most secret and possibly the most important mission of World War II. She was dispatched to San Francisco to pick up an important cargo. Two crates were loaded and locked in the hangar deck. No one aboard the ship–including Captain McVay–knew the contents of the crates. We then set sail for the Island of Tinian. On arrival the crates were unloaded and taken to Tinian Airfield.

After completing our mission we were ordered to set sail for Guam and then to Leyte to take part in gunnery practice with the USS *Idaho* in preparation for the invasion of Japan. We were sent unescorted, and about halfway a Japanese submarine spotted us and sent our ship and many of our crew to a watery grave. This began our fight for survival in the waters of the Pacific Ocean. Captain McVay had received no information of any enemy activity near our route of travel.

On July 29, I began my day by attending church. As this was Sunday, my watch did not start until 8:00 p.m. The guys and I were shooting dice and I won a few dollars. When we finished I kissed the dice and threw them overboard. I stood watch from 8:00 p.m. to midnight on the number five gun starboard side. There was no moon and it was very dark. I got off watch and returned to my compartment. We were talking about my winnings and I put my money in one of my socks.

About 12:15 a.m. on July 30, we heard a very loud explosion and one of the guys yelled, "We have been hit," and we all started running topside. I told my buddy, Hank McKlin, that the ship was going to sink as it was listing toward starboard side and water was on the quarterdeck. We went up the ladder toward my division, grabbed four cargo nets and loaded them on the railing. About that time they yelled, "Abandon ship!" We slid down the side of the ship (along with the cargo nets that were still rolled up) and started to swim away from the ship as it was going down.

When we looked back the ship was gone, which started our struggle for survival in the waters of the Pacific Ocean. We started praying and tried to calm each other and stay together. I would say out of a crew of 1200 only 800 were believed to have made it off the ship. Our first day in the water we prayed and hoped for rescue and were confident we would be reported missing when we failed to arrive at our destination.

Then the sharks arrived, and one by one the men began to disappear. Some began to drink the sea water and hallucinate and disappear. We had no water or food and the sun was very hot. One day turned into two, then three, and then four. We never gave up hope of being rescued.

In despair and our prayers still unanswered, a plane—a PV-1 Ventura bomber piloted by Lt. Wilbur Gwinn on a routine submarine patrol—spotted an oil slick in the water, flew down to take a closer look and discovered us in the water. He reported to the American base at Peleliu that there were many men in the water; it was unknown whether we were friend or foe.

A seaplane—navy PBY piloted by Lt. Adrian Marks—was dispatched to the scene and began circling and dropping rubber rafts. Against orders he landed his plane, loading as many men on his plane as he could. It wasn't until Lt. Marks started the rescue that it was learned that the USS *Indianapolis* had been sunk four days earlier. The USS *Doyle* and USS *Bassett* arrived after dark. Many men were incoherent and didn't even realize we were being rescued. Many died trying to swim to rescue boats.

I was rescued by the USS *Bassett,* along with my buddy Hank McKlin and others of our crew. The members of the *Bassett's* crew gave up their bunks for us and cared for us while we were transported to hospitals. Only 317 men survived this horrible ordeal.

On August 6, 1945, the *Enola Gay* dropped the atomic bomb on Hiroshima and a second on Nagasaki, which ended the war with Japan.

After the war, I returned to Shinnston, West Virginia to resume my life. It was very hard for me to go and visit the family of my buddy, Harry Linville, who gave his life when the ship went down. We had enlisted and gone through boot camp together. I still think of him often. Upon returning home, I was employed by Consolidation Coal as a shift foreman for many years and retired in 1989.

In 1960 we had our first reunion in Indianapolis, Indiana. I have attended all the reunions to date, and I am looking forward to the next reunion in July 2003. On August 2, 1995, the monument to the USS *Indianapolis* (CA-35) was unveiled. The monument has all of the ship's crew members' names engraved. A piece of the *Arizona* also was placed inside the monument. The ships were the first and last ships sunk in World War II in our fight for freedom for our country.

I am very proud to have been a member of the crew of our great ship, the USS *Indianapolis* and to have served our country. Freedom doesn't come cheap and many of the members of our armed forces gave their life for their country. We must always honor and cherish our memories of them.

God bless the USA.

CHAPTER 162   SURVIVOR LUCAS

NAME	LUCAS, ROBERT A. S2C
STREET	36 Circle Dr
CITY	Streator
STATE	IL 61364
PHONE	815 672 1452
ENTERED SERVICE FROM	Streator, IL
PICKED UP BY	USS *Bassett*
DIVISION	7th Div
DOB	11/30/26

FAMILY
Spouse: Marianne

EXPERIENCE
On July 30, 1945, I was standing gun watch below the bridge. When the first blast came I was knocked down on the deck. I got up to see what had happened and walked toward the front of the ship. I saw the bow had been blown off and went to get life jackets to put on the wounded.

The ship started to sink. All the wounded slipped down and forward. Somebody said, "Abandon ship!" I made it down to the deck, jumped into the water, and started to swim away from the ship. Someone said, "There she goes," and we all stopped and watched her go down.

The rest of the night and morning we looked for men from our division. There were men all over. The men that were in good shape looked after the men who drank the salt water and were sick, and also helped the men who were hurt on the ship before it went down. Every day there were more empty jackets floating around. After the second day we started to change life jackets. If a jacket was high in the water it was empty.

I do not know if it was the third or fourth day when we were spotted and the planes started to come. A PBY landed on the water and picked up men. A plane dropped a life jacket with clean drinking water in it, and I went to get it. Going was easy, but coming back I was going against the current. I couldn't make it back. I had to let the water go. I was tired and I didn't think I could get back. Then I heard a loud noise and looked up. There was a B-17 coming right at me. He dropped a life raft right close to me. I was able to get it and climb in. A little later six or seven men came to the raft. It was now dark and we worried that nobody would find us.

All at once lights were coming our way. The USS *Bassett* came and took us off the raft. When we got to the ship and got aboard a man took our names. They gave us water and a bath and put us in bunks. The men on the *Bassett* took real good care of us.

CHAPTER 163   SURVIVOR LUCCA

NAME	LUCCA, FRANK J. F2C
STREET	
CITY	
STATE	
PHONE	
ENTERED SERVICE FROM	Cleveland, OH
PICKED UP BY	USS *Bassett*
DIVISION	
DOB	Deceased 5/99

FAMILY

EXPERIENCE
   Unable to contact any family members.

NAME	MAAS, MELVIN A. S1C
STREET	
CITY	
STATE	
PHONE	
ENTERED SERVICE FROM	Los Angeles, CA
PICKED UP BY	USS *Bassett*
DIVISION	
DOB	Deceased 9/85

FAMILY
Widow: Ruth

EXPERIENCE
Unable to contact any family members.

NAME	MACE, HAROLD S2C
STREET	
CITY	
STATE	
PHONE	
ENTERED SERVICE FROM	Lansing, MI
PICKED UP BY	USS *Bassett*
DIVISION	
DOB	Deceased 9/96

FAMILY

EXPERIENCE
Unable to contact any family members.

NAME	MACK, DONALD F. Bugler 1
STREET	RD 2 Box 304P
CITY	Greentown
STATE	PA 18426
PHONE	570 857 0048
ENTERED SERVICE FROM	New York, NY
PICKED UP BY	USS *Doyle*
DIVISION	N Div
DOB	10/31/25

FAMILY

Spouse: Dorothy J.
Children: Linda Lee, David Bruce Mack
Grandchildren: Kristin Lee Mooney
Great–Grandchildren: Kerian Joseph Mooney

EXPERIENCE

I was born in Easton, Pennsylvania, the youngest of five children. I went to school in Wilson Boro and graduated from high school in 1943. I played the trumpet from age nine and played in the school band for six years.

When the navy learned that I played the trumpet, they sent me to a service school in San Diego to learn bugle calls. I graduated from there in January 1944 and was sent to Pearl Harbor to wait for the USS *Indianapolis* to return from the Aleutian Island campaign. I boarded the *Indianapolis* in February and my first campaign was the Guam, Saipan and Tinian operation. From there I was aboard for the operations of Palau, Eniwetok, Battle of the Philippine Sea, Iwo Jima and Okinawa.

I was fortunate in many ways to have been on watch when we were hit by Japanese suicide attacks and also when we were hit by torpedoes from the Japanese submarine *I-58*. Being on the navigation bridge where all the action was taking place, I was in the middle of everything.

After being hit by the torpedoes, I waited for the order to sound the call to "abandon ship." This order was never given to me by the "OOD." The captain, quartermaster, coxswain, and the yeoman of the watch all went overboard about the same time.

I was picked up by the USS *Doyle* after being in the water for four days and five nights. I saw many of my friends and shipmates go to their deaths from sharks and mostly from exposure.

I finally was honorably discharged from the navy in March 1946 from the Baimbridge, Maryland naval station.

My wife and I have attended most of the Indianapolis reunions. I always enjoy seeing many of my old friends there.

Keep smiling and God bless America.

CHAPTER 167   SURVIVOR MADAY

NAME	MADAY, ANTHONY Avia Mach Mate 1C
STREET	
CITY	
STATE	
PHONE	
ENTERED SERVICE FROM	Chicago, IL
PICKED UP BY	USS *Doyle*
DIVISION	
DOB	Deceased

FAMILY

EXPERIENCE

Unable to contact any family members.

NAME	MAKAROFF, CHESTER Gunner Mate 3C
STREET	
CITY	
STATE	
PHONE	
ENTERED SERVICE FROM	Chicago, IL
PICKED UP BY	USS *Bassett*
DIVISION	
DOB	Deceased 93

FAMILY

EXPERIENCE

Unable to contact any family members.

NAME	MALDONADO, SALVADOR V.
	Baker 3C
STREET	495 W Paisley Ave
CITY	Hemet
STATE	CA 92545
PHONE	909 765 9181
ENTERED SERVICE FROM	Los Angeles, CA
PICKED UP BY	USS *Bassett*
DIVISION	5th Division
DOB	6/13/22

FAMILY

Spouse: Consuelo

EXPERIENCE

My name is Sal Maldonado. I am a survivor of the USS *Indianapolis*. I went into the navy October 28, 1942. I took my training in San Diego, California and boarded the *Indianapolis* at Mare Island, California on April 24, 1943.

The ship had just got back from the South Pacific. I boarded the ship and went on my first invasion which was Attu. Next were the Kiska invasion in the

Aleutian Islands, the invasion of Tarawa, the Marshall Islands and then the invasion of Okinawa. Our ship was hit by a kamikaze suicide plane, which killed nine of our shipmates. We then headed back to Mare Island for repairs.

After the ship was repaired, we went on leave for a bit until they called us back to the ship. They told us we were going on a top-secret mission so we headed to Hunters Point. There we loaded a box that was guarded by marines. At that time we were unaware that the box contained the main parts for the atomic bomb that would be dropped on Hiroshima. We carried the box to Tinian Island and dropped it off. The other parts of the atomic bomb would be delivered by airplane.

We left Tinian without a ship escort. Our captain, Captain McVay, had requested an escort but his request was denied. We were sailing on July 30, 1945, when suddenly at about midnight, we were torpedoed two times. The ship sank in 12 minutes. I jumped overboard, hit the water, and began swimming for my life. It was very dark and I was not able to see anything.

I was in the water for five days with only a life jacket. By daylight the sharks began to attack the group of swimmers I had found. We fought them off by kicking and screaming. We had no food or water for five days. The sharks would attack daily, and little by little men were disappearing. On the fifth day we were rescued and were found barely alive with the sharks still attacking. The plane that spotted us found us by accident when flying maneuvers. Of the 1,197 crew members, only 317 survived. I thank God that I am still alive. That's my story and thank you for your time and interest.

CHAPTER 170   SURVIVOR MALENA

NAME	MALENA, JOSEPH Gunners Mate 2C
STREET	
CITY	
STATE	
PHONE	
ENTERED SERVICE FROM	Dayton, OH
PICKED UP BY	USS *Bassett*
DIVISION	
DOB	Deceased

FAMILY

EXPERIENCE
   Unable to contact any family members.

NAME	MALSKI, JOSEPH S1C
STREET	Unknown
CITY	
STATE	
PHONE	
ENTERED SERVICE FROM	Grand Rapids, MI
PICKED UP BY	USS *Bassett*
DIVISION	
DOB	

FAMILY

EXPERIENCE

Unable to contact any family members.

CHAPTER 172 SURVIVOR MATRULLA

NAME	MATRULLA, JOHN S1C
STREET	
CITY	
STATE	
PHONE	
ENTERED SERVICE FROM	Bloomsburg, PA
PICKED UP BY	USS *Doyle*
DIVISION	Fire Control
DOB	Deceased 8/00

FAMILY

EXPERIENCE

Unable to contact any family members.

NAME	MAXWELL, FARRELL S1C
STREET	
CITY	
STATE	
PHONE	
ENTERED SERVICE FROM	Peoria, IL
PICKED UP BY	USS *Ringness*
DIVISION	
DOB	Deceased 12/92

FAMILY

EXPERIENCE
Unable to contact any family members.

NAME	McCALL, DONALD C. S2C
STREET	1814 Broadmoor
CITY	Champaign
STATE	IL 61821
PHONE	
ENTERED SERVICE FROM	Champaign, IL
PICKED UP BY	USS *Bassett*
DIVISION	
DOB	2/2/25

FAMILY
Spouse: Helen
Children: Peggy Campo, Don McCall, Jeff McCall, Fred McCall
Grandchildren: Scott McCall, Brett McCall, Charles Campo, Mike Campo, Pete McCall, Kevin McCall, Steve McCall, Jennifer Conrad, Laine McCall
Great-Grandchildren: Carter McCall

EXPERIENCE
Respectfully submitted by Survivor McCall's son, Jeff McCall.
My dad tried twice to volunteer for military service during the early months

of World War II, but he was rejected each time because of chronic bronchitis. Much to his surprise, however, he then was drafted and accepted into the U.S. Navy in early 1943. Soon thereafter, at 18 years of age, he reported to Great Lakes naval station near Chicago for training.

It was quite a shock for a teenager from low-income means in rural Mansfield, Illinois to see Lake Michigan and a big city like Chicago. "It was the first pond I've ever seen that I couldn't see across," he recounted. Indeed, before reporting for training at Great Lakes, McCall had never traveled further than 50 miles from his home in central Illinois.

McCall's eye-opening continued after basic training, with a train ride across the United States. Eventually he arrived in the bay area of California, where he first saw the USS *Indianapolis* at anchor. The USS *Indianapolis*, the only ship on which McCall would serve, was an impressive sight. "I couldn't believe that much metal could float," McCall said, "I was awestruck and dumbfounded. So much had happened so fast for a kid from Mansfield."

After receiving foul-weather gear for a short stint to the Aleutian Islands, McCall and his crewmates turned their cold weather clothes back in and headed for an undisclosed location in the South Pacific. "They never told us much," McCall said. From that point, the USS *Indianapolis* was in near constant action and McCall, as an air-sea lookout, had a close-up view of the seemingly unbelievable action.

McCall's first action was at Tarawa. "When we pulled in at Tarawa, it looked like an emerald in a blue sea. But when we left, it looked like somebody had taken a weed-whacker to it—it was all stumps and smoke," McCall remembered. "With my binoculars as an air-sea lookout, I could see the marines hitting the beaches and I was shocked to see such an inhumane thing happening."

"Then we did this at all the other islands," McCall continued, "and they were all the same." Other campaigns during this time for the USS *Indianapolis* included Saipan, Tinian, the Philippine Sea, Iwo Jima, and Okinawa.

McCall believes he was assigned as an air-sea lookout because of his 20/20 vision. "We had to be very aware of what we saw out there. We were drilled and updated frequently on what we were looking for—different kinds of Japanese planes and ships—and we had to be able to distinguish instantly from American planes."

From his lookout position on the starboard side of the bridge, McCall was at times able to observe the USS *Indianapolis's* skipper, Captain Charles McVay, and fleet commander Admiral Spruance, in action. Speaking of Spruance, McCall said, "Nothing ever shook him up and he was always calm under pressure." McCall held McVay in high regard. "He was a good skipper and concerned for his men. Everybody loved him and he didn't deserve what all happened to him after the sinking," McCall said, referring to the navy's eventual disciplinary action and court-martial of McVay.

When not doing duty as air-sea lookout, McCall served as a loader on a 20-

mm gun. He enjoyed playing cards with shipmates while not on duty, and "did some mess cookin', too, when I got into trouble a time or two." His two best friends on the *Indy* were S2C Carroll Gove and S1C Andrew Reynolds, but both were lost at sea as a result of the tragedy.

McCall had just got off gun watch when the USS *Indianapolis* was struck by torpedoes on July 30, 1945. "I had decided to sleep up top even though that circumvented the rules, but it was hot down below and I had a blanket stashed up top behind a gun and was settling in for the night," McCall said. That decision likely kept him from being trapped below, ultimately saving his life.

"My first thought was that one of our boilers had blown up. I didn't think we had been torpedoed," McCall said. McCall received a shrapnel wound in the back of his leg from the explosion. "Then I went to get myself a life jacket, using my knife to cut open a bag of jackets on the deck. I handed them out to some of the other guys," he continued.

"We were always taught to throw our life jackets into the water first and then jump in, but I looked below and saw the confusion and was afraid I wouldn't find it, so I jumped in with my life jacket on," McCall said, recalling that he jumped off the tail of the ship. "I never heard an order to abandon ship, but we all knew the ship was going down."

McCall spent most of his time during the ordeal drifting alone with just his life jacket. He used an additional life jacket he had recovered to cover his head during the heat of the day.

McCall finally got out of the water when an airplane dropped a rescue boat near him. The boat landed so close to McCall that the splash of the boat on the water washed over him. He was the first survivor to crawl in, and he was soon joined by other shipmates. He was picked up and treated by the destroyer USS *Bassett,* a fact he never knew until years later when he saw his name in the *Bassett*'s records, displayed at a survivors' reunion in Indianapolis.

McCall remembers with great thankfulness the care and consideration provided the survivors by the crew of the USS *Bassett* and the medical personnel in the Philippines, where he and other survivors were taken after rescue. McCall's first-ever plane ride came when he and other survivors were later transported to Guam for further rehabilitation. At Guam, McCall received his Purple Heart medal from Admiral Spruance.

Upon McCall's return to the States, he received his honorable discharge at Great Lakes station. Prior to the sinking of his ship, McCall had considered making the navy his career. "The navy was the best life I'd ever had up until that time. It was my first real job, I was getting paid, and I had plenty to eat for the first time in my life," McCall said. "But after the ship sank, I couldn't see myself in the navy as a career because I didn't think I could have ever gone back to sea."

McCall returned to central Illinois and has lived there ever since. McCall took up a career as a brickmason. He married Rita Mattingly and together they raised four children. Rita died in 1975. McCall later remarried and now lives with his wife, Helen. He enjoys spending time with his nine grandchildren and one great-grandchild. In addition, he is an avid golfer and gardener. McCall and his family have attended each of the crew's reunions in Indianapolis over the years.

CHAPTER 175   SURVIVOR McCLAIN

NAME	McCLAIN, RAYMOND Boats Mate 2C
STREET	
CITY	
STATE	
PHONE	
ENTERED SERVICE FROM	LaRue, TX
PICKED UP BY	PBY tr USS *Doyle*
DIVISION	
DOB	Deceased 8/95

FAMILY

EXPERIENCE
   Unable to contact any family members.

NAME	McCOY, GILES G. PVT 1 C USMC
STREET	5 Wills Pl
CITY	Palm Coast
STATE	FL 32164
PHONE	
ENTERED SERVICE FROM	St Louis, MO
PICKED UP BY	USS *Ringness*
DIVISION	Marine
DOB	3/30/26

FAMILY
Spouse: Betty

EXPERIENCE

No response.

Respectfully submitted by Survivor Paul J. Murphy, Chairman, USS Indianapolis Survivors Organization.

Survivor McCoy and his lovely wife, Betty, devoted many years to organizing our very first reunion, serving in various positions, as well as helping with the beautiful memorial in Indianapolis. We all will be forever grateful.

NAME	McCRORY, MILLARD V. Jr Water Tender 3C
STREET	
CITY	
STATE	
PHONE	
ENTERED SERVICE FROM	Ponchatoula, LA
PICKED UP BY	USS *Bassett*
DIVISION	
DOB	Deceased 8/92

FAMILY

EXPERIENCE

Unable to contact any family members.

CHAPTER 178 — SURVIVOR McELROY

NAME	McELROY, CLARENCE S1C
STREET	
CITY	
STATE	
PHONE	
ENTERED SERVICE FROM	Baldwin Pk, CA
PICKED UP BY	
DIVISION	
DOB	Deceased 2/83

FAMILY

EXPERIENCE

Unable to contact any family members.

CHAPTER 179 — SURVIVOR McFALL

NAME	McFALL, WALTER E. S2C
STREET	
CITY	
STATE	
PHONE	
ENTERED SERVICE FROM	Cloquet, MN
PICKED UP BY	USS *Doyle*
DIVISION	
DOB	Deceased 10/86

FAMILY

EXPERIENCE

Unable to contact any family members.

NAME   McGINNIS, PAUL W.
                          SM3 Signalman
STREET   4 Meadow Dr
CITY   Wheeling
STATE   WV 26003
PHONE   304 242 0597
ENTERED SERVICE FROM   Elm Grove, WV
PICKED UP BY   PBY Tr USS *Doyle*
DIVISION   SM3 Signalman
DOB   12/13/25

FAMILY
Spouse: Marcella
Children: Kathleen Ann Gompers (Joe)
Grandchildren: Kelly Gompers, Michael Gompers

EXPERIENCE

I was born December 13, 1925 in Wheeling, West Virginia, the fourth of six children. My family and I lived on Marshall Avenue in a duplex house shared with my paternal grandmother who taught classical piano. My childhood spanned the Great Depression era when many families kept gardens for canning and raised chickens for eggs and meat. I did my share of hoeing corn. I attended St. Vincent's Catholic School for eight grades then attended Triadelphia High School, a public school.

My first near-death experience occurred during the winter of my sophomore year of high school, when I missed—by five minutes—being caught, crushed and taken out with thawing ice I had unsuccessfully tried to skate on.

During my junior year at Triadelphia High, I participated in an optional body development program for all junior and senior boys anticipating serving their country. In September of my senior year, I decided to enlist in the United States navy and become a sailor. My father didn't hesitate signing the necessary documents for my enlistment since I would become eligible for the draft on my eighteenth birthday in December.

By October 1, 1943, I found myself at Great Lakes naval training station in Illinois. I was now a boot with skinned head, double-soled shoes and leggings. While there, I marched what seemed to be miles, steel wooled the black shoe marks from the barracks' wooden floor, cleaned windows, and was given my share of "happy hours," which was punishment for some or any minor infraction.

In early December, after approximately nine weeks of training, I graduated as seaman second class and was given boot leave.

I had always enjoyed working with my hands building model airplanes, repairing bicycles, etc. as a young kid and had hoped to be assigned to a naval motor or machinist school, but that was not to be. From 2000 hours until midnight Christmas Eve 1943 (my first Christmas away from home), I found myself on guard duty, carrying a dummy rifle on my shoulder and walking inside the fence of the Navy Signal School at the University of Illinois campus in Champaign, Illinois. The navy had decided to make me a signalman.

My training at signal school lasted four months. While there, I learned to send and receive semaphore, send and receive Morse code by light and equally important, to identify all those pretty colored flags one normally sees hanging from a ship's yard-arm and waving in the breeze. Upon completion of signal training, I graduated seaman first class (more money) and was given a short leave.

Sometime in early May 1944, some of us were sent to Shoemaker naval station in California where sailors were billeted while awaiting assignment to a ship or shore station. In short order, Ken Lanter (another signalman) and I were assigned to the USS *Indianapolis* which was docked somewhere in San Francisco.

The navy transported Lanter and me, along with other young sailors, to the *Indianapolis*. We went aboard via gangplank and were directed by the officer of the deck to the compartment immediately beneath the quarterdeck where we stowed our hammocks and sea bags. Immediately we all were put to work loading ammunition, which consisted of shells in long metal containers.

We loaded ammunition all day until early evening, somehow missing lunch. Having worked up quite an appetite, we had to ask about chow and only then were we shown to the mess hall and our first meal aboard. I thought the meal good, particularly the fresh bread. Most of us decided then we had found a good home.

After a couple days of living out of our sea bags and sleeping in our hammocks, Wojiechowski, a ship's company signalman, found and escorted Lanter and me to the signal bridge. There, we were assigned a sleeping compartment, a sleeping rack, a locker, and given our watch schedule. Following several days of becoming acquainted with other signalmen, standing watch, inspection, and the like, we finally sailed out of Frisco Bay for Pearl Harbor and beyond.

It was only a short time after leaving port that the gyrations of the ship caused me to become extremely seasick. Someone on the signal bridge handed me a bucket to use and this I did while kneeling on the signal bridge deck.

My first introduction to actual warfare was during the invasion of Saipan in the Marianas. We were bombarding Japanese installations ashore while being shelled by enemy artillery located somewhere high in the hills. Captain Johnson cleverly maneuvered our ship, moving it slowly starboard or port while at the same time going forward or reverse. The enemy shells would land where we had just been. I can remember the sound of their shells as they passed overhead and recall how most everyone instinctively crouched down. I believe we all were quite apprehensive at the time and I recall particularly one older signalman who took shelter in a bulkhead recess, sitting on the deck with knees pulled to his chest and looking petrified with fear. I learned later he had survived the hell of the Pearl Harbor attack by the Japanese. We did take a hit that day; fortunately, the shell failed to explode.

Another admiral who had previously come aboard and was on the signal bridge with Admiral Spruance was trying to persuade Spruance to have the high smokestack of the sugar mill ashore blown up just to see it tumble down. Admiral Spruance wouldn't comply—at least not that day. Sometime after the war, it was reported the Japanese spotter for the artillery that had shelled us was inside the stack; however, I never heard how we found this out and or whether the smokestack was blown away.

Our ship was stationed off Saipan for a considerable time after the invasion. Many nights while fighting was still in progress ashore, we illuminated the battle area with star shells. During the day, I can't recall much (if any) activity involving the firing of our guns.

In the waning days of the Saipan invasion, the putrid stench of decaying bodies hung in the air far out from shore. The flies, which were quite large and not very skittish, were everywhere. The ship's carpenter shop manufactured a hundred or more fly swatters which consisted of a 4-inch by 6-inch piece of canvas attached to a stick. All watches were issued a fly swatter and many hundreds of flies met their demise.

My last vivid memory of Saipan occurred when leaving the area. I was looking at the water near the shore and noticed a man in the water with his arm raised. At first, I thought this man was waving for help. Immediately I looked through the telescope and realized he was a dead bloated Japanese man, floating with legs and torso submerged with his shoulders, head, and raised right arm above the water. Sayonara!

The *Indianapolis* was soon involved in the invasions of Tinian, Guam, Palau, and carrier raids on Tokyo where our ships at night turned searchlights to the sky so our returning aircraft, which were running low on fuel, could easily find our carriers. Some of our aviators did have to ditch after running out of fuel.

Iwo Jima was our next engagement. There the *Indianapolis,* with Admiral Spruance aboard, participated in pre-invasion bombardment. There again, I looked down into a landing craft loaded with marines and felt fortunate not to be one of them. Admiral Spruance who was on the signal bridge, asked me how I would feel if I were in those marines shoes? I answered, "I would be scared to death, sir." He replied, "I'm sure they are too." That was the only time the admiral had ever spoken to me directly.

A short time after the Iwo invasion, with fighting still going on, I was involved with a message saying that a B-29 bomber returning from a bombing run on Japan was going to have to land on the unsecured island's airfield. We all watched that B-29 come in and go out of our sight as it landed on the Iwo airfield. To this day, I never have heard if that B-29 survived the landing or the gunfire.

Our next port of call was Okinawa with its green vegetation and mountains. I paid particular attention to the horseshoe-shaped tombs, which I observed through field glasses and telescope. These tombs were not destroyed by our gunfire if my memory is correct.

Our invasion fleet would bombard during the day and retire to sea at night.

Sometimes it was necessary to lay a smoke screen when Japanese kamikazes (suicide planes) were threatening.

It was March 31, 1945 and I had been on the midnight to 0400 watch. I was asleep in my sack when awakened around 0730 by another signalman and told the watch was being doubled. I was again to go on watch at 0800. Of course I grumbled about just getting off watch, but got up, got dressed and went to the mess hall for breakfast. Halfway through my breakfast of beans and cornbread, two other signalmen joined me. I finished eating several minutes before 0800 and immediately went to the signal bridge and proceeded to shine my shoes prior to taking my station at 0800.

I heard a tremendously loud roar coming from above, looked up, and to my horror saw a kamikaze in a power dive headed directly for me on the port side of the signal bridge. Its engine and spinning propeller looked huge. Immediately I ran forward several feet, dove to the deck, buried my head in my arms, and the plane struck the ship. It felt like the ship had been picked up and was being shaken violently; then shortly, the shaking stopped. Since the ship had been moving forward about 25 feet per second while the plane was in its descent, it didn't hit the signal bridge at all; instead, it struck aft beyond the port hangar near the head. Its bomb went through the ship's main deck, through the mess hall area where I had just finished breakfast, on through the mess hall deck, the sleeping compartment below, the fuel oil tanks, and finally the ship's hull, before exploding in the water directly beneath the ship, damaging the hull and the number four screw shaft.

The seawater rushed into the ruptured fuel tank, forcing its contents up into my sleeping compartment (where I had just been sleeping) flooding it with oil and seawater, and drowning several sailors. We had many casualties—nine men dead. Oh, what a somber experience when we buried them. John Diamond, one of the signalmen who had joined me at breakfast, was wounded and sent somewhere off the ship for care. This kamikaze incident was the second time in my life that I knowingly missed certain death by a few minutes. Had I not been called for doubling of the watch, that fuel oil and water would have drowned me also. Hatches had been closed and dogged to prevent additional flooding and eventual sinking; however, our stern was quite low in the water.

We were detached from the Task Unit and preceded on various courses and speed under our own power off Okinawa, eventually steaming at about 8 knots to anchorage at Kerama Retto.

We were anchored at Kerama Retto for a full week while a salvage tug tied alongside our port stern investigated the damage and made temporary repairs to our hull. While there, the entire fleet of ships (many of which were damaged) was constantly on alert for and often under attack by kamikazes. I witnessed several ships hit and particularly recall the atomic-bomb-like explosion of one of our tankers when struck by one of those devils.

We left Kerama Retto on Saturday, April 7, 1945 in convoy with nine APA's and five anti-submarine vessels sailing for Guam. Everyone aboard felt relief from the extreme stress of being under attack by kamikazes.

We arrived at APRA Harbor Guam on Wednesday, April 11, 1945 and stayed until Sunday, April 15, 1945. While there, further repair to the ship's damaged hull was made, passengers disembarked, nearly 50 crew members transferred off, and several replacement crew members came aboard. About one third of the crew went ashore on a recreation party. We even had two crew members returned to ship under arrest by shore patrol and made prisoners at large. The ship unloaded some aviation gasoline and took on fuel oil and thousands of gallons of fresh water, etc.

Underway again on Sunday, April 15, 1945, we headed for Pearl Harbor alone, except for the USS *Adams* DM27, our anti-submarine screen. Our ship held AA target practice that morning and five minutes of silence in commemoration of our late president and commander-in-chief, Franklin D. Roosevelt. The following day memorial services were held for him. (Taken from ship's log.)

During our voyage to Pearl via Eniwetok, we launched and recovered our plane several times for anti-submarine patrol and held gunnery exercises. We had picked up a second escort, the USS *Cochlan* DD606, which with the *Adams* accompanied us to Pearl Harbor. We arrived there Tuesday, April 24, 1945. We departed Pearl Thursday, April 26, 1945 and sailed independently for the States arriving Wednesday, May 2, 1945 at San Francisco, where we went into dry dock at Mare Island on May 5, 1945 for approximately 49 days. Then our ship was relocated and moored at Pier 22S navy yard at Mare Island for completion of repairs and overhaul.

Approximately 400 sailors and officers (one-third of the crew) were given 15 days' leave plus some travel time. Upon their return, the second third of the crew would be given their 15 days plus travel. I elected to be in the last third to go on shore leave and lucked out. When on leave at home, I received a telegram saying my leave was extended 5 days. I surmised this extension was granted because we had done most of the initial work, such as chipping paint, and were now being rewarded.

After my leave, I returned to my ship at Mare Island and was surprised and saddened that our signal officer, Mr. Fisher whom we all thought a lot of, had transferred. Mr. Hill, a young ensign who was later lost at sea, replaced him.

The *Indianapolis* was looking like a queen. She had been repaired, repainted, and fitted with the latest weaponry and associated equipment in preparation for the forthcoming invasion of the Japanese mainland, and I was proud and happy to be one of her crew.

We had heard the *Indianapolis* was to sail for Leyte in the Philippines and there join with other ships of the fleet for maneuvers in preparation for that invasion.

We left Mare Island and shortly afterwards again docked at Hunters Point. There we took on a huge wooden crate, which I watched hoisted aboard by the ship's crane, placed upon the quarterdeck, then moved into the port hangar where it remained under 24-hour marine guard to its destination.

It was reported another container or two was brought aboard and placed in a cabin in officer country; however, I wasn't a witness.

We sailed out of Frisco and were immediately under the surveillance of a navy blimp, which stayed with us for an extremely long time acting as anti-submarine patrol. We were churning up quite a wake doing something like 30 knots continuously, the entire way to Pearl Harbor. We arrived there in record time.

With little delay, after having her fuel tanks topped off, the *Indianapolis* was again on her way at high speed for the far reaches of the Pacific and arrived at Tinian where the B-29 air base was located—again in record time. We anchored and soon were visited by an LCI full of brass hats. In short order, the huge crate was loaded into the LCI, which soon thereafter, shoved off for the island. Unknown to us, we had just delivered some of the components of the atomic bomb that which was to be dropped on Hiroshima.

Shortly we weighed anchor and again were underway. After a little anti-aircraft gunnery, we headed for Guam, arriving there the next morning, Friday, July 25, 1945. Captain McVay had gone ashore for briefing, and while there had requested an escort but was informed none was necessary. The ship was again refueled in preparation for our departure.

We departed APRA Harbor, Guam on Saturday morning, July 28, 1945 for Leyte in the Philippines, where we were to arrive Tuesday morning, July 31, 1945. Unescorted, we were cruising at a leisurely 17 knots, which to all appearances, would make this a pleasure cruise. For wasn't it true the Japanese fleet had lost practically all its major ships in previous engagements with our fleet and—other than a few submarines—presented very little threat to our ships in this theater?

Sunday night, July 29, 1945, the *Indianapolis* was several hundred miles west of Guam in the middle of the Philippine Sea. I had showered late, dressed, and with my bedding, had gone to the signal bridge where we signalmen not on watch were permitted to sleep on the deck at night. In the tropics, sleeping on the deck topside was done by much of the crew because most sleeping compartments were like saunas.

Around midnight, I was awakened by the most violent shaking and explosions that one could imagine. It was as though some giant was using this 15,000-ton, 610-foot-long cruiser for a cocktail shaker and we were the ingredients. After what seemed ages, the violent gyrations ceased along with most of the explosions. It was then I heard the agonizing screams of men who were being burned alive in the internal fires below. Their screams seemed to last forever...then they suddenly ceased.

Not knowing how extensively the ship had been damaged, we signalmen who were on the signal bridge high above the main deck immediately donned kapok life jackets. Some of the signalmen prepared the classified material in a weighted bag for jettison.

The ship was still moving forward on an even keel at what seemed the same speed as earlier in the evening. Off our port side, I distinctly noticed the frothy foam of our wake and thought we must have made a U-turn or the ship was running in a large circle. Also I noticed some of the gun crews were manning their guns. Most of the noise, screams, and shouting had subsided and Carpenter, a signalman, was sweeping up the spilled sugar and coffee from the signal bridge coffee station. I thought everything was going to be okay.

Suddenly, the ship listed sharply starboard and immediately we all knew for certain that we were in for real trouble. I vaguely remember Captain McVay had come down to the signal bridge and met Mr. Flynn, the executive officer who just then was returning from down below where he apparently evaluated the damage and was now at the top of the bridge ladder. They talked out of my hearing, but the order to abandon ship was given shortly and passed by word of mouth, since all communication by phone or speaker was impossible.

The ship continued rolling slowly starboard while simultaneously going down by the bow. Along with other signalmen, I hurried down the long ladder to the deck immediately beneath the signal bridge. The ship was rolling onto her starboard side at an increased rate now, and everything was mass confusion. Sailors were rushing to the port rail and going over the side into the water. It certainly wasn't an orderly abandonment, for everyone's heart was filled with fear of being sucked under with the ship.

I recall Lt. Hill, clad only in his underwear, trying in vain to release a life raft and requesting us to give him a hand. He said, "You'll never make it without a raft." Having just gone over the poop deck rail and starting down to the last deck when he said those words, I hesitated momentarily in my descent but could feel the ship rolling and decided not to climb back up to assist him, nor did I look back to see if he succeeded in getting help.

The ship was now listing at least 30 degrees. Another signalman and I climbed over the last life line and literally half jumped, half slid down the port hull deep into the water. Normally, when one goes under the water, the expectation is to come up through water, breaking the surface. However, we came up through what seemed to be a couple inches of thick black fuel oil that had leaked profusely from the ship's ruptured tanks and was now floating on the surface. Unfortunately, the oil covered my body with some going into my nose and eyes. Fortunately, the oil did not catch fire; otherwise, in all probability, no one would have survived.

I swam away from the ship as fast as possible; luckily the surface current was going my way. Soon I exited the heavy oil slick and continued swimming away until I was a safe distance from our sinking ship. Only then did I stop and turn to look at her. She was standing straight up on end with her bow down under, and she had revolved 180 degrees. It appeared at least half of her was still above the water line—just standing there like a tall building, the ship's black silhouette on this black-ink sea cast against the background of an extremely overcast and poorly moonlit sky. Momentarily, she continued to stand there, seemingly motionless; then slowly, ever so slowly, she started to descend, picking up speed and then, with that final plunge, disappearing beneath the surface.

Although I didn't then, I later wondered and oh yes, still do wonder about the horrifying ordeal faced by those sailors who were still aboard when our ship went down. Those trapped men maybe hurt or maybe not, sealed in a dogged-closed hatch compartment surrounded by total darkness, possibly only hearing the cries and sobs of others or the pounding of their own hearts and then, the loud groaning of the compartment steel as the ever-increasing water pressure prepared its crushing blow of that compartment tomb. I think and dwell on this, placing myself there. Then, imagining the horror they must have felt, I begin to cry and say, "Oh my God, what a terrible way to die!"

What a shock—beyond belief! I had been comfortably asleep on the signal bridge deck just 15 or so minutes prior, and now my ship was gone. I was in the ocean among very large white capping swells, all wet, covered with smelly fuel oil and hearing distant cries for help coming out of the darkness.

Eventually a group of 25 or more survivors gathered around a floater net and I was happy to be one of them. At first some of the group related what they had experienced aboard after the explosions. Then the possibility of a distress signal having gotten off was discussed, but no one seemed to know. We all knew and agreed the ship was due in Leyte Tuesday morning and all felt assured the navy would come looking for us when we didn't show. This was our hope, our "ace in the hole!"

Actually, an SOS had been successfully transmitted from the ship's radio shack 2 and was received in the Philippines; however, it was discounted by NAVY BRASS as a Japanese ruse.

Someone in the group suggested we pray, so all of us prayed the "Our Father" aloud, then all went silent. I decided to maybe help morale by singing all the marching songs we signal trainees learned while marching to classes at the University of Illinois. So I sang, and as expected when I finished, no one clapped, no one spoke a word, nothing but complete silence was the order of the day. For sometime that Sunday night, our group had been silently swaying back and forth and bobbing up and down with the ocean swells. Then someone regurgitated, then another and another; finally I too, along with most all the others, became seasick and vomited or had the dry heaves. I heard no other sound from anyone through the night except the retching, for all of us had become like zombies. Time stood still.

Dawn, and then morning finally came. We scattered somewhat from our cluster around the floating net but remained relatively close to one another. Someone hollered, "SHARK!" Immediately we all thrashed the water and screamed, thinking the noise and commotion would frighten the shark away. We had four shark alarms that Monday morning, each accompanied with thrashing and screaming, but I never saw the sharks.

We all seemed to scatter more, and I swam some, looking for whatever. I ran into Fred Kouski, who was from Bridgeport, Ohio just across the river from my hometown. Fred had been burned badly by fire below deck, leaving him in bad shape, and there was no way to help him. Years later, I learned that Fred had died on Tuesday.

As Monday wore on, the sun's direct heat as well as that reflected from the water's mirror surface was starting to have disastrous effect, for there was no escaping its merciless fire. What a relief when it dipped into the ocean at horizon's edge and was gone.

The evening became night and the night became chilly and seemed to last for eternity. I recall it was during this Monday night that an unexplained round green light which appeared to be quite steady was seen. It reminded me of the standard signal bridge light with a green filter. When this light was seen, word was passed to remain silent for fear it might be a Japanese sub, which we thought would machine-gun us. Several minutes passed and the light disappeared.

When dawn came that Tuesday morning, we waited with great anticipation for the sun with all its fiery brilliance to again rise and warm our shivering bodies. This was the morning of our ship's scheduled arrival at Leyte, and when she didn't show there, the navy would come looking for us and we would be rescued. (Dream on sailor boy!)

Sometime around midday, I was swimming a slow breast stroke and going somewhat with the current when I came down from the top of a huge swell and ran into several scattered survivors, one of whom was Father Conway, our chaplain. Being Catholic, I was most happy to see him since I hadn't been to confession for some time. I asked Father Conway if he would hear my confession; however, due to the extreme circumstances, he waived confession and gave me absolution. It is difficult to explain the feeling of relief that came over me when he finished with the sign of the cross. I was elated and religiously prepared to die. In this group also were Dr. Haynes, the ship's medical doctor and the marine commander, Captain Parke.

With this group there also were cries of "SHARK" several times. Once again I didn't see any sharks or shark fins that day or any day out there. Years after the rescue, Dr. Haynes stated in a published article he had counted eighty-eight shark attacks on cadavers in two days; rescue vessels recovering bodies refer to many as being mutilated or skeletonized, and fellow survivors tell me of witnessing actual attacks on live survivors and also say sharks were always beneath us. Thank God I looked down only twice.

At some point Tuesday I ran into Frank, another signalman with whom I spent considerable time exploring the area; that is, we swam to other groups, which we could see when atop swells at the same time. Our thinking was that they might have food or water, for we certainly had nothing and the hunger and thirst were always there.

Father Conway was constantly swimming from one injured or suffering survivor to another trying to comfort them. Eventually he exhausted himself, became incoherent, and died.

Captain Parke also was constantly trying to assist and comfort his marines who were suffering from injuries or burns and were incessantly, with pleading voices, calling out, "Captain Parke, Captain Parke." Captain Parke eventually exhausted himself physically and mentally and finally succumbed.

All during Tuesday, we kept watching for those rescue planes the navy would send out searching for the *Indianapolis*. Evening arrived and still no planes; darkness fell and they never showed; of course, we were overcome with despair, knowing then, they would never come.

Sometime Tuesday night I found myself all alone in the darkness, having drifted away from the other survivors. The sea was its usual blackness but seemed to emit minute flashes of light, which I did not question.

For the first time since being immersed in that liquid grave, my mind became slightly, just slightly, veiled; however, the fear of being all alone in that vast sea prevailed and I began calling out, "Anybody out there, anybody out there?" Eventually I got an answer and requested whoever it was to come for me—but to no avail. So I contrived a story of floating boxes and eventually a lone survivor swam to me. It was Todd Hickey, a radioman whom I was well acquainted with, having done 30 days mess duty together. He asked about the boxes and I pointed saying, "Out there." Without hesitation, he swam the direction I had pointed. Todd Hickey wasn't rescued but his body was found and buried Sunday, August 5, 1945, two days after the 317 were rescued. I still wonder if I was responsible for him not being rescued.

Harry Todd Hickey, radioman third class was a very likeable, congenial, out-going person and an accomplished cartoonist who frequently produced cartoon drawings of many different shipboard functions and situations. In 1944 he drew a cartoon of activity on the signal bridge and presented it to me. That cartoon is still in my possession and is treasured. Had Hickey survived, he could have been a very successful cartoonist. (A copy of the cartoon is in the middle of this book.)

Somehow the chilly night turned into day with the usual welcoming of the sun. Besides being hungry, thirsty, and sunburned that Wednesday morning, my vision had become somewhat blurred and my eyes felt full of grit, which I attributed to oil and salt residue.

Sometime during late morning I had lost contact with Frank but chanced upon another signalman, John Diamond, who had been wounded at Okinawa by the kamikaze attack. John also was having similar eye problems. Since trying to wipe the oil and salt residue from our eyes with our hands only worsened the condition, we decided to lick each other's eyes out. This was a crude but very effective remedy providing nearly complete relief.

As the day wore on, more survivors became delirious and were like unmanageable drunks; others wanted to remove their jackets and swim for some figment of their imagination.

I came across a marine with whom I started a conversation (big mistake)! He asked me to swim to Pearl Harbor with him and when I told him "No, it's too far," he firmly grabbed my throat with both hands. He didn't squeeze, but continued to hold on. While I was pleading my case, out of the blue popped good old Frank saying, "Hey friend, what's going on?" Man was I ever glad to see Frank! Almost immediately, the marine released me and with no more discussion, Frank and I departed the area of that deranged marine. Had Frank not intervened, I might have had a battle for life and possibly met my demise, for I wasn't sharp enough to have told the marine, "OK, lead the way!"

One cannot sleep in a life jacket, at least not for very long. On several occasions, upon dozing off and before my face would fall forward into the water awakening me, I dreamed of being in some restaurant (one time at Coney Island, where I had never been) drinking ice tea, lemonade or even beer, and always in my dream the drink was salty. In reality, I had been sipping salt water.

My first hallucination occurred that Wednesday with the realness of life. Several Arabs on as many camels were circling me and gradually closing in for the capture. I was cursing them in sound naval profanity (which I had learned aboard ship) but they continued closing in on me. Just when I could have reached out and touched them, they vanished and I—completely in shock—looked around and saw only my fellow survivors in oil-stained clothes and life jackets and on some, oil-stained headgear. (Long before this time, that heavy mask of oil that had covered many of us had been washed away from our head and hands by agitating seawater.)

Whether with Frank or alone, I was almost constantly swimming slowly. It gave me something to do, for time just stood still; however, in the end, the swimming proved exhausting.

During my swimming, I chanced upon another signalman who was receptive to any suggestion. I asked if he wished me to baptize him and he concurred. So, I proceeded with the ritual by scooping up seawater with a cupped hand, pouring it onto his uncapped head while saying the words, "I baptize you, etc...". When finished with the baptism, I asked him if he wanted me to drown him and again he answered "yes." So with both my hands atop his head, I pushed him under and momentarily held him there. Suddenly all hell broke loose, for he struggled free and came up fighting and striking, which aroused me from my stupor. I couldn't avoid his wrath, for when trying to escape by backing away, the current shoved me right back. After a few failed tries, the light came on and I realized it was necessary for me to circle him 180 degrees, then back off going with the current. The strategy was successful and I watched him become smaller as I back paddled away.

In early evening, Frank and I were again together. A short distance away, a survivor suddenly began frantically flailing his arms, striking the water and screaming. He continued this while we approached and stopped only when we shouted and placed our arms about him saying words of comfort and encouragement. With this man between us, Frank and I must have momentarily fallen asleep. We both awakened with a start, and Frank asked, "What happened?" The survivor we had calmed was no longer between us, that is, above the water. He was now dead, still between us, but below the surface. Had he died and our weight (from hanging onto him) forced him under, or had our weight (from holding him) forced him under and drowned him? If the latter, he struggled not, for that certainly would have awakened us, and with this reasoning, I take solace. When Frank and I parted, the survivor's body rose to the surface between us. We removed his jacket and watched as his body sank slowly into the depths.

Darkness fell and eventually the night turned into dawn and dawn into morning. I have absolutely no recollection of that Wednesday night.

Thursday morning Frank was still in the area and apparently in better shape than I. Realizing my strength and stamina were quickly dwindling and that I couldn't last another day, I related this to Frank. I added, "I am only 19 and I don't want to die," then for the first time, broke down and cried. Frank immediately spoke his usual famous words of encouragement, "You talk like a man with a __ _ _ !" That helped a lot.

Sometime later that morning, a huge, black, transparent ship appeared among us and stayed for quite awhile. I could see survivors floating beyond it and in it and then it was gone.

The sun was now high and getting mighty hot when suddenly we heard a roar and turned our heads toward the sound. There, quite close to the water, coming lickety split was an American bomber with bomb bay doors open. We cheered, waved our arms, and shouted, "We're saved, we're saved."

In reality, the plane's crew only saw unidentifiable bumps on the water. The plane made a second pass at the same altitude and we again yelled and waved as he passed, but there was no sign of recognition. The plane then gained altitude, circled and finally waved its wings. "Thank God!" we had finally been spotted.

The plane, piloted by Wilbur Gwinn, continued circling for a considerable time before being relieved by another plane. Other planes dropped rubber rafts and some were recovered, but most were too far away for retrieval since most of us had grown too weak to swim that distance.

I recall that a raft was recovered close by and Dr. Haynes was elected to get into it, possibly with a survivor who was badly injured. The raft had some fresh water and an extremely small ration of it was doled out to each survivor surrounding the raft. Later, a single cracker was being passed to each man. Being near the raft, I asked for and got an extra cracker to take to Frank who was on the far-side outer perimeter of the survivors. I placed the cracker in my mouth, intending to retrieve it for Frank upon arriving at his location. While swimming to him, the cracker grew soft in my mouth, and being extremely hungry, I was overcome with temptation and swallowed the cracker. Boy was Frank ever ticked when I arrived without that cracker!

Very early in the evening, we saw a PBY (which had landed) taxi by our group some fifty yards away and go out of sight beyond the swells.

An occasional plane would fly overhead and drop supplies into the water. In my weakened condition, I slowly drifted away from the survivors around Dr. Haynes' raft and ended up some distance away from them. I was watching a plane (possibly a PBM) circle when one of its crew tossed out something which struck the water about three to four feet in front of me. It was a sack-like container which had split open upon striking the water quickly expelling a green can of something. I grabbed for the green can, missed it, and watched in dismay as it slowly sank. Then a small miracle happened–rather a big miracle. Those in the plane must have observed what happened for when the plane circled again, another package was tossed out. It landed in the same way (bursting open) and at the same distance from me; however, this time knowing what to expect, I immediately grabbed the can when it exited the sack. Again, the can was green and contained water which I readily drank–"the whole thing."

How is it possible for an object being tossed from an airplane to hit the bull's-eye twice in a row? The odds are astronomical!

I was a good distance away from the group of survivors with Dr. Haynes. With my body growing weaker and my mind less clear, I felt like I was in a trance. Then it happened...I saw that PBY taxiing ahead of me, going to my left only to disappear behind the ocean swells. It had to turn around, but shortly it again appeared ahead of me passing to my right, towing a buoy with a long line. The buoy was moving on top of the water and was a few feet ahead and to my left. I swam forward as fast as possible and just as the buoy was passing in front of me I reached out to hook my right arm into the buoy and missed. I then despaired and became completely bewildered.

Sometime during the night, I awoke and found myself lying on and secured to the wing of that PBY with many other survivors. Some plane crew members were walking among us, doling out rations of water that I refused, already having had more than my share when I drank that can of water previously.

I–and I'm sure most of us–again fell asleep and upon awakening saw reflected light coming from the overcast sky. We were told it was the reflected light from the oncoming rescue vessel's searchlight.

The USS *Cecil J Doyle* arrived in our area a little after midnight and removed all 56 survivors from the PBY, plus one from the rubber raft tied to the plane. Adrian Marks, pilot of the PBY, having been guided by a second plane in the air as spotter, had taxied about retrieving isolated survivors until darkness fell and his operation had to cease.

I remember being placed in a steel-framed wire body stretcher, lowered to the *Doyle's* motor whaleboat, transported to the *Doyle* and hoisted aboard. Thereafter we were medically examined and our conditions recorded as serious to acute, and we were placed in a crew member's sack and watched over by one of the *Doyle's* crew while we slept.

The *Doyle* had taken 2 1/2 hours to remove us from the plane, and then spent several more hours searching for and retrieving 35 or more survivors in the vicinity of Mark's PBY.

Around 0730 Friday morning, we were alarmingly aroused by gunfire from the *Doyle's* guns. We survivors were quieted and told Marks' badly damaged plane was being sunk.

With a minimum of 92 survivors aboard, the *Doyle* set course for Peleliu in the Palau Islands. En route, those able to eat were given soft ice cream, but somehow I was missed. When the *Doyle* crewman watching over us came in and sat down on the upside-down bucket and proceeded to eat his ice cream, I inquired if there was any more ice cream, he said "No." When I told him that I didn't get any, he immediately got up, came over, and gave me his. Oh what a heavenly delight to eat, so smooth and refreshing and my first nourishment since the previous Sunday. I thank that man from the bottom of my heart.

The *Doyle* arrived at Peleliu Saturday, August 4, 1945, and all the survivors were transferred to the base hospital where we stayed two days. It was there at Peleliu that survivor Robert Shipman, who had been picked up by the USS *Register* APD 92, died. All the survivors from all the rescue vessels except the USS *Bassett* had been brought to Peleliu, and with the exception of Harold Shearer (who had been blinded) were transferred to the hospital ship *Tranquility* on Monday, August 6, 1945.

On the *Tranquility*, I stood up for the first time since my rescue, took my first shower, washed off the oil residue, had my saltwater ulcers treated, and my injured back looked at. We were given a wonderful full meal of which most was wasted because our stomachs had shrunk.

We arrived at Guam on Wednesday, August 8, 1945 and were admitted to Base Hospital 18 for treatment and recovery. Later, those able were transferred to the submarine rest camp for R & R. Finally, we were shipped via CVE *Hollandia* to San Diego and there given 30 days' survivor leave.

Should you ever sail the Pacific and cross that great trench, where wet hell reigned and many deaths met, go ever so quietly and softly pray, for you're o'er the graves of my buddies who died there one day.

FOOD FOR THOUGHT...

In San Francisco, just prior to our high-speed run to Tinian, Davis, our 310-pound second class signalman and ex-boxer, was memorizing a poem about sailors being buried at sea...HE WAS!

Saturday en route to Leyte, Singerman, a second class signalman spoke of his dream concerning an enemy submarine...HE MET HIS DEATH BY ONE!

Sometime during my four days and five nights in the ocean, my mother–back home in West Virginia–awakened from a dream during the night, sat up in bed, woke my father and said, "Paul's in trouble and he's swimming"... AND I WAS!

Front row: Survivor McGinnis, Marcella McGinnis, Kelly Gompers
Back row: Joe Gompers, Michael Gompers, Kathleen Gompers

NAME	McGUIGGAN, ROBERT M. S1C
STREET	3438 N Ottawa Ave
CITY	Chicago
STATE	IL 60634
PHONE	773 625 4994
ENTERED SERVICE FROM	Chicago, IL
PICKED UP BY	USS *Talbot* Tr USS *Register*
DIVISION	4th Division
DOB	9/29/22

FAMILY
Spouse: Gloria
Children: Mel McGuiggan (Kathy), Thomas McGuiggan (Joyce)
Grandchildren: Mel McGuiggan Jr., Traci Lynn McGuiggan

EXPERIENCE

I was born in Minneapolis, Minnesota but moved to McHenry and then to Chicago. I enlisted in the navy in November 1942 and was sent to boot camp in San Diego, California. While there I was sent to cook and baker school. After three weeks I was transferred to Treasure Island to be stationed aboard a ship. In the navy yard there were two ships: the USS *Indianapolis* and the USS *Minneapolis*. I took one look at the *Indy* and knew she was MY SHIP.

While aboard, I was transferred to the gunner's gang. The USS *Indianapolis* was an honorable ship. She was named President Roosevelt's ship of state and the flagship of the Fifth Fleet. My experience on the *Indy* took me to nine of the ten battles she participated in.

In March of 1945, a Japanese suicide plane hit the ship. Nine crewmen died. She limped to Mare Island for repairs. After repairs were made the ship and crew were to go on a shakedown cruise which was normally done after a ship was damaged. That's what the men were told. While at Hunters Point, the ship took on a secret cargo—so secret that even the crew didn't know what it was. The *Indy* was chosen because she was a fast ship. After dropping off the secret cargo at Tinian, the *Indy* was on her way to meet with the USS *Idaho* for target practice. At midnight, July 30, 1945, the ship was hit by two Japanese torpedoes. She sank in twelve minutes.

My nightmare was soon to begin...I had just finished the 8:00-12:00 a.m. watch. I took a shower, put on fresh dungarees, and went back to my hammock, which I had strung up on deck due to the stifling conditions below. When the first torpedo struck, I went to my battle station. A battery officer told me to launch one of the ship's aircraft. The aircraft had no fuel, and water was rising fast with the ship listing at a 30-degree angle on the starboard side. The aircraft couldn't be launched. I was one of the last to leave the ship. Several of the men were still aboard and I helped as many as I could get off the ship while trying to avoid the screws.

Despite being hit by two torpedoes, the ship was moving forward fast. I slid down the side of the ship and jumped into the water. I felt something hit me, which stunned me for a minute. When I came up for air, I could taste the oil in my mouth and felt a pain in my side. The ship was about to sink and I swam away as fast as I could. I was wearing a life jacket and carried a rubber one around my waist, which I blew up and gave to a man who didn't have one. I saw a large number of men in the distance. I turned around to see what was happening to my ship. She was slowly sinking into the water. I swam to the group I had seen before. We were to be together for the next five days.

We formed a circle, tying ourselves together using the straps of the life jackets and putting the most injured and those without life jackets in the center. At first none of us knew what was going on. At daylight we saw sharks circling us. They kept dragging men down. There was a man next to me with his head forward in the water. I thought he was asleep but when I pulled his head up he turned over and was gone from the waist down. From then on, I pulled my legs up and tried to hold myself in cannon ball position. This was hard to do but I was conscious of the sharks and couldn't bear to have my legs hanging down.

Some of the guys were delirious. They kept breaking away from the group and diving in an attempt to stab the sharks. We tried to stop them but they were going crazy. They didn't know what they were doing. A few of us led the group in prayers. It was all we could do. One of the most awful things we heard was planes overhead. They were too high to see us in the water. I had high hopes of being picked up. I had gotten engaged to Gloria while home on leave in November of 1944. I had to get back to her and the thought of that kept me going.

Finally, on the fourth day, I heard the roar of an aircraft. I was a trained spotter and recognized it as one of ours. It was Lt. Wilbur Gwinn. He had seen the men in the water and radioed to his base for help. A B-17 dropped rafts in the water. I decided to make a move even though I was weak. I tried to get my life jacket off but the knots were too tight. I managed to slide underneath it and swam to a raft. Two other guys swam with me but when I reached the raft they were gone.

I pulled the cord on the raft. I found another guy in the water. He was Hamer Campbell and I picked him up. I looked in the water for the first time. There were layers and layers of sharks. We took the paddles and started to hit at the water but stopped when we realized it would make them more frenzied. We went back to the group with the raft and found there were only 15 men left in our group of what had been about 150. We pulled them into the raft. We all fell asleep for the first time in days.

Suddenly a ship appeared. It was the USS *Talbot*. Coming alongside, they threw us a rope but we were too worn out to reach for it. Marksmen on the ship began shooting in the water. We didn't know what was happening. It seemed the ship put a man in the water to swim with a line to the raft. There were sharks in the water and they were shooting at them to protect him.

The *Talbot* picked up 23 of the 317 survivors. The *Talbot* didn't have a doctor aboard so we were transferred to the USS *Register*. It was there that I found my good buddy, Mike Kuryla, also a survivor. We had become good friends, both coming from Chicago. We still are good friends today, having stood up for each other's weddings and being godparents to each other's sons. We hugged and were glad we both survived.

When we got to Base 18 Hospital for care, nurse Louise Budrey took special care of all of us—such good care that she remained in my memory all these years. John Wassell, who lives in Fort Wayne, Indiana, located her for me, as she lives in Huntertown, Indiana. We have since become good friends and keep in touch regularly.

The USS *Hollandia* brought the survivors to the States.

After my honorable discharge in February 1946, I became a brick-layer. I helped to build the skyline of Chicago including the John Hancock Building and the Sears Tower, to name a few. On May 25, 1946 I married Gloria. We had two sons, Mel and Tom, and have two grandchildren, Mel Jr. and Traci Lynn.

My one regret—and I think about it all the time—is whether there was more I could have done to help the other men who didn't make it. I still have nightmares about it all, and I can't escape from my dreams.

Being co-treasurer of the USS *Indianapolis* Survivors Organization from 1960-2001 has meant a great deal to me. Being part of this great organization is very special to me.

NAME   McHENRY, LOREN S1C Radioman
STREET
CITY
STATE
PHONE
ENTERED SERVICE FROM   Chicago, IL
PICKED UP BY   USS *Bassett*
DIVISION
DOB   Deceased 2/85 Farmington, MO

FAMILY
Widow: Norma
Children: Charles McHenry
Grandchildren: Loren Charles McHenry IV, Jessica Erin McHenry

EXPERIENCE
Respectfully submitted by Survivor McHenry's son, Charles.

Dad never talked much about it until *Jaws* (the movie) came out. A reporter from the *St. Louis Post Dispatch* interviewed him for a story.

He was in the water the entire time. A shark took a guy right beside him. Dad was given a Bronze Star because he helped put men onto the plane when help arrived. I talked to a fellow at the survivors' reunion in 1995 (50th anniversary) who remembered being helped by my dad.

He was in the radio room and was among the last to leave the ship as they stayed and tried to get an SOS out. As the ship listed, the radio equipment threatened to fall on them. A radioman held the equipment up for them until they left. Dad didn't know what happened to that man but thought he did not leave the ship.

NAME McKENZIE, ERNEST S1C
STREET
CITY
STATE
PHONE
ENTERED SERVICE FROM Columbia, MO
PICKED UP BY USS *Bassett*
DIVISION
DOB Deceased

FAMILY

EXPERIENCE

Unable to contact any family members.

CHAPTER 184 SURVIVOR McKISSICK

NAME McKISSICK, CHARLES B. Lt. (jg)
STREET
CITY
STATE
PHONE
ENTERED SERVICE FROM McKinney, TX
PICKED UP BY USS *Doyle*
DIVISION
DOB Deceased 10/95 McKinney, TX

FAMILY

Widow: Loraine

EXPERIENCE

No response from family.

Respectfully submitted by Survivor Paul J. Murphy, Chairman, USS Indianapolis Survivors Organization.

Survivor McKissick devoted many years in the early stages of organizing our group. He was the first vice chairman and served as our chaplain for numerous years. We will be forever grateful. May he rest in peace.

NAME	McKLIN, HENRY T. S1C
STREET	
CITY	
STATE	
PHONE	
ENTERED SERVICE FROM	Madison Heights, MI
PICKED UP BY	USS *Bassett*
DIVISION	
DOB	Deceased

FAMILY

EXPERIENCE

Unable to contact any family members.

CHAPTER 186 SURVIVOR McLAIN

NAME	McLAIN, PATRICK S2C
STREET	18245 Hamann
CITY	Riverview
STATE	MI 48192
PHONE	734 285 0999
ENTERED SERVICE FROM	Detroit, MI
PICKED UP BY	USS *Register*
DIVISION	4th Division 5" Gun Crew
DOB	10/11/27

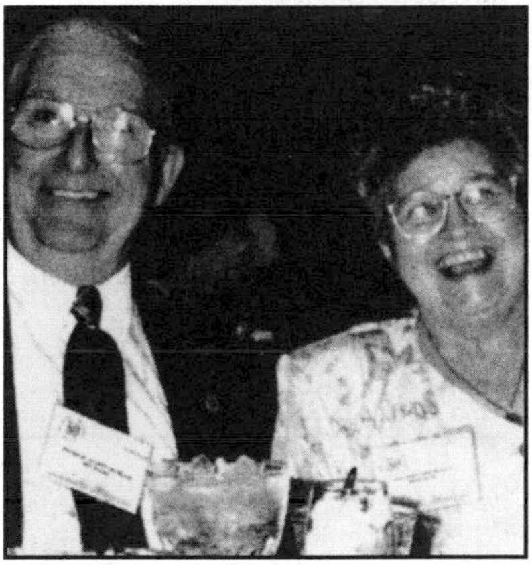

FAMILY

Spouse: Deloris
Children: Six
Grandchildren: Six

EXPERIENCE

I was standing on gun watch on hangar deck when we were hit on the starboard side. I could see the flash from torpedoes, left hangar deck, when we smelled gasoline. I went down to boat deck until the gasoline smell passed, then returned to the hangar deck to man the 5-inch gun. The ship began to list and was going down by the bow. We couldn't man guns anymore, so we passed life jackets and shifted to the starboard side of the hangar deck. The ship began to roll to starboard so fast we couldn't do anything. I washed overboard and came back up, maybe 50 yards away. The tail was pointed straight up and the screws were still turning.

We found four rafts, and survivors helped tie them together. Then we started to pick up a bunch of survivors who were in the water with life jackets. We also tried to pick up anything we could find. We found no water in the raft, but did find a bottle of malt pills and a can of Spam.

We survived the first night but had trouble with sharks the next day. They were trying to tear the rafts apart. We couldn't reach other survivors, so we decided to cut the rafts loose so we could be spotted more easily. There were four men on our raft. Jerry Mitchell, a yeoman, a radioman, and myself. It was decided to transfer the radioman and yeoman to another raft. We got Mike Kuryla and Giles McCoy. We began having trouble with sharks again and the other rafts were now out of sight.

On the fourth night, lights began signaling back and forth. McCoy, being a marine, had a gun and fired at the lights thinking it was a Japanese sub. The next day we prayed a lot. Mike had a rosary. A big storm came up in the afternoon and we were able to get a little water. After the storm, we spotted a plane and the pilot spotted us and waved to us. He made a circle and dropped markers, dipped his wings, and took off.

The USS *Register* picked us up in a landing craft. Mitchell and I were on the first craft and Mike and McCoy were in the second craft. We were then taken to Peleliu.

I am so grateful to God for letting me survive. I still have memories of what all of us went through and I still have nightmares, even after all these years.

CHAPTER 187   SURVIVOR McVAY

NAME	McVAY, CHARLES BUTLER III	
	CAPTAIN	
STREET		
CITY		
STATE		
PHONE		
ENTERED SERVICE FROM	New Orleans, LA	
PICKED UP BY	USS *Ringness*	
DIVISION		
DOB	Deceased 68	

FAMILY
Children: Charles Butler McVay IV (Elaine), Kimo Wilder McVay (Deceased) (Betsy)

EXPERIENCE
Respectfully submitted by Survivor McVay's son, Charles IV.

The first thing I noticed about my father upon his return to Washington, D.C. after the sinking of the *Indy* was the absence of the smile never far from his lips or his eyes. He had never been one to talk about himself, and now was no exception. I never questioned his silence on the tragedy, for he, as well as I, had been born navy juniors. After all, we'd been raised in the navy tradition. There was the right way, the wrong way and the "navy way" of doing things. Therefore, I found nothing wrong with this tradition until long after Dad's death.

I believe the first crack in the armor of my conviction of the navy's infallibility happened after my brother, Kimo, got a letter from the radioman on Leyte who received the SOS from the sinking *Indy*. Since Dad's court-martial had established that no SOS had ever been sent, the information on this cornerstone of the trial took me some time to digest. Of course, this was only the beginning of my disillusionment. Subsequently, Dan Kurzman's research and the publication of *Fatal Voyage* did much to further my reeducation about the navy way.

The final crumbling of my belief in this tradition occurred over the next few years while attending the survivors' reunions in Indianapolis. Their unanimous belief in the navy's culpability for this tragedy and their undying loyalty to my father was an inspiration to me. Ultimately, the objective of the survivors of this, the greatest tragedy in the history of the United States Navy, was met. Spearheaded by a young student, Hunter Scott of Florida, the miscarriage of justice finally reached the ears of the U.S. Congress. Senate hearings were held under the dedicated and skillful direction of Senators Warner and Smith of the Armed Services Committee. A join resolution was passed which stated the "Sense of Congress" that Dad should never have been court martialed. At long last, the USS *Indianapolis* and her crew had been recognized and honored, and her commanding officer, Charles B McVay III, Captain, USN had been exonerated.

Under most circumstances, the story would end here—after an appropriate period of celebration. Not so, for one more chapter would be added to the tale. Shortly after the survivors' meeting in August of 2001, I got a phone call from Captain Bill Toti, who had just been assigned to duty as aide to Secretary of the Navy England. Bill told me that he had related the events leading up to the Joint Resolution, and that Secretary England had expressed a desire to meet Senator Smith. Accordingly, Bill arranged the introduction. After the meeting, Secretary England immediately contacted the Navy JAG to insist that the Joint Resolution, in its entirety, be attached to my father's record ASAP.

Secretary England, apparently wanting to be sure his wishes were carried out, sent Captain Toti to read Dad's record and ascertain that the secretary's wishes

had been carried out. The
resolution had been
appended to Dad's service
record in its entirety.
However, Bill Toti
discovered something else
in Dad's record,
something we both found
utterly unbelievable.

This notation, dated
November 1945, stated
that Captain McVay had
been awarded the Bronze
Star and could not be
located. The award had
been returned for later
disposition. Bill asked me
if Dad had ever gotten this
award to which I
answered, "not to my
knowledge." I also told
Bill that, to my
knowledge, my father
went to his grave without

ever knowing he had ever been awarded this honor! After this information had
sunk in, it became apparent to me that the navy never intended to decorate my
father because the highly publicized court martial was being held less than five
miles away at the Washington Navy Yard.

The text of the award is as follows:

The President of the United States takes pleasure in presenting the BRONZE
STAR MEDAL to

CAPTAIN CHARLES B MCVAY III
UNITED STATES NAVY

For services as set forth in the following

CITATION:

For heroic achievement in connection with operations against the enemy while
serving as Commanding Officer of a United States Cruiser during the assault on
Okinawa from 21 March to 7 April 1945. Displaying outstanding leadership and
courage, Captain McVay caused his ship to successfully bombard enemy shore

installations and inflict heavy damage on the enemy. On 31 March 1945, his ship was attacked and seriously damaged by enemy aircraft, through his capable direction and skill, he caused the vessel to withdraw to a forward base without further damage. With determination and courage in combat, Captain McVay proved to be an inspiration to his crew and contributed materially to the success of the assault operations. Captain McVay's conduct throughout distinguished him among those performing duties of the same character.

The Combat Distinguishing Device is Authorized.

> For the President,
> Secretary of the Navy

Secretary England made sure that the award was reinstated and physically delivered to me. I will forever regret that my father died without knowledge of this honor.

CHAPTER 188   SURVIVOR McVAY

NAME	McVAY, RICHARD C. Yeoman 3C
STREET	
CITY	
STATE	
PHONE	
ENTERED SERVICE FROM	Logansport, IN
PICKED UP BY	USS *Bassett*
DIVISION	
DOB	Deceased 12/87 W. Lafayette, IN

FAMILY
Widow: Wilma McVay
Children: Charlotte Ann McVay Hicks, Gary Richard McVay and Brian Wayne McVay
Grandchildren: Stephanie Hicks

EXPERIENCE
Respectfully submitted by Survivor McVay's son, Gary McVay.
There were two McVays aboard the USS *Indianapolis*. One was the captain, and the other was a farm boy from Burnettsville, Indiana. The latter was my

father and I couldn't be prouder. When I was growing up my dad couldn't speak of his navy experience. It was too troubling. He had nightmares of sharks attacking him.

As the years passed he finally was able to speak of his experiences. In 1985, two years before his death, I recorded my father's story as he related it to a friend and me. These are his memories, and as in all memories, they aren't always factually correct. We hope you enjoy, "The Memories of Richard C. McVay."

I went in the navy February 22, 1944, spent six weeks in boot camp and back to Great Lakes. I was sent to California and picked up a troop ship that was sent to Honolulu. I remember seeing all of these beautiful, beautiful ships docked and of course I being a farm boy, this was something for me. A big guy comes along and says, "Can anybody down there type?" I had also heard that you never volunteer for anything, but that sounded pretty good to me. So I held up my hand. He said, "Okay, come with me."

His name was Homer Stone, and later he turned out to be one of the best friends that I've ever had. He took me to the ship (this was the first time I was ever aboard a ship) and said, "Let's see you type." Well, I couldn't even type the speed sentence. He said, "Well, you are a farm boy and you're probably a pretty good worker, so I will keep you and we will make a yeoman striker out of you."

In 1944 we participated in the Kwajelin and Eniwetok operation which included the Battle of the Philippine Sea, called the Marianas Turkey Shoot. Planes from our carriers and the fleet shot down 402 enemy planes. During this period we operated in the bombardment of Saipan, Guam, and later in the capture of Tinian Island. In February 1945, the Fifth Fleet, which the USS *Indianapolis* was part of, escorted the aircraft carriers to the Japanese home islands and the capture of Iwo Jima, then on to the Okinawa operation.

March 31, 1945, a Japanese suicide plane approached us. It was less than 2,000 feet away. We were not allowed to shoot unless the captain gave the order to shoot. Pretty soon, it sounded like a pop gun going off. The plane went through four decks. It didn't explode until it hit one of the shafts on the propeller underneath. It tore a big hole in the bottom of the ship, flooded seven compartments, and killed nine men. We went to a placed called Kerama Retto for temporary repairs, then back to California.

After repairs, we were told to make this real fast speed run. A large crate was brought aboard and guarded by marines. We unloaded the crate and proceeded to Leyte. On the night of July 30, a few minutes after midnight, Japanese submarine *I-58* fired several torpedoes and two hit us.

I was asleep in my office as there was a cold air duct that came down from the outside and it was cooler there. Ordinarily I would have been sleeping two decks below as I was just a seaman. I heard a terrific explosion and the door blew in. Fire swept through our office and when I put my bare feet on the deck I couldn't stand because the deck was so hot. I found my shoes–my eyebrows and hair were singed–and I walked out on the quarterdeck. I could not find a life jacket. I waited until the ship turned over on its side and I crawled off the top deck, over the railing, walked down the side of it and stuck a toe in the water. I remember what I thought, "I'm good and fat. I'll last a long time because I can swim." I then began swimming around in thousands and thousands of gallons of real heavy diesel fuel.

Finally Maurice Bell from Mobile, Alabama said, "Is that you, McVay?" He said, "I have a life jacket, hang on with me." I hung on with him until daybreak. Men were dying fast. I soon got a kapok jacket from a dead man. We found a group of about 120 men in one life raft. They also had a floater net. The water barrels were already diluted with salt water. There were two or three cans of Spam on this life raft. We found a flare gun and some malted pills. The extent of my eating and drinking during the 105 hours in the water was one malted pill. No water at all. I kept thinking that I was going to be sunburned to death. I had a quarter of an inch of oil all over my body, which actually saved my life. I kept saying prayers with our group. When there is nothing left, you pray. We thought surely a message got off. Many airplanes flew over us and guys would yell and scream.

Finally a plane was flying over and his antenna was not working. The pilot, Lt. Chuck Gwinn, saw this huge oil slick and opened his bomb bay doors. When he got down low, he saw hundreds of heads bobbing in the water. Lt. Gwinn called for help and a PBY came and dropped food, water, and whaleboats. Some marine kept slapping me and telling me to crank this thing. To this day, I don't remember who that marine was but I am sure he is alive today.

The next morning another PBY piloted by Adrian Marks who lived thirty miles from where I lived in Frankfurt, Indiana, landed in the water. The swells were very big for him to land. He taxied around and picked up 56 men. He then broke radio silence and asked for help.

I was picked up by the USS *Bassett*. They sent down wire baskets as we were too exhausted to climb the rope ladder. The man that took care of me was marvelous. He took me in and gave me a shower, some water in a glass, and an orange. I laid down and thought I was in heaven. It was a bed like an officer would have. Later I learned that the man was J. D. Arthur.

We were picked up and taken to the Fleet Hospital 18 in the Philippines. I was too sick to go with most of the men when they left the hospital. Later I joined them at a submarine rest camp on Guam. I'm telling you the submarine boys get treated great because we had ice cream on the table at every meal and everything that Mom would fix you at home during a holiday.

Finally we got to go home. I went on a train to Joliet, Illinois. I got off the train and hitchhiked to Lafayette, Indiana. I was so glad to see my wife. About 30 minutes went by and she said, "Would you like to see your new baby?" I was excited.

I was honorably discharged on April 6, 1946 and got to go home for good.

NAME	MEREDITH, CHARLES S1C
STREET	
CITY	
STATE	
PHONE	
ENTERED SERVICE FROM	Sylvania, OH
PICKED UP BY	USS *Bassett*
DIVISION	
DOB	Deceased 12/78

FAMILY

EXPERIENCE

Unable to contact any family members.

NAME	MESTAS, NESTOR A. WT 3C
STREET	
CITY	
STATE	
PHONE	
ENTERED SERVICE FROM	Walsenberg, CO
PICKED UP BY	USS *Talbot* tr USS *Register*
DIVISION	
DOB	1/22/21
	Deceased 8/01 Albany, CA

FAMILY

EXPERIENCE

Respectfully submitted by Survivor Mestas's dear friend Joan Lebow (wife of Survivor Cleatus Lebow).

July 30, 2000 at the mini-reunion in Broomfield, Colorado, I was sitting on the couch and Nestor came over and introduced himself. He said Cleatus was the only person he remembered from the ship. Their paths crossed coming and going from their duty on watch. He had been on the ship a few weeks when it was sunk.

Nestor began telling me his personal story of being on the USS *Indianapolis*. He was 17 years old and had been assigned to the USS *Honolulu*. The *Honolulu* was damaged, decommissioned, and taken out of service. He was not assigned to another ship at that time.

After two weeks his cousin talked him into taking an underwater demolition course. When he signed up for the course, the commanding officer could not find any papers on him. He was assigned immediately to the USS *Indianapolis*.

Nestor said the minute he stepped on board the *Indianapolis*, he had a premonition that something was going to happen. It scared him so bad that he got off the ship and went AWOL. After a week he was afraid he would be court-martialed so he went back and gave himself up. He said he had the same premonition when he got back on the ship, but he stayed this time. At this point, I asked him if he had told this to anyone and he replied, "No," that it was too awful and he began to cry.

I told him that Cleatus had had a feeling like something was going to happen and we had wondered if anyone else had had a premonition that the ship was going down. He continued, saying that he was in the group that was killing each other for their life jackets. I said, "Oh dear God, you mean you were in that group." He said that he went to sleep clutching his life jacket so no one could get it. I then replied, "You know the Lord was really protecting you to live through that ordeal."

He said his mother came to him in a dream and asked him if he would like to have a drink of water. He said, "Yes, I would like that more than anything in the world." He said he suddenly woke up and his mouth was full of water, so he spit it out immediately. I said, "Well, your mother saved your life." We were called in to eat, so that was the end of our conversation.

I have been haunted by his story ever since. Can you imagine the fright this young 17-year-old boy went through? It was bad enough being in the ocean four or five days, but seeing your comrades killing each other must have been horrifying.

I was so stunned I couldn't ask any questions at that time. I kept thinking about him and was looking forward to seeing him again at the reunion in 2001. I wanted to ask him some questions.

Upon our arrival in *Indianapolis*, the first thing we were told was that Nestor had passed away a few days before. I stood there in disbelief. My thoughts went back to the mini-reunion in Colorado...Nestor sharing his story with me. I asked Cleatus, "Why do you think he chose me to tell his story?" Cleatus said, "Because you are easy to talk to and you have compassion."

Nestor, thank you for sharing your story with me. I hope it brought healing and inner peace to you. This is my way of honoring you...by telling your story so the world will know.

Now you have heard the rest of the story. "May you rest in peace."

Joan Lebow, your friend (wife of survivor Cleatus Lebow)

Survivor Riggins, Rescue Crew Goodfriend, Survivor Bray, Survivor Stamm, Survivor Mestas, Marilyn Andrews. Colorado Mini-Reunion, July 2000.

CHAPTER 191   SURVIVOR MEYER

NAME	MEYER, CHARLES T. S2C
STREET	
CITY	
STATE	
PHONE	
ENTERED SERVICE FROM	Houston, TX
PICKED UP BY	USS *Bassett*
DIVISION	
DOB	Deceased 73

FAMILY

EXPERIENCE

Unable to contact any family members.

NAME   MIKLOAYEK, JOSEPH COX
STREET
CITY
STATE
PHONE
ENTERED SERVICE FROM   Detroit, MI
PICKED UP BY   USS *Bassett*
DIVISION
DOB   Deceased

FAMILY

EXPERIENCE
   Unable to contact any family members.

NAME   MILBRODT, GLEN L. S2C
STREET
CITY
STATE
PHONE
ENTERED SERVICE FROM   Akron, IA
PICKED UP BY   USS *Ringness*
DIVISION
DOB   2/1/27
                            Deceased 4/00 Akron, IA

FAMILY
Widow: Deloris Oltmanns Milbrodt
Children: Ken Milbrodt (Lynette), Arlen Milbrodt (Arlene),
Grandchildren: Matt Milbrodt, Mark Milbrodt, Michael Dickey

EXPERIENCE
   Respectfully submitted by Survivor Milbrodt's widow, Deloris, and family.
   Glen L. Milbrodt S2C was born February 1, 1927 on a farm near LeMars,
Iowa. His family then moved to Akron, where they settled permanently. In

January 1945 at the age of 17, Glen enlisted in the United States Navy. He completed boot camp training at the Great Lakes Naval Training Center in Illinois. He then was assigned to the USS *Indianapolis* on May 12, 1945.

On the evening of July 30, 1945, the USS *Indianapolis* was torpedoed. It was a very hot and humid July evening that was only cooled by an occasional breeze from the ocean. Glen was relieved of his watch by shipmate and best friend Kenny Beukema. Because it was so hot, Glen decided to stay on the top deck, to cool off and have a cigarette.

At the time the torpedo hit and following the many explosions, Glen's best friend Kenny Beukema was killed in action. For many years, as with many veterans, Glen asked the question, "Why did I live and why did he die?"

Within twelve minutes of being torpedoed, Glen and many of his shipmates had to abandon ship and jump into the ocean. He began swimming through sea water, diesel fuel, and debris. Fortunately, Glen swam into a life raft and was the first one to climb aboard the raft. Another shipmate climbed into the raft with no clothes on. Since Glen had just completed his watch and was fully clothed, he provided the survivor with his shirt. He literally gave him "the shirt off of his back."

For most of his life, Glen was unwilling and hesitant to discuss what he had experienced for the next five days in the life raft. On August 3, 1945, Glen's life raft was discovered by the crew of the USS *Ringness*. Glen was then taken by the *Ringness* to Peleliu. At Peleliu, he was treated for exposure and dehydration and responded quickly to the medical treatment.

As Glen was recuperating, a man from his hometown (Iowa) found him and sent an airmail letter to his parents about his health condition. The airmail letter, dated August 13, 1945, read as follows:

Dear Sir:

It gives me great pleasure to be able to be the person of the old hometown to give you the news of your son, Glen. As you must have been informed via official sources, Glen's ship had been sunk by enemy action. He among others, after several days in the waters of the war area, was picked up by an American warship and later transferred to a base hospital upon the island that my ship is at present stationed. I found Glen, or I should say, was informed that he was here by the Red Cross, so I immediately came ashore to see him. I am very pleased to say that, with the exception of a severe case of sunburn, he is in the best of health. You as a father can be very proud of his courage in carrying on through the hardships he has witnessed. Please do not worry about his health, as I assure you he is plenty healthy, and, with a little rest, he will be like he always was. It sure seems good to meet friends from the hometown. Another Akron man, Richard Bean is here also, so we will see he is not lonesome.

Respectfully

F. H. Myers, Lt. USN

Glen talked a lot about how amazing it was to have two men from his hometown find him while he was recuperating. It was great to see familiar faces after what he had experienced. A very special bond was formed for many years with these two men.

After recuperation and a short leave from the navy, Glen was stationed at the U.S. naval air base about 20 miles from Detroit, Michigan. He received an honorable discharge on July 12, 1946 and was awarded the Purple Heart. Upon returning home he sought employment with his father in the Plymouth CO-OP gas station. He was married to Deloris Oltmanns and they had two sons, Ken (Lynette) and Arlin (Arlene), and three grandsons. Glen worked for the Akron-Westfield School District as a custodial engineer for 23 years before his retirement. He passed away on April 20, 2000.

Glen and his family attended all the reunions (except one, because of his son's wedding) held in Indianapolis. It has been very beneficial and supportive to get together with other survivors and their families as all of us try to understand and comprehend what it was like being forgotten by the navy and spending four days in the ocean.

When interviewed by a television reporter in Indianapolis, Glen was asked the following question, "How often do you think of your *Indianapolis* experience?" Glen replied by saying, "Every time I see the blue sky, water, airplanes, boats, and men in uniform, I think of my experience and the sinking of the USS *Indianapolis*." The reporter stated, "Glen that is all the time." And Glen replied, "You are right."

This statement shows the powerful impact this experience had on Glen's life. It also demonstrates the physical and mental sacrifice that Glen, other survivors of the *Indianapolis,* and the many veterans of World War II have made for their country.

NAME	MINER, HERBERT J. II (Jack) RT2C
STREET	1309 Ridgewood Dr
CITY	Northbrook
STATE	IL 60062
PHONE	847 272 5630
ENTERED SERVICE FROM	Glencoe, IL
PICKED UP BY	USS *Bassett*
DIVISION	Radio
DOB	3/7/26

FAMILY

Spouse: Gloria (Muffy)
Children: Catherine, Nancy, David
Grandchildren: Rachel Guenther, Elizabeth
Guenther, David Guenther, Alexandra Miner, Jay Miner,
Christian Miner

EXPERIENCE

My career in the navy: I enlisted the day before my
18th birthday, March 7, 1944 after completing one semester at Yale University. I
was sent to radio technician school after boot camp, finishing in the spring of
1945 as a radio technician second-class.

On or about July 1, 1945 I was assigned to the USS *Indianapolis*, then in dry-
dock at Mare Island, California where it was being repaired after severe damage
at Okinawa. We went to sea on or about July 16, were torpedoed July 30 and
rescued in the predawn hours of August 3. So my "sea duty" during World War
II amounted to about 17 days–13 days were aboard ship and the balance up to
my chin in the ocean.

Our rescue ship, the USS *Bassett*, took us to Samar in the Philippines, where
we were immediately hospitalized. After a few days I was flown to Guam, first to
testify (see next paragraph regarding SOS message from ship) before CINCPAC
(Commander in Chief, Pacific), a board consisting of commanders, captains, and
admirals–all very intimidating to a second class petty officer–and second, to
recuperate at a rest camp for submariners–unlimited sleep and ice cream. Then it
was home for a survivor's leave, a trip to Washington, D.C. (this time to testify at
the Pentagon), and back out to the Pacific for radio duty on Carlson's Island (a
suburb of the island Kwajalein). Finally, in June of 1946, I was returned to
civilian life from Great Lakes naval base (North Chicago, Illinois) to my home in
Glencoe, Illinois, in time to make it back to college for a summer term to
complete my freshman year.

While we were in the water, I went through the same fear, thirst, general misery, and dementia as the rest of our bunch (perhaps 300 the first night, but only 158 or 159 left alive to be picked up the last night). However, there was one unique factor during this drama that made me slightly different from the rest; namely, a <u>certainty</u> that we would be picked up.

Right after the torpedoes hit, we radio technicians assembled in radio shack 2, where all the radio transmitters (as opposed to the receivers, which were all located in radio shack 1, the main radio shack, from where all messages were normally sent and received) were located. There were, I think, seven or eight of us, and we had no idea what had happened or what to do next. It was a little after midnight, and most of us had been asleep. Within a very short time, we were joined by Mr. Leonard Woods, our boss, a communications warrant officer. He was burned and covered with soot, but thoroughly in command of the situation. He had been sleeping in the forward part of the ship, near where the torpedoes hit. He knew that the cables connecting radio shack 1 with radio shack 2 had been severed, so no kind of message could be sent from radio shack 1.

He told me to warm up a certain transmitter, then he told us all to inflate our life belts and put them on. He then began to send an SOS message by using an emergency key attached to the transmitter. I <u>know</u> the message went out, because I stood right beside him and watched the needle jump in the power meter in the antenna circuit. I cannot remember how long he keyed–maybe 15 seconds or maybe two minutes–I don't know. By the time he finished, the ship had rolled at least 20 degrees to starboard, (the direction we were facing), and it was almost impossible to stand. He gave the "abandon ship!" order.

By the time I turned around, the shack was empty. As rapidly as I could, I left the shack, crawled down a ladder to the main deck (on the "low" side), and abandoned ship in what turned out to be a very awkward and un–seamanlike manner. Then the four days of horror began, but <u>I</u> knew that a distress message had been sent and that we would be found. I believe that my certainty of rescue gave me the little edge that assured my survival. I passed the word to all the men around me, making a major effort to keep up morale.

Only many years later did I learn that the SOS message had indeed been received by at least three stations, but for various reasons no action had been taken by any of them. At the time of the inquiries, the navy rejected my testimony. Being the only survivor of radio shack 2, there was no one to corroborate my story.

To what do I attribute my survival? To the above-mentioned radio message of course, but the three chief reasons were luck, luck, and luck. For example, my bunk was located about three decks below the main deck. If I had been in it, I would still be there. A few days before the sinking, my mattress had been stolen. Rather than sleep on bare springs, I was able to set up a cot in Battle II, a command post to be used in the event that Battle I (on the bridge) became unusable. Battle II was located just forward of radio shack 2. The two rooms formed a "doughnut" around the afterstack, above the main deck. When the torpedoes hit, I was two steps from radio shack 2.

Another example: when I reached the main deck while abandoning ship, I was on the "wrong" side. In trying to get to the high side, I had to grab the leg of a shipmate who had already begun to cross the deck, and pull myself up to get a new handhold. Well, this shipmate would have none of it. With a curse he kicked me loose, and I slid down the deck and directly into the water, without so much as a splash. The timing was such that the low side of the deck was awash just as I reached it.

I swam away as fast I could. When I stopped for breath, I turned to watch the silhouette of the ship, which had turned turtle, silently slip out of sight, bow first. If I had not been kicked overboard, so to speak, I would likely have been directly under the ship, pulled down with it.

Additional factors were that I was barely 19 years old, and thanks to the special war-time training at my high school and college, in top-notch physical condition. I was a good swimmer and had no fear of the water; life had treated me well up until then, probably much better than I deserved, and I strongly wanted it to continue.

What did I think about while in the water? Foremost were thoughts related to basic survival. These included such things as keeping my socks on so the sharks wouldn't bite, keeping a piece of shirt tied around my head for protection from the sun, keeping my good eye (the other was clogged with diesel oil) out of the water, resting in the life net when squares became available, avoiding men who had gone berserk sooner than I, and wondering why the many planes that flew overhead did not appear to see us. I did try to help some friends who weakened sooner than I.

How did the experience affect my life? It gave me a greater degree of self-confidence. It also made me more tolerant of life's many unimportant problems and more appreciative of life's simple pleasures. In all the intervening years I dreamed about it only once, a nightmare that recreated my worst memory–that of a dying friend slipping out of my grasp and slowly sinking through the crystal–clear water until he faded from sight. One dream like that is enough.

NAME	MITCHELL, JAMES E. S2C
STREET	
CITY	
STATE	
PHONE	
ENTERED SERVICE FROM	Savannah, GA
PICKED UP BY	USS *Bassett*
DIVISION	
DOB	Deceased

FAMILY

EXPERIENCE

Unable to contact any family members.

CHAPTER 196 SURVIVOR MITCHELL

NAME	MITCHELL, KENNETH E. S1C
STREET	
CITY	
STATE	
PHONE	
ENTERED SERVICE FROM	Mishawaka, IN
PICKED UP BY	USS *Bassett*
DIVISION	
DOB	Deceased

FAMILY

EXPERIENCE

Unable to contact any family members.

NAME	MITCHELL, NORVAL J. S2C
STREET	7206 Medallioni
CITY	Lansing
STATE	MI 48917
PHONE	517 323 1736
ENTERED SERVICE FROM	Lansing, MI
PICKED UP BY	USS *Register*
DIVISION	4th Division
DOB	12/25/27

FAMILY
Spouse: Doris
Children: Kathy Jacobs, Karen Ewing
Grandchildren: Anita, Jerry, Brent, Boe, Blake
Great–Grandchildren: Kristina, Jillisa

EXPERIENCE

I was a pot loader on a five inch gun, just coming on a midnight to four a.m. watch on the night of July 30. I was alone as the rest of the crew had not come up yet. There was a tremendous explosion on the front part of the ship. As I stood in the doorway to the number one stack, I stepped out and saw a big ball of fire coming right at me. There was no time to do anything. I fell flat on the deck as the fireball passed over the top of me. After the fireball passed, I got up and put on a life jacket. There were other life jackets in the storage room under the stack and I threw some of them out. The ship was starting to list heavily to starboard but I walked back to my gun and stayed with my gun.

The ship continued to list and I finally knew I had to leave. I got off my gun, reached up, grabbed the side of the ship and pulled myself onto the side of the ship. By the time I had done that, the ship was on its side and continuing to roll over. As it came bottom side up, I was walking up the ship. A rope fell from somewhere and wrapped around my right leg. I was trying to take the rope off my leg when the ship rolled all the way over. When I was thrown into the water, the rope came off my leg somehow, along with my shoe. At first I held my breath under water but finally just decided to breath normally. While I was under water I saw a great bright light. I know you see a great bright light just before death.

I do not know how long I was under water but when I came up there was a crate of potatoes and I wrapped my arm around it. As I looked at the ship, it came right straight up and down, the screws were still turning, and it sank from sight. Floating alone, I could hear voices but I could see no one. After a time, I do not know how long, Mike Kuryla came along in a life raft. I got on but I don't know if there was anybody else in the raft as I was so sick from all the oil and sea water I had swallowed. As we found other rafts we tied them together. At one time there were four or five rafts tied together. After about three days, we decided that we would improve our chances of being found if we cut the rafts apart. At no time did we think we would not be found or that the navy was not looking for us.

The rafts had a wooden grating for the bottom which was tied to a kapok ring, so we were always in the water. We had trouble with the bottoms of some of the rafts rotting out and the kapoks becoming water-logged. We were constantly surrounded by sharks. One afternoon it rained and we collected rain water in our shirts and drank it, forgetting that our clothes were soaked with salt water. I was completely blind for about 1 1/2 days, probably because of the fuel oil covering my body and the hot, glaring sun. Gradually my sight returned. I remember it being very cold at night.

On the fourth or fifth day we saw the PBY land and knew we would be picked up eventually. The next morning the waves were really high and it was raining but a PBY flew over and dropped dye and more rafts into the water. We did not try to get another raft because of the sharks that were around us.

When the USS *Register* picked us up, the sea boiled from the activity of the sharks; the sharks acted as if they knew we were leaving. The *Register* took us to an island where we were picked up by a hospital ship and taken to the submarine rests camp on Guam. From Guam, we went to San Diego.

CHAPTER 198   SURVIVOR MLADY

NAME	MLADY, CLARENCE C. S1C
STREET	
CITY	
STATE	
PHONE	
ENTERED SERVICE FROM	Cleveland, OH
PICKED UP BY	USS *Doyle*
DIVISION	
DOB	Deceased

FAMILY

EXPERIENCE

Unable to contact any family members.

NAME   MODESITT, GARL E. S2C
STREET
CITY
STATE
PHONE
ENTERED SERVICE FROM   Galloway, WV
PICKED UP BY   USS *Bassett*
DIVISION
DOB   Deceased 5/94

FAMILY

EXPERIENCE
Unable to contact any family members.

NAME   MODISHER, MELVIN
                        W. Lt.
STREET   2404 Loring St
CITY   San Diego
STATE   CA 92109
PHONE   858 581 8605
ENTERED SERVICE FROM   Erie, PA
PICKED UP BY   USS *Doyle*
DIVISION   Medical Division
DOB   5/9/16

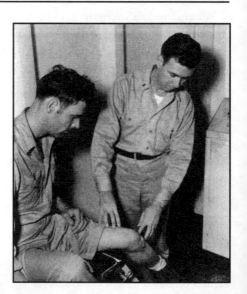

FAMILY
Spouse: Corla Lackland Modisher
(married 6/26/42)
Children: Brian George Modisher, Nua
Modisher Shores
Grandchildren: Scott Modisher, Craig Modisher

EXPERIENCE
The attack on Pearl Harbor found me halfway through medical school at
Temple University in Philadelphia. I joined a part of the navy V12 program and

was allowed to finish my studies, graduating December 16, 1943. I chose a civilian internship in a Philadelphia hospital which I completed the end of September 1944. The navy allowed me time to take my medical boards before arriving at Camp Perry, Virginia (near Williamsburg).

On October 9, 1944 I was in a pool of 40–50 new doctors waiting for permanent assignment. My orders arrived November 3, 1944, directing me to report to the flagship heavy cruiser, USS *Indianapolis* (CA-35). I arrived in San Francisco November 11, 1944, only to find that the ship was in dry-dock at nearby Mare Island, California.

When I arrived I found that I completed the medical staff of senior medical officer Lt. Comdr. L. L. Haynes, Lt. Cmdr. Earl Henry (dentist) and me, as junior medical officer. Fifteen hospital corpsmen, including the chief, completed the medical staff. I had relieved Lt. Bonar.

The *Indy* had trial runs off San Francisco in early December 1944 then headed south to San Diego for more training and exercises until January 3, 1945, when the ship headed for Pearl Harbor and points west. We spent Christmas and New Year in San Diego that year--little did I realize then it would be my home for 32 years (now 2002). I served on the *Indy* from that point until she sank July 30, 1945.

While recovering from our wounds on Guam, Admiral Spruance asked Dr. Haynes and me if he could help us get special orders for our next duty. We had taken care of the admiral and his staff medically when they were aboard. The result was that Dr. Haynes was sent to the Naval Hospital in Philadelphia for training in surgery. My orders were the same except at the Naval Hospital in Norfolk, Virginia. While I was at Norfolk, I was ordered to testify at Captain McVay's court-martial trial in Washington, D.C. (in December 1945-January 1946). My testimony helped to clear him on the charge of failing to give the orders to "abandon ship." I was discharged from the navy on June 8, 1946.

After that I had three years of special training in obstetrics–gynecology at the University of Cincinnati, followed by 17 years of private practice in Erie, Pennsylvania. We finally moved to California, where I have worked as a gynecologist for the state for five and one half years at their women's state prison. Since 1970 I have worked for the San Diego County Health Department and UCSD Medical School. I am currently Associate Clinical Professor of Reproductive Medicine at UCSD Medical School.

I have never been an active member of the USS Indianapolis Survivors Organization but have attended three reunions–the first in 1960, the second in 1970, and the third in 1985. The first two were wonderful but by 1985, we were getting older, affecting our memories, but our imaginations were running wild–more than I could take–so I promised myself, NO MORE REUNIONS. God bless you ALL!

NAME   MORAN, JOSEPH J. Radio1C
STREET
CITY
STATE
PHONE
ENTERED SERVICE FROM   Johnstown, PA
PICKED UP BY   USS *Ringness*
DIVISION
DOB   Deceased

FAMILY

EXPERIENCE
   Unable to contact any family members.

NAME   MORGAN, EUGENE S. S2
STREET   7936 10th Ave SW
CITY   Seattle
STATE   WA 98106
PHONE   206 767 4587
ENTERED SERVICE FROM   Seattle, WA
PICKED UP BY   USS *Bassett*
DIVISION   5th Div Master at Arms Force
DOB   9/14/20

FAMILY
Spouse: Elain Wavel Morgan (deceased 3/99)
Children: Julie, Bob, Mary Beth, Scott, Kelly
Grandchildren: 9
Great-Grandchildren: 2

EXPERIENCE
   I was born in Seattle, Washington on September 14,
1920 and graduated from Queen Anne High School in

1939. I was working at King County Courthouse when the war broke out. I enlisted in the navy on December 7, 1941 and left for San Diego Navy boot camp on December 13. Boot camp lasted about three weeks, and then I was sent to Bilboa Park Zoo which opened as a naval training school.

One reason I joined the navy was that one of my brothers was a baker first class aboard the USS *Indianapolis,* which was stationed at Pearl Harbor. We served together until my brother was transferred off the ship after the five Sullivan brothers lost their lives in the sinking of the USS *Juneau.*

I was aboard the USS *Indianapolis* for all ten battle stars that the ship earned. I also survived all the terror and suffering of five days in the shark-infested waters with no food or water.

The Purple Heart was given to me by Admiral Spruance for injuries suffered from the sinking and for being in the water for five days.

I was honorably discharged from the navy on November 27, 1945 in Brementon Navy Ship Yard in Washington.

After I got out of the navy, I joined the Seattle Fire Department on December 4, 1945 and retired from that job on December 13, 1972. I married Elain November 8, 1945 and we raised five children. Since retiring, I have enjoyed traveling in my trailer. I also enjoy attending the reunions of my shipmates as well as spending time with my children, grandchildren and great-grandchildren. I have one grandson in the navy, and he is serving on the USS *Brementon* SSN 698. One brother was also in the navy as a radioman in China.

CHAPTER 203   SURVIVOR MORGAN

NAME	MORGAN, GLENN G. BGM3
STREET	Rt 3 L 42
CITY	Franklin
STATE	TX 77856
PHONE	979 828 3936
ENTERED SERVICE FROM	Salem, Il
PICKED UP BY	USS *Ringness*
DIVISION	NAN Navigation Division
DOB	10/14/23

FAMILY

Spouse: Mertie Jo Lowe Morgan
Children: Thomas Michael Morgan
Grandchildren: Michele Aimee Morgan, Blaine Michael Morgan

EXPERIENCE

My association with the USS *Indianapolis* really began when I wrote my draft board in Great Bend, Kansas. Most of my friends had already been drafted yet, I had not received any "greetings" and thus became concerned. This did it, for I received my draft notice almost immediately.

I reported with two other draftees. We met at the railroad station in Salem, Illinois, and we were in Chicago the next morning on a short walk to the army center. The few minutes after we arrived may have changed my life completely. We entered a large room where a line of naked men were in line for a "short arm" inspection. One look left me somewhat dismayed and a little humiliated. Through the spaces between these naked bodies, I spotted a navy officer making his way down the hall. Quickly I asked my two friends whether they would like to join the Coast Guard. "How can we?" one replied. I sped around the end of the line and made my way down the hall.

Sure enough, the officer was sitting in his office and I asked if we might speak to him. He invited us in, and we explained that we would like to join the Coast Guard. He told us he doubted we could get in the Coast Guard but that if we went down the stairs and over to the next block we could join the navy or the marines. All three of us joined the navy and went to boot camp in the same company.

We were called to the Great Lakes naval training station to start our boot camp training. Here another interesting event took place. I took my nineteen dollar cornet to boot camp. My shipmates made it clear that they preferred that I practice in the "head." This was okay because the reverberation made me think I was really better than I was. That is when a series of events took place that I shall try to condense the best I can. Someone from the drum and bugle corps heard me and asked me if I would like to play in the corps. He told me I would get out of a lot of marching. I read some music for them and they signed me up.

When I was out of boot camp at last, Mertie Jo Lowe and I got married. A thirty-seven-dollar wedding ring, a twenty-mile bus ride, a J.P. and by golly, Mertie and I tied the knot. The J.P. was quite old and frail and spoke almost in a whisper. Later on reflection, Mertie and I wondered if those famous lasts words, "I now pronounce you man and wife" were perhaps his last. We took a bus ride back to Salem with joy in our hearts and adventure ahead.

I returned to boot camp and found that to my surprise I was rated a second-class bugler and surprise, surprise, I found also that I was in charge of a drum and bugle corps in the Thirty-first Regiment. I also had a counterpart, a drummer by the name of Vernon L. Turko. I was stationed there for three months then transferred to Treasure Island, California, where I was attached to a troop transport, the general tasker *H. Bliss*. While they were assembling a crew, I was sent to the gunnery and fire-fighting schools.

Mertie Jo then came to San Francisco and was employed by the army under a civil service contract. It was great to have Mertie Jo with me and everything was just fine when suddenly, after I returned from liberty, I was told to pack my gear—I was being transferred. I told these people they were mistaken. I was already attached to a ship. It was difficult to believe this simply made no difference to them. Off to Vallejo, California I went.

I was accompanied by another bugler, a fine fellow named Calvin Ball. We became good friends and little did we know what lay ahead. Mare Island naval repair base looked ominous and forbidding. The navy bus let us off at the end of a pier. With some feeling of apprehension we were directed to move down the pier alongside a sleek heavy cruiser. I had never been near a large "man of war" before. It had an awesome and almost majestic appearance. We were told to salute the flag as we crossed the gangplank and stepped onto the quarterdeck. Now my great adventure was really starting.

I was aboard the USS *Indianapolis* (CA-35). It had just returned from the invasion of Tarawa, a small island in the Pacific. It was commanded by Captain Johnson and was the flagship of the Fifth Fleet commanded by a three-star admiral by the name of Raymond A. Spruance.

Calvin Ball Emory and I were the only buglers on the ship, and we were under the direction of an articulate and knowledgeable quartermaster first class whose name I no longer remember. He told us our duties and after general quarters were sounded, I was to report to the bridge and Calvin to Battle II. I was to relieve the JL telephone talker. All necessary points of operation were on this circuit and all information received at this station was to be reported to the captain. I was first assigned to the bridge, and there I remained until the end.

During my first excursion into battle, the Fifth Fleet under the command of Admiral Spruance made successful operations against many Japanese island strongholds. In the meantime two new buglers came aboard, Earl Procia and Donald F. Mack. The two were a welcome improvement in the way Calvin and I stood our watches, for this allowed us to stand watches of 4/4/2/2 during the setting of condition three, a normal provision with no enemy action.

The USS *Indianapolis* returned to the United States and at that time I decided to keep a diary. I entered the first page of my diary on January 1, 1945, and I wrote:

Monday, January 1, 1945

Today is a significant day for it was on a New Year's Day when I first started going with Mertie Jo. We celebrated today quietly. We went to the zoo and sure had fun. Some other of the fellows were with us.

Tuesday, January 2, 1945

I saw Mertie Jo for the last time before going to Pearl Harbor. All day I wondered what fate had in store for all of the boys on the *Indy*. Day uneventful.

Scuttlebutt had it we were going to Saipan but that was erroneous. Instead we wound up in the northern anchorage of the Ulithi atoll. According to my diary, we remained there from January 29 to February 14. We were issued foul-weather gear because we were headed for Japan. On February 14 we were again warned not to keep a diary. I ordinarily obeyed all commands but somehow I took my chances and wrote on.

What a sight. War ships everywhere you looked. From horizon to horizon, nothing but ships. I would guess probably the greatest armada of ships ever assembled then and since. On February 15 we were some 200 to 300 miles off of the Japanese coast. Our planes sank three fishing boats and shot down one aircraft. Our carrier-based planes carried our message to Japan. Returning pilots reported we caught the Japanese completely by surprise. Japanese airmen were out on the fields doing calisthenics. This raid was considered a success though some of our planes ran out of fuel and ditched in the ocean. We launched our float planes, "Curtis SOC Seagulls" to search for the downed pilots. Many were rescued.

We returned to Ulithi on Friday, March 9 and took on provisions. We were headed for the invasion of Iwo Jima. It was a bloody battle for a little island and a rock mountain. It was here that my heart went out to the United States marines. What courage and what training these stalwart soldiers had. I love marines. How lucky, I thought, that I was aboard a ship and only painfully watched these fine fellows die for their country.

Another raid ensued on the mainland of Japan, and many Japanese suicide planes were encountered. Aircraft carriers were their prime targets, though later they took any vessel they could hit. The firepower these ships put up defending themselves was enormous; nevertheless, many suicide planes hit their mark. We moved to the invasion of Okinawa, an island to the south of Japan deemed necessary for the invasion of Japan, which we all thought would come next.

Friday, March 30

Today we bombarded Okinawa but at noon we quit and went to a little harbor in some island (Kerama Retto) already taken and about 15 miles from Okinawa. We replenished our ammunition and proceeded to retire (move out to sea). The islands are very beautiful. I love you, Mertie Jo.

Saturday, March 31

Today is one of the saddest days I have known for sometime. This morning, as I was on the bridge, we were attacked by a Japanese suicide plane which hit us in the main deck aft. The bomb exploded and killed nine crewmen. Six of them were in my division, C.B. Emory being one of them as he was my dear friend. Four quartermasters, two buglers, two machinist mates, and one yeoman. When the plane hit it shook the ship violently even where I was. I'm glad I wasn't eating because I had just finished for it was right in the mess hall the plane went. I love you, Mertie Jo.

Actually, the plane remained on the first deck, the bomb went through a two-inch armor deck, which was the mess hall deck. It cleaved what appeared to be a neat eight-inch hole and didn't stop until it came out the bottom of the ship and exploded when it hit one of the screw shafts.

We were forced to return to Kerama Retto for some kind of repair. Of necessity, watertight hatches were closed immediately after the attack to keep the ship from flooding. Eight of the nine personnel killed were locked in their compartments until repairs could be made and the water pumped from the compartments. Only Earl Procia, one of the two buglers, made it out before the hatches were sealed. He died shortly thereafter.

Easter Sunday, April 1

I sounded taps for Earl Procia, my dear friend. It is indeed a crime for him to have to die as he did as he lived about seven minutes after he was found. The other quartermasters and bugler, Calvin Ball Emory, have not been removed as yet from the compartments. Earl was buried on one of the little islands. (I wrote more on this sad day but it just pains me to mention it.)

We remained in the bay at Kerama Retto for approximately seven days. All but two of the remaining crew members were recovered from their compartments. Again I sounded taps. The two remaining victims were then recovered and this time I was a pall bearer and Donald F. Mack sounded taps. When these bodies were recovered, I was asked to identify Richard Kuckenback. His body had been placed in a shower stall so the fuel oil could be washed from his body. It appeared that his back had been broken. It is a memory that so saddened me, I shall never forget it. This time as one of the pall bearers, I was selected to take Richard and the other crew member over to the island for burial.

Finally, we were considered seaworthy and sailed from Kerama Retto on April 7, 1945. We returned to Pearl Harbor, and the last entry I made in my diary was that we were to leave to go stateside the next day. This was on Wednesday, April 25, 1945. We arrived in Vallejo naval yards for overhaul and on my first liberty to Frisco, I gave my diary to Mertie Jo before I was reprimanded for breaking the rules. Thus my diary did not later go to the bottom of the ocean.

The overhaul period allowed some quality time for Mertie Jo and me. Upon completion of the overhaul, we were told we were expected to have a shakedown cruise. Then suddenly this information was reversed. The USS *Indianapolis* sailed from Vallejo to San Francisco and docked at Hunters Point naval base. There a secret cargo was loaded and the ship sailed at flank speed to Pearl Harbor. Little did we know that we carried an atomic bomb.

The large wooden box that had been placed in the port aircraft hangar held some of the main parts of the atomic bomb "Little Boy" that was later dropped on the city of Hiroshima, Japan. The uranium needed to produce nuclear fission for "Little Boy" was secreted very securely elsewhere aboard the USS *Indianapolis*. Armed U.S. Marine guards watched carefully (twenty-four hours a day) over this large box until it was removed upon our arrival at the island of Tinian. Though we knew not what we had, we knew it was serious business.

Each day as I walked by this large box, I could not help but wonder what in the world it could hold. It appeared to be about the size of an automobile van. The wood was quite pretty, and the screws that held it together were countersunk, covered with a red sealing material, and neatly smoothed flush with the wood. Rumors, of course, were rampant. In jest, some claimed it was toilet paper for General MacArthur. Some claimed the box held maps and charts for the invasion of Japan, but in our wildest imagination, how could we possibly have guessed its contents?

We made a record speed run to Pearl Harbor, a record that still stands today for sea going vessels. We refueled and set off for the island of Tinian. Much has been written in many books and I shall not dwell on the details of the Tinian delivery.

Orders directed the USS *Indianapolis* to depart from Guam and conduct gunnery practice in the Philippines. The second night out from Guam, the USS *Indianapolis* was struck by two torpedoes. (Even though our Captain McVay had requested an escort vessel with submarine detection gear, the request was denied.) I had retired from my 6:00 to 8:00 watch on the bridge, and I was asleep in conning tower. This was an armored area just beneath the bridge where control of the ship could be established in case personnel on the bridge needed protection from small-arms or machine-gun fire. This was my housekeeping area and I chose to sleep there instead of a hot bunk in a compartment below deck. There was no activity in this area while condition three was set, and my good friend Ralph Guye was sleeping there also.

The blast of exploding torpedoes seemed to momentarily make us weightless after the jarring explosion. I grabbed a red-lens flashlight and looked at my watch. I could see it was ten minutes after midnight. Neither Ralph nor myself immediately believed we had been torpedoed. Some internal explosion seemed more logical, for the navy would not have allowed us into enemy waters knowing we had no submarine detection gear, no way of defending ourselves from one. This is exactly what they did. Later, when our captain was court-martialed there should have been several others in line for a court-martial—for many more plausible reasons than those thrust upon Captain McVay.

Momentarily, Ralph and I were at a loss as to what to do. The ship was already listing to starboard. We decided to report to the bridge. Then we thought somebody was shouting my name. The bridge was sloping at a 45-degree angle, and we climbed to the port side. There were only two other people on the bridge—Lt. Orr, the officer of deck, and Donald Mack, the bugler of the watch. I asked Lt. Orr what action we should take and he told us that word already had been passed to abandon ship since electrical power was no longer available. With a voice-powered megaphone, Lt. Orr shouted instructions to anybody below who might be in earshot to throw all life rafts over, because we would be needing them.

I asked Mack if he was going to sound "abandon ship" and he said, "Just as soon as I get the orders." He never sounded "abandon ship." I saluted Lt. Orr and told him I would see him later. I proceeded to crawl over the bridge railing, sliding down at an angle that by now had a friendlier slope, then jumped to the signal bridge. I looked up but Ralph was nowhere to be seen. We had previously agreed to stick together. I never thought of asking him if he wanted to go my way. Ralph was not particularly athletic, and I suppose he did not think too much of my method of escape. I never saw Ralph again nor have I talked to any survivor who was with him or saw him in the water. Ralph was such a nice person and I always get a guilty feeling when I think back to the events of that morning. I wonder if I had said, "Come on Ralph, this is the way," he may have followed me. Then too, he may have convinced me that another way was better. It's a memory I review in my mind quite often.

I can remember that after rescue some survivors were taken to Samar in the Philippines, while some of us wound up in the hospital on Guam. We on Guam didn't know for some time who the survivors were on Samar. I waited anxiously for news. When I finally received a list of the Samar survivors, Ralph's name was not among them and to this day, I cannot forget the events that led to that tragic loss of a friend. "If you're watching from somewhere out there Ralph, please, please forgive me."

Well, I had a way to go. I could see the bulkhead that formed the side of the ship that would take me to the 40-mm gun mounts. I scooted safely down, skidding along on my rear end. As I slid to the bottom, water surged like a river, pinning me momentarily to the breech of the forward gun. Then for some reason, the pressure against me subsided and I was bouyed up by my life belt as the gun barrels were beginning to submerge. I felt the barrel slide through my hands then felt the funnel-like flash-cover pass my hands, and I was free of the ship.

I had heard that large vessels could pull you under if you were too close. I put some distance between me and the stricken vessel then watched as the stern rose high in the air, screws still turning. I watched my home of the last two years plunge into the ocean depths. A mountain of bubbles boiled to the surface, aglow with phosphorus light. As the bubbles subsided I turned away and scanned the area. In the distance I could see the silhouette of an airplane. That was for me, and I struck out toward it with a sturdy Australian crawl. When I arrived at the plane, I could see it was sinking fast. This, I reasoned, was the plane we kept on our catapult. It was a Curtis SC1 single-wing Seahawk that had recently replaced the old Curtis SOC biplanes, and it had apparently fallen when the torpedoes struck. The large pontoon under its body must have had a gaping hole, for the plane sank quickly to join the ship to which it had so recently been attached.

As I approached the plane, a life raft blocked my progress. As it turned out, it was just as well. I climbed into the raft. Other heads popped up and survivors climbed in. Another raft was close by, and I tied the rafts together with little lengths of line that were hanging around the perimeter for just such purposes. Soon two more rafts appeared, and we ended with four rafts tied in a large rectangle.

Standard navy life rafts were simply rectangular or oval pieces of wood with a lattice bottom (also made of wood) hung on short lines under the wooden frames. Essentially, you simply sat in water up to your navel. Not too impressive, but I suppose it was adequate for short periods of time. Soon out of the darkness came a floater net still rolled up like a cigar, with a sailor astride on his stomach, paddling with his hands. I tied the net to the raft and asked if he would like to board the raft. He decided to stay where he was until daylight.

Come the dawn, we found we had 20 men. Nothing and no one else was in sight. No debris, absolutely nothing but ocean. Could we be the only survivors? It hardly seemed possible. By now we were highly suspicious that we had been sunk by Japanese torpedoes. The first night—even though we had flashlights—somebody suggested we not use them for fear of a surfacing submarine that might decide to shoot us.

The next morning was a welcome sight. The waves were white-capping under a stiff breeze. A can of what appeared to be pyrotechnics was swiftly sailing away. I had shed my greasy life belt and was preparing to swim out and capture the runaway container. I was about to disembark when a fellow I did not know as yet suggested that I might like to make other plans. This man's name was Joseph J. Moran, a radioman first class. He pointed out and there for all to behold was the classic shark fin, just like you saw in the movies. It was slicing through the waves as I watched the container I was going to recover fade from view.

Soon after the lost canister episode I felt myself getting sick. It was difficult to believe that a swimmer such as I could swallow fuel oil during my excursion to the airplane and rafts. I vomited until the late afternoon, and then up came some material of a different color...green. Perhaps a tablespoon full. It tasted horrendous but I was glad, because I began to feel much better.

Now if only my eyes would quit stinging. It was difficult to open your eyes. I could occasionally stand and search the horizon, but I could only hold my eyes open for a few seconds. Fuel oil had managed to commingle my eyes and stomach into a condition that was making me wonder why it was not better to die. However, my eyes began to recover the next day and I actually was beginning to feel much better.

Lt. J. G. Freeze was the senior ranking person aboard our flotilla. He sat in another raft opposite me and appeared to have a severe flash burn. His body was pink but I could detect no seared or burned skin. He was in his skivvies and said he had escaped through a porthole. He seemed calm and reserved and suggested we shoot our flares, but it was broad daylight and thus the visibility of the flares was severely diminished. I suggested we wait until dark and he concurred. I stood watch with Lt. Freeze and found him to be a fine officer.

It was toward evening when I glanced at him again. It was still the first day, and I only opened my eyes when I felt it was necessary. The sun was behind him as I looked across to his raft. I smiled at him but I received what appeared to be a dazed look. He lay down on several kapok life jackets that were in that raft. Sometime during the night, Lt. Freeze died. Those in his raft removed his ring and watch and gently slipped his body over the side. I could not look.

After the death of Lt. Freeze, the senior ranking member of our flotilla was Joseph J. Moran. He was next to me in our raft and we became good friends. He took the initiative, calling on everyone for attention. He pointed to the fact that some were drinking water at random. So that distribution of food and water would be fair, the rules would be thus: Since our gear had enameled cups marked in ounces, we would distribute one ounce to each person in the morning and one in the afternoon, one slice of Spam in the morning and one in the afternoon. There were no objections. (Malt tablets were not rationed because nobody cared for them.) Soon all looked forward to our morning and afternoon snacks.

When would we be rescued? Had an SOS been sent? I relied heavily on J.J.'s opinion, "There's no doubt an SOS message was sent," J.J. said. He knew this to be true because he had sent it. "Sure, you tapped out the message but how do you know it left the antenna?" J.J. looked askance. "Morgan, I know when I'm sending because I have a meter that says so. When the needle pops over, it's going. We should be rescued soon if somebody received the signal." I felt much better.

As previously mentioned, out of the darkness came a survivor astride a floater net. He stayed on it until daylight then came in the raft. The floater net would bump the raft and then back away. This did not seem to bother anything until it was my turn to sit up and out of the water on my corner of the raft. Then it would bump me where I hung over the edge. (It was nice to get most of your body out of the water but everybody could not sit on the main frame at the same time, for this would sink the raft lower in the water, putting the others even deeper.) None of the others wanted the net tied in their area, and someone suggested I just cut it loose. I really hated to do this and was glad I did not for I suggested to J.J. that we simply roll the net out flat and pull it inside the raft, lacing it back and forth. Then we could clamber atop and be out of the water.

J.J. agreed that this might work. After some grumbling by others in the raft, we put this plan into effect. It worked splendidly. A four-by-eight-foot canvas was spread over the net to take the sharp corners off the little wheels and for the first time we were completely out of the water. This was an immense help, because ordinarily we shivered all night. I did not get a medal for this brilliant suggestion.

As one stared into the depths of this great blue ocean, many fish could be seen. This was especially true of sharks. In between the rafts was a space of two feet or so, as the waves and currents pushed the rafts to and fro. There was a calm in this area that allowed a better view into the depths. There were several variety of fish, so I opened the navy's version of a fishing kit. It contained a large white piece of cloth stabbed by several fish hooks with string attached. There were pieces of dried bacon rind, colored pieces of yarn, and a little wire dip net, that when opened was about the size of a coffee cup.

My piscatorial escapade was a total failure. The bacon rind was so hard that a hole had to be punched in it with a knife to get it on the hook. As I hung the bait down into the water, several fish approached it but backed away. The colored yarn proved to be a failure also. I quit.

It was shortly after my fishing endeavor that I saw ingenuity functioning at its fullest. In the raft opposite was a young fellow lying length-wise and partially submerged. His elbow rested on the top of the raft, his head on his left hand and his right hand poised in a striking position above the water between the rafts. I watched as he chewed a malt tablet, then spit it into the water with saliva. In his hand was the little dip net from the fishing kit. A little purplish fish would come in close, hesitate, then grab the glob and dart away. Each time the sailor would swipe at the little fish and miss–but not by much. Perseverance paid off, and soon he held a wiggling fish aloft in the ridiculously small dip net.

Kenley Lanter picked up on the action sacrificing the little fish for bait to catch four beautiful silvery blue fish. Kenley proceeded to fillet them and made an offering of nice white pieces of fish stacked in a pile to the rest of the survivors. Some accepted the offering, including myself. The fish had a pleasant taste, and I envisioned life-extending possibilities if rescue failed to materialize.

Somewhere in this narrative I should mention Charlie. Charlie was a good-sized shark that seemed to be around all the time. I do not know if it was the same shark whose fin I saw the first morning or even whether Charlie was the same shark we saw each day, but when a greasy Spam can was thrown away it was evident that this excited Charlie. He would come in for a closer look but generally refrained from getting too close. Then one time I was sitting on the corner of the raft watching Charlie when he began to maneuver closer to the raft. Strangely he came straight for our raft. I watched without moving until I realized he was getting too close. With some consternation, I swiftly shifted my position to the opposite side of the raft. Astonished, I watched this fellow gracefully slide his entire head out of the water and onto the side of the raft. With only slight hesitation, Charlie slid backwards and swam away. I only wish I knew what he was thinking.

Signal mirrors were also part of standard navy gear and considered important for survival in a life raft. A clever arrangement allowed you to aim the mirror so you could be reasonably sure the flash was headed for the target. The mirror came with a line attached. I had tied mine to the corner of the raft and left it hanging in the water. These mirrors would later prove to be a valuable asset.

I would shoot a flare at night, for they were almost worthless in the daytime. These flares looked like ten-gauge shotgun shells but were filled with powder that produced various colors. The flares gave off puffs of light similar to those shot from Roman candles. Of course there never seemed to be any response to these flares.

Harold Shearer sat in the raft with Kenley Lanter. Harold's bare arms were severely burned, and charred flesh hung from them so that Harold held his arms aloft. The pain must have been unbearable, but Harold never complained. He never said much but just sat there in misery. Kenley Lanter suggested that perhaps we could wrap his arms in bandages. This sounded logical, so I pulled the rafts together and Kenley found a first-aid kit, took out the oil-soaked bandages and unrolled them until clean but water-soaked bandages appeared. I also found some mineral oil in the gear. We poured this on Harold's arms, folded the loose flesh around his arms and wrapped them in the bandages. I do not know whether Harold felt any better, but I know that Kenley and I did.

Four days were about gone. The sun was setting and quiet reigned within our group of rafts. I do not remember what I was thinking at the time, but I was aroused from my lethargy by hearing my name called by Kenley Lanter in the next raft. He told me to look and pointed in a southerly direction. (We knew the direction by the sun setting in the west.) As I looked I saw a black dot just above the horizon. It seemed to float back and forth. Was it a plane or just a bird? As we both pondered, a flash of sunlight glinted from its fuselage. "It's a plane," Kenley said. The back and forth motion proved to be a plane flying in huge circles. We knew that rescue must be close at hand.

As darkness came, so did a series of Morse code. It came from the sky and Kenley Lanter answered it with "Roger Wilco." Kenley was a signalman and told us he had sent "Help," to which the plane responded, "Roger Wilco." Then the plane was gone. Shortly thereafter, we saw pencils of blue light piercing the sky. They seemed to be far away, as if made with a small flashlight, weaving to and fro, reflecting light from the various cloud formations. There could be only one reason for this; they were letting us know that help was on the way and not to give up. At that time we did not know of the survivors still floating in kapok life jackets, struggling to stay alive for a few more hours. How their spirits must have been raised, how they must have thanked the good Lord. Soon the blue lights dwindled and again we were left alone.

As daylight came, we found the water was getting rough. A rain squall was just ahead of us, and it looked as if we would wind up in the middle of it. By now the waves were beginning to whitecap. For some reason Harold Shearer rolled out of his raft, mumbling something about body bags. Kenley and another survivor quickly grabbed him and pulled him back inside the raft. He then sat still but began to shiver. Now it was raining cats and dogs.

Quickly we grabbed the canvas that had served as the buffer between our raft's occupants and the ocean beneath. We stretched it in a manner we thought best to catch rainwater. Catch it we did, and when the rain stopped we had a bulging canvas full of water. Joyously we took a sip. To our dismay it was too salty to drink. We took the water and with our hands used it to rinse the canvas. We then folded the canvas and laid it atop some gear, away from salt water—the idea being that in scrubbing the canvas with just half-salty water, the next time the water collected would be potable. There was a reason for this: there was another rain squall just ahead.

Sure enough it started raining again, though not as much as the first time. We did catch more water, and this time we could drink it even though it had a slightly salty taste. Several of us sipped a little, and there was not enough to save or put into a wooden water keg. Somehow I think we just felt like we had conquered the elements a tiny bit.

By this time the rain had stopped and the sun was making an appearance. It was still early in the morning. Harold Shearer was again holding his arms away from his body. He was shivering violently after the cold rain. Observing Harold's predicament, J.J. Moran mandated that he be moved to our raft saying that Harold might get pneumonia and in our raft he would be high and dry. Kenley Lanter found a morphine syrette and unloaded it into Harold. He laid down and went to sleep, probably at peace for the first time since he was burned.

It was now around 0900. Someone suddenly exclaimed, "Look a plane!" Sure enough, there on the horizon was a plane making large circles. It was a good way off so I grabbed my mirror and aimed it at the plane. The sun was in the right direction for a good shot. A couple of other mirrors from the other rafts were in operation also, and to our amazement, the distant plane straightened and came directly toward us. It was a PV-1 Ventura, and it swooped low. A crew member waved and then a color marker was ejected from the plane. The marker hit the water close by, turning a spot in the blue Pacific into a large circular spot of green.

The Ventura flew away and then came a PBY Catalina. It too flew over low, somebody waved, and then it flew on–but we just knew that rescue was at hand.

Between noon and one o'clock the USS *Ringness* (APD 100) performed an excellent maneuver. Her skipper Captain Bill Meyer reversed the screws, backing down and stopping with a broad cargo net hanging over the side, dangling so close alongside our life rafts one could easily grab the net and climb it like a ladder. I scrambled up, since the cargo net was right beside me. I was immediately escorted into the starboard passageway, a section filled with bunks. As a *Ringness* crew member was stripping my greasy clothing from me, I heard a cheerful voice from the far end of the passageway shout, "Hey Morgan, welcome aboard." A pleasant sensation came over me, for I never had to look to see who it was. I knew it was my good friend Vincent Jerome "Luke" Allard.

Time enough later to talk; the matter at hand was getting me scrubbed down. Into a shower I went. I was scrubbed mercilessly to remove the fuel oil embedded in my pores. When I passed inspection, I was escorted to a nice clean bunk and told to rest. I was asked what I would like to eat. I suggested two eggs over easy, and by golly, I got 'em. The *Ringness* crew members gave us their clothing, because in the navy you bought your own and we had no money.

There was an exception–Vincent Allard who had been in Captain McVay's group. Vincent had abandoned ship with money in his pocket. He unraveled a bill and said, "Look Glenn, I've got money, we can buy some skivvies." The bill he produced was almost white–for most of the ink had been washed away and the amount could barely be discerned. Good old Luke bought both of us a pair of skivvies, and we were never in want until the USS *Ringness* discharged us to the hospital on the island of Peleliu.

At that time, I never had a chance to thank the *Ringness* crew for their kindness and generosity, and I never saw any of the *Ringness* crew until some 56 years later at one of their reunions in Nashville. T'was then and there I got to thank them for the consideration they had given 39 miserable looking survivors, lo those many years ago. By the way, as an honorary member, I have not missed one of their reunions since.

The *Ringness* picked up Captain McVay and his group as well. Once I was up and about, Captain McVay asked to see me. I suppose it was because he probably knew me better than most at that point since I was always on the bridge and he certainly knew my name. Captain McVay greeted me, saying he was glad to see that I was apparently okay. He asked me to get the names of all the survivors and their rates. I did so and gave the list to him. I didn't see him again until some fifteen years later.

I believe there should be a word here about Captain McVay and Admiral Spruance. As I have mentioned, during regular watches and general quarters I was assigned to the bridge. This was where many decisions were made; thus I had the opportunity to see and sometimes hear things. Here I had seen two men operating with a rapport of almost classic proportions. Their movements were almost majestic with a military flair. It was just one of those things you do not forget.

About Admiral Spruance, it has been said he was one of America's most brilliant strategists. He selected subordinates with care. He was not as well known as Nimitz or Halsey simply because he refused the center of attention. Though he never received a fifth star, it was not because he did not deserve one.

Perhaps here I should tell a simple little story which gives an infinitesimal insight into the character of Admiral Spruance. While anchored at Majuro Atoll, I was standing on the bridge early one morning. Not much going on and I was just standing there looking over the vast array of ships that surrounded us. Vincent Jerome Allard was a quartermaster who liked to fish. I looked down and there Vincent was, with rod and reel in hand, diligently trying to get some kind of a fish to bite. He was standing on a little platform projecting from the side of the ship. Ordinarily, this little platform was used to heave a lead line for the purpose of measuring depth when the ship was in shallow water. Admiral Spruance's cabin was on this deck and each morning, when he could, he would take a walk from one end of the forecastle to the other.

On this morning the admiral exited his cabin and started his walk. Vincent saw him and began to reel in his line. I then saw the admiral stop and say something to Vincent. Vincent let his line down again. The Admiral continued his walk. While I watched this action and the admiral had reached the far end of his walk, a commander that just happened to be on the bridge also suddenly called, "Allard, get out of there." Vincent began to reel in once again. The admiral

overheard and loudly told the commander that it was okay, that he had told Allard he could fish there. "Aye aye sir," said the commander. Allard once again began letting his line down.

Many years later, during our first reunion in Indianapolis, I remember the following story that Captain McVay told us about Admiral Spruance. He told us that Admiral Spruance was aware that either he or Halsey was to be awarded a fifth star. He said that Admiral Spruance went to those who handled such matters and told them not to consider himself over Halsey, for he felt that Halsey deserved it and besides, it would break his heart if he did not receive it.

It makes me mighty proud to have served under men such as these.

I shall end my narrative here because of time and space, but fifty-seven years have yet to bring this story to an end. All that I have written here is only a small part of the many stories that have developed and come to light over the years. I still have Mertie Jo and I still love her.

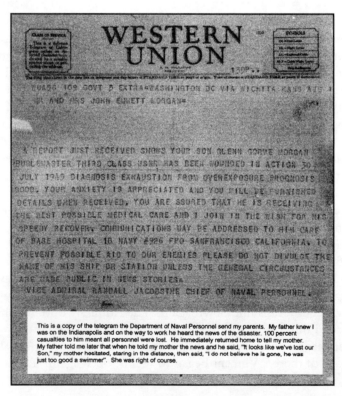

This is a copy of the telegram the Department of Naval Personnel send my parents. My father knew I was on the Indianapolis and on the way to work he heard the news of the disaster. 100 percent casualties to him meant all personnel were lost. He immediately returned home to tell my mother. My father told me later that when he told my mother the news and he said, "It looks like we've lost our Son," my mother hesitated, staring in the distance, then said, "I do not believe he is gone, he was just too good a swimmer". She was right of course.

NAME	MORRIS, ALBERT O. S1C
STREET	2619 Nesmith Lake Blvd
CITY	Akron
STATE	OH 44314
PHONE	330 753 4827
ENTERED SERVICE FROM	Akron, OH
PICKED UP BY	USS *Bassett*
DIVISION	4th Division
DOB	7/28/25

FAMILY
Spouse: Ethel

EXPERIENCE
No response.

NAME	MOSELEY, MORGAN M. S1C
STREET	331 Mosely Ln
CITY	DeFreniak Springs
STATE	FL 32433
PHONE	850 892 5720
ENTERED SERVICE FROM	Opp, AL
PICKED UP BY	USS *Bassett*
DIVISION	4th Division
DOB	11/16/21

FAMILY
Spouse: Joy
Children: Janna, Zanda, Tanya, Landa
Grandchildren: Bart, Mindi, Kelly

EXPERIENCE
   After I was honorably discharged from the navy in November 1945, I returned
to work for the L & N Railroad Company. I was in my last promotion as road
master, a position I held for the last 18 years of service with the railroad. I retired
in 1978 after 39 years with the railroad.

NAME MOWREY, TED Storekeeper 3C
STREET
CITY
STATE
PHONE
ENTERED SERVICE FROM Long Beach, CA
PICKED UP BY USS *Doyle*
DIVISION
DOB

FAMILY

EXPERIENCE

Unable to contact any family members.

CHAPTER 207 SURVIVOR MULDOON

NAME MULDOON, JOHN J. Machinist Mate 1C
STREET
CITY
STATE
PHONE
ENTERED SERVICE FROM New Bedford, MA
PICKED UP BY
DIVISION
DOB 9/1/15 Deceased 3/92 Narragansett, RI

FAMILY

Widow: Kathleen
Children: John J. Muldoon Jr., Kathleen Muldoon Sullivan (Paul)
Grandchildren: John Patrick Muldoon

EXPERIENCE

Respectfully submitted by Survivor Muldoon's family.

John J. Muldoon was born in New Bedford, Massachusetts, on September 1, 1915. One of six children, he was educated in the public school of New Bedford and in 1941 enlisted in the navy to serve in the Second World War.

After basic training and "skills school" as a machinist, he was assigned as a machinist mate aboard the USS *Indianapolis*. John saw combat aboard *Indy* on an earlier deployment, when the ship was attacked by a kamikaze on Easter Sunday morning of 1945. The attack occurred during breakfast, and great damage was done to the *Indianapolis*. She put in for repairs in San Francisco. It was after the repairs that the *Indianapolis* set out on her final voyage.

The story of the attack on the *Indianapolis* is well known, but for each individual there were personal and horrific stories of that event. Men were mutilated and killed after the sinking in such horrible ways that the images were coped with by being hidden. John never talked much about what happened on the *Indy* until he witnessed the launching of the new SSN *Indianapolis* nuclear-powered submarine. He and the family members that witnessed the launching described it as an incredibly emotional event.

What he did talk about was his decision as to which side he would jump from as the *Indy* was sinking. He also told us how he had to swim with all his might to escape the "draft" of the ship as she went down and how he swam toward a voice in the dark. The voice was that of John Spinelli, who was aboard a life raft that was his salvation.

John made it to that life raft, which was more like an oversized life ring or tube-like device that had no bottom. He dangled in the water, holding dear to this flotation device to endure the ordeal. His life raft was connected to the one Captain McVay was on.

During the course of the ordeal at sea, John heard Captain McVay on many occasions express dismay for those lost in the attack and his personal distress that he had survived, for the captain is supposed to go down with his ship. The pain of the captain's expressions over those "that he had lost" gnawed at John until the day he died. He knew how good a man Captain McVay was. He knew this for near the end of the ordeal at sea, he remembered hearing the captain cry out, "Oh Lord! Muldoon is gone!" thinking that like so many others he had swum off to be taken by sharks. John then stood on the raft to see the approaching rescue ships, and when the captain realized that John was still with them, he prayed again, "Thank you, Lord."

Machinist Mate First Class Muldoon was rescued by the USS *Ringness* and taken to the hospital to recover and be treated for his exposure during that ordeal at sea.

He returned home and sought employment, which he found at General Electric's River Works facility in Lynn, Massachusetts. John moved to the north side of Boston to Lynn, where he made his home. He married the love of his life, Kathleen Ryan, with whom he had two children. After his time at GE, John worked for the Boston and Main Railroad for 25 years, finishing as a machine shop supervisor at the Massachusetts Bay Transportation Authority (MBTA), the metropolitan Boston rail and subway service.

NAME	MULVEY, WILLIAM R. BM1
STREET	Wyoming
STATE	MI 49509
PHONE	616 534 4223
ENTERED SERVICE FROM	Grand Rapids, MI
PICKED UP BY	USS *Doyle*
DIVISION	Chief Master At Arms
DOB	6/5/18

FAMILY
Spouse: Donna
Children: Michael, Jeffrey, and Jamie
Grandchildren: Heather Siskonen, Robin
Wilson, Roderick Wilson
Great-Grandchildren: Sarah Siskonen

EXPERIENCE
I joined the navy in 1937. After boot
camp, I was assigned to the USS *Texas* and
became a real navy salt on a midshipman
cruise to Europe in 1938. My tour of duty
on the USS *Indianapolis* began in October
1943 in Pearl Harbor. I was assigned duties
as chief master-at-arms.

On July 30, 1945 at midnight, I was asleep in the starboard hangar when I felt
two thuds below decks. My first thought was that a boiler had blown up. I
started to get dressed but did not finish. I had only my skivvies on as I stepped
onto the quarterdeck. Commander Flynn was coming down from the bridge.
He wanted me to go up on the focsle to see why men were screaming with pain.
He was ordered below decks to investigate damages. That was the last I saw of
the commander.

The ship started lurching to starboard and listing. I never got to go forward.
When it got up to water's edge, the life line was even with the water. I just
stepped off into the sea. As I went into the water, the sky aft caught me in the
back and pushed me farther under water. I kicked myself free and came up
under an oil slick and could see the ship. I was about a block away from the
focsle, which was under water. The ship was almost standing on end with the
screws still turning. That was the end of the USS *Indianapolis*.

Then I realized I had no life jacket. There were several 5-inch ammo cans
floating by, so I put one under each arm and floated until daylight. I found I was
near several men. One had two kapok life jackets, and he gave one to me. As

daylight grew brighter, I found that I was the senior man in a group of 38. Soon we saw that singles could not stay together, so we tied the long cords of our life jackets together so we would not drift apart. Many of the 38 men were just young recruits that had just come aboard in San Francisco. They were more afraid than the seasoned men with experience in service.

The ship was supposed to arrive in Leyte in the Philippines at 11:00 a.m. on Tuesday. We all assumed that an SOS had got off, but I knew that was impossible, as we lost all power when the ship was hit. I still figured that when we didn't show up, help would come.

After a day in the water, some men became disoriented. The sun was very hot on our heads, and we needed fresh water. Some men thought that the ship had come apart and part of it was just below us. One sailor thought he could dive down and get a drink of cold water from the scuttlebutt. As he went down, the cold water brought the blood rushing back to his brain and he realized that he was in trouble. He came thrashing back up. It took several of us to get him back into a life jacket. He was fighting us, as he thought he was going to drown. Sometime in the night I heard him call, "Mulvey! Mulvey! Mulvey! Save me." But with the water splashing over us you couldn't figure out which direction his call was coming from. In the morning his life jacket was still tied to ours, but he was not in it.

On the third or fourth day, our life jackets became saturated. More men were lost. We had to turn their life lines loose, as they would have pulled us down. More and more men turned to prayer. Several sang the "Navy Hymn" which we had sung every Sunday morning aboard ship... "for those in peril on the sea."

Several men had given their dog chains to me. Some chains we took off as the men went below the sea. I in turn lost theirs and mine.

On Thursday, the good Lord performed a miracle. One of the radiomen aboard a patrol plane saw splashing in the sea and told the pilot. The pilot said it might be fish. He took the plane lower to have a look and spotted 50 men, with no oil slick to locate where they came from. He radioed back to his home port. He was told that there had been no report of American ships lost in the area. It might be Japanese in the water. They didn't find out about us until more planes arrived and they dropped life rafts. They never found out until Adrian Marks, pilot of a PBY, learned that the sailors they rescued were from the USS *Indianapolis*.

I was picked up by the USS *Doyle* and taken to Peleliu. Later I was transferred to the hospital ship USS *Tranquility*, which took us to Guam. I was taken to San Diego later and honorably discharged in Shoemaker, California. In 1950 I was recalled for Korea, stayed in for Vietnam and was honorably discharged again in 1964. I went into the Fleet Reserves and completed my obligated service for 30 years.

NAME   MURPHY, PAUL J. FC3
STREET   1030 W 4th Ave
CITY   Broomfield
STATE   CO 80020
PHONE   303 469 9503
ENTERED SERVICE FROM   Chillicothe, MO
PICKED UP BY   USS *Bassett*
DIVISION   Fox Division
DOB   9/18/24

FAMILY
Spouse: Mary Lou Walz Murphy
Children: Mary Welch (Rob); Virginia Geidt
(Steve); Paula Watkins (Michael); Michael
Murphy (Kim); Leonard Murphy (Sue); Tammy
Brown (Larry)
Grandchildren: Erica Welch, Bria Welch,
Abby Welch, Bryan Geidt, Jason Geidt, Peter
Watkins, Brandon Murphy, Cara Tonnell, Molly
Tonnell, Lauren Brown

EXPERIENCE
I was born in Chillicothe, Missouri. My parents were Robert Joseph Murphy
Sr. and MaryVictoria Obrecht Murphy. They raised four boys: Robert Jr.
(Gladys), Paul (Mary Lou), John (Miriam), and William (Sue). (Mother liked me
best!) Two weeks after I graduated from high school in 1943, I was drafted into
the navy.

My boot camp was at Camp Hill, Company #453, in Farragut, Idaho. One of
my memorable experiences in boot camp was jumping off an 80-foot tower with
a life jacket on. I grabbed the collar of my life jacket with one hand, my family
jewels with the other, and jumped...wondering if I would be sucking air in or
blowing air out when I hit the water.

After boot camp, I was sent to fire control school on Treasure Island, then later
to advanced fire control school in San Diego. This training involved learning to
calibrate fire control instrumentation on all gunnery...no red fire trucks.

In early June of 1944, I was assigned to the navy's most beautiful ship, the USS
Indianapolis. I participated in five of the ten campaigns. These included battle
stars for Saipan and Guam and the Battle of the Philippine Sea, the capture of
Tinian Island, Peleliu in Palau Islands, raids on Honshu and Nansei Shoto and
Iwo Jima, and on Saturday, March 31, the day before D-Day (Easter Sunday), we
were hit by a kamikaze as we participated in attacks on Okinawa.

On March 31, 1945 several Japanese kamikazes were headed for us. One got through and landed on the port-side after deck. Nine men lost their lives and 27 were injured. We were towed back to Kerama Retto where a temporary concrete bottom was installed. We then limped back to Mare Island, California and spent eight weeks in dry dock. I went home on leave. When I returned to San Francisco and boarded the ship again, a large crate was brought aboard, stored on the hangar deck, and guarded by marines. No one knew what it was. In the navy, if you don't know something, you hear scuttlebutt. The best scuttlebutt I heard was that it contained 50,000 rolls of scented toilet paper for General MacArthur.

July 16, 1945, we left on a speed run to Hawaii and then to Tinian Island. This trip took ten days...a record which still stands today. We unloaded the crate and on July 26, we went to Guam. Captain McVay went ashore to receive orders for the forward area.

Captain McVay asked for an escort as he knew we were going through enemy waters. He was declined such. He also was told to zigzag at his own discretion. We were told to meet the USS *Idaho* for gunnery practice prior to arriving at Leyte in the Philippines. This meeting was scheduled on July 31. He was not told that just four days earlier the USS *Underhill* had been sunk by Japanese torpedoes.

We left Guam on July 28. On Sunday, July 29, I had the 8:00 p.m. to midnight watch. About 10:30 p.m. Captain McVay got ready to retire for the night and told the officer in charge to cease zigzagging. It was a cloudy night; you could see the moon only intermittently.

Just before midnight, Japanese submarine *I-58*, commanded by Captain Hashimoto, was searching for enemy ships. He noticed this little "blimp" some 15,000 yards away, turned his periscope 360 degrees, and noticed there were no escorts. He waited until we passed, which was shortly after midnight, and fired six torpedoes. Two hit us. The first one blew about 40 feet of the bow off, and the second hit under the eight-inch gun turret in the powder room. This knocked out all power and it was dark. There was no way to tell the engine room to turn off the engines; therefore, we took on water rapidly.

My quarters were one deck below the fantail just above the brig compartment. I was knocked out of my bunk, dressed quickly, took two extra life jackets, and went to my general quarters. When I arrived at the 8-inch after control tower and opened the door, there was one of my good buddies, Paul Boone Mitchell. He was sound asleep...he had slept through the whole thing. I gave him a life jacket and told him to go to his general quarters. I never saw him again. Some of my buddies told me they saw him in the water but he died the second day or third day. Paul had had rheumatic fever in boot camp and I believe he was not in the best physical condition.

Since I was in the after-part of the ship, I was unable to see and know what damage was done at the bow and the first 8-inch gun turret. The ship began to list to the starboard side. I saw many men holding on to the life lines on the port side, and I just knew that all that weight would right the ship. However, no more than a few minutes later the 5-inch guns on the starboard side were under water, and all I had to do was step into the water and swim. (No jumping 80 feet!!) As I was swimming, I found another life jacket. Later I found Concepcion Bernacil ("Bernie") swimming without a life jacket, and I gave him the extra one I had.

I swam as fast as I could...you don't go very fast with a life jacket on...and after I got away from the ship about 100 feet or so, I looked back and saw the ship had rolled over on its topside and was going down, bow first. Soon the screws were the only thing I could see, and they were still turning as the ship disappeared.

WOW! It was dark and the water was cold. We had all swallowed oil so we vomited then waited for the sun to rise so we could see what was what. We knew someone would come looking for us–after all, the USS *Indianapolis* was the most beautiful ship and also President Roosevelt's ship of state. As the sun rose higher, it began to get very hot. We were hoping someone would come soon. When the sun set and the night got long, the water was very cold. Our teeth chattered.

Tuesday morning came and we knew for sure someone would be looking for us, as we were to meet the USS *Idaho* for gunnery practice. Well, when we didn't show up, the port director just removed us from the plotting board. It was navy policy if a major vessel didn't show up on schedule, you did nothing...the ship's orders might have been changed. (So we found out later.)

This was the beginning of four days and five nights without food or water. Planes flew over us daily, but they were too high. I spent the entire time in a life jacket and occasional rest on top of a floater net. My group had three floater nets and two life rafts. We tried to keep the rafts for the most severely wounded. There were approximately 200 or more in this group. Sharks swam below us, bumping our legs. I am often asked about sharks. My reply, "They don't like Irishmen!" Most of us were Christians or became Christians. We prayed daily. God was with me always.

Our group was spotted by Wilbur Gwinn in his PV-1 Ventura bomber and later his home base sent out a PBY flown by Adrian Marks. Adrian dropped supplies...the water kegs broke when they hit the water! Later another PBY came out. Adrian decided to make an open sea landing. He landed in 8- to 12-foot swells. He and his crew picked up 56 men. It was the first time the navy knew that the USS *Indianapolis* had been sunk. Now you know the rest of the story.

I was picked up by the USS *Bassett*. I will be forever grateful to all the rescue men. They treated us like royalty...lifted our near-death and weak bodies out of the water, showered us, dressed us in clean clothes, gave us water to drink, and oranges to eat, and let us sleep in their beautiful white bunks. When the *Bassett* arrived at Samar in the Philippines, we were taken to a new hospital base. I remember being placed on a rubber-sheeted bed and the nurse pouring liquid penicillin over my entire body. After 9 or 10 days, we were flown to Base

Hospital 18 on Guam. Further recovery for me was at the submarine rest camp. There we got steak, ice cream in gallon buckets, and beer if we wanted.

I am also most grateful to the many other men on rescue ships and planes who participated in our rescue and those who helped with identifying dead bodies, burials at sea, and clean up. The book, *We Were There* by L. Peter Wren (LCDR on the USS *Bassett*) goes into much detail on the rescue as well as the retrieval of corpses, their identification, and burial at sea.

I was honorably discharged from the navy in March 1946 at Great Lakes naval station. Thanks to the GI Bill, I was able to attend college at Missouri School of Mines and Metallurgy at Rolla, Missouri, graduating with a mechanical engineering degree. During my first marriage, we had five children: Mary, Ginger, Paula, Mike, and Leonard. After my divorce in 1973, I moved to Colorado. In 1987 I married Mary Lou and she had one daughter, Tammy.

I have been active in the USS Indianapolis Survivors Organization and was elected vice-chairman in 1985 and chairman in 1995. I'm like a former president...I too sleep with my secretary. However, I'm legal. My wife, Mary Lou, is the secretary of the USS Indianapolis Survivors Organization. Several survivors were discussing the need for a book which included ALL SURVIVORS. She enthusiastically volunteered to prepare all the "chapters" for this book. I thank her and all those who have participated to make this possible.

WE ARE THE SURVIVORS...THE REAL HEROES DIED AT SEA

Survivor Paul J Murphy, Lost At Sea Thomas L Barksdale, Lost At Sea Samuel G Miller Jr.

NAME MYERS, H. B. Fireman 1C
STREET
CITY
STATE
PHONE
ENTERED SERVICE FROM Harden City, OK
PICKED UP BY USS *Bassett*
DIVISION
DOB Deceased 7/94

FAMILY
Widow: Helen

EXPERIENCE
Unable to contact any family members.

CHAPTER 211 SURVIVOR NASPINI

NAME NASPINI, JOSEPH A. Fireman 1C
STREET
CITY
STATE
PHONE
ENTERED SERVICE FROM Cudahy, WI
PICKED UP BY USS *Talbot* tr USS *Register*
DIVISION
DOB Deceased 5/81

FAMILY

EXPERIENCE
Unable to contact any family members.

NAME   NELSEN, EDWARD J. GM1C
STREET   12402 N 177th E Ave
CITY   Collinsville
STATE   OK 74201
PHONE   918 371 8859
ENTERED SERVICE FROM   Omaha, NE
PICKED UP BY   USS *Bassett*
DIVISION   4th Division GM1C
DOB   4/3/20

FAMILY
Spouse: Ethel Nadine
Children: Bonnie, Michael, Dane, Roxanne
Stepchildren: Joanne, Gordon, Stuart, Michelle
Grandchildren: Michelle, Jamie, Brandi, Joshua, Hannah
Great-Grandchildren: Makayla, Justin

EXPERIENCE

I was born in Omaha, Nebraska, one of five children: Mabel, Margaret, me, Dorothy, and Virginia. My parents came from Denmark. I grew up on a farm near Fremont, Nebraska and graduated from South High School in 1938. As a young boy, I delivered newspapers and did odd jobs. I joined the navy in Omaha, August 1940. After I attended boot camp at Great Lakes near Chicago, I was sent to San Diego and boarded the USS *Indianapolis*. During my time on the *Indianapolis*, I participated in ten of her campaigns: Pacific Raids, Aleutians Operations, Gilbert Islands Operation, Marshall Islands Operation, Asiatic-Pacific Raids, Marianas Operation, Tinian, Western Caroline Islands Operation, Iwo Jima, and Okinawa.

While at Okinawa, we were hit on the port side by a Japanese kamikaze. Nine men were killed and 26 injured. We were towed back to Kerama Retto for temporary repairs and then returned to San Francisco. A large crate was brought aboard, placed on the hangar deck, and guarded by marines. No one knew what it was. Some thought it was toilet paper for General MacArthur.

On July 16, 1945, we left on a special run for Hawaii and arrived at Tinian on July 26. The crate was unloaded, and later we found out it was the atomic bomb. Captain McVay received orders and we left for Guam where we were to meet the USS *Idaho* for gunnery practice. Captain McVay asked for an escort but his request was denied. He wasn't told that four days before, the USS *Underhill* had been sunk. About 10:30 p.m. on July 29, he told the officer of the deck to cease zigzagging. It was a cloudy night but you could see the moon at times.

I had just finished my evening shift on the forward part of the deck, and I decided to talk a few minutes to the man that had just relieved me. (I don't remember his name.) About ten minutes after midnight a Japanese submarine (*I-58* commanded by Captain Hashimoto) was searching for enemy ships and saw one. They fired six torpedoes and two hit us. The first torpedo blew off 40 feet of the bow and the second torpedo hit under the 8-inch gun turret in the powder room. All power was knocked out. It was dark and there was no way to turn off the engines. We took on water very rapidly. I remember commenting when I knew we had been hit, "Here we go back to the navy repair yard again."

The next thing I knew the ship started to list very quickly. We had to climb over the side of the gun platform. I still had on my life jacket from night duty. Being where I was and with my life jacket on is probably what saved me. I crawled down the side and swam as fast as I could. I clung to parts of things from the ship that were floating in the water. I looked back and the ship had rolled on its side and going down, bow first. I saw that the screws were still turning.

It was dark and the water was very cold. We had swallowed oil and salt water and started to vomit. We were chin deep in water and covered with oil and could not tell who was who. We had no food or water. All I could think of was, "I sure hope they find us soon." Even today, I still wonder how we made it!

Planes flew over us daily. We encountered heat, cold, hunger, sharks, oil, dehydration, thirst, and being scared. We also drifted in and out of consciousness during our days and nights in the water. Some men panicked and drank water and then went crazy. It took a lot of prayers and perseverance to make it. We were scattered over such a large area.

By the grace of God, we were spotted by Lt. Wilbur Gwinn in his PV-1 Ventura bomber and we call him our "angel." They then sent a PBY flown by Lt. Adrian Marks. He dropped supplies. It was the first time the navy knew we had been sunk. I was picked up by the USS *Bassett* and taken to a hospital.

After the war was over, I went back to sea. I spent time all over the world: China, South America, Mediterranean Sea, Africa, Italy, Spain, Sweden, England, France, Portugal, Aleutian Islands, and eight trips through the Panama Canal. I also spent time on *Maddox*, an LST tanker, USS *Missouri* BB81 and *Fargo*. I spent three years at the Navy ROTC at the University of Nebraska. I retired September 1960 after 20-plus years of navy life. I worked for the U.S. Post Office in Lincoln as a clerk and mechanic until I retired in 1983. We moved to Mitchell, Nebraska in 1983 and in 1998, we moved to Oklahoma.

NAME	NELSON, FRANK H. S2C
STREET	
CITY	
STATE	
PHONE	
ENTERED SERVICE FROM	Greenville, MI
PICKED UP BY	USS *Bassett*
DIVISION	
DOB	Deceased 87

FAMILY
Widow: LaVon Edwards

EXPERIENCE
No response from family.

NAME	NEWHALL, JAMES F. S1C Gunner Mate	
STREET		
CITY		
STATE		
PHONE		
ENTERED SERVICE FROM	Phoenix, AZ	
PICKED UP BY	USS *Doyle*	
DIVISION		
DOB	12/10/23	Deceased 8/95 Phoenix, AZ

FAMILY
Children: Jeanne Newhall-Nofi, James F. Newhall, Jr.
Grandchildren: Edward Ornelas, Rhianna Newhall, Emery Newhall

EXPERIENCE
Respectfully submitted by Survivor Newhall's daughter, Jeanne, and son, James.
As told in a personal narrative dictated to our mother in the 1950s and a transcript of a video filmed in the 1990s.

I was born on a 640-acre homestead in Congress, Arizona, the middle child and only son among four daughters, Mary, Margaret, Lois and Phyllis. My father and mother, Franklin Day Newhall and Esther Carney Newhall, moved the family to Phoenix when I was two years old. I went to school in Phoenix, graduating from Phoenix Union High School.

I was on the USS *Indianapolis* before the kamikaze plane hit us in Okinawa. It was morning and I was on gun watch on a 5-inch gun. There had been some aerial attacks by kamikaze planes. It was kind of cloudy and there were mountains around. I guess the radar didn't work well in the mountains. This plane came in over the bow and somebody on the bow of the ship on a 20-mm gun started shooting at it. Then somebody said over the loud speaker, "Who's that gun happy so-and-so shooting at that plane?" You weren't supposed to shoot until you had orders but this guy recognized the plane. The plane was flying pretty low towards the back of the ship. It just turned and dove straight down. The wing sheared off and went on our deck. There was an explosion and nine men were killed and several wounded. We went to Kerama Retto for temporary repairs. After we got patched up, we went to Hunters Point at Mare Island near Frisco.

When all the repairs were made, a crate (which was the atomic bomb) was loaded and we left on a speed run for Tinian. We thought something was up as no one knew what was in the big wooden container. It looked like a couple of piano boxes and was guarded by marines. It took us 68 hours to get to Pearl Harbor. The ship went so fast it vibrated. Ordinarily, you don't go that fast on a ship.

When we arrived at Pearl Harbor, we refueled, took on supplies and continued to Tinian. On Sunday night, July 29, 1945, I had just got off watch about midnight. I remember going down to the mess hall to get a real big drink of water. Then, I slept in the Potter's Circle. This is under the guns under the first turret.

When I was almost asleep, I heard a big explosion. I was stunned and shocked. I remember getting on my feet but about halfway up, I heard another explosion. There was fire in my area, and I decided it was time to get out of there. (In fact, I was naked.) I tried to get out a passageway there and other people said it was full of smoke and fire. The stairway was red hot. Everything was burning and smelled and I couldn't get out that way.

Then I remembered I could get up through Potter's Circle where the ammunition went up. There was an emergency-use little narrow passageway that went up through the Potter's Circle and through the trainer's booth. I was worried about that little hatch being closed. They did close it sometimes but it was open and I got out of there. I saw some other men down where I had been and they couldn't get out. They didn't know about this passageway through the gun turret. One or two of them tried to run through the smoke and fire. They got twenty or thirty feet and they just collapsed.

As soon as I got out of there, I was really relieved. I went back and rescued a

couple of officers—one was Lt. McKissick and the other man died later. They had
been trapped down below. As soon as I got out, I knew I had found a way out
and then I got those guys out. Lt. McKissick died in October 1995. The other
guy died in the water. I made two trips. It didn't take long to get down there.

We waited on the deck for the word to abandon ship. We never heard it, of
course, because communications were knocked out. As the ship started listing
more and more—even though we didn't hear the words "abandon ship"— a bunch
of us started getting off because we knew it was going to sink.

The bow was not blown off, although others claim that it was blown off. It
was ruptured and sank down so that when we left the ship, it was listing maybe
ninety degrees. In fact it was so steep you could hardly crawl up over it. After
encouraging young boots who were frozen to the spot to jump, my buddy
Woodie James and I jumped from the shattered bow into the water. We tried to
jump way clear of the ship, but we hit the water as we went down.

I swam away from the ship as fast as I could. That's what we were taught
because a ship has the tendency to suck you down when it goes under. I swam
on my back because that was supposed to protect your lungs. I was a pretty
good swimmer and got a lot of distance between the ship and me. Then I
watched the ship, nose down, turn on its side. The screws were up in the air and
I could see a few guys on the bottom of the ship. As the ship turned over, the
screws were barely turning as it went down and it made a silhouette. I was
between the ship and the moon.

I swam as hard as I could and as fast as I could. There were guys all around me
in a group. The water was real rough the first night. There were a lot of waves
and a lot of oil. I had a hard time because I did not have a kapok on the first
night. Later that night, I heard somebody say, "There's a light and it's a sub and
they are going to start strafing." I decided if they did any strafing, they would
strafe where a group of people would be, so I left all the guys and swam way out
by myself. Later, I swam back to the group and held on to different guys with
kapok life jackets on, to help hold myself up. Being burned and having no life
jacket, I needed moral and physical support. Other groups of men and stragglers
huddled in one large bunch. There were 137 men in our group. During five
days, I saw 128 of my buddies die, leaving only 9 of us left.

There were a couple of wounded guys in the group. They died later in the
night. I got clothes and a kapok from them. None of the guys in my group had
floater nets or life rafts, just the kapoks. It was awful rough the first night. The
salt water and glare from the sun each day burned our eyes so badly we all
thought we would be blinded. In the middle of the day the temperature was
extremely hot; at night we shivered until we became numb.

Men kept dying. As they died, we took them away from the group, removed
their kapok, and they would go down between our legs. Then we had extra
kapoks. At the last I had three or four from the dead guys. My hands and legs
had been burned. My hands were burned when I touched the bulkhead when I
lost my balance. I still have scars where I got burned. My feet were burned from

the deck, and my stomach was messed up from drinking the salt water and oil. I vomited blood and yellow stuff.

After one day and night in the Pacific Ocean, morale began to fade. Most of the guys died. Many got delirious. They came up with all kinds of stories. They drank salt water and believed the *Indianapolis* was only a few feet below. They could be so persuasive that others would follow and soon met their fate. After they drank the water, they frothed at the mouth, their eyes rolled back, their lips turned purple and they would silently pass away.

If I saw anything on the surface, I tried to swim and get it. I found a crate of potatoes. Later I saw a gallon can floating. I swam out, got it, and thought it would be something to eat...maybe juice, maybe peaches, or plums. Another guy named DeMent from Tennessee had a knife and we poked a hole in the bottom. We were all waiting for something to drink or eat...it turned out to be lard.

Sometimes I wondered how I would die if I did not drink salt water or swim off to the unknown. My heart was beating hard, but weak. Perhaps it would stop. Maybe a shark would get me or I would fall asleep and drift away. Sharks were around us, and at first we splashed water to frighten them away. Eventually we became too weak to bother. They seemed more interested in the dead bodies of men who had strayed away from the group. One guy got bitten and I saw the wound from it, but they did not bite me. I think in my group there were so many dead guys around, they got them.

I tried to talk everybody else into living and surviving. I tried to use the old psychology that the longer they stayed out there, the better the chance they would get picked up. The odds were better in their favor every day. Some of the guys would try to give up, and I'd tell them I was going to tell their kids and their wife they gave up. If a guy came from Tennessee I would tell him, "I thought you ole' hillbillies were tough and could make it. Here I am from Arizona and I'm not that tough and I'm gonna make it." I tried to use all the psychology I could, but not being too educated, I did the best I could. Many of them just got disgusted and disappointed and thought that they were not going to get picked up anyway and why suffer.

Yes, I am mad they didn't pick us up. If you go on leave or liberty and you're ten minutes late, you are court-martialed. But here is a ship, a quarter of a mile long, weighing ten thousand tons, with twelve hundred people...the thing is missing for days, and nobody looks for it. Yes, I am still bitter about that. I feel sorry for the guys that died. I figured maybe the good Lord had his arm around me.

The last day, regardless of what they say in the books, the water was really, really calm. If it hadn't been calm we wouldn't have gotten picked up. If there had been twelve foot swells, it would have dumped the raft over and we wouldn't have lived. As a plane flew overhead, it circled, circled once more, very low, and we knew we had been spotted. We were just too tired to become overjoyed. Furthermore, we did not know when we would be rescued. The seaplane finally landed on the water, a long distance from our group. Shortly before dark, a raft was dropped from another plane in our vicinity. It was a long way from where I was. I was out of energy and could hardly swim. We all tried to make our way toward it, using every ounce of strength left in our weak bodies.

After dark, I finally made it to the raft. After much struggling and bickering, a few boys decided the raft was theirs. I finally got enough strength to get on the raft. I was concerned about picking up the guys that I had passed on my way. The other guys didn't want to pick up anybody. They finally agreed and we went back and got all nine survivors on it. The raft was equipped with water and some candy, which we quickly consumed.

I felt relieved and grateful that we were going to be rescued but I was so weak and tired that it wasn't that big of a deal. When I saw that last plane, I knew all I had to do was just hang on. I sure didn't want to blow it now. I tried to keep peace among the other men.

Later that night, the USS *Doyle* turned on its big spotlight. I was taken aboard the USS *Doyle* on Friday morning, August 3 and taken to the hospital at Peleliu. Then I was transferred to the USS *Tranquility* hospital ship. I was nervous on that ship as it was all lit up like a Christmas tree. We had to go across the ocean and would be a perfect target. The nurses were very good to us. The *Tranquility* took us to the hospital at Guam.

Eventually, I was brought back to the States from the hospital in Guam. I was sent to the U.S. Naval Hospital at San Diego for several weeks to recuperate from severe burns on my hands and legs. I had lost 68 pounds in the water.

It took so long to get rescued. I couldn't figure it out. I thought they were looking for us but in the wrong area. It was kind of tough because a lot of guys held on for a couple of more days after that Tuesday and they still died. It was not a very good feeling. My idea was that the longer we toughed this thing out, the better our chances would be. Most of the guys made it into the water. I think the navy blew it. I can't understand why they didn't look for us. I just can't comprehend it.

As far as the captain, I have nothing against him. He was really well liked. I don't know enough about zigzag courses, but I think he got a raw deal. Everybody liked the guy. In fact, at the first reunion, we gave him a standing ovation. I know he didn't announce "abandon ship" because all the communications were knocked out.

This experience has affected my life because you think about it a lot. I wonder why I made it and the other people didn't make it. I thank my folks for giving me a good body. They taught me healthy living. I worked quite a bit and was pretty strong. I feel sorry for the guys that didn't make it and especially the ones that tried and then died at the last. Those are the ones you feel sorry for. I feel lucky. It keeps you from being so money-oriented and gives you other values.

Different people are going to have different versions according to their experience. At the time they looked back at the ship from the water, there are going to be different versions about if the clouds were covered in darkness or not. Some guys had floater nets and some guys had rafts and they all had different experiences. In our group of 137 men, as fate would have it, only 9 survived. They were mostly young guys, in pretty good health. They were not the youngest and not the oldest. Married guys in our group didn't survive because they worried about their families a lot. One guy in our group lived partly because of his family. He wanted to see his kids again. I knew him really well and he had said he didn't much care whether he lived or not. He had had a lot of disappointments in his life. Later I saw him and asked why he had hung on and didn't give up. He said he started thinking about those four little kids. So, you get compensated in this world in a lot of different ways.

CHAPTER 215   SURVIVOR NICHOLS

NAME	NICHOLS, JAMES C. S2C
STREET	3899 OLD Samburg Rd
CITY	Hornbeak
STATE	TN 38232
PHONE	901 538 3480
ENTERED SERVICE FROM	Hornbeak, TN
PICKED UP BY	USS *Bassett*
DIVISION	7th Division
DOB	12/8/25

FAMILY
Spouse: Mary

EXPERIENCE

I was raised on a farm in northwest Tennessee and attended schools in Obion County. I was drafted in February 1944 and chose the navy. I received my four weeks of basic training at Great Lakes naval station. After a short leave, I was sent to San Francisco and boarded a transport ship to Pearl Harbor. What an experience for an 18 year-old farm boy! I was sick the five days over.

In April I boarded the USS *Indianapolis* and headed for the Marianas. Captain McVay was in charge of our ship and was very much respected. I was on the *Indy* for five battles, the last being at Okinawa. On March 31, 1945–two days before the invasion of Okinawa–the *Indy* was hit by a kamikaze plane. It hit on the port-aft portion of the ship and splashed over the side. Nine of our crew were killed. After the hit we went into Kerama Retto for repairs and then made the long trip back to Mare Island in California.

After repairs were made we were chosen to go on a secret mission to deliver two boxes to Tinian Island. No one knew what they contained, not even the captain. These were delivered under heavy guard and we left there July 28, headed for Guam. We headed across the Philippine Sea without an escort. We had delivered the atomic bomb and were headed for Leyte Island.

My position on the ship was loader for a 20-mm anti-aircraft gun. On July 30, shortly after midnight, my buddy and I had just got off watch. We left the second deck from the main deck and went to our compartment. I sat on my bunk for a short while and suddenly decided to go take a shower. I had shaved and was in my shorts when the first torpedo hit. I tried to get back to my compartment but was unable to because of the flames. The second torpedo had hit that area. I did not see my friend or anyone from that compartment after that. I went to my gun station, which was under the aft radar station. I was able to find a life jacket there. The ship started to roll and there was a mad scramble to get overboard. As the ship turned on its side, I slid down the hull, climbed over the screw shaft and jumped overboard as far as possible. I was a very poor swimmer and was fighting for my life. I swam into a bunch of guys who had a floater net and I hung on. I stayed with this group the entire time.

We had no water or food. Someone gave me one malt ball the second day. We were covered in black oil. Some were lucky to have clothes on. I had nothing to cover my upper body. The sharks were the worst at night. Each morning we would have a few guys missing. In the daytime you could see the sharks in the swells. Some of the guys would swim off or swim down to the gedunk stand and we would never see them again.

We saw several planes and prayed they would see us, but we were disappointed. After being in the water for 108 hours we were finally spotted. We owe our lives to Adrian Marks, Chuck Gwinn, and the rescue crews.

I was picked up by the USS *Bassett*. I felt sure I could climb the ladder up to the barge but discovered I could not stand. We were taken back to the *Bassett* where we were cleaned up, treated for oil sores, given one teaspoon of water at a

time, and treated like babies until we were stronger. The *Bassett* crew even gave up their bunks for us. I thank them for all they did for me. I was taken to the hospital in Samar in the Philippines for treatment.

I was only 19 years old at that time. This was quite an ordeal for a young farm boy from Tennessee. I lost my two best friends who didn't make it, James Thomas King and Jimmy Jones. They were excellent swimmers and I could hardly swim at all. I think of them so often and wonder how I could have survived and not them. They were not on the floater net with me. We had great times together while on the *Indy*. I consider them heroes.

After my honorable discharge in January 1946, I moved to Michigan and worked in the auto factories for 26 years. I married my wife, Mary, in 1950 and we just celebrated our 52nd anniversary. In 1970 we moved to Clearwater, Florida and lived there for 21 years. We loved the beaches and good fishing. In 1991 we moved back to northwest Tennessee and built our retirement home near Reelfoot Lake. We are back near family, and this is beautiful country.

The Lord has been good to us.

CHAPTER 216   SURVIVOR NIGHTINGALE

NAME	NIGHTINGALE, WILLIAM O. Mach Mate 1C
STREET	
CITY	
STATE	
PHONE	
ENTERED SERVICE FROM	Deer Island, OR
PICKED UP BY	USS *Bassett*
DIVISION	
DOB	Deceased

FAMILY

EXPERIENCE
Unable to contact any family members.

NAME	NIXON, DANIEL S2C
STREET	366 Beatrice Ave
CITY	Johnston
STATE	PA 15906
PHONE	Robinson, PA
PICKED UP BY	USS *Talbot* Tr USS *Register*
DIVISION	3rd Division
DOB	9/15/23

FAMILY
Spouse: Joann M. Antal Nixon

EXPERIENCE

In 1943, I was 20 years old and drafted into the army. Since my twin brother Dave was in the navy, I requested a transfer into the navy. I was assigned to the USS *Indianapolis*.

On July 30, 1945, I was on watch at midship when the torpedoes hit us. I was blown from the ship into the water. I was unconscious for two days. My friend saved my life by putting a life jacket on me. I was in the water for 5 days and 5 nights. There were a lot of sharks swimming around us and I tried to knife a small shark so I could eat it, but I couldn't catch it. I have a newspaper clipping showing me on board the USS *Tranquility*, talking to a crew member and telling him I killed an 8-foot shark, but I do not remember doing that. There were about 25 men in our group, and only five survived. I saw many of my buddies die. Some men thought they saw the mess hall, dove under, and never came back up. Some thought they saw a beautiful island, and they too would dive under and we would never see them again. Some were killed by sharks and others by exposure. Drinking the salt water would kill you, so I just wet my lips with the salt water. But the salt water was a blessing in some ways—it kept my wounds from bleeding. We had nothing in our group to eat or drink. We also survived by taking the life jackets of those who died and putting them on ourselves. I saw five or six planes but they were too high to see us.

Finally the PBY dropped dye markers around our group and another plane eventually came and dropped rafts into the water. I was able to get in with four other guys. I was picked up on the fifth day by a ship and then transferred onto the USS *Tranquility*. From there I went to the hospital in Guam and to the hospital in San Diego. I was unable to walk; I had fractured my ankle in several places and injured my back. I had other wounds. I was eventually sent home with an honorable discharge. I didn't know Jesus Christ as my Savior then. I thank God that he heard my cries for help. He saved my life and gave me the chance to accept him as my Savior. I praise God that I was one of those that survived.

One more thing! Captain McVay loved his men and took good care of them.

CHAPTER 218 SURVIVOR NORBERG

NAME	NORBERG, JAMES A. CBM
STREET	
CITY	
STATE	
PHONE	
ENTERED SERVICE FROM	Duluth, MN
PICKED UP BY	USS *Bassett*
DIVISION	
DOB	Deceased 76

FAMILY

EXPERIENCE

Unable to contact any family members.

NAME	NUNLEY, TROY A. S2
STREET	7338 Donna Dr
CITY	New Port Richey
STATE	FL 34652
PHONE	
ENTERED SERVICE FROM	Bellwood, IL
PICKED UP BY	USS *Register*
DIVISION	4th Division
DOB	10/25/25

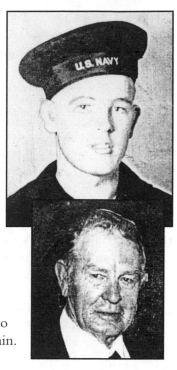

FAMILY
Spouse: Alice
Children: 4
Grandchildren: 7

EXPERIENCE
   Survivor Nunley said he spent many years trying to forget the nightmare and did not care to relive it again.

NAME	NUTTALL, ALEXANDER C. S1C	
STREET		
CITY		
STATE		
PHONE		
ENTERED SERVICE FROM	Cordova, NC	
PICKED UP BY	USS *Bassett*	
DIVISION		
DOB	9/3/17	Deceased 3/00

FAMILY
Widow: Lois Williams Nuttall
Children: Robert Alexander Nuttall (Lauranne)
Grandchildren: Blaine Nuttall Maples (Jim), Robin Nuttall Rakes (Mike)
Great-Grandchildren: Megan Shea Maples and Matthew McKinley Rakes

EXPERIENCE

Respectfully submitted by Survivor Nuttall's widow, Lois.

Alexander was born September 3, 1917 and in January 1944, he was called to serve his country.

In the fall of 1944, Alex came home on leave and I returned with him to Mare Island, where we lived in a quonset hut for the duration of his leave.   In the spring of 1945, the *Indy* returned for repairs and Alex was granted a leave. After his leave, Alex, I, and our son Robert made the long trip back to California to reside in the quonset hut. Of course in July, Alex returned to the *Indianapolis* and she sailed away for the last time. He spent his entire enlistment on the *Indianapolis*.

Alex and I were able to retire at a relatively young age and enjoyed traveling. Although we traveled to many parts of the country, Alex would never entertain the notion of sailing again. Therefore, we never went on a cruise. Of the ten battle stars she earned, Alex fought for seven of them. For many years, Alex would talk very little about his experience on the *Indianapolis*. In his last year, he finally spoke more about the traumatic event and even visited a fifth grade class in a local school to tell the children about that fateful time. When Alex was hospitalized, the children all sent get-well cards to him. This touched him very much.

Like many of his shipmates, Alex is no longer with us. He died in March of 2000 as a result of physical ailments he had developed over a lifetime of living through his ordeal. Our family has a lifetime of wonderful memories to sustain us and we know that we will, one day, see him again.

CHAPTER 221   SURVIVOR O'DONNELL

NAME	O'DONNELL, JAMES E. WT3	
STREET	7602 Derrek Pl	
CITY	Indianapolis	
STATE	IN 46219	
PHONE	317 357 9343	
ENTERED SERVICE FROM	Indianapolis, IN	
PICKED UP BY	USS *Bassett*	
DIVISION	No 2 Fire Room B Division	
DOB	7/8/20	

FAMILY

Spouse: Mary Alice O'Donnell
Children: James M. O'Donnell (Cindy), Thomas
J. O'Donnell (Jo Ann), Timothy G. O'Donnell
(Suzy), Mary T. O'Donnell Hofmeister (Eric)
Grandchildren: Kathleen O'Donnell, Colleen
O'Donnell, James P. O'Donnell, Kelly O'Donnell,
Thomas O'Donnell, Sean O'Donnell, Shannon
O'Donnell, Haley O'Donnell, Connor Hofmeister,
Kevin Hofmeister, Kyle Hofmeister

EXPERIENCE

I was raised in Indianapolis and graduated from Arsenal Technical High School.
After graduation I landed a job at Allison's. In 1944 at the age of 23, I was
drafted into the United States Navy. On April 27, 1944, I boarded the ship that
would take me and the crew into history...the USS *Indianapolis*.

The heavy cruiser was the pride of the United States Navy. She was so grand
that Admiral Spruance chose her to be the flagship of the Pacific Fifth Fleet. I
worked as a "water tender" aboard this great vessel. My job was to toil in the
heat of the boiler room. It wasn't a glamorous job but it was a job they wanted
us to do, so we did it.

The USS *Indianapolis* had seen combat in the battles for Saipan, Tinian, Guam,
Iwo Jima and Okinawa. She also had participated in the key battles of Midway
and the Philippine Sea. In all, she was adorned with ten battle stars. I
participated in five.

On March 31, 1945, while engaged in the Battle of Okinawa, the USS
Indianapolis was hit by a Japanese kamikaze pilot. When the plane hit, it rocked
the entire ship. Damage to the ship was extensive, and nine members of the crew
were killed. The USS *Indianapolis* was pulled from Okinawa for repairs.

On July 16, 1945, she was assigned the most secret and possibly most important
mission of World War II. She was dispatched to pick up important cargo in San
Francisco. Two crates were carried onto the ship and locked in the hangar deck.
No one aboard the ship, including Captain McVay, knew the contents of the
crates. The USS *Indianapolis* then set sail for the island of Tinian. On arrival the
crates were unloaded and taken to Tinian Airfield. During the mission, I worked
my shifts in the boiler room. No one aboard the USS *Indianapolis* knew that
when they docked at Tinian, a series of events were to be set in motion that
would forever change the world. The USS *Indianapolis* had delivered the most
powerful weapon mankind had ever known...the atomic bomb.

After unloading her payload, the USS *Indianapolis* set sail for the island of
Guam and then sailed toward Leyte to participate in gunnery practice with the
USS *Idaho* in preparation for the invasion of Japan.

On July 29, 1945, I worked my usual shift and was scheduled to return at 0400 hours the following morning. I located a place to sleep on the main deck near the aft gun turret. It was very hot near the boiler room. The higher up you went on the ship, the better chances you had of getting a breeze.

The USS *Indianapolis*, traveling alone on this journey, had reached the halfway point between the Philippines and Guam. The waters were calm that night. The men aboard the ship were either sleeping or casually manning their stations. Captain McVay had received no information of enemy activity near our travel route. Shortly before midnight, the Japanese submarine *I-58* made contact with a large vessel. The submarine moved closer and raised its periscope. At 12:14 am, two Japanese torpedoes struck the unsuspecting USS *Indianapolis*. The first torpedo hit the bow, and I was awakened. The second torpedo hit midship, igniting the ammunition magazine. The enormous ship was mortally wounded. The damage caused a complete electrical failure–lights were out and communications were rendered useless. The USS *Indianapolis* had no chance to call for help. Unfortunately the engines continued to run and the mighty ship maintained its speed and course. In its forward movement, the USS *Indianapolis* was scooping water into the damaged bow.

Despite the damage, many members of the crew were able to make it topside in the darkness when the order to abandon ship was given. I had time to reach a bag containing a kapok life jacket. Soon the ship rolled over on its starboard side. I walked along the side of the ship to the area of the keel and I jumped into the oil-filled water.

It is estimated that it took only 12 minutes for the USS *Indianapolis* to sink. It is believed that some 800 men successfully made it into the water before the sinking. The fortunate crew members that made it safely off the ship were floating in the pitch black Pacific Ocean. Many of the men had time to secure life vests, but some did not. The sinking happened so quickly that few lifeboats were launched. Yes, the survivors were in a dilemma, but they had one comfort...help was coming. If they could just stay afloat a few more hours the "cavalry" would arrive.

My eyes were burning from the oil. As the sun brought daylight to July 30, we were finally able to visually inspect our surroundings. We searched the horizon and the sky but saw no salvation. We were alone with no food, no water, no means of communication. Daylight also revealed that some of the survivors had disappeared during the night. Those that had been badly injured or had no flotation device were the first to succumb to the harsh Pacific Ocean.

We faced our worst nemesis the first morning in the sea. Sharks were in the area and had started to attack the defenseless men. The crew was scattered. We were in groups of ten or fifteen. You had to stay in a group. If you didn't, the sharks would get you. The groups were miles apart at some points. As the current carried us, it also brought along the oil and gasoline that floated on the surface.

By the evening of the first day, hope of a rescue had not diminished. Surely the navy was coming. We were due in for gunnery practice; surely someone realized we were missing. We had been without water and food for almost 24 hours.

On the second day, we started praying out loud. Once in a while we would see a plane fly overhead. It would be up so high it couldn't see us. The sharks were still following the men. One by one, they would attack. I could look down into the water and see the sharks swimming underneath us.

By the end of the third day, the elements and the sharks had exacted their toll on the survivors. Now after 72 hours, nearly half were gone. After so much time in the water, some of the men gave up. They would duck their head under the water and drink the salt water. After about four hours, they were gone. Men began to hallucinate. In other groups men were found lifeless in their vests. Removing the life vests from the dead and passing them to the living was common. On one occasion, a sailor found that his best friend had died. He clung to his friend's lifeless body, refusing the suggestion that he remove the life vest for his own use.

I maintained my position in the group. My kapok life vest was water-logged by now. It just kept my head and shoulders above the water. I continued to pray as hour upon hour passed. Despite the circumstances, the thought of giving up was inconceivable. I wasn't going to give up no matter what. I wanted to live. No matter how tight the spot, you can never give up.

On August 2, the crew had been drifting helplessly for 100 hours. Hope no longer existed for some. About 11:00 a.m., a PV-1 Ventura bomber was in the area on routine submarine patrol. The pilot, Lt. Wilbur C. Gwinn, spotted an oil slick and circled over to take a close look. What he saw caused an urgent radio broadcast to the American base at Peleliu. "Many men in the water." No one knew at the time who the men were and whether they were friend or foe. A navy PBY (seaplane) piloted by Lt. Adrian Marks was dispatched to the area. The destroyer USS *Cecil Doyle* was alerted by Marks and also responded to the area.

The aircraft piloted by Marks was the first rescue craft to arrive. He circled overhead, dropping rubber rafts. Against standing orders, Marks landed the PBY after seeing men attacked by sharks. For hours, the crew gathered as many men as the aircraft could hold. It wasn't until Marks started the rescue that it was learned that the USS *Indianapolis* had been sunk four days earlier. The USS *Doyle* and USS *Bassett* arrived after dark and survivors were pulled from the sea throughout the night. The men were too weak after nearly five days in the elements to rejoice or celebrate. Some were incoherent and did not realize they were being rescued. Some drowned while attempting to swim to rescue boats.

A rescue boat from the USS *Bassett* located my group. We had been in the water 108 hours. I don't remember seeing the rescue boat. I don't remember knowing that they had finally come for us. I just remember men pulling me from the water into the boat. I knew that when they got me in the boat, I was a lot better off than where I had been.

I was 25 years old during this disastrous event. I, along with 316 other shipmates, shared one powerful and steadfast quality...we would not give up. Once aboard the USS *Bassett*, I was placed in a bunk. All crew members of the USS *Bassett* volunteered to give up their bunks for us. They also had two or three guys to watch over each survivor. After lying in the bunk for a while, I decided I needed to go to the bathroom. The guys assigned to me said they would help. I said "No, I'm o.k."...I took two steps and hit the deck.

On August 6, 1945, the *Enola Gay* dropped an atomic bomb on the Japanese city of Hiroshima. The bomb dropped on Hiroshima and a second dropped on Nagasaki brought an end to World War II. The bombs used to force peace throughout the world had been the secret contents of the crates transported on the USS *Indianapolis*.

I returned to Indianapolis in the fall of 1945 and took a position with the Indianapolis Fire Department. My wife Mary Alice and I had three sons and a daughter.

In 1960 the crew members of the USS *Indianapolis* felt it important to have a reunion. My wife and I attended. Through the years the reunions have continued. Once held every five years, they are now held every other year in the city that shares the ship's name.

I remained with the Indianapolis Fire Department until 1981. In 1990, I was asked to help lead the efforts to build a national memorial dedicated to the USS *Indianapolis*. The decision to say yes was not an easy one. Agreeing to this task would mean I would be forced to speak about and revisit the experience. I agreed to do this for all of the 1,196 other men. I then set off on a speaking tour in which a million dollars would need to be raised. Groups of businessmen would gather up and I would talk in front of them. At the end of the evening, they would open up their checkbooks and donate to the fund. These engagements continued for five years.

On August 2, 1995, the monument to the USS *Indianapolis* (CA-35) was unveiled. A piece of the USS *Arizona* was placed inside the monument. The ships were the first and last American vessels to sink during the struggle for freedom. Building the monument was not only a proud moment for me and the other crewmembers; it was also an opportunity for me to come to grips with that tragic event that happened so long ago.

Over the years, the USS *Indianapolis* has become one of the best known World War II stories.

Freedom doesn't come cheap...never give up...**you can never give up!**

THE USS *INDIANAPOLIS*

Once there was a great U.S. ship,
That went out to the sea
There were many young men aboard this vessel
Many who soon would see
Some of these men were very scared,
Some were fearless and brave.
But many of these men however,
Would take their emotions to the grave.
A mission in the Second World War,
To deliver the first atomic bomb.
Who would have thought that aboard this ship,
something would go wrong.
That one fateful morning,
At a little past midnight,
Torpedoes struck the ship,
Filling everyone with fright.
In the shark infested water,
The men would float and wait.
As God above them,
Would soon decide their fate.
So here's to all the heroes,
Who lost their lives at sea.
And to my grandpa, James O'Donnell,
Water tender number three.

By Connor Hofmeister (age 11),
Grandson of Survivor O'Donnell

★ ★ ★ ★ ★ ★ ★ ★ ★ ★

Respectfully submitted by Paul J. Murphy, Chairman, USS Indianapolis
Survivors Organization.
    On behalf of all the crew of the USS *Indianapolis*, thanks, Jimmy and Mary
Alice, for the many hours you have dedicated to our organization. You were one
of the founding fathers of our organization, and still today serve on the board of
directors and reunion committee. Your charm with many people in the city of

Indianapolis helped get our beautiful national monument built. You continually spend hours each week selling our merchandise at the City Market, Westin Hotel and various other locations in Indianapolis. Thanks for continually sharing your experience and keeping our story alive. Some of the many honors given to this great hero (that I am aware of) are, Indianapolis Star Man of the Year Award, 1996; Hanson Anderson Award at Tech High School, 1996; Sagamores of the Wabash, 1998; Irishman of the Year Hibernians, 2001; Honorary Co-Chairman of Irish Festival, 2002; and August 2, 2002 was proclaimed "Jimmy O'Donnell Day" by Mayor Bart Peterson of Indianapolis. Thanks, Jimmy...you are very special to us!

CHAPTER 222   SURVIVOR OBLEDO

NAME	OBLEDO, MIKE G. S1C
STREET	
CITY	
STATE	
PHONE	
ENTERED SERVICE FROM	San Antonio, TX
PICKED UP BY	USS *Doyle*
DIVISION	
DOB	Deceased 10/01

FAMILY

EXPERIENCE

No response.

NAME	OLIJAR, JOHN S1C
STREET	
CITY	
STATE	
PHONE	
ENTERED SERVICE FROM	Chicago, IL
PICKED UP BY	PBY Tr USS *Doyle*
DIVISION	
DOB	Deceased 12/85

FAMILY

EXPERIENCE

Unable to contact any family members.

CHAPTER 224 SURVIVOR ORSBURN

NAME	ORSBURN, FRANK Ship Serv 2C
STREET	
CITY	
STATE	
PHONE	
ENTERED SERVICE FROM	Manilla, AR
PICKED UP BY	USS *Talbot* tr USS *Register*
DIVISION	
DOB	Deceased 9/90

FAMILY

EXPERIENCE

Unable to contact any family members.

NAME	OUTLAND, FELTON J. S1
STREET	1669 HWY 158 E
CITY	Sunbury
STATE	NC 27979
PHONE	
ENTERED SERVICE FROM	Sunbury, NC
PICKED UP BY	USS *Ringness*
DIVISION	5th Division
DOB	3/17/26

FAMILY

Spouse: Viola Brown

Children: Felton Outland Jr. (Janice), Teresa Outland Dail (Broughton Jr.), Ed Outland (Kim King), Cheryl Outland Moore (Master Sgt. Garry)

Grandchildren: Travis Outland, Kristen Outland, Chad Outland, Greg Dail, Tim Dail, Sara Dail, Brooke Outland, Carly Outland, Lee Outland, Rachel Moore, Caleb Moore

Step-Grandchildren: Ken Cowper (Jenny Foutz), Brandow Cowper (Donna Price)

EXPERIENCE

In 1943, I graduated from Sunbury High School and immediately enlisted in the navy in Raleigh, North Carolina on July 12, 1943. I was sent to the Great Lakes Training Station in Illinois. I was there for eight weeks and then was given leave to come home, and then it was back to Great Lakes. A few days after, I was sent by train to San Diego, California. I was there a couple of weeks and then put on the USS *Portland* for passage to the naval base at Pearl Harbor. After another week or two at Pearl Harbor, I was assigned to the USS *Indianapolis* as one of her crew. In a short time I was placed in the Fifth Division and in two weeks I was assigned to 40-mm anti-aircraft guns. This would be my workstation, battle station and watch station, until the sinking of the ship July 30, 1945.

The ship had no air conditioning, and we stayed around the equator a lot of the time. It was so hot below that we slept topside most of the time—on a blanket or kapok life jacket. We had a four-hour watch during the day, a four-hour watch at night, and a one-hour watch before sunrise and a one-hour watch before sunset. We worked on the guns during our spare time. We were always busy and worked hard. I will try to tell part of what went on from November 1943 until July 31, 1945. I am glad I could do my part for this great country of ours.

I saw my first action on November 20, 1943. This was the Gilbert Islands operation. We lost an aircraft carrier and lots of marines. This is when I realized what a terrible situation I had gotten myself into. (I was 17 years old and would be 18 on March 17, 1944.) The ship earned a total of ten battle stars and I was aboard for eight of them.

On June 19, 1944 we were in the battle of the Philippine Sea. We went to Saipan to help with the invasion of Saipan. We were at Saipan when we heard that the Japanese fleet was headed our way. Part of our fleet left Saipan to meet the Japanese fleet. We met the fleet in the Philippine Sea. As we got in range for the carrier planes to strike, they were launched. This was a very tense time and lots of planes were lost. Some ran out of fuel and it was dark before some of the planes got back. We turned on searchlights to help them find their ship. (Remember the ships had been blacked out.) Some were damaged and landed in the water; others had landing gear collapse when they hit the deck of the carrier and caught fire. These planes were pushed overboard. Pilots were picked up when possible. In all we sank one carrier, two destroyers, and one tanker and damaged other ships. There were more than 400 planes shot down, and we lost 30 planes.

When we got back to Saipan the Japanese had tried to reinforce Saipan from Tinian. There were bodies floating all around–everywhere we looked. We bombarded the island of Saipan. The shore battery was firing at the ships. In the book (*American Cruisers of WWII*), you can see that my side of the ship (port side) was next to the island. I could see the shore-batteries fire (flash) and just waited to see where it would hit next. They hit in the water all around us; one hit the ship but didn't cause damage, another projectile cut the flag line on the bridge just above my head. After Saipan we went in and took Guam and Tinian.

We were the flagship of the Fifth Fleet, commanded by Admiral Spruance. He was aboard our ship most of the time. We were cruising around the Carolina Islands one night and general quarters were sounded. After we got to our battle stations we found out a Japanese plane was heading our way. We were told to hold our fire...soon we heard the plane as it flew across our bow, about 1000 feet high, a perfect target. We could see the light or fire from the exhaust pipes. It flew on across the fleet and didn't know we were there. If we had fired, we would have given our position away. That patrol plane did not do a very good job.

In the Pacific during 1944 the Fifth Fleet was cruising around looking for trouble when a destroyer contacted a Japanese submarine and dropped depth charges. In a few minutes the submarine surfaced and the ship's guns took over. The submarine was destroyed. The survivors were picked up and ended up on our ship. There was always something going on.

In February 1945 the Fifth Fleet was sent to strike the homeland of Japan. Before we got off the coast of Japan we were issued cold weather gear, and we put antifreeze in the water jacket around the gun barrels. The guns fired 140 rounds per minute and were cooled by water. The sea was very rough and sometimes you could not see the ship next to you, but the navy would strike as planned. The aircraft carriers would launch planes when the bow was high and the stern down. They were recovered opposite from launching. It was cold and rough. We could see the snow-covered mountains of Japan. We carried the war to the homeland the second time (the first one being Doolittle in 1943). Some of the ships were damaged from the rough waters.

Okinawa was another hot spot. There were ships as far as you could see, anywhere you looked. We bombarded Okinawa for several days and on March 31, 1945 we were hit by a suicide pilot and his plane. We were damaged very badly, fuel tanks flooded, two propeller shafts damaged and water distilling equipment destroyed. We lost 9 men and 26 were wounded. We then headed back to the Mare Island navy yard in Vallejo, California. We had saltwater baths until May 2, 1945, when we arrived in California. We were repaired and left the yard on July 16, 1945. We knew we had secret cargo on board but no one knew what. We were to travel at top speed to Tinian and deliver the cargo, which was part of the atomic bomb. From Tinian we went to Guam and there got our orders to join the fleet in the Philippine Islands.

On July 30, 1945, George Abbott from Kentucky and I went on midnight watch. I had put on headphones and we were just beginning our duty when we heard an explosion. The ship shook terribly. We were on 40-mm guns by the aft stack. My watch was always on 40-mm guns under the bridge on port side. I'll never know why that particular watch I was by the aft stack. (A guardian angel was present.)

After the explosion I could not make any contact on the phone. We tried for a minute or so and I told George to go for life jackets. Remember it was very dark. He came back with one life jacket saying it did not look good. Still no word by phone. At that point the ship was listing to starboard. George gave me the one life jacket and said he was going for another, and I never saw him again. I did hear from others later that he did get a life jacket and lasted about three days in the water.

As for me I looked over the 40-mm guns where the ammunition was stored and saw it falling out of the gun-shield and I figured it was time to go. I took off the phone and started off the ship on port side. The water met me on the main deck and I went down with the ship. I was sucked under the water and on the way down my feet got tangled in a line or phone wire, but they came loose in a few seconds. I had to let go of the air I had in my lungs, and I thought to myself, "Oh Lord...not now."

In a short time that good old kapok life jacket shot me right out of the water. The ship was gone. I wonder how long I stayed under the water. I do know that George saved my life. Without the life jacket I would have gone with the ship. I came up about six to eight feet from four life rafts still tied together. They had broken away from the ship. Don't forget that it was very dark. There was one other man on these rafts, and he and I untied the four rafts. We called to others that there were life rafts. We got them separated and then tied the four rafts to keep us together.

Men started coming, and we ended up with 17 men, which made one extra man for one of the rafts. We had five men on the raft that I was on. The last man on our raft was Giles McCoy. I pulled him on our raft, as he was exhausted from swimming. Giles was a marine who had been on watch at the brig. He had a .45 automatic pistol around his waist and wore big heavy shoes. Some were just in their nightclothes. The others on our raft were David Kemp, Willis Gray, and Robert Brundige. For the next two or three hours I was sick from swallowing fuel oil and salt water and from bobbing up and down in the raft.

When the sun came up in the morning it was a welcome sight. We found some Spam and dry crackers and two water kegs that were empty. We ate very little due to the fact we had no water. It was hot during the day and cold at night. The raft was only two or three inches above the water. We stayed wet from the chest down all the time. At night we would slip down in the water to stay warm. When the waves would break over our heads, we would raise up and turn our heads to the side and let the water out of our ears.

The sharks were there on the first day and kept us company all the time. They swam around the raft constantly three to eight feet away. By the end of the first day we were getting sore bottoms from the rafts rubbing and bumping on one another. We talked about how when we got back to San Francisco, we would get ice-cold watermelon and eat in the middle of Market Street. (We eventually came home to San Diego, and not San Francisco.)

Our life jackets were hard from the salt they had absorbed and for those of us who had shoes, they became hard and we threw them out. We had to untie the rafts and let each one go on its own. I had been fully dressed when the ship went down, so I had my cap in my pocket. We used it to pour water over our heads to help keep cool during the day.

The raft was sinking down in the water about one inch a day. We had hoped for rain and the sight of a ship. The sharks stayed with us and nothing changed. Each day we talked a little less and on the fourth day things were getting bad...no rain, no ship, and we were losing hope. That day one of our men jumped over and another one who was a good swimmer went after him. The man who had jumped was delirious and talked very little after that. At this time we divided a can of Spam between us. One survivor took the can the Spam had been in, urinated in it, then drank the urine. We all were despondent and finding it harder to hold on.

On the evening of the fifth day we heard an airplane flying real low. It spotted us and dropped dye markers about 3:00 or 4:00 p.m. We saw the bow of a ship coming toward us–a beautiful sight. The USS *Ringness* would pick us up.

We were helped onto the ship by the crew, and then two crew members would take a man into the shower to clean the oil and salt from his body. They then gave us dry clothes and their bunks to sleep on. At first they gave us water to drink but nothing to eat. We went to sleep and they would awaken us every hour or two with more water, but not all we wanted. The next morning we had a full breakfast with fresh eggs. The crew of the *Ringness* was very good to us, and I want to thank them.

I learned from some of the other survivors about the lights shining on the clouds the night before we were rescued. We never saw anything until the ship appeared in our view. I understand we were the last group to be picked up.

We were taken to the hospital on the island of Palau. We stayed there for a few days and then were put on a hospital ship to Guam. We remained in the hospital there for three or four weeks. From there we were moved to a submarine base on Guam. We were treated really well and the food was delicious. We finally got passage back to San Diego on an aircraft carrier. There we were paid and issued new clothes and given thirty days' leave. It was nice to get home after a long hard trip. I had wondered during those months at sea what one would do if his ship was sinking. Now I can assure you that you can never prepare or make plans for such an occasion. Our ship was sunk in about 12 minutes after we were hit, and we never had a chance to fire our guns.

When my leave was up, I was to report to Norfolk naval base. I was sent to Camp Perry, Virginia to finish my navy career. I was honorably discharged in March 1946 as a GM third-class. In 1946 I worked at different jobs trying to decide what kind of work I wanted to do. I did some bricklaying, carpentry, and some farm work. In 1947 I got a tractor and tried farming. It did not work out too well, as I did not put my best in to it.

In the winter of 1947, I got a job with the National Screen Co in Suffolk, Virginia. In 1947, I met Viola Brown from Colerain, North Carolina. She was in nursing school at Lakeview in Suffolk, Virginia. She graduated in 1947. We got along fine (still do), fell in love, and were married in January 1948. We lived in Suffolk for three years and had a wonderful time. We were both working.

In 1950 we decided to move back to Sunbury to a small farm my parents gave me. From 1950 to 1988 I farmed and raised four children—Felton, Teresa, Ed, and Cheryl. We had some good times and some tight times. It has been a good life for us and it was a good life for the children. We worked together and played together. In 1982 we sold our house to our son Felton, the older son and the farmer of the family. We built a new house across the road, where we reside now. I have a good wife, a good partner and it has been great all the way. No complaints.

In the summer of 1959, after the book *Abandon Ship* was published, we decided to visit the family of George Abbott. The Abbotts were very nice to us and from their house we tried to contact the survivors that were on the raft with me. We had no phone numbers, and trying to find someone in St. Louis, Missouri with no address or number is not easy. I called the operator in St. Louis and told her what I was trying to do. There were about 200 McCoys in St. Louis, and she said we would start at the top of the list and work our way down. The first call she made was to McCoy's mother, and I talked with her. She gave me her son's number in Boonville, Missouri.

We left Kentucky and headed for Boonville the next day. We arrived at Giles

McCoy's house late that day. We sat around the table that night and talked. He suggested we have a reunion of all the survivors. He said if I thought enough of him to look him up then he would like to see us all get together. He asked where I thought we should meet, and I suggested Indianapolis, Indiana. McCoy did lots of hard work toward getting a reunion started, and in 1960 we met for the first time. We have been meeting every five years since then until 1995. At that time we decided to meet every two years, since we were getting older. He also worked hard to get a site in the city of Indianapolis on which to erect a memorial. The city finally gave the organization a location, which is a very pretty spot. The survivors–along with many others–had to raise the money to erect a memorial, and in 1995 it was dedicated. This is a memorial to all men lost at sea.

CHAPTER 226   SURVIVOR OVERMAN

NAME	OVERMAN, THURMAN D. S2C
STREET	
CITY	
STATE	
PHONE	
ENTERED SERVICE FROM	Canton, NC
PICKED UP BY	USS *Bassett*
DIVISION	
DOB	Deceased

FAMILY

EXPERIENCE

Unable to contact any family members.

CHAPTER 227 — SURVIVOR OWEN

NAME	OWEN, KEITH N. COOK 3C
STREET	
CITY	
STATE	
PHONE	
ENTERED SERVICE FROM	Chula Vista, CA
PICKED UP BY	USS *Bassett*
DIVISION	
DOB	Deceased 12/88

FAMILY

EXPERIENCE

Unable to contact any family members.

CHAPTER 228 — SURVIVOR PACE

NAME	PACE, CURTIS S2C
STREET	
CITY	
STATE	
PHONE	
ENTERED SERVICE FROM	Ashford, AL
PICKED UP BY	USS *Talbot* tr USS *Register*
DIVISION	
DOB	Deceased 6/69

FAMILY

EXPERIENCE

Unable to contact any family members.

NAME	PACHECO, JOSE S1C
STREET	
CITY	
STATE	
PHONE	
ENTERED SERVICE FROM	Wagon Mound, NM
PICKED UP BY	USS *Bassett*
DIVISION	
DOB	Deceased

FAMILY

EXPERIENCE

Unable to contact any family members.

CHAPTER 230 SURVIVOR PALMITER

NAME	PALMITER, ADELORE A. S2C
STREET	P O Box 293
CITY	Whitaker
STATE	MI 48160
PHONE	
ENTERED SERVICE FROM	Monroe, MI
PICKED UP BY	USS *Ringness*
DIVISION	
DOB	

FAMILY

Spouse: Wilma
Children: three sons and one daughter
Grandchildren: four grandsons and four granddaughters
Great-Grandchildren: seven

EXPERIENCE

No response.

NAME	PAROUBEK, RICHARD A. Y1
STREET	126 Henry Tyler Dr
CITY	Williamsburg
STATE	VA 23188
PHONE	757 258 0266
ENTERED SERVICE FROM	Skokie, IL
PICKED UP BY	USS *Doyle*
DIVISION	Engineering (Log Room)
DOB	10/31/22

FAMILY
Spouse: Ann Clendenin
Children: Richard, Mary, Ellen
Grandchildren: Zak, Ross, Joseph, Emma, Nina, Chelsea

EXPERIENCE

I was raised in a family of eight children, five boys and three girls. All the boys were in the service—four in the navy and one in the army. Fortunately, we all came back home. I graduated from Niles Township High School in 1941, after which I attended Walton School of Commerce, hoping to become a court reporter. During the depression that job was always in demand and the pay was good. After one year of that study, I obtained a position with the U.S. Army Corps of Engineers, Procurement Department, working in the Merchandise Mart in Chicago.

While commuting to work on the El one morning, my friend Bob Reiland and I met a sailor who was sitting close by but soon came over to us. "How would both of you like a good job in the navy?" Since our draft numbers were coming up, we said, "Tell us more." He explained we would be working in Chicago in the Office of Naval Officer Procurement, the night shift, but would be given a second class rating if we passed the office test and physical. We looked at each other and decided we would "show up."

After passing the tests, we were sworn in on October 5, 1942 and given uniform acquisition vouchers and a car to proceed to Great Lakes for our uniforms. No boot camp...would you believe?

We reported to the Office of Naval Officer Procurement in the Board of Trade Building the next day. Since we lived at home we were given subsistence and assigned to a recruiting team for navy, marines, and army. We visited colleges and universities in Illinois, Wisconsin, Michigan, and Minnesota. Great duty! After returning from this tour, I was sent to Kansas City and Bob was sent to Milwaukee.

While in Kansas City, I was assigned to recruiting Waves (Women Accepted for Volunteer Emergency Servcice). Well, you know someone had to do it! This duty consisted of one Wave officer, two enlisted Waves and myself. We set up store-front offices, rented on a monthly basis, in Topeka, Wichita, Hutchinson, and Lawrence, Kansas. The ladies would talk to social clubs and other ladies' groups and I would process the paperwork.

After returning from this trip, I made application for entry in the V-5 program, flight training. I was accepted and sent to three months of training at Cornell College in Mount Vernon, Iowa. I then was sent to WTS flight training in Grand Junction, Colorado. Basic flight training was in a small two-seat Taylorcraft plane.

Although I soloed and completed 25 hours, I did not make the cut. One-third of each class had to be terminated. I returned to Great Lakes for reassignment, was restored to my second class rating and assigned to the personnel office at Alameda Air Station in California. After six months, a directive from Washington said, "All personnel who have over twenty months' shore duty must be rotated overseas."

My working contact at the Twelfth Naval District in San Francisco asked me to come in and talk about my new assignment. He said he had an aircraft carrier, a destroyer, and a heavy cruiser currently under repair at Mare Island. He said the cruiser was also the flagship of the Fifth Fleet. Since two of my good friends had been lost on the USS *Franklin*, I did not like the prospects of a carrier. The destroyers also were having heavy losses around the Philippines, so a flagship, sounded good to me. "I'll take it."

I reported to the USS *Indianapolis* during the latter part of June 1945. I was told I would be in charge of the log room and my battle station would be on the damage-control phone in the forward engine room. Ensign Twible showed me how to get to the engine room. The log room is the administration office of the engineering department, and I was to report to Lt. Richard Redmayne, chief engineer. In addition to the daily routine, I was directed to be Captain McVay's yeoman on his inspection rounds. I also served as court recorder during Captain's Mast.

Sea duty is much different than shore duty. First, you have to find the mess hall and head. It took several days to become orientated, especially developing sea legs and getting information over the PA system and the shrill of piping code. Not having been at sea before, I thought it was not unusual for ships to travel at such high speeds.

After stopping in Hawaii for refueling and supplies, we immediately proceeded to the island of Tinian at flank speed. We arrived on Friday morning and dropped anchor. Because of the large crowd on the quarterdeck, I made my way up to the forecastle, proceeding to the port side opposite number one turret.

While watching the small boats and barges coming alongside, Commander Flynn came over and ordered the last three men on the rail to follow him. I was the last of the three. We followed him to the cabin referred to as a guest cabin on the port side. As we entered the cabin, three men were already there. We saw two lead canisters, about knee-high, with long steel pipes through rings on top. As I made my way to the opposite side, I said, "This looks like it has to do with radiation." Silence...the two escorts, later identified as Captain Nolan and Major Furman, looked at each other, but said nothing. These canisters I was later told, contained the uranium–235 slugs which were used in the atomic bomb dropped on Hiroshima.

Commander Flynn then ordered us to take the canisters out to the forecastle where a boom was used to lower the first one to a barge below. We then returned for the other canister, which was about the same size, but square in the body, rather than round like the first. Then the large crate which had been stored in one of the hangars was lowered, with difficulty, onto a barge below.

With the cargo delivered, we were directed to proceed to Guam for refueling, and ten days of off-shore training and gunnery practice. Shore leave also was scheduled. When we reached Guam, we were notified over the PA system that all crew members were to remain on board and that a movie would be shown on the quarterdeck at 2100 hours. We left Guam's Apra Harbor the next morning.

The sleeping quarters for the log room personnel were in the log room, located just below the quarterdeck on the starboard side, but above the water line. Strangely, I did not hear or feel the explosions from the torpedo hits, but I found myself on the deck in complete darkness. Moments later the door was opened and smoke came pouring in. I felt my slippers under me, and I put them on. I went to the door. As we moved quickly (Longwell, myself and the third shipmate's name I do not remember), we saw cable draping down and sparking and the battle lamp glowed dimly through the smoke. We quickly made our way up the ladder to the quarterdeck and saw heavy smoke coming from the forward part of the ship. The ship already was listing to starboard but still moving forward. Men were leaving the ship, having already heard "abandon ship."

Abandon ship!! Life belts!! We had left our life belts below. Rather than go below to get them, we remembered new life jackets were stored along the rail at the after-stack. Longwell and I rushed to climb the ladder to that gangway. The other man did not follow. He went below to get personal items, having received word from his wife just before leaving San Francisco that he was to become a father. He was never seen again.

As we reached the top of the ladder, someone–I believe it was Mike Kuryla–was already cutting the jackets from the railing and passing them out. As I was going to the port side, the ship took a strong list to starboard. As it was going over, I put my legs over the rail and slid down the hull. The last ten or twelve feet was free fall. I swam away as quickly as I could.

When I turned around, the ship was still moving forward, with the fantail rising higher into the air. Just then the moonlight came through the clouds; it seemed almost overhead. I was stunned at what I saw. Men were jumping or being dumped overboard from a height of a hundred feet or more. As the ship was rolling on its side and rising in the air, it continued turning to the point of being almost upside down. There was a low rumble coming from inside the ship, as gear and munitions rolled and slammed against the bulkheads. The ship hesitated at the top of its height before slowly at first, then more quickly driving itself into the sea. After the ship disappeared, there were two heavy underwater explosions. I do not know what caused them.

In a survival course while a naval air cadet, we were told as a precaution to prevent abdominal injury, to bring your knees to your chest. This fetal position was more comfortable than any other and tended to keep my head back and kept my legs from dangling. I kept this position most of the time until rescue.

When the ship disappeared, many men were in the general area, some in great pain and others calling for friends. Some were badly burned or had suffered broken bones. Those who left the ship with just life belts–or left with nothing at all–were in a serious way. I believe some did not last until morning.

We soon became aware of the oil covering us. Scared? Yes! Bewildered? Yes! How did I ever get here in the middle of the Pacific Ocean? Within the first 20 minutes, however, Father Conway identified himself and asked all Catholics to gather around. He said he was going to give the last rites for all who had just died and all who were about to die. During the grueling days which followed, he went from man to man giving help and comfort to all those who were in the group. He did not survive but he served his fellow man graciously and in a heroic manner. This group was later referred to as Dr. Haynes' group.

Still frightened and cold, it was reassuring that I was not alone, but that feeling did not last long. A loud voice called out, "Submarine!" and a sudden quiet came over the entire area. The Japanese had been known to machine-gun survivors of other ships they had sunk.

It must have been an hour before the men began talking and calling again for their buddies. The sub (if in fact it had been there) mercifully missed us. Dawn seemed to take forever to arrive, but when the sun it slowly came over the horizon in the east, we could see the problems we were facing. The oil slick was between one and two inches thick, and along with the salt water made it difficult to see and breathe. The oil slick did dissipate over time but did not entirely leave us. This was fortunate because it was the reflection of the sun off the oil slick which ultimately saved those of us who survived.

At daybreak, I found I was in a group of about 300. I believe it was the largest group. We managed to keep fairly well together. By chance, someone found a long line. Those on the outer perimeter of the circle would hold the line by bringing it behind our backs. Even with this line, we felt better. The expectation was of course that we would soon be rescued, so there was no real panic or deep concern. Each man helped others where he could. In addition to Dr. Haynes and Father Conway, in this group was Commander Lipski, gunnery officer, who was badly burned around the face and arms. His eyes seemed to be burned shut and Dr. Haynes was helpless to do anything. Those of us around

him tried to keep his legs flat so they
would not dangle. Dr. Haynes was near
him when he mercifully died. His jacket
was cut off and he slipped away.

No rescue ships on Monday. We were
due at Leyte Tuesday morning. Surely we
would be missed and a search would be
started. The days in the water were both
hot and cold, but in either case, time
seemed never to pass. This was especially
so at night. During this time, there were a
lot of prayers and thoughts of family and
home. I started making promises that if I survived, I would never do such and
such again. If I survived, I promised to do many good things. If I had kept all
my promises, I would have been bishop by now. We thought for sure we would
see some help on Tuesday, because if we did not report at Leyte, a search would
surely begin. Toward nightfall, the men began to use the second language of the
navy. I will not repeat this here.

Although we were hungry the first day and night, that feeling soon left, and
thirst became the major concern. I believe that was the major reason why so
many men were lost. Also, I believe most of the men died on the third day.
Drinking the salt water was the major factor.

While I did see shark fins, I did not see any attacks on the men, just body parts
and dead bodies. I kept telling myself, "DO NOT DRINK THE SALT
WATER!" The urge to drink the water was overwhelming. Another concern
was changes in the mental condition we were experiencing. The hot sun,
combined with drinking the water, caused various slow changes in our
behavior...having strange delusions, seeing things that were not there. On two
occasions when my eyes were closed, someone grabbed me and climbed on my
back. I'm sure he felt I was something to help him float. To free myself of this
weight, I fought to go deeper so his head was also below water, which caused
him to release me. From then on, I tried to keep my distance from everyone.

Looking back, human behavior was changing on a daily basis. It went from
joint help and cooperation to expectation, to anger, then to the strongest instinct
of all...the will to survive.

Finally, a beautiful plane came overhead. HAPPY DAY! Help was now on the
way. Lt. Adrian Marks' Catalina soon landed near our group, but I was not able
to get on the plane. I did manage to reach a three-man life raft which eventually
held seven men. This group, Dr. Haynes' group, was picked up by the USS *Doyle*.

We were sent to Palau for much-needed medical attention, a bath, clothes, and
much-needed sleep. It was wonderful to be alive!

NAME	PASKET, LYLE M. S2C
STREET	1756 Walnut Ln
CITY	Eagan
STATE	MN 55122
PHONE	651 452 4513
ENTERED SERVICE FROM	St Paul, MN
PICKED UP BY	USS *Talbot* Tr USS *Register*
DIVISION	S Division
DOB	8/17/27

FAMILY

Spouse: Evelyn
Children: Lance Pasket, Lynnette Pasket
Grandchildren: Amber, Ashley, Jacob, Sarah, Temery
Great-Grandchildren: Grace

EXPERIENCE

I was born and raised in St Paul, Minnesota in a family of six children. I was the oldest. At the age of 16, I dropped out of high school and started working for Northwest Airlines on November 11, 1943. I stayed with the airlines until my retirement in 1989, with time off for military service in World War II and the Korean War.

In March 1945, I joined the navy and went to the Great Lakes naval station in Illinois for boot camp. I was assigned to the USS *Indianapolis* on June 21, 1945 as an aviation storekeeper. In that position, I kept track of parts and materials for repair of aircraft the ship carried.

On July 30, 1945, I was on duty for the midnight to 0400 watch on the boat deck, starboard side, 5-inch gun. I recall it was a cloudy night. The ship took its first hit around ten after twelve. I was able to grab a life jacket (kapok), and I stayed at my post until the ship started to list to starboard. I crawled on my hands and knees to the portside and laid against the bulkhead until the ship was completely on its side. I then jumped overboard in the complete darkness and swam about 200 feet away from the ship. Having been in the Navy only a short time (and it was my first sea duty), I remembered from boot camp, "If your ship sinks, get away from the ship as suction will take you down."

I joined up with a group of about 75 men. The first thing we did was pray and as for myself, I also thought of my mother and what a horrible birthday present this would be for her to receive a telegram saying "KIA" or "MIA". She and I shared the same birthday in mid-August.

After praying, we hooked arm-to-arm in a circle formation until daylight. When we found a life net, we spread it out and put the wounded inside, while the rest of us stayed on the outside edge. Someone had found a can of malted milk tablets. We formed a sort of line, and we all received one tablet. I believe it was a chief who passed them out.

On Monday morning, I heard screaming and someone shouted, "Sharks!" We all started to kick our legs, as when you looked beneath the water, a shark would pass. They did not attack inside our ring but waited outside of the circle, as if they knew a few men would leave, which they did due to hallucination and various dementia, which stemmed from thirst, hunger, and other ordeals. The weather was very hot during the day and chilly to cold at night.

I stayed with the group until Wednesday. That's when I passed out. When I came to, it was a sunny day and I was alone. Why the sharks didn't get me, I don't know, but I suppose it was the praying I did. After drifting by myself for about an hour or so, I joined two other stragglers, but they both died shortly afterwards.

Later that day, our fourth, I looked up and saw an aircraft flying low. It dropped a raft. I swam to it, pulled the ring to inflate it, but unfortunately it inflated upside down. I tried to turn it right side up, but I lacked the strength to do it. So I fought and was able to get on it while it was upside down. By now, I was so very weak and the backs of my legs were chafed from my pants rubbing during the hours spent treading water.

After a while on the raft, I came upon another raft with three men in it. We righted my raft and then went two men per raft. They had used all their raft rations, and mine had been lost when the raft was inflated upside down.

In the very early hours of Friday morning a rain squall came up. We caught the rain by holding a rubberized tarp over our heads and funneling the water into our mouths for our first drink, which helped our thirst a bit. Just before daylight, we saw a searchlight and knew help and rescue were on the way.

Several hours later the USS *Ralph Talbot* (DD 390) picked me up, along with the other men on our rafts. A sailor from the *Talbot* jumped in the water with a life line to help pull our rafts to the ship. This was done with caution, because it was not known whether we were Japanese or Americans on the rafts. I had the good fortune to meet my rescuer in 1987 at the USS *Talbot* reunion in Long Beach, California, when he told me that he was the sailor who swam to the raft to retrieve us.

I was transferred to the USS *Register* that took me to Palau. From there, I was transferred to a hospital in Guam for convalescing. I returned to the States in September 1945. I stayed in the navy until August 1948, spending most of the time in the Philippine Islands. After returning home from military duty, I went back to work at Northwest Airlines in aircraft maintenance and remained in the Navy Air Reserves.

On April 10, 1950, I was on a routine flight from Bermuda to Minneapolis Naval Air Station when we encountered electrical troubles. We were running low on fuel in a severe thunderstorm with zero visibility. We ditched the plane, and it happened to be in Lake Michigan. Fortunately, we were about 300 yards offshore and I swam to shore to get help for the rest of the crew.

I was recalled to active duty June 1950 when the Korean War broke out. I was a flight mechanic on a P2V, and we flew on patrol missions out of Kodiak, Alaska.

Losing one ship and one aircraft was enough for me to settle down and get married in May 1955. Prior to the birth of our first child, I resigned from the Navy Air Reserves. We have raised a son and daughter who have in turn presented us with five grandchildren and one great-grandchild. Since May 1976, we have lived in our present home in the suburbs of Eagan, south of the Twin Cities.

I have maintained a close bond with the other survivors of the ship through the reunions over the years, most of which I have attended. I am a member of the USS Indianapolis Survivors Organization and at the present time hold the position of master of arms.

Since my retirement from Northwest Airlines in 1989, I have spoken to and shared my *Indy* experience with many school groups, clubs, military reunions, churches, and associations in the private and public sectors. I also have taken part in signing many books and in newspaper and TV interviews.

To this day, I still wonder WHY the sharks never attacked me when I passed out and left the group. To me, each day is a blessed event and I thank God for it. I am proud to have served aboard such a great ship as the USS *Indianapolis* (CA-35).

CHAPTER 233   SURVIVOR PAULK

NAME	PAULK, LUTHER D. S2C
STREET	
CITY	
STATE	
PHONE	
ENTERED SERVICE FROM	Dothan, AL
PICKED UP BY	USS *Doyle*
DIVISION	
DOB	Deceased 8/95

FAMILY

EXPERIENCE
    Unable to contact any family members.

NAME	PAYNE, EDWARD G. S2C
STREET	
CITY	
STATE	
PHONE	
ENTERED SERVICE FROM	Berkeley Springs, WV
PICKED UP BY	USS *Ringness*
DIVISION	
DOB	Deceased

FAMILY

EXPERIENCE

Unable to contact any family members.

NAME	PENA, SANTOS S1C
STREET	502 N Shawnee Ave
CITY	Tucson
STATE	AZ 85745
PHONE	520 622 5003
ENTERED SERVICE FROM	Tucson, AZ
PICKED UP BY	USS *Bassett*
DIVISION	7th Division
DOB	11/1/25

FAMILY
Spouse: Erlinda Pena
Children: Four
Grandchildren: Seven
Great-Grandchildren: Three

EXPERIENCE

I was the last watchman on the bow of the *Indy*. On that fateful night, I arose from my bunk and prepared to stand watch from 0000 to 0400. With my life jacket on, I walked from the aft number three 8-inch gun turret forward past the number one 8-inch gun turret and relieved the previous watch stander at the 20-mm guns.

Only minutes into my watch, I was blown straight up in the air from the blast of the first torpedo, which struck below and a few feet in front of me. I had experienced kamikaze strikes in the past, but there was no doubt that this time the *Indy* would soon go under. Getting to my feet, I went aft.

My buddy Celaya had been sleeping topside, as many shipmates did, because of the heat below decks. He frantically said he would go below to retrieve a life jacket, but I yelled back at him that he would never make it back if he did. I told him to stick with me, as my life jacket would keep both of us afloat for awhile. If he had ignored my warning, it is very likely I would not have seen him again. Celaya and I were not only shipmates, but friends and fellow Arizonians. We abandoned ship together at the port side, slightly forward of the number three gun turret. Although we both knew we had survived the sinking, we did not know whether we had both survived the following five days until after our rescue.

On the first night, one shipmate seemed more like the enemy than a friend. Soon after abandoning ship, I swam toward this lone sailor who was on a life raft and was shocked that he was striking me on the head to prevent me from climbing on. So I hung on the side. By morning, many survivors had succeeded in getting on the raft, and others joined me in hanging on the sides.

During the nights and days that followed, my only reality besides the endless expanse of the sea was the sun and clouds, moon and stars, shipmates and sharks, oil and blood. In my mind, I could see my loved ones back home. I held on to good memories while I floated and held onto the life raft—waiting, hoping, and praying that I would see them all again.

I'll never forget the moment I saw Lt. Gwinn's plane flying over us. It was then that I knew God would surely rescue those of us that remained alive. Neither will I forget the moment Lt. Marks landed his plane on the open sea. Those two lieutenants were the real heroes of this ordeal. The crew of the great ship USS *Bassett* picked me up. They took good care of me and my shipmates. May God bless each and every one of them.

50th Wedding Anniversary

NAME PEREZ, BASILLO S2C
STREET
CITY
STATE
PHONE
ENTERED SERVICE FROM Pearsall, TX
PICKED UP BY USS *Bassett*
DIVISION
DOB Deceased 4/01

FAMILY

EXPERIENCE

Unable to contact any family members.

CHAPTER 237 SURVIVOR PERKINS

NAME PERKINS, EDWARD Fireman 2C
STREET
CITY
STATE
PHONE
ENTERED SERVICE FROM Steubenville, OH
PICKED UP BY USS *Bassett*
DIVISION
DOB Deceased

FAMILY

EXPERIENCE

Unable to contact any family members.

CHAPTER 238 SURVIVOR PETERSON

NAME	PETERSON, AVERY C. S2C
STREET	
CITY	
STATE	
PHONE	
ENTERED SERVICE FROM	Waupun, WI
PICKED UP BY	USS *Bassett*
DIVISION	
DOB	Deceased 87

FAMILY

EXPERIENCE

Unable to contact family members.

CHAPTER 239 SURVIVOR PHILLIPS

NAME	PHILLIPS, HUIE H. S1C
STREET	
CITY	
STATE	
PHONE	
ENTERED SERVICE FROM	Dothan, AL
PICKED UP BY	USS *Doyle*
DIVISION	
DOB	Deceased

FAMILY

EXPERIENCE

Unable to contact any family members.

CHAPTER 240 SURVIVOR PODISH

NAME PODISH, PAUL S2C
STREET
CITY
STATE
PHONE
ENTERED SERVICE FROM Eight Four, PA
PICKED UP BY USS *Doyle*
DIVISION
DOB Deceased 7/83

FAMILY

EXPERIENCE

Unable to contact any family members.

CHAPTER 241 SURVIVOR PODSCHUN

NAME PODSCHUN, CLIFFORD S1C
STREET
CITY
STATE
PHONE
ENTERED SERVICE FROM Wichita, KS
PICKED UP BY USS *Doyle*
DIVISION
DOB Deceased 75

FAMILY

EXPERIENCE

Unable to contact any family members.

NAME   POGUE, HERMAN G. S2C
STREET
CITY
STATE
PHONE
ENTERED SERVICE FROM   Roff, OK
PICKED UP BY   USS *Bassett*
DIVISION
DOB   Deceased 94

FAMILY

EXPERIENCE
Unable to contact any family members.

NAME   POOR, GERALD S2C
STREET   10625 Highway E
CITY   Rolla
STATE   MO 65401
PHONE   314 364 3452
ENTERED SERVICE FROM   Vienna, MO
PICKED UP BY   USS *Bassett*
DIVISION   Fox Division
DOB   4/2/27

FAMILY
Spouse: Mildred
Children: Homer Poor and Thelma Poor Bailey
Grandchildren: Cody Poor, Blake Poor, Sonya
Lamerson, James M. Coe, James W. Coe, Michael Bailey
Great-Grandchildren: Kylee Bailey, Michael
Lamberson, Janice Bailey, Christina Bailey

EXPERIENCE

Respectfully submitted by Survivor Poor and his younger sister, Billie Ann. When Billie Ann asked Jerry if she could help him with his chapter, his comment was, "I don't have anything exciting to tell." The following is what he agreed to share.

I was born April 2, 1927 in Maries County, Missouri, one of eight children. Our mother died when I was seven years old. We went to live with my grandparents on their farm. I was too young to join the navy and Dad was hesitant because my three older brothers were already in the service. My older sister convinced him and in January of 1945 I joined the navy. My boot camp was at Great Lakes naval base in Illinois.

When I finished boot camp, I was assigned to the USS *Indianapolis* in June of 1945. I had only been on board a short time when shortly after midnight on July 30, 1945, the ship was sunk by two Japanese torpedoes.

I became good friends of Alfred Jurgensmeyer and Norbert Boss. I remember Jurgensmeyer became disoriented, and I was holding him in my arms when he died. There were officers and corpsmen who would come and help "bury" someone when they passed away. Finally, there were only corpsmen left. When I called for help to "bury" Alfred, I was told there were no more corpsmen left and I would have to do it myself. Norbert helped me and all we could do was take off his life jacket, say a prayer, and let him slip into the water. Later Norbert became disoriented and kept asking about Alfred. He started to cry, started to swim away, and I never saw him again.

I saw the PBY land on the water. I remember seeing a beam of light about the size of a stove pipe shining from the water. I really thought it was God coming to get me. Of course by this time, I was very disoriented myself. The USS *Bassett* picked me up and I remember someone saying, "this one is alive, this one is dead." I couldn't talk and was very relieved when I heard them say I was alive.

From there we were taken to the Philippines and then to Guam.

Quote from Jerry's sister, Billie Ann. "I remember Jerry as being very tall and handsome in his uniform—very different from the farm boy in bib overalls. We always credited his survival to the fact that he was a big, sturdy farm boy."

NAME   POTTS, DALE S2C
STREET
CITY
STATE
PHONE
ENTERED SERVICE FROM   St. Paul, MN
PICKED UP BY   USS *Doyle*
DIVISION
DOB   Deceased 3/94

FAMILY

EXPERIENCE
  Unable to contact any family members.

NAME   PRICE, JAMES D. S1C
STREET   Rt 1 Box 99
CITY   Telephone
STATE   TX 75488
PHONE   903 664 3773
ENTERED SERVICE FROM   Ravenna, TX
PICKED UP BY   USS *Talbot* Tr USS *Register*
DIVISION   3rd Division
DOB   3/25/20

FAMILY
Widow: Estelle (Crickett) Price
Children: Alton Ray Chesser
Grandchildren: Glenn Chesser, Judy Thomas, Darrell Chesser
Great-Grandchildren: Carmen Chesser Turner, Jeffrey Chesser, James Chesser,
Bradley Thomas, Dustin Thomas, Kacie Thomas, Erica Chesser, and Brandon
Chesser
Great-Great-Grandchildren: Alexis Turner

EXPERIENCE

I was born in Ravenna, Texas on March 25, 1920. I was one of six children and only finished the eighth grade. I worked on the family farm and at various odd jobs until I was 24 years old, when I was drafted into the navy. I went to boot camp in San Diego, California.

My account of the sinking of the USS *Indianapolis* begins early July 30, 1945. On that night I had strung a hammock between two railings near midship and was sleeping peacefully. The lack of air conditioning belowdecks made it very hot, so many sailors chose to escape the heat by moving topside. It was much better than the noise and heat down below.

About a quarter past midnight, I was awakened by a rather large jolt that knocked me to the deck. When I got to my feet I was unaware of what had happened. The ship began to list. I knew then we had been torpedoed. We had been trained in these situations, but nothing could have prepared us for what we were about to experience. Knowing my duties, I ran to number three turret, grabbed life jackets, and began to hand them out to anyone who did not have one. When I felt everyone had been taken care of, I put one on myself. Now the ship was listing very badly and I thought it was about to sink. I grabbed onto the next available thing I could to keep from going into the water. I climbed onto one of the barrels of the number three turret and jumped as far as I could away from the ship.

Hitting the water, I swam fast to escape the "suction" the ship would create when it went under. When I was at a safe distance, I stopped swimming momentarily and looked back. I saw the stern of the ship pointing skyward with the screws still turning slowly. I turned back and began to swim away again. That was my last view of the ship.

The next day was hot because there was no shade from the sun. There was a layer of engine oil coating the top part of the water and everyone in it. During the day and night we tried to stay in large groups to help the weaker ones. We also thought the sharks would not attack large groups. I noticed that the water was very clear. I thought you could see a mile down. I also saw hundreds of sharks that swarmed below, attracted to the blood that was floating in the water.

The next four days brought few changes. The only thing that changed was the number of men that were left by the end of each day. Many would swim off, believing that they had seen a ship or island off in the distance. Most did not come back; others were eaten by sharks. Sometimes a man would swim off several feet from the group, then scream and disappear under the water. There was nothing we could do. Others would swim downward thinking the water was fresh below. Many drank the salt water but it would make them hallucinate. It was ironic to know that there was all that water but none to drink. Despite this, many of us tried to keep men from wondering off.

My particular story is of James King. I became friends with him on the *Indy* because of his youth, and I took care of him in the water. He had been wounded on the ship and I tried to keep him from swimming away, which he did a couple of times. He would swim out a ways, get tired, and then come back. To keep him from giving up I grabbed a loose life jacket and wrapped it, (and myself), around him and held onto him. It was not until Dr. Haynes told me that he had died that I let him go. He sank slowly down with his head tilted back, eyes open, staring upwards. I often, to this day, remember that.

During the last couple of days our hope of being found slowly diminished. We often saw airplanes fly over and we thought we saw ships. We even gave up trying to prevent men from swimming off. I guess we thought if they found something that could help us they would come back and tell us, but they did not.

On the fourth day a PBY flying over threw out life rafts and various other supplies. A life raft landed upside down near us. By this time many of us were so weak we could hardly lift our arms out of the water. It took us a long time to turn the boat over, but we managed to and then we got into it.

On Friday, August 3, 1945 about 0720, I was in a large group that was picked up by the USS *Talbot*. I stayed on the *Talbot* until I was transferred to the USS *Register*. Finally, I felt as if I was safe. It was not until later that I learned that the war had ended.

One thing I can attribute my survival to was the hope that someone was looking for us. If we had known that we had not been missed, conditions would have been worse. We always held out hope that someone was looking for us...Later I found out that we weren't even missed.

CHAPTER 246   SURVIVOR QUEALY

NAME	QUEALY, WILLIAM C. Jr. PR2
STREET	1431 Ocean Ave Unit 709
CITY	Santa Monica
STATE	CA 90401
PHONE	310 393 3905
ENTERED SERVICE FROM	Santa Monica, CA
PICKED UP BY	USS *Doyle*
DIVISION	Victor Division
DOB	10/14/20

FAMILY

EXPERIENCE
   No response.

NAME   RAMIREZ, RICARDO S1C
STREET
CITY
STATE
PHONE
ENTERED SERVICE FROM   El Paso, TX
PICKED UP BY   USS *Doyle*
DIVISION
DOB   Deceased 2/01 Hayward, CA

FAMILY

EXPERIENCE
Unable to contact any family members.

NAME   RATHBONE, WILSON S2
STREET   1168 Hyatt Cr Rd
CITY   Waynesville
STATE   NC 28786
PHONE   828 456 5047
ENTERED SERVICE FROM   Waynesville, NC
PICKED UP BY   USS *Doyle*
DIVISION
DOB   8/13/18

FAMILY
Spouse: Lottie London Rathbone
Children: Catherine Rathbone Williams, Sherman Rathbone, Jackie Rathbone Sutton, James Rathbone, Emma Jean Rathbone Speck
Grandchildren: Cindy, Eddie, Tonia, Dewayne, Angela, Rhonda, Michelle
Great-Grandchildren: Marc, Christy Ann, Dawn, Tiffany, C J, Christopher, Alex, Hayden, Brittany, Marissa

EXPERIENCE
Wilson Rathbone sent the following newspaper article.
When Wilson Rathbone jumped into an oil-slicked sea from the sinking USS *Indianapolis* just after midnight on July 30, 1945, he wondered if he would ever

see his wife and two children again. He also wondered if he would be able to survive in the shark-filled sea.

When the *I-58* Japanese submarine slammed two torpedoes into the 610 foot long heavy cruiser on that fateful night, 1,197 men went into the water. When they were rescued five days later only 317 remained alive. They had survived watching fellow shipmates be attacked by sharks or drink salt water and die, or just simply give up, too tired to keep hanging on to their inadequate life jackets.

Rathbone, now 83, was drafted into the service February 24, 1944. He was a young father of two children, Catherine, who was 4, and Sherman 2. He worked at the A.C. Lawrence Tannery in Hazelwood and going to war was the last thing on his mind. "I didn't want to go, but what could I do about it," he said. In December 1938 while he was working at a local sawmill, he met his future wife, Lottie London, and they were married in June 1939. She was 16 years old and he was 20.

Rathbone was drafted into the navy and sent to Great Lakes, Illinois for basic training. As it was for other veterans, training was only four weeks, as the armed forces were in a hurry to get men into combat and on ships. "They just wanted the men and for them to be able to pull a trigger on a gun," Rathbone said.

The USS *Indianapolis* was kept in the heat of many battles. He took part in five major operations during his three years in the navy, including the battle of Iwo Jima. He remembers that well. For six days and six nights his ship and others in the fleet shelled the island in an effort to let the marines who had landed on the beach get to the enemy troops. Rathbone's ship was often a target for kamikaze missions and when that was happening he was stationed topside in front of a 40-mm anti-aircraft gun. "You would see a plane coming in on you and you know it's going to hit you. You gotta do something," he said. "They would come so close you could see their faces and you know he's going to dive right on you, so you would shoot at them and they would land in the water near the ship."

Rathbone said he and his shipmates were able to thwart many of the suicide attempts on the *Indianapolis*, but on March 31, 1945, the ship was struck on the portside of the fantail. Divers went over the side and made a temporary patch until the ship could get to port for repairs.

The world's first operational atomic bomb was delivered by the *Indianapolis* to the island of Tinian on July 26, 1945. The *Indianapolis* then reported to its headquarters in Guam for further orders. The ship was directed to join the battleship USS *Idaho* at Leyte Gulf in the Philippines to prepare for the invasion of Japan. Rathbone had just finished his watch on July 29 when he went down to the mess hall for a cup of coffee. It was 14 minutes past midnight.

"I had just sat down for a cup of coffee when the first torpedo hit. Then another hit and I raced up to the top deck. I walked across the deck, went over the railing and into the water." The first torpedo blew away the bow, and the second struck near midship on the starboard side adjacent to a fuel tank and a powder magazine. The ship only took 12 minutes to sink to the bottom of the ocean. Shark attacks began by the next sunrise and continued until the men were physically removed from the water five days later. Because the ship had so much fuel the men were covered in oil.

"Some of the men held on to tater crates," he said, "There was a net that tore loose when the ship went down and there was about 70 men hanging on to that, but not for long." The men shed their clothes and boots to help stay afloat as the life jackets became water-logged. They used their shirts to tie a headdress on their heads to help protect them from the sun and the salt water. Sleep was rare as the sea was rough and the sharks kept their vigil.

The men held hands as best they could and tried to form a circle. They used the circle to help fend off shark attacks. When the fins would come into the circle, they would beat the water and holler and scream just like they had been taught. But it only worked for a few. Now down to his underwear, and his shirt wrapped around his head, Rathbone just kept hoping for a rescue. He had one other item in his possession which he hung onto the entire time, a small Bible that he always carried with him. "We prayed in that circle," Rathbone said. "We prayed and prayed." Between the prayers, screams could be heard of men in pain, being eaten by sharks, and just simply giving up. "Each morning there would be more empty life jackets," he said, "the ones that didn't make it through the night."

The men also didn't know if the Japanese submarine was still in the area and if it was, would it come after them again. "We didn't know if it was coming back to sink us or not," Rathbone said. "I didn't give up hope, but after four days I began to wonder if we were ever going to be picked up."

Then there was the salt water. Men would drink it and hallucinate and eventually die. "It was awful because you knew when they drank it they were going to die," Rathbone said.

The men were spotted in the water the fourth day by a pilot who was on an anti-submarine patrol, who in turn alerted his base in Peleliu. The navy had not looked for them despite the fact it knew they had not joined the USS *Idaho*. Because of its secret mission, no distress call had been sent before the ship had gone down.

Lt. Adrian Marks was dispatched to the scene in a seaplane and upon arriving saw the men under attack by sharks. Disregarding his orders to not land at sea, he landed and began picking up the men who were at greatest risk of shark attack.

When Rathbone was pulled aboard the USS *Cecil Doyle* he weighed 50 pounds less than he had five days before. He shook hands with Marks and was given little bits of water at a time. The first thing he ate was a Spam sandwich and he said, "it was the best thing I have ever eaten."

Rathbone received the Purple Heart for his bravery at sea and is proud that he defended his country.

And standing behind that proud man is a proud family of five children and a wife he has been married to for 62 years. "He has taken care of us all of our lives," Lottie (his wife) said.

CHAPTER 249 SURVIVOR RAWDON

NAME	RAWDON, JOHN H. EM3
STREET	P O Box178
CITY	Obion
STATE	TN 38240
PHONE	310 393 3905
ENTERED SERVICE FROM	Obion, TN
PICKED UP BY	USS *Doyle*
DIVISION	E Division
DOB	1/20/19

FAMILY

Spouse: Mary

EXPERIENCE

No response.

CHAPTER 250 SURVIVOR REDMAYNE

NAME	REDMAYNE, RICHARD B. Lt.
STREET	3025 NE 137 St #203B
CITY	Seattle
STATE	WA 98125
PHONE	
ENTERED SERVICE FROM	FPO NY, NY
PICKED UP BY	USS *Bassett*
DIVISION	
DOB	

FAMILY

Spouse: Mary

EXPERIENCE

No response.

NAME   REEVES, CHESTER O. B. S1C
STREET
CITY
STATE
PHONE
ENTERED SERVICE FROM Paris, TX
PICKED UP BY   USS *Talbot* tr USS *Register*
DIVISION   7th Division
DOB   3/6/14
                      Deceased 4/02 Portales, NM

FAMILY
Widow: Maxcine
Children: Joyce Ward, Lewis Reeves (Cheryl), Raymond Reeves, Dickie Reeves (Yolanda), Paul Reeves (Donna)
Grandchildren: 9
Great-Grandchildren: 12
Great-Great-Grandchildren: 2

EXPERIENCE
Survivor Reeves' chapter is submitted by several members of his family.

Chester O. B. Reeves was born March 6, 1914 in Madrill, Texas. He grew up in Slate Shoales, Texas, near Paris. During World War II, Chester served aboard the USS *Indianapolis*.

The *Indianapolis*, a heavy cruiser, served as the flagship of the Scouting Force and later the Scouting Fleet. On several occasions prior to World War II, she had served as the ship of state for President Franklin D. Roosevelt. During the ship's career in the Pacific, she earned ten battle stars. Outside Okinawa, the ship was hit by a kamikaze plane, resulting in 38 casualties. Following repairs, she was chosen to deliver the world's first operational atomic bomb. After delivering the atomic bomb, she was ordered to join the USS *Idaho* at Leyte Gulf in the Philippine Islands in preparation for the invasion of Japan.

On July 30, 1945, she was struck by two Japanese submarine torpedoes. The ship sank within twelve minutes, leaving 900 of 1,197 men originally aboard ship in the warm, shark-infested waters for five days. By the time they were rescued, only 317 remained alive, with the rest being victims of shark attack or exhaustion and exposure. He, along with all the men, was awarded the Purple Heart.

At the end of the war, he came to visit his sister in Floydada and worked for his brother-in-law at his gas station. It was there that he met Maxcine Archer, and the couple married on August 19, 1947. He was a member of the Disabled American Veterans and a lifetime member of VFW Post 3299 in Portales, New

Mexico. He also was a member of the USS Indianapolis Survivors Organization and attended several reunions in Indianapolis. The last reunion he attended was in Broomfield, Colorado in 2000. Before his death in 2002, he was the second-oldest living survivor.

Submitted by his widow Maxcine

I met Chester, "the big guy," on a blind date in Floydada, Texas. I was a young widow with a four-year-old daughter, Joyce Kay Ellerd, whose father was killed in action in France on August 4, 1944. One of Alvin's cousins had been visiting in Portales, New Mexico and invited me to go home with them. They already knew "Check", as he was living there with his sister and her family. After a brief courtship, we were married in Paris, Texas on August 22, 1947. We soon returned to Portales, New Mexico, where I had a house. As far as living places, the rest is history. Chester lived the remainder of his life here and passed away April 6, 2002. He had several jobs, first as a butcher in a small grocery store; he then spent the next 18 years working for the REA, first as a hole digger then as a lineman for about 15 years. Later he worked at a peanut processing plant.

He went to the USS *Indianapolis* reunion in Indianapolis in 1965 riding the Greyhound bus. Chester made two trips to Washington, D.C. to testify in defense of Captain McVay. He was not one to talk about the ordeal very much. He had a friend that was a marine during the same time and they would talk about their experiences once in a while. In December of 1990 he developed a severe heart condition which limited his travel. We went to the USS *Indianapolis* mini-reunion in Broomfield, Colorado in 2000...the last one he was able to attend. Our son Lewis went with us, along with Larry (his brother) and Barbara Reeves.

We had five children: Joyce, Lewis, Raymond, Dick, and Paul. Chester enjoyed gardening, reading, dominoes and fishing. He grew up fishing in the Red River in Texas. After he moved to New Mexico his fishing was limited to occasional trips to one of the lakes about 75 miles away. Later he enjoyed trout fishing at Oasis Lake State Park near Portales.

Submitted by step-daughter Joyce

My first contact with Chester, whom I learned to call "my daddy," was when I was four years old. My mother met him and married him in Texas. They had four more children (all boys); however, he instilled in us the love of fishing, baseball, and gardening. As we got older, we learned about his time in the navy. I was grown with grandchildren of my own when Daddy got very sick. At that time, he began to open up to us and tell us of the sinking of the ship. The time finally came when he just couldn't go on anymore and died on April 6, 2002. "Daddy, this chapter is to you, and my chance to tell you I love you very much and will miss you." Joyce Kay Ward

Submitted by son Raymond Reeves

What I find remarkable about my dad was how little I knew about his experience in the war. I knew about the *Indy* being sunk from a book my brother brought home from the library when I was ten years old. Dad went to the first *Indy* reunion in 1965. I don't remember anything about the ship until I saw the movie *Jaws* when I was 25 years old. When the captain talked about being on the *Indy* and being in the water four days and five nights and about sailors getting taking by the tiger sharks–this was really the first time I understood that something terrible had happened. I came home and asked Dad about what happened. He didn't have much to say. Dad put this behind him and went on with his life. I wonder how the other survivors dealt with their memories?

Submitted by son Lewis Reeves

When I was first asked to submit my contribution for my dad's chapter, I was unsure how to begin. After a lifetime of memories, what stands out? Do I write about how I feel or what I think others thought about my Dad? I decided it must be all of these things.

In conversation with others, I always had the feeling that Dad was well liked. He had a very good sense of humor and a love of a good joke. While some of the jokes were kind of silly, I will always remember them with a smile. One of the most memorable things about Dad was how he had such a calm demeanor. I am not sure that you could have excited him with a hand grenade.

As a youth, I knew about his experiences aboard the USS *Indianapolis* and its sinking, but Dad never spoke much about those times when my siblings and I were kids. Any information we got had to be on our own. I first read the book *Abandon Ship* when I was in junior high school. I have since read all the other books and watched the various made-for-television shows about the sinking. I am still amazed at how the men of the USS *Indianapolis* survived their ordeal. While I served in the navy, I would think about how it must have felt to be floating in a life vest in the middle of nowhere. I don't think anyone who has not experienced that kind of challenge to survive could ever relate to what kind of great strength it took to survive. And that is one thing my Dad was. He was a survivor.

Submitted by son Dick Reeves

When I think about my father, Chester Reeves, two things come to mind: jokes and dominoes. Dad loved to fish and watch baseball, but he really came alive when he played 42 or 88 in dominoes. I don't know which was worse, being his partner or playing against him. He knew what I had in my hand better than I did. He just seemed to sense what everyone was going to play. If you were his partner and you played the wrong domino, you got that look. It wasn't any better if you played against him. I never played the game for any other purpose than to enjoy sharing time with him and my mother and my other family members.

Dad always loved to tell sly little jokes. Sometimes they were risque, drawing a glare from Mom, and sometimes they were dry-word jokes that made you think. "Did you know that blueberries are red when they're green?" I use that jewel myself in the high school English classes I teach. I tell my students that most of them will grow up to be their parents. I know that is what has happened to me, and I wouldn't have it any other way.

Submitted by son Paul Reeves

My Dad exemplified the true meaning of being a survivor. When the USS *Indianapolis* was torpedoed in World War II, he spent nearly five days floating in the Pacific Ocean waiting to be rescued. He and his shipmates had to survive shark attacks as well as food and water deprivation. Dad saw many of his crew members succumb to the elements, but he held on and was rescued eventually.

Dad's personal life was filled with many instances of his will to survive. He had a heart condition for many years. There were times when his physicians did not hold out much hope, but somehow Dad found the strength to pull through. His abiding love for his long-time wife, Maxcine, my mother, was one of the reasons that Dad held on as long as he did.

Dad never glorified his involvement as a survivor of the USS *Indianapolis*. He generally was reluctant to tell his story, even to his family members.

Submitted by granddaughter Alicia Zion Lee

One of my favorite memories of my Grandpa Reeves is going to visit him at the peanut mill with Grandma. I would get fresh peanuts while they would talk. The other memory that I see very clearly is him working in his garden. He always had a big garden, until his health kept him from doing so. He loved to go fishing. When he got to where he couldn't fish, he would sit and work on his rods and reels. They still had to be able to cast, even if he couldn't take them out and use them. I am going to miss my grandpa very much! I thought it would be easier because of his age, but it has only made it harder. The longer you know someone the harder it is, because there are so many more years of memories.

Submitted by granddaughter Janice Bisset

My Grandfather Reeves was a survivor of the USS *Indianapolis*, which sank in WWII. He was a war HERO. It was very painful for him to talk about the five days he spent in shark-infested waters. The man I knew and respected was a man who kissed his wife every day before he went to work, kissed her again every night before he went to bed, and stole sweet, secret glances at her whenever he thought no one was looking. He was a man who loved fishing, baseball, and gardening. He could tell a joke and make up a rhyme, riddle, or pun for every occasion. I always laughed at his jokes, and I never stopped being delighted at hearing him say things like, "Pass the cheese, please, to Chester Reeves."

My grandpa was a hero in my eyes because he "rescued" my hamburger from an unexpected torrential rainstorm by pushing the barbecue grill up close to the back door and standing there with a big black umbrella protecting my hamburger until it was cooked and delivered to my plate. My grandfather was a hero in my eyes long before I knew anything at all about the war. My love, respect, and admiration for him continue to grow, even after his death, as I learn more about his war experiences from books and documentaries on that period of American history.

Submitted by sister Peggy Reeves Rothwell

My brother Chester was a well-traveled man with a strong sense of humor. It was a joy to be around him. He traveled from Texas to California in search of employment to better his finances. He enlisted in the navy in 1942 because he felt it was his duty to serve his country. The day we received a telegram from the War Department telling us he was missing in action was a sad day for his family, but in a few days we received another telegram saying he was in the hospital and recovering. We all rejoiced at this word. In my opinion my brother has always been special and greatly loved by his family and friends.

Submitted by Survivor Reeves' younger brother

When I was three, my oldest brother came home from California. He taught me how to tie my shoestrings the way he did, and he taught me how to shoot marbles—even though I thought I was good at that before. His way made me better.

While he did not stay at home very long, I knew what he was like to be around. It was always thrilling to be where "Check" was, partly because he had a certain presence that made it comforting and exciting to be in his company. When he returned from the war, we had lost our mother and moved to Paris, Texas. He did not stay with us there, except for a short visit. Then he married a war widow with a small daughter and lived in New Mexico.

Chester would not talk about his experience in surviving the sinking of the USS *Indianapolis* for many years, but finally during one of our trips to Arkansas to visit our sister he spoke about some of the things that had happened and the loss of many of his shipmates. Chester was very quick-witted, and his memory of people he had known and past events was remarkable. During the last ten or twelve years of his life, when his health was seriously compromised, he continued to amaze with his continued zest for living. We enjoyed coming to visit, playing 80, and watching baseball on television with him. He was my oldest brother and I loved him very much!

Submitted by friend D. L. Hankins

This concerns my best friend, Chester O. B. Reeves. We were best friends from

1947 on. Our families grew up together as best friends. I never knew a person that was more dedicated, faithful, and loyal to his family and friends. He will be missed greatly by all.

CHAPTER 252   SURVIVOR REHNER

NAME	REHNER, HERBERT S1C Signalman
STREET	
CITY	
STATE	
PHONE	
ENTERED SERVICE FROM	Chicago, IL
PICKED UP BY	USS *Ringness*
DIVISION	
DOB	Deceased 7/81

FAMILY

EXPERIENCE
   Unable to contact any family members.

NAME REID, CURTIS F. S2C
STREET
CITY
STATE
PHONE
ENTERED SERVICE FROM Trafford, AL
PICKED UP BY USS *Doyle*
DIVISION
DOB Deceased 9/01 Trafford, AL

FAMILY
Widow: Inolene

EXPERIENCE
Unable to contact any family members.

CHAPTER 254 SURVIVOR REID

NAME REID, JAMES E. Boat Mate 2C
STREET
CITY
STATE
PHONE
ENTERED SERVICE FROM Middletown, OH
PICKED UP BY USS *Bassett*
DIVISION
DOB Deceased 1/96

FAMILY

EXPERIENCE
Unable to contact any family members.

NAME	REID, JOHN III LCDR
STREET	830 W 40th St #461
CITY	Baltimore
STATE	MD 21211
PHONE	
ENTERED SERVICE FROM	Mexico City, Mexico
PICKED UP BY	USS *Doyle*
DIVISION	Supply Officer
DOB	4/8/19

FAMILY
Spouse: Elizabeth

EXPERIENCE
No response.

NAME	REID, TOMMY L. Radar 2C
STREET	
CITY	
STATE	
PHONE	
ENTERED SERVICE FROM	Bell, CA
PICKED UP BY	USS *Bassett*
DIVISION	
DOB	Deceased 78

FAMILY

EXPERIENCE
Unable to contact any family members.

NAME REYNOLDS, ALFORD Gunner Mate 2C
STREET
CITY
STATE
PHONE
ENTERED SERVICE FROM Wanette, OK
PICKED UP BY USS *Bassett*
DIVISION
DOB Deceased

FAMILY

EXPERIENCE

Unable to contact any family members.

CHAPTER 258 SURVIVOR RICH

NAME RICH, RAYMOND A. PFC USMC
STREET
CITY
STATE
PHONE
ENTERED SERVICE FROM Mansfield, OH
PICKED UP BY USS *Doyle*
DIVISION USMC
DOB Deceased

FAMILY

EXPERIENCE

Unable to contact any family members.

NAME	RIGGINS, EARL W. PFC USMC
STREET	470 N CO RD 2125 E
CITY	Oakland
STATE	IL 61943
PHONE	217 346 3110
ENTERED SERVICE FROM	Champaign, IL
PICKED UP BY	USS *Bassett*
DIVISION	Sea Going Marine
DOB	11/16/24

FAMILY
Spouse: Dorothy
Children: Steve, Linda (deceased) and Judy

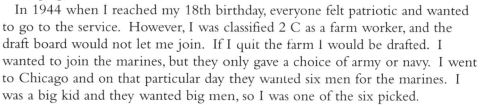

EXPERIENCE
I am a retired farmer in the Oakland area, and I raise quarter horses. This is sort of returning to my roots. In the 1940s I was a resident of Champaign, Illinois, and spent much time working on relatives' farms in the Champaign area.

In 1944 when I reached my 18th birthday, everyone felt patriotic and wanted to go to the service. However, I was classified 2 C as a farm worker, and the draft board would not let me join. If I quit the farm I would be drafted. I wanted to join the marines, but they only gave a choice of army or navy. I went to Chicago and on that particular day they wanted six men for the marines. I was a big kid and they wanted big men, so I was one of the six picked.

I was sent to Paris Island, South Carolina for boot camp. The next stop was Camp LeJeune, North Carolina for infantry training. I was a runner for the company and happened to be taking messages when headquarters called and asked for three volunteers to go to San Diego, California for sea school. It sounded like a good way to get out of the mud. I asked two of my buddies, Robert Redd and Howard Martilla, who didn't like mud either. We all three were shipped to San Diego in the spring of 1945.

We were assigned to the cruiser the USS *Indianapolis*. It came into port with a lot of battle damage. It was amazing how quickly repairs were made. The marine complement was 39 men under Captain Parke. We stood watches onboard the ship, which included 5-inch gun mounts and 40-mm guns.

We all knew we were carrying high-security cargo. It was brought aboard under armed guard. As we found out later, the core of the atomic bomb was in a lead box that was welded to the deck in officers' quarters. The rest of the bomb was placed on the plane hangar deck. It was approximately 12 x 8 x 5 feet. The planes were left on the catapults so the hangar could be used for this storage. Two marines guarded it around the clock.

We didn't find out what the cargo really was until we were in the naval hospital and it was announced that we had carried the atomic bomb that was dropped on Hiroshima. This was the bomb that ended the war. The uranium-235 core was the main component of "Little Boy" (the atomic bomb) destined for Hiroshima.

We sank just after midnight, July 30 1945. I was asleep on deck in the main forward turret. It was so hot below you couldn't sleep, and it rained every night, so I was in the turret for protection from the rain.

The torpedo explosion awakened me. I climbed out from under the turret and was disoriented. Everyone was gone. I had a knot on my head. I almost walked off into the sea. Thirty feet of the bow was gone. I think that's why we sank so fast. We were still going forward and the ship was like a big funnel scooping in water. My first thought was to get a life belt. We were supposed to wear them, but no one did. I started down for my locker and my rifle but after a few steps I was in water. I headed back up to get a life jacket. By that time, the ship was lying on its side. I knew I had to get off or go down with it.

The master of arms, whose name was Jack, said, "I can't swim. Will you help me?" We put his life jacket on but left it unbuttoned because the pressure of hitting the water could break your neck. He and I held hands and jumped. We got separated and I never saw him again. He didn't make it.

I landed among a lot of people and we ultimately ended up in a large group. People were drifting in different directions. We had been trained to get away from the ship so we wouldn't get caught in the undertow when it went down. I swam as hard as I could. I turned around. It had been a dark night, but the moon came out and I saw the ship standing straight up in the water. The propellers were still turning. Then it went straight down. There was no undertow because it had taken on so much water.

By morning we had formed a group of 60 to 70 people. I had a life jacket and the group had a couple of rafts and a cork floater net. Almost everyone had wounds of some kind. The men in the engine rooms had received the worst wounds. When the torpedo hit, it burst the boilers and many men were scalded. Some survived as long as three days. LCDR Haynes, the ship's doctor, was in my group. He consoled the officer in charge of the engine room, who took a long time to die. The salt water was pure torture and there was no morphine to relieve the pain.

We tied the strings of our life jackets to the net so we wouldn't drift away. Everyone slept or became delirious. We didn't want to drift. We had no water and no food. The rafts had a few malted tablets and I got one or two of them. One group had a crate of potatoes. They chewed the oil off the outside and ate the centers. Survival took will power and hope. As the days went on, many men lost their minds and just swam off.

The afternoon we were sighted, a friend came over and said, "Earl, I found a ship. It's right over here. The scuttlebutts (water fountains) still work, and the water is cold. Come on! Let's go!" I said, "There is no ship out there!" He said, "If you won't come with me, I'm going anyway." I never saw him again. Everyone had stories like that. My two friends from camp ended up in different groups. Redd had a broken foot, in a cast. Other men said he survived three days...he never made it either.

The sharks were always beneath us. They seldom bothered the groups, but when people got separated, they got them. You got used to the fact that they were there, but it was still a hair-raising experience.

At times, everyone lost their sanity. It would come and go. Planes flew over constantly, but they were flying at 10,000 feet and had a hard time seeing us. We fired flare pistols, but they didn't see us. We spent our time discussing why they didn't rescue us. We wondered why they didn't send rescue ships. Surely they would miss us.

You see your buddies, then sharks would get them, the sun would get them, and salt water would get them. More than one guy would drink the water and think he was drinking water from the ship.

When people died, we took their jackets off and gave them to someone else. The bodies just drifted away. We were all virtually naked when we were picked up. We tore off our clothes to cover our faces. If we hadn't, we would have been blinded from the sun.

The last day, when they finally spotted us, we were almost able to get up and walk on water—even though we were near dead. Anyhow, that was probably the most exciting day of my life. You figure you are going to get saved after four or five days of swimming in water. You are ready to get out.

Obviously we weren't in very good shape. We were down to just a few people in our group. After we were spotted by the plane, it wasn't long till all kinds of rescue planes came over and dropped survival gear and stuff. One of them dropped a string of cans of water out away from us about 50 to 100 yards. Of course they didn't want to drop them right on us. I figured I was strong enough to swim out to that, so I untied the front net but left my jacket on and swam out there, just ready to grab a can of water. I looked down and there was a shark that looked like it was 40 feet long. I am sure he wasn't that big. I never did get the water but I got back pretty quick to the group.

On the way back there was a rubber raft picked up by a couple of guys after one of the planes dropped it. I got up in the rubber raft and I spent the rest of the afternoon and evening there, so the last part wasn't too bad.

The pilot, Wilbur Gwinn, had been on sub patrol and had an antenna that wasn't working right. We called him our angel! They were trying to fix the trailing antenna, turned the plane so it was facing away from the sun, and saw the oil slick. They went down to have a better look. Gwinn realized there were a lot men there. He reported back to the base, "Many men in the water." The base said there were no ships reported missing so they must be Japanese. They denied permission. Gwinn went back to the base because he was low on fuel. Another pilot, Adrian Marks from Franklin, Indiana, was in the area. He asked for permission to land his airplane in the water. It was denied, but he said, "I'm going to land anyway."

It was getting dark when Marks arrived. Before Gwinn left he had dropped survival gear in the water. Marks arrived, set his plane down, and picked up the stragglers around the edge, the most vulnerable. He sent a transmission saying,

"These are the survivors of the *Indianapolis*...send rescuers." Marks had survivors on the wings, the fuselage, the pontoons, every place he could put them. We knew help was on the way. When Marks called to say he'd found the survivors of the *Indianapolis* and they were in terrible shape, all ships within striking distance headed our way. They started arriving about 2:00 a.m.

The first ship wanted to give us encouragement, so it turned on its searchlights...one to the sky and one to the water. It was like an invitation to the Japanese. But you talk about a thrill seeing that! I am convinced that action saved some lives, because we then knew help was coming.

Crew members came out in power boats to pick us up. We were so covered with grease you couldn't recognize your closest buddies. One sailor said to me, "You look strong; I believe you can get up to the ship by yourself." They had cargo nets hanging over the sides and you climbed up. I said, "I think I can," but when he wanted me to take the jacket off, I said, "Not until I get on that ship." One of the sailors had to help me up. They took us to the showers to get the grease washed off. The next thing I knew, someone was saying, "Hey, wake up. You're wasting fresh water." I'd fallen asleep in the shower.

After five days on Samar, they put us on planes to Guam where all the survivors were reunited and sent to a submarine rest camp. It was fantastic. You wore swim trunks all the time, but at chow, you had to put on a t-shirt. We had three kinds of meat and dessert at every meal. We had trap shooting, pool, and free beer. The beer was a popular thing. We then were sent back to the States for a 30-day leave.

NAME   RINEAY, FRANCIS S2C
STREET
CITY
STATE
PHONE
ENTERED SERVICE FROM   New Orleans, LA
PICKED UP BY   USS Dufilho tr USS *Register*
DIVISION
DOB   Deceased

FAMILY

EXPERIENCE
. Unable to contact any family members.

CHAPTER 261   SURVIVOR ROBERTS

NAME   ROBERTS, NORMAN H.
                          Machinist Mate 1C
STREET
CITY
STATE
PHONE
ENTERED SERVICE FROM   New Boston, OH
PICKED UP BY   USS Bassett
DIVISION
DOB   6/16/20   Deceased 1/00

FAMILY
Widow: Garnet
Children: Norman L. Roberts, Bernadine Roberts Weddington, Teresa L.
Stallard, Scott E. Roberts
Grandchildren: Brian L. Roberts, Norman Todd Roberts, Kelli Roberts Moss,
Kerrie Sue Roberts, Chelsea Weddington Doerger, Erin Weddington, Erica
Stallard Ray, Melissa Stallard Hall, Jessica Roberts, Janna Roberts, Scott E.
Roberts, Jr.
Great-Grandchildren: Amber Roberts, Michelle Roberts, Steven Roberts,
Ryan Roberts, Shaun Moss, Shane Moss, Ethan Doerger, Abby Doerger, Baylee
Klingel, Aurora Hall

EXPERIENCE

Submitted by Survivor Roberts' daughter, Bernadine Roberts Weddington.

My father died before his story could be written. I compiled this story from a recording of a speech he made at a local high school. During his life he spoke at several schools and churches and at a youth prison in Texas. Please forgive any factual errors. My father was a wonderful man and is sadly missed by all who knew him.

In May 1945 the ship was sitting in dry dock at Mare Island in San Francisco, California. The ship had been hit by a suicide plane and had a large hole in it; refrigeration and evaporators which kept our food cold and provided our water to drink had been destroyed.

We were divided into three sections for leave, and I drew the first section. I had 23 days of leave and I had not been on land in 18 months...home was good. I took off for home and spent five days and nights traveling on a train. In the short time I had, I visited family and friends and then picked up my wife and young son and headed back to Mare Island, where we lived for the remaining part of this time in dock.

After repairs the ship was ready for a shakedown cruise, which was a trial run to see if it was in good shape. Surprisingly, all leaves for everyone were canceled and the crew was ordered to return to the ship immediately. We knew something important was up. I got my bags aboard ship, told my wife goodbye, and told her she would have to find her way back home.

The ship took off and went down to Hunters Point, which was a place across the bay from San Francisco. When we pulled in there the place was surrounded by heavily armed marines. Two crates were taken aboard and set in one of the hangars. Two men carried another container aboard and placed it in the captain's battle cabin. Two big posts were welded to the deck in the middle of his quarters and big springs were attached; part of the atomic bomb was suspended in mid-air on the springs. Of course, at this time we had no idea what this was. We had orders to get it to Tinian, which was a little island halfway around the world, and we were ordered to get there at top speed.

We pulled out of Hunters Point on the 16th day of July in 1945 and opened up the ship at top speed, which was about 32 knots per hour. With the ship's weight being 10,000 tons, that was really moving in the water. We arrived at Pearl Harbor in 74 hours, which was a world's speed record at sea. When we pulled into Diamondhead at Pearl Harbor there were no ships in the harbor. We pulled next to the submarine dock, which was full of men to help load supplies and ammunition aboard the ship. The crew of the *Indianapolis* was not allowed to leave the ship.

We pulled out of Pearl Harbor and immediately headed for Tinian at the top speed of 32 knots. As an engineer, 32 knots was a difficult speed to maintain and kept the engine room where I worked very hot. We arrived at Tinian ahead of schedule. Two LST landing crafts pulled up alongside of us, and the two crates and the container of uranium-235 were set aboard the crafts. Several naval officers who had been aboard our ship also left on the LST.

We headed for Guam. Guam was the navy headquarters of the Pacific and we were the flagship of the Fifth Fleet. We carried Admiral Spruance, who was one of only three-star admirals. We had left the admiral in Guam on our previous trip, so we were headed to Guam to pick him up. He was not yet ready to leave when we arrived, so they sent us to the Philippines.

On the stroke of midnight on the morning of July 30, a Japanese submarine hit us with two torpedoes. The torpedoes blew 40 feet off the front of the ship and we started toward the bottom. I was in the bottom of the ship in the forward engine room standing watch, which was nothing more than taking care of the machinery in the engine room. When the torpedoes hit the ship, I remember I was holding a cup of coffee. I was knocked high enough that I hit the ceiling of the room and the coffee went all over me. I had charge of the crew in the forward engine room and I had headphones on which connected me to the bridge. Our engine room started going dead. We knew that the fire room directly in front of us had been hit. We generated all the power for the electricity of the forward part of the ship so the lights all went out. The only lights we had were battery lanterns attached to the walls around the engine room.

The ship started listing badly, and things started flying around the engine room. We knew we had to get out of there. We started towards the ladder. We quickly found out we could not get out of the engine room because of the water pouring through the hatch. We got behind the ladder and stayed there until the engine room nearly filled up with water. When the water was several inches from the top of the room we blew up our life jackets and waited until the room filled up with water. By this time the ship was nearly on its side. We got into the air locker above the engine room and then we went on into the mess hall which was directly above.

The marine unit had been in the compartment directly in front of the mess hall, and most of them had been severely burned when the original torpedo hit the ship. Many of the marines were lying hurt in the mess hall. A corpsman was circulating among them giving morphine and doing what he could to relieve their pain. I took my crew and went over behind the ladder that went up to the quarterdeck and waited for the mess hall to fill up with water. When the mess hall filled up with water, we floated onto the quarter-deck and out into the sea. We knew that we had to get away from the ship as quickly as possible. We had been taught that the ship would pull us under as she went down. The ship was turning over fast and was sinking quickly. My last sight of the ship was the rear end of the ship above the water with the two screws from the after engine room still turning. I knew that all the crew in the after engine room were still aboard the ship. We got off into the sea and started swimming. That was the last I ever saw of the seven men in my engine room.

I was a really strong swimmer. The sea was choppy and heavy and there were big waves. There was fuel oil all around me. It was heavy and thick like molasses. You swallowed it, it got in your eyes, and you breathed it. At that time I was not thinking about how sick I was from swallowing the fuel oil. Instead I was concerned about finding someone else.

At dawn I found a group of men holding onto a floater net, which was a big net with corks around the outside. We tried to count the men hanging onto the net, and at that time there were 147. We spaced ourselves all around the net and hung on. I had a pneumatic life jacket which was like an inner tube. It was made of a rubberized cloth and you carried it around you all the time. As I had left the engine room I had grabbed an extra life jacket. I placed one around my waist and put a second one under my legs. At first I laid back nice and comfortable. I floated like that for two days and nights.

During the first day we all vomited nothing but fuel oil. The fuel oil was still all around us. We did have hope that when the ship did not show up as scheduled at Leyte in the Philippines at 11:00 a.m. on Tuesday that we would be missed. On the second day we were expecting help. No help arrived. The days were very hot and we were all covered with massive sores. We were blind from the fuel oil and the sun. By the end of the second day we were all miserable.

Then the sharks arrived. There were six or eight to start with. I could push the fuel oil away from my body, look down into the water, and see two or three twenty-foot sharks. You prayed if one took your leg off it would go ahead and take all of you. At night we were so scared of the sharks we kept our legs pulled up into our chests hoping they could not reach us as easily. At night we were freezing cold, even though we were only 12 degrees north of the equator. Most of us had no clothes and we were almost totally submerged in the water. If we stayed in a compact group and stayed quiet the sharks did not bother us. But if one person swam off 10 or 15 feet all you heard was a big scream.

One group decided they knew where we were. They thought we were close to Leyte. They swam off and that was the last we saw of them. A group of officers knew there was an island just over the horizon. They also swam away and were never seen again. And if you drank the sea water your throat would swell closed and you would suffocate.

I had found two very good friends, Glenn Myers and Ralph Lane. Glenn had a nice diamond ring. He told me he had lost his mind the previous night and thought the ship was under us. He dove down and drank the sea water. He asked me to see that his mother got his diamond ring. I encouraged him that he would make it home but he died a couple of hours later in my arms. All I could do at that point was take off his life jacket and push him away. I was never able to give the ring to his mother, since it slipped off of my finger while I was in the water. My other close friend, Ralph Lane, lived to see home again. We spent many hours in the water encouraging each other. We even held each other above water so we could take turns getting some sleep. I mention these two guys because they were the only men I was close to in the group I was in.

A doctor in our group swam around to help people until he got too weak to swim. Our chaplain also swam around the group, praying and consoling and encouraging the men.

During the third day the men started to have hallucinations. They actually lost their minds. They started to kill each other since some of their life jackets started going down after 72 hours. They started to fight for the pneumatic life jackets which had a longer life. A lot of men died that night.

During the afternoon of the fourth day we heard a plane. We had heard planes go over before but they were too far away to see us. The plane was a Ventura bomber and Chuck Gwinn was the pilot. He had antenna trouble and opened his bomber doors to check on the problem. The sun glistened off the fuel oil and he saw us, but he thought we were an enemy submarine. He went back to his pilot seat and started into a dive. He had the bomb release button in his hands when he happened to see men waving and shouting. He found men scattered for fifty miles away. He called for help in code. When no one answered he broke regulation and sent in for help in plain English. He made it clear that there were a lot of men floating in water that needed help.

A pilot named Adrian Marks received the message and flew his seaplane to the vicinity. As he circled the group of men he could see them being eaten by the sharks. He finally decided to land his plane in the middle of a group of men in the ocean. He managed to take 56 men aboard the plane by knocking holes in the wings. He rationed the water and food he had aboard the aircraft. He sat in the ocean and waited for more help to arrive. That was Thursday night.

My strength and hope were gone. I was not near the seaplane, and I had not seen it land. I had used all my strength to keep away from sharks and to stay alive. The USS *Doyle* arrived on the scene and Captain Claytor thought we were going down too fast. He turned on the *Doyle's* spotlights and the light bounced off the clouds. Renewed hope went through my group since we knew the ship wasn't very far away. We held on even though many men were dying fast. If Captain Claytor had not turned on those lights I do not believe I would have survived the night. I know one of the reasons I survived was that I was in good physical condition and I did not smoke or drink. I really believe the main reason I was among the survivors was that I had a Christian wife at home who was praying for me as well as a praying mother and mother-in-law.

On Friday morning other ships arrived at the scene to help with the rescue. Near me the USS *Bassett* put some landing craft into the sea. When the craft pulled up alongside us there were only 37 men left in my group. When the landing craft pulled up next to me, I reached up to get into the boat. The craft was only about three feet out of the water. I was young, healthy, and I thought I was full of strength. I did not even have enough strength to get out of the water. I asked one of the guys in the craft to give me a hand. He said if they did that for everyone they would be there all day. He had no idea how long we had been in the water. I do not remember anything after that.

I woke up once on the USS *Bassett* for a few minutes and remember being in one of the bunks. The next time I woke up I was in the naval hospital in the Philippines. I had sores all over my body. I was taken to Guam where I was put in the hospital and treated like royalty. We were given everything we asked for.

My eyes were in bad shape and my legs were in bad shape from the exploding ship. My sores began to heal and since I was immersed in sea water I was left nearly scar-free. I do remember a nurse coming and telling us our sores would not heal unless we shaved off the five or six days of beard which we had grown. She shaved us all and pulled the hide from our faces. That was a bloody ward of men that day. The only permanent scars I was left with were under my arms and on my legs.

I was given the Purple Heart by Admiral Spruance while I was in Guam. I then boarded an aircraft carrier which brought me back to San Diego. My group was taken to a hospital in San Bernardino. I was only there a few days when I was told I could go home. After about 30 to 40 days, I received a radiogram to report to Washington, D.C. I was taken to navy headquarters, where an admiral sat me down and told me they were going to court-martial my captain, who was a 30-year veteran of the navy. He had served his country honorably. In order to get the people off of the navy's back, the captain was held responsible. He was charged because he had not zigzagged the ship, which was customary during war time. The night the ship sank it was as dark as pitch and the sea was choppy. We were doing 16 knots and were supposedly in a cleared area. A ship of this size was usually escorted. We were alone.

In Washington the admiral started to ask me questions. I soon found out that they had brought the captain of the submarine that sank us over from Japan to testify against our captain. I was bitter against the United States Navy because I knew our captain was guilty of nothing. He also was charged with not ordering abandon ship. If anyone had come to tell us to abandon ship, he would not have gotten out of the ship. The captain was eventually found guilty of not zigzagging. I left the navy and returned home to New Boston, Ohio. I spent over thirty years as a maintenance foreman in a steel plant and then another ten years as a foreman in an atomic energy plant.

I had a total of four children and have spent many happy years with my wife, Garnet.

CHAPTER 262 — SURVIVOR ROBISON

NAME — ROBISON, JOHN D. COX
STREET
CITY
STATE
PHONE
ENTERED SERVICE FROM — Tulsa, OK
PICKED UP BY — USS *Bassett*
DIVISION
DOB — Deceased 7/83

FAMILY

EXPERIENCE

Unable to contact any family members.

CHAPTER 263 — SURVIVOR ROGERS

NAME — ROGERS, RALPH G. Radar 3C
STREET
CITY
STATE
PHONE
ENTERED SERVICE FROM — Stout, OH
PICKED UP BY — USS *Doyle*
DIVISION
DOB — Deceased

FAMILY

EXPERIENCE

Unable to contact any family members.

NAME   ROGERS, ROSS Jr. ENS
STREET
CITY
STATE
PHONE
ENTERED SERVICE FROM   Garden City, NY
PICKED UP BY   USS *Register*
DIVISION
DOB   Deceased

FAMILY

EXPERIENCE
   Unable to contact any family members.

NAME   RUSSELL, VIRGIL M. COX
STREET   25001 Blood River Rd
CITY   Springfield
STATE   LA 70462
PHONE   225 294 5761
ENTERED SERVICE FROM   San Benito, TX
PICKED UP BY   USS *Bassett*
DIVISION   2nd Division
DOB   9/9/23

FAMILY

EXPERIENCE
   No response.

CHAPTER 266 SURVIVOR SAATHOFF

NAME	SAATHOFF, DON W. S2C
STREET	
CITY	
STATE	
PHONE	
ENTERED SERVICE FROM	Los Angeles, CA
PICKED UP BY	USS *Bassett*
DIVISION	
DOB	Deceased 5/98

FAMILY

EXPERIENCE

Unable to contact any family members.

CHAPTER 267 SURVIVOR SANCHEZ

NAME	SANCHEZ, FERNANDO S. Cook 3C
STREET	
CITY	
STATE	
PHONE	
ENTERED SERVICE FROM	Tucson, AZ
PICKED UP BY	USS *Bassett*
DIVISION	
DOB	Deceased

FAMILY

EXPERIENCE

Unable to contact any family members.

NAME SCANLAN, OSCEOLA C. S1C
STREET
CITY
STATE
PHONE
ENTERED SERVICE FROM New Orleans, LA
PICKED UP BY USS *Bassett*
DIVISION
DOB Deceased

FAMILY

EXPERIENCE

Unable to contact any family members.

CHAPTER 269 SURVIVOR SCHECHTERLE

NAME SCHECHTERLE, HAROLD J. Radar 3C
STREET
CITY
STATE
PHONE
ENTERED SERVICE FROM Shattuckville, MA
PICKED UP BY USS *Doyle*
DIVISION
DOB Deceased 4/00

FAMILY

EXPERIENCE

Unable to contact any family members.

CHAPTER 270 — SURVIVOR SCHMUECK

NAME	SCHMUECK, JOHN A. Chief Phar Mate
STREET	
CITY	
STATE	
PHONE	
ENTERED SERVICE FROM	Steger, IL
PICKED UP BY	USS *Doyle*
DIVISION	
DOB	Deceased 12/81

FAMILY

EXPERIENCE

Unable to contact any family members.

CHAPTER 271 — SURVIVOR SEABERT

NAME	SEABERT, CLARKE W. S2C
STREET	3070 Ogenaw Tr
CITY	West Branch
STATE	MI 48661
PHONE	517 873 5683
ENTERED SERVICE FROM	Dearborn, MI
PICKED UP BY	USS *Ringness*
DIVISION	2nd Division
DOB	

FAMILY

EXPERIENCE

No response.

CHAPTER 272 — SURVIVOR SETCHFIELD

NAME	SETCHFIELD, ARTHUR COX
STREET	
CITY	
STATE	
PHONE	
ENTERED SERVICE FROM	St Louis, MO
PICKED UP BY	USS *Doyle*
DIVISION	
DOB	Deceased 2/88

FAMILY

Widow: Jackie

EXPERIENCE

No response from family.

CHAPTER 273 — SURVIVOR SHAFFER

NAME	SHAFFER, ROBERT P. Gunner Mate 3C
STREET	
CITY	
STATE	
PHONE	
ENTERED SERVICE FROM	Ontario, CA
PICKED UP BY	PBY tr USS *Doyle*
DIVISION	
DOB	Deceased 1/99

FAMILY

EXPERIENCE

Unable to contact any family members.

NAME	SHARP, WILLIAM H. S2C
STREET	4157 Tarkiln Rd
CITY	Jacksonville
STATE	FL 32223
PHONE	904 268 7239
ENTERED SERVICE FROM	Decatur, AL
PICKED UP BY	USS *Doyle*
DIVISION	5th Division
DOB	4/26/26

FAMILY
Spouse: Helen

EXPERIENCE
No response.

NAME	SHEARER, HAROLD J. S2C
STREET	2921 Indian Run Ave SE
CITY	East Canton
STATE	OH 44730
PHONE	330 488 1981
ENTERED SERVICE FROM	Canton, OH
PICKED UP BY	USS *Ringness*
DIVISION	Damage Control
DOB	8/3/20

FAMILY
Spouse: Mary L. Carpenter Shearer
Children: Ronald Shearer, Richard Shearer, Russell Shearer
Grandchildren: Brian Shearer, Angela Shearer, Richard Shearer, Jaime Shearer, Ryan Shearer, Baron Shearer, Christina Shearer

EXPERIENCE

Respectfully submitted by Survivor Shearer's wife, Mary.

Harold has macular degeneration and cannot see. He was born August 3, 1920 at Lafferty, Ohio to William and Martha (Beal) Shearer. He joined the navy September 12, 1942 and his boot camp was at Great Lakes. He was wounded when the USS *Indianapolis* was sunk on July 30, 1945 and spent several months in the hospital at San Diego Naval Hospital. Harold was aboard the USS *Indianapolis* for all ten major battles she participated in. He received the Bronze Star, Good Conduct Ribbon, Victory Medal, Purple Heart, Combat Action Ribbon and the Navy Unit Commendation Ribbon. Harold is most thankful that the good Lord saved his life.

After the war, he and his brother Edward opened their own business in a garage in Waco, Ohio, called the "Shearer Brothers Garage." Harold and Mary raised three sons and have seven grandchildren. He has enjoyed fishing, photography and traveling.

CHAPTER 276   SURVIVOR SHOWN

NAME	SHOWN, DONALD H. CFC
STREET	352 Springs Rd
CITY	Vallejo
STATE	CA 94590
PHONE	707 644 7282
ENTERED SERVICE FROM	Olympia, WA
PICKED UP BY	USS *Bassett*
DIVISION	Fox Division
DOB	11/23/20

FAMILY

Spouse: Nenora K. Shown (deceased 1995)

EXPERIENCE

I joined the navy September 15, 1939 in Seattle, Washington. I was sent to boot camp in San Diego, California. After boot camp (a draft of ten men) I was assigned to the USS *Indianapolis,* which was at Mare Island naval shipyard for repairs (dry dock number two).

After the shipyard, the USS *Indianapolis* went to sea for sea trials, then proceeded down the coast to Long Beach, California. At that time, Long Beach was home port for the Pacific Fleet. Next the USS *Indianapolis* was assigned to the Hawaiian Islands area as scouting force flagship, early in 1940. She operated in the vicinity of the Hawaiian Islands until after December 7, 1941 and was at sea when Pearl Harbor was attacked. The *Indianapolis* operated in all of the major theaters in the Pacific: South, Central, and North Pacific. I served under six commanding officers while I was a member of the crew.

In March 1945 the USS *Indianapolis* was off Okinawa, beginning the pre-invasion bombardment. She was hit by a Japanese single-engine plane (kamikaze). It dove into the ship and damaged it. The ship had to return to the U.S. West Coast for repairs.

After repairs, we left the West Coast with the atomic bomb components aboard. We delivered them to the B-29 on Tinian (Marianas Islands) and proceeded to Guam. The next day we departed for Leyte Island, and on July 30, 1945, just past midnight, the USS *Indianapolis* was struck by two Japanese torpedoes, and she sank in the Philippine Sea. The ship sank in about 15 minutes.

I had been in the chief petty officers quarters, main deck aft, second deck. I got out of my bunk, got dressed and proceeded forward on the second deck toward my battle station, which was forward in the main battery plotting room. This is the area the second torpedo hit. As I stepped into the number three mess hall, marine Captain Parke was coming aft from forward on the second deck telling us to "get topside," which I did and then proceeded up the ladder to the boat deck. When I arrived on the boat deck, the ship was listing badly to starboard. There was no word to "abandon ship." The ship continued to list farther to starboard. I knew from experience in rough weather that the ship would not right itself. I proceeded to go over the port side, encouraging members of the crew in the area to do likewise.

I swam away from the ship after I hit the water. I looked back and saw the ship standing straight up in the water, bow down, screws were still turning...then she disappeared below the waves.

I spent the next four days and five nights in the Pacific Ocean, covered with fuel oil that also covered a large area surrounding the survivors in the water. The group I was in consisted of about 150 men to start. I was completely submerged except for my head. I was wearing a kapok life jacket, which was designed for approximately 72 hours of flotation. We had no food or drinking water. There were a large number of sharks in the water below us most of the time. At various times high-flying aircraft would pass over us. We tried to attract their attention but to no avail.

On the fourth day, one of our anti–sub patrol aircraft out of Ulithi spotted an oil slick in the water, came down to a lower altitude to investigate, and saw people in the water. He reported it to his base. Later another patrol aircraft (a PBY) came out and after that, ships began to appear. They did not know who we were or what ship we had been on.

I was picked up by the USS *Bassett* and taken to a naval hospital on the island of Samar in the Philippines. About a week or so later, I was flown to Base Hospital 18 on the island of Guam. I was there for about one month and then returned to San Diego, California aboard the USS *Hollandia,* a baby flattop.

I was given a 30-day leave and then returned to Bremerton navy yard in Washington to be discharged. My enlistment was up September 15, 1945, and I was honorably discharged in late November 1945.

NAME   SHOWS, AUDIE B. COX
STREET   1112 W 23RD ST
CITY   Odessa
STATE   TX 79763
PHONE
ENTERED SERVICE FROM   Odessa, TX
PICKED UP BY   USS *Bassett*
DIVISION
DOB

FAMILY

EXPERIENCE
No response.

CHAPTER 278 SURVIVOR SIMPSON

NAME	SIMPSON, WILLIAM E. Boats Mate 2C
STREET	
CITY	
STATE	
PHONE	
ENTERED SERVICE FROM	Oquawka, IL
PICKED UP BY	USS *Bassett*
DIVISION	
DOB	Deceased 2/81

FAMILY

EXPERIENCE

Unable to contact any family members.

CHAPTER 279 SURVIVOR SINCLAIR

NAME	SINCLAIR, JAMES R. S1C
STREET	
CITY	
STATE	
PHONE	
ENTERED SERVICE FROM	Detroit, MI
PICKED UP BY	USS *Bassett*
DIVISION	
DOB	Deceased

FAMILY

EXPERIENCE

Unable to contact any family members.

NAME SITEK, HENRY J. S1C
STREET
CITY
STATE
PHONE
ENTERED SERVICE FROM Detroit, MI
PICKED UP BY USS *Bassett*
DIVISION
DOB Deceased 4/92

FAMILY

EXPERIENCE

Unable to contact any family members.

CHAPTER 281 SURVIVOR SLADEK

NAME SLADEK, WAYNE L. Boats Mate 1C
STREET
CITY
STATE
PHONE
ENTERED SERVICE FROM Cleveland, OH
PICKED UP BY USS *Bassett*
DIVISION
DOB Deceased 8/86

FAMILY

EXPERIENCE

Unable to contact any family members.

NAME	SLANKARD, JOHN (JACK) C. S1C
STREET	850 NE Lakewood Dr
CITY	Newport
STATE	OR 97365
PHONE	541 574 1047
ENTERED SERVICE FROM	Phoenix, AZ
PICKED UP BY	USS *Bassett*
DIVISION	2nd Division
DOB	9/27/25

FAMILY
Spouse: Una
Children: Kirby Slankard
Grandchildren: Kara

EXPERIENCE

My date of entry into active service was July 6, 1943 at 17 years of age. I received my basic training at San Diego naval training station and then was assigned to Submarine Base, Torpedo Section, Pearl Harbor. I worked under the supervision of the men assigned to solve the problem with the navy's submarine torpedos.

I was transferred to the USS *Indianapolis* October 1943. I served aboard her until July 30, 1945. My watch station was number five gun mount and my battle station was the powder room for number five gun. I was assigned to the deck crew.

On July 30, 1945 (age 19), I had just stepped out on the deck for the midnight watch. Very shortly thereafter, the first torpedo hit and the guys around me thought it was a mine—until the second torpedo hit the ship. We tried to take the wounded to sickbay but were turned back by men coming up from below. They told us the sickbay was on fire. The word was passed to abandon ship. We put life jackets on as many wounded men as we could. I went to get my jacket from the gun mount but someone had taken it. Therefore, I went into the water without a jacket.

I swam as far as I could away from the ship, but I still was pulled down by the suction. I was down so long, I had given up. There was an underwater explosion, and then a second. The second explosion blew me out of the water. My last view of the *Indianapolis* was bow down, flag still flying on the stern, and men jumping into the turning screws. Their screams still haunt me today.

I floated until a shipmate with a jacket floated by and held me up until we were able to take a life jacket off a deceased shipmate.

The next morning we assembled into work divisions. I found my best friend, Harry Kirby S1C. He was badly burned and blind from his eye injuries. He needed help, so he was one of the men we floated in the middle of the circle on the life jackets we took off the deceased men. He died in my arms on the third day.

I was picked up by the USS *Bassett* and taken to Samar in the Philippines. The men from the *Bassett* were superb in their efforts to rescue the 152 men they picked up. They came into the water with us to lift us out of the water on their shoulders into the boats without pulling the skin off our

Survivor Slankard July 2000, Nye Beach, Newport, Oregon

arms. They were lifting about 250 pounds—a water soaked-kapok life jacket plus the man's body weight. We were lifted in cargo nets to the *Bassett*'s deck. Our clothes were cut off, then we were taken to the shower to be scrubbed with diesel oil to remove the crude oil. Everybody was black with oil. This made it very difficult to recognize anyone. Our first food was cut-up fresh oranges, then liquids, followed by soup. The *Bassett* crew gave us their clothes, bunks, and food and carried us off their ship on stretchers at Samar. There were 149 survivors in a 3000-bed hospital built for expected casualties of the invasion of Japan.

After convalescent leave, I was assigned to a destroyer base in San Diego, California, where I was honorably discharged March 1, 1946. Awards I received: Asiatic Pacific Area - 8 Stars, Purple Heart, American Area, Philippine Liberation, Victory Medal World War II, Combat Action Ribbon, and Navy Unit Commendation.

NAME	SMELTZER, CHARLES H. S2C
STREET	
CITY	
STATE	
PHONE	
ENTERED SERVICE FROM	Cornstock, MI
PICKED UP BY	USS *Bassett*
DIVISION	
DOB	Deceased

FAMILY

EXPERIENCE

Unable to contact any family members.

NAME	SMITH, COZELL L. Jr. COX
STREET	
CITY	
STATE	
PHONE	
ENTERED SERVICE FROM	Eufaula, OK
PICKED UP BY	USS *Talbot* tr USS *Register*
DIVISION	7th Division
DOB	Deceased 10/96

FAMILY

EXPERIENCE

"For Peace of Mind" was written by Survivor Cozell L. Smith prior to his death. It was respectfully submitted by a shipmate and close friend.

For Peace of Mind

In an attempt to help clear my mind of the fear, terror, and horror of my experience in World War II, I am putting down on paper because I cannot convey in words the horror I have seen and experienced before my 21st birthday. I am presently going on 70 years of age. To this day I relive these happenings almost on a daily basis.

I enlisted in the navy the summer of 1943 after completing the tenth grade of school. I had 21 days' training in San Diego, California. I had a nine-day leave, returned to my base, and was transferred to Bremerton, Washington. From there I was sent out with many others on civilian ships up the coast of Alaska, where we transferred to the USS *Indianapolis*, a heavy cruiser. We patrolled and guarded and assisted in the retaking of Atu and Kiska. We patrolled the Bering Sea all the way to the Russian territory. For months we did not see the sun. We were in the area called the "land of the midnight sun." It was daylight 24 hours a day–very confusing at times and very cold. After securing Attu and Kiska we headed for the central Pacific. The USS *Indianapolis*, a heavy cruiser, the flagship of Admiral Spruance, commander of the Fifth Fleet and at times, commander of both the Third and Fifth Fleets.

We participated in all landings in the south and south-central Pacific and the invasions of Tarawa in the Gilbert Islands, Marshall Islands, and Eniwetok. We were in the Battle of the Eastern Philippines known as the "Mariana Turkey Shoot," one of the largest battles of the South Pacific. We covered the invasions of Saipan, Tinian, Guam, and the Palau Islands. We encountered strafing, shelling and air raids, including Kamikaze planes month after month, which seemed like years.

We were battle weary, but the war in the Pacific raged on. The Japanese kept coming and coming, with every one shot down there seemed to be two to take their place. At this point I began to wonder if I would see the States, Oklahoma, or my loved ones ever again.

While participating in the invasion of Okinawa we witnessed hundreds of Japanese jumping from cliffs, committing suicide. We shelled the beach and island for seven straight days, at the same time fighting off suicide kamikaze planes. This was the first of April 1945. We were hit by one of these planes during the operation. Nine men were killed and 27 seriously wounded, and many received minor injuries. This hit happened early in the morning right after general quarters, which were held each morning and evening just before dark. This was the time the suicide planes were most active, at daylight and dark. My division had charge of 20-mm automatic guns. We had secured from our guns a few minutes and I was on the main deck supervising a crew. Sweeping the aft port side of the ship, I heard a 20-mm gun chattering from the bow of the ship. I looked up and saw tracer bullets reaching far into the sky. Above the tracers I saw a Japenese fighter plane. I ran for a steel ladder that led up to what we called the "bathtub." We had several 20-mm guns that we manned during attack. I reached the top of the ladder (steps), the ship swerved in a maneuver, and I fell back across the ladder rails injuring my leg, shoulder and hand. I quickly got up, went back up the ladder and as I looked up the dive bomber had started his dive on the ship. On a 20-mm you strap yourself onto the gun for stabilization. With no time for this, I swung the gun up toward the plane and started firing. The plane was coming right on top of me. I saw the pilot's face-full view just before he hit. I will never forget that face. Knowing the plane was going to hit by or on me, I knew by instinct that his bomb and plane would explode, killing me. My life flashed through my mind in a mere second. Flashes of childhood, my teen years, my dad and my grandmother who had raised me.

By sheer luck or providence the plane's wing hit the edge of this so-called bathtub, the motor went through the main deck and the other wing off the port side of the ship. Instead of a contact bomb the plane was carrying an armor-piercing type that went through three decks and upon striking the port screw shaft exploded, knocking a screw off and heavily damaging the bottom of the ship. My leg, shoulder, and hand were numb and hurting somewhat; however, I was not cut or bleeding. Due to the deaths and other wounded the medical crew was busy for days. I ignored my hurt and went about my duties.

A repair ship fixed us up to travel and the *Indianapolis* headed for San Francisco navy yard for major repairs.

While in dry dock for repairs (which took about 6 to 8 weeks) we were granted a 12-day leave to go home. I was home 8 days and during this time I married my childhood sweetheart. I was 20 years of age.

Upon returning to the ship in Mare Island navy yard, we made the ship seaworthy and sailed for the South Pacific. Just before we left the States a secret cargo was loaded onto the ship. This was July 16, 1945. Little did we know we were transporting the heart of two atom bombs sealed in a small lead-lined container. This material was welded to the deck of the admiral's cabin. This cargo was a strict secret and was guarded by several marines on a 24-hour basis. There was a much larger container sitting in the port aircraft hangar also guarded by several marines with machine guns. I believe this held the bomb components. We had never heard of an atomic bomb. Our ship made a record run for Tinian Island, stopping for a very short time in Hawaii to refuel.

When we arrived at Tinian I never saw so many army and navy generals and admirals, plus a large group of civilians. We unloaded our cargo under strict guard of marines and army MPs.

We anchored at Tinian for a couple of days. Our captain was ordered to proceed to the Philippines for gunnery practice in preparation for landing on the mainland of Japan, which had been scheduled for the fall of 1945. As we slipped through the sea, I thought gunnery practice! I had three years of actual practice covering all the landings in the central and south Pacific. This practice was not for the old salts; it was for the approximately 400 new raw recruits. We had taken them on the ship when we sailed out of San Francisco.

I was weary of war and killing. I would look at the swirling water around the ship and at times felt it would just swallow us up. Little did I realize this was about to happen. I began to think what my dad said to me when he signed the navy application for me to join. He said, "Do you know what I am signing?" I said, "Yes, your permission for me to join." I was only 17 years old. He said, "NO, I am signing your death warrant."

The night the *Indianapolis* was sunk, at about midnight on July 30, 1945, I was scheduled for the midnight to 4:00 a.m. watch. I was to stand watch at our usual battle station, known as the "bathtub." Because of the extreme heat below deck I decided to sleep in the bathtub where I was to stand watch. Someone awoke me about 11:30 to give me a chance to go to the mess hall for a cup of coffee before my watch began. About 11:50 I went to my watch station and was visiting with James Reid, another coxswain in my division. In a few minutes there were large explosions, fire was shooting skyward. The ship shuddered and James Reid said a boiler evidently exploded and he said, "Oh boy, we will go back to the States for repair." Immediately the ship started to list starboard. Fear set in. I never dreamed the ship was going to sink. It began to list more, at about a thirty percent list. I then knew it was going to roll over.

People were running everywhere shouting for a life jacket. I left the bathtub and with difficulty made it to the main deck. It was listing more. I made it to the safety cable at the edge of the ship, where I held on until it rolled more and I could get on the side of the ship where I could abandon her. I watched as many shipmates who had not made it to the cable slipped and fell backward into the number three gun turret. I could hear their heads and bones crack as they hit the turret, evidently killing them on contact with the steel. As the ship rolled I followed the roll until she was on her side. People were then running down the side and jumping off the keel, which at this time was ocean level. I had no life jacket and was about to jump into the water when someone grabbed me and was screaming he had no life jacket. I said I didn't either, but that we had better get off and move away from the ship before she tilted upward and sucked us down with her. I knew this man; he was in my division and worked under my supervision. He screamed, "I cannot swim!" I thought this odd; however, stranger things happen than being in the navy and unable to swim.

This shipmate was Dronet from Louisiana. I told Dronet when we were going into the water to hold onto my shoulders and kick the water like hell as I used my arms. I told him not to get more scared and grab me around the neck; if he did, I would drown him and leave him in the water. We went off the keel and I swam as hard as I could. He was kicking and never tried to grab me around the neck. I expected to experience the suction and possible death as the ship tilted and started down. I looked back and saw the fantail of the ship, which was about 200 feet away. She had swung away from us on her final plunge. She slowly went straight down, taking several hundred of my shipmates with her. When the fantail was straight up I saw about 20 people jump at a height of around 200 feet from the fantail, and I am sure they went down with the final suction if they survived the jump.

The water was covered with black fuel oil that made us sick, and we almost heaved our guts out. The black oil covering our bodies turned out to be a blessing in the coming days. It helped protect us from the sun.

We came upon a group of men. Screams filled the air from their pain and injuries. Two were holding onto a third who was so badly burned his arms were bare of flesh–the bones were shining in the moonlight. He was begging them to let him go so he could get out of the pain. After a few minutes his head tilted into the water. I don't think he was dead. I feel he did this so they would let him go. They did and he floated away toward Dronet and me. He had a life jacket on; neither Dronet nor I had one. I removed the life jacket from this man and helped Dronet into it. I was relieved because I was getting tired of supporting Dronet and felt we would both drown. Until morning I held onto Dronet to relieve my exhaustion. The life vest supported both of us.

The screams went on through the night and come morning bodies were floating everywhere. Many had died and the sharks started coming into devour them. This next morning I saw a group of about 150 men hanging onto something. They were about 100 yards away. I left Dronet and swam to the group hoping there was something more stable to hang onto. The item turned out to be what we called a floater net, similar to a cargo net with cork floats about two feet apart. They were not very large, maybe 20 feet square. You could only hang on, and even if you were on it, you were still in the water. It was filled with people and others were clustered around the net just holding on the edge and holding onto each other. I caught the edge of the floater net and held on so I could rest. I still had no life jacket. About one half of the group were without jackets. I classify these four days and five nights in the water in four stages: FEAR, TERROR, HORROR AND MADNESS WITH INSANITY.

This first morning the terror started. We worked together putting the most severely wounded on the net, provided someone would make way. Many would not give up their space. It was becoming survival of the fittest. Sharks were around all the time, waiting to eat the dead or someone who drifted away from the group a few feet. Around noon the sharks started attacking the outer circle of the group. Screams filled the air. The screams were those of dying men...confusion, panic, and hell.

Many sailors had no life jackets and they were climbing on top of each other. If a man was in a life jacket, three or four men would be trying to climb on top of him. It was like rats swimming in a bathtub, with no way out and nothing to cling to. I was surrounded by screaming and panic. The ocean was a swirling pit of blood and oil. My buddies' screams were blood-curdling as they gasped and died in agony. I was alive in hell. I thought I was dreaming but it was real. All the horrors we knew about hell were happening before my eyes, and I was in horror and helpless to aid anyone. Small fish of all kinds were swarming around the bodies until a larger fish would tear the body in half and swim off. The small fish would eat what was left. They ate all the flesh off the bone. It was a battle of size as sharks swept the half eaten bodies out of sight.

All of the five days I was in the water, sharks attacked men next to me, pulling them under. We tried splashing and screaming to scare them away, but a hungry shark would grab someone and pull him under or, if a shark took only a piece of the body, we soon learned he would be back for the rest. We tried to stay away from the burned and anyone who was bleeding, realizing this was a sure invitation for a shark attack. As soon as someone died, we shoved the body away for the sharks in the hopes they would not come back for us.

The screams of someone being pulled away by a shark is like nothing you have ever heard of will ever forget. Late the first afternoon, without warning, a shark grabed my left hand. I went down so fast I did not have time to scream. He pulled me down about 10 to 12 feet. I knew I was going to be eaten alive. With my free right hand I tried to free my left hand. I could not get my hand out of his mouth. I was pushing his snout and he kept jerking, trying to tear the hand off. While pushing, my right hand slipped on his slick skin and I felt my middle finger go into a soft spot all the way. He turned me loose and I fought my way to the surface expecting him to grab my legs or whole body. I have always figured I had stuck my finger deep into his eye, hurting him enough he released me.

I popped to the surface, my hand badly torn and bleeding. I swam toward the floater net while my shipmates were yelling for me to get away. They were afraid of the blood. I was so horrified I fought my way through kicks and fists to my head and body by these people. I was all over the top of these men trying to get in the middle of this floater net. After getting there one sailor started slashing at me with his knife. Trying to protect my face and body I held my arms up and was stabbed in my arms several times. Realizing they would kill me, I fought my way back into the water. Luckily the sharks gave up for a while. I held my wrist tight to stop the blood. I held it for a long time while kicking my feet to keep my head above water. The salt water helped stop the blood; however, my left hand was useless. The shark had torn away the tendons to my fingers. I was about 100 feet from the group and a body floated by me face down. He was dead. He had on a life jacket which with much difficulty I removed and worked my arms into it. I could not tie the strings due to the damaged hand; however, I had some support. I had been swimming most of the previous 18 hours.

After dark that night I slowly worked my way back to the group without incident. The second day I found a personal friend in the group and he tore part of my shirt tail and bandaged my hand.

Panic about the sharks was still evident, and many sailors still were fighting for position on the floater net. If the badly burned and injured were near death, they were starting to be ignored and allowed to float away to the ever-present sharks. This part of the Pacific is scorching in the day, but at night it was cold. We alternated between freezing and severe dehydration from the sun's heat and the lack of water. We wondered if an SOS had been sent. We were looking for a rescue. As we waited we began to realize the ship had sunk so fast that no SOS had been sent. But we were due to join the battleship USS *Idaho* at 10:00 a.m. on August 2 at Leyte Gulf for practice in preparation for landing on mainland Japan. We were sure that if we did not join the *Idaho* on time, a search would begin for our ship. As history shows this was a false hope.

Someone mentioned prayer and we prayed or some just said holy words. On this day there were no atheists in the group. All believed in a supreme power and asked for mercy.

The third day we were terribly exhausted. More terror was evident as we realized our kapok life jackets were absorbing water and our heads were getting closer to the surface of the ocean. We realized we must get out of the life jackets or be dragged below the surface. My friend who helped me bandage my hand was able to untie the strings on our vests and we just held on to them for support, just keeping our heads above water.

The night brought more horror as men began to have delusions about an island nearby. Many swam for this island, never to return. Someone said they had found the ship and it was just below our group and the scuttlebutts had ice water in them. Many started diving for this water. I could feel my mind going in and out, and I dived down to get my share. A few feet into my dive I hit a cold current that brought my senses back to reality. Several had drunk the salt water and their death was slow and agonizing. The fourth day was the start of madness and insanity.

All of us talked out of our heads with only moments of sanity. Some killed their shipmates thinking they were Japs. The sharks were still around to clean up the unfortunates. Pure horror was evident with no end in sight. This horror has seared my mind like a hot poker and I cannot forget it. A man in my division cut the throat of another sailor to drink his blood to quench his thirst. This incident was witnessed by me and others. I saw a man cut the wrist of another who was dead and try to suck out blood. Many said, "Look, he is eating that arm." I witnessed several acts of cannibalism. The waves and swells of the ocean were so high you could not see straight across, but every so often I could see one person eating another. Sometimes I would only be a few feet from them. I cannot describe the horror in the acts of cannibalism. To this day, I relive many of these scenes in my nightmares and my daily living. Being half-crazed or insane, the time slipped by. Many just gave up and died. This group was now down to about 25.

The evening of the fourth day our "angel" of mercy appeared, an army bomber on sub patrol. The plane had trouble with a new antenna and a man was lying down in the plane in an attempt to fix the antenna. He was looking straight down to the water. He saw an oil slick and advised the pilot that something had been sunk. The plane circled down low and could see survivors all over the ocean. The crew began throwing things out of the plane into the water. The waves and swells were about 10 to 12 feet high this day.

I saw a bundle hit the water about 300 yards from our group. I made a decision to swim for it, because I could see the bundle as the swells and waves would peak. I started out and with my injured hand made slow progress. I began to think I had made a terrible mistake. I swam and fought the waves for what seemed an eternity. I was making headway and this gave me encouragement. As fate or providence would have it, the waves were coming toward me and I finally reached the object. It was a two-man raft in a bundle. I pulled a handle and it started to inflate upside down. Having only one good hand and a stub, I had a struggle trying to upright it. With the help of the waves I was able to get it upright. I held on to it for about an hour before I could catch my breath and work my way onto the boat.

It was getting dark. I could not see another person in any direction. There was no water on this small boat. If there had been any, it would have fallen out as I tried to inflate the thing. About the middle of the night I heard someone gasping for breath. I shouted and he shouted back. I worked my way to him and helped him onto the boat. We just rested throughout the rest of the night. This was the first time we had been out of the water for better than four days and nights.

We were picked up by a destroyer the next morning. Due to my damaged hand and wounds to my arms from the knife attack I could not climb up the net they had thrown over the side of the destroyer. A sailor came down the net, put his head between my legs and carried me aboard on his shoulders. I do not recall much of the next few days. We were all out of it. We were transferred to a hospital ship and taken to a hospital on Guam. They could not operate on my hand for about 30 days due to the swelling. We were later taken to the States.

I know that only death will bring peace to me by blocking my mind of these horrors. I sometimes think that my shipmates who were killed or eaten by sharks were the lucky ones. We who were left have had almost fifty years of mental pain. After 50 years, dates and faces lose their distinction, but the horror never goes away. I suffer long periods of depression and I cannot shake the feeling. The older I get the more it bothers me.

When I came home after being honorably discharged, no one would come near me or touch me while I was sleeping because I would attack them. I can still hear the screams of the injured and dying.

CHAPTER 285   SURVIVOR SMITH

NAME	SMITH, FREDRICK C. Fireman 2C
STREET	
CITY	
STATE	
PHONE	
ENTERED SERVICE FROM	Gorham, KS
PICKED UP BY	USS *Bassett*
DIVISION	
DOB	Deceased

FAMILY

EXPERIENCE

Unable to contact any family members.

NAME	SMITH, JAMES W. S2C
STREET	3668 St Rt 14
CITY	Rootstown
STATE	OH 44272
PHONE	330 325 1051
ENTERED SERVICE FROM	Pontotoc, MS
PICKED UP BY	USS *Doyle*
DIVISION	4th Division
DOB	7/10/24

FAMILY

Children: Andrea, James Jr., David, John, Barbra, and Donna
Grandchildren: 16

EXPERIENCE

My name is James Smith and I grew up in a small town in Mississippi called Pontotoc. I was drafted into the army my senior year of high school with only six months to go until graduation. But knowing that in the army you got shot at a lot, I wanted to go into the navy. So much for that idea! I went on the USS *Indianapolis* the last of December 1943, and that was my home for 19 months. I turned 21 on July 10. I had a pretty good time on the ship, got three hot meals a day.

My job was the 5-inch guns during my duty, and I participated in seven battle stars. I was very proud of my duty with the navy; however, I am not proud of the fact that I was in the brig on bread and water for five days prior to our sinking. I got out on Sunday and had one good meal before we were sunk that night.

I was asleep in my bunk when the torpedo hit, and I thought we were having a raid. There were no lights on so I went to my gun on the number two by the hangar deck. The ship was already turning over, so several of us tried to get a raft off. I put a life jacket on and just walked off the ship into the water. I swam as fast as I could because I knew it would suck me in when it completely went under. The moon was so bright you could see the ship until it completely disappeared. There was no one around me and after swimming a while, I came across a group of men. The oil was everywhere and I was covered with it. Oil was up my nose and in my mouth. You couldn't recognize anyone because everyone was covered.

I made it through the first night because I knew we would be rescued the next morning. However, the sun came up and went down and we were watching our friends slowly die right in front of our eyes. Some were so badly injured that they couldn't survive without medical attention. When the sun went down, the water became very chilly and we wished the sun would rise. The minute the sun came up we were wishing for the sun to go down because it was so hot.

The second day was just like the first...nowhere to go, nothing to eat or drink, but our group was getting smaller. Someone would yell, "Shark!" and I would raise my legs up as far as I could, hold my breath, and pray that I would not get bitten. We just floated around knowing that someone would find us. For 90-plus hours, I hadn't slept, and after that long you get into a daze. I was afraid to sleep in the water for fear of not waking up. I would try to catch small fish that were swimming around me, but I couldn't catch them. You always heard the saying about water everywhere but not a drop to drink. People would take off for islands that were not there; we never saw them again.

Finally, an angel flew over and spotted us. He was on a routine patrol and was having antenna trouble. By the grace of God he spotted us. We all yelled and waved as he came down for a closer look. Adrian Marks came in later that afternoon and landed on the water. I tried to get on one of the rafts that was dropped but a marine wouldn't let me on. So I swam over to the plane and was one of the first on. They gave me a small cup of juice and I went to sleep. I woke up on the USS *Doyle* and thanked God that I was alive. I had to do without food for a few days...they gave us broth. My nipples had been eaten off by salt water and I had lost quite a few pounds. But I was alive and going to see my mom. I guess someone was watching out for my fellow survivors and me.

CHAPTER 287   SURVIVOR SOSPIZIO

NAME	SOSPIZIO, ANDRE EM3
STREET	12714 Oak Park Ave
CITY	Palos Heights
STATE	IL 60463
PHONE	708 361 3793
ENTERED SERVICE FROM	Chicago, IL
PICKED UP BY	USS *Bassett*
DIVISION	3rd Division & E Division
DOB	4/8/24

FAMILY
Spouse: Margaret Sospizio
Children: Donna Sospizio and Andrew Sospizio (Barbara)
Grandchildren: Amanda Sospizio, Scott Simpson, Tina Simpson

EXPERIENCE

I usually don't speak much of our last victories at the end of World War II, but I will write a few lines to tell a bit about myself. I was born in the city of Chicago but was raised as a child in Italy and France.

In 1940, when I was 16 years old, I said good-bye to the Nazis in France and headed to Lisbon, Portugal. While I was there, an American ship arrived and with the orders of President Roosevelt that all Americans from 15 to 30 years old had priority on the ship, I made it aboard! The journey was a dangerous one. Our good United States flag saved us from submarine attack, because we were not yet at war. We made it safely to New York!

From there I made my way to Chicago and in late 1942, at the age of 18, I volunteered and joined the United States Navy. In 1943 I was assigned to the USS *Indianapolis* and was off to Alaska. From there we headed for the South Pacific, fighting our enemies that occupied that territory. When we reached Okinawa we were hit by a suicide plane. I was one of ten sailors in the bunks that early morning and the only one that was able to escape the area.

We returned to the United States where our ship was repaired, and in San Francisco we received a very heavy, large, and mysterious box. We shoved off immediately at full speed in the dark of the night. We were on a secret mission. We arrived at our destination ten days later, and I was one of a crew that helped to remove that mysterious box. It took 1000 amps at 250 DC volts to do the job! Afterward we sailed to Guam, then to the Philippines. I was on watch when two torpedoes hit our ship and sank it in the dark of the night in just twelve short minutes.

I was helping some burned sailors when another explosion knocked me off my feet. I directed another sailor, whom I later saw in the water, as to how to get off the ship. Later I ran by the third gun turret to look for a raft; there were none. As I waited for the light of the moon, I heard sailors cry out for help as they were getting pulled back into the ship by the strong waters. The ship was going down fast so I decided I had to abandon ship!

Once in the water I could hear the roaring of our ship being swallowed by the Pacific. Then there was an awesome quiet as we listened for the possibility of a submarine in our area. No sub in site. We called to our shipmates to join together. We thanked God that we were alive but had many days of trial and tribulation ahead of us, until the fateful day that our angel, Chuck Gwinn, flew over and spotted us in the water.

The memories of my fellow shipmates and friends who did not make it live in my heart each and every day...alas.

NAME	SPENCER, DANIEL F. S1C
STREET	
CITY	
STATE	
PHONE	
ENTERED SERVICE FROM	Morris, IL
PICKED UP BY	USS *Doyle*
DIVISION	
DOB	10/31/14
	Deceased 3/87

FAMILY

Widow: Esther (Sis) Spencer
Children: Ervin Spencer (deceased) (Ann), Dolores Spencer Ehret, Carol
Spencer Johnson (Richard), Neal Spencer (Le)
Grandchildren: Don, Lois, Mark, Michell, Frank, Royce, Lisa, Daniel, Joe, Tina,
Kelly, LeAnn, Lee, Guy
Great-Grandchildren: 15

EXPERIENCE

Respectfully submitted by Survivor Spencer's daughter Carol.

I am writing this chapter about my dad, Daniel F. Spencer, the loving husband
of Esther (Sis) Spencer, the father of Ervin, Dolores, and Carol, then later of Neal
Adrian. He joined the navy January 7, 1944. He was a proud American, who
with a wife and 3 kids volunteered to fight for his country. Dad was 29 at the
time of his enlistment. He reported to the naval training station in Farragut,
Idaho. After his training was over, he was attached to the USS *Indianapolis* (CA-
35). He always talked about his time aboard the ship. He was first loader on the
5-inch guns and he always said that he liked shooting them.

The night the *Indy* went down, dad was lying on the deck because it was such
a hot night. When the torpedo hit he said he didn't know what was happening.
There was a lot of noise and yelling. The ship was going down so fast, he said.
He went over the side and into a pool of oil. He said when he looked back the
ship was sinking so fast that it was gone in 12 minutes. My dad was one of the
lucky ones as he had a life jacket on. After hooking up with some of the others
that went overboard, they formed a life line by hooking up with each other.

Dad would tell us about the sounds of the other men screaming because of the
wounds they received when the ship was hit. When someone would pass on
they would release him from his jacket and let him go so someone else could use
it. He said many times how hard it was to lose someone that had made it off the
ship. Dad told us about all the sharks that were swimming around them and
about losing his buddies to them. When he would see the sharks coming or feel

them under his feet, he would pull his feet up so they would not bite him. Dad had many nightmares about sharks–right up to the time of his death in 1987. At one point in the water, with all the sores and the oil burning into his skin and the lack of food and water, dad was ready to commit suicide. He said it was more than he could bear. A buddy in his group, Ed Brown, told dad to hang on just one more day, that there was still hope they would be found. Dad said he told Ed, "Just one more day," and that he was going to do it.

Dad looked into heaven and was saying a prayer when he saw a vision of my mom, brother Ervie, sister Dolores, and myself, Carol. He cried and asked God to find them and not let him die out there. The next day when he thought all was lost and it was his time to go, he heard an airplane overhead. It was Chuck Gwinn in his PV-1 Ventura. After the report was out that there was a large group of men floating in a pool of oil, Lt. Gwinn flew over the men to let them know they were all found. Dad said he thanked God for answering his prayers.

Dad was picked up by the USS *Doyle* and then taken to a base hospital. I can remember the day my mom received the telegram that Dad was wounded in action, July 30, 1945. Mom stood by the radio with a dear neighbor waiting for word that dad was okay. I can still see her crying as she read the telegram that our dad was going to be okay. We all went to the depot to meet the train when he came home. Mom said we waited five hours for the train, but we were never so glad to see it when it finally arrived. Mom said he was the best sight she had ever seen.

The day after he got home, he got Quincy throat. Mom said he was so sick with it. Dad was so happy to get his honorable discharge that he went to town and bought a brand-new brown suit. He took it easy for a while and then moved us all to Durand, Illinois where he took up farming as a hired hand.

We moved back to Morris, Illinois, where he went to work for Caterpillar Tractor. He took an early medical retirement due to a stroke after going through open-heart surgery. We lost Mom in 1979 to cancer and buried her on their 44th wedding anniversary. Dad moved in with my brother, Ervie, for a while, then spent the next 8 years with my family. Dad died March 26, 1987 and was laid to rest with full military honors.

I am so proud to be the daughter of an American hero and that is what my dad was to me, a HERO. May God bless the USS *Indianapolis* (CA-35) and all that were lost at sea or have since passed on.

* * * * * * * * * *

A personal note from Paul J. Murphy, Chairman of the USS Indianapolis Survivors Organization.

Dan was secretary of our organization for years. He and his wife, Sis, volunteered many hours in helping organize and support our organization. Sis edited the organization's "Wagging Tongue" newsletters. We are most grateful!

NAME	SPENCER, ROGER S1C Radio
STREET	
CITY	
STATE	
PHONE	
ENTERED SERVICE FROM	Baltimore, MD
PICKED UP BY	USS *Doyle*
DIVISION	
DOB	Deceased 65

FAMILY

EXPERIENCE

Unable to contact any family members.

NAME	SPINELLI, JOHN A. Cook 2C
STREET	
CITY	
STATE	
PHONE	
ENTERED SERVICE FROM	San Diego, CA
PICKED UP BY	USS *Ringness*
DIVISION	
DOB	1/18/23
	Deceased 5/01 Gallup, NM

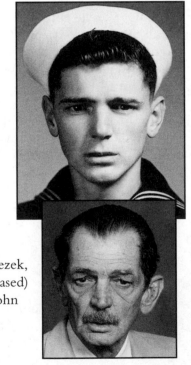

FAMILY

Wife: Ruby Foreman Spinelli (deceased 11/93)
Children: Esther Spinelli Wiley, Bruna Spinelli Bezek,
Marge Spinelli Tomada, Nino (Skip) Spinelli (deceased)
Grandchildren: Peter Basgal, Karen Matthews, John
Hiskey, Katerina Montoya, Brian Tomada, Mark
Tomada, Annette Mauldin, Nino Spinelli, Robert
Spinelli
Great-Grandchildren: 8

EXPERIENCE

Respectfully submitted by Survivor Spinelli's daughters.

Dad was born on January 18, 1923 in Gallup, New Mexico. He was the only child of Nino and Esterina (Mazocca) Spinelli. He joined the navy in 1942 and went to boot camp in San Diego, California. After boot camp, he was assigned to the USS *Indianapolis,* which was undergoing repairs at Mare Island naval shipyard in Vallejo, California. This is where Dad met Ruby (Mom), his wife of 49 years. While on the *Indy*, he went to the Alaskan coast and in the South Pacific to the islands of Tarawa, Saipan, Tinian, Okinawa and Iwo Jima. He served on the USS *Indianapolis* until it was sunk on July 30, 1945.

On the ship, dad was a cook. He really enjoyed being a cook as he always said, "The cooks always got the best food first, because we had to do the ordering and cooking. We could hide and sneak some really good stuff for ourselves." When the torpedoes struck, dad remembers he was in the bake shop, one of the hangouts. He had just finished winning a game of pinochle! "After the torpedo struck the ship, it lurched to its side. Then the men donned life jackets and jumped into oil-covered waters, polluted by the ship's ruptured oil tank," he told us.

Captain McVay was in his small group of survivors on the rafts, while hundreds of others treaded water, trying to avoid shark attacks. "The captain tried to calm the men. At that time, he was more like a father to us than a captain of a ship. We would keep normal conversation...like what are we going to do after we get picked up. After four days it was... ARE WE GOING TO GET PICKED UP?" He remembered with a laugh, "We only had some Spam and malted tablets as our daily rations on board the rafts." He kept thinking of the delicious candied Bing cherries his mother had sent from New Mexico and how good they would taste about now! Then he would think of his mother, dad, wife Ruby, and their newborn baby girl whom he had only seen two days before leaving on the *Indy*. These wonderful thoughts kept his spirits up.

Eighty-four hours after the Indianapolis was sunk, a pilot by the name of Lt. Wilbur "Chuck" Gwinn spotted the men in the water, called for help, and the rescue began. From then on, Lt. Gwinn was known as their "angel."

Dad always enjoyed attending the ship reunions and keeping in touch with his shipmates. He developed a cancerous lung tumor in 1999 but still made it to the 1999 reunion for many reasons but most of all because he had promised to bring some of his famous New Mexico green chili to everyone, especially Indiana Congresswoman Julia Carson. In turn, she had promised him she would bring her famous fried chicken. They both kept their promises, and in John's room everyone helped themselves to fried chicken and green chili.

In the summer of 2000 we took Dad to the mini-reunion in Broomfield, Colorado. It was one of the best times Dad ever had. He sipped his Coors Light and stayed up late visiting with his friends and shipmates. He said he knew he would not make it to the next reunion in Indianapolis, so he had the best time that could be had there. One thing Dad did do was take pictures of everything and everyone everywhere he went. We have plenty of them to remember him by.

After his rescue and recovery, Dad returned to Gallup, where he and mother raised three daughters and one son. He was a butcher for a few years and then worked for the city of Gallup for 37 years. He also served as a volunteer fireman. He was a member of the Elks Lodge, Principi Luigi Lodge, Knights of Columbus, Veterans of Foreign Wars, Disabled Veterans, and many more organizations to which he gave much of his time.

On May 7th and 8th, 2001 Dad got on the phone and called several of his shipmates and said "goodbye," because he said he was going to leave them in a few days. Dad passed away May 10, 2001 with his family and friends beside him at his home in Gallup. Surivor Paul Murphy and his wife, Mary Lou, came to Gallup for his funeral.

Dad was a very religious man and a true friend to all. He loved life and had a good time while here. He wanted everyone to remember him as a happy, fun-loving man. He loved fishing and dancing. But more than anything he wanted to be remembered as **The Kissing Bandit!**

Thank you, Dad. May you rest in peace.

Survivor John Spinelli at dedication of memorial in Broomfield, Colorado 2000.

NAME	SPOONER, MILES PFC USMC
STREET	
CITY	
STATE	
PHONE	
ENTERED SERVICE FROM	Bayard, FL
PICKED UP BY	USMC
DIVISION	
DOB	Deceased 12/96

FAMILY

EXPERIENCE
  Unable to contact any family members.

NAME	STAMM, FLORIAN M. S2C
STREET	209 Hanneman
CITY	Mt Horeb
STATE	WI 53572
PHONE	608 437 5622
ENTERED SERVICE FROM	Strongs Prairie, WI
PICKED UP BY	USS *Bassett*
DIVISION	4th Division
DOB	1/17/24

FAMILY
Spouse: Mary
Children: Terrance Stamm (Ann); Larry Stamm; Sharon Stamm; Timothy Stamm (Lisa); James Stamm; David Stamm (Barbara); Vicki Taylor Heideman (Jordan); Terri Taylor Reis (David)
Grandchildren: Diane Day (Kevin); Dodi O'Connor (Michael); Sidney Stamm; Tamara DeVoe; Jason Stamm; Margaret Stamm; Mitchell Stamm
Great-Grandchildren: Mathew Day; James Stuart; Candace Stuart; Coleman Stuart; David Archer; Amber Archer

461

EXPERIENCE

I enlisted and took my basic training at Great Lakes Naval Training Station. My entire navy career was served on the USS *Indianapolis*. I was on board when we were hit by a kamikaze pilot. We then had to be taken in for repairs. We then were dispatched to San Francisco to pick up cargo for our secret mission.

I had just come on watch. I had the 12:00 to 4:00 a.m. watch. I heard and felt the two explosions. Then all hell broke loose. Someone told me to get a life jacket on. I didn't think the *Indy* would sink. It is a good thing I put a life jacket on because I more or less swam off the ship, it was listing that far over. Once in the water, we were covered by thick oil from the ship. It was like molasses but it probably saved us.

I was spared from the sharks. I didn't have enough meat on me to interest them. They went after the bigger guys. I remember being so thirsty I tried to drink the salt water, but I was stopped by my fellow shipmates. I remember guys hallucinating and thinking fresh water was just beneath them. They would swim down to get a drink, and you would never see them again.

The last day and the rescue are pretty much a blur to me. I do know my kapok life jacket was giving out so that I was floating with just my nose above water.

I went to Washington, D.C. to testify in Captain McVay's trial. He was a fine captain and was unfairly singled out for blame.

After being honorably discharged in California, I hitchhiked to Wisconsin with eight dollars in my pocket. My four brothers and I all were in the service at the same time during the war. We were in different branches and all survived.

I am a member of the VFW and the American Legion and at one time was commander of our Legion post in Phoenix.

My work career was spent as an electrician, mostly in the Madison area. We have attended most of the USS *Indianapolis* reunions along with several members of our family.

NAME	STEPHENS, RICHARD P. S2C
STREET	3275 Cottage Grove Ave
CITY	Naples
STATE	FL 33962
PHONE	941 775 4589
ENTERED SERVICE FROM	Birmingham, AL
PICKED UP BY	USS *Bassett*
DIVISION	5th Division
DOB	1/25/27

FAMILY
Spouse: Mary

EXPERIENCE
No response.

NAME	STEVENS, GEORGE G. Water 2C
STREET	
CITY	
STATE	
PHONE	
ENTERED SERVICE FROM	Humphrey, ID
PICKED UP BY	USS *Talbot* tr USS *Register*
DIVISION	
DOB	Deceased 1/90

FAMILY

EXPERIENCE
Unable to contact any family members.

CHAPTER 295 SURVIVOR STEWART

NAME STEWART, GLENN W. Chief Fire Control
STREET
CITY
STATE
PHONE
ENTERED SERVICE FROM Ft Worth, TX
PICKED UP BY USS *Bassett*
DIVISION
DOB Deceased 2/86

FAMILY

EXPERIENCE

Unable to contact any family members.

CHAPTER 296 SURVIVOR STURTEVANT

NAME STURTEVANT, ELWYN L. Radio 2C
STREET
CITY
STATE
PHONE
ENTERED SERVICE FROM Los Angeles, CA
PICKED UP BY USS *Ringness*
DIVISION
DOB

FAMILY

EXPERIENCE

Unable to contact any family members.

NAME	SUTER, FRANK E. Storekeeper 3C
STREET	
CITY	
STATE	
PHONE	
ENTERED SERVICE FROM	Hartshorne, OK
PICKED UP BY	USS *Bassett*
DIVISION	
DOB	Deceased 87

FAMILY

EXPERIENCE

Unable to contact any family members.

CHAPTER 298 SURVIVOR TAWATER

NAME	TAWATER, CHARLES Fireman 1C
STREET	
CITY	
STATE	
PHONE	
ENTERED SERVICE FROM	Chickaska, OK
PICKED UP BY	USS *Bassett*
DIVISION	
DOB	Deceased

FAMILY

EXPERIENCE

Unable to contact any family members.

NAME	THELEN, RICHARD P. S2C
STREET	1323 Comfort St
CITY	Lansing
STATE	MI 48195
PHONE	517 482 2519
ENTERED SERVICE FROM	Lansing, MI
PICKED UP BY	USS *Doyle*
DIVISION	7th Division
DOB	3/14/27

FAMILY

Spouse: JoAnne
Children: Mike Thelen (Debbie), Larry Thelen (Ella), Dave Thelen (Pam), Barbara Thelen Ketchem (Al), Cathy Thelen Moore (Randy), Karen Thelen
Grandchildren: Adam Thelen, Monica Thelen, Christsy Thelen, Dawn Thelen, Daniel Thelen, Kelliann Thelen, Kaci Thelen, Nikki Cady, Matt Cady, Jacki Sheaffer and Allison Moore
Great–Grandchildren: Austin Thelen

EXPERIENCE

Federal law made it mandatory to enroll in the draft by your 18th birthday. I liked being around water and I decided to enlist in the navy in December 1944. I was called to Detroit for a physical on January 18, 1945. After passing the physical I was sent to the Great Lakes. I had just turned 18 in March. Otto Andrews and Jerry Mitchell went into the service at the same time. They both lived down the road from me.

When training was completed in April, I was given a seven day–pass and then reported back to Great Lakes for classes and testing. Approximately 200 to 300 of us traveled by military train to Shoemaker, California. I spent two weeks working in the mess hall there.

My fate was decided one day when 100 to 200 sailors standing in rows were asked to count off one-two-one-two down the line. All the "ones" were sent to the USS *New Jersey* at Bremerton, Washington and the "twos" went to the USS *Indianapolis* at Mare Island. Otto went to the *New Jersey*; Jerry and I went to the *Indianapolis* the first week of May, where it was in dry dock being repaired after an enemy plane crashed into it a few weeks earlier.

My duty was to accompany civilian welders working on the ship, standing by with a fire extinguisher during repairs. This was interrupted by a week of gunnery school where I trained on Mark 14 sight, twin-20 and 40-mm guns. When welding was through I chipped paint and cleaned various compartments.

On Saturday, July 14, 1945 the *Indy* left port on a shakedown cruise. On

Monday, July 16 a large crate was lifted from the docks and placed on the hangar deck. Four hours later, at 8:00 a.m., the *Indy* pulled up anchors and sailed.

I saw the box, but no one knew what it contained or why marines were on 24-hour guard around it. I stood muster in the seaplane hangar where the crate had been placed. There were some discussions about what it could contain, but most talk revolved around the speed we were traveling. I didn't know any difference and thought all ships vibrated so much. We traveled at top speed.

Our days were spent on watch, and we also were occupied with cleaning and drills. I had air watch 2 + 4 on starboard super-structure and twin millimeter guns on bow four hours on and eight off.

Joe Jacquemot, Eric Anderson, and I had become friends at Mare Island and went on leave together. Eric—15 or 16 years older than Joe and me—took charge of us—"father duties." Both Joe and Eric had been on the *Indy* before I arrived. Joe stood watch just prior to my watch in the same area.

We went from the States to Pearl Harbor, spent eight hours there, and then it was on to Tinian. No leaves were granted at Pearl. We refueled and took on supplies. We set a new speed record between the U.S. and Tinian.

On July 26, the *Indy* reached Tinian island and its cargo (a bomb) was removed. That same night the ship left for Guam, where it arrived the next morning. We left Saturday morning for Leyte Gulf in the Philippines, expecting to arrive there about 6:00 a.m. Tuesday for gunnery practice.

I started sleeping topside because it was too hot below. My sleeping quarters were two levels below (aft), the mess hall.

I stood watch Sunday from noon to 4:00 p.m. and was off until 4:00 a.m. Before Joe was going on watch at midnight, I had coffee with him and reminded him to wake me up on time. I couldn't have been asleep long when the first torpedo hit the bow. The blast moved me over from the 8-inch gun approximately 10 to 12 feet to where I laid against the cowls that run around the ship. I tried but couldn't find my clothes or shoes. I attempted to go to general quarters, but because the hangar deck was on fire the officer wouldn't let us cross.

I then returned to the bow area and looked for Joe. I saw that approximately 40 feet of the bow was gone, and it was tilting downward. I knew we were in trouble and with others, we started to cut down the life rafts and laid them on the deck. They floated away. After the second explosion we cut down life jackets that were stored topside and I put one on.

The second explosion knocked me down. It hit the 8-inch powder magazine and avation gasoline storage area and blew a hole in the ship's bottom. It was one hell of a rumble! The ship pitched to starboard side and continued to go down. When the water on deck got to my knees I swam off and away from the ship. I was about 200 feet away when the ship went down. Its hull raised straight up out of the water, stood for a moment, then slid into the water.

There were about 25 to 30 men in the water near me, all covered in oil. The water was very choppy. Someone in the darkness said to spread the oil on your body and life jackets "as we may be here longer than we think." We rode 8 to 10-foot swells all night and all Monday. At daylight I discovered I was in a group of 50 to 75, all in life jackets. Some had been burned. Those seriously injured didn't live long in the salt water. The combination of the salt water, oil, and motion of the waves had everyone vomiting.

Father Conway was in our group and asked any Catholics in the group to swim toward him. He gave us the last sacrament. Then he swam away. I was told later that he continued to administer to the men and exhausted himself and died.

MONDAY: There wasn't any panic that day, although one sailor, Bob Suhr, had his shoes on, and being afraid of the water refused to remove them. He did not survive. The talk was positive because we were due in Leyte on Tuesday and would be missed and rescue operations would begin. The day was hot—90 to 100 degrees. I was wearing only a pair of shorts. Someone suggested placing a piece of clothing on your head as a sunscreen, then putting it back on at night so you wouldn't lose it. This is what I did each day. I didn't experience any hunger pains that day. When the sun went down it was very chilly and your teeth chattered. I didn't sleep any that night.

TUESDAY: The sun was out about 6:00 a.m. The waves lessened to about two to three feet. We all talked about being missed and how soon we would be rescued. In the afternoon I saw the first sharks swimming below us. The group was spread about 40 yards; we tried to stay grouped to scare them off. They took some of our group that day—the injured and those on the perimeter.

I began to feel hungry and thirsty, but no one was thinking of drinking salt water. I also discovered Robert Terry in the group. We had stood muster in California and had become friends. We stayed together after that, watching out for each other. I could only doze in intervals with thoughts of sharks going through my mind, and the bobbing would force salt water up your nose and wake you up. By late afternoon the talk was about why the rescue planes and ships weren't on the scene. Why?? Hope was still alive. During the night, I heard someone yell out, "Sharks!" or heard screams when they were taken.

WEDNESDAY: Waves were now three to four feet, and I felt very hungry and thirsty. My thinking was becoming cloudy; some were out of their heads, drinking salt water. They would gulp more and more, start foaming at the mouth, become delirious and die. Disagreements and fighting began. Our group of about 25 began drifting off. Terry and I stayed together. Sharks ate the loners that swam off away from the group. The life jackets started to come apart, causing you to sink further into the water. We were now thinking we were all going to die. Survivors took jackets off the dead and put them on over original jackets. Terry and I took turns sleeping, watching, and preventing the others from drowning.

THURSDAY: Mental condition worsening. A few that had jackknives began to threaten others, although I never saw anyone being stabbed. I began to doze off more and more. Terry and I tried to keep watch over each other by letting one sleep for a short period and keeping our head out of the water. Only 12 to 20 remained in our group. All hope of rescue gone! Every time I reached the point of giving up I would think of my dad and how this would affect him. Because I was only 17 he had had to sign for me to enlist. He told me, "You had better come back."

A little before noon, a plane flew over us again this once a little lower than previous flights. Chuck Gwinn on a routine flight had had problems with a radio antenna, and while attempting to reel it in, he spotted an oil slick. Believing it could be an enemy submarine, he came back over the area with bomb bay doors open, ready to drop a bomb. What he saw were bodies bobbing in the water, spread over a wide area, 2 miles by 20 miles. He began to drop rafts and survivor gear. It was difficult to see, as my eyes were swollen almost shut from the sun, salt, and oil, but a raft appeared about 100 yards from us. Terry and I and two others started swimming toward it. I was the only one that made it. The others died of exhaustion on the way.

When I reached the raft there were already five or six men there, mostly delirious. The food and water was ruined. I attempted to get on the raft but I was too weak to do so. One tried to help me but the tugging hurt my skin so much we had to stop. I tied the strap from my jacket around the cord on the raft to secure myself and help to stay afloat. The plane continued to circle above us. Later several other planes arrived and dropped gear and left. A seaplane piloted by Adrian Marks arrived about 4:00 a.m., dropping lots of gear. I saw what looked like an attempted landing in the water but lost sight of the plane once it was down. We were now hopeful although everyone was only semiconscious, slipping in and out of reality.

THURSDAY EVENING: Sometime after dark, a light could be seen shining into the clouds, coming from the south. There was little reaction from anyone in our group.

FRIDAY: After daylight, the USS *Doyle* picked us up. It dropped a net and a raft over the side. Ship's crew climbed down and helped us up. They put a strap or something around us and hauled us up with some sailors pushing from below. Once on deck I thought I could walk. When I tried to stand I had such severe cramps in my legs and was so weak I nearly fell down. Someone asked my name, and then I was helped below and was given clear liquid, bullion, and water. Later I was told it had been 100 percent alcohol. I felt my heart pick up and my head cleared some. Two sailors put me in the shower. I couldn't stand. My legs were drawn up and I was unable to straighten them. They cleaned as much of the oil off as they could. I was helped to a bunk that the crew gave up for us. I was placed in the second level of three, where I caught sight of Joe Jacquemot across the aisle in the bottom bunk. I told my helpers to wake me up when he woke up. I guess I passed out and never got to talk to him on the *Doyle*. I have no recollection of being transferred off the *Doyle*. After picking up 93 survivors, the ship left the area about noon and headed to Peleliu, arriving at midnight Saturday, August 4. We were transferred to the hospital there.

I have a vague memory of someone making me drink, but full consciousness didn't return until Sunday. On Monday, August 6, I was transferred to the hospital ship *Tranquility*. I was taken out on a landing barge and put in a wire basket to be lifted aboard. It was a day or so before I was allowed up. I still needed assistance going down the gangplank when the ship reached Guam on Wednesday.

We were placed in a submarine rest camp. There we had plenty of delicious food and all you wanted to eat any time of the day. We stayed there approximately two weeks. We then were transported to San Diego on a small carrier escort, the *Hollandia*. On September 26, we were met by a brass band and paraded in Jeeps downtown.

I finished the remaining time in the service at the Grosse Isle Navy Station in Detroit. There were 17 of the 39 Michigan survivors at that location with me. Robert Terry and I made a promise while in the water that if only one of us survived the other would visit his family. I didn't go until spring; I put it off all winter. I never did tell her the full story. In later years, my wife and I visited Terry's sister and husband several times in Muncie, Indiana.

I left the navy but Joe Jacquemot re-enlisted and served in the submarine corps for four years. He married and lived in New Jersey until his death in 1995 from cancer. He attended all reunions from 1960 to 1990. My wife and I visited him twice at his home in New Jersey.

Eric Andrews lived in California and died in December of 1996. We looked forward to seeing him at each reunion and kept in touch by letters.

Every two years a reunion is held in Indianapolis for all the survivors, family and friends. The next reunion will be in July 2003.

★ ★ ★ ★ ★ ★ ★ ★ ★ ★

A personal note from Paul J. Murphy, Chairman, USS Indianapolis Survivors Organization.

The Thelen family have been wonderful supporters of the organization. Richard and his lovely wife Joann worked on the original committee to help organize our group. Their daughter, Cathy, organized and was elected the first president of the "Second Watch." This organization is for family or friends of any crew member, or anyone interested in preserving the history of the USS *Indianapolis*. At the 2001 reunion, a plaque from the organization was given to the Thelen family recognizing their many contributions. Unfortunately, Joann was very ill with cancer and died in January 2002. May she rest in peace. Richard still is very active in the organization and at the present time holds the position of co-master of arms.

CHAPTER 300   SURVIVOR THOMAS

NAME	THOMAS, IVAN M. S1C
STREET	
CITY	
STATE	
PHONE	
ENTERED SERVICE FROM	Boise, ID
PICKED UP BY	USS *Bassett*
DIVISION	
DOB	Deceased

FAMILY

EXPERIENCE

Unable to contact any family members.

NAME	THOMPSON, DAVID A. Elect Mate 3C
STREET	
CITY	
STATE	
PHONE	
ENTERED SERVICE FROM	Glouster, OH
PICKED UP BY	USS *Talbot* tr USS *Register*
DIVISION	
DOB	Deceased 9/90

FAMILY

EXPERIENCE
   Unable to contact any family members.

NAME	THURKETTLE, WILLIAM C S2C
STREET	205 So Maple Rd
CITY	Branch
STATE	MI 49402
PHONE	231 757 0453
ENTERED SERVICE FROM	Muskegan, MI
PICKED UP BY	USS *Bassett*
DIVISION	
DOB	1/11/28

FAMILY

EXPERIENCE
   No response.

NAME	TORRETTA, JOHN M. Fireman 1C
STREET	
CITY	
STATE	
PHONE	
ENTERED SERVICE FROM	St Louis, MO
PICKED UP BY	USS *Bassett*
DIVISION	
DOB	Deceased 11/84 St Louis, MO

FAMILY

Widow: Rose

Children: Gary Torretta (Karen); Karen Klemmer (Jon); Nancy Zoia (Mike); Janet Mohler (Andy)

Grandchildren: Sarah Torretta; Jenni Torretta; Jamie Klemmer; Michael (Abby) Zoia; Mark Zoia; Matt Zoia; John Mohler; and Maria Mohler

EXPERIENCE

John "Mickey" Torretta's experience is being submitted by his widow, Rose.

Mickey, an 18-year-old fireman first class, decided to enjoy the soft Pacific breezes and sleep on deck. Torretta slept only two hours. Two tremendous explosions on the starboard side shook him awake. He thinks he may have been the last man off the ship.

After the explosion he scrambled to his battle station, which was in the front of the ship. By the time he returned to the middle, she was on her side and the front half under water. When he reached the tail of the ship, he saw only two other men on board. "The two fellas jumped, then I took a few steps and jumped. They must have hit something. That's the last I ever saw them."

At first light Monday morning, he found himself in a group of about 145 men. "We spent a lot of the night praying, Catholics, Jews, Protestants—we all prayed together." Each day took its toll. The men grew too weak to respond emotionally to anything. But when they sighted sharks, the whole group was charged with fear.

A few times the sharks swam beneath the group and once, Mickey felt one go through his legs. The group was lucky, for up to Wednesday they hadn't suffered a shark attack. But Wednesday afternoon their luck ran out. They put the bitten man on the raft and tried to tie a tourniquet on his leg with a belt. But he died during the night. Mickey recalled that, "You'd say to yourself, 'How can I stand it? How can I stay out here? Is this it? Is someone going to pick us up or are we going to dwindle every day until there are no more of us?'"

Mickey lost his fingernails and eyebrows from the salt water and sun. His throat burned and he had constant cramps in his stomach. He was semiconscious and events began to lose form. Only one thing remained constant–his craving for water. Of the men in Mickey's group, only half remained when the group was spotted by Chuck Gwinn. "None of us could have lasted another night." Torretta said.

"When I went in the navy I weighed 165 pounds. And after a few days of eating regular in the hospital I weighed 105. You can imagine the shape we were in when they rescued us. The thing that gave us the stamina to last another night was the beacon shining in the sky from the USS *Cecil Doyle*. We knew then that help had arrived." He was picked up by the USS *Bassett*.

Mickey was one of the founding members of the USS Indianapolis survivors' memorial reunion and served as its secretary for many years.

* * * * * * * * * *

A personal comment from Paul J. Murphy, Chairman, USS Indianapolis Survivors Organization.

Mickey's widow, Rose, assumed Mickey's secretarial duties after his death. She volunteered countless hours for years as our secretary and continues to serve on various committees. Rose was given the distinctive title of "Honorary Survivor." We are forever grateful!

CHAPTER 304   SURVIVOR TURNER

NAME	TURNER, CHARLES M. S2C
STREET	
CITY	
STATE	
PHONE	
ENTERED SERVICE FROM	LaGrange, IL
PICKED UP BY	USS *Ringness*
DIVISION	
DOB	Deceased 2/87

FAMILY

EXPERIENCE
Unable to contact any family members.

NAME	TWIBLE, HARLAN M. ENS
STREET	323 Hernando Ave
CITY	Sarasota
STATE	FL 34243
PHONE	941 355 3524
ENTERED SERVICE FROM	Michigan City, IN
PICKED UP BY	USS *Bassett*
DIVISION	Gunnery
DOB	3/10/22

FAMILY

Spouse: Alice Bradford Southworth Twible
Children: Pamela, Susan Lestock, Barbara, David Twible
Grandchildren: James

EXPERIENCE

United States Navy in World War II and Korean War in various line billets. Most notable experience was aboard the USS *Indianapolis*, which delivered the first atomic bomb to Tinian. The bomb was dropped on Hiroshima by the U.S. Army Air Force. Upon completion of the mission, the ship was sunk off Yap Island as it sailed to join the fleet that was to invade Japan. After four days and five nights in the water we were spotted by a navy plane on anti-submarine patrol. One of 317 survivors out of a crew of 1197. Awarded the Navy and Marine Corps Medal for Heroism and the Purple Heart for wounds received in action.

NAME   UFFELMAN, PAUL R. PFC USMC
STREET
CITY
STATE
PHONE
ENTERED SERVICE FROM
PICKED UP BY   USS *Doyle*
DIVISION   Marine
DOB   Deceased 12/96

FAMILY

EXPERIENCE
    Unable to contact any family members.

NAME   UMENHOFFER, LYLE S1C
STREET   8925 E Greenwood
CITY   San Gabrel
STATE   CA 91775
PHONE   626 286 8079
ENTERED SERVICE FROM   Rosemead, CA
PICKED UP BY   USS *Doyle*
DIVISION   3rd Division
DOB   5/27/23

FAMILY
Spouse: Mary
Children: Caren Umenhoffer Gonser
Grandchildren: Kenneth Gonser, Brian Gonser, Jeffrey Gonser

EXPERIENCE
    In February 1942, I joined the navy to serve my country during the war. My
orders came in March and the training period was three weeks in boot camp in
San Diego, California. We were sent to San Francisco by train, then taken to

Mare Island to go aboard the USS *Indianapolis*. I was assigned to the Third Division Deck Force.

Leaving San Francisco we escorted Matson Line ships, loaded with troops, to Australia. After leaving Australia we sailed to Alaska to assist in the Aleutians Campaign. I joined the Gunners Gang on the number three turret. During our time of service there we sank a Japanese transport ship loaded with troops preparing to make a landing on one of the islands.

We were in the Bering Straits for almost a year. The weather was extremely harsh during the winter months. The sea was so rough that the ship would go over two waves and under one wave.

When we left the Aleutians we sailed to the South Pacific. There we were in many battles—bombarding islands, and giving support to troops on the islands. At one time we were firing at one of the islands and our sister ship, the USS *Portland*, was on the opposite side of the island firing as well. The island was so flat we almost hit the *Portland*; they quickly left.

While we were engaged in a battle at Okinawa on Easter Sunday, 1944, we were hit by a kamikaze airplane carrying two 500-pound bombs. One bomb went through a gun deck then through the mess hall where the diving gear was stored. I was sitting at a table eating breakfast with six other men. The impact knocked all of us off our chairs and onto the deck. It then went through the compartment deck where nine men lost their lives, then into the engine room where it exploded. The other bomb hit the screw shaft on the port side, leaving a huge hole in the side of the ship. We had a memorial service on board for the men who were lost. I was part of the burial party, and we transported the bodies to the island of Kerama Retto. The army told us to leave and that they would bury the bodies because there were Japanese snipers on the island.

We returned to the States for repairs to our ship. We limped back with only two starboard screws at a seventeen degree list. We were in dry dock for ninety days. Then we went to Hunters Point. Some of us helped carry the components of the atomic bomb onboard. We didn't know what we were bringing on, as it was all top secret. We sailed for a world-record run to Tiniain island at approximately 32 knots. It was difficult to stand or walk on deck because the ship was vibrating from going at such high speed. At Tinian we unloaded the atom bomb onto a barge. There was one large crate and smaller containers.

We then sailed to Guam for further orders. The following morning we left Guam, and shortly after midnight we were hit by two torpedoes. I had just finished standing watch at midnight and laid down on deck to go to sleep. When the first torpedo hit, I jumped up and put on my clothes, and walked to the port side of the ship to wait for instructions. My best friend Gene Ragsdale was standing by me. He said he was going below deck to see what was going on. I said, "Gene, don't go down there," but he did and that was the last time I saw him.

When the ship rolled over on the starboard side, I slid off of the deck and into the water without a life jacket. When I slid off the deck I hit a hatch and injured both of my legs. I swam for what seemed like a long time, and then a man came by with an empty 20-mm can and gave it to me. I hung on to it until a man floated by with an extra life jacket, which he gave to me. I was still swimming with it when I was picked up. The water was covered with oil, which made everyone sick.

I was in a group with about 35 men. We formed a circle and put the men who were severely injured in the middle of the group. Every day there were always many sharks swimming around us. When one would get close to me, I would just kick it away. They always came back and got kicked away many times.

During our five days in the water we saw many planes fly over. We waved and yelled but they were too high to see us.

We tried to keep the men together, but as time passed some died, others swam away, giving in to hallucinations of ships, islands, and other things. You could hear men screaming while being dragged under and eaten by sharks. Some wanted fresh water and would dive down looking for the ship; of course they drowned. There were only three in our group when we were found.

We were excited when we knew we had been spotted by Lt. Wilbur Gwinn, pilot of the PV-1 Ventura airplane. He radioed for help. Then many planes could be seen. They dropped life rafts and supplies.

When Lt. Adrian Marks' PBY plane landed on the water and started picking up men, he came by once and said I will come back. Of the three of us that were together, I was assisting the other two men to stay afloat as they were both very weak. When he picked us up, I was placed on the wing of the plane.

The USS *Doyle* was the first ship to arrive at the scene. They sent out boats, took us off the plane, and transferred us to the ship. We were covered with oil. The crew scrubbed us and gave us their bunks.

We were taken to the Island of Peleliu and stayed there two days. We were then transferred to the hospital ship USS *Tranquility*. While I was on the hospital ship lying on a bed, my legs had big sores on them caused by hitting the hatch when I went off the ship. All of us had saltwater ulcers. A nurse came by to check on me and after seeing the sores on my legs, she came back with a pink ribbon and tied it on my toe.

We were transferred from the hospital ship to Base 18 Hospital on the island of Guam. We were there for one month. The USS *Hollandia* arrived at Guam and transported us back to the States.

I am grateful to my Lord and Savior, Jesus Christ, for bringing me through this ordeal and giving me the strength and will power to put it behind me and go on with my life.

CHAPTER 308 SURVIVOR UNDERWOOD

NAME UNDERWOOD, RALPH E. Radar S1C
STREET
CITY
STATE
PHONE
ENTERED SERVICE FROM Louisville, KY
PICKED UP BY USS *Bassett*
DIVISION
DOB Deceased 4/99

FAMILY

EXPERIENCE

Unable to contact any family members.

CHAPTER 309 SURVIVOR VanMETER

NAME VanMETER, JOSEPH W. Water 3C
STREET
CITY
STATE
PHONE
ENTERED SERVICE FROM Bowling Green, KY
PICKED UP BY USS *Register*
DIVISION
DOB Deceased

FAMILY

EXPERIENCE

Unable to contact any family members.

NAME   WALKER, VERNER B. F2
STREET   918 So Jackson
CITY   Tucumcari
STATE   NM 88401
PHONE
ENTERED SERVICE FROM   Tucumcari, NM
PICKED UP BY   USS *Bassett*
DIVISION   E Division
DOB   9/9/26

FAMILY

EXPERIENCE
No response.

NAME   WELLS, CHARLES O. S1C Radar
STREET
CITY
STATE
PHONE
ENTERED SERVICE FROM   Camanche, IA
PICKED UP BY   USS *Bassett*
DIVISION
DOB   08/01/08
                        Deceased 2/52

FAMILY
Widow: Olive Harrington Wells (deceased)
Children: Jerry Wells (Jinette), Jimmy Charles Wells (deceased)

EXPERIENCE
   Respectfully submitted by Survivor Wells' son Jerry and his two sisters Darlyne
Dickinson and Natalie Shadle.
   Charles Orville Wells was born in Waynoka, Oklahoma on August 1, 1908 to

Reverend Charles Wells and Minnie Gordon Wells. He was married in 1935 to Olive Harrington and they had two sons: Jimmy Charles and Jerry. His wife Olive died in 1955 and his son Jimmy died in 1982. Son Jerry lives in San Antonio, Texas with his wife, Jinette.

Orville, as we called him, lived in Camanche, Iowa, where he had a painting and decorating business. Hometown folks called him "dobber" because in addition to contracting, he also painted lovely art work as a hobby. He was the happiest, most cheerful person and we remember him as always singing and whistling. Orville had one brother, four half-sisters, and a half-brother. He was dearly loved by his family and friends. His son Jerry remembers many happy times with his dad and brother, fishing on the Mississippi River after the war.

Orville joined the navy in 1944 and because he was 36 years old–considerably older than the other men aboard ship–his nickname was "Pappy Wells." Orville rarely talked about his experience during the USS *Indianapolis* tragedy. We do remember him telling us of the severe saltwater ulcers on his body. One of his most painful memories was seeing his shipmates swim away in their delirium and losing his buddy to sharks.

Orville tragically lost his life in an automobile accident in February 1952, seven years after the USS *Indianapolis* tragedy.

LAS Knott, Survivor Paul Murphy, Survivor Orville Wells, LAS Peterson.

NAME   WHITING, GEORGE A. F2
STREET   978 N 2075 E Circle
CITY   St. George
STATE   UT 84770
PHONE   435 673 5400
ENTERED SERVICE FROM   Salmon, ID
PICKED UP BY   USS *Bassett*
DIVISION   Fireman Second Class Engine Room
DOB   3/2/26

FAMILY
Spouse: Nina
Children: Carl, Hal, and Janene
Grandchildren: 11 grandsons and 2 granddaughters

EXPERIENCE

I grew up in the beautiful Salmon River Mountains of Idaho with my several brothers and cousins. We had a great life hunting, fishing, exploring, motorcycle riding and enjoying every day.

World War II came along and I was drafted into the navy when I turned 18. From boot training in Farragut, I went on to the USS *Indianapolis*, a heavy cruiser with 8-inch, 5-inch, 50-mm, 30-mm and 20-mm guns. I worked in the engine room and in most ways really enjoyed being in the navy. I served in the Pacific, Hawaii, where I saw the ships that were sunk at Pearl Harbor, and I was at Iwo Jima. Near Okinawa, the *Indianapolis* was hit by a suicide plane and we were sent back stateside for repairs.

When we sailed again, there was a large box in the hangar with a 24-hour marine guard. We sailed to Honolulu and on to Tinian, where we off-loaded the box. We then proceeded to Guam where Captain McVay received orders for the forward area. Before going to Guam, my bunk was in the forward part of the ship near the bow. I was told to move my bunk to the rear of the ship, which I did not do until the night we left Guam and headed for the Philippines.

The first or second night after leaving Guam, on July 30, 1945, we were torpedoed by a Japanese submarine. The forward part of the ship (where I had just moved my bunk from) was hit. The first torpedo woke me up. I bumped my head on a post at the second explosion. I hurriedly dressed and went to the forward part of the ship where it was dark and smoky. I heard, "Abandon ship," although all communications had been knocked out. When I got to the top deck the ship was listing to starboard side at an angle that made standing upright almost impossible.

I got the last kapok life jacket from a box on deck. I watched men jump off the ship—some were getting hurt as they landed on the top propellers. I walked forward and sat on the almost vertical deck and slid down the side of the ship. I hit into a propeller shaft that flipped me backward. I was in the water and a man who had injured his own back when he jumped climbed onto my back. He was hysterical and wouldn't listen to me. I couldn't hold him up. He was pushing me down under the water. I knew if I did not get help I would die. I prayed for my life to be spared so I could be married and raise a family. As I said, "Amen," I was raised up out of the water and was then able to support myself as well as the man on my back.

I was so close to the ship, I could have touched it with my hand. I was going to stay near in case it didn't sink. The ship began to lurch and I knew it would sink soon. I began to swim away but it didn't seem as if I could make any distance. When I looked back, I was almost a block away, and the man was still clinging to my shoulders. I watched the ship sink—bow first. There was moonlight and there was a heavy oil slick on the water. There was a man standing silhouetted on the fantail as it disappeared into the dark water.

A wooden support that had held a small boat on our ship was floating near us. I asked the man who was still clinging to my back to get on to this support. I saw him later on a raft. I swam over to the raft. There were so many men on the raft that it would sink until the water came up around them. Many of us stayed in the water clinging to a cargo net. There were other rafts as heavily loaded as ours.

I was never worried the four days and five nights we were in the water. A small voice gave me constant assurance I would be picked up.

There were sharks around us. We had a few dry biscuit rations, but I couldn't keep the one or two I ate down. When we opened the one can of Spam we had and divided it, I got a piece the size of my smallest fingernail. The sharks smelled the Spam and were all around us.

There was no way to sleep and there was no drinking water. Many men died from drinking the salt water, and men died in the water from exposure and fear. Some were suddenly getting religious and began repeating the Lord's Prayer. I did not fear.

We shook from the cold at night and burned from the oil, water, and sun combination by day. The first day, a plane went over but we didn't get a flare shot in time. He did not see us although he wasn't very high.

The fourth night, I remember hanging onto the side of the raft but then I drifted out of my mind and have no further recollection of that night. The next morning I became alert and was sitting on one side of the raft, totally alone on that side. I do not know how I got there or what happened to the men who had been there. The men started moving back and I returned to my place in the water. There were still too many men for me to have a place on the raft. I feel the hand of God helped me.

In the late afternoon of the fourth day, we were spotted by a plane that dropped us several messages and radioed our location. I swam out and picked up one of the messages. It said that a ship from the Philippines would be there to pick us up at 2400 hours. We were instructed to gather our rafts together.

Two seaplanes landed and loaded a few men but did not leave. Lifeboats and a hand-cranked signal device were dropped from another plane.

The *Indianapolis* had been cruising in radio silence, the communications were knocked out with the first torpedo, and higher commands did not realize we were in trouble. A B-29 came over and dropped a motor whaleboat and more rafts. Tension was growing among the few survivors and fights erupted.

I got on a boat and found water. The ship picked us up at 2400 hours. The men on the rescue ship were wonderful to us. They even went into the showers with us and scrubbed our bodies that were covered with saltwater sores.

Some of the survivors were taken to Guam. I went with a group to Samar in the Philippines to a hospital. We had a constant guard around our building, and I wondered why. A few days later we found out we had been carrying the atomic bomb on the *Indianapolis* and it was this that had warranted the marine guard. The box carrying the part of the A-bomb had been unloaded at Tinian.

The atomic bomb was dropped on Japan while I was in the hospital in the Philippines. We were flown to Guam to be with the other survivors and found out that of the 1,197 men only 317 of us had survived. We were given Purple Hearts while at Guam.

I was shipped home for a 30-day leave, where I went deer hunting almost every day with an older brother.

Great Therapy!!!

CHAPTER 313 SURVIVOR WILCOX

NAME	WILCOX, LINDSEY Z. WT2C
STREET	300 Long Dr
CITY	Baytown
STATE	TX 77521
PHONE	281 422 4487
ENTERED SERVICE FROM	Dequincy, LA
PICKED UP BY	USS *Bassett*
DIVISION	B Division Fire Rm #2
DOB	2/14/25

FAMILY

Spouse: Colleen Marie Wilcox
Children: Charlotte Wilcox, Cathleen Wilcox Auld
Grandchildren: Daniel Wilcox Auld

EXPERIENCE

The USS *Indianapolis* was in the navy yard, Mare Island during May 1945, after getting heavy underwater damage from a kamikaze hit off Okinawa on March 31, 1945. During this time each section of the B Division was given leave for several weeks. I was in love with my childhood sweetheart and she was visiting her mother in Seattle, Washington and we thought this was a good time to get married. So we were married on May 22, in a Methodist Church chapel. My best man was Kenneth W. Shand WT2C and his date was a Navy Wave; they also were married during that week.

On July 12 we received orders that the USS *Indianapolis* was going to perform a special task. On July 15, 1945, the ship sailed to Hunters Point near San Francisco, California. On July 16 we began preparing to sail and by noon they had loaded the "special cargo," which was later known as the atomic bomb! Our orders were to proceed as fast as possible to Pearl Harbor. We were told that whatever time we saved would shorten the war by that amount. The USS *Omaha* had made the trip in 1932 in 75.4 hours. We broke that record, making the trip in 74.5 hours at 18 to 19 knots.

Two scientists were on board with the atomic bomb and as we pulled away from the Golden Gate Bridge they had their eyes looking toward the east horizon. They had witnessed the glow of the mushroom produced by the testing of the first atomic bomb in New Mexico.

On the morning of July 26, 1945 at Tinian, an island located in the Marinas, the components of the "special cargo"–the atomic bomb–were unloaded and later would be dropped over Hiroshima.

We left Tinian that afternoon and headed for Guam, which was an overnight trip. We had never tried our new anti-aircraft guns, but they were tested during gunnery practice that morning. We left Guam on Saturday morning, July 28 at 0930, and were to arrive in Leyte at 1100 Tuesday, July 31, 1945.

I was on the 1800 to 2400 watch in fire room 2 on July 29 and was relieved at 5 minutes before midnight. I had just left fire room 2 and headed for the deck to sleep in the port aircraft hangar. As I was starting to lie down, there was an explosion, and fire came out of the forward starboard and port passageways, extending half the distance of the quarterdeck. The Japanese submarine *I-58* under the command of Hashimoto had just fired six torpedoes with two hitting the USS *Indianapolis*. The first torpedo broke off part of the ship's bow and the second torpedo hit fire room 2 or the forward ammunition magazine.

Within five minutes the ship had a 25 degree list to starboard. I was making my way back to the fantail. When I reached the fantail, the ship had a 90 degree list to starboard. I stood on the port side of the eight-inch gun turret and stepped into the water on the starboard. Less than 30 feet of the ship was left at the time.

I swam out about 50 feet and blew up my life jacket. The ship's propellers were between me and the moon as I watched her sink into the ocean. One of the things you expect when a ship this large (615 feet in length) sinks, is that there will be a great suction. This suction will pull you under water approximately 12 feet and hold you there for a while. But if the ship fills up with water, there will be no suction. There was no suction when the USS *Indianapolis* went down into the sea. The USS *Indianapolis* took approximately 15 minutes to go down after receiving the two torpedoes.

I then noticed a life raft several feet away and swam over to it. After getting on the life raft I floated over to another raft and several floater nets. There was some confusion, but soon we started to pick up shipmates that were hurt (injured backs and burns). I gave up my place on the life raft for the wounded. The life raft was the safest place to be, but in the floater nets, the most important thing for me was to conserve my energy, not knowing how long we would be in the water.

On the morning of July 30, we had about 150 men on the two life rafts and several floater nets. We all had different stories and questions to ask. The most common question was whether an SOS message had been sent? The answer was that not anyone knew for sure.

The first day was not too bad; we had the sharks and we took care of the wounded. We also found the wooden water kegs had taken on salt water. On this day we all prayed for God to give us strength to overcome this ordeal. The things that I had done in my younger years passed in my mind before me. I had to think about what I must do to become a survivor. We all were born with an intuition at birth. We develop this during our childhood with the help of our family, friends, our church, and God. I am talking about the brain that we all have. The message we must send our brain: "I am a survivor."

Years later, I had an interview with a magazine company from Los Angeles, California regarding how I survived the tragedy and the sharks. Also present was Dr. Martin Nemiroff, chief of health services for Coast Guard training. His answer for survival was that, "It's the will to live, and that's hard to measure. It transcends lack of food and water. It overcomes body size, health conditions, even lack of skills, it's an intangible, basically, the message you give your brain: "I am a survivor."

Second Day

On the morning of July 31, some of my shipmates started to see islands and airplanes. We could see neither of these. During the late evening, several took one raft and set off to see if they could find help or other survivors. We lost several shipmates from fighting with each other, because one would think another was the enemy. Some survivors would sink below the surface of the water and come back up to tell us they had been to chow to eat and to get a drink of water. In time, this would convince others they were telling the truth. The number of survivors we had on the first day was slowly decreasing. You could look down between your legs in the water and see sharks at any time during the day. We were providing an umbrella for them to get out of the sun.

Third Day

On this day, August 1, things were starting to get very bad. Some of the men were starting to lose their minds. When a person starts to lose his mind, he wants to swim off and when he becomes too exhausted he dies and the sharks get him. You could stretch your arms around someone to try to hold them in the floater net. I did this for my shipmate Carl Nielson, fireman first class. After his continued persistence to leave, he swam away and I had to let him go. You have to remember you had to conserve your own energy if you were to survive. Others did not want to swim away, but they decided to drink the sea water. This caused their throats to swell and in time they died. I do not know why we did this, but when a person died from drinking salt water, we would say a prayer, remove his life jacket and let him sink into the sea. The life jacket would then be given to someone whose life jacket was starting to take on sea water.

I took a nap late in the afternoon on this day and woke up just before sunset. I asked an officer what had happened and he told me we were to be picked up in four hours. I finally realized his mind was playing tricks on him but I almost believed him. I then moved to a position next to the outside row of squares on the floater net. Every day we did lots of praying, asking forgiveness of our sins as our lives passed before us.

We repented several times on the big and small things that we should have not done. I even ask forgiveness in taking a pie from my grandmother's kitchen window.

Fourth Day

On this day, August 2, I was awakened by being taken underwater by one or two sharks. I came up fighting and I was staring at two gray sharks lying on top of the water. They were about 10 to 12 feet in length about 10 feet from me. I did not believe the sharks were going to attack me; they were just seeing if I was dead. In my teenage years I was taught how to catch small fish; if you throw a crumb of bread in the water, minnows will come up and bump the bread. The next time the minnows come in contact, they would eat the bread. This is what the sharks did to me to see if I was dead or alive. The group of survivors were now nowhere in sight. I was more concerned with the sharks than the group of survivors. The waves had swells about four feet in high and I could not see very far, with just my head sticking out of the water. All the time I was talking to the sharks saying, "You don't bother me and I will not bother you." I was watching the two sharks when in the distance between them the waves brought into sight the head of one of the survivors. The next thing I did was to swim between the two sharks, brushing them with my legs. They turned to follow me as I swam towards the survivor. The sharks followed me all the way back to the floater net. The two sharks had to be in this specific, exact spot for me to have looked between them and seen that one survivor's head sticking out of the water.

On this day Lt. Wilbur Gwinn accidentally sighted a group of survivors. He was testing a new sonar antenna, and the antenna cable broke. Lt. Gwinn's PV-1 Ventura bomber then returned to base for another sonar and antenna and cable. They had the same problem with this antenna cable as the first one. Lt. Gwinn went back to see what was causing all the problems with the cable. Lt. Gwinn was inspecting the broken cable and then noticed an oil slick on the water; in his mind he was thinking about a crippled Japanese submarine. He saw that it was men floating in the oil-slicked water and sent a message back to his base about men in the water.

The survivors were scattered over ten square miles. The group I was in never did see Lt. Gwinn's plane or Lt. Adrian Marks' PBY, which he landed in the water. We did have several planes fly over our group of survivors. A B-17 came over us with a motor launch boat tied to the underside of the plane. After circling several times this motor launch was parachuted into the water. It took three parachutes to get the motor launch into the water and several survivors in the group swam out to it. I started to swim out to the motor launch and turned back.

Several minutes later a C-47 flew over and dropped an emergency package in the water. I swam out to pick up the package and there was one can of water and a package dye marking. After recovering the water and dye package, I swam back to the group. Someone in the group yelled out he was going to court martial me if I did not bring over to him the case of beer that the C-47 had dropped into the water. I did not give up the one can of water, but divided it among several of my shipmates in the group.

Another C-47 later in the day dropped a small rubber raft into the water, and I swam out and recovered the raft. I brought the raft back to the group and I picked up a shipmate and Lt. Redmayne (engineering officer of the USS *Indianapolis*). We then paddled over to the motor launch, let the engineering officer off, and picked up a supply of water to take back to the group of survivors. After leaving the water with the group we started paddling back to the motor launch for more water. We had no idea how far the motor launch was from us or if it was drifting in the same direction as before. Darkness was appearing, and we never saw the motor launch again. We stopped paddling the raft and soon fell asleep in the night.

Fifth Day

I was rescued around 4:00 a.m. on August 3, 1945 by the USS *Bassett* (APD 73). The USS *Register*, USS *Cecil J Doyle*, USS *Madison*, USS *Ralph Talbot*, and USS *Ringness* rescued others. My group was taken to a hospital at Samar; the rest of the survivors were taken to a hospital at Palau or Ulithi. Some of the group gave thanks to God for the ships that were sent to rescue us. We stayed in the hospital two weeks and then were flown to Guam. The war was over and we were all sent back to the United States. I had enlisted at age 17 in the regular navy and left at 21. I was honorably discharged February 14, 1946 at the naval air station, New Orleans, Louisiana.

I frequently think of my shipmates who did not make it. Kenneth Shand WT 2/C; Walter Miller Boilermaker 1/C; Ray Brooks CWTA; Robert Makowski CWTA; Charles Linden WT 2/C; Forrest Pursel WT 2/C; Elwood Dale F1; Charles Barry LT (jg)—and some of the little things that happened aboard the USS *Indianapolis* (CA-35).

I never knew Captain Charles Butler McVay III while aboard the USS *Indianapolis*. He held many personnel inspections on Saturday mornings because we were the flagship with Admiral Spruance aboard (but I had not gotten to meet him). March of 1951 was the first time I met Captain McVay. I had joined the Navy Reserve and had been called up to leave for San Diego, California in May of that year. I made a trip to New Orleans in March to get a deferment. This required going through the different departments of the navy and finally coming before the three-man board. Several navy men told me how awful Captain McVay had been treated while he was stationed in New Orleans.

A chief machinist mate wrote the captain's phone number on a piece of paper and put it in my shirt pocket. He said to find the time to call the captain TODAY! That afternoon I called the captain, and we met at the front of the Roosevelt Hotel and then we went out to the naval air station. He told me about the court martial and the things that bothered him most about the sinking. I felt then the same way I do today; he was not guilty of the charges brought against him. Captain McVay was a person most children need as a father in growing up to manhood in today's world. My opinion—and mine alone—is that the loss of the USS *Indianapolis* (CA-35) did not cause him to take his own life.

CHAPTER 314   SURVIVOR WISNIEWSKI

NAME	WISNIEWSKI, STANLEY F2C
STREET	
CITY	
STATE	
PHONE	
ENTERED SERVICE FROM	Detroit, MI
PICKED UP BY	PBY Tr USS *Doyle*
DIVISION	
DOB	7/31/26 Deceased 6/95

FAMILY
Widow: Barbara
Children: David Wisniewski (Mary), Daniel Wisniewski (Mary), Douglas
Wisniewski (Lori)
Grandchildren: Bridget Wisniewski, Max Wisniewski, Kurtis Wisniewski

EXPERIENCE

Respectfully submitted by Survivor Wisniewski's widow Barbara and family.

Stanley Wisniewski was the son of Polish immigrants living in Detroit and was 18 years old when he signed up for the navy. He completed training and his first assignment was on the USS *Indianapolis*. He was on the ship only one week before it set sail on what would be its final mission. Stanley served as a fireman, second class.

The boiler room was the hottest part of the ship so when he had completed his shift he went up onto the deck clad only in his undershorts to get some fresh air and find a cool place to sleep. That was where he was when the ship was torpedoed. He recounted to family that he literally half-walked, half-slid down the side of the ship as it sank and swam away as the *Indianapolis* slipped below the water.

Stanley went into the water alone but joined up with a group of about 20 other sailors floating in the water. They formed a large ring and tried to stay together. He was wearing the standard-issue kapok cork life jacket and knew they were only guaranteed to float for 48 hours. He tore his undershorts into pieces in order to wipe the oil from the ship out of his eyes and spent his five days in the water "as naked as a baby."

As days wore on without fresh water or food, some of the sailors removed their life jackets in an attempt to dive down to the sunken ship where they were sure there were supplies of fresh water. He was never sure whether these sailors were hallucinating or committing suicide. When he found himself repeatedly untying and retying his life jacket, he deliberately tied the cords in knots to prevent himself from removing it should he also begin to hallucinate.

Stanley turned 19 years old during those five days in the water, watching as his shipmates slowly dwindled in number. He did not talk to his family about the shark attacks, but he did say that of the 20 or so sailors he was with in a big ring when the ship first sank, he was the only one who was pulled from the water alive.

His face barely above the sea surface, he was pulled from the water by Adrian Marks' PBY and was tied to the wing of the plane. Massive sores, infections all over his oil-coated body and ulcerated corneas caused blindness. He remembered overhearing two navy doctors discussing with a nurse, "I don't think he's going to make it." Last rites were administered. He received 120 injections of antibiotic. However, Stanley did survive. He said he spent much of his time in the water praying and was lucky to be alive.

After recovering from his injuries, he was shipped out to continue serving out his term of enlistment. It was decades later that he finally discussed his experience with his family. He married, raised three sons, and worked for Ford Motor Company for most of his life. Stan had made three promises while he was in the water. One was to stop smoking; another was to attend church regularly, and he fulfilled these two promises. The third promise we are unsure of. We believe it was never to swear. If indeed it was, that promise was also kept. After his family was nearly grown, he began to attend survivors' reunions.

In coming to terms with his experience at sea, Stanley said, "The object is to carry on afterwards. I tried to live a good life after this. I tried to do the right thing." Unfortunately, he passed away at age 68 only one month before the memorial in Indianapolis was dedicated.

CHAPTER 315   SURVIVOR WITZIG

NAME	WITZIG, ROBERT M. FC3
STREET	4808 Greenwood Rd
CITY	Fennimore
STATE	WI 53809
PHONE	608 822 6610
ENTERED SERVICE FROM	Stitzer, WI
PICKED UP BY	USS *Bassett*
DIVISION	Fox Division
DOB	8/24/24

FAMILY

EXPERIENCE

I am Robert M. Witzig, fire control man third class living in Wisconsin. This event never dies. It is always in the life of the leftover men. Special reminders: frequent reunions, the movie *Jaws*, dedication of a nuclear submarine USN 697 *Indianapolis*; dedication of national monument in Indianapolis (1995), which was built with NO TAX DOLLARS; eleven books, several television documentaries; and numerous documents from the city of Indianapolis signed by governors, congressional people, as well as mayors and other leaders of the city of Indianapolis, as well as other states. The USS *Indianapolis* was President Franklin D. Roosevelt's flagship as well as being the flagship of Admiral Spruance's Fifth Fleet.

Her final 13 minutes...

On July 29, 1945, I was sound asleep in my work area, the main battery director, 97 feet to the water line. There was no cool air or drinking water. Ice cubes were unheard of. Men slept topside with shoes and clothing on, a blanket and pillow was always with you. The blanket served as your mattress on the steel deck.   Shortly after midnight, July 30, I was thrown on my feet and out the rear hatch to the surrounding catwalk. I never actually heard the explosion. The greatest damage was on the forward bow. All this happened so fast. The forward decks and second decks where the big guns were mounted were crowded with men asleep.   Directly above about 60-70 feet, I heard the death cries of these men, left motionless. Mainly cries for help with the last air in their lungs, broken bones unable to rise up. The impact of the explosion was fierce.

This fast moving, massive event delivered you to the next source of life...the Pacific Ocean. Life beyond all dimensions. We were intruders of the deep.

I stayed right there in the main battery director station, right to the aft, the yard arm. There was the large smokestack with the heavy explosives, the oil fumes and worst of all, the big guns, powder bags, mainly with the bags of nitroglycerin. Not giving up my personal part of this fabulous ship, its steel body, I thought this point would land me outward as far as any point. I had a better view of what was going on than anyone. Walking around the catwalk of this main battery director provided a front line view. The events are very set in my mind to this day.

Now as this massive hunk of steel was losing its life so fast, the forward bow was sinking very fast, listing starboard at a heavy angle. After all, I was up there in height watching all of this. My heart beat like a jungle drum...breathing just as fast. After all, I was way out in the rough sea, as all men; kapok life jackets were not everyday gear. We also had the Mae West rubber belt, folded with some air; in the event of need it could be taken off and air blown into it. In the rough water, that was almost impossible to do and reinstall.

The greatest act of "God" or as I also say, an act of "Mother Nature"—I was hardly in the water when I started to swim as far away from the ship as possible. I turned around for the last view. The great ship turned 180 degrees and went straight down, the stern yet to go. Timeless, the stern submerged. It left a water wall circle so many feet high. It was a perfect circle. Then, that water came down returning the great ocean to a level surface. I started to vomit. Somehow, I kept count—over seventeen times.

As the darkness of this tragic night began to let us see the day, a thought came to mind. "We're not done yet!" One more great threat! "These people may be back. If we can make it through the break of light to sunup, we'll have a chance." The men that heard my voice thought I was way out. Not really. This is the time when the enemy will come and machine gun the leftovers.

I was left with my Mae West life preserver. Somehow, I was just there with my right arm straight out in the rough water and all at once, a life preserver floated right on my arm. All I did was shift myself, the other arm, and tie the closures. This milkweed-stuffed hunk of canvas, sewn into a vest fashion, guaranteed for 48 hours and good for 72 hours, pulled my life through the night and all five days and nights. My group of 126 men had two floater nets which were only to hold our legs together under the water line above ankles. Now, on top of that...no food or water Our method of beating sharks away was yelling and splashing water. Don't let any blood run loose. That can call sharks in for 8 miles.

The first day about noon, the sun's heat, full blast, men were coated with crude oil, you begin to realize the Pacific Ocean had no land boundaries for us men. Outside of our own voices and the tremendous sound of the relentless ocean, there was nothing else to be heard or seen. The first night came and we made it through. Now, in my aftermath, I'm going to leave out the next four days of ocean life.

I was recovered by the USS *Bassett*, a high speed transport, long after midnight on day number five. The ship pulled near, dropped a landing craft and located our group of men. It took four trips to gather all those close by. I was included in the last run. They pulled 122 men in my group. I remember the stern of this landing craft. About 24 to 30 inches above the water line. That is where I came aboard. The first try, I couldn't make it. But the second try took all I could do to make it. I laid on the steel deck, whatever time, the last man. I could feel the men putting me on the wire stretcher and tying me down. Then they hand-pulled up the bow on the basket, through the life lines. The rope slipped some. To come all this way and lose out on a drop. But the rope was secured and pulled through the life lines. Lines were untied and the next thing I remember was coming awake on white sheets. After no "shut eye" for the past five nights and days, we were tired, worn men.

The *Bassett* delivered us to a field hospital in the Philippine islands, God only knows where. We were taken to a compound enclosed in barbed wire with the sky as the roof; machine gun fire outside was a common event, mostly at night. It was almost like we traded one place for another. We each had an army cot, a sheet and a small canvas to cover us. The first ten days we used the same sheet, and then we received clean sheets that lasted four days. We then were shipped to Guam.

Later during Captain McVay's court martial in Washington, D.C., Captain Hashimoto said, "I was only doing for my country, like your men did for your country. I would do nothing to add more distress."

I want to share a letter I received from a young lady, Andi Lynn Welch, of Morristown, NJ.

Dear Mr. Witzig:
My name is Andi Lynn Welch and I'm fifteen years old. I got your address

from Mr. Paul Murphy, the Chairman of the USS Indianapolis Survivors Organization. You may think that kids these days can't comprehend and don't appreciate the sacrifices made by you and the others in World War II. You have every right to think that if you do...we teenagers have proven ourselves to be pretty empty-headed! But Mr. Witzig, though I will never fully understand war, since I've never fought in one, I can and do appreciate the strength and dedication of those who have. I just wanted to write to you, thanking you from the bottom of my heart for the sacrifices you have made to preserve a heritage of freedom and honor for our country.

We live with so many blessings here in America today, and when I hear stories of the brave men like you who secured them, I am determined to never take these privileges for granted. I know that they did not come without cost. Just knowing that you and the other boys and men would stand up and pay that price so that I could be free today, makes me proud to be an American.

Sir, you have no idea how your dedication has impacted my life and inspired me personally. So thank you, Mr. Witzig, and may God bless you always.

Respectfully,
Andi Lynn Welch

In 1951, the Veteran Medical Center ruled me with service Post Traumatic Stress Disorder, which carries on to this day. The Center has personal programs that assist me. With that aid, during the last four years the pattern of my life has excelled. Thank heavens. In my final ending, this story is so enormous, no one man can tell it all. After all, as considered by the United States Navy, this was the worst naval sea disaster in history.

NAME	WOOLSTON, JOHN ENS
STREET	1015 Wilder #A804
CITY	Honolulu
STATE	HI 96822
PHONE	808 533 6567
ENTERED SERVICE FROM	Seattle, WA
PICKED UP BY	PBY Tr USS *Doyle*
DIVISION	Repair Div
DOB	8/11/24

FAMILY

Spouse: Laura Woolston

Children: Peter Woolston, Lynn Sambueno, Alfred Streck, Jr.

Grandchildren: Christopher Woolston, Courtney Woolston, Lisa Sambueno, Michael Sambueno

EXPERIENCE

I was born and brought up in Seattle, between the magnificent Cascade and Olympic mountain ranges and beside the deep sea waters of Puget Sound. When I was four, my parents took a 15-month voyage around the world. To me that was two birthdays and one Christmas, a period to develop self-reliance and independence.

I spent many of my summers in the San Juan Islands at a homestead where my grandmother had established a lime company when she and my grandfather returned from the Alaska gold rush. I aspired to become the captain of one of the Black Ball line ferries that tied the islands to the mainland. When I was nine and starting fifth grade, we had an assignment to write a paper on what we wanted to be when we grew up. I wrote about becoming a ferry boat captain, but as I got up to read the paper, it hit me - that's not what I want - I'm going to design and build ships! I settled on MIT as the place to go, got their catalog in the seventh grade to plan high school courses, worked in the engineering department of a shipyard building navy ships when I graduated from high school, and entered MIT in September 1941 with a modest scholarship.

At about the time of my future profession revelation I had another adventure. A good friend had a much older sister who was married to a naval officer. One day he invited my friend and me to visit his ship. We took the ferry across the Sound to Bremerton, entered the naval base and thoroughly toured his wonderful ship - the USS *Indianapolis*. Navy ships often visited Seattle and there were always several at the naval base but this was the first time I had ever been aboard and it was most exciting. I found a model kit for *Indy* and that was the first and the most treasured of my models. I saw her again on a high speed run in the

Straits of Juan de Fuca; impressive even from a distance in a rowboat.

The news of Pearl Harbor made life and education at MIT much more serious. I was picked up in Navy V 12, earned my BS in naval architecture and marine engineering in October 1944, and went to midshipman school. When orders were issued, I was most pleased to be assigned to the *Indianapolis*.

After being commissioned March 9, 1945, I entered damage control school, married, traveled to San Francisco, then reported to *Indy* in Mare Island May 2. I was assigned as damage control watch and junior repair division officer and concentrated on learning the ship and my duties.

At sea, damage control watches were stood in damage control central from dusk to dawn with the usual turnovers at 2000, 2400, and 0400. Four of us rotated in these watches and Lt. Hurst, the assistant damage control officer joined the watch from 2000 to 2400 each night. On July 29, I had the 2000 to 2400 watch and was relieved at almost exactly midnight. I climbed up to the wardroom, got coffee and a ham sandwich from the steward and sat down to eat. Almost immediately there was a loud, hollow, metallic boom from forward. The ship shook and great whirling caterpillars of orange flame flew aft into the wardroom. About three seconds later, there was a much greater explosion from directly below, more whirling flames from aft filling the wardroom, and I was singed and thrown to the deck. All lights were out. Flames flickered outside the wardroom and I heard screams from the deck below and the passageways leading aft to the weather deck amidship. I slid through the serving window into the pantry, and fighting the smoke and fumes to maintain consciousness searched with the steward for the wrench to open the ports.

We found it, opened two ports, and leaned out to breathe much-needed clean air. The steward wanted to rest awhile but I climbed out the port and up to the forecastle deck. The bow was under and the list close to 30 degrees to starboard – it looked like the end. I picked up a life preserver and since my battle station was where the second fish hit, I looked for a place to assist where needed but found good supervision from forward to the afterstack area. I returned to the well deck and crawled to the port deck edge. Another steward with a life jacket joined me and I took him down the side and into the water. I found a life jacket, helped him into it and started him towards a group of men. Nobody else reported seeing either steward.

I ended up in the large group with Dr. Haynes, the marine captain, the chaplain, and a couple of hundred others. This group has been written about several times.

I never gave up hope (even expectation) of rescue, though it was depressing when aircraft flew over without seeing us and there were no signs of search when we became overdue in port. The night many of the men took off their life jackets and tried to drown others was the worst. I would hear a scream, swim over, pull the attacker off his victim and calm both of them. Often they had drifted away from the group and had to be brought back. I don't know how many times I did that before I passed out (or fell asleep). I was dreaming of walking in the passageway of the wardroom to get a drink from the scuttlebutt when my eyes opened and the view of the seas merged with the dream of the ship and I said: "The interior decorator of this ship had a lousy sense of humor." The sharks were horrible but I wasn't bothered even when I took off my sock and wiggled my toes at them to bring them up so I could take a bite – not too rational!!

Adrian Marks described my rescue as follows: "One of the survivors slipped out of his life jacket when we threw him the ring and then he missed grabbing the ring! We were closing rapidly on him but it was obvious that if we missed him on the first pass he would never have the strength to survive while we came about for a second try. Morgan was standing by the port blister and as the man passed under it, he reached down, grabbed the man under the armpits and then straightened up on one movement, lifting the man out of the water and pitching him over his head into the airplane."

I had quite a bruise across my chest but was mighty grateful. I was transferred to the USS *Doyle* then the hospital in Peleliu, then from the USS *Tranquility* to the hospital in Guam. I had pneumonia and saltwater ulcers but recovered quickly. As sole surviving damage control department officer, I wrote much of the draft War Damage Report (which was never published). I was not called for the investigation on Guam but did testify at the one held in Washington navy yard and at the court martial.

For years after the tragedy, I answered hundreds of letters from families of our lost shipmates. Usually I could say nothing specific but put the best light I could on dying swift or falling asleep in the deep. I tried also with early authors to downplay horrors. I lost contact with the survivors group (hence later authors) when evacuated from Iran in early 1979 and did not reestablish it until 1990. I attended the 1995 memorial dedication.

Back to 1945 and the rest of my life. I was ordered to the precommissioning detail for USS *Philippine Sea* (CV 47), which was commissioned in 1946, and served for two years as auxiliaries division and engineering watch officer and qualified as chief engineer. We had a fun trip taking Admiral Byrd to Antarctica and launching six DC-3 aircraft. I then had three years at MIT for the naval engineer degree and was designated engineering duty officer. I reported to Hunters Point to manage a DDG conversion but was selected to go into submarines. Six months in submarine school and 18 months aboard USS *Remora* (SS 487) and submarine qualification followed. The next three years were in Charleston Naval Shipyard on the waterfront and in planning.

Next I spent five years in Portsmouth Naval Shipyard as design project officer for *Thresher* class SSN–ships that would go deeper than previous submarines but more important be much quieter–a generation ahead of all others. This earned me a Legion of Merit. Three years in the Bureau of Ships followed as program manager for constructing 51 *Thresher/Permit/Sturgeon*-class submarines in seven shipyards.

I then went to Pearl Harbor to be material officer for Commander, Submarine Force Pacific Fleet for three years; I also was divorced and remarried in Honolulu. I then returned to Charleston Naval Shipyard, a 7,000 employee shipyard overhauling and converting SSN, SSBN, and surface-guided missile ships as repair superintendent then planning officer. I then was selected to command the shipyard for the next three years. My last year on active duty was in the Ships Systems Command as acting deputy and Sea Systems Command as deputy commander. I retired as captain with 32 years of service.

Laura and I then moved to Tehran, Iran where I was technical advisor to their navy for a year; then for three and a half years I was in Bandar Abbas overseeing design and construction and putting into commission their first naval shipyard. We went from five shipyard people and a large construction effort to 135 U.S., 350 Filipino, and 1,500 Iranian personnel overhauling ships. When the revolution heated up in early 1979 we were evacuated thanks to the Iranian, U.K., and U.S. navies.

I then went to work for Bechtel in San Francisco for ten years on government projects, though my last assignment was general manager of Australian warship systems in Sydney, competing for a frigate design/construct project. We decided to parlay this trip into a retirement move to Honolulu. So here we live and try to catch up on all the trips we couldn't take before—mostly cruising as I am still a sailor!

CHAPTER 317   SURVIVOR ZINK

NAME	ZINK, CHARLES W Elect 3C
STREET	
CITY	
STATE	
PHONE	
ENTERED SERVICE FROM	So Zanesville, OH
PICKED UP BY	USS *Talbot* tr USS *Register*
DIVISION	
DOB	Deceased 6/00

FAMILY

EXPERIENCE

Unable to contact any family members.

USS *Indianapolis* (CA-35) earned ten battle stars on the Asiatic-Pacific Aisa Service Medal for participating in the following operations and engagements:

 Star/Pacific Raids-1942.
Air Action off Bougainville--20 February 1942. Salamaus-Lal Raid-10 March 1942.

 Star/Aleutians Operation.
Attu Occupation-25 May to 2 June 1943.

 Star/Gilbert Islands Operation-20 November to 8 December 1943.

 Star/Marshall Islands Operation.
Occupation of Kwajalein and Majuro Atolls-29 January to 8 February 1944.
Occupation of Eniwetok Atoll-17 February to 2 March 1944.

 Star/Asiatic-Pacific Raids-1944.
Palau, Yap, Ulithi, Woleai Raid-30 March to 1 April 1944.

 Star/Marianas Operation.
Capture and Occupation of Saipan-11 June to 10 August 1944.
Battle of Philippine Sea-19-20 June 1944.
Capture and Occupation of Guam-21-23 July 1944.

 Star/Tinian Capture and Occupation-24-25 July 1944.

 Star/Western Caroline Islands Operation.
Capture and Occupation of Southern Palau Islands-6 September to 14 October 1944.

 Star/Iwo Jima Operation.
FIFTH Fleet Raids against Honshu and the Nansei Shoto 15-16, 25 February; 1 March 1945.
Assault and Occupation of Iwo Jima-15 February to 6 March 1945.

 Star/Okinawa Gunto Operation.
Assault and Occupation of Okinawa Gunto 17-25 March Operation–26 March to 5 April 1945.

STATISTICS

Displacement ....9,800 tons
Length Overall...610 feet
Beam..66 feet
Speed ....32 knots
Complement...excess of 1,200

USS INDIANAPOLIS (CA-35) SURVIVORS ORGANIZATION
OFFICERS AND BOARD OF DIRECTORS
2001-2003

CHAIRMAN
Paul J. Murphy
1030 W 4th Ave
Broomfield, CO 80020
(303) 469-9503
Fax: (303) 469-9503
Email: murphyindy@aol.com

VICE CHAIRMAN
Glenn G. Morgan
Rt 3 L 42
Franklin, TX 77856
(979) 828-3936

SECRETARY
Marylou Murphy
1030 W 4th Ave
Broomfield, CO 80020
(303) 469-9503

TREASURER
Lindsey Z. Wilcox
300 Long Dr
Baytown, TX 77521-4509
(281) 422-4487

CO-MASTER OF ARMS
Lyle M. Pasket
1756 Walnut Ln
Eagan, MN 55233-2420
(651) 452-4513

Richard P. Thelen
1323 Comfort St
Lansing, MI 48915-1407
(517) 482-2519

BOARD OF DIRECTORS
Harold J. Bray, Jr.
400 Vista Ct
Benicia, CA 94510
(707) 745-5706

Frank J. Centazzo
158 Park Ave
Warwick, RI 02889
(401) 738-6035

James E. O'Donnell
7602 Derreck Pl
Indianapolis, IN 46219
(317) 357-9343

CHAPLAIN
Cleatus A. Lebow
Box 96
Memphis, TX 79245
(806) 259-2427

USS INDIANAPOLIS SURVIVORS ORGANIZATION OFFICERS AND COMMITTEE MEMBERS 1960-2003

CHAIRMAN
Survivor Giles McCoy
Survivor Felton Outland
Survivor Glenn G Morgan
Survivor Paul J Murphy

VICE CHAIRMAN
Survivor Charles McKissick
Survivor Glenn G. Morgan
Survivor Paul J. Murphy

TREASURER
Survivor Michael N. Kuryla Jr.
survivor Robert G. McGuiggan
Survivor Lindsey Z. Wilcox

SECRETARY
Survivor Daniel Spencer
Esther Spencer
Survivor John M. Torretta
Rose Torretta
Lindsey Z. Wilcox
Mary Lou Murphy

MASTER OF ARMS
Survivor Richard P. Thelen
Survivor Lyle M. Pasket
Survivor Harold A. Eck
Survivor Earl W. Riggins

BOARD OF DIRECTORS
Survivor James E. O'Donnell
Survivor Paul W. McGinnis
Survivor Donald L. Beaty
Survivor Richard A. Paroubek
Survivor Lindsey Z. Wilcox
Survivor Harold J. Bray Jr.
Survivor Frank J. Centazzo

CHAPLAIN
Survivor Charles McKissick
Survivor Cleatus A. Lebow

COMMITTEE MEMBERS
Adrian Barksdale
Lucille Barksdale
Red Bolduc
Joan Bolduc
Beatrice Carver
Survivor Grover Carver
Genevieve Eck
Survivor Harold A. Eck
Survivor Albert Ferguson
Survivor William Gooch
Survivor Edgar Harrell
Ola Harrell
Survivor Clarence Hershberger
Estelle Houck
Survivor Richard Houck
Lorain Kuryla
Survivor Michael N. Kuryla Jr.
Julia Magana
"Mac" Magana
Betty McCoy
Survivor Giles McCoy
Gloria McGuiggan
Survivor Robert G. McGuiggan
Survivor Richard McVay
Survivor Kenneth Mitchell
Survivor Glenn G. Morgan
Mertie Jo Morgan
Mary Lou Murphy
Survivor Paul J. Murphy
Lois O'Banion
Survivor Keith Owen
Survivor James O'Donnell
Mary Alice O'Donnell
Dorothy Riggins
Survivor Earl W. Riggins
Survivor Arthur Setchfield
Jackie Setchfield
Survivor Daniel Spencer
Esther Spencer
Marge Stepp
Joan Thelen
Survivor Richard P. Thelen
Gene Toffolo
Survivor John M Torretta
Rose Torretta
Survivor Ralph E. Underwood
Survivor Joseph VanMeter

A

ABBOTT, George S., S1
ACOSTA, Charles M., MM3
*ADAMS, Leo H., S1
ADAMS, Pat L., S2
ADORANTE, Dante W., S2
*AKINES, William R., S2
ALBRIGHT, Charles E Jr ., COX
*ALLARD, Vincent J., QM3
ALLEN, Paul F., S1
ALLMARAS, Harold D., F2
*ALTSCHULER, Allan H., S2
ALVEY, Edward W., Jr. AerM2
AMICK, Homer I., S2
ANDERSON, Lawrence J., SK2
*ANDERSON, Erick T., S2
ANDERSON, Leonard O., MM3
ANDERSON, RICHARD L., F2
ANDERSON, Sam G., S2
ANDERSON, Vincent U., BM1
*ANDREWS, William R., S2
ANNIS, James B., Jr., CEMA
ANTHONY, Harold R., PHM3
ANTONIE, Charles J., F2
*ANUNTI, John M., M2
ARMENTA , Lorenzo., SC2
*ARMISTEAD, John H., S2
ARNOLD, Carl Lloyd., AMM3
ASHFORD, Chester W., WT2
*ASHFORD, John T., Jr., RT3
ATKINSON, J.P., COX
AULL, Joseph Harry, S2
*AULT, William F., S2
AYOTTE, Lester J., S2

B

BACKUS, Thomas H., LT (jg)
BAKER, Daniel Albert, S2
BAKER, Frederick H., S2
BAKER, William M., Jr., EM1

*BALDRIDGE, Clovis R., EM2
BALL, Emmet Edwin, S2
BALLARD, Courtney J., SSM3
BARENTHIN, Leonard W., S2
BARKER, Robert C., Jr., RT1
BARKSDALE, Thomas Leon., FC3
BARNES, Paul C., F2
BARNES, Willard M., MM1
BARRA, Raymond James, CGMA
BARRETT, James B., S2
BARRY, Charles., LT (jg)
*BARTO, Lloyd Peter, S1
BARTON, George S., Y3
*BATEMAN, Bernard B., F2
BATENHORST, Wilfred J., MM3
BATSON, Eugene C., S2
BATTEN, Robert Edmon, S1
BATTS, Edward Daniel, STM1
*BEANE, James Albert, F2
*BEATY, Donald Lee, S1
BECKER, Myron Melvin, WT2
BEDDINGTON, Charles E., S1
BEDSTED, Leo A. K., F1
BEISTER, Richard J., WT3
*BELCHER, James R., S1
*BELL, Maurice Glenn, S1
BENNETT, Dean R., HA1
BENNETT, Ernest F., B3
BENNETT, Toney W., ST3
BENNING, Harry, S1
*BENTON, Clarence U., CFCP
*BERNACIL, Concepcion P., FC3
BERRY, Joseph, Jr., STM1
BERRY, William Henry, ST3
BEUKEMA, Kenneth Jay, S2
BEUSCHLEIN, Joseph C., S2
BIDDISON, Charles L., S1
BILLINGS, Robert B., ENS
BILLINGSLEY, Robert F., GM3
BILZ, Robert Eugene, S2
BISHOP, Arthur Jr., S2
*BITONTI, Louis P., S1
BLACKWELL, Fermon M., SSML3
*BLANTHORN, BRYAN, S1

*BLUM, DONALD J., ENS
BOEGE, Raymond R., S2
BOGAN, Jack R., RM1
BOLLINGER, Richard H., S1
*BOOTH, Sherman C., S1
BORTON, Herbert E., SC2
BOSS, Norbert George, S2
BOTT, Wilbur Melvin, S2
BOWLES, Eldridge W., S1
BOWMAN, Charles E., CTC
BOYD, Troy Howard, GM3
BRADLEY, William H., S2
BRAKE, John Jr., S2
*BRANDT, Russell L., F2
BRAUN, Neal F., S2
*BRAY, HAROLD J. JR., S2
BRICE, R. V., S2
BRIDGE, Wayne A., S2
BRIGHT, Chester L., S2
BRILEY, Harold V., MAM 3
BROOKS, Ulysess R., CWTA
BROPHY, Thomas D'Arcy Jr., ENS
BROWN, Edward A., WT3
*BROWN, Edward J., S1
BRUCE, Russell W., S2
BRULE, Maurice J., S2
*BRUNDIGE, Robert H., S1
BRUNEAU, Charles A., GM3
*BUCKETT, Victor R., Y2
BUDISH, David, S2
*BULLARD, John K., S1
*BUNAI, Robert P., SM1
BUNN, Horace G., S2
*BURDORF, Wilbert J., COX
BURKHARTSMEIER, Anton T., S1
BURKHOLTZ, Frank, Jr., EM3
BURLESON, Martin L., S1
BURRS, John W., S1
BURT, William George A., QM3
*BURTON, Curtis H., S1
BUSHONG, John R., GM3

C

CADWALLADER, John J., RT3
CAIN, Alfred B., RT3

CAIRO, William G., BUG1
CALL, James E., RM3
CAMERON, John W., GM2
CAMP, Garrison, STM2
CAMPANA, Paul, RDM3
*CAMPBELL, Hamer E. Jr., GM3
*CAMPBELL, Louis D., AOM3
CAMPBELL, Wayland D., SF3
CANDALINO, Paul L., LT (jg)
CANTRELL, Billy G., F2
CARNELL, Lois W., S2
CARPENTER, Willard A., SM3
CARR, Harry L., S2
CARROLL, Gregory K., S1
CARROLL, Rachel W., COX
CARSON, Clifford, F1
CARSTENSEN, Richard, S2
*CARTER, Grover C., S1
*CARTER, Lindsey L., S2
*CARTER, Lloyd G., COX
*CARVER, Grover C., S1
*CASSIDY, John C., S1
CASTALDO, Patrick P., GM2
CASTIAUX, Ray V., S2
CASTO, William H., S1
CAVIL, Robert R., MM2
CAVITT, Clinton C., WT3
*CELAYA, Adolph V., F2
*CENTAZZO, Frank J., SM3
*CHAMNESS, John D., S2
CHANDLER, Lloyd N., S2
CHART, Joseph, EM3
CHRISTIAN, Lewis E. Jr., WO
CLARK, Eugene, CK3
*CLARK, Orsen N., S2
CLEMENTS, Harold P., S2
*CLINTON, George W., S1
CLINTON, Leland, J., LT (jg)
COBB, William L., MOMM3
COLE, Walter H., CRMA
COLEMAN, Cedric F., LCDR
*COLEMAN, Robert E., F2
*COLLIER, Charles R., RM2
COLLINS, James, STM1
COLVIN, Frankie L., SSMT2

504

CONDON, Barna T., RDM1
CONNELLY, David F., ENS
CONRAD, James P., EM3
CONSER, Donald L., SC2
CONSIGLIO, Joseph W., FC2
CONWAY, Thomas M., Rev. LT
COOK, Floyd E., SF3
COOPER, Dale, Jr., F2
COPELAND, Willard J., S2
*COSTNER, Homer J., COX
COUNTRYMAN, Robert E., S2
*COWEN, Donald R., FC3
COX, Alford E., GM3
*COX, Loel Dene, S2
CRABB, Donald C., RM2
*CRANE, Granville S. Jr., MM2
CREWS, Hugh C., Lt. (jg)
CRITES, Orval D., WT1
CROUCH, Edwin M., CAPT (Passenger)
CRUM, Charles J., S2
CRUZ, Jose S., CCKA
CURTIS, Erwin E., CTCP

D
DAGENBART. Charles R. Jr., PHM2
DALE, Elwood R., F1
*DANIEL, Harold W., CBMA
DANIELLO, Anthony G., S1
DAVIS, James C., RM3
DAVIS, Kenneth G., F1
DAVIS, Stanley G., LT (jg)
DAVIS, Thomas E., SM2
DAY, Richard R. Jr., S2
DEAN, John T. Jr., S2
*DeBERNARDI, Louie, BM1
DeFOOR, Walton, RDM3
DeMARS, Edgar J., CBMA
DeMENT, Dayle P., S1
DENNEY, Lloyd, Jr., S2
*DEWING, Ralph O., FC3
*DIZELSKE, William B., MM2
DIMOND, John N., S2
DOLLINS, Paul, RM2
DONALD, Lyle H., EM1
DONEY, William Jr., F2

*DONNER, Clarence W., RT3
DORMAN, William B., S1
DORNETTO, Frank P., WT1
DOSS, James M., S2
DOUCETT, Roland O., S2
*DOUGLAS, Gene D., F2
DOVE, Bassil R., SKD2
DOWDY, Lowell S., CWO
DRANE, James A., GM3
*DRAYTON, Wiliam H., EM2
DRISCOLL, David L., LT (jg)
*DRONET, Joseph E. J., S2
DRUMMOND, James J., F2
DRURY, Richard E., S2
*DRYDEN, William H., MM1
DUFRAINE, Delbert E., S1
DUNBAR, Jess L., F2
DURAND, Ralph J. Jr., S2
DYCUS, Donald, S2

E
EAKINS, Morris B., F2
EAMES, Paul H. Jr., ENS
EASTMAN, Chester S., S2
*ECK, Harold A., S2
EDDINGER, John W., S1
EDDY, Richard L., RM3
EDWARDS, Alwyn C., F2
EDWARDS, Roland J., BM1
E'GOLF, Harold W., S2
ELLIOTT, Harry W., S2
ELLIOTT, Kenneth A., S1
EMERY, William F., S1
EMSLEY, William J., S1
ENGELSMAN, Ralph, S2
EPPERSON, Ewell, S2
EPPERSON, George L., S1
*ERICKSON, Theodore M., S2
ERNST, Robert C., F2
*ERWIN, Louis H., COX
*ETHIER, Eugene E., EM3
EUBANKS, James H., S1
Evans, Arthur J., PHM2
*EVANS, Claudus, GM3
EVERETT, Charles N., EM2

EVERS, Lawrence L., CMMA
EYET, Donald A., S1

F
FANTASIA, Frank A., F2
FARBER, Sheldon L., S2
FARLEY, James W., S1
*FARMER, Archie C., COX
*FARRIS, Eugene F., S1
FAST HORSE, Vincent, S2
*FEAKES, Fred A., AOM1
*FEDORSKI, Nicholas W., S1
FEENEY, Paul R., S2
*FELTS, Donald J., BM1
*FERGUSON, Albert E., CMMA
FERGUSON, Russell M., RT3
FIGGINS, Harley D., WT2
FIRESTONE, Kenneth F., FC2
FIRMIN, John A. H., S2
*FITTING, JOHNNY W., GM1
*FLATEN, HAROLD J., WT2
FLEISCHAUER, Donald W., S1
FLESHMAN, Vern L., S2
FLYNN, James M. Jr., S1
FLYNN, Joseph A., CDR
FOELL, Cecil D., ENS
*FORTIN, Verlin L., WT3
*FOSTER, Verne E., F2
*FOX, William H. Jr., F2
*FRANCOIS, Norbert E., F1
FRANK, Rudolph A., S2
FRANKLIN, Jack R., RDM3
FREEZE, Howard B., LT (jg)
FRENCH, Douglas O., FC3
FRENCH, Jimmy Jr., QM3
FRITZ, Leonard A., MM3
FRONTINO, Vincent F., MOMM3
FRORATH, Donald H S2
FUCHS, Herman F., CWO
FULLER, Arnold A., F2
FULTON, William C., CRMA
*FUNKHOUSER, Robert M., ART2

G
*GABRILLO, Juan, S2

Gaither, Forest M., FC2
*GALANTE, Angelo, S2
*GALBRAITH, Norman S., MM2
*GARDNER, Roscoe W., F2
Gardner, Russell T., F2
Garner, Glenn R., MM2
*GAUSE, Robert P., QM1
GAUSE, Rubin C. Jr., ENS
*GEMZA, Rudolph A., FC3
*GEORGE, Gabriel V., MM3
GERNGROSS, Frederick J. Jr., ENS
*GETTLEMAN, Robert A., S2
*GIBSON, Buck W., GM3
GIBSON, Curtis W., S2
GIBSON, Ganola F., MM3
GILBERT, Warner, Jr., S1
*GILCREASE, James, S2
GILL, Paul E., WT2
GILMORE, Wilbur A., S2
GISMONDI, Michael V., S1
*GLADD, Millard, Jr., MM2
GLAUB, Francis A., GM2
*GLENN, Jay R., AMM3
GLOVKA, Erwin S., S2
GODFREY, Marlo R., RM3
GOECKEL, Ernest S., Lt. (jg)
*GOFF, Thomas G., SF3
GOLDEN, Curry, STM1
GOLDEN, James L., S1
GONZALES, Ray A., S2
*GOOCH, WILLIAM L., F2
GOOD, Robert K., MM3
GOODWIN, Oliver A., CRTA
GORE, Leonard F., S2
GORECKI, Joseph W., SK3
GOTTMANN, Paul J., S2
GOVE, Carroll L., S2
*GRAY, Willis L., S1
GREATHOUSE, Bud R., S1
GREEN, Robert U., S2
*GREEN, Tolbert, Jr., S1
GREENE, Samuel G., S1
*GREENLEE, Charles I., S2
GREER, Bob E., S2
GREGORY, Garland G., F1

506

GREIF, Matthias D., WT3
GRIES, Richard C., F2
GRIEST, Frank D., GM2
GRIFFIN, Jackie D., S1
*GRIFFITH, Robert S., S1
GRIFFITHS, Leonard S., S2
GRIGGS, Donald R., F1
GRIMES, David E., S2
GRIMES, James F., S2
GROCE, Floyd V., RDM2
GROCH, John T., MM3
GUENTHER, Morgan E., EM3
GUERRERO, John G., S1
GUILLOT, Murphy U., F1
GUYE, Ralph L. Jr., QM3
GUYON, Harold L., F1

H
HABEREMAN, Bernard, S2
HADUCH, John M., S1
HALE, Robert B., LT
HALE, William F., S2
HALL, Pressie, F1
HALLORAN, Edward G., MM3
HAM, Saul A., S1
HAMBO, William P., PHM3
HAMMEN, Robert, PHOM3
HAMRICK, James J., S2
HANCOCK, William A., GM3
HANKINSON, Clarence W., F2
HANSEN, Henry, S2
*HANSON, Harley C., WO
HARLAND, George A., S2
HARP, Charlie H., S1
HARPER, Vasco, STM1
HARRIS, James D., F2
HARRIS, Willard E., F2
*HARRISON, Cecil M., CWO
HARRISON, Frederick E., S2
HARRISON, James M., S1
*HART, Fred Jr., RT2
HARTRICK, Willis B., MM1
*HATFIELD, Willie N., S2
HAUBRICH, Cloud D., S2
HAUSER, Jack I., SK2

*HAVENER, Harlan C., F2
*HAVINS, Otha A., Y3
HAYES, Charles D., LCDR
HAYLES, Felix, CK3
*HAYNES, Lewis L., MC., LCDR
HAYNES, Robert A., LT
HAYNES, William A., S1
HEERDT, Raymond E., F2
HEGGIE, William A., RDM3
HEINZ, Richard A., HA1
*HELLER, John, S2
HELLER, Robert J. Jr., S2
HELSCHER, Ralph J., S1
HELT, Jack E., F2
HENDERSON, Ralph L., S1
HENDRON, James R. Jr., F2
HENRY, Earl O., DC, LCDR
*HENSCH, Erwin F., LT
HENSLEY, Clifford, SSMB2
HERBERT, Jack E., BM1
HERNDON, Duane, S2
*HERSHBERGER, Clarence L., S1
HERSTINE, James F., ENS
HICKEY, Harry T., RM3
HICKS, Clarence, S1
HIEBERT, Lloyd H., GM1
HILL, Clarence M., CWTP
HILL, Joe W., STM1
HILL, Nelson P. Jr., LT
HILL, Richard N., ENS
*HIND, Lyle L., S2
HINES, Lionel G., WT1
*HINKEN, John R. Jr., F2
HOBBS, Melvin D., S1
*HODGE, Howard H., RM2
HODGINS, Lester B., S2
HODSHIRE, John W., S2
HOERRES, George J., S2
HOLDEN, Punciano A., ST1
HOLLINGSWORTH, Jimmie L., STM2
HOLLOWAY, Andrew J., S2
HOLLOWAY, Ralph H., COX
HOOGERWERF, John Jr., F1
*HOOPES, Gordon H., S2
Hopper, Prentice W., S1

507

HOOPER, Roy L., AMM1
*HORNER, Durward R., WO
HORR, Wesley A., F2
HORRIGAN, John G., F1
*HORVATH, George J., F1
*HOSKINS, William O., Y3
*HOUCK, Richard E., EM3
HOUSTON, Robert G., F1
HOUSTON, William H., PHM2
HOV, Donald A., S1
*HOWISON, John D., ENS
*HUBELI, Joseph F., S2
HUEBNER, Harry H., S1
HUGHES, Lawrence E., F2
HUGHES, Robert A., FC3
HUGHES, William E., SSML2
HUMPHREY, Maynard L., S2
HUNTER, Arthur R. Jr., QM1
HUNTLEY, Virgil C., CWO
*HUPKA, CLarence E., BKR1
*HURLEY, Woodrow, GM2
HURST, Robert H., LT
HURT, James E., S2
HUTCHISON, Merle B., S2

I
IGOU, Floyd Jr., RM2
IZOR, Walter E., F1

J
JACKSON, Henry, STML
*JACQUEMOT, Joseph A., S2
JADLOSKI, George K., S2
JAKUBISIN, Joseph S., S2
*JAMES, Woodie E., COX
JANNEY, John Hopkins, CDR
*JARVIS, James K., AM3
JEFFERS, Wallace M., COX
JENNEY, Charles I., LT
JENSEN, Chris A., S2
*JENSEN, Eugene W., S2
JEWELL, Floyd R., SK1
JOHNSON, Bernard J., S2
JOHNSON, Elwood W., S2
JOHNSON, George G., S2

JOHNSON, Harold B., S1
JOHNSON, Sidney B., S1
JOHNSON, Walter M., Jr., S1
*JOHNSON, William A., S1
JOHNSTON, Earl R., BM2
JOHNSTON, Lewis E., S1
JOHNSTON, Ray F., MM1
JOHNSTON, Scott A., F2
*JONES, Clinton L., COX
JONES, Georege E., S2
JONES, Jim, S2
JONES, Kenneth M., F1 MoMM
*JONES, Sidney, S1
JONES, Stanley F., S2
JORDAN, Henry, STM2
JORDON, Thomas H., S2
JOSEY, Clifford O., S2
JUMP, Davis A., ENS
JURGENSMEYER, Alfred J., S2
*JURKIEWICZ, Raymond S., S1
*JUSTICE, Robert E., S2

K
KARPEL, Dan L., BM1
KARTER, Leo C. Jr., S2
KASTEN, Stanley O., HA1
KAWA, Raymond P., Sk3
*KAY, Gust C., S1
*KAZMIERSKI, Walter, S1
KEENEY, Robert A., ENS
*KEES, Shalous E., EM2
KEITH, Everette E., EM2
KELLY, Albert R., S2
*KEMP, David P. Jr., SC3
*KENLY, Oliver W., RDM3
KENNEDY, Andrew J. Jr., S2
KENNEDY, Robert A., S1
KENNY, Francis J.P., S2
KEPHART, Paul, S1
*KERBY, Deo E., S1
KERN, Harry G., S1
KEY, S.T., EM2
*KEYES, Edward H., COX
KIGHT, Audy C., S1
KILGORE, Archie C., F2

KILLMAN, Robert E., GM3
KINARD, Nolan D., S1
KINCAID, Joseph E., FC2
*KING, A.C., S1
KING, Clarence Jr., STM2
KING, James T., S1
KING, Richard E., S2
KING, Robert H., S2
KINNAMAN, Robert L., S2
*KINZLE, Raymond A., BKR2
KIRBY, Harry, S1
KIRK, James R., SC3
*KIRKLAND, Marvin F., S1
KIRKMAN, Walter W., SF1
*KISELICA, JOSEPH F., AMM2
*KITTOE, James W., F2
*KLAPPA, Ralph D., S2
*KLAUS,Joseph F., S1
KLEIN, Raymond J., S1
KLEIN, Theil J., SK3
KNERNSCHIELD, Andrew N., S1
KNOLL, Paul E., COX
KNOTT, Elbern L., S1
KNUDTSON, Raymond A., S1
KNUPKE, Richard R., MM3
*KOCH, Edward C., EM3
KOEGLER, Albert, S1
KOEGLER, William, SC3
KOLAKOWSKI, Ceslaus, SM3
KOLLINGER, Robert E., S1
KONESNY, John M., S1
KOOPMAN, Walter F., F2
KOPPANG, Raymond I., LT (jg)
KOUSKI, Fred, GM3
KOVALICK, George R., S2
*KOZIARA, George, S2
KOZIK, Raymond, S1
KRAWITZ, Henry J., MM3
*KREIS, Clifford E., S1
KRON, Herman E., Jr., GM3
KRONENBERGER, William M., GM3
*KRUEGER, Dale F., F2
*KRUEGER, Norman F., S2
KRUSE, Darwin G., S2
KRZYZEWSKI, John M., S2

KUHN, Clair J., S1
KULOVITZ, Raymond J., S2
*KURLICH, George R., FC3
*KURYLA, Michael N. Jr., COX
KUSIAK, Alfred M., S2
KWIATKOWSKI, Marion J., S2

L
LABUDA, Arthur A., QM3
LaFONTAINE, Paul S., S1
LAKATOS, Emil J., MM3
LAKE, Murl C., S1
LAMB, Robert C., EM3
LAMBERT, Leonard F., S1
LANDON, William W. Jr., FC2\
*LANE, Ralph, CMMA
*LANTER, Kenley M., S1
*LaPAGLIA, Carlos, GM2
LaPARL, Lawrence E., Jr., S2
LAPCZYNSKI, Edward W., S1
LARSEN, Melvin R., S2
LATIGUE, Jackson, STM1
LATIMER, Billy F., S1
LATZER, Solomon, S2
LAUGHLIN, Fain H., SK3
*LAWS, George E., S1
LEATHERS, William B., MM3
LeBARON, Robert W., S2
*LEBOW, Cleatus A., FC3
*LEENERMAN, Arthur L., RDM3
LELUIKA, Paul P., S2
LESTINA, Francis J., S1
LETIZIA, Vincencio, S2
LETZ, Wilbert J., SK1
LeVALLEY, Wiliam D., EM2
LEVENTON< Mervin C., MM2
LeVIEUX, John J., F2
LEWELLEN, Thomas E., S2
LEWIS, James R., F2
LEWIS, John R., GM3
LINDEN, Charles G., WT2
LINDSAY, Norman L., SF3
LINK, George C., S1
LINN, Roy, S1
LINVILLE, Cecil H., SF2

LINVILLE, Harry J., S1
LIPPERT, Robert G., S1
LIPSKI, Stanley W., CDR
LITTLE, Frank E., MM2
LIVERMORE, Raymond I., S2
LOCH, Edwin P., S1
*LOCKWOOD, Thomas H., S2
LOEFFLER, Paul E. Jr., S2
*LOFTIS, James B. Jr., S1
LOFTUS, Ralph D., F2
LOHR, Leo W., S1
LOMBARDI, Ralph, S1
LONG, Joseph W., S1
LONGWELL, Donald J., S1
*LOPEZ, Daniel B., F2
*LOPEZ, Sam, S1
LORENC, Edward R., S2
LOYD, John F., WT2
*LUCAS, Robert A., S2
*LUCCA, Frank J., F2
LUHMAN, Emerson D., MM3
LUNDGREN, Albert D., S1
LUTTRULL, Claud A., COX
LUTZ, Charles H., S1

M
*MAAS, Melvin A., S1
MABEE, Kenneth C., F2
*MACE, Harold A., S2
MacFARLAND, Keith L., LT (jg)
MACHADO, Clarence J., WT2
*MACK, Donald F., Bugler 1
*MADAY, Antony F., AMM1
MADIGAN, Harry F., BM2
MAGDICS, Steve Jr., F2
MAGRAY, Dwain F., S2
*MAKAROFF, Chester J., GM3
MAKOWSKI, Robert T., CWTA
*MALDONADO, Salvador, BKR3
*MALENA, Joseph J. Jr., GM2
MALONE, Cecil E., S2
MALONE, Elvin C., S1
MALONE, Michael L. Jr., LT (jg)
*MALSKI, Joseph J., S1
MANESS, Charles F., F2

MANKIN, Howard J., GM3
MANN, Clifford E., S1
MANSKER, LaVoice, S2
MANTZ, Keith H., S1
MARCIULAITIS, Charles, S1
MARKMANN, Frederick H., WT1
MARPLE, Paul T., ENS
MARSHALL, John L., WT2
MARSHALL, Robert W., S2
MARTIN, Albert, S2
MARTIN, Everett G., S1
MASSIER< George A., S1
MASTRECOLA, Michael M., S2
MATHESON, Richard R., PHM3
*MATRULLA, John, S1
MAUNTEL, Paul J., S2
*MAXWELL, Farrell J., S1
McBRIDE, Ronald G., S1
McBRYDE, Frank E., S2
*McCALL, Donald C., S2
*McCLAIN, Raymond B., BM2
McCLARY, Lester E., S2
McCLURE, David L., EM2
McCOMB, Everett A., F1
McCORD, Edward Franklin, Jr., EM3
McCORKLE, Ray R., S1
McCORMICK, Earl W., MOMM2
McCOSKEY, Paul F., S1
McCOY, John S. Jr., M2
*McCRORY, Millard V., Jr., WT2
McDANIEL, Johnny A., S1
McDONALD, Franklin G. Jr., F2
McDONNER, David P. Jr., F1
McDOWELL, Robert E., S1
*McELROY, Clarence E., S1
*McFALL, Walter E., S2
McFEE, Carl S., SC1
*McGinnis, Paul W., SM3
McGINTY, John M., S1
*McGuiggan, Robert M., S1
McGUIRE, Denis, S2
McGUIRK, Philip A., LT (jg)
*McHENRY, Loren C. Jr., S1
McHONE, Ollie, F1
McKEE, George E. Jr., S1

510

McKENNA, Michael J., S1
*McKenzie, Ernest E., S1
McKINNON,, Francis M., Y3
*McKISSICK, Charles B., LT (jg)
*McKLIN, Henry T., S1
*McLAIN, Patrick J., S2
McLEAN, Douglas B., EM3
McNABB, Thomas, Jr., F2
McNICKLE, Arthur S., F1
McQUITTY, Roy E., COX
*McVAY, Charles Butler, III, CAPT
*McVAY, Richard C., Y3
MEADE, Sidney H., S1
MEHLBAUM, Raymond A., S1
MEIER, Harold E., S2
MELICHAR, Charles H., EM3
MELVIN, Carl L., F1
MENCHEFF, Manual A., S2
*MEREDITH, Charles E., S1
MERGLER, Charles M., RDM2
*MESTAS, Nestor A., WT2
METCALF, David W., GM3
*MEYER, Charles T., S2
MICHAEL, Bertrand F., BKR3
MICHAEL, Elmer O., S1
MICHNO, Arthur R., S2
MIKESKA, Willie W., S2
*MIKOLAYEK, Joseph, COX
*MILBRODT, Glen L. S2
Miles, Theodore K., LT
Miller, Artie R., GM2
MILLER, George E., F1
MILLER, Glenn E., S2
MILLER, Samuel George Jr., FC3
MILLER, Walter R., S2
MILLER, Walter W., B1
MILLER, Wilbur H., CMM
MILLS, William H., EM3
*MINER, Herbert J. II, RT2
MINOR, Richard L., S1
MINOR, Robert W., S2
MIRES, Carl E., S2
MIRICH, Wally M., S1
MISKOWIEC, Theoodore F., S1
*MITCHELL, James E., S2

MITCHELL, James H. Jr., SK1
*MITCHELL, Kenneth E., S1
*MITCHELL, Norval Jerry Jr., S1
MITCHELL, Paul B., FC3
Mitchell, Winston C., S1
MITTLER, Peter John Jr., GM3
MIXON, Malcom L., GM2
*Mlady, Clarence C., S1
*MODESITT, Carl E., S2
*MODISHER, Melvin W., MC, LT (jg)
MONCRIEF, Mack D., S2
MONKS, Robert B., GM3
MONTOYA, Frank E., S1
MOORE, Donald G., S2
MOORE, Elbert, S2
MOORE, Harley E., S1
MOORE, Kyle C., LCDR
MOORE, Wyatt P., BKR1
*MORAN, Joseph J., RM1
*MORGAN, Eugene S., BM2
*MORGAN, Glenn G., BGM3
MORGAN, Lewis E., S2
MORGAN, Telford F., ENS
*MORRIS, ALBERT O., S1
MORSE, Kendall H., LT (jg)
MORTON, Charles W., S2
MORTON, Marion E., SK2
*MOSELEY, Morgan M., SC1
MOULTON, Charles C., S2
*MOWREY, Ted E., SK3
MOYNELO, Francis A., S2
MROSZAK, Francis A., S2
*MULDOON, John J., MM1
*MULVEY, William R., BM1
MURILLO, Sammy, S2
Murphy, Allen, S2
*MURPHY, Paul J., FC3
MUSARRA, Joseph, S1
MYERS, Charles Lee Jr., S2
MYERS, Glen A., MM2
*MYERS, H. B., F1

N
NABERS, Neal A., S2
*NASPINI, Joseph A., F2

NEAL, Charles K., S2
NEAL, George M., S2
NEALE, Harlan B., S2
*NELSEN, Eward J., GM1
*NELSON, Frank H., S2
NEU, Hugh H., S2
NEUBAUER, Richard, S2
NEUMAN, Jerome C., F1
NEVILLE, Bobby G., S2
NEWCOMER, Lewis W., MM3
NEWELL, James T., EM1
*NEWHALL, James F., S1
*NICHOLS, James C., S2
NICHOLS, Joseph L., BM2
NICHOLS, Paul V., MM3
NIELSEN, Carl Aage Chor Jr., F1
NIETO, Baltazar P., GM3
*Nightingale, William O., MM1
NISKANEN, John H., F2
*NIXON, Daniel M., S2
*NORBERG, James A., CBMP
NORMAN, Theodore R., GM2
NOWAK, George J., F2
NUGENT, William G., S2
NUNLEY, James P., F1
*NUNLEY, Troy A., S2
NUTT, Raymond A., S2
*NUTTALL, Alexander C., S1

O
*OBLEDO, Mike G., S1
O'BRIEN, Arthur J., S2
O'CALLAGHAN, Del R., WT2
OCHOA, Ernest, FC3
*O'DONNELL, James E., WT3
OLDERON, Bernhard G., S1
*OLIJAR, John, S1
O'NEIL, Eugene E., S1
ORR, Holmer L., HA1
ORR, John Irwin, Jr., LT
*ORSBURN, Frank H., SSML2
ORTIZ, Orlando R., Y3
OSBURN, Charles W., S2
OTT, Theodore G., Y1
*OUTLAND, Felton J., S1

*OVERMAN, Thurman D., S2
*OWEN, Keith N., SC3
OWENS, Robert Sheldon Jr., QM3
OWENSBY, Clifford C., F2

P
*PACE, Curtis, S2
*PACHECO, Jose C., S2
PAGITT, Eldon E., F2
PAIT, Robert E., BM2
*PALMITER, Adelore A., S2
PANE, Francis W., S2
PARHAM, Fred, ST2
PARK, David E., ENS
*PAROUBEK, Richard A., Y1
*PASKET, Lyle M., S2
PATTERSON, Alfred T., S2
PATTERSON, Kenneth G., S1
PATZER, Herman L., EM1
*PAULK, Luther D., S2
*PAYNE, Edward G., S2
PAYNE, George D., S2
*PENA, Santos A., S1
PENDER, Welburn M., F2
*PEREZ, Basilio, S2
*PERKINS, Edward C., F2
PERRY, Robert J., S2
PESSOLANO, Michael R., LT
PETERS, Earl J., S2
*PETERSON, Avery C., S2
PETERSON, Darrel E., S1
PETERSON, Frederick A., MAM3
PETERSON, Glenn H., S1
PETERSON, Ralph R., S2
PETRINCIC, John Nicholas Jr., FC3
PEYTON, Robert C., STM1
PHILLIPS, Aulton N. Sr., F2
*PHILLIPS, Huie H., S2
PIERCE, Clyde A., CWTA
PIERCE, Robert W., S2
PIPERATA, Alfred J., MM1
PITMAN, Robert F., S2
PITTMAN, Almire Jr., ST3
PLEISS, Roger D., F2
*PODISH, Paul, S2

*PODSCHUN, Clifford A., S2
*POGUE, Herman C., S2
POHL, Theodore, F2
POKRYFKA, Donald M., S2
*POOR, Gerald M., S2
POORE, Albert F., S2
POTRYKUS, Frank P., F2
*POTTS, Dale F., S2
POWELL, Howard W., F1
POWERS, R. C. Ottis, S2
POYNTER, Raymond L., S2
PRAAY, William T., S2
PRATHER, Clarence J., CMMA
PRATT, George R., F1
*PRICE, James D., S1
PRIESTLE, Ralph A., S2
PRIOR, Walter M., S2
PUCKETT, William C., S2
PUPUIS, John A., S1
PURCEL, Franklin W., S2
PURSEL, Forest V., WT2
PYRON, Freddie H., S1

Q
*QUEALY, William C. Jr., PR2

R
RABB, John R., SC1
RAGSDALE, Jean O., S1
RAHN, Alvin W., SK3
RAINES, Clifford Jr., S2
RAINS, Rufus B., S1
*RAMIREZ, Ricardo, S1
RAMSEYER, Raymond C., RT3
RANDOLPH, Cleo, STM1
*RATHBONE, Wilson, S2
RATHMAN, Frank Jr., S1
*RAWDON, John H., EM3
REALING, Lyle O., FC2
*REDMAYNE, Richard B., LT
REED, Thomas W., EM3
REEMTS, Alvan T., S1
REESE, Jesse E., S2
*REEVES, Chester O.B., S1

REEVES, Robert A., F2
REGALADO, Robert H., S1
*REHNER, Herbert A., S1
*REID, Curtis F., S2
*REID, James E., BM2
*REID, John, LCDR
*REID, Tommy L., RDM3
Reilly, James F., Y1
REINERT, Leroy, F1
REMONDET, Edward J. Jr., S2
*Reynolds, Alford, GM2
REYNOLDS, Andrew E., S1
REYNOLDS, Carleton C., F1
RHEA, Clifford, F2
RHODES, Vernon L., F1
RHOTEN, Roy E., F2
RICE, Albert, STM1
RICH, Garland L., S1
RICHARDSON, John R., S2
RICHARDSON, Joseph G., S2
RIDER, Francis A., RDM3
RILEY, Junior Thomas, BM2
*RINEAY, Frances Henry Jr., S2
ROBERTS, Benjamin E., WT1
ROBERTS, Charles, S1
*ROBERTS, Norman H., MM1
ROBISON, Gerald E., RT3
*ROBISON, John D., COX
ROBISON, Marzie J., S2
ROCHE, Joseph M., LT
ROCKENBACH, Earl A., SC2
ROESBERRY, Jack R., S1
ROGELL, Henry T., F1
*ROGERS, Ralph G., RDM3
*ROGERS, Ross, Jr., ENS
ROLAND, Jack A., PHM1
ROLLINS, Willard E., RM3
ROMANI, Frank J., HA1
ROOF, Charles W., S2
ROSE, Berson H., GM2
ROSS, Glen E., F2
ROTHMAN, Aaron, RDM3
ROWDEN, Joseph G., F1
ROZZANO, John, Jr., S2

RUDOMANSKI, Eugaene W., RT2
RUE, William G., MM1
Russell, Robert A., S2
*RUSSELL, Virgil M., COX
RUST, Edwin L., S1
RUTHERFORD, Robert A., RM2
RYDZESKI, Frank W., F1

S
*SAATHOFF, Don W., S2
SAENZ, Jose A., SC3
SAIN, Albert F., S1
SALINAS, Alfredo A., S1
SAMANO, Nuraldo, S2
SAMPSON, Joseph R., S2
SAMS, Robert C., STM2
SANCHEZ, ALEJANDRO V., S2
*SANCHEZ, FERNANDO S., SC3
SAND, Cyrus H., BM1
SANDERS, Everett R., MOMM1
SASSMAN, Gordon W., COX
*SCANLAN, Osceola C., S2
SCARBROUGH, Fred R., COX
SCHAAP, Marion J., QM1
SCHAEFER, Harry W., S2
SCHAFFER, Edward J., S1
SCHARTON, Elmer D., S1
*SCHECHTERLE, Harold J., RDM3
SCHEIB, Albert E., F2
SCHEWE, Alfred P., S1
SCHLATTER, Robert L., AOM3
SCHLOTTER, James R., RDM3
*SCHMUECK, John A., CPHMP
SCHNAPPAUF, Harold J., SK3
SCHOOLEY, Dillard A., COX
SCHUMACHER, Arthur J. Jr., CEMA
SCOGGINS, Millard, SM2
SCOTT, Burl D., STM2
SCOTT, Curtis M., S1
SCOTT, Hilliard, STM1
*SEABERT, Clarke W., S2
SEBASTIAN, Clifford H., RM2
SEDIVI, Alfred J., PHOM2
SELBACH, Walter H., WT2
SELL, Ernest F., EM2

SELLERS, Leonard E., SF3
SELMAN, Amos, S2
*SETCHFIELD, Arthur L., COX
SEWELL, Loris E., S2
*SHAFER, Robert P., GM3
SHAND, Kenneth W., WT2
*SHARP, William H., S2
SHAW, Calvin P., GM2
*SHEARER, Harold J., S2
SHELTON, William E. Jr., SM2
SHIELDS, Cecil N., SM2
SHIPMAN, Robert L., GM3
*SHOWN, Donald H., CFC
*SHOWS, Audie B., COX
SIKES, Theodore A., ENS
SILCOX, Burnice R., S1
SILVA, Phillip G., S1
SIMCOX, Gordon W., EM3
SIMCOX, John A., F1
*SIMPSON, William E., BM2
SIMS, Clarence, CK2
*SINCLAIR, J. Ray, S2
SINGERMAN, David, SM2
SIPES, John L., S1
*SITEK, Henry J., S2
SITZLAR, William C., F1
*SLADEK, Wayne L., BM1
*SLANKARD, Jack C., S1
SMALLEY, Howard E., S1
*SMELTZER, Charles H., S2
SMERAGLIA, Michael, RM3
SMITH, Carl M., SM2
SMITH, Charles A., S1
*SMITH, Cozell Lee Jr., COX
SMITH, Edwin L., S2
SMITH, Eugene G., BM2
*SMITH, Frederick C., F2
SMITH, George R., S1
SMITH, Guy N., FC2
SMITH, Henry A., F1
SMITH, Homer L., F2
*SMITH, James W., S2
SMITH, Kenneth D., S2
SMITH, Olen E., CM3
SNYDER, John N., SF2

SNYDER, Richiard R., S1
SOLOMON, William Jr., S2
SORDIA, Ralph, S2
*SOSPIZIO, Andre, EM3
SPARKS, Charles B., COX
SPEER, Lowell E., RT3
*SPENCER, Daniel F., S1
SPENCER, James D., LT
*SPENCER, Roger, S1
SPENCER, Sidney A., WO
SPINDLE, Orval A., S1
*SPINELLI, John A., SC2
SPOMER, Elmer J., SF2
STADLER, Robert H., WT3
*STAMM, Florian M., S2
STANFORTH, David E., F2
STANKOWSKI, Archie J., S2
STANTURF, Frederick R., MM2
STEIGERWALD, Fred, GM2
*STEPHENS, Richard P., S2
*STEVENS, George G., WT2
STEVENS, Wayne A., MM2
*STEWART, Glenn W., CFCP
STEWART, Thomas A., SK2
STICKLEY, Charles B., GM3
STIER, William G., S1
STIMSON, David, ENS
STONE, Dale E., S2
STONE, Homer B., Y1
STOUT, Kenneth I., LCDR
St. PIERRE, Leslie R., MM2
STRAIN, Joseph M., S2
STREICH, Allen C., RM2
STRICKLAND, George T., S2
STRIETER, Robert C., S2
STRIPE, William S., S2
STROM, Donald A., S2
STROMKO, Joseph A., F2
STRYFFELER, Virgil L., F2
STUECKLE, Robert L., S2
*STURTEVANT, Elwyn L., RM2
SUDANO, Angelo A., SSML3
SUHR, Jerome R., S2
SULLIVAN, James P., S2

SULLIVAN, William D., PTR2
*SUTER, FRNK E., S1
SWANSON, Robert H., MM2
SWART, Robert L., LT (jg)
SWINDELL, Jerome H., F2

T

TAGGART, Thomas H., S1
TALLEY, Dewell E., RM2
*TAWATER, Charles H., F1
TEERLINK, David S., CWO
TELFORD, Arno J., RT3
TERRY, Robert W., S1
*THELEN, Richard P., S2
THIELSCHER, Robert T., CRTP
*THOMAS, Ivan M., S1
*THOMPSON, David A., EM3
THORPE, Everett N., WT3
*THURKETTLE, William C., S2
TIDWELL, James F., S2
TISTHAMMER, Bernard E., CGMA
TOCE, Nicolo, S2
TODD, Harold O., CM3
*TORRETTA, John Mickey, F1
TOSH, Bill H., RDM3
TRIEMER, Ernst A., ENS
TROTTER, Arthur C., RM2
TRUDEAU, Edmond A., LT
TRUE, Roger G., S2
TRUITT, Robert E., RM2
TRYON, Frederick B., BUG2
TULL, James A., S1
*TURNER, Charles M., S2
Turner, William C., MM2
Turner, William H. Jr., ACMMA
*TWIBLE, Harlan M., ENS

U

ULIBARRI, Antonio D., S2
ULLMANN, Paul E., LT (jg)
*UMENHOFFER, Lyle E., S1
UNDERWOOD, Caray L., S1
*UNDERWOOD, Ralph E., S1

515

V
*VAN METER, Joseph W., WT3

W
WAKEFIELD, James N., S1
WALKER, A. W., STM1
WALKER, Jack E., RM2
*WALKER, Verner B., F2
WALLACE, Earl J., RDM3
WALLACE, John, RDM3
WALTERS, Donald H., F1
WARREN, William R., RT3
WATERS, Jack L., CYA
WATSON, Winston H., F2
*WELLS, Charles O., S1
WELLS, Gerald Lloyd, EM3
Wennerholm, Wayne L., COX
WENZEL, Ray G., RT3
WHALEN, Stuart D., GM2
WHALLON, Louis F. Jr., LT (jg)
WHITE, Earl C., TC1
WHITE, Howard M., CWTP
*WHITING, George A., F2
WHITEMAN, Robert T., LT
*WILCOX, Lindsey Z., WT2
WILEMAN, Roy W., PHM3
WILLARD, MERRIMAN D., PHM2
WILLIAMS, Billie J., MM2
WILLIAMS, Mageilan, STM1
WILLIAMS, Robert L., WO
WILSON, Frank, F2
WILSON, Thomas B., S1
*WISNIEWSKI, Stanley, F2
WITTMER, Milton R., EM2
*WITZIG, Robert M., FC3
WOJCIECHOWSKI, Maryian J., GM2
WOLFE, Floyd R., GM3
WOODS, Leonard T., CWO
*WOOLSTON, John, ENS

Y
YEAPLE, Jack T., Y3

Z
*ZINK, Charles W., EM2
ZOBAL, Francis J., S2

MARINE DETACHMENT ABOARD

BRINKER, David A., PFC
BROWN, Orlo N., PFC
BUSH, John R., PVT
CROMLIONG, Charles J. Jr., PLTSGT
DAVIS, William H., PFC
DUPECK, Albert Jr., PFC
*GREENWALD, Jacob, lst SGT
GRIMM, Loren E., PFC
HANCOCK, Thomas A., PFC
*HARRELL, Edgar A., CPL
HOLLAND, John F. Jr., PFC
HUBBARD, Gordon R., PFC
HUBBARD, Leland R., PFC
*HUGHES, Max M., PFC
*JACOB, Melvin C., PFC
KENWORTHY, Glenn W., CPL
KIRCHNER, John H., PVT
LARSEN, Harlan D., PFC
LEES, Henry W., PFC
MARTTILA, Howard W., PVT
*McCOY, Giles G., PFC
MESSENGER, Leonard J., PFC
MUNSON, Bryan C., PFC
MURPHY, Charles T., PFC
NEAL, William F., PFC
PARKE, Edward L., CAPT
REDD, Robert F., PVT
REINOLD, George H., PFC
*RICH, Raymond A., PFC
*RIGGINS, Earl, PVT
ROSE, Francis E., PFC
SPINO, Frank J., PFC
*SPOONER, Miles L., PVT
STAUFFER, Edward H., lst LT
STRAUGHN, Howard V. Jr., CPL
THOMSEN, Arthur A., PFC
TRACY, Richiard I. Jr., SGT
*UFFELMAN, Paul R., PFC
WYCH, Robert A., PFC

517